Communications
in Computer and Information Science   **2262**

Series Editors

Gang Li ⓘ, *School of Information Technology, Deakin University, Burwood, VIC, Australia*
Joaquim Filipe ⓘ, *Polytechnic Institute of Setúbal, Setúbal, Portugal*
Zhiwei Xu, *Chinese Academy of Sciences, Beijing, China*

AF173190

Rationale

The CCIS series is devoted to the publication of proceedings of computer science conferences. Its aim is to efficiently disseminate original research results in informatics in printed and electronic form. While the focus is on publication of peer-reviewed full papers presenting mature work, inclusion of reviewed short papers reporting on work in progress is welcome, too. Besides globally relevant meetings with internationally representative program committees guaranteeing a strict peer-reviewing and paper selection process, conferences run by societies or of high regional or national relevance are also considered for publication.

Topics

The topical scope of CCIS spans the entire spectrum of informatics ranging from foundational topics in the theory of computing to information and communications science and technology and a broad variety of interdisciplinary application fields.

Information for Volume Editors and Authors

Publication in CCIS is free of charge. No royalties are paid, however, we offer registered conference participants temporary free access to the online version of the conference proceedings on SpringerLink (http://link.springer.com) by means of an http referrer from the conference website and/or a number of complimentary printed copies, as specified in the official acceptance email of the event.

CCIS proceedings can be published in time for distribution at conferences or as post-proceedings, and delivered in the form of printed books and/or electronically as USBs and/or e-content licenses for accessing proceedings at SpringerLink. Furthermore, CCIS proceedings are included in the CCIS electronic book series hosted in the SpringerLink digital library at http://link.springer.com/bookseries/7899. Conferences publishing in CCIS are allowed to use Online Conference Service (OCS) for managing the whole proceedings lifecycle (from submission and reviewing to preparing for publication) free of charge.

Publication process

The language of publication is exclusively English. Authors publishing in CCIS have to sign the Springer CCIS copyright transfer form, however, they are free to use their material published in CCIS for substantially changed, more elaborate subsequent publications elsewhere. For the preparation of the camera-ready papers/files, authors have to strictly adhere to the Springer CCIS Authors' Instructions and are strongly encouraged to use the CCIS LaTeX style files or templates.

Abstracting/Indexing

CCIS is abstracted/indexed in DBLP, Google Scholar, EI-Compendex, Mathematical Reviews, SCImago, Scopus. CCIS volumes are also submitted for the inclusion in ISI Proceedings.

How to start

To start the evaluation of your proposal for inclusion in the CCIS series, please send an e-mail to ccis@springer.com

Leonidas Deligiannidis ·
Farid Ghareh Mohammadi ·
Farzan Shenavarmasouleh · Soheyla Amirian ·
Hamid R. Arabnia
Editors

Image Processing, Computer Vision, and Pattern Recognition and Information and Knowledge Engineering

28th International Conference, IPCV 2024
and 23rd International Conference, IKE 2024
Held as Part of the World Congress in Computer Science
Computer Engineering and Applied Computing, CSCE 2024
Las Vegas, NV, USA, July 22–25, 2024
Revised Selected Papers

 Springer

Editors
Leonidas Deligiannidis ⓘ
Wentworth Institute of Technology
Boston, MA, USA

Farid Ghareh Mohammadi ⓘ
Mayo Clinic
Athens, GA, USA

Farzan Shenavarmasouleh ⓘ
Medialab Inc.
Lawrenceville, GA, USA

Soheyla Amirian ⓘ
Pace University
Athens, GA, USA

Hamid R. Arabnia ⓘ
University of Georgia
Athens, GA, USA

ISSN 1865-0929   ISSN 1865-0937 (electronic)
Communications in Computer and Information Science
ISBN 978-3-031-85932-8   ISBN 978-3-031-85933-5 (eBook)
https://doi.org/10.1007/978-3-031-85933-5

This Springer imprint is published by the registered company Springer Nature Switzerland AG
The registered company address is: Gewerbestrasse 11, 6330 Cham, Switzerland

If disposing of this product, please recycle the paper.

Preface

It is our great pleasure to introduce this collection of selected papers presented at the 28th International Conference on Image Processing, Computer Vision, & Pattern Recognition (IPCV 2024) and the 23rd International Conference on Information & Knowledge Engineering (IKE 2024). Both conferences were held as part of the federated 2024 Congress on Computer Science, Computer Engineering, and Applied Computing (CSCE 2024), which took place from July 22 to July 25, 2024, in Las Vegas, Nevada, USA.

The CSCE 2024 Congress brought together papers from a diverse array of communities, including researchers from universities, corporations, and government agencies. Accepted papers are published by Springer Nature, and the proceedings showcase solutions to key challenges in various critical areas of Computer Science, Computer Engineering, and Applied Computing.

Computer Science (CS) is the study of computational systems, data processing, information management, and automation. Many applications in CS focus on solving problems that would be impossible or extremely difficult to address without the use of computers. It serves as a bridge between computational science and other scientific fields. The interdisciplinary nature of CS involves leveraging computers to understand and solve complex challenges, making it the science of using computers to advance scientific discovery. Computer Engineering (CE), on the other hand, integrates aspects of computer science, electronic engineering, and electrical engineering. It encompasses the design and production of computer hardware, such as chips, servers, supercomputers, embedded systems, and communication systems, among others.

Considering the above broad outline, the CSCE 2024 Congress was composed of the following focused conferences:

Applied Cognitive Computing (ACC); Bioinformatics & Computational Biology (BIOCOMP); Biomedical Engineering (BIOENG); Scientific Computing (CSC); e-Learning, e-Business, Enterprise Information Systems, & e-Government (EEE); Embedded Systems, Cyber-physical Systems, & Applications (ESCS); Foundations of Computer Science (FCS); Frontiers in Education (FECS); Grid, Cloud, & Cluster Computing (GCC); Health Informatics (HIMS); Artificial Intelligence (ICAI); Data Science (ICDATA); Emergent Quantum Technologies (ICEQT); Internet Computing & IoT (ICOMP); Wireless Networks (ICWN); Information & Knowledge Engineering (IKE); Image Processing, Computer Vision, & Pattern Recognition (IPCV); Modeling, Simulation & Visualization Methods (MSV); Parallel & Distributed Processing Techniques & Applications (PDPTA); Security & Management (SAM); and Software Engineering Research & Practice (SERP). The scope of each track can be found at: https://www.american-cse.org/csce2024/conferences

The primary objective of the CSCE Congress and its associated conferences is to foster opportunities for cross-fertilization between the fields of Computer Science (CS) and Computer Engineering (CE). The CSCE Congress is deeply committed to promoting diversity and eliminating discrimination, both in its role as a conference organizer and as a service provider. Our goal is to create an inclusive culture that respects and values differences, promotes dignity, equality, and diversity, and encourages individuals to reach their full potential. We are also dedicated, wherever possible, to organizing a conference that represents the global community. We sincerely hope that we have succeeded in achieving these important objectives.

The Steering Committee and the Program Committees would like to extend their gratitude to all the authors who submitted papers for consideration. This year's conferences received submissions from 46 countries, with approximately 52% of them coming from outside the USA. Each submitted paper underwent a rigorous peer-review process, with at least two experts (an average of 2.2 referees per paper) evaluating the submissions based on originality, significance, clarity, impact, and soundness. In cases where reviewers' recommendations were contradictory, a program committee member was tasked with making the final decision, often consulting additional referees for further guidance. The Congress followed the guidelines of COPE (Committee on Publication Ethics):

- Typical submissions underwent a single-blind peer review process, in which the authors remained unaware of the identities of the reviewers, while the reviewers were informed of the authors' identities.
- Papers authored by one or more members of the program committee, including co-chairs, were subjected to a double-blind peer review process, ensuring that neither the authors nor the reviewers were aware of each other's identities or affiliations.

The IPCV 2024 Conference received 98 submissions, of which 19 papers were accepted, resulting in a paper acceptance rate of 19.4%. The IKE 2024 Conference received 40 submissions, of which 10 papers were accepted, resulting in a paper acceptance rate of 25.0%. This volume includes the 29 accepted papers from IPCV 2024 and IKE 2024.

We are deeply grateful to the many colleagues who contributed their time and effort to organizing the Congress. In particular, we extend our thanks to the members of the Program Committees, the Steering Committee, the referees, and the Chairs and organizers of individual sessions and conferences. We would also like to express our appreciation to the primary sponsor of the conference, the American Council on Science & Education. The list of members of the Program Committee for each track can be found at: https://www.american-cse.org/csce2024/committees

We extend our heartfelt gratitude to all the speakers and authors for their valuable contributions. We would also like to thank the following individuals and organizations for their support: the staff at the Luxor Hotel, the staff of Springer Nature for assistance during the publication process, Ranis Ibragimovin (Walter De Gruyter, Inc.) for his assistance in publishing multiple books, and many Departments and Universities for their assistance in various aspects of the event.

We are pleased to present a curated selection of papers from IPCV 2024 and IKE 2024 conferences. These proceedings represent a collection of outstanding research contributions that reflect the diversity and depth of work in core areas of applied computer science and computer engineering.

August 2024

Leonidas Deligiannidis
Farid Ghareh Mohammadi
Farzan Shenavarmasouleh
Soheyla Amirian
Hamid R. Arabnia

Organization

Steering Committee – Co-chairs (CSCE 2024)

Hamid R. Arabnia	University of Georgia, USA
Leonidas Deligiannidis	Wentworth Institute of Technology, USA
Fernando G. Tinetti	Universidad Nacional de La Plata, Argentina
Quoc-Nam Tran	Southeastern Louisiana University, USA

Co-Editors of IPCV 2024 and IKE 2024 Proceedings – Publication Co-chairs

Leonidas Deligiannidis (Co-chair, IPCV 2024 & IKE 2024)	Wentworth Institute of Technology, USA
Farid Ghareh Mohammadi (Co-chair, IPCV 2024 & IKE 2024)	Mayo Clinic, USA
Farzan Shenavarmasouleh (Co-chair, IPCV 2024 & IKE 2024)	Medialab Inc., USA
Soheyla Amirian (Co-chair, IPCV 2024 & IKE 2024)	Pace University, USA
Hamid R. Arabnia (Co-chair, IPCV 2024 & IKE 2024)	University of Georgia, USA

Members of Steering Committee (CSCE 2024)

Babak Akhgar	Sheffield Hallam University, UK
Abbas M. Al-Bakry	University of IT & Communications, Iraq
Nizar Al-Holou	University of Detroit Mercy, USA
Hamid R. Arabnia	University of Georgia, USA
Rajab Challoo	Texas A&M University-Kingsville, USA
Chien-Fu Cheng	Tamkang University, Taiwan
Hyunseung Choo	Sungkyunkwan University, South Korea
Kevin Daimi	University of Detroit Mercy, USA
Leonidas Deligiannidis	Wentworth Institute of Technology, USA
Eman M. El-Sheikh	University of West Florida, USA

Mary Mehrnoosh Eshaghian-Wilner	University of California Los Angeles, USA
David L. Foster	Kettering University, USA
Henry Hexmoor	Southern Illinois University at Carbondale, USA
Ching-Hsien (Robert) Hsu	Chung Hua University, Taiwan; and Tianjin University of Technology, China
James J. (Jong Hyuk) Park	SeoulTech, South Korea
Mohammad S. Obaidat	University of Jordan, Jordan
Marwan Omar	Illinois Institute of Technology, USA
Shahram Rahimi	Mississippi State University, USA
Gerald Schaefer	Loughborough University, UK
Fernando G. Tinetti	Universidad Nacional de La Plata, Argentina
Quoc-Nam Tran	Southeastern Louisiana University, USA
Shiuh-Jeng Wang	Central Police University, Taiwan
Layne T. Watson	Virginia Polytechnic Institute & State University, USA
Chao-Tung Yang	Tunghai University, Taiwan
Mary Yang	University of Arkansas, USA

Research Tracks – Co-chairs (CSCE 2024)

Abeer Alsadoon (Co-chair, Health Informatics)	Charles Sturt University, Australia
Soheyla Amirian (Co-chair, Computer Vision & AI)	Pace University, USA
Hamid R. Arabnia (Co-chair, HPC)	University of Georgia, USA
Kevin Daimi (Co-chair, Security)	University of Detroit Mercy, USA
Leonidas Deligiannidis (Co-chair, Imaging Science, AI)	Wentworth Institute of Technology, USA
Richard Dill (Co-chair, Military and Defense Modeling)	US Air Force Institute of Technology, USA
Ken Ferens (Co-chair, Cognitive Computing & AI)	University of Manitoba, Canada
David de la Fuente (Co-chair, Information Management)	University of Oviedo, Spain
Farid Ghareh Mohammadi (Co-chair, Computer Vision & AI)	Mayo Clinic, USA
Michael R. Grimaila (Co-chair, Military and Defense Modeling)	US Air Force Institute of Technology, USA

Douglas D. Hodson (Co-chair, Military and Defense Modeling)	US Air Force Institute of Technology, USA
Masahito Ohue (Co-chair, Mathematical Modeling)	Tokyo Institute of Technology, Japan
Jose A. Olivas (Co-chair, Information Management)	University of Castilla - La Mancha, Spain
Javier Ordus (Co-chair, Quantum Computing & AI)	Baylor University, USA
Pablo Rivas (Chair, Quantum Computing & AI)	Baylor University, USA
Farzan Shenavarmasouleh (Co-chair, Computer Vision & AI)	MediaLab Inc, USA
Robert Stahlbock (Co-chair, Data Mining)	Universität Hamburg, Germany
Masami Takata (Co-chair, Mathematical Modeling)	Nara Women's University, Japan
Quoc-Nam Tran (Co-chair, Education & Bioinformatics)	Southeastern Louisiana University, USA
Nobuaki Yasuo (Co-chair, Mathematical Modeling)	Tokyo Institute of Technology, Japan

IPCV 2024 Program Committee – Image Processing, Computer Vision, and Pattern Recognition

Nizar Al-Holou	University of Detroit Mercy, USA
Mahmood Al-khassaweneh	Lewis University, USA
Soheyla Amirian	Pace University, USA
Hamid R. Arabnia	University of Georgia, USA
Alireza Bagheri Rajeoni	University of South Carolina, USA
Azita Bahrami (Vice-chair)	IT Consult, USA
Juan-Vicente Capella-Hernandez	Universitat Politècnica de València, Spain
Juan Jose Martinez Castillo	Director, Universidad Nacional Abierta, Venezuela
Kevin Daimi	University of Detroit Mercy, USA
Zhangisina Gulnur Davletzhanovna	Central Asian University, Kazakhstan; and International Academy of Informatization, Kazakhstan
Leonidas Deligiannidis	Wentworth Institute of Technology, USA
Trung Duong	Rutgers University, USA

Mary Mehrnoosh Eshaghian-Wilner	University of Southern California, USA; and University of California Los Angeles, USA
Farid Ghareh Mohammadi	Mayo Clinic, USA
Ray Hashemi (Vice-chair)	Georgia Southern University, USA
Byung-Gyu Kim	Sun Moon University, South Korea
Tai-hoon Kim	University of Tasmania, Australia
Guoming Lai	Sun Yat-sen University, China
Hyo Jong Lee	Chonbuk National University, South Korea
Muhammad Naufal Bin Mansor	Universiti Malaysia Perlis, Malaysia
Andrew Marsh	HoIP Telecom Ltd, UK
Aree Ali Mohammed	University of Sulaimani, Iraq
Robert Ehimen Okonigene	Ambrose Alli University, Nigeria
James J. (Jong Hyuk) Park	SeoulTech, South Korea
Farzan Shenavarmasouleh	Medialab Inc., USA
Hayaru Shouno	University of Electro-Communications, Japan
Ashu M. G. Solo (Publicity)	Maverick Technologies America Inc., USA
Sim Kok Swee	Multimedia University, Malaysia
Fernando G. Tinetti	Universidad Nacional de La Plata, Argentina
Hahanov Vladimir	Kharkiv National University of Radio Electronics, Ukraine
Haoxiang Harry Wang	Cornell University, USA; and GoPerception Laboratory, USA
Shiuh-Jeng Wang	Central Police University, Taiwan
Layne T. Watson	Virginia Polytechnic Institute & State University, USA
Jane You	Hong Kong Polytechnic University, China

IKE 2024 Program Committee – Information and Knowledge Engineering

Nizar Al-Holou	University of Detroit Mercy, USA
Soheyla Amirian	Pace University, USA
Hamid R. Arabnia	University of Georgia, USA
Travis Atkison	University of Alabama, USA
Kevin Daimi	University of Detroit Mercy, USA
Zhangisina Gulnur Davletzhanovna	Central Asian University, Kazakhstan; and International Academy of Informatization, Kazakhstan
Leonidas Deligiannidis	Wentworth Institute of Technology, USA
Mary Mehrnoosh Eshaghian-Wilner	University of Southern California, USA; and University of California Los Angeles, USA

Contents

**Image Processing, Computer Vision, and Pattern Recognition (IPCV)
- Detection Methods**

Information and Knowledge Engineering (IKE)

Image Processing, Computer Vision, and Pattern Recognition (IPCV)

Improving Accuracy of Image Clustering Using Convolutional Neural Network and Learning from Confusion

Md Farhad Mokter and Jung Hwan Oh[(✉)]

Department of Computer Science and Engineering, University of North Texas, Denton, TX, USA
Mdfarhadmoker@my.unt.edu, Junghwan.oh@unt.edu

Abstract. Image clustering is a very useful but difficult task in machine learning and computer vision. Recently, convolutional neural network (CNN) is taking a major role in image clustering in which it is used to extract features to be used for an objective function of similarity or dissimilarity measures. There are two problems in the image clustering methods using CNN. First, it is still challenging to estimate a correct number of clusters initially, which decides the quality of the clustering result mostly. Second, a clustering algorithm frequently clusters some images with semantically different contents, into a same cluster (due to their similar color distributions) and generates incorrect clustering result. In this paper we propose a framework for image clustering with CNN and learning from confusion, which can address these problems. The experiments show that the proposed framework increases image clustering effectiveness significantly.

Keywords: Deep Learning · Image clustering · Learning from confusion · ImageNet

1 Introduction

Image clustering is an essential analysis tool in machine learning and computer vision. Many applications such as content-based image annotation [1] and image retrieval [2] can be viewed as different instances of image clustering [3]. Traditionally, various clustering methods have been explored, including K-means [4, 5], agglomerative clustering [9], and so on. When the number of clusters is unknown initially, validity indices can be used to find a cluster number where they are supposed to be independent of clustering algorithms [6]. Many cluster validity indices had been proposed in the literature, such as Bayesian information criterion (BIC) [7], Akaike information criterion (AIC) [8], Dunn's index [9], Davies-Bouldin index (DB) [10], Silhouette Width (SW) [11], Calinski and Harabasz index (CH) [12], Gap statistic [13], generalized Dunn's index (DNg) [14], modified Dunn's index (DNs) [15], extended k-means called X-means [16], and Elbow method [17].

Clustering methods are mostly based on an objective function of similarity or dissimilarity measures, which uses features extracted from each image. Recently, efforts

L. Deligiannidis et al. (Eds.): CSCE 2024, CCIS 2262, pp. 3–17, 2025.
https://doi.org/10.1007/978-3-031-85933-5_1

have focused on deep feature learning methods, such as the autoencoder [18] or the auto-encoding variational bayes [19] for extracting the features. There are two problems in the image clustering using CNN. First, it is still difficult to find a correct number of clusters initially. The quality of the clustering result heavily depends on the accurate selection of initial number of clusters. Second, there are two images with semantically different contents but have a similar color distribution. So, a clustering algorithm clusters these two images into a same cluster and generates incorrect clustering result. In this paper we propose a framework (see Fig. 1) for image clustering with CNN and learning from confusion, which can address these problems.

As seen in Fig. 1, Step 1 of the proposed framework is to extract a feature from each image in an image dataset using a pretrained CNN [20]. For convenience, we call the image dataset as $D_{initial}$, which is given initially. Since the proposed framework performs multiple iterations where this image dataset is updated in each iteration, we call this updated image dataset as D_{sure} ($D_{sure} = D_{initial}$ initially in the first iteration). The feature is a result of the fully connected layer of a pretrained CNN. Typically, the size of result of the fully connected layer is very large, so we apply Principal Component Analysis (PCA) [21] to reduce it. The results of Step 1 are the feature values to be used further. Now each image has a feature value, so we can do the clustering. Most clustering algorithms need to know how many clusters there in the dataset to start the actual clustering. In Step 2, the number of clusters for the image dataset, D_{sure} is estimated using one of the methods mentioned above (i.e., Silhouette Width (SW) [11], ...). Now it is ready to apply an actual clustering algorithm.

In Step 3, a clustering method [4, 5] is applied to D_{sure}, and generates C number of clusters. In Step 4, a CNN with C number of classes is trained using the clustering result in the previous step. In Step 5, all images in D_{sure} are fed into the CNN trained in the previous step, and a classification result with C number of classes from D_{sure} is obtained. During the classification, *not-sure* images are identified and collected to a set, $D_{not-sure}$. The images that do not have any dominant probability in the final *softmax* layer in the CNN is called *not-sure* images. If the exit condition ($D_{not-sure}$ has less than a certain number (T) of images) is satisfied, then Step 6, the final clustering for the initially given image dataset, $D_{initial}$ is performed. Otherwise (if the exit condition above is not satisfied), Steps 2 to 5 are performed again in the second iteration. Repeating iteration will be continued until the exit condition above, which is that $D_{not-sure}$ has less than a certain number (T) of images, is satisfied. The value of T can either zero or very small number. In each iteration, new clusters (C_i) and new CNN (CNN_i), where i = iteration number, are generated, and D_{sure} is updated using the following Eq. (1).

$$D_{sure} = D_{sure} - D_{not-sure} \qquad (1)$$

We assume that the CNN and the number of classes (clusters) obtained from the last iteration is called CNN_S and C_S respectively, which means that CNN_S has C_S number of classes (clusters). In the final step (Step 6), all images in $D_{initial}$ are fed into CNN_S, and its result becomes the final clustering result. Our contribution is summarized as follows. First, the proposed framework is very flexible, any clustering and classification methods can be used. Second, the clustering accuracy is significantly improved when compared with that of single major clustering method. The rest of the paper is organized as follows.

Section 2 discusses the related work. Section 3 describes the proposed methodology. Section 4 shows our experimental results. Finally, Sect. 5 summarizes our concluding remarks.

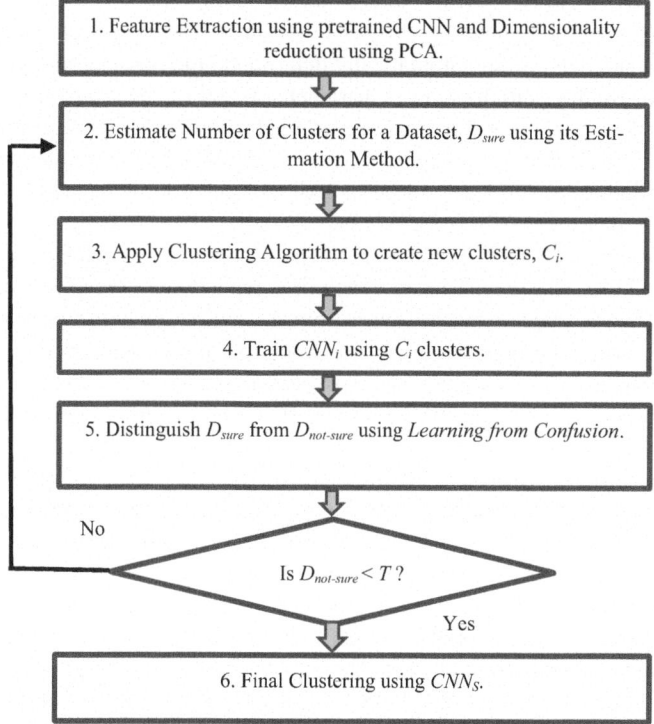

Fig. 1. Overview of the proposed framework

2 Related Works

In this section, we discuss some recent works that involve clustering of images. An image clustering algorithm was proposed, which uses multi-feature extraction of images [22]. The algorithm first applied some preprocessing i.e., cropping, graying, bilateral filtering and LaPlace filtering on the target images. Then the preprocessed images were used for multi-features (i.e., SIFT, ORB and color histogram) extraction and fusion. A set of 60 images was used for the experiment. Multiple experiments were carried out on the same dataset with different combination of feature extractions. The proposed study reported an accuracy of 89.9%, 95.8%, 96.5% and 99.0% in four different experiments.

Another study introduced Deep Adaptive Clustering (DAC) [3] for an image clustering. DAC transformed the problem into a binary pairwise classification framework using a deep ConvNet to generate label features. An Adaptive Learning algorithm trained the ConvNet on labeled samples. DAC achieved 97.75% of clustering accuracy on MNIST,

52.18% on CIFAR-10, and 46.99% on STL-10. The lack of ground-truth similarities in image clustering was addressed in this study by proposing Adaptive Learning algorithm which relied on an iterative process with labeled samples.

A study of unsupervised learning schema based the k-means clustering algorithm (U-kmeans) [23] was proposed for addressing the common challenge of initialization which is to specify the number of clusters in advance. The proposed unsupervised k-means (U-kmeans) algorithm automatically determined the optimal number of clusters without requiring any initialization or parameter selection. The algorithm employed entropy-type penalty terms and a competition schema to determine the optimal number of clusters. The experiments used both synthesized and real datasets which included Iris dataset and Wine dataset. The accuracy rate (AR) for the proposed method was reported as 89% for Iris dataset, and 70% for Wine dataset.

A multi-view-based learning model performed image clustering and local structure learning simultaneously [24]. This approach first generated a graph for each view and then weighted each graph to build a unified representation for K-means to produce the final clusters. Once the optimal graph was obtained, it was partitioned into specific clusters without using any parameters. Experimental results showed that this approach achieved 78% of accuracy, an NMI score of 0.78, and a purity score of 0.89 using Caltech101 dataset.

An Autoencoder based Deep Convolutional Embedded Clustering (DCEC) [25] algorithm was presented, which combined convolutional neural networks and local structure preservation for enhanced deep clustering. Using a convolutional autoencoder structure, the algorithm learned embedded features from image datasets and incorporated a clustering-oriented loss directly on the CovNet features. The process refined the features and assigned clusters by using feature maps and corresponding embedded points, while maintaining local structure through decoder retention. The proposed approach was performed on three datasets: MNIST-full dataset with 7,000 hand-written digits, MNIST-test dataset with 10,000 images, and USPS dataset with 9,298 Gy-scale hand-written images. The DCEC reports an accuracy of 88.97%, 85.29% and 79.00% on MNIST-full, MNIST-test and USPS dataset respectively.

3   Proposed Framework

We discuss the details of the six steps in Fig. 1 in this section.

3.1   Feature Extraction

A pretrained model [26] is used as a feature extractor for the proposed framework. Some example models are ResNet18 [27], VGG19 [21], Inception v3 [28], etc. We use ResNet18 with some modifications. We remove the batch normalization from the last two residual blocks of the model, and the stride from the convolutional layer to preserve the spatial resolution of the feature map. As all the images in the given image dataset ($D_{initial}$ initially, and D_{sure} after the first iteration as discussed in Introduction) are passed through the model, it generates a feature for each image. A result obtained from the fully connected layer of the model is considered as a feature.

After the feature extraction, we apply Principal Component Analysis (PCA [21]) to the features for dimensionality reduction. Reducing the feature can contribute to the model efficiency by saving memory requirements and computational time, and by retaining only meaningful information in the feature space rather than redundant ones.

3.2 Estimation of Number of Clusters

To estimate the number of clusters, we discuss Silhouette method [19] which is a technique of determining the optimal number of clusters in a dataset. The process begins by applying k-means clustering to the dataset multiple times, each with a different number of clusters (k). This variation allows an exploration of different clustering configurations, starting from k = 2 and increasing incrementally. For each data point in every clustering solution, the silhouette coefficient is calculated. This coefficient ($S(i)$) is a critical measure that evaluates how similar a data point is to its own cluster compared to other clusters. It is calculated using the following formula:

$$S(i) = \frac{b(i) - a(i)}{\max\{a(i), b(i)\}} \tag{2}$$

where $a(i)$ is the average distance of the i-th data point from other points in the same cluster, and $b(i)$ is the average distance of the i-th data point from the points in other clusters. The silhouette coefficient values range from -1 to +1. The effectiveness of each k-value is then assessed by averaging the silhouette coefficients of all data points in the dataset. The average silhouette coefficient is used to determine the number of clusters. The value that yields highest average silhouette coefficient is considered as the optimal number of clusters.

3.3 Clustering Images

In this step, we perform the unsupervised part of the proposed framework. Using the extracted features and the estimated number (i.e., C_i) of clusters in the previous steps, we can perform the clustering of images. We use K-means clustering with Euclidean Distance as the distance function. As a result, there are Ci clusters. The clustering result is used to train a new CNN in the next step.

3.4 Training CNN

The clustering result (i.e., C_i clusters in which each cluster has a certain number of similar images. $i = 1$ initially and it will increase by 1 for each iteration) from the previous step is used as a training image dataset to train a CNN. For better illustration, we name it CNN_i. To train CNN_i, we treat each cluster as a single class. We use the clustering result without any further preprocessing, hence the number of classes for CNN_i is same as C_i. The CNN_i starts with an initial block which contains a convolutional layer with 64 filters in which their size is 7x7 with a stride of 2. This convolutional layer is followed by a 3x3 max pooling layer with the same sized stride. This block is followed by another block which consists of two convolutional layers with 64 filters in which their size is 3x3 with a stride of 2. The convolutional layer is followed by a batch normalization layer and a ReLU activation function. The CNN_i has two more blocks that consist of two convolutional layers followed by batch normalization layer and ReLU activation function. The numbers of filters in these two blocks are 128 and 256 respectively. These blocks help extracting important features from the samples. After these blocks, an average pooling function is applied to reduce the feature map before the final layer. The final layer concludes the network by returning the final number (C_i)) of classes with predictive values.

We use the data augmentation [29] for CNN_i. Since the number of images is limited overall, we try to evaluate different views of each image throughout the training. We apply Random-rotation and Flipping of the images for the augmentation which helps the model to generalize the data better during training process.

3.5 Learning from Confusion

In this step, all the images in D_{sure} ($D_{sure} = D_{initial}$ in the first iteration, and $D_{sure} = D_{sure} - D_{not\text{-}sure}$ from the second iteration and after) are fed into the CNN trained in the previous step, and a classification result with C number of classes from D_{sure} is obtained. A set of *not-sure* images is identified in this process, which is referred as $D_{not\text{-}sure}$. During the evaluation, we can find some images that do not have any dominant probability in the final *softmax* layer in the CNN. When an image is evaluated by the CNN, the CNN generates probability values for each target class for that image. If the CNN is trained properly, the CNN is confident in the classification, which means a probability value of a certain class is remarkably higher than those values of all other classes. But sometimes, the CNN generates very close probability values in which there is no remarkably higher one. For example, consider a 4-class classification problem. For a test image, the CNN returns four probability values: $P_1 = 0.25$, $P_2 = 0.20$, $P_3 = 0.30$ and $P_4 = 0.25$. While the classification function can make final decision based on highest probability value of p3 = 0.30, the model is not confident enough about the score. The other probability values are very close to the highest one, which indicates the model is not confident about its choice returned for the image. The images for which the model is not confident in the classification is called the *not-sure* images. *Not-sure* images can be distinguished using the algorithm 1 below. For our experiment, we mark an image as *not-sure* if the highest probability value is less than a certain threshold ($P_{threshold}$).

Algorithm 1: *Not-sure* Image Determination

| **Input:** | A set of Images, D. |
| **Output:** | Classification Result for each image, "class label" or *not sure* |

1.	For Each Image I in the dataset D:
2.	- Evaluate I using the CNN.
3.	- Generate probability values $P_1, P_2...P_n$ for each class.
4.	- Calculate the highest probability P_{max} from $P_1, P_2...P_n$.
5.	- If : P_{max} < a certain threshold $(P_{threshold})$;
6.	Mark the Image I as *not-sure*
7.	- Else:
8.	Assign the class corresponding to P_{max}
9.	Repeat for next Image.

If the exit condition ($D_{not\text{-}sure}$ has less than a certain number (T) of images) is satisfied, then the final clustering for the image dataset, $D_{initial}$ is performed in Step 6. Otherwise (if the exit condition above is not satisfied), Steps 2 to 5 are performed again in the second iteration. Repeating iteration will be continued until the exit condition above, which is that $D_{not\text{-}sure}$ has less than a certain number (T) of images is satisfied. The value of T can be either zero or very small number. In each iteration, new clusters (C_i) and new CNN (CNN_i) (where i = iteration number) are generated, and D_{sure} is updated using the Eq. (1).

3.6 Final Clustering

As discussed above, Steps 2 to 5 are repeated in each iteration which generates a new CNN trained with a new clustering result. We consider the number of images in $D_{not\text{-}sure}$ as the key factor to control the iteration. We stop the iteration if we have less than T number of images in $D_{not\text{-}sure}$. The value of T shall be zero or very small in this case. Once the iteration is terminated, we initiate the final clustering. The number of classes (clusters) obtained after the last iteration is denoted as C_s as discussed in Introduction. We train the final CNN using C_s number of classes. This CNN is called CNN_s. Finally, all the images from $D_{initial}$ are fed into the final CNN (CNN_s) and the result of this evaluation is the final clustering result.

4 Experimental Results

In this section, we discuss the datasets used for the experiments, and the performance evaluations of the proposed framework. The experiments were implemented in a Linux environment using NVIDIA GTX 1650 4GB GPU on a system of 32 GB RAM and core-i7 8th generation with 3.20 GHz processor. Keras, a python package, was used as the framework for all the networks.

4.1 Description of Dataset

We use a subset of ILSVRC dataset [30] for the experiments. Our image dataset consists of 15,600 images, has 12 distinct classes, in which each class contains 1300 images. Their sizes are various ranging from 100 × 120 to 1200 × 1600 pixels. All images were resized to 224 × 224 pixels before passing into the model. We chose a balanced dataset with equal number of images in each class to ensure that each class and their representative features are equally treated by the model to avoid any possible biases. The images in each class of the dataset are visually different from others shown in Fig. 2. Most of the images in the dataset clearly shows the main object with different variations of scales and angles. Some images also contain unclear objects and backgrounds. We keep those images to make the model robust to different outliers. For our experiment, we divide this dataset into the smaller datasets with various combinations of the classes as follows:

Dataset 1 – Class 4, Class 5, and Class 6.
Dataset 2 – Class 1, class 2, Class 3, and Class 4.
Dataset 3 – Class 9, class 10, Class 11, and Class 12.
Dataset 4 – Class 6, Class 7, Class 8, Class 9, and Class 10.

(a)   (b)   (c)   (d)   (e)   (f)

(g)   (h)   (i)   (j)   (k)   (l)

Fig. 2. Sample Images from each class in the Image Dataset. (a) Class 1-whale, (b) Class 2-newtt, (c) Class 3-owl, (d) Class 4-parrot, (e) Class 5-duck, (f) Class 6-dog, (g) Class 7-meerkat, (h) Class 8-butterfly, (i) Class 9-starfish, (j) Class 10-rabbit, (k) Class 11-panda and (l) Class 12-Rock beauty fish.

As described in Sect. 3.1, the modified ResNet18 is used to extract the features from the images in each of the dataset. The model returns a feature vector of 2,048 values for each of the images. We apply PCA to reduce the dimension of feature vector. The PCA returns a feature vector of 1,024 values, which is used in the next steps. The number of clusters is estimated using Silhouette method as discussed in Sect. 3.2. For our experiments we set Silhouette method to generate the number of clusters between 2 to 10, which means it only returns the number of clusters between this range for a given dataset. Once we obtain the number of clusters C_i, we plug that value to clustering algorithm (K-means) and generate actual clusters as described in Sect. 3.3. A new CNN is trained using those clusters and *not-sure* images are distinguished from the initial Dataset of the images as discussed in Sects. 3.4 and 3.5. We repeat the same process until we have a number of *not-sure* images, which is less than a certain threshold value, T. We set T

value as 10 which was determined experimentally. We stop the iterations if we have less than T number of images in the $D_{not\text{-}sure}$. Once the iteration is terminated, we perform the final clustering step as discussed in Sect. 3.6. The number of classes obtained after the last iteration is denoted as C_s. We train the final CNN using C_s number of classes. The CNN is called CNN_s. Finally, all images from $D_{initial}$ are fed into the final CNN (CNN_s) and the result of this evaluation is the final clustering result.

4.2 Evaluation with Precision and Recall

The experiments were carried out in each of the dataset above and the results are reported in terms of typical *Precision* and *Recall*. The results for Dataset 1 are shown in Table 1. Dataset 1 consists of Class 4, Class 5 and Class 6. The proposed framework returns an average precision and recall of 0.92 for this dataset. It takes only one iteration to generate this result. The number of *not-sure* images in the first iteration is a zero (T = 0). The first iteration returned three clusters.

Table 2 shows the results of Dataset 2 which consists of four classes. The proposed framework took two iterations for Dataset 2. The first iteration returned 36 not-sure images, so it repeated the second iteration which returned 9 *not-sure* images. The first and second iterations returned four clusters. It shows that an average precision and recall of 0.89 and 0.88 respectively. Class 3 yielded the highest precision and recall of 0.90 and 0.93, whereas Class 4 returned the lowest ones of 0.87 and 0.81.

Table 1. Results for Dataset 1.

Classes	Class 4	Class 5	Class 6	Average
Correct	1,204	1,209	1,198	
Incorrect	113	96	80	
Total	1,317	1,305	1,278	
Precision	0.91	0.92	0.93	0.92
Recall	0.92	0.93	0.92	0.92

Table 2. Results for Dataset 2.

Classes	Class 1	Class 2	Class 3	Class 4	Average
Correct	1,189	1,181	1,219	1,065	
Incorrect	146	117	128	155	
Total	1,335	1,298	1,347	1,220	
Precision	0.89	0.90	0.90	0.87	0.89
Recall	0.91	0.90	0.93	0.81	0.88

Table 3. Results for Dataset 3.

Classes	Class 9	Class 10	Class 11	Class 12	Average
Correct	1,143	1,170	1,113	1,139	
Incorrect	156	159	163	157	
Total	1,299	1,329	1,276	1,296	
Precision	0.87	0.88	0.87	0.87	0.87
Recall	0.87	0.90	0.85	0.87	0.87

Table 4. Results for Dataset 4.

Classes	Class 6	Class 7	Class 8	Class 9	Class 10	Average
Correct	1,082	1,142	1,077	1,143	1,124	
Incorrect	206	199	189	155	183	
Total	1,288	1,341	1,266	1,298	1,307	
Precision	0.84	0.85	0.85	0.88	0.85	0.85
Recall	0.90	0.87	0.82	0.87	0.86	0.86

The proposed framework returned an average precision and recall of 0.87 for Dataset 3. It took two iterations to reach this conclusion. The first iteration returned five clusters. It returned 29 images as *not-sure*. The second iteration returned 4 clusters where the number of *not-sure* images dropped down to 8 (Table 3).

Datasets 4 consist of five classes. It also took three iterations to generate the final clustering results. The first iterations generated 53 *not-sure* images, and returned six clusters. The next iteration was initiated after discarding the *not-sure* images, and returned five clusters. The number of *not-sure* images in the second iteration was 27. So, the third iteration was done, and it returned 6 *not-sure* images and the accuracy was calculated using new clusters. The average precision for Dataset 8 was 0.85 and the average recall was 0.86 (Table 4).

As seen from the tables above, the number of iterations increases as the number of classes in a dataset increases. While the first three dataset took only one iteration with no *not-sure* images, the number of iterations increased to three with the increase of the classes in Dataset 8. Also, as the number of classes increases, the precision and recall drop.

Figure 3 shows some examples of images that are classified incorrectly. As seen from the images, most of them do not clearly portray the target objects from their backgrounds. Sample (a) belongs to Class 3 ("owl") but was misclassified as Class 7 ("meerkat"). The main object ("owl") is zoomed out further which makes it smaller than the other object. Due to the lack of light on the frame, the object gets less attention by the feature extractor. Sample (b) belongs to Class 2 ("newt") but was misclassified as Class 8 ("butterfly"). Sample (c) belongs to Class 4 ("parrot") but was misclassified as Class 8 ("butterfly").

There is not much color difference between the object and background in these two images, therefore the CNN fails to capture the necessary information to distinguish them. Sample (d) belongs to Class 7 ("meerkat") but was misclassified as Class 10 ("rabbit"). Sample (g) belongs to Class 10 ("rabbit") but was misclassified as Class 7 ("meerkat"). As seen in these two images, the different objects look similar with each other. Sample (e) belongs to Class 8 ("butterfly") but was misclassified as Class 4 ("parrot"). Sample (e) contains the target object for a very small area compared to the entire image area. In this sample, the flower gets more attention by the feature extractor compared to the object. Sample (f) belongs to Class 6 ("dog") but was misclassified as Class 11 ("panda") due to the lack of light and the different angle of the object. Sample (h) belongs to Class 9 ("starfish") but was misclassified as Class 2 ("newt"). It shows an example of starfish, that looks different for its angle and position in the image. To summarize, we observe that, there are many factors that can lead to incorrect classification which include, lack of lights, position, angle of object, and visual similarities of images among different classes.

4.3 Evaluation with NMI and ARI

We also evaluated the quality and robustness of the clustering results by calculating the Normalized Mutual Index (NMI) [31] and Adjusted Random Index (ARI) [32]. NMI calculates the mutual information among the predicted clusters and actual ground-truth clusters, and expresses the amount of mutual information that is shared by the clusters. It can be calculated as follows:

$$\text{NMI}(X, Y) = \frac{2 \times I(X, Y)}{H(X) + H(Y)} \tag{3}$$

where I (X, Y) is the Mutual information between two cluster X and Y. It calculates the amount of information shared by X and Y, and can be described by the calculation:

$$\text{I}(X, Y) = \sum_{i=0}^{|X|} (\sum_{j=1}^{|Y|} (\frac{|X_i \cap Y_j|}{N} \text{Log} \frac{\log(N|X_i \cap Y_j|)}{|X_i \times Y_j|})) \tag{3}$$

where, $|X_i|$ and $|Y_j|$ refer to the size of clusters X_i and Y_j, and N is the number of total data points for clusters. H(X) and H(Y) refer the entropy, a measure of uncertainty of the cluster X and Y, and can be defined as follows. The NMI score is derived from the context of Mutual information theory.

$$H(X) = \sum_{i=0}^{|X|} (\frac{|X_i|}{N} \log(\frac{|X_i|}{N})) \tag{4}$$

$$H(Y) = \sum_{j=0}^{|Y|} (\frac{|Y_j|}{N} \log(\frac{|Y_j|}{N})) \tag{5}$$

The Adjusted Rand Index (ARI) calculates a similarity between clusters by counting pairs of samples that are assigned to same or different clusters in predicted and actual ground-truth clusters. ARI ranges from -1 to + 1. ARI can be derived as follows:

$$ARI = \frac{Rand\ Index - Expected\ Index}{Max\ Index - Expeced\ Index} \qquad (6)$$

Here, Rand Index is computed from data based on decisions of pairing elements. Max Index is the maximum possible value of the index, which is 1. Rand Index can be defined as follows:

$$Rand\ Index,\ E_{rand} = \frac{a + d}{a + b + c + d} \qquad (7)$$

(a)   (b)   (c)   (d)

(e)   (f)   (g)   (h)

Fig. 3. Examples of Incorrectly classified images.

Expected Index is calculated by the following equation:

$$Expected\ Index,\ E_{exp} = \frac{(a + b)(a + c) + (c + d)(b + d)}{a + b + c + d} \qquad (8)$$

Those parameters, a, b c, and d in the above two equations are defined as follows using ground truth clusters $G = (G_1, G_2,....G_n)$ and predicted clusters $P = (P_1, P_2,....P_n)$.

- a = number of data that get same cluster in both G and P (true positive).
- b = number of data that get same cluster in P, but has different clusters in G. (false negative)
- c = number of data that has same clusters in G, but get different cluster in P. (false positive)
- d = number of data that get different clusters in both G and P (true negative).

The comparison results of NMI and ARI scores are shown in Tables 5 and 6. The second columns in those two tables indicate the comparison results of "Initial Clustering" (the clustering result after the first iteration) with the actual ground-truth clustering. And the third columns in those two tables indicate the comparison results of "Final Clustering" (the clustering result after the last iteration) with the actual ground-truth clustering. As seen in the tables, the initial clustering returns lower NMI and ARI scores compared to those from the final clustering. It means that the scores from the final clustering outperformed those from the initial clustering for all datasets.

Table 5. Comparison Initial Clustering to Final Clustering using Normalized Mutual Index (NMI).

Dataset	Initial	Final
Dataset 1	0.66	0.89
Dataset 2	0.56	0.86
Dataset 3	0.51	0.84
Dataset 4	0.45	0.82
Average	0.568	0.851

Table 6. Comparison Initial Clustering to Final Clustering using Adjusted Random Index (ARI).

Dataset	Initial	Final
Dataset 1	0.75	0.87
Dataset 2	0.69	0.86
Dataset 3	0.68	0.86
Dataset 4	0.67	0.86
Average	0.712	0.865

Moreover, the scores of the initial clustering for both NMI and ARI are decreasing when the number of clusters are increasing from Dataset 1 towards Dataset 4. For Dataset 1, the scores of NMI and ARI after the initial clustering is 0.66 and 0.75 respectively, which drop down to 0.45 and 0.67 for Dataset 4. This trend in the scores indicates that a typical clustering struggles when the number of clusters is increasing.

With more iterations, the final clustering shows more consistent numbers with higher scores of NMI and ARI. The min-max difference of NMI scores in the initial clustering is 0.21 (0.66–0.45) while that in the final clustering is 0.07 (0.89–0.82). The min-max difference of ARI scores in the initial clustering is 0.08 (0.75–0.67) while that in the final clustering is 0.01 (0.87–0.86). It shows that the proposed iterative clustering can produce more robust and consistent result, even with the increase on number of clusters (classes) in the datasets.

5 Concluding Remarks

There are two problems in the image clustering. First, it is still challenging to estimate a correct number of clusters initially, which decides the quality of the clustering result mostly. Second, a clustering algorithm frequently (due to the similar color distributions of the images in the given dataset) clusters some images with semantically different contents, into a same cluster and generates incorrect clustering result. In this paper we proposed a framework for image clustering with CNN and learning from confusion, which can address these problems. The experiment empirically demonstrates the effectiveness of the proposed framework on image clustering task and validates that both CNN and learning from confusion are vital to clustering images. More investigation is necessary for the iteration stop condition (i.e., $D_{not\text{-}sure}$ has less than a certain number (T) of images).

References

1. Qi, G., Liu, W., Aggarwal, C., Huang, T.: Joint intermodal and intramodal label transfers for extremely rare or unseen classes. T-PAMI, pp.1360–1373 (2016)

2. Jégou, H., Chum, O.: Negative evidences and co-occurences in image retrieval: the benefit of PCA and whitening. In: Fitzgibbon, A., Lazebnik, S., Perona, P., Sato, Y., Schmid, C. (eds.) Computer Vision – ECCV 2012: 12th European Conference on Computer Vision, Florence, Italy, 7–13 Oct 2012, Proceedings, Part II, pp. 774–787. Springer, Berlin, Heidelberg (2012). https://doi.org/10.1007/978-3-642-33709-3_55

3. Chang, J., Wang, L., Meng, G., Xiang, S., Pan, C.: Deep adaptive image clustering. In: 2017 IEEE International Conference on Computer Vision (ICCV), pp. 5880–5888. Venice, Italy (2017)

4. Gowda, K., Krishna, G.: Agglomerative clustering using the concept of mutual nearest neighbourhood. Pattern Recogn. 10(2), 105–112 (1978)

5. Wang, J., Wang, J., Song, X., Xu, H., Shen, Li. S.: Optimized cartesian k-means. IEEE Trans. Knowl. Data Eng. 27(1), 180–192 (2015). https://doi.org/10.1109/TKDE.2014.2324592

6. Halkidi, M., Batistakis, Y., Vazirgiannis, M.: On clustering validation techniques. J. Intell. Inform. Syst. 17(2/3), 107–145 (2001)

7. Kass, R.E., Raftery, A.E.: Bayes factors. J. Am. Stat. Assoc. 90(430), 773–795 (1995)

8. Bozdogan, H.: Model selection and Akaike's information criterion (AIC): the general theory and its analytical extensions. Psychometrika 52(3), 345–370 (1987)

9. Dunn, J.C.: A fuzzy relative of the ISODATA process and its use in detecting compact well-separated clusters. J. Cybern. 3(3), 32–57 (1973)

10. Davies, D.L., Bouldin, D.W.: A cluster separation measure. IEEE Trans. Pattern Anal. Mach. Intell. $\mathbf{PAMI\text{-}1}$(2), 224–227 (1979)

11. Rousseeuw, P.J.: Silhouettes: A graphical aid to the interpretation and validation of cluster analysis. J. Comput. Appl. Math. 20, 53–65 (1987). https://doi.org/10.1016/0377-042 7(87)90125-7

12. Calinski, T., Harabasz, J.: A dendrite method for cluster analysis. Commun. Statist. Theory Methods 3(1), 1–27 (1974)

13. Tibshirani, R., Walther, G., Hastie, T.: Estimating the number of clusters in a data set via the gap statistic. J. Roy. Stat. Soc., Ser. B, Stat. Methodol. 63(2), 411–423 (2001)

14. Pal, N.R., Biswas, J.: Cluster validation using graph theoretic concepts. Pattern Recognit. 30(6), 847–857 (1997)

15. Ilc, N.: Modi_ed Dunn's cluster validity index based on graph theory. Przeglad Elektrotechniczny (Elect. Rev.) 88(2), 126–131 (2012)

16. Pelleg, D., Moore, A.: X-Means: extending k-means with efficient estimation of the number of clusters. In: Proceedings of the 17th International Conference on Machinery Learning, pp. 727–734. San Francisco, CA, USA (2000)

17. Ketchen, D.J., Jr., Shook, C.L.: The application of cluster analysis in Strategic Management Research: An analysis and critique". Strat. Manage. J. 17(6), 441–458 (1996)

18. Bengio, Y., Lamblin, P., Popovici, D., Larochelle, H.: Greedy layer-wise training of deep networks. In: Schölkopf, B., Platt, J., Hofmann, T. (eds.) Advances in Neural Information Processing Systems 19: Proceedings of the 2006 Conference, pp. 153–160. The MIT Press (2007). https://doi.org/10.7551/mitpress/7503.003.0024

19. Kingma, D., Welling, M.: Auto-encoding variational bayes. CoRR, abs/1312.6114 (2013).

20. Sarwinda, D., Paradisa, R.H., Bustamam, A., Anggia, P.: Deep learning in image classification using residual network (ResNet) variants for detection of colorectal cancer. Procedia Comput. Sci. 179, 423–431 (2021)

21. Bajwa, I.S., Naweed, M., Asif, M.N., Hyder, S.I.: Feature based image classification by using principal component analysis. ICGST Int. J. Graph. Vis. Image Process. GVIP 9, 11–17 (2009).

22. Huang, P., Pan, X., Tao, J.: Research on image clustering algorithm based on multi-features extraction. In: 2021 33rd Chinese Control and Decision Conference (CCDC), pp. 7272–7276 (2021).

23. Sinaga, K.P., Yang, M.S.: Unsupervised K-means clustering algorithm. IEEE Access **8**, 80716–80727 (2020)
24. Nie, F., Cai, G., Li, J., Li, X.: Auto-weighted multi-view learning for image clustering and semi-supervised classification. IEEE Trans. Image Process. **27**(3), 1501–1511 (2017)
25. Guo, X., Liu, X., Zhu, E., Yin, J.: Deep clustering with convolutional autoencoders. In: Neural Information Processing: 24th International Conference, ICONIP 2017, Guangzhou, China, 14–18 Nov 2017, Proceedings, Part II 24, pp. 373–382 (2017).
26. Deng, J., Dong, W., Socher, R., Li, L.J., Li, K., Fei-Fei, L.: Imagenet: A large-scale hierarchical image database. In: 2009 IEEE Conference on Computer Vision and Pattern Recognition, pp. 248–255 (2009).
27. Awan, M.J., et al.: Image-based malware classification using VGG19 network and spatial convolutional attention. Electronics **10**(19), 2444 (2021)
28. Joshi, K., Tripathi, V., Bose, C., Bhardwaj, C.: Robust sports image classification using InceptionV3 and neural networks. Procedia Comput. Sci. **167**, 2374–2381 (2020)
29. Rebuffi, S.A., Gowal, S., Calian, D.A., Stimberg, F., Wiles, O., Mann, T.A.: Data augmentation can improve robustness. Adv. Neural Inform. Process. Syst. **34**, 29935–29948 (2021)
30. Russakovsky, O., Deng, J., Su, H., Krause, J., Satheesh, S., Ma, S., Fei-Fei, L.: Imagenet large scale visual recognition Challenge. Int. J. Comput. Vis. **115**, 211–252 (2015)
31. Akbarpour, N., Akbari, E., Motameni, H.: External clustering validity index based on extended similarity measures. J. Comput. Sci. **72**, 102116 (2023)
32. Li, Y., Peng, H., Liu, Z., Peng, D., Zhou, J.T., Peng, X.: Contrastive clustering. Proc. AAAI Conf. Artific. Intell. **35**(10), 8547–8555 (2021). https://doi.org/10.1609/aaai.v35i10.17037

Analysis of Driver Attention to Objects While Driving

Kolby Sarson and Michael Bauer[(✉)] [iD]

Department of Computer Science, The University of Western Ontario,
London, ON N6A5B7, Canada
{ksarson2,bauer}@uwo.ca

Abstract. A driver's gaze has often been used to estimate driver attentiveness or focus during driving. These works often rely on simple definitions of what it means to "see", namely, a driver's gaze falling on an object for a single frame. In this work, we consider a definition of "seen" which requires an object to be gazed upon for a set length of time, or frames, before it can be considered as seen by the driver. This is done by examining consecutive frames to find those where the driver's gaze remains uninterrupted within a bounding box of a given tracked object over a series of frames. Reliance on multiple frames allows enough time for a driver to process the object gazed upon. We analyze driver gaze on traffic-related objects identified in frames from actual driving sequences. We then consider the impact of different lengths of frame sequences and the size of bounding box overlap across frames on which objects can be taken as "seen" by the driver.

Keywords: Object Recognition · Object Tracking · Point of Gaze · Advanced Driving Systems

1 Introduction

1.25 million. This is the estimated number of fatalities caused by automotive accidents worldwide each year, with these accidents being the leading cause of death for young people, ranging in age from 15–29 [25]. These fatal accidents also account for approximately 3% of government GDP annually [25]. With such significant numbers, intelligent driving systems, including both autonomous vehicles and Advanced Driver Assistance Systems (ADAS), have the potential to significantly reduce serious accidents. ADAS in particular have and continue to be developed with the purpose of reducing driver error. ADAS often consist of a variety of tasks to assist drivers in driving more safely. Some examples include adaptive cruise control, forward collision warnings, lane departure warnings, and traction control.

According to the U.S. Department of Transportation, National Highway Traffic Safety Association (NHTSA), lack of driver attention is cited as the number one cause of accidents, specifying drowsiness and distractions as sources of attention breakers [24]. Drivers also pay less attention to driving activities due to an excessive trust in driving assistance and car safety features [22].

L. Deligiannidis et al. (Eds.): CSCE 2024, CCIS 2262, pp. 18–30, 2025.
https://doi.org/10.1007/978-3-031-85933-5_2

When a driver is on the road it is assumed that they will take in and process their surroundings. Unfortunately, humans are not capable of seeing everything, and must actively choose to pay attention to important objects and events in the driving arena. Research in human perception has established that there is a strong association between what a driver is gazing at and what their mind is engaged with [13, 17]. Human gaze behavior consists of saccades and fixations. Saccades are very fast movements adjusting the eyes from one fixation to another. Objects are only recognized during fixation phases. Eye fixation falls into pre-attentive and attentive fixations phases [4]. During pre-attentive fixations, the driver explores the surroundings to discover crucial objects. This type of eye fixation usually takes 150 ms to 250 ms. On the other hand, attentive fixations are estimated to between 250 ms and 500 ms. Thus, a driver "sees" what they gaze at for a sufficient period of time.

To gain a better understanding of what drivers are aware of during actual driving, we analyze what drivers see and do not see while driving. To know if a driver has "seen" an object we consider two factors, whether the driver's gaze has fallen onto the object and how long their gaze remained on said object. As for the object in question, we will utilize a predetermined set of common traffic objects, including various vehicles (cars, buses, trucks, bicycles), traffic signs, and pedestrians. We perform object detection on a dataset collected from drivers during actual driving activities and consider the driver's observation of objects during the driving sequence to identify those objects which are both "seen" and "missed" given our definitions of "seen".

This paper is organized as such: In Sect. 2 we look at some prior work in the fields of advance driver assistance systems, traffic object detection, driver's gaze, and other related topics. In Sect. 3 we describe our data and present the our overall approach. Results are presented and discussed in Sects. 4 and 5 provides a conclusion and directions for future work.

2 Related Work

In this Section we briefly review related work, specifically, Advanced Driver Assistance Systems (ADAS), driver gaze and perception.

2.1 Advanced Driver Assistance Systems

Advanced Driver Assistance Systems, or ADAS, are systems implemented to "enhance, among other things, active and integrated safety" [7, 19]. With the success of ADAS, research has focused on advancing it in a variety of areas, ranging from improvement of current systems, to ideas for whole new ADAS which could benefit drivers. Nidamanuri et al. [15] provides a review of these research areas including automotive electronics, vehicle-to-vehicle (V2V) and vehicle-to-infrastructure (V2I) communication, RADAR, LIDAR, computer vision, and machine learning. This review outlines areas where more research is required for some of the existing ADAS technologies, such as collision avoidance systems, traffic sign recognition, and lane change assistance.

Other research has looked to address some of the other challenges for ADAS. These include approaches for dealing with driver drowsiness and distraction, handling varied illumination and occlusions. The problems of inconsistent illumination and occlusion of objects are sub-problems in the object detection domain. While in the drowsiness and distraction category, driver perception of objects may well benefit from the knowledge of a driver's object of attention. Dong et al. [9] proposed an approach for determining drowsiness or distraction of the driver. Various factors which may indicate drowsiness or distraction are collected and these factors are then searched for during testing, ultimately contributing to the classification of driver fatigue (utilizing a Random Forest) and driver distraction (utilizing an CNN). Of these factors, the driver's attention on objects, either inside or outside of the vehicle, is not considered, though the approach does consider gaze directions (left, right, center) and blink frequency. Another attempt to recognize driver distraction is presented by Banerjee et al. [3]. In this work, the gaze direction was utilized but divided into 6 categories instead of the 3 used in the previous work discussed. This work also considers "down", "rearview mirror", and "instrument cluster" as gaze directions. Although this work does not handle the driver distraction itself, it does tackle glance estimation which is an important part of distraction. Like the previously discussed work, this research also does not account for the driver's attention on objects.

2.2 Driver Gaze

Driver's gaze is a term used to describe where a driver is looking while driving. Past approaches relied on either vision-based methods or learning-based methods. Vision-based methods focus more on the driver and their head/eye positions to estimate gaze while learning-based methods focus on the use of machine or deep learning practices, with or without driver head/eye data to estimate gaze.

Looking at vision-based approaches, Murphy-Chutorian et al. [14] and Baker et al. [2] provide early work in the area of head pose estimation while Hansen et al. [11] provide a summary of eye detection frameworks as well as the gaze estimation prior to 2010. Sugano et al. [21] proposed a gaze estimation framework which auto-calibrates through the use of saliency maps. This work provides solid groundwork in the area of gaze estimation, but is limited to stationary head position.

For learning-based approaches, with the help of eye gaze tracking, Bublea et al. [8] produce two Deep Neural Networks (DNN) which can determine the driver's behavior (drowsiness, distracted, etc.) during a driving sequence. They proposed two methods for eye gaze estimation, a geometric approach and an auto-keras approach, ultimately producing almost identical results. Sugano et al. [21] used saliency maps on eye imagery to estimate the gaze of users watching a video.

Other research looks to combine vision and learning based approaches to estimate gaze. This is exemplified in the work done by Shirpour et al. [20], considering the position of the driver's head in relation to a forward stereo system implemented within an experimental vehicle. Gaussian process regression is then implemented using this head pose to estimate the gaze direction as a confidence interval. This approach is less hardware intensive and does not require eye tracking capabilities. During further investigation, Shirpour et al. integrate eye tracker data to determine a singular point of gaze in the driving scene. With these two sets of data (the gaze estimation and the eye tracker data) the eye fixation is then estimated. This final driver's eye fixation estimation is exhibited as a confidence region on the frame image.

2.3 Driver Perception

Previous research on what a driver is or was looking at has made use of driver gaze or head position to try to determine on what a driver is focusing. Approaches have used computation of gaze or area of focus to do this.

Huang et al. [12] consider driver focus of attention (DFoA) and True DFoA (TDFoA) to produce a driver distraction detection (DDD) method. They developed a tool to predict TDFoA along with determining the DFoA to determine whether a driver is distracted or not. They focus on the driver's attention in a singular frame and only consider the attention area, not whether the object is seen or not. Work by Tang et al. [23] combines driver gaze data and a car's perception of the environment to accentuate the objects of concern only if they are deemed as "not perceived" by the driver. This research assumes that perception is defined by a point of gaze on the environment within a single frame.

In the DR(eye)VE project, Palazzi et al. [16], look to predict what drivers will pay attention to while driving. Rather than focusing on the driver's gaze in a frame, a series of frames is considered. These frames are analyzed and in the final frame of the series, a fixation map is produced to show the areas most likely to be looked at by the driver. The work does not look to identify the specific objects that a driver may be gazing at. Doshi and Tivedi [10] examined gaze patters and the relationship to driver intent.

Research closest to the work presented here is by Bär, et al. [4] and by Shabani, et al. [18]. Bär presented an approach to determine the driver's attention to different types of traffic objects: bikes, cars, trucks, pedestrians. They make use of a database of feature vectors for traffic objects extracted from a laser-scanner unit. The feature vector includes information on the object, such as the object's velocity, distance to the ego-vehicle, dimensions, heading, type, color, etc. Objects are considered as "seen" if they are attentively fixated for longer than 250ms and an awareness confidence exceeds 0.5 for each traffic object. Using this data they build a decision tree representing the gaze behavior of the driver for different driving contexts, e.g. driving a curve or driving a car through a narrow gap. This can then be used to assess how well the driver pays attention to certain critical objects in those situations. The work does not specifically address objects "seen" by the driver over a drive and does not consider other traffic objects, such as signs or lights.

The work by Shabani et al. looks to assess whether drivers are seeing traffic signs present during driving sequences. The definition of "seen" used is one which looks for the driver's point of gaze and whether it intersects with a traffic sign over a number of frames. The work analyzes the sequence of images from drives with an instrumented vehicle; a point of gaze is associated with each frame as determined by onboard cameras on the driver. Each frame is analyzed for traffic signs and their bounding boxes are recorded. Consecutive frames are analyzed to determine how long the point of gaze remains on a particular sign. If the gaze remains on a sign beyond a threshold, the sign is considered "seen". Our work extends this approach by considering more diverse objects as well as well as how consecutive signs are determined.

3 Methodology

The data used in our analysis consisted of actual driving sequences from a single driver. This data was collected from an instrumented vehicle equipped with a variety of sensors and cameras capturing driving data during actual drives [5]. The data collected includes frontal stereoscopic video, driver head position and angle, and driver ocular parameters. The OBD-II system provides various vehicle subsystem information, including the current speed and acceleration (longitudinal and lateral), steering wheel rotation, state of accelerator and brake pedals.

For the work presented here, the analysis focused on the video and driver gaze data. The video frames provide a visual image displaying the area in front of the vehicle and the driver; the videos sequence consisted of 101,220 frames of data after removing a small number of noisy frames from the beginning and end of the sequence. In terms of gaze data, a Point of Gaze (PoG) of the driver was associated with each video frame. This PoG is presented as a coordinate (x,y) which may fall within or outside of the current frame, as the driver may not always be looking straight ahead (or in frame). To determine the Point of Gaze, cameras which focus on the driver's eyes were utilized to determine the position and direction of the eye, and then software was used to compute the gaze vector. The gaze vector was then mapped to the same coordinate system as the video images of the visual environment which was finally used to determine the point of gaze. The details on how this was done is described Beauchemin et al. [6].

To determine what a driver "sees" or does not "see", we analyze the video and gaze data in three steps. Our first step is to analyze the video frames to identify the relevant objects of interest, i.e., those of some importance during drives. In our work we considered traffic signs (10 different signs), vehicles (cars, trucks, buses), traffic signs (green, red, yellow and unclear) and pedestrians. Each identified object in frame is represented by a bounding box with coordinates defining its position in the frame. The second step is then to determine for each frame whether the driver's PoG falls on to one of the identified objects. Finally, the sequence of frames, with identified objects and PoG, are analyzed to identify consecutive frames where the same object is under the gaze of the driver. We briefly describe these steps in the following.

3.1 Object Detection

The object detection method used for this research was based on the work of Shirpour [25], which utilized a neural net to detect bounding boxes and label them. The neural net is a compilation of two separate models, model A and model B. Each of these models provided benefits to the final neural net; model A provided better results on smaller or further objects while model B provided better results for larger or closer objects. Model A consisted of two parts, a multi-scale HOG-SVM and a ResNet-101 network, whereas Model B utilized a Faster R-CNN. Evaluating the neural net object detection framework on sets of available images resulted in classification accuracies of 96.1%, 96.2%, and 94.8% for traffic signs, traffic lights, and vehicles respectively.

3.2   Determining Point of Gaze in Each Frame

The next step was to link the PoG coordinates to the bounding box data. The gaze data is used to compute a gaze vector directed outward from the eye. The gaze vector is then mapped to the same coordinate system as the video, producing an intersection between the two. This intersection determines the Point of Gaze on an individual frame.

Upon completion of this step, there was a single file containing all pertinent data: frame number, the PoG coordinates, bounding box measurements (top-left coordinate, width, and height) and object label for each bounding box in the frame. This output could also be visualized to ensure correct processing; Fig. 1 illustrates the labeled output; the " +" indicates the Point of Gaze which, in this case, is on the background.

Fig. 1. Driver PoG represented by a cross in the frame.

3.3   Consecutive Frame Analysis

The final step was to find all series of images in which the driver gazed at a bounding box for a number of consecutive frames. To do this we first find all frames in which the PoG falls within any bounding box for that frame. Then we look for sequences of consecutive frames where the gaze fell on the "same" bounding box in each frame. Starting with the first frame in a sequence, the bounding box containing the PoG was compared to the bounding box containing the PoG in the following frame. The upper left corner of the bounding boxes (an arbitrary choice) were compared and if the difference (in pixels) exceeded a threshold in either direction, the two boxes were considered different; otherwise the two boxes were considered to be the same object. Our analyses considered different thresholds (see Sect. 4).

The result of this processing was a table containing information on the sequences where the PoG remained in the same bounding box for the entire sequence **and** of a minimum length. In our analysis we examine several different lengths.

Table 1. Object Types Considered in Analysis

Category	Object Type	Category	Object Type
Backgrounds	Background	*Traffic Signs (continued)*	Keep to Right
Pedestrians	Pedestrian		Lane Turns Right
Vehicles	Bus		Maximum Speed Limit
	Car		No Trucks
	Truck		No Turns
Traffic Lights	Traffic Light Green		Not a Through Street
	Traffic Light Not Clear		Parking
	Traffic Light Red		Pedestrian Crossover
	Traffic Light Yellow		Railroad Crossing
Traffic Signs	Arrow		Right Lane Ends Ahead
	Bicycle Lane		Stop
	Construction		Traffic Light Ahead
	Do Not Enter		Watch For Pedestrian
	Exit Only		Yield

4 Analysis and Results

In this section we provide some of the results of our analyses. For our purposes we will define "seen" as an object which has been gazed upon for a minimum number of frames during the driving sequence. This number must be large enough that the driver could be considered to have acknowledged the object. As noted in the Introduction, attentive fixation is assumed to be at least 250 ms, or about 8 frames and pre-attentive fixation to be at least 150 ms, or about 5 frames. In our full analysis we considered frame sequences from 3 to 30 (0.1 to 1 s). Due to space considerations, we report on frames sequences of 5 to 10. We also considered different thresholds for differences between bounding boxes in two consecutive frames. This is an important threshold in determining which bounding boxes are considered to be the same object. We investigated thresholds ranging from 10 pixels to 30 pixels, but limit our focus on thresholds of 10, 20 and 30 for this paper.

4.1 On Objects Seen

The goals of this research were to understand what objects were seen or not seen by drivers and whether there were differences in the types of traffic objects seen or not seen by a driver. Our processing of the images considered 28 different types of objects (see Table 1) which formed 5 categories: Background (1), Pedestrians (1), Vehicles (3), Traffic Signs (18) and Traffic Lights (4); in some situations the traffic light could be identified but its color was obscured or not clear and so it was classified as an "unclear"

Table 2. Categories of Objects Gazed at for Different Minimum Frame Sequence Lengths and Thresholds for Matching Bounding Boxes.

Threshold 10	Minimum Sequence Length					
Category	**5**	**6**	**7**	**8**	**9**	**10**
Backgrounds	1	1	1	1	1	1
Pedestrians	26	18	12	9	9	6
Vehicles	1410	1017	737	560	438	331
Traffic Lights	27	22	13	10	9	8
Traffic Signs	14	8	7	5	3	2
Objects "Seen"	1478	1066	770	585	460	348
Threshold 20	**Minimum Sequence Length**					
Category	**5**	**6**	**7**	**8**	**9**	**10**
Backgrounds	2	2	2	2	2	2
Pedestrians	33	27	18	14	13	11
Vehicles	1436	1182	977	819	716	609
Traffic Lights	42	38	30	28	25	21
Traffic Signs	18	13	9	8	7	5
Objects "Seen"	1531	1262	1036	871	763	648
Threshold 30	**Minimum Sequence Length**					
Category	**5**	**6**	**7**	**8**	**9**	**10**
Backgrounds	0	0	0	0	0	0
Pedestrians	2	2	2	2	2	2
Vehicles	1318	1102	915	781	605	595
Traffic Lights	44	40	32	30	27	23
Traffic Signs	20	16	22	9	8	6
Objects "Seen"	1418	1189	979	837	746	638

traffic light. For Backgrounds and Pedestrians, there were no distinguishing types, i.e., a road, a building, a tree, the car's dashboard, were all treated as background. Similarly, there was no distinguishing among different classes of pedestrians.

Table 2 summarizes the results of driver gaze at objects for different frame sequences and for different thresholds used to match bounding boxes in consecutive frames. As is evident from the table, the driver's gaze is primarily on vehicles, significantly more often than on other types of objects. This trend is observed across the thresholds used. The number of objects in a category does drop, for object types, as the minimum length of the frame sequence increases, i.e., gaze on the same object in more consecutive frames is required. Given that that this is an urban environment where there is a significant number vehicles on the road, a driver's focus on vehicles while driving makes sense. A breakdown of the percent of cars, trucks and buses and total vehicles compared to the total number of objects gazed at is presented in Table 3.

Table 3. Percentages of Vehicles Gazed at for Different Minimum Frame Sequence Lengths and Thresholds.

Threshold 10	Minimum Sequence Length					
Category	5	6	7	8	9	10
Cars	80.11	81.14	80.90	80.00	78.91	78.45
Trucks	6.56	6.19	6.36	6.50	6.74	6.61
Buses	8.73	8.07	8.44	9.23	9.57	10.06
All Vehicles	95.40	95.40	95.71	95.73	95.22	95.11
Threshold 20	Minimum Sequence Length					
Category	5	6	7	8	9	10
Cars	76.22	77.02	76.74	76.00	76.02	75.77
Trucks	8.23	7.45	8.20	8.50	8.26	7.56
Buses	9.34	9.19	9.36	9.53	9.57	10.65
Objects "Seen"	93.79	93.66	94.31	94.03	93.84	93.98
Threshold 30	Minimum Sequence Length					
Category	5	6	7	8	9	10
Cars	75.54	78.79	78.02	76.89	77.19	77.32
Trucks	9.32	8.53	9.27	9.61	8.47	7.83
Buses	7.37	7.67	8.02	8.52	9.29	9.90
Objects "Seen"	95.23	95.00	95.31	95.01	94.95	95.05

The impact of sequence length and threshold is illustrated in the graph of Fig. 2. A sequence length that is too short creates a larger number of objects though in fact many of these are the result of breaking up images of a single object across multiple frames, e.g. an object actually appearing in 10 consecutive frames would be considered 2 separate objects with a sequence length of 5. Similarly, a restrictive threshold for matching bounding boxes across frames creates objects of shorter length, some of which then fall below the threshold number of frames for being "seen". For example, if an objects exists in an 8 frame sequence, but because of the threshold 10 it becomes two objects each in 4 frame sequences, then these would not be counted as they would fall below the threshold set base on attentive fixation, which would be about 7–8 frames.

We also computed the total number of objects during the drive using the same thresholding method to determine matching objects in consecutive frames. For thresholds of 10, 20 and 30, the number of objects determined were 113,790, 91,967, and 89,134, respectively. This would mean that the driver gazed at roughly 0.5% to 1.6% of the objects. While this may seem like a small number of the total objects recall that: 1) We are only counting objects where the driver's gaze was on the same object for at least

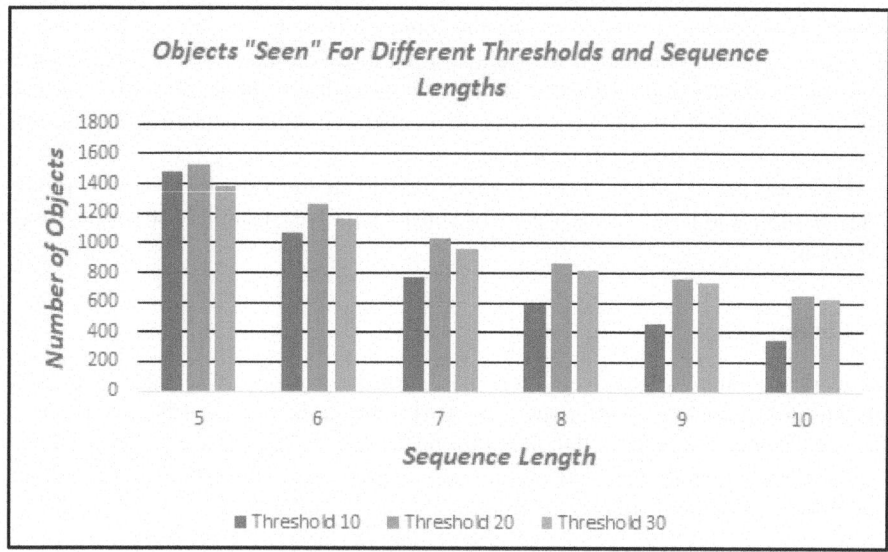

Fig. 2. Comparing Objects "Seen".

some minimum number of frames, e.g., 5, 6, etc.; objects where the gaze was on an object for fewer frames were not counted. 2) Within the field of view of the driver there are many objects that will be picked up by the cameras, some appearing in only few frames. The driver's gaze is focused on one particular object and so others are ignored. Many of these objects, of course, are not relevant, e.g. many signs on the side of the road are not relevant to the driving activity, e.g. advertisements. 3) The driver's gaze is not always on objects in the external environment. The driver may gaze at the dashboard, the rear view mirror, side mirror, telephone, etc. which means that their gaze is not on the environment for some period of time. Yet the objects in the environment are being captured by the cameras.

4.2 Discussion

As discussed, vehicles were the objects most often gazed at by the driver. The driver did gaze at traffic signs. The route had 44 physical traffic lights and so drivers gazed at roughly a quarter to half of the lights. This may seem low, but there are other cues that drivers can use. For example, in some situations the driver might not even look at a traffic light if they are focused on the vehicles in front of them, e.g. if a vehicle is stopped the driver would simply stop. The number of traffic signs suggests that the driver has not looked at many of the signs during the drive. This may not be an issue, since many signs may be irrelevant for the driving activity; as with the traffic light there may be other cues, such as the behavior of other vehicles, that would suggest the action that the driver should take.

The computation depends on the minimum length of the frame sequence and the matching of objects between consecutive frames. Computation of objects considered the same is dependent on the matching threshold. In looking at Table 2}, for each of the sequence lengths considered we see that using threshold 20 results in more objects identified than for those for threshold 10. This suggests that threshold 20 may be a better bound; a threshold of 10 may be too restrictive, resulting in fragmentation. Similarly, a threshold of 30 seems to be a little to generous.

The results presented have focused on a single driver and a single driver of approximately 50 min. Additional drives need to be considered to see if similar patterns in driver gaze occur.

4.3 Limitations

This work examines what drivers "see" based on the analysis of actual driving data collected during real on-road drives. The work introduces a method for determining what a driver gazes at under different constraints based on frame sequence length and a bounding box matching threshold. While successful, there are limitations to the current study which can be addressed in the future.

The analysis was based on actual driving data but from a single driver and single driving sequence. While substantial data was collected, there are occasional gaps in the actual driving data, e.g. driver gaze is not always on the environment, head position or movement can result in missing gaze information. These data gaps can result in a sequence of frames being broken or a frame without a corresponding point of gaze. Examining the gaze behavior of additional drivers would help determine whether this gaze behavior is similar across drivers or whether there are different behaviors.

A bounding box threshold was utilized to identify whether a bounding box was the same object or not between frames. A threshold of 20 seemed to work best, but is was employed uniformly without consideration of object size, distance from ego vehicle etc. Alternative approaches taking size and distance into consideration where the threshold is more dynamic may result in better methods. The work done in [1] proposes a novel bounding box tracking approach which may act as a good starting point for this research.

5 Conclusions and Directions

The results of the study provide insight into what a driver gazes at during drives under different analysis thresholds. For all combinations of the thresholds tested, vehicles were the most common type of object gazed at and with cars being the most common type of vehicle. Given that the drive took place in an urban environment this is not surprising. A consequence of this is that many signs are ignored by the driver. This could be critical in certain driving situations and likely some contextual analysis needs to be considered.

As noted in the introduction, attentive fixation is estimated to be between 250 ms and 500 ms; attentive fixation is needed for object recognition. Thus, the minimum sequence would be 7–8 frames. Thus, the approach can be used to determine what object a driver is likely gazing at and what they are not. Such information could be useful in advanced driving systems to assess whether a driver has missed something critical, e.g. a pedestrian stepping onto the road, or whether a driver is distracted, e.g. looking at a billboard on the side of the road and not paying attention to the vehicle in front.

The focus in this paper has been on driver gaze on objects external to the ego vehicle. What a driver gazes at in the interior of the vehicle and how often is also important as it means that the driver's eyes are not on the external environment. The method proposed could be used to measure this but would require additional data on gaze within the vehicle.

Finally, it would be useful to consider objects gazed at within specific driving contexts. A driver's gaze behavior while driving on a straight road with no vehicle in front would likely be different than the gaze behavior at a busy intersection while trying to make a turn. It would be useful to understand gaze behavior within a number of different driving contexts.

References

1. An, J., Kim, E.: Novel vehicle bounding box tracking using a low-end 3D laser scanner. IEEE Trans. Intell. Transp. Syst. **22**(6), 3403–3419 (2021). https://doi.org/10.1109/TITS.2020.299 4624
2. Baker, S., Matthews, I., Xiao, J., Gross, R., Ishikawa, T., Kanade T.; Real-time non-rigid driver head tracking for driver mental state estimation. Report CMU-RI-TR-04-10, Carnegie Mellon University, Pittsburgh, Pennsylvania (2004)
3. Banerjee, S., Joshi, A., Turcot, J., Reimer, B., Mishra, T.: Driver glance classification in-the-wild: towards generalization across domains and subjects, In: Proceedings 16th IEEE International Conference on Automatic Face and Gesture Recognition (FG 2021), pp. 1–8. IEEE, New York (2021). https://doi.org/10.1109/FG52635.2021.9667084
4. Bär, T., Linke, D., Nienhüser, D., Zöllner, J.M.: Seen and missed traffic objects: A traffic object-specific awareness estimation, In: Proceedings 2013 IEEE Intelligent Vehicles Symposium (IV), pp. 31—36. IEEE, New York (2013). https://doi.org/10.1109/IVWorkshops. 2013.6615222
5. Beauchemin, S., et al.: Roadlab: An in-vehicle laboratory for developing cognitive cars. In: Proceedings. 23rd International Conference on Computer Applications in Industry and Engineering (CAINE), International Society for Computers and Their Applications, Cary, North Carolina, USA (2010). https://api.semanticscholar.org/CorpusID:2921526
6. Beauchemin, S.S., Bauer, M.A., Kowsari, T., Cho, J.: Portable and scalable vision-based vehicular instrumentation for the analysis of driver intentionality. IEEE Trans. Instrum. Meas. **61**(2), 391–401 (2012). https://doi.org/10.1109/TIM.2011.2164854
7. Bengler, K., Dietmayer, K., Farber, B., Maurer, M., Stiller, C., Winner, H.: Three decades of driver assistance systems: Review and future perspectives. IEEE Intell. Transport. Syst. Mag. **6**(4), 6–22 (2014). https://doi.org/10.1109/MITS.2014.2336271
8. Bublea, A., Căleanu, C.: Deep learning based eye gaze tracking for automotive applications: an auto-keras approach. In: Proceedings 2020 International Symposium on Electronics and Telecommunications (ISETC), pp. 1–4. IEEE, New York (2020), https://doi.org/10.1109/ISE TC50328.2020.9301091
9. Dong, B., Lin, H.: An on-board monitoring system for driving fatigue and distraction detection, In: Proceedings 2021 22nd IEEE International Conference on Industrial Technology (ICIT), pp. 850–855. IEEE, New York (2021). https://doi.org/10.1109/ICIT46573.2021.945 3676
10. Doshi, A., Trivedi, M.: Investigating the relationships between gaze patterns, dynamic vehicle surround analysis, and driver intentions, In: Proceedings 2009 IEEE Intelligent Vehicles Symposium, pp. 887–892. IEEE, New York (2009). https://doi.org/10.1109/IVS.2009.516 4397

11. Hansen, D.W., Ji, Q.: In the eye of the beholder: a survey of models for eyes and Gaze. IEEE Trans. Pattern Anal. Mach. Intell. **32**(3), 478–500 (2010). https://doi.org/10.1109/TPAMI. 2009.30
12. Huang, T., Fu, R.: Driver distraction detection based on the true driver's focus of attention. IEEE Trans. Intell. Transp. Syst. **23**(10), 19374–19386 (2022). https://doi.org/10.1109/TITS. 2022.3166208
13. Just, M., Carpenter, P.: A theory of reading: from eye fixations to comprehension. Psychol. Rev. **87**(4), 329–3545 (1980). https://doi.org/10.1037/0033-295X.87.4.329
14. Murphy-Chutorian, E., Doshi, A., Trivedi, M.: Head pose estimation for driver assistance systems: a robust algorithm and experimental evaluation. In: Proceedings 2007 IEEE Intelligent Transportation Systems Conference, pp. 709–714. IEEE, New York (2007). https://doi.org/ 10.1109/ITSC.2007.4357803
15. Nidamanuri, J., Nibhanupudi, C., Assfalg, R., Venkataraman, H.: A progressive review: emerging technologies for ADAS driven solutions. IEEE Trans. Intell. Veh. **7**(2), 326–341 (2022). https://doi.org/10.1109/TIV.2021.3122898
16. Palazzi, A., Abati, D., Calderara, S., Solera, F., Cucchiara, R.: Predicting the driver's focus of attention: the DR(eye)VE project. IEEE Trans. Pattern Anal. Mach. Intell. **41**(7), 1720–1733 (2019). https://doi.org/10.1109/TPAMI.2018.2845370
17. Rucci, M., McGraw, P., Krauzlis, R.: Fixational eye movements and perception. Vision. Res. **100**(118), 1–4 (2016). https://doi.org/10.1038/nrn1348
18. Shabani, S., Beauchemin, S., Bauer, M.: Analysis of Driver Gaze and Attention to Traffic Signs. J. Adv. Transport. 1–13 (2022), https://api.semanticscholar.org/CorpusID:248225290
19. Shadeed, F., Wallaschek, S.: Concept of an intelligent adaptive vehicle front-lighting assistance system. In: Proceedings 2007 IEEE Intelligent Vehicles Symposium, pp. 1118–1121. IEEE, New York (2007). https://doi.org/10.1109/IVS.2007.4290267
20. Shirpour, M.; Predictive Model of Driver's Eye Fixation for Maneuver Prediction in the Design of Advanced Driving Assistance Systems. Electronic Thesis and Dissertation Repository. 7706. The University of Western Ontario (2021)
21. Sugano, Y., Matsushita, Y., Sato, Y.: Appearance-based gaze estimation using visual saliency. IEEE Trans. Pattern Anal. Mach. Intell. **35**(2), 329–341 (2013). https://doi.org/10.1109/ TPAMI.2012.101
22. Suzuki, K., Yamada, K.: Method for evaluating the collision mitigation ratio when using collision avoidance alarm at intersection: Effects of the driver's mental situation on the integrated error of driver and system, In: Proceedings of the Society of Instrument and Control Engineers (SICE) Annual Conference 2010, pp. 1374–1379. IEEE, New York (2010)
23. Tang, R., Jiang, J.: Driver's perception model in driving assist. In: 2020 IEEE 20th International Conference on Software Quality, Reliability and Security Companion (QRS-C), pp. 237–240. IEEE, New York (2020). https://doi.org/10.1109/QRS-C51114.2020.00047
24. U.S. Department of Transportation, National Highway Traffic Safety Association, Critical reasons for crashes investigated in the national motor vehicle crash causation survey, Traffic Safety Facts – Crash Stats (2015). https://www.nhtsa.gov/sites/nhtsa.gov/files/documents/812 409_tsf2015dataspeeding.pdf. Last accessed 19 Aug 2024
25. World Health Organization. Global status report on road safety 2015. World Health Organization, pp. 7–12. https://iris.who.int/handle/10665/189242 (2015). Last accessed 19 Aug 2024

Image-Based Seal Recognition: Approaches and Challenges in Current Automated Systems

Jorge Yero Salazar[1] ⓘ, Renato Borras-Chavez[2] ⓘ, Sarah Kienle[2] ⓘ, and Pablo Rivas[1(✉)] ⓘ

[1] Department of Computer Science, Baylor University, Waco, TX, USA
{Jorge_Yero1,Pablo_Rivas}@Baylor.edu
[2] Department of Biology, Baylor University, Waco, TX, USA
{Renato_Borras-Chavez,Sarah_Kienle}@Baylor.edu

Abstract. This paper examines the challenges and advancements in recognizing seals within their natural habitats using conventional photography, underscored by the emergence of machine learning technologies. We used the leopard seal, *Hydrurga leptonyx*, a key species within Antarctic ecosystems, as our model to review the different available methods found. As apex predators, Leopard seals are characterized by their significant ecological role and elusive nature so studying them is crucial to understand the health of their ecosystem. Traditional methods of monitoring seal species are often constrained by the labor-intensive and time-consuming processes required for collecting data, compounded by the limited insights these methods provide. The advent of machine learning, particularly through the application of vision transformers, heralds a new era of efficiency and precision in species monitoring. By leveraging state-of-the-art approaches in detection, segmentation, and recognition within digital imaging, this paper presents a synthesis of the current landscape, highlighting both the cutting-edge methodologies and the predominant challenges faced in accurately identifying seals through photographic data.

Keywords: Vision Transformer · Object Detection · Semantic Segmentation · Leopard Seals · Seals Detection · Computer Vision

1 Introduction

Like other apex predators, leopard seals, *Hydrurga leptonyx* plays a crucial role in Antarctic ecosystems and has captivated researchers with its distinctive ecological functions and behaviors. Nonetheless, Leopard seals are found in remote locations and research on the species is challenging. Conventional methods of monitoring and gathering data are labor-intensive, time-consuming, and tend to provide restricted information because of the leopard seal's elusive nature. The advent of machine learning has provided a breakthrough in overcoming

L. Deligiannidis et al. (Eds.): CSCE 2024, CCIS 2262, pp. 31–48, 2025.
https://doi.org/10.1007/978-3-031-85933-5_3

these limitations. By integrating machine learning techniques, wildlife research has embraced automated recognition methods that significantly improve the efficiency and accuracy of species monitoring.

Building upon this technological advancement, projects focusing on the recognition of seals have predominantly utilized conventional photographs as the primary data source. We characterize these conventional photographs based on three criteria: they are composed of the standard Red-Green-Blue three-channel color model; their resolution is typical of images taken with handheld cameras; and the focal subject (i.e. Leopard seals) occupies at least 20% of the image area. This categorization generally encompasses images captured by handheld devices and some drone-operated cameras, excluding satellite imagery. Satellite photographs are typically omitted due to their incorporation of additional spectral channels, ultra-high resolution, and a relatively small representation of objects of interest, needing distinct analytical approaches [30]. Within the scope of digital image recognition, accurately identifying the location of seals hinges on the critical processes of detection and segmentation.

Developing any project centered on recognition, along with the essential detection and segmentation stages, fundamentally begins with an examination of the existing state of the art (SOTA) of this area. Therefore, this paper presents a detailed synthesis of the latest advancements in seal recognition through conventional photographs, elucidating the most cutting-edge models and methodologies in the field and highlighting the principal challenges and limitations inherent to the aforementioned processes. To accomplish this, the subsequent sections are organized and presented in a manner that addresses three fundamental questions:

1. What are the most successful SOTA approaches for detecting and segmenting seals using conventional photographs? How do these approaches compare, and what are the biggest challenges?
2. Why have vision transformers (ViT) gained popularity recently compared to other SOTA models in image recognition tasks, and what is their potential application for recognizing seals in surface marine environments?
3. What are the primary challenges associated with recognizing seals from Computer Vision (CV) and Machine Learning (ML)? How do these challenges impact the development and performance of automated detection systems?

We provide examples of some of the revised methodologies and approaches, using leopard seals as our main model and our own photographic dataset of the species.

2   Approaches for Detecting and Segmenting Seals in Conventional Photos

In the rapidly evolving field of CV, object detection and image segmentation are foundational tasks that enable machines to interpret and understand visual data accurately and in-depth. Object detection refers to identifying and locating objects within an image. This involves classifying the types of objects present and pinpointing their positions with bounding boxes or similar markers. Image segmentation takes this further by partitioning an image into multiple segments or pixels to simplify its representation or make it more meaningful. It is a critical step in distinguishing between the object of interest and the background or between different objects in an image.

This section will examine the latest advancements in object detection and image segmentation techniques for seals in conventional photographs. The section also explores image segmentation strategies used in previous studies.

2.1 Seals Detection

This revision focuses on studies incorporating object detection with pinnipeds (true and ear seals) as study models. We found that Pinniped's studies often focus either on seals using non-traditional imagery, like satellite photos [11,12,32], or on different species using conventional images [4,5,27], and rarely tackling both simultaneously. We found only one study that examines seals in conventional photographs and relies on manual face landmark detection [3].

We identified three studies using non/conventional photographs employing Convolutional Neural Networks (CNNs [21]) for object detection in seal species [11,12,32]. When expanding the search to include other species, additional studies emerge. From these, we selected four relevant examples: three that utilize manual detection methods, and one that employs both You Only Look Once (YOLO) [31] and Detector with image classes (Detic) [36] technologies. For a more precise overview of the research landscape and how it intersects with our interests, refer to Table 1, which organizes these studies based on the two critical aspects of our inquiry.

Table 1. Overview of Research Studies on Object Detection in Different Species and Using Different Photographic Domains

Paper	Study Object	Photography Domain	Methodology
[3]	**seals**	**conventional**	Manual
[5]	primates	**conventional**	Manual
[4]	lemur	**conventional**	Manual
[27]	cetacean	**conventional**	YOLO v5, Detic
[32]	**seals**	satellite	R-CNN
[12]	**seals**	satellite	U-Net
[11]	**seals**	satellite	Fast R-CNN

While there are indeed studies focusing on seal detection in non-conventional images [11,12,32], we excluded these studies due to the significant differences in the domain images and the specific pre-processing that is required for them. The images used in these studies typically have very high resolution, resulting in the region containing the seal proportionally much smaller than what is found in conventional photos. Additionally, these non-conventional images often feature more than three color channels in contrast to conventional ones that contain only three. A prevalent method in handling such high-resolution images is to segment them into smaller patches before feeding them into the detection model. This patch-based approach is necessary to manage the large image sizes and the detailed information content, which is not directly applicable to the domain of conventional photography that our research is focused on. Thus, we focus on studies that align with our criteria of using conventional images as their primary domain with different species (ref. Table 1).

Seal Detection on Conventional Photographs. As previously noted, the sole study identified that applies object detection to seals in conventional photographs is the work in [3]. This research aims to establish a model capable of recognizing individual seals by their facial features. Although facial recognition does not directly correspond to the main objective of this section, the initial phase of their approach, which involves detecting seal faces, bears relevance.

The detection phase employs a CNN, details of which were not extensively described in the paper. The methodology includes downscaling the image to reduce dimensionality and augmenting the number of channels using a series of filters. This is followed by applying convolutional layers normalized in batches and utilizing the ReLU activation function.

The study in question underscores the significance of eye landmarks in orienting seal face images for consistent recognition. It's important to highlight that accurate facial recognition, particularly in humans, has been shown to rely heavily on the positioning of the eyes [18]. This investigation successfully culminates in a model that automates the detection of seal faces, marking a significant stride toward individual seal recognition. However, manual intervention is required during data preparation. Following the initial automatic detection of faces, researchers must manually pinpoint the eyes, nose, and mouth locations. The resultant coordinates are critical for the software to perform subsequent image alignment and cropping tasks automatically.

Other Species Detection on Conventional Photographs. The methodology proposed in [3] is similar to the one used in other studies [4,5] that maintain the conventional photography domain but focus their attention on different species, such as lemurs and primates respectively. The primary goal of these works was to identify individuals through facial recognition, in which face detection is also necessary as part of the process. Unlike the seal face detection approach [3], these studies do not employ automatic face detection methods but rely on manually annotated landmarks for the face location. Furthermore, estimating the face's width and height is based on the inter-pupil distance, which is the distance between the centers of the two eyes. This measurement is then used to scale the image so that the eyes are positioned at specific proportions relative to the edges of the cropped face image. Both studies implement a face alignment as a pre-processing step similar to the previously mentioned work.

Furthermore, using conventional photographs from cetaceans, studies have implemented automatic full-body object detection [27]. This research introduces a multi-species individual identification model leveraging two ArcFace heads, a cutting-edge technique in human facial recognition [6,7]. These heads perform dual functions, classifying species and individual identities, thus allowing species to share information and parameters within the network.

The study employs an object detection phase pertinent to our research question as a component of the identification process. This phase aims to crop the image, effectively reducing background noise that may hinder the identification-matching process. The researchers integrated four distinct detectors, each activated according to a specific probability-three based on YOLOv5 [31] and one based on Detic [36].

Comparing Approaches and Identifying Challenges. Comparing state-of-the-art (SOTA) approaches for detecting seals in conventional photographs reveals a landscape where very specific methodologies are applied, each tailored to the unique challenges presented by the subject matter and the medium. The primary difference among the approaches is the balance between manual and automated detection methods. The manual face landmark detection approach suffers from scalability issues due to its manual nature. In contrast, automatic full-body detection offers a more scalable and less labor-intensive solution.

In addressing our specific objective of detecting seals in conventional photographs, the task simplifies to a binary classification problem within a bounding box, where the model must discern whether the box contains a seal or not. This framing does not align with the core strength of Detic, which is designed to manage a wide array of classes for bounding boxes and to identify objects outside the predefined vocabulary. Consequently, our focused application may only partially utilize Detic's ability to handle extensive class variety and predict out-of-vocabulary objects. Conversely, YOLOv5 is celebrated for its optimal balance between speed and accuracy, making it an ideal candidate for applications that demand rapid processing without significantly compromising precision. This attribute of YOLOv5 could be particularly beneficial for scenarios requiring real-time monitoring or immediate analysis.

Seal detection on conventional photographs has many challenges, but the biggest one is the lack of previous work that does not rely on manual annotations. Also, conventional photographs vary widely in quality and resolution, posing significant challenges in identifying small or subtle features crucial for species identification. Manual methods, while precise, are not scalable and require substantial human effort. Automated methods must be adaptable to different species and contexts, which can be challenging given the variability in animal appearances and environmental conditions. Furthermore, high-quality, annotated datasets are crucial for training effective models, yet such datasets are often scarce or difficult to compile for wildlife studies.

The YOLO framework, noted for its agility and accuracy, emerges as a promising solution to these constraints. However, YOLO's true efficacy and applicability over manual and automated approaches like Detic can only be accurately gauged through direct application and comparative analysis. Such empirical testing is crucial to validate YOLO's potential advantages in speed and scalability and explore its adaptability to the diverse quality and resolution in conventional photographs, which pose challenges in accurately identifying seals. In conclusion, while manual and automated detection methods offer valuable insights into seal detection in conventional photographs, their efficacy and applicability vary based on the research objectives, available resources, and specific challenges of working with wildlife imagery.

2.2   Image Segmentation of Seals

In the context of image segmentation, two primary tasks exist: semantic segmentation and instance segmentation. Although both tasks can differentiate between pixels that represent a seal and those that do not in an image, our focus will be on instance segmentation. This choice is motivated by its ability to identify and segment individual instances of the same object separately. In contrast, semantic segmentation treats multiple objects of the same category as a single, unified segment if they are in close proximity or touching. This distinction makes instance segmentation particularly valuable for applications requiring precise identification and differentiation of each object, regardless of its category similarity to others in the image.

Image Segmentation of Seals on Conventional Photographs. A single study emerges from reviewing methodologies for image segmentation of seals [35] emerges as a primary reference. This research explicitly targets the accurate identification of Saimaa ringed seals (*Pusa hispida*). While the focus on individual seal recognition does not directly correlate with our scope, the methodology proposed in [35] is noteworthy. Their approach involves an initial segmentation phase to isolate the seal from the background, followed by applying a separate recognition algorithm to the segmented image. We used our own dataset and provide an enhanced visualization of the methodology described Fig. 1 in [35].

Zhelezniakov et al. [35] highlights the utility of segmentation, mainly because all images are captured during the same seasonal period each year with stationary cameras. This consistency in imaging conditions allows the algorithm to potentially rely on highly similar backgrounds for identification when analyzing the entire image or specific bounding boxes rather than the seals themselves. Zhelezniakov et al. [35] prefer semantic segmentation rather than instance segmentation based on the assumption that each input image contains only a single seal. Given this specific constraint, the task can effectively be treated as instance segmentation since each image contains only one instance for segmentation.

As previously stated, the segmentation process for identifying Saimaa ringed seals in images employs a sophisticated methodology that begins with unsupervised segmentation to divide the image into superpixels or minor, coherent pixel

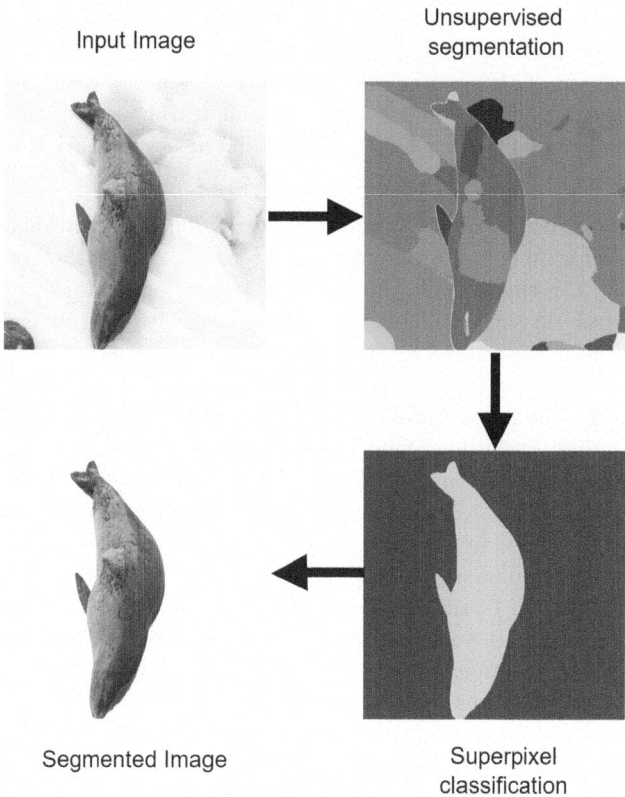

Fig. 1. Methodology for segmentation following the work in [35]. The image was created based on their image methodology but only the part aligned with our question was kept.

clusters. This initial step utilizes a state-of-the-art algorithm combining a Globalized Probability of Boundary (gPb) detector, Oriented Watershed Transform (OWT), and Ultrametric Contour Map (UCM), which together generate superpixels by thresholding a weighted contour image [1,2]. Adjusting the threshold value, the size of the superpixels can be controlled. This adjustment helps pick sufficiently large superpixels for reliable classification while preventing the seal and background from being combined into a single superpixel.

Following unsupervised segmentation, texture features are extracted from the superpixels using Blur Invariant Local Phase Quantization (LPQ) descriptors [26]. These features are particularly suited for processing camera trap images, which often exhibit blur and significant variations in illumination, as they are based on phase information that is invariant to such distortions.

The final step involves classifying each superpixel as either seal or background using a Support Vector Machine (SVM) classifier trained on manually labeled superpixels. This supervised classification process effectively distinguishes seal segments from the background, with the combined seal-classified superpixels forming the final segmented image of the seal for further identification processes. The classification accuracy is determined by intersection over union (IoU) over a certain threshold. This ensures that only those segments with significant conformity to the actual shape and location of the seal are considered accurately classified, thereby maintaining high precision in the segmentation process.

Segment Anything Model. Two studies were identified that discuss segmentation methods for images of different species (see [22, 29]). Although these investigations enrich the theoretical foundation of image segmentation, they diverge from our research objectives. The first study concentrates on images of animals swimming at the water's surface, while the latter uses underwater imagery as its domain.

Consequently, our focus shifts towards one research encompassing a broader range of domains, including conventional imagery. The research conducted by [19] has established a foundational model in segmentation, named Segment Anything Model (SAM), earning widespread recognition within the scientific community as evidenced by its impressive tally of 2,298 citations within the first eleven months post-publication. Although this research is not directly related to image segmentation of seals, the innovative approach of the model suggests that it can be adapted to various tasks through zero-shot transfer using prompt engineering. This advantage enables the application of the model for image segmentation of seals without the need for fine-tuning or manual annotation of seal segments, thereby demonstrating its adaptability and potential for expansive applications across different domains (Fig. 2).

The SAM architecture, illustrated in Fig. 2, processes an input image through an image encoder to generate an embedding. This embedding is then used to produce object masks responding to input prompts. The encoder's core is a Mask Auto Encoder (MAE), leveraging a pre-trained ViT for image encoding [9,16]. Notably, the approach to querying with text diverges from other methods. It serves primarily as a conceptual demonstration for converting text to masks, though the models for this specific functionality have not been made public.

The image encoder remains consistent for other types of queries-points, boxes, and masks. Points and box queries are translated into positional encodings. Mask embeddings are generated through a CNN encoder added to the image embedding. The model outputs a list of pairs, each consisting of a mask and the associated confidence level for that mask.

The model is noteworthy for its versatility and efficiency in segmenting a wide range of objects within images, even those not pre-defined or labeled in existing datasets. This is a significant advancement since traditional segmentation models often require extensive training on large, labeled datasets that cover all possible objects and scenarios they might encounter. Such requirements make them less adaptable to new or rare objects. SAM aims to overcome these limitations by using an approach that can generalize from known objects to novel ones, allowing it to perform segmentation tasks on a broader array of images without needing specific training for each new object type.

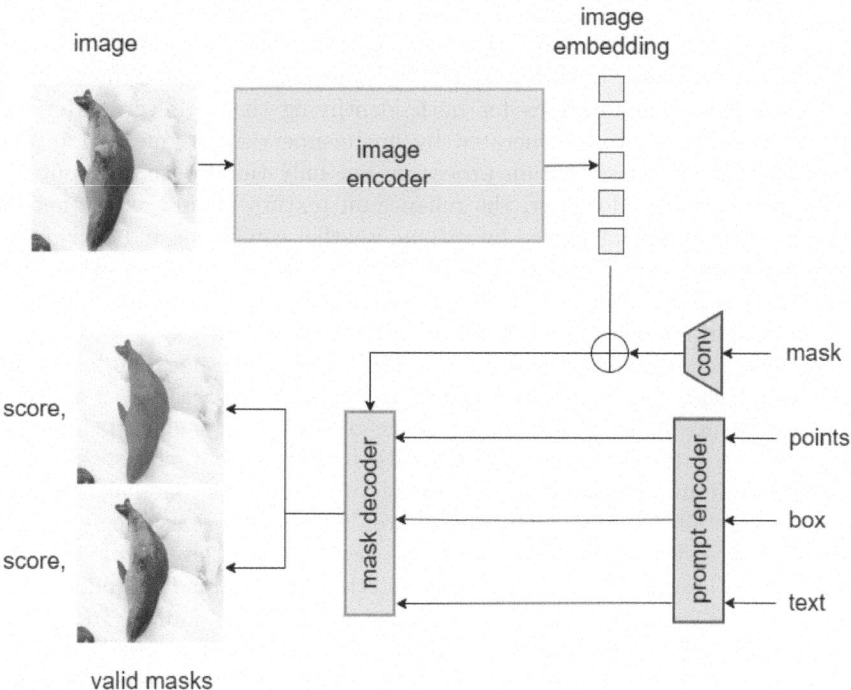

Fig. 2. Segment Anything Model (SAM) overview. Image was based on the architecture figure from [19] using our database.

Further evidence of the model's superiority over existing research is its outstanding performance in interactive segmentation, surpassing state-of-the-art models on 23 distinct datasets [19]. Superior outcomes in human evaluation underscore this achievement and mean intersection over union (mIoU), particularly noting the model's accuracy in segmenting an object given its central point. Additionally, the model demonstrates comparable performance to the advanced ViTDet-H [23] model across various datasets, including COCO [25] and LVIS v1 [14], in terms of average precision (AP). This is notable given that ViTDet-H was specifically trained on these datasets, whereas the Segmenting Anything Model was not. Additionally, in the realm of instance segmentation, where SAM was prompted with the bounding box of the target object, it not only matched but, based on human evaluations, exceeded the performance of ViTDet-H. This suggests that while ViTDet-H may rely on biases inherent in the COCO and LVIS datasets, the SAM approach, free from such training data biases, offers a more generalized and accurate segmentation capability.

Comparing Segmentation Approaches and Identifying Challenges. The superior capabilities of the Segment Anything Model are evident not only because of its innovative approach to image segmentation but also because of its ability to address issues that other studies in this field have yet to be able to overcome. For instance, the study of [35] relies heavily on manual intervention, requiring extensive annotations for both identifying the seals (ground truth) and classifying superpixels generated by an unsupervised segmentation algorithm. This manual classification process is not only time-consuming but also susceptible to errors. Moreover, the reliance on texture feature extraction can lead to inconsistencies influenced by varying weather conditions and background elements. The Segment Anything Model addresses these limitations using zero-shot instance segmentation, which eliminates the need for detailed image segment annotations and requires only the provision of bounding boxes.

Conversely, despite its successes, the SAM [19] can sometimes produce small, disconnected segments within the seal imagery. It also falls short of real-time processing when employing a complex image encoder, thus lagging behind previous methods in terms of speed. SAM tends to over-segment when tasked with straightforward image segmentation of the picture containing the seal, capturing unnecessary details like skin patterns that aren't required for basic segmentation tasks. A proposed solution to mitigate this issue involves leveraging zero-shot transfer with a specified bounding box around the seal, guiding the model to generate a singular, comprehensive segmentation within this boundary. To evaluate this approach and its limitations, we experimented using both methods, with the results depicted in Fig. 3. As illustrated, Fig. 3b includes extraneous segments, whereas providing a bounding box in Fig. 3c results in a singular, accurate segmentation of the seal, aligning with expectations. Although conclusions from a single image are not definitive, they are consistent with anticipated outcomes based on the model's training to detect object subparts.

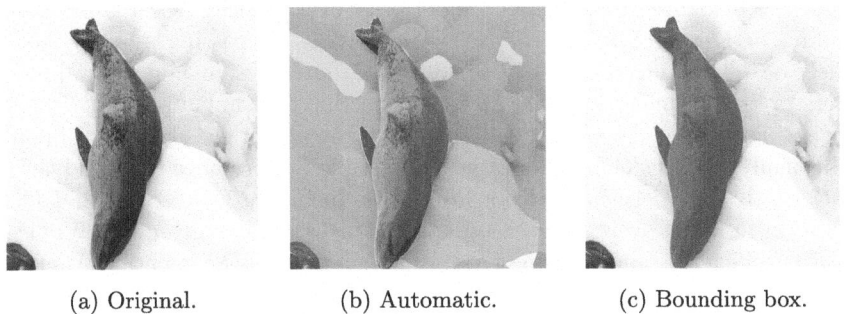

(a) Original.   (b) Automatic.   (c) Bounding box.

Fig. 3. Seal image segmentation using SAM [19].

Altogether, image segmentation of seals still presents significant challenges similar to those encountered in object detection, as outlined in Sect. 2.1. The primary obstacle is the lack of prior research in this area, with limited studies addressing specifically image segmentation of seals methodologies. Compounding this issue is the critical shortage of annotated datasets, which are essential for training robust models. These datasets are particularly rare or challenging to compile, especially in the context of wildlife research. Although employing bounding boxes as input for the SAM represents a promising strategy for image segmentation of seals, the effective implementation of this approach still hinges on the availability of annotated datasets. These datasets, containing bounding boxes as ground truth, and are necessary to train object detection models. Consequently, the challenges previously identified for automatic detectors in Sect. 2.1 remain relevant and apply to the task of image segmentation of seals as well.

Despite these challenges, SAM's demonstrated effectiveness and flexibility make it the preferred method for achieving our objectives of segmenting seals from conventional photographs, offering a promising avenue for advancing image segmentation of seals research.

3   Vision Transformers in SOTA Image Recognition: Applications for Seal Detection

The introduction of Vision Transformer (ViT, [9]) marked a critical milestone in the evolution of deep learning architectures. This innovation was heavily influenced by the unprecedented success of the Transformer model [34] in natural language processing (NLP). The essence of ViT's innovation lies in its application of the standard Transformer architecture to the visual domain, which is implemented with minimal modifications. This approach underscores the versatility of the Transformer model, making an understanding of the original Transformer framework essential for fully appreciating the impact and functionality of ViT.

The Transformer model [34] revolutionized the field of machine translation. This success led to its rapid adoption across various NLP tasks. The profound impact of the Transformer model is evident when examining leading models across various NLP challenges. An outstanding example of its wide-ranging implications constitutes its dominance in the Multi-task Language Understanding (MMLU) benchmark [17], a comprehensive and challenging assessment covering 57 subjects from elementary to advanced professional levels, evaluating world knowledge and problem-solving abilities.

The Transformer architecture includes both an encoder and a decoder. We focus here on the encoder because of its use in ViT. It turns input tokens, x_i, into embeddings, z_i, of a specific size D. It adds positional information to these embeddings to keep track of the order of input, which is essential for understanding language and images. This positional information can be learned or set by rules to avoid looking ahead in the input. These enhanced embeddings then proceed to the multi-head attention layer, where the model calculates attention scores based on queries Q, keys K, and values V, as detailed in (1) below. This part of the model decides how much focus to give each input part by comparing it against all other parts. It uses a mathematical operation (dot product) to calculate attention scores, which are turned into probabilities. These probabilities help select the essential parts of the input to produce an output relevant to the task being performed; attention is generally calculated as:

$$\text{Attention}(Q, K, V) = \text{softmax}(\frac{QK^T}{\sqrt{D}})V. \tag{1}$$

A key factor behind the Transformer's success is its self-attention mechanism, which empowers the model with selective attention capabilities. This means that, following the self-attention process, the model has the potential to "see" all the input at once, understanding the context and the relationships between different parts of the input. Furthermore, the architecture presents significant capabilities for concurrent processing. Each attention head operates independently, allowing for simultaneous computation across heads. After computing attention, the representation of each token in the sequence becomes independent of others, enabling parallel processing across all tokens.

The ViT seeks to adhere closely to the original Transformer architecture. However, an unavoidable adaptation concerns the nature of the inputs; while the Transformer is designed for 1D sequences of tokens, ViT must handle 2D images. ViT divides an image into a sequence of N patches, each of size (P, P), to bridge this gap. These image patches, represented as $x_p \in \mathbb{R}^{N \times (P^2C)}$ where C denotes the number of image channels, are then mapped to a dimension of $N \times D$, aligning with the encoder's dimensionality D. Similar to BERT's approach [8], a particular x_{class} token is a prefix to this sequence. This token is designed to capture the overall representation of the image. The mapping of image patches to the model's dimension and their positional encoding within the image are described by (2) below, where E performs the dimensional mapping, and E_{pos} applies positional encoding. A classification head is attached to the output representation of the artificial x_{class} token for classification tasks. Formally, the process is defined as:

$$z_0 = [x_{class}; x_p^1E; x_p^2E; \cdots ; x_p^NE] + E_{pos}, \tag{2}$$

where $E \in \mathbb{R}^{(P^2C) \times D}$ and $E_{pos} \in \mathbb{R}^{(N+1) \times D}$.

Vision Transformer; the Popular Option. Since the advent of AlexNet [20], Convolutional Neural Networks (CNNs) have been the gold standard in computer vision, dominating the field with their state-of-the-art performance. However, the emergence of ViTs has introduced a paradigm shift. Unlike CNNs, which rely on local receptive fields to process images incrementally, ViTs leverage self-attention mechanisms to analyze entire images holistically. Achieving a similar level of global attention with CNNs would require stacking multiple layers, a process that significantly restrains efficiency compared to the streamlined performance of transformers. This global approach allows ViTs to capture long-range dependencies within the data, a feature especially beneficial for complex recognition tasks where understanding context and spatial relationships is critical.

ViTs have challenged the supremacy of CNNs and showcased exceptional scalability and computational efficiency. As the size of the model scales, ViTs tend to exhibit improved performance, making them exceptionally well-suited for handling large datasets. This scalability, combined with the inherent parallelizability of self-attention mechanisms-more so than convolution operations-positions ViTs as a more computationally efficient choice for extensive tasks [20].

Furthermore, ViTs have demonstrated significant expertise in transfer learning scenarios. They excel at adapting knowledge from extensive datasets to specific tasks with limited data, maintaining high-performance levels. This versatility is invaluable in wildlife monitoring, where obtaining labeled data can be challenging. The availability of pre-trained ViT models of various sizes (82M, 307M, and 632M) further simplifies fine-tuning for specific applications. Collectively, these attributes underscore the growing popularity and potential of ViTs to redefine the landscape of image recognition and beyond, marking a significant milestone in the evolution of computer vision technologies.

3.1   Potential of ViT for Recognizing/Identifying Seals in Surface Marine Environments

The potential of ViTs for recognizing and identifying seals in surface marine environments extend across several key areas:

Fine-grained Classification: ViTs excel in fine-grained classification tasks [15], making them highly effective at distinguishing between closely related seal species or identifying individual seals within a species. This is due to their ability to focus on fine details across the entire image, capturing subtle differences that might elude other models.

Robustness to Environmental Variability: The inherent global perspective of ViTs equips them with a significant advantage in dealing with the environmental variability typical of marine settings, such as changes in lighting, background, and weather conditions [28]. This robustness enhances their reliability and accuracy in real-world applications.

Transfer Learning for Rare Species: ViTs demonstrate exceptional transfer learning capabilities, which can be particularly valuable for recognizing rare or endangered seal species [24]. By fine-tuning pre-trained models on more common species or related tasks, researchers can develop effective recognition systems even with scarce training data for specific rare species [27].

High-Quality Image Embeddings: Utilizing a methodology similar to the image encoder for SAM [19] or for ImageBind [10], a ViT can generate high-quality image embeddings. These embeddings can serve as a robust foundation for seal recognition tasks, offering a sophisticated approach to understanding and classifying marine wildlife imagery.

ViTs are popular because they efficiently process and understand complex image data at once through the attention mechanism [9], making them particularly promising for specialized applications like recognizing seals in marine environments.

4   Challenges in Seal Recognition: Impact on Automated Detection Systems

From the perspectives of Computer Vision (CV) and Machine Learning (ML), several primary challenges are associated with the recognition and identification of seals, impacting both the development and performance of automated detection systems. These challenges include:

Data: High-quality, annotated datasets of seals are crucial for training effective ML models. However, collecting and annotating such datasets is labor-intensive and challenging, particularly for less common species or those living in remote locations. To alleviate this issue, data augmentation techniques using Generative Adversarial Networks (GANs) [13] or Diffusion Models [33] are used to increase the size of the dataset for training time.

Pose Variation: Seals can adopt various poses. The pose of the seal is essential for individual recognition; if we have the right side of a seal, we don't want to try to match it with the left side of a seal. A potential solution is to detect the pose of the seal and combine the pose and the features of the seal; a possible approach is using learnable embedding that represents the pose of the seal and applies it to the seal itself. Figure 4 shows various angles of the same seal, which appear dissimilar due to the images capturing different sides of its body.

(a) Leopard Seal left side of face.   (b) Leopard seal right side of full body.

Fig. 4. Examples of the same leopard seal showing different poses and body sides.

Background and Occlusion: The natural habitats of seals vary from glacial habitats with icebergs acting as the main haul-out substrates for the animals to sandy or rocky beaches. Also, they may be partially occluded by objects in their environment or by other seals. These conditions push the automatic algorithm to extract the correct features of the seal and ignore the background or object in front of the seal. An approach to mitigate this issue is to segment the seal, removing all the background noise and the occluded objects. Figure 5c illustrates a seal in a non-ice background, while Fig. 5a depicts an example of a seal occluded by an object.

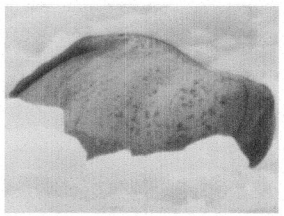  

(a) Leopard seal occluded by ice.

(b) Leopard seal image affected by sunlight.

(c) Leopard seal hauling-out onshore in Antarctica and not on ice.

Fig. 5. Examples of pictures that represent different data challenges.

Weather Conditions: Lighting conditions can dramatically affect the appearance of seals in images, particularly for those captured in the wild. Variations in weather, time of day, and water reflections can alter how seals are visualized, affecting detection consistency. To reduce this issue, data augmentation techniques can augment the dataset by applying different filters to the image, like blurring and sepia. Figure 5b shows an example of a seal where the colors are different due to sunlight.

Variability: Seals can vary significantly in color, size, and shape due to age, species, molting stage, and environmental factors. To effectively address this variability, an ideal approach would involve using a comprehensive dataset with sufficient samples for each seal individual captured across different conditions. Still, if we don't possess enough samples from all the conditions, we can try an approach similar to [27] where we add an additional head to the model. Hence, it can produce species besides the identification. In this way, the idea of the model is that it can transfer learning from similar species to the ones that contain just a few images. Figure 6 illustrates an example of a different seal species (a southern elephant seal, *Mirouga Leonina*) compared to our model species used in Figs. 4 and 5 with specific features in the body and the face that differentiate them.

Fig. 6. Southern elephant seal (*Mirounga leonina*) a different species than our model species leopard seals.

5   Conclusion

Our investigation highlights the transformative potential of machine learning, particularly vision transformers, for seal recognition when using conventional photography. Although traditional methods of seal monitoring present challenges in scalability and adaptability, machine learning emerges as a robust solution, effectively bridging these gaps. Despite their precision, manual detection methods are limited by their lack of scalability. In contrast, automated approaches like the YOLO framework offer scalability and potential for real-time application, yet their efficacy across diverse environmental settings warrants further empirical exploration.

One of the primary obstacles in this domain is the variability inherent in conventional photographic data, influenced by factors like image quality and environmental conditions. Despite these challenges, the advent of machine learning and, specifically, vision transformers, signals a promising avenue for advancing seal monitoring processes. These technologies have the potential to significantly enhance the precision and efficiency of species identification efforts, providing a pathway to more effective, non-intrusive wildlife monitoring.

This research contributes to the broader understanding of applying image processing techniques within wildlife monitoring and conservation science, suggesting that integrating CV and ML could revolutionize environmental conservation practices. Through the lens of ML, we envision a future where monitoring and protecting seal species in their natural habitats is more effective and less intrusive.

Acknowledgments. Part of this work was funded by the National Science Foundation under grants CNS-2210091, OPP-2146068, CHE-1905043, and CNS-2136961.

Disclosure of Interests. The authors have no competing interests to declare that are relevant to the content of this article.

References

1. Arbelaez, P., Maire, M., Fowlkes, C., Malik, J.: From contours to regions: an empirical evaluation. In: 2009 IEEE Conference on Computer Vision and Pattern Recognition, pp. 2294–2301. IEEE (2009)
2. Arbelaez, P., Maire, M., Fowlkes, C., Malik, J.: Contour detection and hierarchical image segmentation. IEEE Trans. Pattern Anal. Mach. Intell. **33**(5), 898–916 (2010)
3. Birenbaum, Z., Do, H., Horstmyer, L., Orff, H., Ingram, K., Ay, A.: Sealnet: facial recognition software for ecological studies of harbor seals. Ecol. Evol. **12**(5), e8851 (2022)
4. Crouse, D., et al.: Lemurfaceid: a face recognition system to facilitate individual identification of lemurs. Bmc Zool. **2**(1), 1–14 (2017)
5. Deb, D., et al.: Face recognition: Primates in the wild. In: 2018 IEEE 9th International Conference on Biometrics Theory, Applications and Systems (BTAS), pp. 1–10. IEEE (2018)
6. Deng, J., Guo, J., Liu, T., Gong, M., Zafeiriou, S.: Sub-center arcface: boosting face recognition by large-scale noisy web faces. In: Vedaldi, A., Bischof, H., Brox, T., Frahm, J.-M. (eds.) ECCV 2020. LNCS, vol. 12356, pp. 741–757. Springer, Cham (2020). https://doi.org/10.1007/978-3-030-58621-8_43
7. Deng, J., Guo, J., Xue, N., Zafeiriou, S.: Arcface: additive angular margin loss for deep face recognition. In: Proceedings of the IEEE/CVF Conference on Computer Vision and Pattern Recognition, pp. 4690–4699 (2019)
8. Devlin, J., Chang, M.W., Lee, K., Toutanova, K.: Bert: pre-training of deep bidirectional transformers for language understanding. arXiv preprint arXiv:1810.04805 (2018)
9. Dosovitskiy, A., et al.: An image is worth 16×16 words: transformers for image recognition at scale. arXiv preprint arXiv:2010.11929 (2020)
10. Girdhar, R., et al.: Imagebind: one embedding space to bind them all. In: Proceedings of the IEEE/CVF Conference on Computer Vision and Pattern Recognition, pp. 15180–15190 (2023)
11. Gonçalves, B.C., Wethington, M., Lynch, H.J.: Sealnet 2.0: human-level fully-automated pack-ice seal detection in very-high-resolution satellite imagery with cnn model ensembles. Remote Sens. **14**(22), 5655 (2022)
12. Gonçalves, B.C., Spitzbart, B., Lynch, H.J.: Sealnet: a fully-automated pack-ice seal detection pipeline for sub-meter satellite imagery. Remote Sens. Environ. **239**, 111617 (2020)
13. Goodfellow, I., et al.: Generative adversarial nets. Adv. Neural Inf. Process. Syst. **27** (2014)
14. Gupta, A., Dollar, P., Girshick, R.: Lvis: a dataset for large vocabulary instance segmentation. In: Proceedings of the IEEE/CVF Conference on Computer Vision and Pattern Recognition, pp. 5356–5364 (2019)
15. He, J., et al.: Transfg: a transformer architecture for fine-grained recognition. In: Proceedings of the AAAI Conference on Artificial Intelligence, vol. 36, pp. 852–860 (2022). https://doi.org/10.1609/aaai.v36i1.19967
16. He, K., Chen, X., Xie, S., Li, Y., Dollár, P., Girshick, R.: Masked autoencoders are scalable vision learners. In: Proceedings of the IEEE/CVF Conference on Computer Vision and Pattern Recognition, pp. 16000–16009 (2022)
17. Hendrycks, D., et al.: Measuring massive multitask language understanding. arXiv preprint arXiv:2009.03300 (2020)

18. Jain, A.K., Li, S.Z.: Handbook of Face Recognition, vol. 1. Springer, Heidelberg (2011)
19. Kirillov, A., et al.: Segment anything. arXiv preprint arXiv:2304.02643 (2023)
20. Krizhevsky, A., Sutskever, I., Hinton, G.E.: Imagenet classification with deep convolutional neural networks. Adv. Neural Inf. Process. Syst. **25** (2012)
21. LeCun, Y., et al.: Backpropagation applied to handwritten zip code recognition. Neural Comput. **1**(4), 541–551 (1989)
22. Li, L., Dong, B., Rigall, E., Zhou, T., Dong, J., Chen, G.: Marine animal segmentation. IEEE Trans. Circuits Syst. Video Technol. **32**(4), 2303–2314 (2021)
23. Li, Y., Mao, H., Girshick, R., He, K.: Exploring plain vision transformer backbones for object detection. In: European Conference on Computer Vision, pp. 280–296. Springer, Heidelberg (2022). https://doi.org/10.1007/978-3-031-20077-9_17
24. Li, Y., Xie, S., Chen, X., Dollar, P., He, K., Girshick, R.: Benchmarking detection transfer learning with vision transformers. arXiv preprint arXiv:2111.11429 (2021)
25. Lin, T.-Y., et al.: Microsoft COCO: common objects in context. In: Fleet, D., Pajdla, T., Schiele, B., Tuytelaars, T. (eds.) ECCV 2014. LNCS, vol. 8693, pp. 740–755. Springer, Cham (2014). https://doi.org/10.1007/978-3-319-10602-1_48
26. Ojansivu, V., Heikkilä, J.: Blur insensitive texture classification using local phase quantization. In: Elmoataz, A., Lezoray, O., Nouboud, F., Mammass, D. (eds.) ICISP 2008. LNCS, vol. 5099, pp. 236–243. Springer, Heidelberg (2008). https://doi.org/10.1007/978-3-540-69905-7_27
27. Patton, P.T., et al.: A deep learning approach to photo-identification demonstrates high performance on two dozen cetacean species. Methods Ecol. Evol. **14**(10), 2611–2625 (2023)
28. Paul, S., Chen, P.Y.: Vision transformers are robust learners. In: Proceedings of the AAAI conference on Artificial Intelligence, vol. 36, pp. 2071–2081 (2022). https://doi.org/10.1609/aaai.v36i2.20103
29. Pollicelli, D., Coscarella, M., Delrieux, C.: Roi detection and segmentation algorithms for marine mammals photo-identification. Eco. Inf. **56**, 101038 (2020)
30. Pritt, M., Chern, G.: Satellite image classification with deep learning. In: 2017 IEEE Applied Imagery Pattern Recognition Workshop (AIPR), pp. 1–7. IEEE (2017)
31. Redmon, J., Divvala, S., Girshick, R., Farhadi, A.: You only look once: unified, real-time object detection. In: Proceedings of the IEEE Conference on Computer Vision and Pattern Recognition, pp. 779–788 (2016)
32. Salberg, A.B.: Detection of seals in remote sensing images using features extracted from deep convolutional neural networks. In: 2015 IEEE International Geoscience and Remote Sensing Symposium (IGARSS), pp. 1893–1896. IEEE (2015)
33. Sohl-Dickstein, J., Weiss, E., Maheswaranathan, N., Ganguli, S.: Deep unsupervised learning using nonequilibrium thermodynamics. In: International Conference on Machine Learning, pp. 2256–2265. PMLR (2015)
34. Vaswani, A., et al.: Attention is all you need. Adv. Neural Inf. Process. Syst. **30** (2017)
35. Zhelezniakov, A., et al.: Segmentation of saimaa ringed seals for identification purposes. In: Bebis, G., et al. (eds.) ISVC 2015. LNCS, vol. 9475, pp. 227–236. Springer, Cham (2015). https://doi.org/10.1007/978-3-319-27863-6_21
36. Zhou, X., Girdhar, R., Joulin, A., Krähenbühl, P., Misra, I.: Detecting twenty-thousand classes using image-level supervision. In: European Conference on Computer Vision, pp. 350–368. Springer, Heidelberg (2022). https://doi.org/10.1007/978-3-031-20077-9_21

Deep Learning Techniques for Lunar Impact Crater Identification Based on CCD and DEM Data

Siyi Chen[1] 📷, Cheng Li[1] 📷, Yueqi Ma[1] 📷, Jiarui Liang[1] 📷, Jionghao Zhu[2] 📷, and Xiaolin Tian[1(✉)] 📷

[1] School of Computer Science and Engineering, Macau University of Science and Technology, Macao, China
xltian@must.edu.mo
[2] School of Science and Engineering, The Chinese University of Hong Kong, Shenzhen, Guangdong, China

Abstract. In recent years, the subject of detection of Lunar impact craters based on deep learning methods has been widely studied with the aim of providing efficient and effective methods for the automatic detection of Lunar impact craters. In this paper, we used the new version in the YOLO series models, YOLO v9, to apply them to the detection of Lunar impact craters based on the CCD and DEM data provided by NASA to obtain accurate detection results. The performance results indicate that YOLOv9-c achieves a precision of 73.42% on CCD data, while YOLOv9-e records a slightly higher precision of 75.27%. On DEM data, their precision is 69.43% and 70.31% respectively. Additionally, the newly developed lightweight networks, GELAN-c and GELAN-e, were tested on the same CCD and DEM datasets. GELAN-c reached a precision of 74.84% on CCD data and 70.82% on DEM data. GELAN-e showed a precision of 75.81% on CCD data and 70.87% on DEM data. The results have proved that the new version of YOLO, YOLO v9, performed effectively and excellently in the task of the Lunar impact crater.

Keywords: YOLO v9 · Lunar impact crater · CCD · DEM · object detection

1 Introduction

In recent years, space exploration has consistently been a topic of keen interest. Among the Lunar surface, one of the most vital geographical and geomorphologic features is the Lunar impact crater, which is typically a bowl-shaped or ring-shaped depression with a central elevated region, surrounded by lower areas, scattered blocks, and debris. Therefore, the detection of Lunar impact craters has long been studied extensively.

Traditionally, the Lunar impact craters were primarily identified through manual annotation by experts [1]. This method not only requires high levels of expertise but

---

S. Chen, C. Li and Y. Ma authors contributed equally to this work.

L. Deligiannidis et al. (Eds.): CSCE 2024, CCIS 2262, pp. 49–59, 2025.
https://doi.org/10.1007/978-3-031-85933-5_4

is also time-consuming and labor-intensive, and sometimes prone to errors. Therefore, the industry has been continually dedicated to developing more efficient and precise automated detection methods. Later, image processing methods are proposed for automatic crater detection. These methods include Hough transformation [2] and Fast Fourier Transform [3]. With the development of artificial intelligence, machine learning techniques have also been employed in the Lunar impact crater detection according to their feature learning like the shape, color, and texture features of the craters [4]. Nowadays, convolutional neural networks have become the mainstream selection for automatic real-time object detection tasks and have also been applied to the Lunar impact crater detection. For example, the two-stage R-CNN is used to detect craters on CE-2 Digital Orthophoto Maps [5]. Also, the one-stage YOLO v7 has been utilized for crater detection based on the charge-coupled device data [6]. They have all illustrated excellent performance on this task.

Recently, a new version of YOLO, YOLO v9, was proposed by Wang et al. that integrates the Programmable Gradient Information and Generalized Efficient Layer Aggregation Network. The YOLO v9 provides greater accuracy and efficiency while maintaining computational overheads, making progress in model lightweight and energy efficiency [7].

In this paper, we present a comprehensive study utilizing the YOLOv9-c, YOLOv9-e, GELAN-c, and GELAN-e models from the YOLOv9 series to detect Lunar impact craters using CCD and DEM data. Our experiments are designed to assess the effectiveness of these YOLO v9 models in accurately identifying crater features under varying imaging conditions. We compare the detection capabilities of YOLO v9 configurations with other YOLO series models to highlight the advancements in accuracy and computational efficiency brought by the YOLO v9 framework. The results aim to provide performance evaluation, offering insights into the suitability of each model variant for Lunar impact crater detection.

2 Methodology

2.1 Data Preparation

The data utilized in this study includes CCD data from the "Lunar LRO LROC-WAC Mosaic global 100m June 2013" and DEM data from the "Moon LRO LOLA DEM 118m v1", both provided by NASA [8, 9]. The CCD data were captured by the LROC Wide Angle Camera (WAC), and the DEM data were obtained from the Lunar Orbiter Laser Altimeter (LOLA), both on the Lunar Reconnaissance Orbiter (LRO). These datasets reflect the topography of the Lunar surface. The CCD and DEM data are illustrated in Figs. 1 and 2 respectively.

Using the ArcGIS Arcpy library, the Lunar maps are cropped with longitude and latitude ranging from -170 to 170 and -80 to 80, respectively, in increments of five degrees. Subsequently, the Plate-Carree projection method is employed for automated labeling. By incorporating the Lunar Robinson database which contains the accurate position information of craters that includes longitude, latitude, and radius [10], these details are mapped onto the cropped images and used to generate corresponding label files.

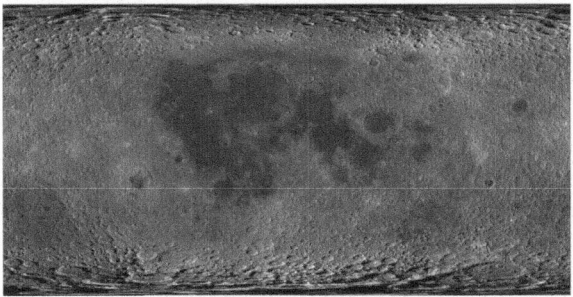

Fig. 1. Lunar LRO LROC-WAC Mosaic global 100m June 2013

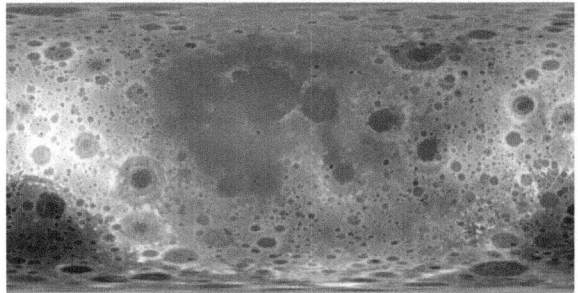

Fig. 2. Moon LRO LOLA DEM 118m v1

Ultimately, from the total pool of cropped images, 250 images containing 56,668 samples of Lunar impact craters were selected as the final image data source. The CCD and DEM cropped images are illustrated in Figs. 3 and 4, respectively.

2.2 YOLO V9 Network Architecture

The YOLO v9 is a new version of YOLO series models with the innovation of Programming Gradient Information and Generalized Efficient Layer Aggregation Network. It improved the detection precision with a decrease in parameter numbers compared to its predecessors. The network architecture of YOLO v9 is illustrated in Fig. 5.

In this paper, we conducted experiments with the four model variants based on the YOLO v9 framework. They are YOLOv9-c, YOLOv9-e, GELAN-c, and GELAN-e.

The YOLOv9-c model is optimized for speed and resource efficiency by utilizing fewer layers and parameters. It combines standard convolutional layers with "RepNC-SPELAN4" blocks for efficient feature extraction and processing while maintaining high detection accuracy. YOLOv9-e provides a deeper network structure and more feature processing power than YOLOv9-c for environments with more adequate computational resources. This model includes more "RepNCSPELAN4" blocks and sophisticated feature fusion techniques such as "CBLinear" and "CBFuse", which are designed to improve the performance and accuracy of the model when processing complex scenes. It is similar that the GELAN-c is a more lightweight design compared with GELAN-e. GELAN-c

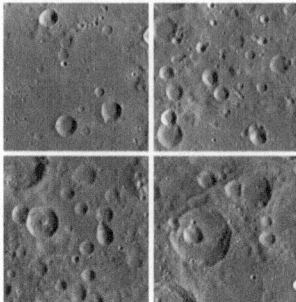

Fig. 3. Cropped CCD images

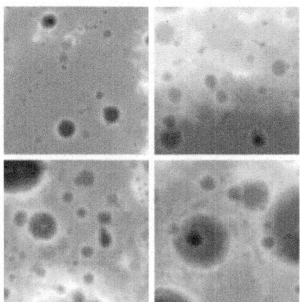

Fig.4. Cropped DEM images

employs Average Downsample to reduce feature map dimensions, whereas GELAN-e uses enhanced "RepNCSPELAN4" blocks to support extensive processing demands. The GELAN-e and GELAN-c mainly focused on optimizing layer aggregation and feature extraction using the GELAN architecture, which is suitable for dealing with deep feature integration. While the YOLOv9-c and YOLOv9-e are mainly combined with PGI techniques that emphasize finding the optimal balance between multi-scale detection and real-time performance.

3 Experiments

3.1 Experiment Environment Configuration

The experiments are conducted under the following settings:

CPU: 16 vCPU AMD EPYC 9654 96-Core Processor
GPU: RTX 4090(24GB) * 1
PyTorch: 2.2.2
Cuda: 12.2
Learning rate: 0.01
Optimizer: SGD
Batch size: 4
Epochs: 300

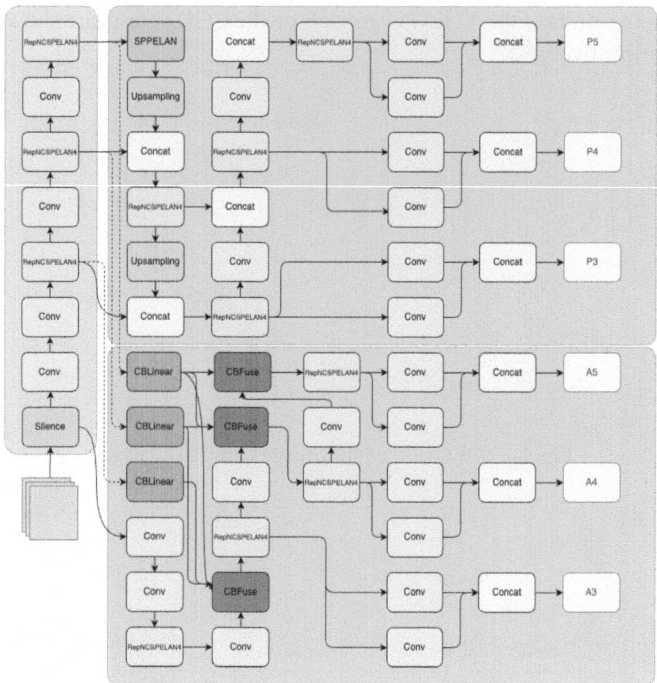

Fig. 5. YOLO v9 Network Architecture

3.2 Evaluation Metrics

The following metrics are used to evaluate and compare the performance of each model on the CCD and DEM datasets.

$$\text{Precision} = \frac{TP}{TP+FP} \tag{1}$$

$$\text{Recall} = \frac{TP}{TP+FN} \tag{2}$$

$$\text{mAP} = \frac{1}{C} \sum_{i=1}^{C} AP_i \tag{3}$$

Besides, the mAP@0.5 equals the mAP at IoU threshold 0.5, and the mAP@0.5 : 0.95 = $\frac{1}{10} \sum_{i=0}^{9} (\text{mAP@0.5} + i \cdot 0.05)$.

3.3 Experiment Results

For each dataset, 250 images featuring the same lunar impact craters are selected from both the CCD and DEM datasets. These images are then randomly divided into a training set and a validation set in a six to four ratio. Consequently, each dataset contains 150 images for training and 100 images for validation, ensuring that both the CCD and DEM datasets are represented equally.

The training results of the YOLO v9 models on the CCD dataset are shown in Figs. 6, 7, 8, and 9, respectively.

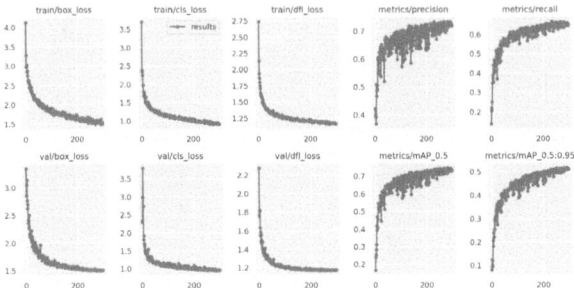

Fig. 6. YOLOv9-c training results on CCD dataset

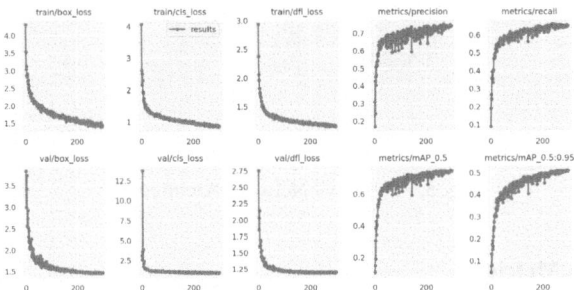

Fig. 7. YOLOv9-e training results on CCD dataset

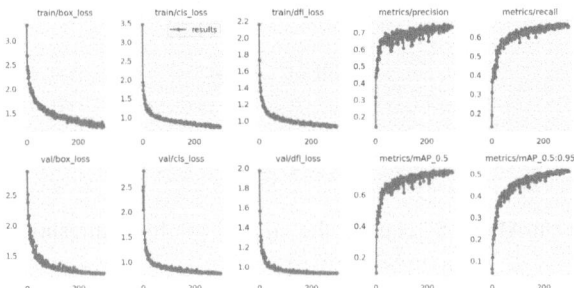

Fig. 8. GELAN-c training results on CCD dataset

The training results indicate that the precision of all four YOLO v9 models exceeds 70% on the CCD dataset. Based on the best training results of these four models, we have obtained their detection results on the CCD dataset. The detection results of the CCD dataset are illustrated in Fig. 10.

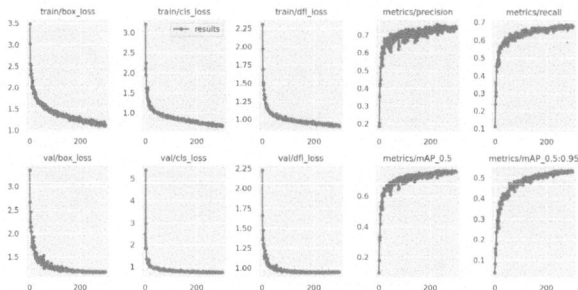

Fig. 9. GELAN-e training results on CCD dataset

For the DEM dataset, the training results are illustrated in Figs. 11, 12, 13, and 14, respectively.

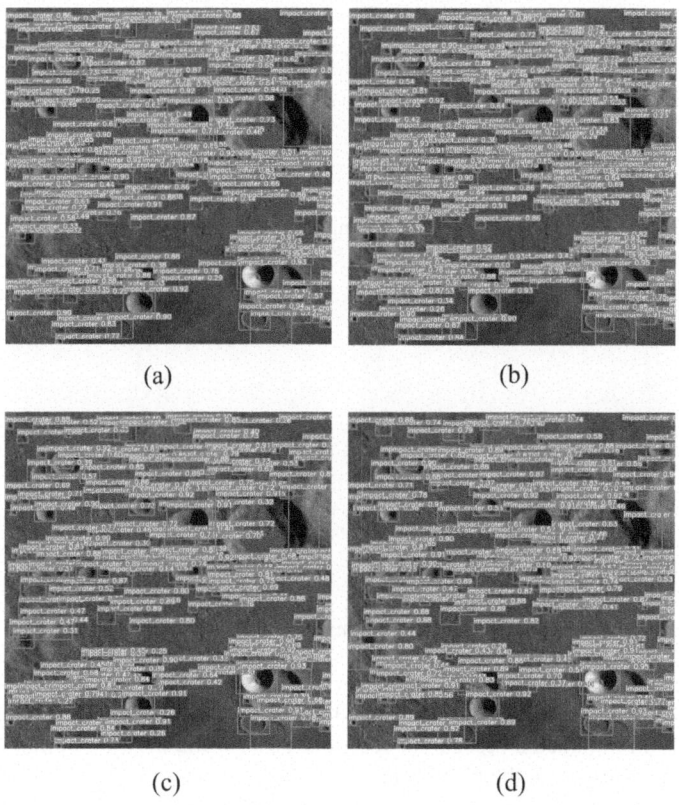

Fig. 10. Detection results on the CCD dataset: (a) YOLOv9-c; (b) YOLOv9-e; (c) GELAN-c; (d) GELAN-e

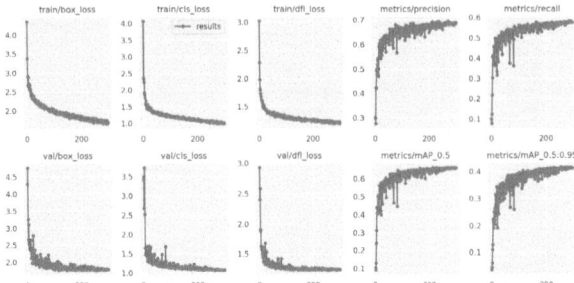

Fig. 11. YOLOv9-c training results on DEM dataset

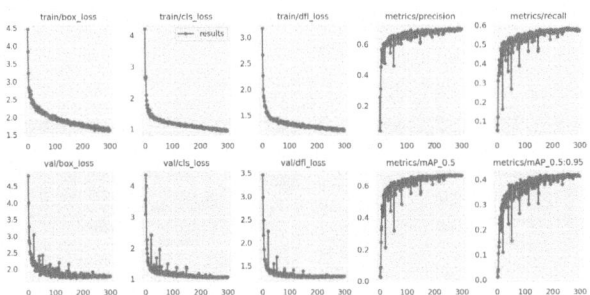

Fig. 12. YOLOv9-e training results on DEM dataset

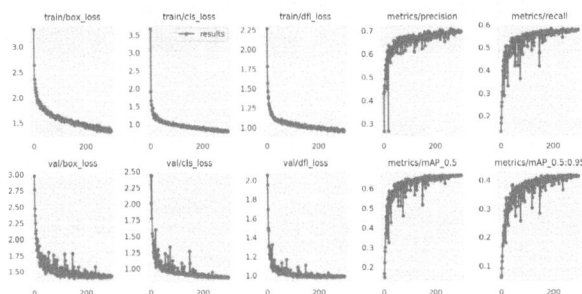

Fig. 13. GELAN-c training results on DEM dataset

According to the training results on the DEM dataset, except for the YOLOv9-e, the other models all obtained a precision exceeding 70%, while they all did not achieve as high precision as those on the CCD dataset.

Based on the best-trained results of the four models, we can obtain their detection results on the DEM dataset. The detection results of these four models are illustrated in Fig. 15.

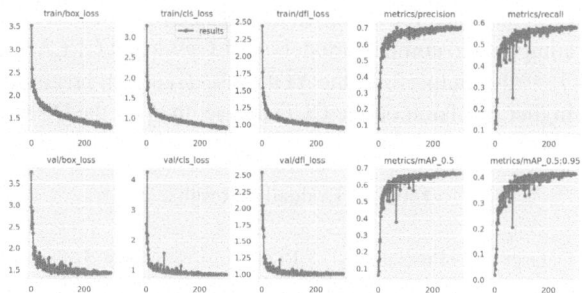

Fig. 14. GELAN-e training results on DEM dataset

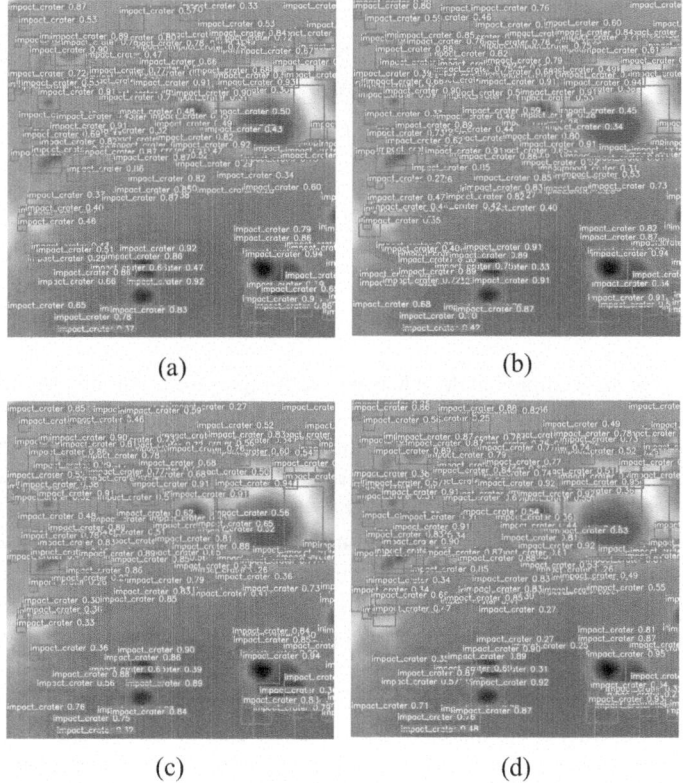

(a)   (b)

(c)   (d)

Fig.15. Detection results on the DEM dataset: (a) YOLOv9-c; (b) YOLOv9-e; (c) GELAN-c; (d) GELAN-e

4   Discussion

The experiments of YOLOv9-c, YOLOv9-e, GELAN-c, and GELAN-e models on the CCD and DEM datasets are conducted with other parameters and settings at the same. Table 1 illustrates the evaluation results of these models on these two datasets.

As observed from the table, the extended models YOLOv9-e and GELAN-e achieve higher precision compared to compact models YOLOv9-c and GELAN-c. The GELAN variants of YOLO v9 also outperform the YOLOv9 variants in precision. Additionally, all models show higher precision on the CCD dataset than on the DEM dataset.

Table 1. Evaluation Results.

Model	Dataset	Precision	Recall	mAP@.5	mAP@.5:.95
YOLOv9-c	CCD	73.42%	66.44%	74.70%	51.65%
YOLOv9-c	DEM	69.43%	56.27%	65.67%	40.79%
YOLOv9-e	CCD	75.27%	65.11%	74.86%	50.86%
YOLOv9-e	DEM	70.31%	56.80%	66.50%	41.43%
GELAN-c	CCD	74.84%	66.28%	75.48%	51.51%
GELAN-c	DEM	70.82%	56.72%	66.61%	41.42%
GELAN-e	CCD	75.81%	65.83%	75.61%	52.86%
GELAN-e	DEM	70.87%	57.11%	66.70%	51.75%

5   Conclusion

In this paper, we have employed deep learning techniques for Lunar impact crater detection based on the CCD and DEM data from NASA using four variants of YOLO v9 models. We have tested the performance of YOLOv9-c, YOLOv9-e, GELAN-c, and GELAN-e on the task of Lunar impact crater detection. The results show that the GELAN-e is the most effective model among these four models, with a precision of 75.81% on the CCD dataset and 70.87% on the DEM dataset. It is also observed that the extended versions of the models achieve higher precision results than the compact versions. The precision of GELAN-c is 74.84% on the CCD dataset and 70.82% on the DEM dataset, which is relatively lower than that of the GELAN-e model. The precision of YOLOv9-c is 73.42% on the CCD dataset and 69.43% on the DEM dataset. The precision of YOLOv9-e is 75.27% on the CCD dataset and 70.31% on the DEM dataset, which is relatively higher compared to the compact version, YOLOv9-c.

These results indicate that YOLOv9 is well-suited for Lunar impact crater detection tasks based on CCD and DEM data, which provides a foundation for future research.

6   Future Work

In the future, we intend to optimize the YOLO v9 network architecture with attention mechanisms like CBAM [11] and Dynamic Head [12] and attempt to obtain better performance. And compare them with other object detection methods like Transformer [13] and Fast R-CNN [14].

Acknowledgments. This work was supported by the Science and Technology Development Fund of Macau under Grant (No. 0038/2020/A1).

References

1. Howard, K.A.: Fresh lunar impact craters – Review of variations with size. In: Proceedings of the 5th Lunar Science Conference, vol. 1, pp. 61–69. Pergamon Press, Inc., Houston, TX New York, 18–22 Mar 1974
2. Galloway, M.J., Benedix, G.K., Bland, P.A., Paxman, J., Towner, M.C., Tan, T.: Automated crater detection and counting using the hough transform. In: 2014 IEEE International Conference on Image Processing (ICIP), Paris, France, pp. 1579–1583 (2014)
3. Pedrosa, M.M., et al.: Improved automatic impact crater detection on Mars based on morphological image processing and template matching. Geomat. Nat. Hazards Risk **8**(2), 1306–1319 (2017). https://doi.org/10.1080/19475705.2017.1327463
4. Wang, Y., Wu, B.: A new global catalogue of lunar craters (≥ 1 km) with 3D information and preliminary results of global analysis. In: The International Archives of Photogrammetry, Remote Sensing and Spatial Information Sciences, vol. XLIII-B3-2020, pp. 1171–1176 (2020)
5. Zang, S., Mu, L., Xian, L., Zhang, W.: Semi-supervised deep learning for lunar crater detection using CE-2 DOM. Remote Sens. **13**, 2819 (2021)
6. Chen, S., Liang, J., Zhu, J., Tian, X.: New Methods for Lunar Impact Crater Detection Based on YOLO v7 with Deformable ConvNets. In: 2023 IEEE International Conference on Electrical, Automation and Computer Engineering (ICEACE), Changchun, China, pp. 123–127 (2023)
7. Wang, C.Y., Yeh, I.H., Liao, H.Y.M.: YOLOv9: Learning What You Want to Learn Using Programmable Gradient Information. arXiv preprint arXiv:2402.13616 (2024)
8. Arizona State University LROC Team: Moon LRO LROC WAC Global Morphology Mosaic 100m v3 [Map]. USGS Astrogeology Science Center (2013)
9. LOLA Science Team: Moon LRO LOLA DEM 118m v1 [Map]. USGS Astrogeology Science Center (2014)
10. Robbins, S.J.: Developing a global lunar crater database complete for craters $\geq$ 1 km". In: Lunar & Planetary Science Conference. Lunar and Planetary Science Conference (2016)
11. Zhu, J., Liang, J., Tian, X., Yan, P.: A Deep learning approach for lunar impact crater detection based on YOLO v7 and CBAM attention mechanism. In: 2023 8th International Conference on Intelligent Computing and Signal Processing (ICSP), pp. 2078–2081. Xi'an, China (2023)
12. Dai, et al., X.: Dynamic head: unifying object detection heads with attentions. In: 2021 IEEE/CVF Conference on Computer Vision and Pattern Recognition (CVPR), pp. 7369–7378. Nashville, TN, USA (2021)
13. Vaswani, A., et al.: Attention is all you need. In: Proceedings of the 31st International Conference on Neural Information Processing Systems (NIPS 2017), vol. 30, pp. 6000–6010. Long Beach, CA, USA, 4–9 Dec 2017
14. Girshick, R.: Fast R-CNN. In: 2015 IEEE International Conference on Computer Vision (ICCV), pp. 1440–1448. Santiago, Chile (2015)

Silicon Wafer Map Defect Classification Using Artificial Intelligence Models

Rushendar Pilli, Suranjan Panigrahi[✉] [iD], and Miad Faezipour[✉] [iD]

School of Engineering Technology, Electrical and Computer Engineering Technology,
Purdue University, West Lafayette, IN, USA
{vpilli,spanigr,mfaezipo}@purdue.edu

Abstract. This paper presents a comprehensive evaluation of three modified advanced neural network architectures-ResNet-34, EfficientNet-B0, and SqueezeNet-by measuring their accuracy in detecting and classifying defects in silicon wafer maps. The research utilized the WM-811K dataset, consisting of various defect types, to train and test each model under binary and multi-class classification scenarios. A customized image processing algorithm was developed to process the wafer map images, which were then used as inputs to the neural network models. The accuracy of these models was the primary metric used to assess their performance. In binary classification tasks, EfficientNet-B0 demonstrated the highest test accuracy of 94.6% with an average test accuracy of 93.2%. ResNet-34 followed closely with a test accuracy of 93.5% and an average test accuracy of 91.6%. SqueezeNet, while achieving a lower test accuracy of 92.6%, maintained an average test accuracy of 91.4%. For multi-class classification, EfficientNet-B0 again led with a test accuracy of 84.2% and an average test accuracy of 84.1%. ResNet-34 achieved a test accuracy of 83.1% with an average test accuracy of 82.3%, while SqueezeNet had a test accuracy of 82.9% and an average test accuracy of 79.7%. The paper further elaborates on the performance metrics of the models. It also discusses the current research and suggests areas for future work.

Keywords: deep neural networks · silicon wafer · defect detection and classification

1 Introduction

The integration of electronic devices into various aspects of daily life has been a transformative development, largely made possible by advances in semiconductor technology. At the heart of this technological revolution are silicon wafers, which play a crucial role in the manufacturing of semiconductors. These silicon wafers serve as the base for the complex circuits and components that enable the functionality of a wide range of electronic devices, from compact smartphones to sophisticated medical equipment [1]. In the rapidly evolving semiconductor industry, where the demand for smaller, faster, and more powerful electronic

© The Author(s), under exclusive license to Springer Nature Switzerland AG 2025
L. Deligiannidis et al. (Eds.): CSCE 2024, CCIS 2262, pp. 60–72, 2025.
https://doi.org/10.1007/978-3-031-85933-5_5

devices is ever-increasing, maintaining high-quality standards is of paramount importance. Silicon wafers are integral to this process, forming the backbone of semiconductor manufacturing. Any imperfection in these wafers can lead to defects in the final electronic products, emphasizing the critical role of quality control in semiconductor fabrication [2]. Recent advancements in technology have seen the emergence of computer vision as a powerful tool for automating the inspection of semiconductor wafers. However, while computer vision is effective in identifying standard defects, it encounters challenges with complex and novel defect patterns. These limitations can result in overlooking subtle imperfections, potentially leading to increased material waste, unnecessary rework, and concerns about the reliability of the final products [3].

This research project delves into the application of advanced neural network (NN) architectures to enhance the capabilities of machine vision systems in semiconductor manufacturing. Thus, this study investigates the accuracy of three distinct modified neural network models (ResNet-34, EfficientNet-B0, and SqueezeNet) in identifying and classifying defects on wafer maps. Each of these architectures offers unique advantages in processing and analyzing the intricate patterns and anomalies present in wafer map images. ResNet-34, known for its deep residual learning framework, enables the model to learn from vast amounts of data without succumbing to the challenges of training deep neural networks [4]. EfficientNet-B0, designed for efficiency, scales model size in a balanced way to enhance accuracy with minimal computational resources [5]. SqueezeNet, with its compact architecture, provided accuracy similar to that by AlexNet [6]. So, SqueezeNet is a potential candidate for resource constraint applications, such as embedded systems within semiconductor manufacturing facilities.

Numerous studies have employed the WM-811K wafer image dataset, often resizing the input images to 256×256 pixels for neural network defect classification models [7,8]. However, the original images in the WM-811K dataset exhibit a wide range of dimensions. To preserve the originality of the data, we chose to resize all the images to 45×45 pixels, a dimension that represents the majority of the images within the dataset. The specialility of this approachapproach is that the dimentions of all the images (input to the model) are same.

2 Methodology

2.1 Data Collection

The study utilizes the WM-811K dataset as its primary data source, which consists of 811,000 images with 9 different silicon wafers map classes [9]. These defects include categories like Center, Donut, Edge-loc, Edge-ring, Loc, Near-full, Random, Scratch and Non-Defective [10].

2.2 Model Selection and Evaluation

Initial Model Selection. Three selected neural network architectures, (i.e., ResNet-34 [4], EfficientNet-B0 [5], and SqueezeNet [6]) were evaluated in this research. The selection criteria were based on their accuracy levels and architectural efficiency from prior image classification tasks.

Evaluation. In this study, two distinct cases of wafer map image classification were used for evaluation of the classification models, confusion matrix [11] was used in both cases. Our study utilizes Google Colab as the primary platform and Python as the programming language. The key terms of the confusion matrix include [11]:

- True Positives (TP): The number of correctly predicted positive observations.
- False Positives (FP): The number of negative observations incorrectly predicted as positive.
- True Negatives (TN): The number of correctly predicted negative observations.
- False Negatives (FN): The number of positive observations incorrectly predicted as negative.

2.3   Case 1: Binary Classification of Defective and Non-Defective Wafer Map Images

The performances of the models for the binary classifications were analyzed using accuracy, sensitivity, and precision metrics. The overall test accuracy (Eq. 1) provided a single measure of model performance across both the classes. Sensitivity (Eq. 2) and specificity (Eq. 3) offered additional detail by indicating the model's ability to correctly classify defective images (Class 0) and non-defective images (Class 1), respectively.

$$Accuracy = (TP + TN)/(FP + FN + TP + TN) \tag{1}$$

$$\text{Sensitivity} = \frac{TP}{TP + FN} \tag{2}$$

$$\text{Specificity} = \frac{TN}{TN + FP} \tag{3}$$

2.4   Case 2: Multi-class Classification of 8 Defective Classes Along with 1 Non-defective Class

The model's ability to classify multiple defect types along with non-defective class was examined using a confusion matrix. For each class, the total count of "False Negatives" is identified by tallying the observations(within the respective row) the model misclassified into alternative classes. This identification is crucial, as it highlights the occurrences where the model failed to detect the actual condition it was trained to identify. The overall accuracy of the model is determined using the formula (Eq. 4),

$$\text{Overall Accuracy} = \frac{\sum(\text{True Positives for all classes})}{\text{Total number of Observations}} \tag{4}$$

3   Image Preprocessing

The dataset underwent an extensive image preprocessing procedure to standard-ize the inputs and boost the models' performance and accuracy. This included discarding unlabeled wafer map images, resizing all the images to uniform dimen-sions, and applying image augmentation techniques. Figure 1 illustrates the dis-tribution of the wafer index within the WM811k dataset. It is evident that not all wafer map images have the same index, indicating that they are manufactured in different batches. Consequently, this variability led to different dimensions of wafer map images, ranging from 212×84 pixels to 15×3 pixels with 632 different unique wafer map dimensions.

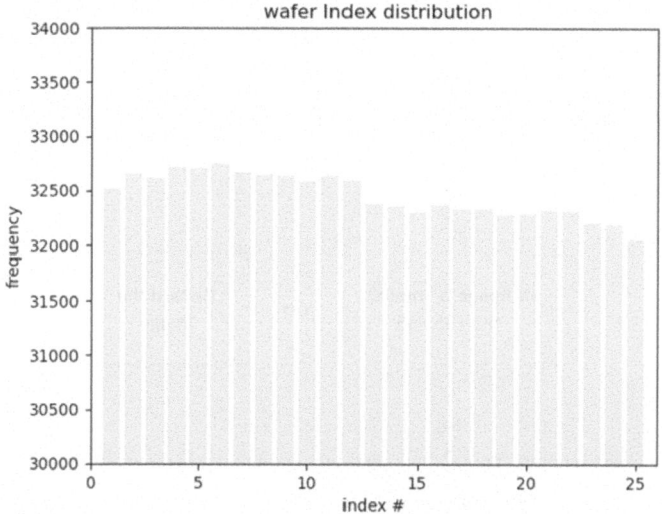

Fig. 1. Bar graph describing unique wafer index across the dataset

Images smaller than 35×35 pixels were removed from the dataset. The rest of the images were resized to 45×45 pixels using bilinear interpolation to achieve consistency throughout the dataset. It is to be noted that the majority of the images originally had dimensions around 45×45 pixels. Table 1 displays the dis-tribution of wafer map images across each category before the implementation of the described process. Figure 2 illustrates the sequence of image preprocessing steps implemented in our study.

3.1   Case 1 (Binary Classification)

To ensure each class has 500 images, we used an image augmentation technique for classes with fewer than 500 images. This technique involved rotating the images at 45-° intervals (45, 90, 135, 180, 225, 270, and 315°) [12]. For classes

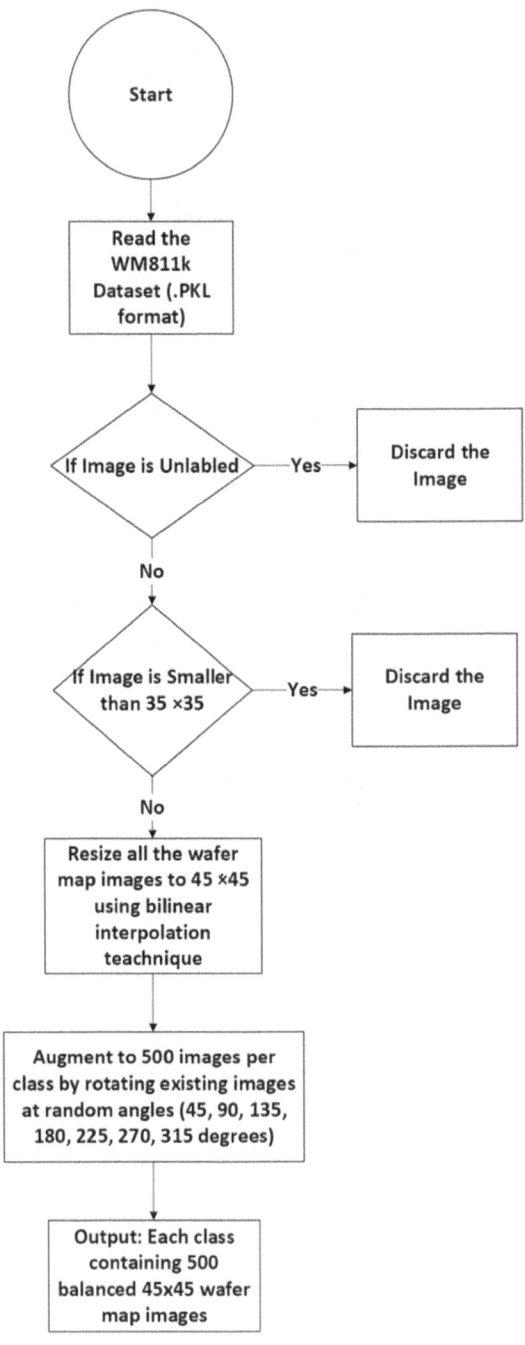

Fig. 2. Flow chart of image preprocessing steps

Table 1. Number of Wafer Map Images in Each Class Before Preprocessing

Wafer Map Type	Number of images
Center	1055
Donut	422
Edge-Loc	2356
Edge-Ring	8880
Loc	1462
Random	498
Scratch	672
Near-Full	39
None (defect free)	48445

with more than 500 images, we reduced their count to 500. The exception was class 8 (non-defective), which started with 48,445 images and was reduced to 4,000 images. Table 2 shows the number of images in each class after this process. Figure 3 shows a sample image before and after preprocessing.

Table 2. Number of Wafer Map Images in 9 Different Classes in Case 1

Wafer Map Class	Number of images
Center (0)	500
Donut (1)	500
Edge-Loc (2)	500
Edge-Ring (3)	500
Loc (4)	500
Random (5)	500
Scratch (6)	500
Near-Full (7)	500
None (8)	4000

All images from classes 0 to 7 were consolidated into a single 'defective' class, and class 8 remains as the 'non-defective' class. Therefore, in this case, we have two categories: defective and non-defective. Table 3 shows the number of images in the defective and non-defective classes.

The dataset has been partitioned into three subsets: 80% for training, and 10% each for validation and testing, as shown in Table 4.

Table 3. Number of Images in Defective Class (0) and Non-Defective Class (1)

Wafer Map Class	Number of Images
Defected (0)	4000
Defect-Free (1)	4000

Table 4. Number of Images in Training, Validation and Test Dataset for Case 1

Dataset	Number of Images
Training Set	6400
Validation Set	800
Testing Set	800

3.2   Case 2 (Multi-class Classification)

To ensure each class has 500 images, we used an image augmentation technique for classes with fewer than 500 images (similar to case 1). This technique involved rotating the images at 45-° intervals (45, 90, 135, 180, 225, 270, and 315°). For classes with more than 500 images, we reduced their count to 500 by randomly dropping the images. The dataset has been partitioned into three subsets: 80% for training, and 10% each for validation and testing, as shown in Table 5.

Table 5. Number of Images in Training, Validation and Test Dataset for Case 2

Dataset	Number of Images
Training Set	3600
Validation Set	450
Testing Set	450

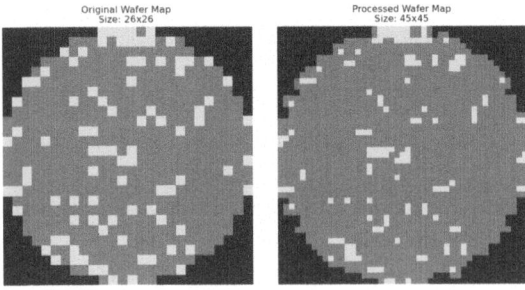

Fig. 3. Wafermap image before (left) and after preprocessing (right)

4   Neural Network Models

4.1   Modified ResNet-34 Architecture

The architecture detailed here is an modified ResNet-34 model [4] designed for classifying 45×45 grayscale wafer map images. It starts with an initial convolution layer followed by batch normalization and rectifier linear unit (ReLU) activation to maintain input dimensions while extracting features. The modified ResNet-34 model used in this study has three Basic Blocks, which are also known as Residual Blocks. These Basic Blocks incorporate skip connections, also known as identity mappings, that allow the original input feature map to bypass the convolutional layers within the block and be directly added to the output. These Basic Blocks incorporate skip connections, also known as identity mappings, that allow the original input feature map to bypass the convolutional layers within the block and be directly added to the output. This is followed by an adaptive average pooling layer that standardizes output size across varying inputs, leading to a fully connected layer and a softmax function for classification. The overview of the architecture is shown in Table 6.

Table 6. Modified ResNet-34 Model to Classify Wafer Map Images

Layer Type	Input Size	Output Size	Filters
Convolution	45×45×1	45×45×16	16
BatchNorm2d	45×45×16	45×45×16	–
ReLU	45×45×16	45×45×16	–
BasicBlock1.0	45×45×16	45×45×16	16, 16
BasicBlock1.1	45×45×16	45×45×16	16, 16
BasicBlock2.0	45×45×16	23×23×32	32, 32, 32
BasicBlock2.1	23×23×32	23×23×32	32, 32
BasicBlock3.0	23×23×32	12×12×64	64, 64
BasicBlock3.1	12×12×64	12×12×64	64, 64
AdaptiveAvgPool2d	12×12×64	1×1×64	–
Fully Connected	1×1×64	case1:2; case2:9	2, 9

4.2   Modified EfficientNetB0 Architecture

The architecture of the second proposed model is a variant of the efficient MobileNet structure [5], which is particularly suited for systems with computational constraints. Our model has been specifically adapted for the task of classifying manufacturing defects, requiring the handling of grayscale images of size 45×45 pixels. The model's architecture is characterized by the use of depth wise separable convolutions, a hallmark of the MobileNet design, which offers a trade-off between efficiency and accuracy. The overview of the architecture is shown in Table 7.

Table 7. Modified EfficientNet-B0 Model Architecture

Layer	Input Size	Output Size	Filters
Convolution	45×45×1	45×45×16	16
BatchNorm2d	45×45×16	45×45×16	–
SiLU	45×45×16	45×45×16	–
InvertedResidualBlock 1	45×45×16	45×45×16	16,4,16,16
InvertedResidualBlock 2	45×45×16	23×23×24	96,96,4,96,24
InvertedResidualBlock 3	23×23×24	12×12×40	144,144,6,144,40
Convolution	12×12×40	12×12×80	80
BatchNorm2d	12×12×80	12×12×80	–
SiLU	12×12×80	12×12×80	–
AdaptiveAvgPool2d	12×12×80	1×1×80	–
Fully Connected	1×1×80	case1:2; case2:9	2,9

4.3   Modified SqueezeNet Model Architecture

The architecture of our third proposed model is a tailored version of the renowned SqueezeNet, optimized for high efficiency and a minimalistic parameter footprint. This architecture is particularly advantageous for computationally restricted plat forms while still providing the necessary capabilities for defect classification from 45×45 pixel grayscale images. The essence of SqueezeNet and FireModules, with

Table 8. Modified SqueezeNet Model Architecture

Layer	Input Size	Output Size	Filters
Covolution Layer	45×45×1	45×45×32	32
BatchNorm2d	45×45×32	45×45×32	–
ReLU	45×45×32	45×45×32	–
FireModule1	45×45×32	45×45×32	sq(8), ex(16+16)
FireModule2	45×45×32	22×22×32	sq(8), ex(16+16)
FireModule3	22×22×32	22×22×32	sq(16), ex(32+32)
FireModule4	22×22×64	22×22×32	sq(16), ex(32+32)
Maxpool2d	22×22×64	11×11×64	–
Conv2d	11×11×64	11×11×2, 9	case1:2, case2:9
AdaptiveAvgPool2d	11×11×9	1×1×××2, 9	–

Note: ex = expansion, and Sq = Squeeze

their squeeze-and-expand operations enables the model to capture complex features without excessive computational demands. MaxPooling layers are strategically placed to reduce dimensionality and capture the most salient features [6]. The network concludes with a classifier that consolidates the features into an 2 classes for case 1 and 9 classes for case 2. This architecture is concisely mapped out in Table 8.

5   Results and Discussion

5.1   Model Performance Evaluation for Case 1 (Binary Classification)

In evaluating defective and non-defective image classification, EfficientNet-B0 demonstrated the highest test accuracy of 94.6% with an average accuracy of 93.2%, highlighting its strong performance in binary classification tasks. ResNet-34 followed closely with a test accuracy of 93.5% and an average accuracy of 91.6%. SqueezeNet, while achieving a lower test accuracy of 92.62% with an average accuracy of 91.4%, remains a viable option, particularly in scenarios where model size and processing speed are more critical than peak accuracy. For ResNet-34, the sensitivity and specificity achieved were 95.8% and 90.9%, respectively. This indicates that the model is 4.9% more effective at identifying defective silicon wafer map images than at identifying defect-free ones. For EfficientNet-B0, both the sensitivity and specificity were 95.8% and 93.3%, respectively. This suggests that the model is 2.5% more effective at identifying defective silicon wafer map images than at identifying defect-free ones.

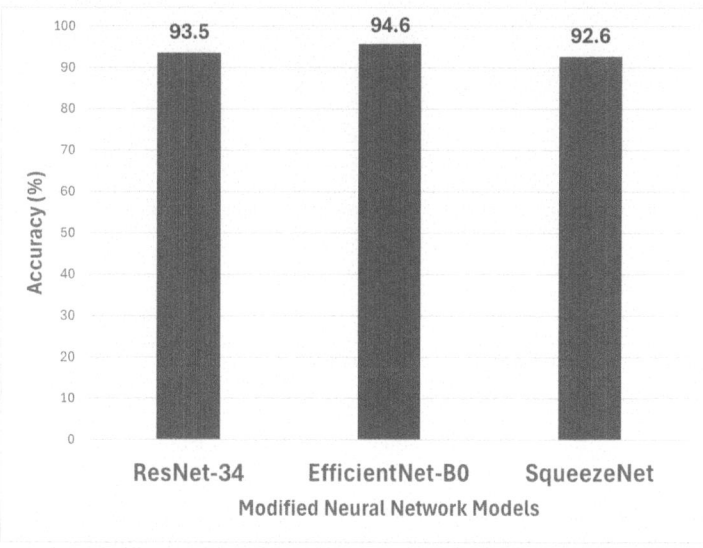

Fig. 4. Test Accuracies of Modified NN Models for Binary Classification of Wafer map images

SqueezeNet exhibited a sensitivity of 90.1% and a specificity of 95.5%, indicating that the model is 5.31% more effective at identifying non-defective silicon wafer map images than at identifying defective ones. Each model's performance varies, with ResNet-34 and EfficientNet-B0 showing high sensitivity, making them particularly effective for applications where detecting defective images is critical. Figure 4 presents a bar graph comparing the test accuracies of the models for binary classification, clearly illustrating the test accuracy of modified EfficientNet-B0, modified ResNet-34, and modified SqueezeNet are within ± 5% of each other.

5.2   Model Performance Evaluation for Case 2 (Multi-class Classification)

In the multi-class classification scenario, EfficientNet-B0 demonstrated the highest test accuracy of 84.2% with an average test accuracy of 84.0%, making it the leading model in identifying the underlying causes of silicon wafer defects. ResNet-34 followed closely, with a test accuracy of 83.1% and an average test accuracy of 82.3%. SqueezeNet achieved the lowest test accuracy of 82.9%, with an average test accuracy of 79.7%, underscoring the variability in effectiveness among the different architectures. Figure 5 illustrates a bar graph showcasing the test accuracies of the models for multi-class classification. This visual representation highlights how the accuracies of EfficientNet-B0, ResNet-34, and SqueezeNet are very similar within ± 5% of each other.

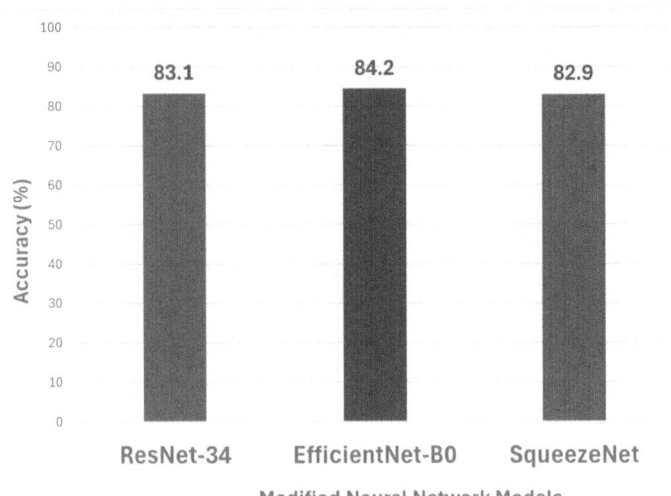

Fig. 5. Test Accuracies of Modified NN Models for Multi-Class Wafer Defect Classification

6   Conclusion and Future Directions

This study systematically evaluated the performance of three advanced neural network models (ResNet-34, EfficientNet-B0, and SqueezeNet) for defect detection in wafer images under two different cases. In binary classification tasks (Case 1), which focused on differentiating defective from non-defective images, EfficientNet-B0 demonstrated the highest test accuracy of 94.6% with an average accuracy of 93.2%, outperforming SqueezeNet's test accuracy of 92.6% and average accuracy of 91.4%. Despite ResNet-34 having a slightly lower test accuracy of 93.5% and an average accuracy of 91.6%, it exhibited the highest sensitivity at 95.8%. Conversely, EfficientNet-B0 led in specificity with a rate of 93.3%, indicating its strength in correctly identifying defect-free images and minimizing false positives. In multi-class classification tasks (Case 2), which involved the identification of nine distinct classes of defects, EfficientNet-B0 delivered the best performance with a test accuracy of 84.2% and an average test accuracy of 84.1%, underscoring its superior capability in handling more complex pattern recognition in wafer map images compared to ResNet-34 and SqueezeNet. ResNet-34 followed closely with a test accuracy of 83.1% and an average test accuracy of 82.3%, while SqueezeNet achieved the lowest performance with a test accuracy of 82.9% and an average test accuracy of 79.7%. These results emphasize the strengths and limitations of each model, suggesting that EfficientNet-B0 is the most balanced model for both binary and multi-class classification tasks, while ResNet-34 excels in sensitivity for defect detection.

The future work will involve incorporating a human-in-the loop system to enhance the model's accuracy in classification tasks. By developing and integrating a human-machine inter action interface, we can systematically record the impact of human interactions on model performance. This initiative is designed to quantify and examine the influence of human input on performance metrics, thereby deepening our understanding of how these interactions can optimize model accuracy. Additionally, we plan to evaluate these models on different datasets that resemble wafer map images, to better gauge their adaptability and performance in diverse contexts.

References

1. Okamoto, K., Sugiyama, M., Mabu, S.: Importance of advanced metrology in semiconductor industry and value-added creation using AI/ML. E-J. Surf. Sci. Nanotechnol. **18**, 214–222 (2020)
2. Wang, P.A.: Industrial challenges for thin wafer manufacturing. In: 2006 IEEE 4th World Conference on Photovoltaic Energy Conference, vol. 1, pp. 1179–1182 (2006)
3. Gelsinger, P.: Semiconductors run the world: hot chips 2022. In: 2022 IEEE Hot Chips 34 Symposium (HCS), pp. 1–19. IEEE Computer Society (2022)
4. He, K., Zhang, X., Ren, S., Sun, J.: Deep residual learning for image recognition. In: Proceedings of the IEEE Conference on Computer Vision and Pattern Recognition (CVPR), pp. 770–778 (2016)

5. Tan, M., Le, Q.V.: EfficientNet: rethinking model scaling for convolutional neural networks. In: International Conference on Machine Learning (ICML), pp. 6105–6114. PMLR (2019)

6. Iandola, F.N., Han, S., Moskewicz, M.W., Ashraf, K., Dally, W.J., Keutzer, K.: SqueezeNet: alexnet-level accuracy with 50x fewer parameters and <0.5 MB model size (2016). arXiv:1602.07360

7. Bhatnagar, P., Arora, T., Chaujar, R.: Semiconductor wafer map defect classification using transfer learning. In: 2022 IEEE Delhi Section Conference (DELCON), New Delhi, India 2022, pp. 1–4 (2022)

8. Zheng, H., Sherazi, S., Son, S.H., Lee, J.Y.: A deep convolutional neural network-based multi-class image classification for automatic wafer map failure recognition in semiconductor manufacturing. Appl. Sci. **11**(20), 9769 (2021)

9. Wu, M.-J., Jang, J.-S.R., Chen, J.-L.: Wafer map failure pattern recognition and similarity ranking for large-scale data sets. IEEE Trans. Semicond. Manuf. **28**(1), 1–12 (2015)

10. Manivannan, S.: Pseudo-labeling and clustering-based active learning for imbalanced classification of wafer bin map defects. SIViP **18**(3), 2391–2401 (2024)

11. Bishop, C.M.: Pattern Recognition and Machine Learning, vol. 2, pp. 1122–1128. Springer, Heidelberg (2006)

12. Sonogashira, M., Shonai, M., Iiyama, M.: High-resolution bathymetry by deep-learning-based image superresolution. PLoS ONE **15**(7), e0235487 (2020)

Low Light Image Enhancement Using Autoencoder-Based Deep Neural Networks

Kuei-Yu Chen and Jin-Jang Leou[✉]

National Chung Cheng University, Chiayi 621, Taiwan
jjleou@cs.ccu.edu.tw

Abstract. In this study, a low light image enhancement approach using autoencoder-based deep neural networks is proposed. The proposed approach consists of two subnets, namely, feature extraction (FE) subnet and color enhancement (CE) subnet. FE subnet extracts image features from the low light image and enhances detailed textures, while CE subnet recovers the color information of the low light image and performs image denoising. A pre-processing technique, namely, relative global histogram stretching (RGHS) is employed in CE subnet. Finally, the processing results of FE and CE subnets are fused to generate the final enhanced image. Based on the experimental results obtained in this study, in terms of two objective performance metrics (PSNR (dB) and SSIM) and subjective evaluation, the performance of the proposed approach is better than those of five comparison approaches.

Keywords: Low light image enhancement · Autoencoder-based deep neural network · Feature extraction (FE) subnet · Color enhancement (CE) subnet · Bottleneck guided channel attention (BGCA) module · U-net

1 Introduction

Recently, low light image enhancement has become an important research topic in image processing and computer vision applications, such as scene classification and image segmentation [1–3]. Conventional histogram equalization based techniques [4–7] are usually employed to enhance image contrast. However, they don't address real-world illumination issues.

The low light images enhancement approaches can be divided into three categories: enhancement-based, illumination-based, and learning-based approaches. For enhancement-based approaches, histogram equalization (HE) and gamma correction are usually used to regulate the dynamic range of image pixels, i.e., to improve image contrast. Ibrahim and Kong [4] proposed a brightness preserving dynamic histogram equalization (BPDHE) approach to enhance image contrast. Histogram for color images, the DHE technique is extended to the processing of color images. Celik and Tjahjadi [5] proposed an image contrast enhancement algorithm, which converts the input image into a 2D histogram using the correlation between each pixel and its neighbors. Nakai, Hoshi, and Taguchi [6] proposed a differential gray-level histogram equalization (DHE)

L. Deligiannidis et al. (Eds.): CSCE 2024, CCIS 2262, pp. 73–84, 2025.
https://doi.org/10.1007/978-3-031-85933-5_6

approach to enhance color images. To recover missing data from color images, Miao and Kou [7] proposed a low-rank quaternion matrix completion approach. Guo, Li, and Ling [8] proposed a low light image enhancement approach via illumination map estimation (LIME). Mukaida, et al. [9] proposed a low-light image enhancement approach. The illumination map is initially estimated using a smoothed local histogram and a soft-closing procedure, and then adjusted in a similar way to LIME [8].

For illumination-based approaches, Land [10] proposed a computational theory of color constancy perception: retinex theory, in which retinex can establish a balance in three areas: dynamic range reduction, edge enhancement, and color constancy. By retinex theory, each image can be decomposed into the illumination and reflectance components. Based on retinex theory, Guo, Li, and Ling [11] proposed a low light image enhancement approach. Fu, et al. [12] proposed a weighted variational model to estimate both the reflectance and the illumination of an image so that the quality of the image can be enhanced with noise reduction. To enhance low light images with intense noise, Li et al. [13] proposed a robust retinex model with noise reduction. Thepade and Shirbhate [14] proposed a low light image enhancement approach with weighted merging of a reliable retinex model and dark channel prior.

For learning-based approaches, Wei, et al. [15] proposed a deep retinex-net with key constraints: the consistent reflectance shared by paired low/normal light images and illumination smoothness. Based on retinex theory, Jiao, Zheng, and Lu [16] decomposed each low light image into illumination and reflectance components, then used an attention-based multi-branch network to perform low light image enhancement. Similarly, Zhang and Wang [17] proposed a multi-scale attention retinex network (MARN) for low light image enhancement. Based on U-net [18] and skip connections, Zang, et al. [19] proposed an attention-based neural network containing spatial attention and channel attention modules. Tang, et al. [20] proposed an integration-and-diffusion network for low light image enhancement. Wang, et al. [21] proposed a deep lightening network (DLN), which consists of several lightening back-projection (LBP) blocks and feature aggregation (FA) blocks for learning the differences between the low and normal light images and exploiting the local and global image features, respectively. Lu and Jung [22] proposed a multi-branch low light image enhancement approach conducting joint illumination control, color enhancement, and denoising. Zhao, et al. [23] proposed an end-to-end color channel fusion network (CCFN) for low light image enhancement. Bow, et al. [24] proposed a low light image enhancement approach containing an illumination boosting network and an image disentanglement network. Qu, Ou, and Xiong [25] proposed an unsupervised low light image enhancement approach, which can restore color information and image details with noise reduction. Ma et al. [26] proposed a generative adversarial network (GAN) based on retinex theory, namely, RetinexGAN for low light image enhancement. Zhang, et al. [27] proposed a histogram equalization prior (HEP) approach for low light image enhancement, which can recover image details with noise reduction. Hai, et al. [28] proposed a retinex-based real-low to real-normal network (R2Rnet) for low light image enhancement, which includes three subnets: a Decom-Net, a Denoise-Net, and a Relight-Net. Zhang, et al. [29] proposed a retinex-based approach with a divide-and-conquer strategy for low light image enhancement. Fan, Liu, and Liu [30] proposed a low light image enhancement approach based on an improved hierarchical model: M-Net +. Zhang, Yuan, Li, Gao, and Li [31] proposed a multi-branch and progressive network for low light image enhancement, which contains four different branches building the mapping relationships among different scales. Sun, et al. [32] proposed a gradient and brightness guilded low light image enhancement with attention-based self-paced learning. Wu, Huang, Ma, Fan, and Ma [33] proposed a low light image enhancement approach via retinex-inline CycleGAN.

This paper is organized as follows. The proposed low light image enhancement approach using autoencoder-based deep neural networks is described in Sect. 2. Experimental results are shown in Sect. 3, followed by concluding remarks.

2 Proposed Approach

2.1 Proposed System Architecture

In this study, a low light image enhancement approach using autoencoder-based deep neural networks is proposed. As shown in Fig. 1, the proposed approach consists of two subnets, namely, feature extraction (FE) subnet and color enhancement (CE) subnet. FE subnet extracts image features from the low light image and enhances detailed textures, while CE subnet recovers the color information of the low light image and performs image denoising. A pre-processing technique, namely, relative global histogram stretching (RGHS) [34] is employed in CE subnet. Finally, the processing results of FE and CE subnets are fused to generate the final enhanced image.

In this study, the input image and enhanced image are denoted as $I(x, y) = \{I_r(x, y), I_g(x, y), I_b(x, y)\}$ and $O(x, y) = \{O_r(x, y), O_g(x, y), O_b(x, y)\}$, respectively, where $I_r(x, y)$, $I_g(x, y)$, and $I_b(x, y)$ are the red, green, and blue components of $I(x, y)$, respectively, $O_r(x, y)$, $O_g(x, y)$, and $O_b(x, y)$ are the red, green, and blue components of $O(x, y)$, respectively, $0 \leq I_r(x, y), I_g(x, y), I_b(x, y), O_r(x, y), O_g(x, y), O_b(x, y) \leq 255$, $1 \leq x \leq W$, $1 \leq y \leq H$, and W and H denote the width and height of images, respectively. In this study, all the input images are normalized as $600 \times 400 \times 3$ in size, where 3 is the number of three (R, G, B) color channels. To speed up the training process, each input low light image is cropped into data processing units $128 \times 128 \times 3$ in size in an overlapping manner.

2.2 Feature Extraction

As shown in Fig. 2, FE subnet consists of an encoder and a decoder, in which bottleneck guided channel attention (BGCA) module [20] can effectively enhance image details and textures. The output of FE subnet is denoted as $I_{FE}(x, y) = \{I_{FE,r}(x, y), I_{FE,g}(x, y), I_{FE,b}(x, y)\}$. The proposed FE subnet architecture is shown in Table 1.

As shown in Fig. 3, Tang, et al. [20] proposed a bottleneck guided channel attention (BGCA) module using the network's bottleneck (a 1×1 convolution structure) so that the amount of computations can be reduced. $BGCA_1$ and $BGCA_2$ in Fig. 1 are $W \times H \times 32$ and $W/2 \times H/2 \times 64$ in sizes, respectively, and separately operate with global average pooling ($1 \times 1 \times 128$ in size). Note that BCGAs with different sizes will generate the corresponding F_{bcga} with different sizes.

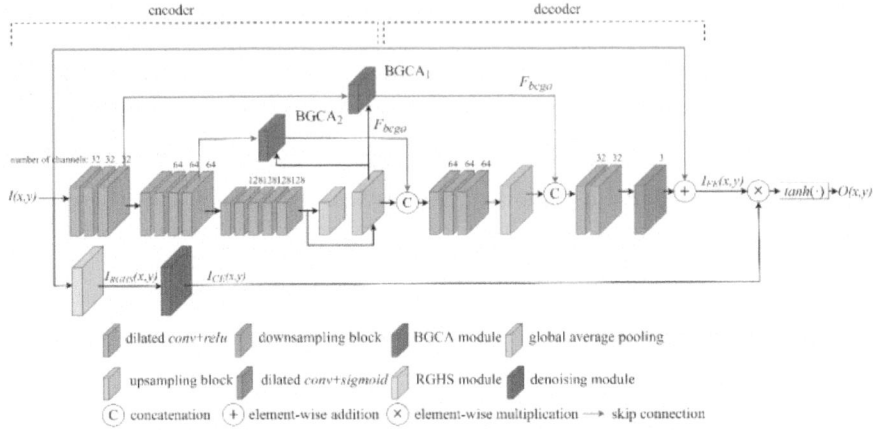

Fig. 1. Framework of the proposed approach.

For U-net, Ronneberger, et al. [18] proposed an encoder-decoder architecture with skip connections, which can perform end-to-end training with a small number of training samples (images). By skip connections, the output of a layer in the encoder can be directly fed into the corresponding layer (same resolution) in the decoder.

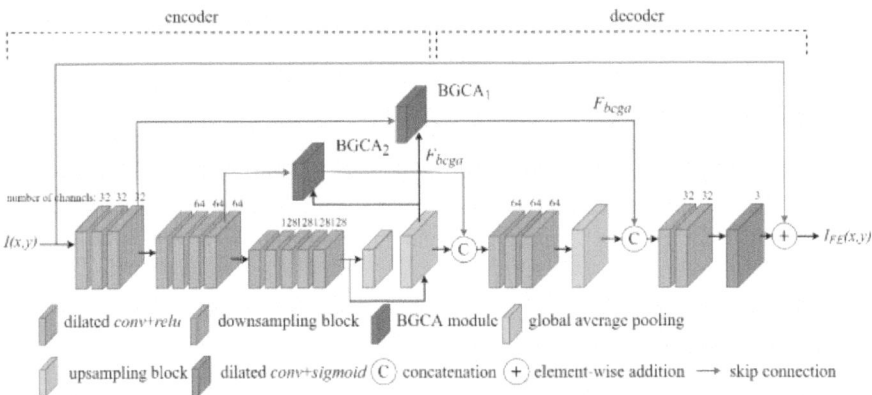

Fig. 2. The proposed FE subnet.

For encoder-decoder structure, to extract image features, various convolution and pooling operations are usually employed with image downsampling and receptive field enlargement at the encoder, and then image upsampling is performed to enlarge image sizes in the decoder. Performing pooling, some image information may be lost. To cope with this problem, dilated convolutions are employed in this study, which can expand receptive fields and maintain image resolutions.

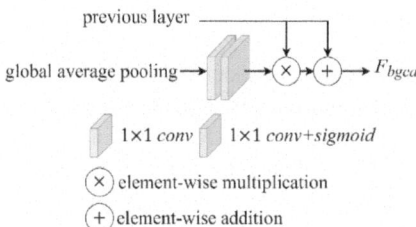

Fig. 3. BCGA module.

Table 1. Proposed FE architecture.

layer index	layer	kernel size	stride	padding	dilated rate	output size
1	dilated *conv*	3 × 3	1 × 1	1	1	H × W × 32
2	dilated *conv*	3 × 3	1 × 1	2	2	H × W × 32
3	dilated *conv*	3 × 3	1 × 1	1	1	H × W × 32
4	downsampling	2 × 2	2 × 2	-	-	H/2 × W/2 × 32
5	dilated *conv*	3 × 3	1 × 1	1	1	H/2 × W/2 × 64
6	dilated *conv*	3 × 3	1 × 1	1	1	H/2 × W2/ × 64
7	dilated *conv*	3 × 3	1 × 1	2	2	H/2 × W/2 × 64
8	downsampling	2 × 2	2 × 2	-	-	H/4 × W/4 × 64
9	dilated *conv*	3 × 3	1 × 1	1	1	H/4 × W/4 × 128
10	dilated *conv*	3 × 3	1 × 1	2	2	H/4 × W/4 × 128
11	dilated *conv*	3 × 3	1 × 1	1	1	H/4 × W/4 × 128
12	dilated *conv*	3 × 3	1 × 1	2	2	H/4 × W/4 × 128
13	upsampling	3 × 3	2 × 2	1	1	H/2 × W/2 × 64
14	concatenation	-	-	-	-	H/2 × W/2 × 128
15	dilated *conv*	3 × 3	1 × 1	1	1	H/2 × W/2 × 64
16	dilated *conv*	3 × 3	1 × 1	2	2	H/2 × W/2 × 64
17	dilated *conv*	3 × 3	1 × 1	1	1	H/2 × W/2 × 64
18	upsampling	3 × 3	2 × 2	1	1	H × W × 32
19	concatenation	-	-	-	-	H × W × 64
20	dilated *conv*	3 × 3	1 × 1	1	1	H × W × 32
21	dilated *conv*	3 × 3	1 × 1	2	2	H × W × 32
22	dilated *conv*	3 × 3	1 × 1	1	1	H × W × 3
23	addition	-	-	-	-	H × W × 3

2.3 Color Enhancement

As show in Fig. 4, the proposed color enhancement (CE) subnet consists of RGHS module and denoising module. RGHS module can improve image quality by global histogram stretching, enhance color saturation due to low light image characteristics, and retain image details and textures, while denoising module will perform noise reduction for the pre-processing image $I_{RGHS}(x, y) = \{I_{RGHS,r}(x, y), I_{RGHS,g}(x, y), I_{RGHS,b}(x, y)\}$, resulting in $I_{CE}(x, y) = \{I_{CE,r}(x, y), I_{CE,g}(x, y), I_{CE,b}(x, y)\}$.

Huang, et al. [34] proposed a relative global histogram stretching (RGHS) approach in both RGB and CIE-Lab color spaces. In the proposed RGHS module, RGHS is first performed in RGB color space, then RGHS is performed again in CIE-Lab color space. Based on Gray-world theory, RGHS in RGB color space performs adaptive histogram stretching by the distribution characteristics of RGB channels. RGHS in CIE-Lab space performs curvilinear and linear adaptive stretchings on the luminance component L and the color (a, b) components, respectively.

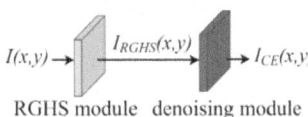

Fig. 4. The proposed CE subnet.

As shown in Fig. 5, in this study, the proposed denoising module consists of 8 consecutive dilated *conv* + *relu* (dilated *conv* followed by *relu* activation function) and 1 dilated *conv* + *sigmoid* (dilated *conv* followed by *sigmoid* activation function). The proposed denoising module architecture is shown in Table 2.

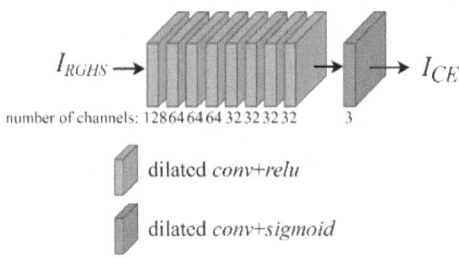

Fig. 5. The proposed denoising module.

2.4 Activation Functions, Loss Functions, and Optimizer

In this study, two activation functions, *sigmoid*$(\cdot)$ and *relu*$(\cdot)$, are employed, where *sigmoid*$(\cdot)$ is a continuous and stable activation function for deep learning and *relu*$(\cdot)$ rectified linear unit is an activation function for reducing the problem of exploding

Table 2. Proposed denoising module architecture.

layer index	layer	kernel size	stride	padding	dilated rate	output size
1	dilated *conv*	3×3	1×1	2	2	H × W × 128
2	dilated *conv*	3×3	1×1	1	1	H × W × 64
3	dilated *conv*	3×3	1×1	2	2	H × W × 64
4	dilated *conv*	5×5	1×1	2	1	H × W × 64
5	dilated *conv*	3×3	1×1	1	1	H × W × 32
6	dilated *conv*	3×3	1×1	2	2	H × W × 32
7	dilated *conv*	5×5	1×1	2	1	H × W × 32
8	dilated *conv*	3×3	1×1	1	1	H × W × 32
9	dilated *conv*	3×3	1×1	1	1	H × W × 3

gradient or vanishing gradient. In this study, mean square error (MSE) and structural similarity index measure (SSIM) [35] are employed as loss functions. The total loss function $Loss_{total}$ is defined as

$$Loss_{total} = \lambda_1 \cdot MSE(GT, O) + \lambda_2(1 - SSIM(GT, O)), \qquad (1)$$

where λ_1 and λ_2 denote two balancing coefficients (empirically set to 0.15 and 0.85, respectively). In this study, to improve gradient descent and reduce the possibility of convergence to local optima, adaptive moment estimation (Adam) optimizer [36] is employed for training.

3   Experimental Results

In this study, the proposed approach is implemented on Microsoft Windows 10 platform with AMD Ryzen 5 5600x 3.70Ghz (CPU), 64 gigabytes main memory (RAM), Nvidia GeForce RTX 3090 (GPU), python version 3.9.7, pytorch version 1.8.0, CUDA version 11.5, and cuDNN version 8.0.5. In this study, LOL dataset [15] and LSRW dataset [28] are employed. LOL dataset contains 500 pairs of low light images, in which 400 image pairs are used for training and 100 image pairs are used for testing. LSRW dataset contains 3170 pairs of low light images, in which 3050 image pairs are used for training and 120 image pairs are used for testing.

To evaluate the performance of the proposed approach, two objective measures, namely, peak signal-to-noise ratio (PSNR) and structural similarity index measure (SSIM) [35], are employed. To evaluate the performance of the proposed approach, in this study, five comparison approaches, namely, R2RNet [28], KinD++ [29], DLN [21], HEP [27], and HWMNet [30], are employed. In terms of average PSNR (dB) and SSIM, performance comparisons between five comparison approaches and the proposed approach on LOL dataset [15] and LSRW dataset [28] are shown in Tables 3 and 4, respectively.

Table 3. In terms of average PSNR (dB) and SSIM, performance comparisons between five comparison approaches and the proposed approach on LOL dataset [15].

Approaches	Metrics	
	PSNR (dB)	SSIM
R2RNet [28]	19.10	0.808
KinD++ [29]	23.43	0.875
DLN [21]	24.20	**0.893**
HEP [27]	22.07	0.850
HWMNet [30]	24.24	0.850
Proposed	**25.99**	0.891

Table 4. In terms of average PSNR (dB) and SSIM, performance comparisons between five comparison approaches and the proposed approach on LSRW dataset [28].

Approaches	Metrics	
	PSNR (dB)	SSIM
R2RNet [28]	16.67	0.643
KinD++ [29]	16.45	0.583
DLN [21]	18.70	**0.641**
HEP [27]	14.93	0.610
HWMNet [30]	17.50	0.634
Proposed	**19.38**	0.658

For subjective quality evaluation, some experimental results of five comparison approaches and the proposed approach on LOL dataset [15] and LSRW dataset [28] are shown in Figs. 6, 7 and 8.

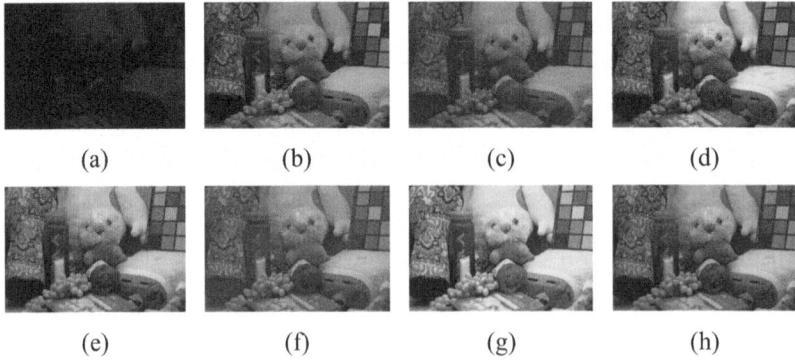

(a)　　　　(b)　　　　(c)　　　　(d)

(e)　　　　(f)　　　　(g)　　　　(h)

Fig. 6. Experimental results on LOL dataset [15]: (a) low light image, (b) ground truth, (c)-(h) processed images by R2RNet [28], KinD ++ [29], DLN [21], HEP [27], HWMNet [30], and the proposed approach, respectively.

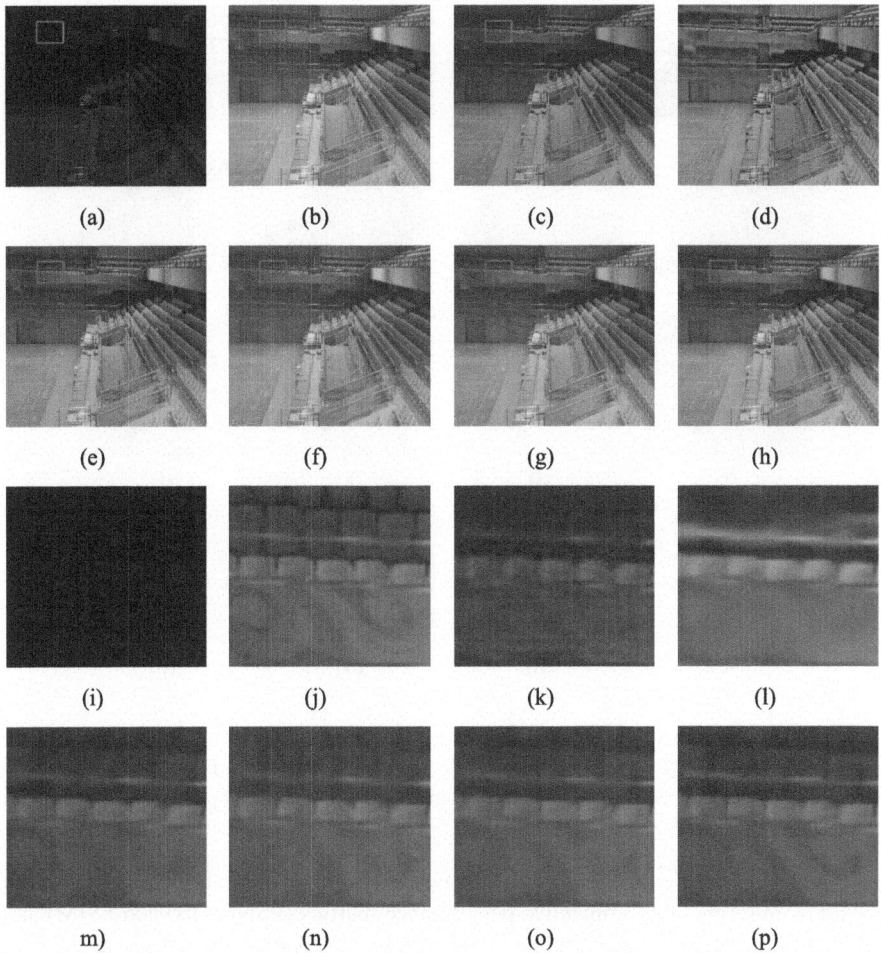

Fig. 7. Experimental results on LOL dataset [15]: (a) low light image, (b) ground truth, (c)-(h) processed images by R2RNet [28], KinD ++ [29], DLN [21], HEP [27], HWMNet [30], and the proposed approach, respectively. (i)–(p) show some corresponding detail parts of images (a)–(h).

4   Concluding Remarks

In this study, a low light image enhancement approach using autoencoder-based deep neural networks is proposed. The proposed approach consists of two subnets, namely, feature extraction (FE) subnet and color enhancement (CE) subnet. FE subnet extracts image features from the low light image and enhances detailed textures, while CE subnet recovers the color information of the low light image and performs image denoising. A pre-processing technique, namely, relative global histogram stretching (RGHS) [34] is employed in CE subnet. Finally, the processing results of FE and CE subnets are fused

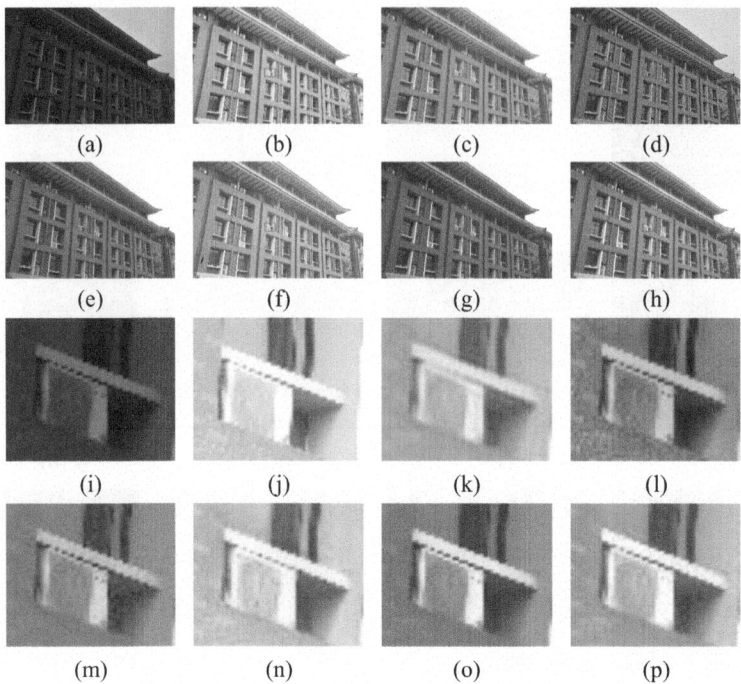

Fig. 8. Experimental results on LSRW dataset [28]: (a) low light image, (b) ground truth, (c)-(h) processed images by R2RNet [28], KinD ++ [29], DLN [21], HEP [27], HWMNet [30], and the proposed approach, respectively. (i)–(p) show some corresponding detail parts of images (a)–(h).

to generate the final enhanced image. Based on the experimental results obtained in this study, in terms of two objective performance metrics (PSNR (dB) and SSIM) and subjective evaluation, the performance of the proposed approach is better than those of five comparison approaches.

Acknowledgements. This work was supported in part by National Science and Technology Council, Taiwan, ROC under Grant NTSC 112-2221-E-194-030.

References

1. Ru, L., Du, B., Wu, C.: Multi-temporal scene classification and scene change detection with correlation based fusion. IEEE Trans. Image Process. **30**, 1382–1394 (2021)
2. Oksuz, I., et al.: Deep learning-based detection and correction of cardiac MR motion artefacts during reconstruction for high-quality segmentation. IEEE Trans. Med. Imag. **39**(12), 4001–4010 (2020)
3. Ning, Z., Zhong, S., Feng, Q., Chen, W., Zhang, Y.: SMU-net: saliency-guided morphology-aware u-net for breast lesion segmentation in ultrasound image. IEEE Trans. Med. Imag. **41**(2), 476–490 (2022)

4. Ibrahim, H., Kong, N.S.P.: Brightness preserving dynamic histogram equalization for image contrast enhancement. IEEE Trans. Consum. Electron. **53**(4), 1752–1758 (2007)
5. Zhang, Y., Bai, X., Wang, T.: Boundary finding based multi-focus image fusion through multi-scale morphological focus-measure. Inform. Fusion **35**, 81–101 (2017)
6. Nakai, K., Hoshi, Y., Taguchi, A.: Color image contrast enhancement method based on differential intensity/saturation gray-levels histograms. In: Proceedings of 2013 International Symposium on Intelligent Signal Processing and Communication Systems, pp. 190–201 (2015)
7. Miao, J., Kou, K.I.: Color image recovery using low-rank quaternion matrix completion algorithm. IEEE Trans. Image Process. **31**, 190–201 (2022)
8. Guo, X., Li, Y., Ling, H.: LIME: low-light image enhancement via illumination map estimation. IEEE Trans. Image Process. **26**(2), 982–993 (2017)
9. Mukaida, M., Kojima, S., Uchino, E., Suetake, N.: Low-light image enhancement method by soft-closing using local histogram. In: Proceedings of 2021 IEEE the 30th International Symposium on Industrial Electronics, pp. 1–6 (2021)
10. Land, E.H.: The retinex theory of color vision. Sci. Am. **237**(6), 108–128 (1977)
11. Guo, X., Li, Y., Ling, H.: LIME: low-light image enhancement via illumination map estimation. IEEE Trans. Image Process. **26**(2), 982–993 (2017)
12. Fu, X., Zeng, D., Huang, Y., Zhang, X.P., Ding, X.: A weighted variational model for simultaneous reflectance and illumination estimation. In: Proceedings of 2016 IEEE/CVF Conf. on Computer Vision and Pattern Recognition, pp. 2780–2790 (2016)
13. Li, M., Liu, J., Yang, W., Sun, X., Guo, Z.: Structure-revealing low-light image enhancement via robust retinex model. IEEE Trans. Image Process. **27**(6), 2828–2841 (2018)
14. Thepade, S.D., Shirhate, A.: Visibility enhancement in low light images with weighted fusion of robust retinex model and dark channel prior. In: Proceedings of 2020 IEEE Bombay Section Signature Conference, pp. 69–73 (2020)
15. Wei, C., Wang, W., Yang, W., Liu, J.: Deep retinex decomposition for low-light enhancement. arXiv: 1808.04560 (2018)
16. Jiao, Y., Zheng, X., Lu, X.: Attention-based multi-branch network for low-light image enhancement. In: Proceedings of 2021 IEEE the 2nd International Conference on Big Data, Artificial Intelligence and Internet of Things Engineering, pp. 401–407 (2021)
17. Zhang, X., Wang, X.: MARN: multi-scale attention retinex network for low-light image enhancement. IEEE Access **9**, 50939–50948 (2021)
18. Ronneberger, O., Fischer, P., Brox, T.: U-net: convolutional networks for biomedical image segmentation. arXiv: 1505.04597 (2015)
19. Zhang, C., Yan, Q., Zhu, Y., Li, X., Sun, J., Zhang, Y.: Attention-based network for low-light image enhancement. In: Proceedings of 2020 IEEE International Conference on Multimedia and Expo, pp. 1–6 (2020)
20. Tang, P., Guo, X., Ju, G., Shen, L., Men, A.: Integration-and-diffusion network for low-light image enhancement. In: Proceedings of 2021 IEEE International Conference on Image Processing, pp. 1664–1668 (2021)
21. Wang, L., Liu, Z., Siu, W., Lun, D.P.K.: Lightening network for low-light image enhancement. IEEE Trans. Image Process. **29**, 7984–7996 (2020)
22. Lu, Y., Jung, S.W.: Progressive joint low-light enhancement and noise removal for raw images. IEEE Trans. Image Process. **31**, 2390–2404 (2022)
23. Zhao, L., Gong, X., Liu, K., Wang, J., Zhao, B., Liu, Y.: Color channel fusion network for low-light image enhancement. In: Proceedings of 2021 IEEE International Conference on Image Processing, pp. 1654–1658 (2021)
24. Bow, N.C.N., Tran, V.H., Kerdsiri, P., Loh, Y.P., Huang, C.C.: DEN: disentanglement and enhancement networks for low illumination images. In: Proceedings of 2020 IEEE International Conf. on Visual Communication and Image Processing, pp. 419–422 (2020)

25. Qu, Y., Ou, Y., Xiong, R.: Low light enhancement by unsupervised network. In: Proceedings of 2020 IEEE International Conference on Real-time Computing and Robotics, pp. 404–409 (2020)

26. Ma, T., et al.: RetinexGAN: unsupervised low-light enhancement with two-layer convolutional decomposition networks. IEEE Access **9**, 56539–56550 (2021)

27. Zhong, F., Shao, Y., Sun, Y., Zhu, K., Gao, C., Sang, N.: Unsupervised low-light image enhancement via histogram equalization prior. arXiv: 2112.01766 (2021)

28. Hai, J., Xuan, Z., Han, S., Yang, R., Hao, Y., Zou, F., Lin, F.: R2RNet: low-light image enhancement via real-low to real-normal network. arXiv: 2106.14501 (2021)

29. Zhang, Y., Guo, X., Ma, J., Liu, W., Zhang, J.: Beyond brightening low-light images. Int. J. Comput. Vision **129**, 1013–1037 (2021)

30. Fan, C.M., Liu, T.J., Liu, K.H.: Half wavelet attention on M-Net+ for low-light image enhancement. arXiv: 2203.01296 (2022)

31. Zhangm, K., Yuan, C., Li, J., Gao, X., Li, M.: Multi-branch and progressive network for low light image enhancement. IEEE Trans. Image Process. **23**, 2295–2308 (2023)

32. Sun, X., et al.: Gradient and brightness guided low-light image enhancement with attention-based self-paced learning. In: Proceedings of 2024 IEEE International Conference on Acoustics, Speech, and Signal Processing, pp. 3434–3439 (2024)

33. Wu, K., Huang, J., Ma, Y., Fan, F., Ma, J.: Cycle-retinex repaired low-light image enhancement via retinex-inline CycleGAN. IEEE Trans. on Multimed. **24**, 1213–1228 (2024)

34. Huang, D., Wang, Y., Song, W., Sequeira, J., Mavromatis, S.: Shallow-water image enhancement using relative global histogram stretching based on adaptive parameter acquisition. In: Proceedings of 2018 the 24th International Conference on MultiMedia Modeling, pp. 453–465 (2018)

35. Wang, Z., Bovik, A.C., Sheikh, H.R., Simoncelli, E.P.: Image quality assessment: from error visibility to structural similarity. IEEE Trans. Image Process. **13**(4), 600–612 (2004)

36. Kingma, D.P., Ba, J.L.: Adam: a method for stochastic optimization. In: Proceedings of 2015 the 3rd International Conference on Learning Representations, pp. 1–15 (2015)

Towards Elephants Intelligent Monitoring in Zakouma National Park, Chad

Hassan Djibrine Oumar[1], Ahmat Daouda[2(✉)], Youssouf Azza[1],
and Ngueilbaye Alladoumbaye[3]

[1] Department of Computer Science, Virtual University of Chad, N'Djamena, Chad
{oumar.hassan,azza.youssouf}@uvt.td
[2] Department of Computer Science, University of N'Djamena, N'Djamena, Chad
daouda.ahmat@uvt.td
[3] Department of Computer Science, Shenzhen University, Shenzhen, China
angueilbaye@szu.edu.cn

Abstract. This paper proposes an approach based on artificial intelligence to open up new prospects for the protection of endangered species in Zakouma National Park, Chad. This paper analyzes a few major algorithm models used in the detection or segmentation process to determine their accuracy when applied to wildlife. An assessment and a benchmarking were carried out on detection and segmentation algorithms such as Faster R-CNN, Mask R-CNN, YOLO V7, YOLO V8, and YOLO NAS. The process of tracking wild animals is handled by the ByteTrack library. A unique ID is assigned to each animal, enabling it to be identified individually after the detection and recognition process. The counting approach derives from the individual animal identification mechanism: when an animal, recognized by YOLO 8, is first detected during the counting process, then the species-specific counter, initialized at 0, is incremented by one unit. The YOLO 8 algorithm yields the most reliable precision rates, and is therefore chosen for animal detection and identification.

Keywords: Computer vision · Machine Learning · Deep Learning · detection · segmentation · wildlife monitoring · wildlife counting

1 Introduction

Zakouma National Park is one of the last intact ecosystems in the Sahel. The park is home to a wide variety of species, some of which are threatened with extinction. Due to the threat posed by poachers, the elephants are one of the park's protected species. The NGO African Parks, which manages the park, has installed a camera every five kilometers to monitor the wildlife. However, the data recorded by these cameras is not processed efficiently. Lacking an effective image management tool, African Parks agents manually analyze the images collected

---

H. D. Oumar, Y. Azza, N. Alladoumbaye—Contributing authors.

L. Deligiannidis et al. (Eds.): CSCE 2024, CCIS 2262, pp. 85–96, 2025.
https://doi.org/10.1007/978-3-031-85933-5_7

from cameras installed in Zakouma Park. Computer vision is a subfield of AI [1–4] that enables machines to visually understand and interpret the world around them, mimicking human intellectual faculties. Authors reviewed the literature on machine learning (ML)-based techniques for wildlife protection [5,6]. Some research work has proposed a review of the literature on machine learning-based or deep learning-based techniques for wildlife protection [7–9]. These scientific contributions support the efforts made by environmental stakeholders to protect wildlife. In this context, numerous methods have been developed to automate animal detection and identification using computer vision, based on data collected by camera traps [10].

The rapid decline of endangered species due to human activities has become a pressing global issue. In response, the development of intelligent control devices has emerged as a promising solution to protect these species from further harm. This paper presents a comprehensive review of the current state of intelligent control devices for the protection of endangered species, including their design, implementation, and potential impact. This paper draws on the concept of computer vision, a subfield of artificial intelligence (AI), to overcome the technical shortcomings observed in processing images collected in the Zakouma Wildlife Park by ensuring the detection/segmentation, recognition, identification, and counting of wild animals. Indeed, a comparative analysis of detection/segmentation algorithms is proposed in order to determine the one with the highest accuracy. An approach is then proposed for monitoring and counting animal populations within the scope of this study.

2   Results

Protecting and monitoring species have always been a priority around the world. Some AI-free innovative approaches are proposed in the literature in order to meet the needs in terms of performance and efficiency in the wildlife monitoring field [11,12]. Nevertheless, computer vision is a field of research that is attracting more and more interest. There is a wide range of research in the literature on animal monitoring and tracking [13–22]. These works are based on various approaches to propose a mechanism for monitoring and tracking wild or domestic animals. Relatively dated papers also address this issue using AI-less approaches [11,12]. Nevertheless, the advent of computer vision in the wake of the development of AI has sparked renewed interest in this field of research [20,23–25]. The authors have thus proposed animal monitoring techniques based on the CNN algorithm [14,23,26–28] and its variants [29]. Many recent papers found in the literature are based on the Mask R-CNN [30] and Faster RCNN variants of the algorithm CNN, for enhanced accuracy, are proposed in the literature [31–34]. The Yolo algorithm, in its various versions, is attracting increasing interest for its high performance and efficiency in images recognition [25,35–39]. In addition to the literature review performed, an evaluation of Deep Learning models in the detection and segmentation process is performed. The assessment is carried out on algorithms such as CNN, R-CNN, D-CNN, SSD, Faster R-CNN and

Yolo, with the aim of measuring their performance through experiments. The Table 1 below summarizes the properties of a few papers and categorizes them by algorithm class. For the purpose of this article, the algorithms are implemented and assessed. The last column shows the accuracies obtained by the various approaches. The results show that the Yolo V8, the latest version of Yolo algorithm, has a higher accuracy than the other algorithms with the same goal.

Table 1. Summary of related work & features comparison

Algorithm	Ref	Task	Model	Precision
AI-less Algo.	[11]	Detect. & recon.	SHIFT	**
	[12]	Detect. & Ident.	Voila jones	**
CNN	[23]	Detect. & Ident.	CNN	***
	[14]	Detect. & Classification	CNN	***
	[26]	Detect. & Classification	CNN	****
	[27]	Detect. & Ident.	CNN	****
	[28]	Detect. & Ident.	DCNN	***
	[40]	Detect. & Ident.	DCNN-VGG	***
	[41]	Detect. & Ident.	DCNN-Inception V3	***
	[42]	Detect. & Ident.	DCNN-Inception V3	***
	[22]	Detect. & Ident.	VGG-19 & Bi-LMST	***
	[43]	Detection & Ident.	Resnet	****
	[17]	Detect. & Ident.	Resnet	***
	[44]	Detect. & Ident.	Mobilenet	***
	[21]	Detect. & Ident.	Inception V3	****
	[45]	Detect. & recon.	Googlenet	***
	[46]	Detect. & recon.	CNN	***
	[47]	Detect. & recon.	CNN trap	***
	[48]	Detect. & recon.	CNN	****
	[29]	Detect. & recon.	D-CNN	****
	[49]	Detect. & track. & count.	CNN	***
	[16]	Detect. & track. & count.	CNN	***
R-CNN	[24]	Detect. & recon.	Faster rcnn	***
	[31]	Detect. & track. & count.	R-cnn	***
	[32]	Detect. & track. & count.	Faster rcnn	***
	[33]	Detect. & track. & count.	Faster rcnn & YOLO	***
	[50]	Detect. & track. & count.	Faster rcnn	****
YOLO&SSD	[51]	Detect. & Ident.	YOLO V3	***
	[35]	Detect. & Ident.	YOLO V3	***
	[52]	Detection & Ident.	YOLO V3	***
	[51]	Detect. & Ident.	EX-YOLO	***
	[18]	Detect. & Ident.	SSD-mobilenet V3	***
	[53]	Detect. & Ident.	SSD-mobilenet V1	***
	[25]	Detect. & track. & count.	YOLO V3	***
	[54]	Detect. & track. & count.	Unet	***
	[55]	Detect. & Ident.	YOLO	***
	[37]	Detect. & recon.	YOLO V5	***
	[56]	Detect. & recon.	YOLO	****

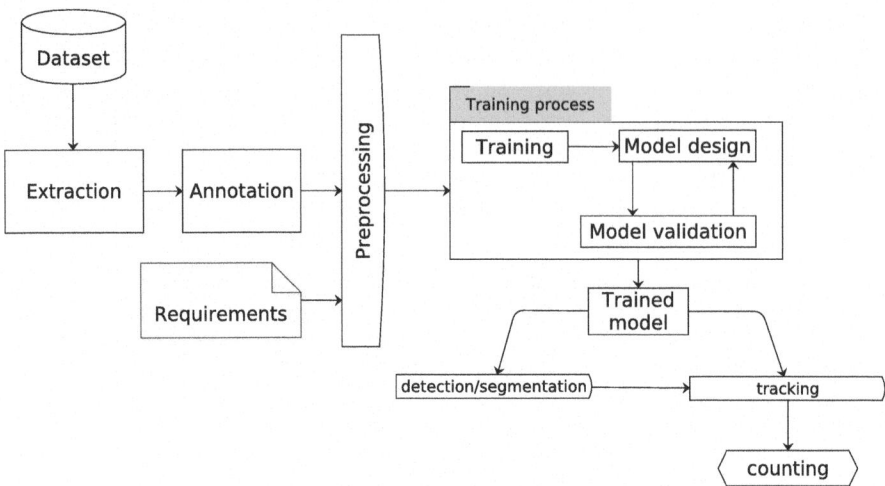

Fig. 1. Proposed scheme.

3   Scheme Design

The Fig. 1 describes the architecture of the proposed model. Indeed, the architecture presents: the pre-processing step in order to prepare the input, the training process in order to improve the model, and the segmentation/detection technique for species recognition. In addition, the architecture proposes a tracking mechanism, using the ByteTrack library, and an animal counting protocol.

3.1   Animal Counting

The Algorithm 1 describes the species counting mechanism from a video content taken as input.

3.2   Detection/Segmentation Process

Based on Deep Learning, the Algorithm 2 defines the detection/segmentation process of animal images. This algorithm is called by previous Algorithm 1 in order to count wild populations of a determined specie.

3.3   Animal Tracking Process

Like Algorithm 1, Algorithm 3 is based on ByteTrack library [57]. Algorithm 3 calls Algorithm 2 in order to provide in real time the itinerary of a specific animal whose image is previously detected or segmented. Bytetrack is a high-performance, lightweight multi-object tracker.

Algorithm 1: animals counting

$\text{count}(\text{algo}(), \text{video}, \text{dataSet})$ **return** $\text{ID}[].size()$

begin

  $\text{ID}[] \longleftarrow \perp$

  if $\text{video}.format = \text{requiredformat}[]$ **then**

    $\text{Frames}[] \longleftarrow \text{extractFramesFrom}(\text{video}, \text{dataSet})$

    foreach $f \in \text{Frames}[]$ **do**

      $\lfloor \quad \text{AnnotatedFrames}[k] \longleftarrow \text{annotate}(f)$

    while $!\text{video}().end$ **do**

      $id \longleftarrow \text{detect\_seg}(\text{algo}(), \text{video}, \text{dataSet})$

      if $id \notin \text{ID}[]$ **then**

        $\lfloor \quad \text{ID}[].add(id)$

Fig. 2. Illustration of detection, tracking and counting.

4   Assessments

This section provides details of the results obtained following the animal detection and segmentation process.

4.1   Image Detection Assessment

The Table 2 propose the assessment of detection models based on Yolo V7, Yolo V8 and Yolo NAS. This table shows that Yolo V8 provides higer pricisions.

The Fig. 2 shows the graphic details inherent of the image detection paradigm. Graphic details include animal ID, counter value and accuracy. The black horizontal line represents the threshold; when it is crossed, the counter value is incremented.

Algorithm 2: detection/segmentation process

```
detect_seg(algo(), video, dataSet) return [precision, animal_ID ]
begin
    k ⟵ 0
    if video.format = requiredformat then
        Frames[] ⟵ extractFramesFrom(video)
        foreach f ∈ Frames[] do
            AnnotatedFrames[k] ⟵ annotate(f)
            k ⟵ k + 1

    for f ∈ AnnotatedFrames[] do
        f' ⟵ preprocessing(f)
        augment(f', dataSet)

    δ ⟵ download()                                    // δ = data
    requirements ⟵ algo().requirements
    weight ⟵ algo().weight
    while δ ≠⊥ do
        train(AnnotatedFrames[], δ, requirements, weight)
        δ ⟵ download()

    precision ⟵ getPrecision()
    animal_ID ⟵ genAnimalID()
```

Algorithm 3: animal tracking process

```
track(detect_seg(), video, POS[])
begin
    ID_DB[] ⟵ ∅
    k ⟵ 0
    while true do
        id ⟵ detect_seg(video).animal_ID
        if id ∉ ID_DB[] then
            ID_DB[]·add(id)
            POS [k++] ⟵ tracker(id)
```

Table 2. Detection models comparison

Epoch	30			100			150		
Metric	precision	MAP 50	F1	precision	MAP 50	F1	precision	MAP50	F1
Yolo V7	0,965	0,961	0,91	0,950	0,983	0,96	0,959	0,987	0,96
Yolo V8	0,931	0,977	0,95	0,934	0,985	0,96	0,961	0,979	0,96
Yolo NAS	0,934	0,94	0,96	56	56	56	56	56	56

Table 3. Segmentation models comparison

Epoch	30			100			150		
Metric	precision	MAP50	F1	precision	MAP50	F1	precision	MAP50	F1
Yolo V7	0,938	0,984	0,96	0,975	0,974	0,95	0.966	0.971	0.95
Yolo V8	0,957	0,979	0,96	0,954	0,980	0,92	0,986	0,984	0,96

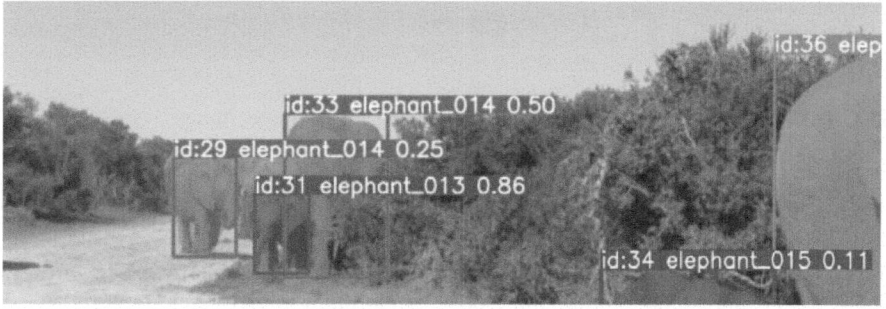

Fig. 3. Illustration of segmentation, tracking and counting.

Table 4. Performances comparison between Faster RCNN & Mask RCNN models

Iteration	300		600	
Metric	Recall	MAP50	Recall	MAP50
Faster RCNN	40%	18%	63%	44%
Mask RCNN	45%	30%	64%	59%

4.2   Image Segmentation Assessment

The Fig. 3 and Table 3 respectively describe the same idea as Fig. 2 and Table 2 defined in the previous sub-section. However, Unlike Table 2 and Fig. 2, Table 3 and Fig. 3 focus on image segmentation.

4.3   Segmentation Vs Detection

The Table 4 provides a comparison between detection (Faster RCNN) and segmentation (Mask RCNN) results. This table shows that segmentation, based on Mask RCNN, presents higher precisions than segmentation, based on Faster RCNN.

4.4   Performance Assessment Results

The Fig. 4 provides details inherent to performances of Yolo 8 obtained from elephant images segmentation. These results are based on 150 epochs for elephant images segmentation.

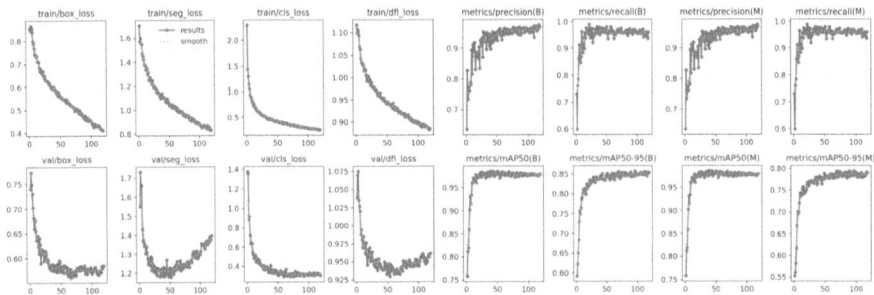

Fig. 4. Performances assessment of Yolo V8 used for elephant images segmentation.

On the one hand, the results shown in the Table 2 are obtained when the Yolo V8 algorithm is used with a fixed number of epochs (150) for elephant detection. Thus, 9/16, or 56.25%, of elephants are detected with 100% accuracy. These experiments also show that 100% of elephant images are detected with 90% accuracy. On the other hand, based on 150 epochs, in the Table 3 presents the segmentation results obtained from Yolo V8 algorithm. The results reach 12/16, or 75%, of elephant images are segmented with 100% accuracy, while 15/16, or 93.75 %, of elephant images reach 98% accuracy.

5   Conclusion

Zakouma National Park, located in Chad, is home to a diverse range of wildlife, including several endangered species such as elephants, Kordofan giraffes, and lions. The protection of these species is of utmost importance to ensure their survival for future generations. This research paper focuses on the implementation of an intelligent control device for the protection of these endangered species within Zakouma National Park. Thus, in order to prevent species disappearances, this paper proposes an approach to wild animals detection/segmentation, tracking and counting in Zakouma National Park, Chad. Major detection and segmentation algorithms, such as Yolo, Yolo NAS, Mask R-CNN and Faster R-CNN, were assessed. These evaluations show that the Yolo V8 algorithm offers the highest accuracies in both cases. The ByteTrack library is used for animal tracking. Animals are uniquely identified, enabling them to be counted. The results presented are based on images of elephants taken from a video downloaded from the Internet. Future work is planned to cover all five species that make up the elephants. In addition, future work will focus in particular on the lastest version of Yolo algorithm, i.e. Yolo V9. The implementation of intelligent control devices in Zakouma National Park has demonstrated positive outcomes in terms of reducing poaching incidents and enhancing wildlife protection. The preservation of endangered species contributes to the overall ecological balance and supports ecotourism, ben- efiting both the local communities and the national economy. Looking ahead, further advancements in technology and data analytics hold potential for refining intelligent control devices and expanding their application to other conservation areas.

References

1. Simonyan, K., Zisserman, A.: Very deep convolutional networks for large-scale image recognition. arXiv preprint arXiv:1409.1556 (2014)
2. Szegedy, C., et al.: Going deeper with convolutions. In: Proceedings of the IEEE Conference on Computer Vision and Pattern Recognition, pp. 1–9 (2015)
3. Stoianov, I.: Connectionist lexical processing. PhD thesis, University Library Groningen][Host] (2001)
4. McCulloch, W.S., Pitts, W.: A logical calculus of the ideas immanent in nervous activity. Bull. Math. Biophys. **5**, 115–133 (1943)
5. Shapiro, S.C.: The turing test and the economist. ACM SIGART Bull. **3**(4), 10–11 (1992)
6. Rosenblatt, F.: The perceptron: a probabilistic model for information storage and organization in the brain. Psychol. Rev. **65**(6), 386 (1958)
7. Krenker, A., Bešter, J., Kos, A.: Introduction to the artificial neural networks. In: Artificial Neural Networks: Methodological Advances and Biomedical Applications, pp. 1–18. InTech (2011)
8. Sharif Razavian, A., Azizpour, H., Sullivan, J., Carlsson, S.: Cnn features off-the-shelf: an astounding baseline for recognition. In: Proceedings of the IEEE Conference on Computer Vision and Pattern Recognition Workshops, pp. 806–813 (2014)
9. He, K., Gkioxari, G., Dollár, P., Girshick, R.: Mask r-cnn: In: Proceedings of the IEEE International Conference on Computer Vision, pp. 2961–2969 (2017)
10. Zou, Z., Chen, K., Shi, Z., Guo, Y., Ye, J.: Object detection in 20 years: a survey. Proc. IEEE **111**, 257–276 (2023)
11. Yu, X., Wang, J., Kays, R., Jansen, P.A., Wang, T., Huang, T.: Automated identification of animal species in camera trap images. EURASIP J. Image Video Process. **2013**(1), 1–10 (2013). https://doi.org/10.1186/1687-5281-2013-52
12. Burghardt, T., Calic, J.: Real-time face detection and tracking of animals. In: 2006 8th Seminar on Neural Network Applications in Electrical Engineering, pp. 27–32. IEEE (2006)
13. Banupriya, N., Saranya, S., Swaminathan, R., Harikumar, S., Palanisamy, S.: Animal detection using deep learning algorithm. J. Crit. Rev **7**(1), 434–439 (2020)
14. Sindhu, V., Alam, A., Thapa, P.: Wild animal detection and warning system using machine learning and deep learning algorithms (2021)
15. Pan, S.J., Yang, Q.: A survey on transfer learning. IEEE Trans. Knowl. Data Eng. **22**(10), 1345–1359 (2009)
16. Brown, L., Schormann, D.: Poacher detection and wildlife counting system. In: Proceedings of Southern Africa Telecommunications on Network Application Conference (SATNAC), pp. 1–6 (2019)
17. Chen, R., Little, R., Mihaylova, L., Delahay, R., Cox, R.: Wildlife surveillance using deep learning methods. Ecol. Evol. **9**(17), 9453–9466 (2019)
18. Gat, A., Gaikwad, H., Giri, R., Sardey, M.P., Gajare, M.P.: Animal detector system for forest monitoring using opencv and raspberry-pi (2020)
19. Singh, P., Lindshield, S.M., Zhu, F., Reibman, A.R.: Animal localization in camera-trap images with complex backgrounds. In: 2020 IEEE Southwest Symposium on Image Analysis and Interpretation (SSIAI), pp. 66–69. IEEE (2020)

20. Lei, J., Gao, S., Rasool, M.A., Fan, R., Jia, Y., Lei, G.: Optimized small waterbird detection method using surveillance videos based on yolov7. Animals **13**(12), 1929 (2023)
21. Gupta, S., Mohan, N., Nayak, P., Nagaraju, K.C., Karanam, M.: Deep vision-based surveillance system to prevent train–elephant collisions. Soft Comput., 1–14 (2022)
22. Natarajan, B., Elakkiya, R., Bhuvaneswari, R., Saleem, K., Chaudhary, D., Samsudeen, S.H.: Creating alert messages based on wild animal activity detection using hybrid deep neural networks. IEEE Access **11**, 67308–67321 (2023)
23. Himawan, I., Towsey, M., Law, B., Roe, P.: Deep learning techniques for koala activity detection. In: INTERSPEECH, pp. 2107–2111 (2018)
24. Cheema, G.S., Anand, S.: Automatic detection and recognition of individuals in patterned species. In: Altun, Y., et al. (eds.) ECML PKDD 2017. LNCS (LNAI), vol. 10536, pp. 27–38. Springer, Cham (2017). https://doi.org/10.1007/978-3-319-71273-4_3
25. Arshad, B., Barthelemy, J., Pilton, E., Perez, P.: Where is my deer?-wildlife tracking and counting via edge computing and deep learning. In: 2020 IEEE SENSORS, pp. 1–4 (2020)
26. Dutta, P.: A deep learning approach for animal breed classification-sheep. Int. J. Res. Appl. Sci. Eng. Technol. **9**(5), 10–22214 (2021)
27. Pan, Y., Jin, H., Gao, J., Rauf, H.T.: Identification of buffalo breeds using self-activated-based improved convolutional neural networks. Agriculture **12**(9), 1386 (2022)
28. El Abbadi, N.K., Alsaadi, E.M.T.A.: An automated vertebrate animals classification using deep convolution neural networks. In: 2020 International Conference on Computer Science and Software Engineering (CSASE), pp. 72–77. IEEE (2020)
29. Chen, G., Han, T.X., He, Z., Kays, R., Forrester, T.: Deep convolutional neural network based species recognition for wild animal monitoring. In: 2014 IEEE International Conference on Image Processing (ICIP), pp. 858–862. IEEE (2014)
30. He, K., Gkioxari, G., Dollár, P., Girshick, R.B.: Mask R-CNN. CoRR (2017). 1703.06870
31. Sarwar, F., Griffin, A., Periasamy, P., Portas, K., Law, J.: Detecting and counting sheep with a convolutional neural network. In: 2018 15th IEEE International Conference on Advanced Video and Signal Based Surveillance (AVSS), pp. 1–6. IEEE (2018)
32. Simões, F., Bouveyron, C., Precioso, F.: Deepwild: wildlife identification, localisation and estimation on camera trap videos using deep learning. Eco. Inf. **75**, 102095 (2023)
33. Schneider, S., Taylor, G.W., Kremer, S.: Deep learning object detection methods for ecological camera trap data. In: 2018 15th Conference on Computer and Robot Vision (CRV), pp. 321–328. IEEE (2018)
34. Norouzzadeh, M.S., Nguyen, A., Kosmala, M., Swanson, A., Packer, C., Clune, J.: Automatically identifying wild animals in camera trap images with deep learning. Proc. Natl. Acad. Sci. **115**, E5716–E5725 (2018)
35. Yudin, D., Sotnikov, A., Krishtopik, A.: Detection of big animals on images with road scenes using deep learning. In: 2019 International Conference on Artificial Intelligence: Applications and Innovations (IC-AIAI), pp. 100–1003. IEEE (2019)
36. Rančić, K., et al.: Animal detection and counting from uav images using convolutional neural networks. Drones **7**(3), 179 (2023)
37. Vishwas, J., Raj, S.P., Anand, M., Puneeth, S., Prajwal, P., et al.: Cnn based animals recognition using advanced yolo v5 and darknet. Int. J. Res. Eng. Sci. Manag. **5**(6), 229–231 (2022)

38. Li, E., Wang, Q., Zhang, J., Zhang, W., Mo, H., Wu, Y.: Fish detection under occlusion using modified you only look once v8 integrating real-time detection transformer features. Appl. Sci. **13**(23), 12645 (2023)
39. Siriani, A.L.R., Miranda, I.B.D.C., Mehdizadeh, S.A., Pereira, D.F.: Chicken tracking and individual bird activity monitoring using the bot-sort algorithm. AgriEngineering **5**(4), 1677–1693 (2023)
40. Nguyen, H., et al.: Animal recognition and identification with deep convolutional neural networks for automated wildlife monitoring. In: 2017 IEEE International Conference on Data Science and Advanced Analytics (DSAA), pp. 40–49. IEEE (2017)
41. Jamil, S., Abbas, M.S., Habib, F., Umair, M., Khan, M.J., et al.: Deep learning and computer vision-based a novel framework for himalayan bear, marco polo sheep and snow leopard detection. In: 2020 International Conference on Information Science and Communication Technology (ICISCT), pp. 1–6. IEEE (2020)
42. Sheikh, N.: Identification and classification of wildlife from camera-trap images using machine learning and computer vision. PhD thesis, Dublin, National College of Ireland (2020)
43. Villa, A.G., Salazar, A., Vargas, F.: Towards automatic wild animal monitoring: identification of animal species in camera-trap images using very deep convolutional neural networks. Eco. Inf. **41**, 24–32 (2017)
44. Ravikumar, S., Vinod, D., Ramesh, G., Pulari, S.R., Mathi, S.: A layered approach to detect elephants in live surveillance video streams using convolution neural networks. J. Intell. Fuzzy Syst. **38**(5), 6291–6298 (2020)
45. Okafor, E., et al.: Comparative study between deep learning and bag of visual words for wild-animal recognition. In: 2016 IEEE Symposium Series on Computational Intelligence (SSCI), pp. 1–8. IEEE (2016)
46. Song, Y., Wang, H., Li, S., Xu, F., Liu, J.: Cnn based wildlife recognition with super-pixel segmentation for ecological surveillance. In: 2018 IEEE 8th Annual International Conference on CYBER Technology in Automation, Control, and Intelligent Systems (CYBER), pp. 132–137 (2018). IEEE
47. CK, S., et al.: Automated wildlife monitoring using deep learning. In: Proceedings of the International Conference on Systems, Energy & Environment (ICSEE) (2019)
48. Ibraheam, M., Gebali, F., Li, K.F., Sielecki, L.: Animal species recognition using deep learning. In: Barolli, L., Amato, F., Moscato, F., Enokido, T., Takizawa, M. (eds.) AINA 2020. AISC, vol. 1151, pp. 523–532. Springer, Cham (2020). https://doi.org/10.1007/978-3-030-44041-1_47
49. Norouzzadeh, M.S., et al.: Automatically identifying, counting, and describing wild animals in camera-trap images with deep learning. Proc. Natl. Acad. Sci. **115**(25), 5716–5725 (2018)
50. Norouzzadeh, M.S., Morris, D., Beery, S., Joshi, N., Jojic, N., Clune, J.: A deep active learning system for species identification and counting in camera trap images. Methods Ecol. Evol. **12**(1), 150–161 (2021)
51. Azizi, E., Zaman, L.: Deep learning pet identification using face and body. Information **14**(5), 278 (2023)
52. Ibraheam, M., Li, K.F., Gebali, F.: An accurate and fast animal species detection system for embedded devices. IEEE Access **11**, 23462–23473 (2023)
53. Alsaadi, E.M.T.A., El Abbadi, N.K.: An automated mammals detection based on ssd-mobile net. In: Journal of Physics: Conference Series, vol. 1879, p. 022086. IOP Publishing (2021)

54. Padubidri, C., Kamilaris, A., Karatsiolis, S., Kamminga, J.: Counting sea lions and elephants from aerial photography using deep learning with density maps. Animal Biotelemetry **9**(1), 1–10 (2021)
55. Körschens, M., Barz, B., Denzler, J.: Towards automatic identification of elephants in the wild. arXiv preprint arXiv:1812.04418 (2018)
56. Sayagavi, A.V., Sudarshan, T., Ravoor, P.C.: Deep learning methods for animal recognition and tracking to detect intrusions. In: Senjyu, T., Mahalle, P.N., Perumal, T., Joshi, A. (eds.) ICTIS 2020. SIST, vol. 196, pp. 617–626. Springer, Singapore (2021). https://doi.org/10.1007/978-981-15-7062-9_62
57. Zhang, Y., et al.: Bytetrack: multi-object tracking by associating every detection box (2022)

A Review of Multi-modal and Multi-view Applications in Hand-Drawn Sketch Images

Yunqi Xu[(✉)] and Ching Y. Suen

Centre for Pattern Recognition and Machine Intelligence (CENPARMI) Gina Cody School of Engineering and Computer Science, Concordia University, Montreal, QC H3G 1M8, Canada
{x_yunq,suen}@encs.concordia.ca

Abstract. Hand-drawn sketches have played a significant role throughout human history, from the ancient world to the present, influencing everything from early childhood education to human psychology. While humans can effortlessly recognize and understand varying abstractions in these sketches, machines find these tasks challenging. Recent advancements in multi-modal models have opened new possibilities for computer vision to interpret hand-drawn sketches more effectively. This survey provides a comprehensive review of the application of multi-modal approaches in the domain of hand-drawn sketches, with a particular focus on generation and recognition tasks.

Keywords: Hand-drawn sketches · Multi-modal models · Sketch generation · Sketch recognition · Computer vision

1 Introduction

Free-hand sketches have been a fundamental means of human expression and communication since prehistoric times, serving as abstract representations of reality that transcend cultural and linguistic barriers. Each artist's unique style, characterized by simplicity and abstraction, reflects personal traits and mindsets, allowing sketches to encapsulate complex ideas and emotions with minimalistic imagery. This universality makes sketching a form of universal language, evident from historical evidence where ancient civilizations used drawings to convey thoughts and concepts. Additionally, free-hand sketching is often a primary form of communication in early childhood, preceding the development of written language and helping children convey complex narratives through basic shapes and contours. This art form plays a crucial role in early education, capturing the essence of the natural world and facilitating initial engagements with learning materials, such as comic books, before children interact with more traditional texts. Even in professional realms such as film making, producers rely on storyboards to articulate and share their ideas during the production process.

L. Deligiannidis et al. (Eds.): CSCE 2024, CCIS 2262, pp. 97–110, 2025.
https://doi.org/10.1007/978-3-031-85933-5_8

Humans can recognize varying abstractions in hand-drawn sketches, a task that has traditionally been challenging for machines. However, advancements in deep learning, particularly in computer vision, have significantly narrowed this gap, enabling more focused research on applying these methods to the interpretation of free-hand sketches. The field of sketch studies, which initially concentrated on recognizing basic elements like lines and curves, evolved dramatically with the 2012 publication of the first large-scale dataset of free-hand sketches, containing 250 categories and 20,000 sketches [9], catalyzing a shift towards developing models specifically tailored for sketch recognition.

Numerous comprehensive surveys have covered deep learning applications in sketch processing, such as [43] and [47]. However, they have not addressed the rapidly developing field of multi-modal or multi-view approaches applied in the recognition and generation of free-drawn sketches over the past three years. This survey aims to provide a thorough overview of the current state of research on the application of multi-modal models and multi-view models to free-hand sketches. We will examine significant contributions, relevant datasets, various models, emphasizing the challenges and potential future directions in this field. The structure of this paper is as follows: Sect. 2 will introduce the datasets and methods traditionally used in free-hand sketch studies. Section 3 will delve into a detailed examination of recent research on multi-modal models in the context of sketches. Finally, Sect. 4 will summarize the current findings and discuss future research avenues in this dynamic field.

2   Review of Previous Work

In this section, we will first introduce the most relevant and recently utilized datasets. Subsequently, we will review studies that have employed single-model deep learning algorithms. Following this, we will discuss the specific challenges associated with working on sketches as compared to natural images, detailing the complexities involved with these datasets.

2.1   Sketch Dataset

Table 1 provides a summary of several significant free-hand sketch datasets that have been widely utilized in recent research. It is obviously that hand-drawn sketches dataset become more and more recently, even some of them includes images comes from machine generation, as the generation task could generate images with high quality, there still are some difficulties we need to face when we process free-hand sketches.

Abstraction and Diversity. Free-hand sketches represent a unique niche within visual representation, characterized by abstraction and the artist's subjective interpretation. Unlike detailed and objective photographs, sketches are stylized simplifications that distill objects down to their essential shapes, often reflecting the artist's unique style and skill. This subjectivity introduces significant variability in sketches of the same object, as each artist's unique interests

Table 1. The Sketch datasets

Datasets	Description	Collection
QuickDraw [13]	50M Sketches across 345 categories. The extended dataset includes SPG, QuickDraw-5-step; SketchSeg-150K; SketchSeg-10K; QuickDrawExtended; DomainNet and SketchyCOCO	Trackpad
TU-Berlin [9]	20K sketches across 250 categories, the extended dataset includes Improved TU-Berlin; SketchFix-160; Extended TU-Berlin and HUST-SI; PACS-DG; SketchCOCO;	Trackpad
Sketch-500 [36]	500 categories	Trackpad
Flickr15K [1]	330 sketches across 33 categories. The extended datasets are Flickr160 and Flick41M	TrackPad
Sketchy [33]	75471 sketches across 125 categories. The extended dataset is SketchCOCO	Trackpad
NicIcon [29]	24441 sketches with 14 categories	Tablet
AerialSI [19]	400 sketches with 10 categories	Tablet
WarteggTest [25]	900 human drawn sketches across more than 30 categories	Pencils and Papers
SEVA [28]	90K human and machine generated sketches	Tablet and machine generated
SFSD [49]	12k sketch-photo pairs over 40 object categories	Trackpad
PSC6K [27]	150k annotations of 6k sketch-photo pairs across 125 object categories	Tablet

and capabilities influence their work, making it difficult to develop a universal model that accurately captures the diversity and abstraction of free-hand sketches. Consequently, these inconsistencies present substantial challenges in creating models that effectively represent the diverse artistic expressions found in sketches.

Lacking Data Information. Free-hand sketches present unique challenges distinct from those of natural images, primarily due to their lack of detailed texture and color, consisting only of simple lines. This sparse signal, stemming from the individual artistic preferences rather than precise physical replication, introduces significant inconsistencies that complicate feature extraction for computational analysis. Despite their minimalistic nature, sketches maintain a level of invariance in human recognition, suggesting that people can consistently interpret these simplified representations. However, this sparsity poses substantial challenges for computer recognition systems, which struggle to process such data effectively. Additionally, the method of collecting sketch data, whether from electronic devices or paper, affects the consistency of time-sequenced stroke information and impacts the recognition process and data quality.

Discussion. The abstraction, diversity, and inherent sparsity of free-hand sketch images, along with the scarcity of comprehensive datasets, highlight the need for innovative methodologies in processing free-hand sketch data to achieve computer understanding comparable to human recognition. As detailed in Table 1, most datasets rely on labor-intensive methods for creating drawings, which, compared to natural photography, require significant investment in terms of time and money and also limit the diversity of the datasets. These factors pose substantial obstacles in effectively training models, underscoring the dual challenges in sketch recognition: managing the sparse nature of the data and assembling a sufficiently large and diverse dataset.

2.2   History of Hand-Drawn Sketch Processing with Deep Learning

Recent advancements in sketch research have been significantly propelled by developments in deep learning, which have revitalized fields such as sketch recognition and sketch-based image synthesis, leading to performance enhancements. This technological breakthrough has not only improved existing methodologies but also introduced new research directions within the sketch domain. For example, Recurrent Neural Networks (RNNs), particularly SketchRNN [13], play a pivotal role in capturing the sequential nature of sketches. Additionally, there are further applications in sketch generation using generative models, sketch abstraction via reinforcement learning, and enhanced sketch recognition techniques.

Recognition of Hand-Drawn Sketches. Recent advancements in sketch recognition have been significantly driven by developments in deep learning [9], with methodologies broadly categorized into offline recognition, analyzing complete sketches post-drawing for class prediction, and online recognition, suitable for real-time applications like drawing guidance. This field is evolving, as evidenced by a shift from raster image analysis to sequence representation [14,18,44], and a transition from traditional CNN arichitectures to Graph Neural Networks(GNNs) [45].

Generation of Hand-Drawn Sketches. Recent years have witnessed significant advancements in sketch generation. A pivotal development in this domain is SketchRNN [13], a sequence-to-sequence variational autoencoder (VAE) that generates vector sketches by simulating human sketching processes, producing key stroke points sequentially. This model employs a bidirectional RNN for encoding and a unidirectional RNN for decoding. The VAE encoder converts input sketches into a Gaussian distribution, from which latent vectors are sampled, allowing the LSTM-based VAE decoder to reconstruct sketches. Building upon SketchRNN, AI-Sketcher [5], another VAE-based model, enhances the capability to generate multi-class sketches. Additionally, other innovative approaches in sketch generation include differentiable rendering [8] and reinforcement learning [2].

New Models of Processing Hand-Drawn Images. Recent research in sketch understanding has increasingly focused on zero-shot and few-shot learning approaches, particularly with the advent of advanced vision-language models like CLIP [32]. CLIP has spurred several innovative applications in sketch generation and recognition, such as CLIPDraw [10], which leverages CLIP's capability to understand and generate images from textual prompt. Additionally, models like CLIPasso [38] and DiffSketcher [41] demonstrate the effective integration of CLIP's vision-language understanding and text-to-image diffusion models to produce high-quality vector sketches. In Sect. 3, we will explore these multi-modal and multi-view algorithms in greater detail.

3   Recent Method in Processing Free-Hand Sketches

3.1   Sketch Generation Tasks

CLIP-Based Sketch Generation. CLIPDraw [10] is a pioneering algorithm that synthesizes drawings from natural language inputs by leveraging a pre-trained CLIP [32] language-image encoder, enhancing the similarity between text descriptions and generated drawings. This method avoids the need for additional training by utilizing the pre-trained CLIP model as a metric to refine the drawings' fidelity to the described prompt. The process starts with a random set of Bézier curves, optimizing both the position and colors iteratively. To increase the accuracy of the match, the drawings undergo augmentation into multiple perspective-shifted copies before being processed by the CLIP encoder. The primary objective of CLIPDraw is to produce an image that closely aligns with the CLIP encoding of the text promptd, effectively narrowing the gap between textual descriptions and visual representations. CLIPDraw demonstrates that CLIP embeddings can bridge semantics between text and drawings despite the domain gap.

Building on CLIPDraw's foundation, StyleCLIPDraw [34] incorporates a style loss into the framework, allowing for artistic control over the synthesized drawings alongside textual content manipulation. Similarly, the paper [6] explores integrating a GAN with a pre-trained CLIP model to convert photographs into sketch drawings, efficiently creating line drawings without the need for paired training data or human evaluation. The method incorporates four distinct types of loss to refine the translation process: adversarial loss ensures that generated images adhere to their respective domains, geometry loss enhances depth in line drawings, semantic loss reduces the distance between CLIP embeddings of the photograph and the drawing, and appearance loss maintains the input appearance through image translation. This innovative approach leverages the strengths of GANs and CLIP to capture domain-specific characteristics and semantic details, facilitating the automated generation of line drawings from photographs. Other studies such as [26,48], and [21] also employ CLIP to transform photographs into sketch-style images.

The papers discussed above focus on transforming photographs into handdrawn sketches. In contrast, CLIPasso [38] is trained on a variety of image styles paired with text, achieving exceptional proficiency in encoding the semantic meanings of visual depictions to guide the sketch image synthesis process. In this model, a sketch is defined as a set of strokes generated from four starting points using Bézier curves. The pre-trained CLIP model is then employed to optimize both semantic and geometric losses. The CLIPasso model is capable of achieving various levels of sketch abstraction, with the degree of abstraction controllable by the user, thus allowing for tailored sketch outputs that meet specific aesthetic or functional requirements. Furthermore, CLIPascene [37] proposes a method that converts a scene image into a sketch with varying types and levels of abstraction by separating abstraction into two dimensions of control: fidelity and simplicity. Learning by Sketching (LBS) [23] transforms an image into a set of colored strokes that capture the geometric information of the scene in a single inference step. A sketch is then generated from these strokes, with a pre-trained CLIP model ensuring the semantic similarity between the final sketch and the original image.

Further extending the application of this technology, the paper [51] proposes a two-stage framework for generating sketches from video. This framework initially decomposes a video into a 2D representation atlas, followed by employing a cross-frame stroke initialization technique to set the initial positions and widths of the curves. The locations of these curves are then optimized using a semantic loss that leverages CLIP features and a novel consistency loss developed from the self-decomposed 2D atlas network. Additionally, [11] synthesizes sketch videos using a sketch image and prompt text as inputs, also achieving high-quality sketch videos. Refremer [22] introduces a human-AI drawing interface that utilizes CLIP-guided synthesis-by-optimization to support real-time synchronous drawing, while CICADA [16] further harnesses pre-trained models to optimize the drawing sketch process, showcasing the diverse applications of CLIP in artistic and creative contexts.

Diffusion-Based Sketch Generation. In VectorFusion [17], the authors enhance a differentiable vector graphics rasterizer by leveraging a pretrained diffusion model to distill abstract semantic knowledge, achieving superior quality compared to previous efforts. The optimization process incorporates Score Distillation Sampling to support both a vector graphics renderer and a latent-space diffusion prior for raster images. This method includes rasterizing SVG paths, applying data augmentations, encoding these into a latent space, calculating the Score Distillation loss on the latents, and employing backpropagation through the encoding, augmentation, and rendering processes to update the paths.

On the other hand, DiffSketcher [41] is an innovative text-prompt-guided model that creates high-quality, free-hand sketches. Unlike some previous generative models, DiffSketcher does not require text-to-sketch pairs or large sketch datasets. This model leverages the impressive capabilities of a pre-trained stable diffusion model to guide sketch synthesis based on input text prompts. DiffSketcher utilizes a differentiable rasterizer to optimize parameters derived from Bezier curves that compose the strokes of sketch images, enabling the synthesis of sketches at multiple levels of abstraction with high fidelity. Additionally, the input text prompt provides guidance, ensuring that the final output sketches are coherent and closely aligned with their corresponding textual inputs. Samilar as DiffSketcher, SketchDreamer [31] integrates a differentiable rasteriser of Bézier curves that optimises an initial input to distil abstract semantic knowledge from a pretrained diffusion model to synthesis free-hand sketches.

The other works related with painting or drawing sketches, such as SVG-Dreamer [42] incorporates a semantic-driven image vectorization process which enables the decomposition of synthesis into foreground objects and backgrounds thereby enhancing editability. DALS [20] utilize the pre-trained Stable Diffusion to synthesis landscape sketches.

Other Multi-modals or Multi-views Based Sketches Generation. Many studies continue to explore the realm of multi-modal algorithms. For instance, PALGAN [24] utilizes a Generative Adversarial Network to generate portrait sketch images, where the portrait images with prior knowledge such as segmentation maps and joint connection diagrams input into the generator. Similarly, [35] introduces a novel multi-modal sketch extraction method that can mimic the style of a given reference sketch using unpaired data training in a semi-supervised manner. This model comprises two encoders to extract features from input images and two domain generators, optimizing both the line loss and sketch style loss to generate sketches from input images effectively. Further advancing the field, SketchINR [3] enhances the representation of vector sketches with implicit neural models. This approach compresses a variable-length vector sketch into a latent space of fixed dimensions that implicitly encodes the underlying shapes as functions of time and strokes, demonstrating a sophisticated use of neural representations for sketch data. Additionally, GGD-GAN [39] proposes a dual-branch GAN framework for high-quality relic sketch generation, showcasing the versatility of GANs in handling complex and specialized artistic tasks. Each of these studies illustrates the ongoing advancements in multi-modal algorithms, leveraging diverse approaches to enhance the fidelity and stylistic diversity of generated sketches.

Results of Sketch Generation. Since it is challenging to evaluate generated sketches using a single metric, we have selectively sampled results from various cited papers. Figure 1 presents detailed outcomes of these sketch generation tasks, with all images sourced from the referenced papers.

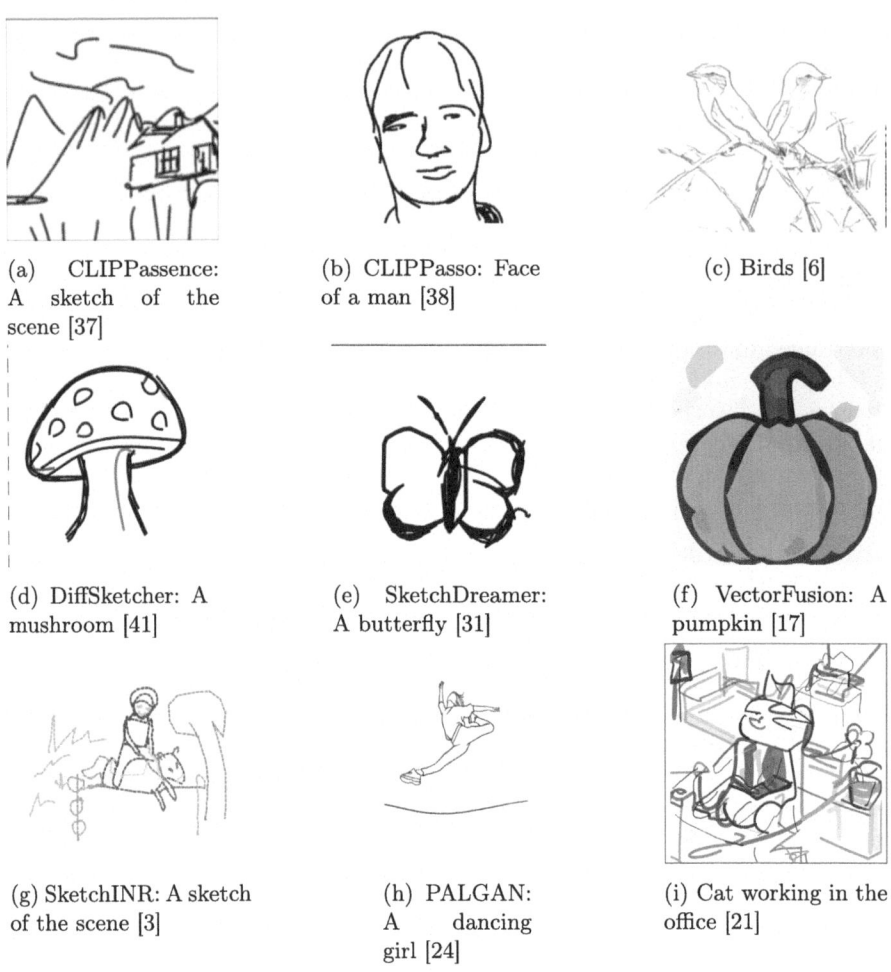

(a) CLIPPassence: A sketch of the scene [37]

(b) CLIPPasso: Face of a man [38]

(c) Birds [6]

(d) DiffSketcher: A mushroom [41]

(e) SketchDreamer: A butterfly [31]

(f) VectorFusion: A pumpkin [17]

(g) SketchINR: A sketch of the scene [3]

(h) PALGAN: A dancing girl [24]

(i) Cat working in the office [21]

Fig. 1. Some Result of the Sketches Generation Tasks

3.2 Sketch Classification Tasks

Sketch Classification Models. Several research efforts have focused on understanding the stroke level of sketches. For instance, PHAL [7] automates the segmentation of sketched objects into parts and constructs multi-level human-like qualitative representations based on Part-based Hierarchical Analogical Learning. This approach facilitates analogical generalization across multiple levels of part descriptions and uses coarse-grained results to refine interpretation at finer levels. The CMPS model [52] integrates inputs from different modalities-sequential stroke sequences and visual images to enhance sketch information processing. The model employs the STAR (Semantic-Temporal Alignment Rasterization) technique, using a convolutional neural network to map high-level semantic and temporal details from strokes into the sketch image, and introduces StrokeFormer to improve local temporal feature extraction and model long-range dependencies within the sketch. Additionally, the four-branch Siamese network described in [40] incorporates a multi-scale weighted bilinear coding module that significantly enhances the capture of discriminative features and the recognition of fine-grained information. This network integrates three newly generated sketches with the original sketch, utilizing a shortcut connection block to fuse features from various depths effectively.

Other notable contributions include the Vision Swin Transformer model used in [12] which detects fine-grained information in free-hand sketches, and Sketch-Segformer [50] which explores feature relationships in sketches by employing cascaded dual self-attention blocks for comprehensive context extraction. Moreover, a stroke-based sequential-spatial neural network proposed in [49] leverages a bidirectional LSTM and GCN to capture both sequential and spatial features of sketches effectively. Lastly, SketchXAI [30] introduces an explainability dimension to sketch recognition by focusing on the network's ability to recover stroke locations in unseen sketches.

Also, [15], which consists of three major functional modules: the feature extraction module, the channel attention module, and the spatial attention module. The sketches are first input to the feature extraction and extracted from shallow to deep, followed by feeding the extracted features into a channel attention module and a spatial attention module in sequence. In the study presented in [4], the authors utilize a vision transformer encoder pretrained with the CLIP model to segment each object in free-hand scene sketches. The text encoder is frozen, and the visual encoder branch is tuned with visual prompts alongside several critical modifications. Notably, classical key-query (k-q) self-attention blocks are augmented with value-value (v-v) self-attention blocks to enhance the model. The framework incorporates a two-level hierarchical training strategy that facilitates efficient semantic disentanglement: the first level aims at holistic scene sketch encoding, while the second level targets individual categories with the introduction of cross-attention between the text and vision branches. These studies collectively underscore the advances in sketch understanding by leveraging deep learning technologies to interpret and classify artistic content effectively.

Results of Sketch Classification. Table 2 shows the results of the sketch classification tasks.

Table 2. Sketch Classification Task Results: In this table, 'SR' in the Task Name column stands for 'Sketch Recognition', and 'SS' stands for 'Sketch Segmentation'.

Model Name	Task Name	Dataset	Accuracy
PHAL [7]	SR	Tu-Berlin	69.85%
CMPS [52]	SR	QuickDraw-141K	79.08%
		Tu-Berlin	80.26%
Four-Branch Siamese Network [40]	SR	TU-Berlin	84.2%
SketchOLS [12]	SR	QuickDraw-141K	78.01%
		QuickDraw-3.8M	81.41%
		QuickDraw-10M	86.45%
SketchXAI [30]	SR	QuickDraw-10M	87.18%
Light-SRNet [15]	SR	Tu-Berlin	72.71%
		Sketchy	84.67%
		QuickDraw	75.40%
Sketch-SegFormer [50]	SS (Stroke level)	SketchSeg-150K	98.95%
		SPG	97.69%
Open Vocabulary Sketch Segmentation [4]	SS (Scene level)	FS-COCO	73.48%
S^3 NN [49]	SS (Scene level)	SFSD	77.65%

4 Future Works

In this paper, we provide an in-depth exploration of the emerging trend of utilizing multi-modal approaches and multi-view models in sketch analysis, particularly focusing on sketch generation and classification. Additionally, we present a comprehensive review of sketch datasets. We hope this survey will offer valuable guidance for future research.

After reviewing recent studies, it is evident that the generation task primarily leverages pre-trained vision-language models or diffusion models to produce high-quality sketches at varying levels of abstraction. However, sketch classification tasks often rely on datasets with a fixed number of images. Therefore, future research in sketch generation may potentially focus on the following areas:

1. Investigating methods for generating high-quality free-hand sketches that can be utilized in classification tasks. This inquiry is inspired by current research demonstrating how generated data can enhance the performance of deep learning models.
2. Most sketch classification models focus on multi-view approaches and rely on fixed training and testing datasets. However, given the diversity of sketches, it is common to encounter unseen data during testing. Thus, exploring the integration of pre-trained vision-language models into sketch classification could represent another fruitful research direction.

3. Developing new methods to generate free-hand sketches in various styles to accommodate diverse preferences.
4. Addressing the gap in captioning sketches into textual descriptions, which could become a significant focus for future research, potentially opening new avenues for interaction between textual and visual data.
5. Linking hand-drawn sketches to the detection of an artist's personality, such as through the use of the Wartegg Test dataset, is the focus of studies like those referenced in [46] and [25]. To effectively process these datasets, it may be necessary to explore or develop zero-shot or few-shot capabilities within multi-modal frameworks.

These directions highlight the evolving nature of sketch-based research and underscore the potential for innovative contributions in this field.

References

1. A performance evaluation of gradient field hog descriptor for sketch based image retrieval. CVIU (2013)
2. Balasubramanian, S., Balasubramanian, V.N., et al.: Teaching gans to sketch in vector format. arXiv preprint arXiv:1904.03620 (2019)
3. Bandyopadhyay, H., et al.: Sketchinr: a first look into sketches as implicit neural representations. In: The IEEE/CVF Conference on Computer Vision and Pattern Recognition 2024. IEEE (2024)
4. Bourouis, A., Fan, J.E., Gryaditskaya, Y.: Open vocabulary semantic scene sketch understanding. arXiv e-prints, pp. arXiv–2312 (2023)
5. Cao, N., Yan, X., Shi, Y., Chen, C.: Ai-sketcher: a deep generative model for producing high-quality sketches. In: Proceedings of the AAAI Conference on Artificial Intelligence, vol. 33, pp. 2564–2571 (2019)
6. Chan, C., Durand, F., Isola, P.: Learning to generate line drawings that convey geometry and semantics. In: Proceedings of the IEEE/CVF Conference on Computer Vision and Pattern Recognition, pp. 7915–7925 (2022)
7. Chen, K., Forbus, K., Srinivasan, B.V., Chhaya, N., Usher, M.: Sketch recognition via part-based hierarchical analogical learning. In: Proceedings of the Thirty-Second International Joint Conference on Artificial Intelligence, pp. 2967–2974 (2023)
8. Das, A., Yang, Y., Hospedales, T., Xiang, T., Song, Y.-Z.: BézierSketch: a generative model for scalable vector sketches. In: Vedaldi, A., Bischof, H., Brox, T., Frahm, J.-M. (eds.) ECCV 2020. LNCS, vol. 12371, pp. 632–647. Springer, Cham (2020). https://doi.org/10.1007/978-3-030-58574-7_38
9. Eitz, M., Hays, J., Alexa, M.: How do humans sketch objects? ACM Trans. Graph. (TOG) **31**(4), 1–10 (2012)
10. Frans, K., Soros, L., Witkowski, O.: Clipdraw: exploring text-to-drawing synthesis through language-image encoders. Adv. Neural. Inf. Process. Syst. **35**, 5207–5218 (2022)
11. Gal, R., et al.: Breathing life into sketches using text-to-video priors. arXiv preprint arXiv:2311.13608 (2023)
12. Guo, W., Liu, S., Yu, Y., Cai, B.: Capture more structured context by vision transformers for free-hand sketch recognition. In: 2023 IEEE International Conference on Systems, Man, and Cybernetics (SMC), pp. 629–634. IEEE (2023)

13. Ha, D., Eck, D.: A neural representation of sketch drawings. In: ICLR (2018)
14. He, J.Y., Wu, X., Jiang, Y.G., Zhao, B., Peng, Q.: Sketch recognition with deep visual-sequential fusion model. In: Proceedings of the 25th ACM International Conference on Multimedia, pp. 448–456 (2017)
15. Hou, X., Rong, X., Yu, X.: Light-srnet: a lightweight dual-attention feature fusion network for hand-drawn sketch recognition. J. Electron. Imaging **32**(1), 013005–013005 (2023)
16. Ibarrola, F., Lawton, T., Grace, K.: A collaborative, interactive and context-aware drawing agent for co-creative design. IEEE Trans. Visualizat. Comput. Graph. (2023)
17. Jain, A., Xie, A., Abbeel, P.: Vectorfusion: text-to-svg by abstracting pixel-based diffusion models. In: Proceedings of the IEEE/CVF Conference on Computer Vision and Pattern Recognition, pp. 1911–1920 (2023)
18. Jia, Q., Yu, M., Fan, X., Li, H.: Sequential dual deep learning with shape and texture features for sketch recognition. arXiv preprint arXiv:1708.02716 (2017)
19. Jiang, T., Xia, G.S., Lu, Q.: Sketch-based aerial image retrieval. In: 2017 IEEE International Conference on Image Processing (ICIP), pp. 3690–3694. IEEE (2017)
20. Kim, J., Yang, H., Min, K.: Dals: diffusion-based artistic landscape sketch. Mathematics **12**(2), 238 (2024)
21. Lawton, T., Grace, K., Ibarrola, F.J.: When is a tool a tool? user perceptions of system agency in human–ai co-creative drawing. In: Proceedings of the 2023 ACM Designing Interactive Systems Conference, pp. 1978–1996 (2023)
22. Lawton, T., Ibarrola, F.J., Ventura, D., Grace, K.: Drawing with reframer: emergence and control in co-creative ai. In: Proceedings of the 28th International Conference on Intelligent User Interfaces, pp. 264–277 (2023)
23. Lee, H., Hwang, I., Go, H., Choi, W.S., Kim, K., Zhang, B.T.: Learning geometry-aware representations by sketching. In: Proceedings of the IEEE/CVF Conference on Computer Vision and Pattern Recognition, pp. 23315–23326 (2023)
24. Li, S., Wu, F., fan, Y., Song, X., Dong, W.: Pldgan: portrait line drawing generation with prior knowledge and conditioning target. Visual Comput. **39**(8), 3507–3518 (2023)
25. Liu, L., Pettinati, G., Suen, C.Y.: Computer-aided wartegg drawing completion test. In: Lu, Y., Vincent, N., Yuen, P.C., Zheng, W.-S., Cheriet, F., Suen, C.Y. (eds.) ICPRAI 2020. LNCS, vol. 12068, pp. 575–580. Springer, Cham (2020). https://doi.org/10.1007/978-3-030-59830-3_50
26. Liu, X.C., Wu, Y.C., Hall, P.: Painterly style transfer with learned brush strokes. IEEE Trans. Visualizat. Comput. Graph. (2023)
27. Lu, X., Wang, X., Fan, J.E.: Learning dense correspondences between photos and sketches. In: Krause, A., Brunskill, E., Cho, K., Engelhardt, B., Sabato, S., Scarlett, J. (eds.) Proceedings of the 40th International Conference on Machine Learning. Proceedings of Machine Learning Research, vol. 202, pp. 22899–22916. PMLR (2023). https://proceedings.mlr.press/v202/lu23g.html
28. Mukherjee, K., et al.: Seva: leveraging sketches to evaluate alignment between human and machine visual abstraction. Adv. Neural Inf. Process. Syst. **36** (2024)
29. Niels, R., Willems, D., Vuurpijl, L.: The nicicon database of handwritten icons for crisis management. Nijmegen Institute for Cognition and Information Radboud University Nijmegen, Nijmegen, The Netherlands **2** (2008)
30. Qu, Z., Gryaditskaya, Y., Li, K., Pang, K., Xiang, T., Song, Y.Z.: Sketchxai: a first look at explainability for human sketches. In: Proceedings of the IEEE/CVF Conference on Computer Vision and Pattern Recognition, pp. 23327–23337 (2023)

31. Qu, Z., Xiang, T., Song, Y.Z.: Sketchdreamer: interactive text-augmented creative sketch ideation. arXiv e-prints, pp. arXiv–2308 (2023)

32. Radford, A., et al.: Learning transferable visual models from natural language supervision. In: Meila, M., Zhang, T. (eds.) Proceedings of the 38th International Conference on Machine Learning. Proceedings of Machine Learning Research, vol. 139, pp. 8748–8763. PMLR (2021). https://proceedings.mlr.press/v139/radford21a.html

33. Sangkloy, P., Burnell, N., Ham, C., Hays, J.: The sketchy database: learning to retrieve badly drawn bunnies. TOG (2016)

34. Schaldenbrand, P., Liu, Z., Oh, J.: Styleclipdraw: coupling content and style in text-to-drawing translation. arXiv e-prints, pp. arXiv–2202 (2022)

35. Seo, C.W., Ashtari, A., Noh, J.: Semi-supervised reference-based sketch extraction using a contrastive learning framework. ACM Trans. Graph. (TOG) **42**(4), 1–12 (2023)

36. Sun, Z., Wang, C., Zhang, L., Zhang, L.: Query-adaptive shape topic mining for hand-drawn sketch recognition. In: Proceedings of the 20th ACM International Conference on Multimedia, pp. 519–528 (2012)

37. Vinker, Y., Alaluf, Y., Cohen-Or, D., Shamir, A.: Clipascene: scene sketching with different types and levels of abstraction. In: Proceedings of the IEEE/CVF International Conference on Computer Vision, pp. 4146–4156 (2023)

38. Vinker, Y., et al.: Clipasso: semantically-aware object sketching. ACM Trans. Graph. (TOG) **41**(4), 1–11 (2022)

39. Wang, J., et al.: Ggd-gan: gradient-guided dual-branch adversarial networks for relic sketch generation. Pattern Recogn. **141**, 109586 (2023)

40. Wang, X., Zhao, Q., Tan, S.: Four-branch siamese network based on sketch-specific data augmentation for sketch recognition. IET Image Proc. **17**(3), 932–943 (2023)

41. Xing, X., Wang, C., Zhou, H., Zhang, J., Yu, Q., Xu, D.: Diffsketcher: text guided vector sketch synthesis through latent diffusion models. Adv. Neural Inf. Process. Syst. **36** (2024)

42. Xing, X., Zhou, H., Wang, C., Zhang, J., Xu, D., Yu, Q.: Svgdreamer: text guided svg generation with diffusion model. arXiv e-prints, pp. arXiv–2312 (2023)

43. Xu, P., Hospedales, T.M., Yin, Q., Song, Y.Z., Xiang, T., Wang, L.: Deep learning for free-hand sketch: a survey. IEEE Trans. Pattern Anal. Mach. Intell. **45**(1), 285–312 (2022)

44. Xu, P., et al.: Sketchmate: deep hashing for million-scale human sketch retrieval. In: Proceedings of the IEEE Conference on Computer Vision and Pattern Recognition, pp. 8090–8098 (2018)

45. Xu, P., Joshi, C.K., Bresson, X.: Multigraph transformer for free-hand sketch recognition. IEEE Trans. Neural Netw. Learn. Syst. **33**(10), 5150–5161 (2021)

46. Xu, Y., Suen, C.Y.: Recognition of graphological wartegg hand-drawings. In: International Graphonomics Conference, pp. 174–186. Springer, Heidelberg (2022). https://doi.org/10.1007/978-3-031-19745-1_13

47. Zhang, X., Li, X., Liu, Y., Feng, F.: A survey on freehand sketch recognition and retrieval. Image Vis. Comput. **89**, 67–87 (2019)

48. Zhang, Z., Chang, M.C.: Two-stage dual augmentation with clip for improved text-to-sketch synthesis. In: 2023 IEEE 6th International Conference on Multimedia Information Processing and Retrieval (MIPR), pp. 1–6. IEEE (2023)

49. Zhang, Z., et al.: Stroke-based semantic segmentation for scene-level free-hand sketches. Vis. Comput. **39**(12), 6309–6321 (2023)

50. Zheng, Y., Xie, J., Sain, A., Song, Y.Z., Ma, Z.: Sketch-segformer: transformer-based segmentation for figurative and creative sketches. IEEE Trans. Image Process. (2023)
51. Zheng, Y., Cun, X., Xia, M., Pun, C.M.: Sketch video synthesis. In: Computer Graphics Forum, p. e15044. Wiley Online Library (2024)
52. Zhou, Y., et al.: Cross-modal pixel-and-stroke representation aligning networks for free-hand sketch recognition. Expert Syst. Appl. **240**, 122505 (2024)

Residential Real Estate Image Classification for Property Valuation

Mehrdad Ziaee Nejad, Mohsen Naderpour$^{(\boxtimes)}$, Vahid Behbood, Fahimeh Ramezani, and Jie Lu

Australian Artificial Intelligence Institute (AAII), Faculty of Engineering and IT, University of Technology Sydney (UTS), 15 Broadway, Ultimo, NSW 2007, Australia
Mehrdad.Ziaeenejad@student.uts.edu.au, {Mohsen.Naderpour, Vahid.Behbood,Fahimeh.Ramezani,Jie.Lu}@uts.edu.au

Abstract. Residential real estate price is one of the key components of our economic developments and has also been a major concern of the public, bank industry, government, and investors. The accurate estimation of the sale price and its changes have an important role in the decision-making of related departments and organizations. In Australia, one of the biggest investments for people is in residential real estate. Therefore, many studies and research works have been carried out to build an automated valuation model to predict sale prices of residential properties accurately as much as possible. Automatic and accurate image classification of residential real estate plays an important role in property valuation and decision making of both sellers and buyers. It can be used in real estate online websites to organize the images for each property or used as a component in a visual decision support system for predicting the property sale prices based on property images. As convolutional image classification models show valuable performance in comparison with traditional models, a convolutional classification model is developed in this paper which creates a highly reliable classification component to be used in the corresponding research areas. The performance of the proposed model is investigated through a real dataset of New Sales Wales, Australia.

Keywords: Image Classification · Property Valuation · Real Estate · Convolutional Neural Network

1 Introduction

Residential real estate price is one of the key components of our economy. The price of residential real estate has been of major importance to the public, bank industry, government and investors. The accurate estimate of sale price has an important role in decision-making in bank, tax and securities industries. Both academics and the real estate industry have attempted to estimate or predict the price of real estate properties accurately and efficiently. The price of residential real estate also affects social equity and affordability [1]. In Australia, one of the biggest investments for people is in residential real estate [2]. The complexity of estimating the residential real estate price is related to

L. Deligiannidis et al. (Eds.): CSCE 2024, CCIS 2262, pp. 111–125, 2025.
https://doi.org/10.1007/978-3-031-85933-5_9

its main characteristics such as immovability, durability and it is highly dependent on location and property structure [3]. Recently, the advanced valuation models (AVMs) have received much attention in industry and academia to estimate the market value of a property automatically, based on its available data and information [4].

The quality and variety of data have a huge impact on the success of valuation application [5]. In literature, there are much research which focus on external features only [6–10]. The main reason for focusing on the external features of residential real estate is that in fact, there is lack of textual and numerical information related to structural features. Most of the structural features are not quantifiable, such as how good the materials are, how good the view of property is, and so on. Quantifying the structural quality features is really a hard task, if not an impossible one. Only the standard structural information is quantifiable, such as the number of bedrooms, number of bathrooms, number of cars paces, floor number, building age, floor area and so on. Developing the valuation system based on the standard structural features only creates an inaccurate model [8]. Therefore, researchers added external features such as locational information to the model. To consider more structural information rather than existing information, an initial suggestion is to use the inside and outside images of residential real estate properties in valuation models which have been neglected in the traditional valuation process. Recently, there have been some attempts to incorporate the images in predicting the sale price of property in AVMs.

To use the property images in the process of sale price prediction, labelling the images is inevitable. The labelling process could be done manually by human which is costly and very time consuming. The aim of this paper is to develop an automatic image classification model that paves the way and feeds the AVMs. To develop the model the capabilities of convolutional neural networks (CNNs) which are the most well-known deep learning methods to solve the classification tasks in computer vision are relied upon.

The rest of this paper is organized as follows. Section 2 reviews the literature. Section 3 presents the proposed model. Section 4 analyzes the results. Section 5 concludes the paper and provides some future research directions.

2   Literature Review

2.1   Property Image Classification Models

Improving the accuracy of AVMs is a major concern in academia and the real estate industry. The differences between physical inspection estimation and AVMs could be based on ignoring visual features in AVMs. Most of the crucial features impacting the accuracy of estimation are visual features that a human valuer uses to estimate the value of property.

Today, sellers and buyers use online real estate websites and check the pictures of property to make decisions. In traditional AVMs only structural data are used such as standard structural, locational and environmental data [6–11]. In recent years several studies have focused on using unstructured data such as images in property valuation problems [11–14].

Due to the difficulty of using visual content from images in AVMs, applying the visual content has been ignored so far. Visual content is very difficult to interpret or quantify by computers as compared with humans. In the real estate industry, images can easily show how the property looks, which is impossible to be described successfully in many ways using text. Given property images, people can easily have an overall feeling for the property. Extracting visual features using a regression model is the problem in this context.

Developing a model that accepts the different types of data such as pictures, video, text and numeric data is necessary to improving the accuracy of the estimation. The traditional AVMs ignore the visual appearance to estimation where it seems these features have an important impact on price and decisions. Having such a model that can handle the visual data as input is the next important step in generating AVMs. The advanced deep learning neural networks can accept all types of data and have good performance with visual and non-visual data and could be used in such visual base AVMs. There are various types of deep learning models regarding image and text inputs as used by a few works [15, 16]. They usually use the pretrained ImageNet models which is a common approach in image classification [17].

2.2   Convolutional Neural Network

The basic CNN consists of convolutions, pooling operators, activation function and dense layers. The neural network can be written as functions $f_i(.)$ that takes vector x_l, W_l and b_l as inputs and returns the x_{l+1} as output. In CNN the x_l is the input image. The overview of building blocks in CNN is described below.

2.2.1   Convolutional Layer

A convolutional layer consists of set of filters (matrix $k * k$ of trainable weights) where each can be applied to the entire input vector. Each filter creates a transformation of the input vector. In the other words, each filter creates a linear combination of pixel values defined by the size of filter in each region of input vector [18]. The main difference between the convolutional layer and the dense layer is the shared weights for pixel values related to the former's filter and its production of the number of outputs based on the number of filters applied. In other words, dense layers learn global patterns in their input feature space, whereas convolutional layers learn local patterns. The output value of convolutional layer $f_i(i, x, y)$ is based on a filter i and data comes from the previous layer centered at position (x, y) by filter size k (Fig. 1). The most common filter sizes are 3, 5 and 7 [19].

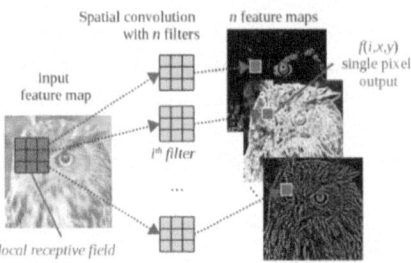

Fig. 1. A convolution process-local information centered in each position (x,y) [19]

2.2.2 Pooling

Pooling is the down sampling image used to reduce the size of image and processing input in a different space scale. The most used pooling is max pooling that selects the maximum values in the region of the pooling center [19].

2.2.3 Dense Layer

After convolutional layers, usually dense layers are applied in order to learn weights for classification tasks. In dense layers, all values of input are considered and global patterns matter, creating a single value based on the activation function. Therefore, the last outputs of a convolutional layer should be flattened as one vector input for a dense layer. For multiclass classification the last layer of CNN output is the probability of belonging to class c using logistic regression [20]:

$$P(y = c|x; w; b) = softmax_c\left(x^T w + b\right) = \frac{e^{x^T w_c + b_c}}{\sum_j e^{x^T w_j + b_j}} \tag{1}$$

where y is the predicted class, x is the input vector coming from the previous layer, w is the weights and b is the bias associated to each neuron in the last layer.

Loss Function

To measure the performance of prediction based on the output of a model and its expected output, the loss or cost function is used. The loss function $l(y, \hat{y})$ calculates the penalty for predicting $\hat{y}$ in respect to true output y. For softmax classifier, usually the cross-entropy loss is used [20].

$$l_j^{(ce)} = -log\left(\frac{e^{f_{y_j}}}{\sum_k e^{f_k}}\right) \tag{2}$$

where $k = 1, \ldots, c$ are the neurons related to each class in output layer with C neurons, one per class. This function maps a real valued vector to a vector of values between 0 and 1 with a unitary sum. By minimizing this function, the Kullback-Leibler divergence between two-class distributions is minimized [21].

2.2.4 Optimization Algorithm

After defining the loss function, the minimization algorithm should be applied. The Gradient Descent (GD) is the standard algorithm for this task. For updating the weights in a network, the backpropagation method is used by applying the chain rule of gradient. Usually the number of weights in CNN is reaches millions and the dataset comprises many examples. Therefore, applying the basic GD algorithm is not efficient. Alternatives of GD include Stochastic Gradient Descent, Momentum, RMSProp and Adam [20].

Stochastic Gradient Descent (SGD): by randomly sampling examples of data in size B (called mini-batch) from the original data to avoid inspecting all data at once, the process is accelerated. It is assumed that, by performing enough iterations, it is possible to approximate the actual GD method.

$$W_{t+1} = W_t - \eta \sum_{j=1}^{B} \nabla \mathcal{L}\left(W; x_j^B\right) \tag{3}$$

where η is the learning rate parameter, W_t is the weights in iteration t and B is the batch size [22].

Momentum: By adding controlling variable α in the parameters W, it is possible to create a momentum to prevent the new weights W_{t+1} from being different in direction to the previous weights W_t.

$$W_{t+1} = W_t + \alpha(W_t - W_{t-1}) + (1 - \alpha)[-\eta \nabla \mathcal{L}(W_t)] \tag{4}$$

where $\mathcal{L}(W_t)$ is the loss computed, based on batch and current weights W_t.

RMSProp: This algorithm calculates the running averages of recent gradient that uses the exponentially decaying average.

$$g_{t+1} = \gamma g_t + (1 - \gamma)\nabla \mathcal{L}(W_t)^2 \tag{5}$$

where g is called the second order moment of $\nabla \mathcal{L}$. The updating formula based on given momentum is:

$$W_{t+1} = W_t + \alpha(W_t - W_{t-1}) + (1 - \alpha)\left[\frac{-\eta \nabla \mathcal{L}(W_t)}{\sqrt{g_{t+1}} + \epsilon}\right] \tag{6}$$

Adam: It is like RMSProp, but the momentum is used to first and second order moment to control the momentum of W and g respectively.

$$m_{t+1} = \alpha_{t+1} g_t + (1 - \alpha_{t+1})\nabla \mathcal{L}(W_t) \tag{7}$$

$$\hat{m}_{t+1} = \frac{m_{t+1}}{1 - \alpha_{t+1}} \tag{8}$$

where m is called the first order moment of $\nabla \mathcal{L}$ and $\hat{m}$ is m after applying the decay factor. Then the gradients g is computed:

$$g_{t+1} = \gamma_{t+1} g_t + (1 - \gamma_{t+1})\nabla \mathcal{L}(W_t)^2 \tag{9}$$

$$\hat{g}_{t+1} = \frac{g_{t+1}}{1 - \gamma_{t+1}} \tag{10}$$

where g is called the second order moment of $\nabla \mathcal{L}$. The final step for updating is given by:

$$W_{t+1} = W_t - \frac{\eta \hat{m}_{t+1}}{\sqrt{\hat{g}_{t+1}} + \epsilon} \tag{11}$$

3 Property Image Classification Model

For an AVM system, it is very important for the arrival images to the system to be labelled and categorized. The categories are bedroom, bathroom, kitchen, balcony, living room and front view. The model presented here, label the arrival images automatically to save time and money, and provides new visual data to be used in the sale prediction models.

3.1 Base Model

The proposed classification model is based on a deep CNN which is comparable to human performance. Several architectures of convolutional network with different parameters and functions are investigated to find the best model.

After trying different network architectures, the baseline classification model is reached via the following architecture. The model is sequential in structure with five convolutional layers and three dense layers. The dense classification layer has six neurons with softmax activation related to each class that is connected to the former dense layer with 512 neurons. The first dense layer after the last convolutional layer has 1024 neurons which is connected to a dense layer with 512 neurons. All activation functions for layers, except the classification layer, are RELU. To avoid overfitting, Dropout layers are used between dense layers with 0.5 dropout ratio. The number of filters used in four convolutional layers are 32, 64, 128, 256 and 512. The filter size of 5*5, the stride size 2 and max pooling size 2*2 are used for all convolutional layers. Based on the proposed network the total number of trainable parameters (weights and biases) is 13,274,886. The input size 128*128 is considered for the model; therefore, images are resized to 128*128 pixels with the rescaled pixels values between 0 and 1. For training, Stochastic Gradient Decent and categorical cross-entropy models are used as an optimizer and loss function respectively. The batch size of 64 and 200 epochs are considered for training.

3.2 Pre-processing

Figure 2 shows an example of images in each category for three properties. Before images are fed to the classification model, they need to be processed into proper format. Images usually have three dimensions: heights, width and color depth (channel).

Color images have three channels called RGB as in red, green and blue channels respectively. Grayscale images have only one channel. Each element of these channels in each location related to its height and width could have integer values between 0 and 255. Neural networks typically show better performance in floating values where absolute values are not large. Therefore, the images should be converted to floating point values before they are scaled. Our property images are in JPEG format. So, the steps for preparing the data are as follows:

Fig. 2. Three samples of images in each category of the dataset Color figure online

1. Read the image files.
2. Decode the JPEG content to RGB forma
3. Convert to floating point vectors
4. Rescale the pixel values to range 0 to 1.

3.3 Dataset

The dataset consists of 8694 property images in 6 classes that are split to train with 5556 images and validation and 3138 images in 6 classes for testing. Images are related to 1749 apartments that had been sold in Sydney in 2017. All images are labelled manually for this research. Different models for real estate classification are developed by different parameters and architectures. All images are resized to (128*128) pixels.

3.4 Implementation

In this research, Keras is used for developing the models. Keras is a high-level neural network API, written in Python and capable of running on top of TensorFlow. The utilities in Keras can handle all the processes.

4 Results Analysis

4.1 Base Classification Model

Based on the images from apartments in Sydney, several classification models are trained. The base model performances regarded to accuracy and loss of training and validation phase are shown in Fig. 3.

The base model can reach 83% accuracy in test data. Tables 1 and 2 present the classification reports in training and test data respectively. In classification with six classes the guess rate is 16.7 percent comparable with 50 percent in two-classes classification. It means prediction accuracy above 16.7 is better than a guess. The confutation matrix of train and test data are presented in Figs. 4 and 5. As can be seen, the model can classify the images reliably. To reach a better performance, the technique of using pretrained convolutional networks is applied which is described in the following.

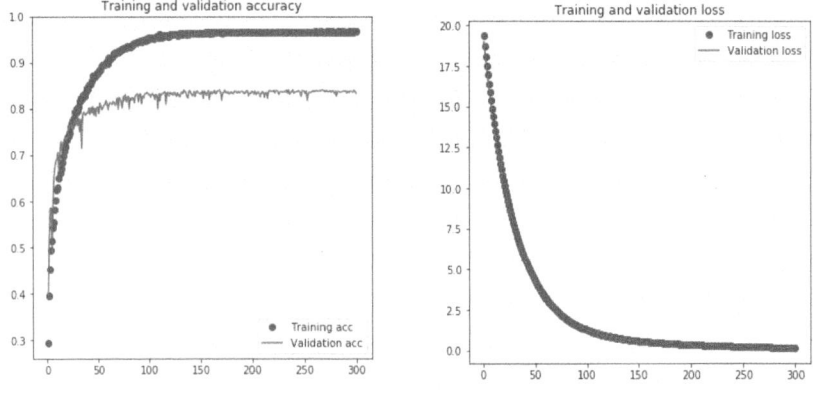

Fig. 3. Base classification model training and validation loss plots repectively

The most errors in training data are related to balcony images and that it is not surprising. The balcony and front images are similar because both include outside view objects such as trees, sky, and front views of other buildings. Another misclassifying related to balcony comes from the bathroom. It is likely because of the likeness in the shape of a balcony and a bathtub and its tiles.

Table 1. Classification report for training data related to base classification model

Category	Precision	Recall	F1-score	Support
Balcony	0.83	1.00	0.91	926
Kitchen	1.00	0.99	0.99	926
Bathroom	1.00	0.89	0.94	926
Living room	1.00	1.00	1.00	926
Front	1.00	0.94	0.97	926
Bedroom	1.00	0.98	0.99	926
Micro avg	0.97	0.97	0.97	5556
Macro avg	0.97	0.97	0.97	5556
Weighted avg	0.97	0.97	0.97	5556
Samples avg	0.97	0.97	0.97	5556

Table 2. Classification report for test data related to base classification model

Category	Precision	Recall	F1-score	Support
Balcony	0.77	0.85	0.81	523
Kitchen	0.85	0.84	0.84	523
Bathroom	0.90	0.79	0.84	523
Living room	0.74	0.88	0.80	523
Front	0.91	0.92	0.92	523
Bedroom	0.86	0.72	0.79	523
Micro avg	0.83	0.83	0.83	3138
Macro avg	0.84	0.83	0.83	3138
Weighted avg	0.84	0.83	0.83	3138
Samples avg	0.83	0.83	0.83	3138

In the test data, another misclassification is linked to bedroom and bathroom images. Although the performance of the base classification model is good it is not sufficient to be applied in the AVS for classification images. To improve the accuracy of prediction, the effective way of using pretrained convolutional image classification models is used.

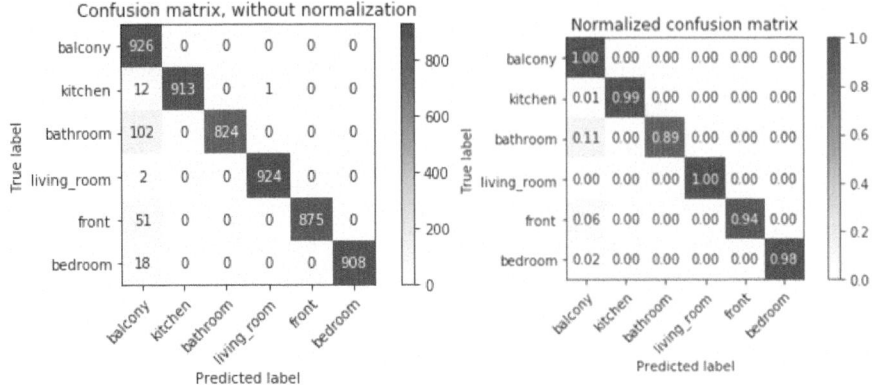

Fig. 4. Confusion matrix of training data related to base model classification.

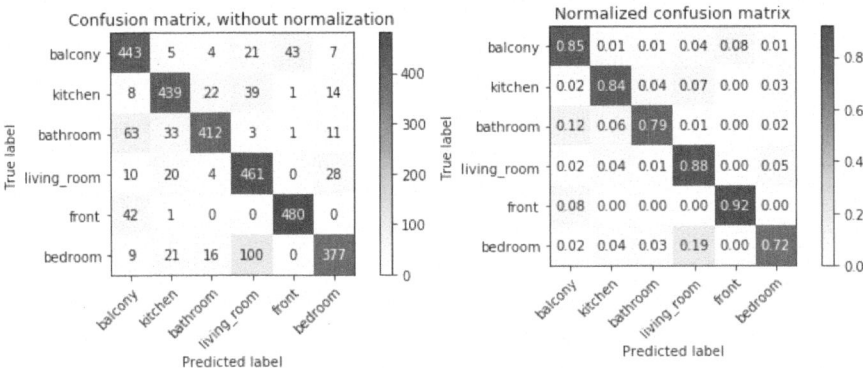

Fig. 5. Confusion matrix of test data related to base model classification.

4.2 Classification Model Using Pretrained Covnet

A common and highly effective approach to increase the accuracy of an image classification deep learning model in small image datasets is to use a pretrained network. A pretrained convolutional model is the saved model that trained on large image dataset and showed good performance. Through large and general datasets with enough classes (1000 classes), the hierarchy of features learned by pretrained convnet can effectively act as a generic model of the visual world. Its features can then be used for other image classification purposes. Even new image classification is completely different to the original pretrained model classification. Here, the image classification is linked to residential real estate images in 6 classes that differ from the original pretrained model used for enhancing prediction accuracy. The model VGG16 that trained on ImageNet dataset with 1.4 million labelled images in 1000 different classes is used for feature extraction and the fine-tune classification model. The VGG16 model was developed by Karen Simonyan and Andrew Zisserman in 2014 [23].

The convolutional base of VGG16 has 14,714,688 parameters. The classifier with two dense layers added on top has 8,395,782 parameters. It is important to freeze the weights of the VGG16 base model before compiling and training the classification model. By freezing the convolutional base model, the weights are not updated during the training process. With this setup, only the weights of the two dense layers are to be trained. The original image size input for VGG16 is 244*244 pixels, but here the input size is changed to 128*128 pixels to suit our image sizes. The outputs of conv base model are 512 feature maps of size 4*4 pixels in respect to one input images. The outputs of conv base model are flattened before feeding into dense layers. The first dense layer in classifier has 1024 neurons with RELU activation. The last classifier layer has 6 neurons associated with each class with softmax activation function. In fact, by freezing conv base model, the features of input image are extracted and fed to dense layers. The architecture of extracted-feature classification model is presented in Fig. 6.

By this setup, the accuracy of real estate image classification increases significantly overall from 83% to 88% in test data. The accuracy and loss results related to training and validation of feature-extracted model are presented in Fig. 7. As can be seen, after 100 epochs the overfitting commences.

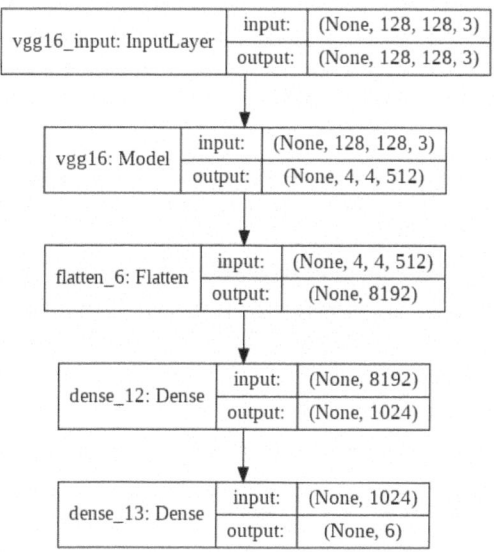

Fig. 6. The feature-extracted classification model for real estate images.

The classification report for test dataset is presented in Table 3. Compared with the base classification model, accuracy has improved in all classes but significantly in living room class because of features extracted from the VGG16 base model. Living room images are more likely have specific objects such as sofa, TV and coffee table which are in 1000 classes in ImageNet dataset classes.

Another technique employed widely in using the pretrained model is fine-tuning. The main difference between the feature-extracted technique and fine-tune technique is

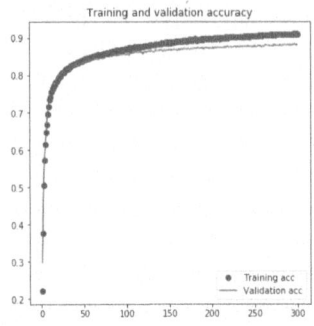 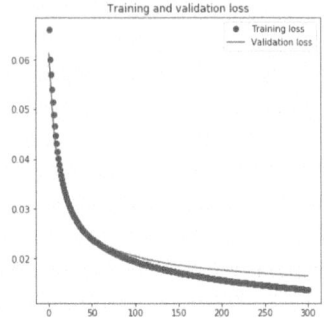

Fig. 7. Accuracy and loss results in training and validation related to feature-extracted

unfreezing a few of top convolutional layers of the pretrained model. Connecting the classifier dense layers on top of pretrained model creates a final network for classification. By unfreezing some convolutional layers, the convolutional features become more relevant for the problem at hand. The steps for fine-tuning a network are as follow [19]:

Add your custom network on top of an already-trained base network.
Freeze the base network.
Train the part you added.
Unfreeze some layers in the base network.
Jointly train both these layers and the part you added.

The architecture of the fine-tune model is the same as that of the feature-extract model in all layers. By applying the fine-tune technique, accuracy of image classification increases and reaches 92% in test data, good enough for using as a final classification model in visual-based real estate sale price system. The classification report of train and test data related to the fine-tune model shows that the living room class has 7% and 13% increase in accuracy compared to feature-extract model and base classification model respectively.

Table 3. Classification report for test data related to feature-extract classification model

Category	Precision	Recall	F1-score	Support
Balcony	0.80	0.89	0.84	523
Kitchen	0.91	0.87	0.89	523
Bathroom	0.93	0.85	0.89	523
Livingroom	0.84	0.88	0.86	523
Front	0.95	0.93	0.94	523

(continued)

Table 3. (*continued*)

Category	Precision	Recall	F1-score	Support
Bedroom	0.88	0.88	0.88	523
Micro avg	0.88	0.88	0.88	3138
Macro avg	0.89	0.88	0.88	3138
Weighted avg	0.89	0.88	0.88	3138
Samples avg	0.88	0.88	0.88	3138

Table 4 concerned with the classification report of test data, based on the fine-tune classification model. As can be seen, the most improvements are related to bathroom and living room compared to base model results.

Table 4. Classification report for test data related to fine-tune classification model

Category	Precision	Recall	F1-score	Support
Balcony	0.80	0.93	0.86	523
Kitchen	0.96	0.92	0.94	523
Bathroom	0.96	0.87	0.91	523
Living room	0.87	0.91	0.89	523
Front	0.97	0.93	0.95	523
Bedroom	0.93	0.90	0.92	523
Micro avg	0.91	0.91	0.91	3138
Macro avg	0.92	0.91	0.91	3138
Weighted avg	0.92	0.91	0.91	3138
Samples avg	0.91	0.91	0.91	3138

5   Conclusion and Future Work

This paper develops a residential real estate image classification model based on CNNs. The main purpose of the model is to be applied in a visual decision support system for sale price prediction or it can be embedded in real estate websites to classify the arrival of images automatically. In this research several convolutional neural networks were examined to find the best model to classify the real estate property images in six classes. The pretrained model was used to increase classification accuracy. The dataset was related to apartments in Sydney, NSW, Australia in 2017. Based on the case study, the highest accuracy was 92% in fine-tuned model. By having a model with 92% accuracy, this model can be used in a prediction process automatically and with confidence.

References

1. Dziauddin, M.F., Ismail, K., Othman, Z.J.B.O.G.S.-E.S.: Analysing the local geography of the relationship between residential property prices and its determinants. **28**:21-35 (2015)
2. Bryant, L.J.J.O.H., Environment, T.B.: Housing affordability in Australia: an empirical study of the impact of infrastructure charges. **32**:559-579 (2017)
3. Li, J., Monkkonen, P.J.P.M.: The value of property management services: an experiment. **32**:213-223 (2014)
4. Schulz, R., Wersing, M., Werwats, A.J.J.O.P.R.; Automated valuation modelling: a specification exercise. **31**:131-153 (2014b)
5. Almy, R.J.C.: Real property assessment systems. 6:11 (2002)
6. Chen, J., Hao, Q.J.J.O.C.E., Studies, B.: The impacts of distance to CBD on housing prices in Shanghai: a hedonic analysis. **6**:291-302 (2008)
7. Kiel, K.A., Zabel, J.E.J.J.O.H.E.: Location, location, location: the 3L approach to house price determination. J. Hous. Econ. **17**(2), 175–190 (2008). https://doi.org/10.1016/j.jhe.2007.12.002
8. Tsai, D.C.-W., Chen, T.-H., Quek, C.L.J.J.O.S., Systems, M.: Analysis on the real estate prices: a perspective of spatial correlation with shopping district. **15**:219-240 (2012)
9. Nejad, M.Z., Lu, J., Behbood, V.: Applying dynamic Bayesian tree in property sales price estimation. In: 2017 12th International Conference on Intelligent Systems and Knowledge Engineering (ISKE) pp. 1–6 IEEE (2017)
10. Nejad, M.Z., Lu, J., Asgari, P., Behbood, V.: The effect of google drive distance and duration in residential property in Sydney, Australia. In: Uncertainty Modelling in Knowledge Engineering and Decision Making: Proceedings of the 12th International FLINS Conference pp. 646–655 (2016)
11. You, Q., Pang, R., Cao, L., Luo, J.: Image-based appraisal of real estate properties. IEEE Trans. Multimedia **19**, 2751–2759 (2017)
12. Law, S., Paige, B., Russell, C.: Take a look around: using street view and satellite images to estimate house prices. ACM Trans. Intell. Syst. Technol. **10**, 1–19 (2019)
13. Ahmed, E., Moustafa, M.: House price estimation from visual and textual features (2016)
14. Poursaeed, O., Matera, T., Belongie, S.: Vision-based real estate price estimation. Machine Vision and Applications (2017)
15. Sermanet, P., Chintala, S., Lecun, Y.: Convolutional neural networks applied to house numbers digit classification. In: Proceedings of the 21st International Conference on Pattern Recognition (ICPR2012), 11–15 Nov 2012 pp. 3288–3291 (2012)
16. Zhu, Y., Newsam, S.: Land use classification using convolutional neural networks applied to ground-level images (2015)
17. Alex, K., Ilia, S., HG, E.: Imagenet classification with deep convolutional neural networks. In: Proceedings of NIPS, IEEE, Neural Information Processing System Foundation, pp. 1097–1105 (2012)
18. KIM, Y.: Convolutional neural networks for sentence classification. arXiv preprint arXiv: 1408.5882 (2014)
19. Chollet, F.: The future of deep learning. Future **8**:2 (2017a)
20. Ponti, M.A., Ribrio, L.S.F., Nazare, T.S., Bui, T., Collomosse, J.: Everything you wanted to know about deep learning for computer vision but were afraid to ask. In: 2017 30th SIBGRAPI Conference on Graphics, Patterns and Images Tutorials (SIBGRAPI-T), 17–18 Oct. 2017 pp. 17–41 (2017)
21. Janocha, K., Czarenkey, W.M.: On loss functions for deep neural networks in classification. arXiv preprint arXiv:1702.05659 (2017)

22. Andrychowicz, M., et al: Learning to learn by gradient descent by gradient descent. Advances in Neural Information Processing Systems, pp. 3981–3989 (2016)
23. Simonyan, K., Zisserman, A.: Very deep convolutional networks for large-scale image recognition. arXiv preprint arXiv:1409.1556 (2014)

Novel Method to Investigate Decay in Rotting Bananas Using RGB Color Images

Unal McLauchlan[1], Mehrube Mehrubeoglu[2(✉)], and Lifford McLauchlan[3]

[1] W.B. Ray, and Del Mar College, Corpus Christi, TX, USA
umclauchlan@webdmc.delmar.edu
[2] Department of Engineering, Texas A&M University-Corpus Christi, Corpus Christi, TX, USA
ruby.mehrubeoglu@tamucc.edu
[3] Department of Electrical Engineering and Computer Science, Texas A&M
University-Kingsville, Kingsville, TX, USA
Lifford.McLauchlan@tamuk.edu

Abstract. Hyperspectral imaging has been used for many years in tandem with image processing to collect data about objects and processes over time based on the reflection of different wavelengths of visible light from these objects. However, hyperspectral imaging requires a hyperspectral camera, which can cost upwards of $50,000 and is unavailable to researchers without university, private, or federal funding. This work serves as a case study to explore an alternative, albeit less advanced method, that can be used to investigate similar objects based on images taken from an average civilian color camera, accessible to the majority of individuals, such as a cell phone camera. Such a method would prove both more affordable and time efficient. The presented method employs programming in MATLAB software to differentiate between red, green, and blue image frames and associated values in temporal images to study color changes in processes over time. In this work, the method is tested during the process of decomposition of bananas over ten days, where color change is simple and obvious; images may then be taken over time to measure for color change during decomposition and then to correlate that change to the degree of rotting. The results of this work showed that in the first few days of the experiment, no observable changes were seen in any of the color frames; however after the sixth day, a linear change in red and green frames were observed suggesting the usefulness of this simple and novel technique to investigate ripening and/or decomposition of bananas over time.

Keywords: Image Processing · Image Segmentation · RGB Color Frames · Agriculture · Fruit Analysis

1 Introduction

Automated determination of fruit or vegetable ripeness will allow efficient crop production, harvesting, and management in agricultural applications. Imaging systems can be used for non-destructive determination of crop or plant health. Hyperspectral imaging systems have been successfully utilized for studying algae [1], seagrass [2] as well as

L. Deligiannidis et al. (Eds.): CSCE 2024, CCIS 2262, pp. 126–137, 2025.
https://doi.org/10.1007/978-3-031-85933-5_10

plant health and coverage in various applications [3–7], such as monitoring the health of trees [3], grapevines [4, 5], forests [6], and cotton [7]. However, hyperspectral systems can be cost prohibitive. As a result, lower cost imaging systems such as visual spectrum RGB cameras can be a viable alternative.

Color features determined using RGB images have been utilized in various fruit, vegetable or plant applications [8–13]. In their work, Arad *et al.* employ flash or no flash for obtaining images for detection of sweet peppers using an RGB camera [8]. Huang *et al.* studied spatiotemporal patterns in seagrass surfaces using RGB image scans of the seagrass, *Thalassia testudinum* [9]. The health of rice plant leaves were studied by Yucky *et al.* [10]. Bagha *et al.* utilized RGB and multispectral imaging to study geranium plant health by analyzing the leaves [11]. Cho *et al.* described using RGB images and machine learning to evaluate water stress in sweet potatoes [12]. The authors were able to identify dry and wet conditions with over 80% accuracy using CNN during preliminary analysis and with limited data. Baek *et al.* investigated classification of external quality in melons using color images and deep-learning [13]. Their work focused on different types of defects on the surface of the melons, differentiating burst and browning with F1 scores of 0.82 and 0.66 in their preliminary results, and requiring additional data to improve their results.

Here, we present the investigation of changes in bananas over ten days, through the use of image segmentation of the red, green and blue color image frames. The simplicity of the methods presented makes them suitable for non-destructive quality assessment and real-time applications at low cost and easy access to required technology. The rest of this paper is organized as follows: Sect. 2. Summarizes the equipment used, Sect. 3. Presents the process of collecting the data, and Sect. 4. Explains the algorithm implemented in MATLAB. Section 5 shows the results of image analysis, and Sect. 6. Summarizes the conclusions.

2 Equipment Used

The equipment used involved a cellular phone as one would have for public use, and a computer with the MATLAB [14] software tool. For reference, though any modern smartphone would meet the criteria of this or a similar experiment, the phone used for this work was that of a Samsung S10+ Android phone, with no changes made to its hardware or software during its use.

3 Data Collection Process

Temporal images were captured to test for color change in the decomposition of the bananas over time. The process is described below:

Five bananas were chosen for use in this study, each of comparable size, shape, and level of ripeness, each also of the same brand and subspecies of banana. Each banana was labelled with an equivalent-sized cut number (one through five) on the banana's posterior. These numbers were used both to label the bananas and kick start the decomposition process as an induced bruise; within five minutes, decomposition (and ripening) occurred such that the cut became a visibly black number, as expected.

Decomposition may originate from this point in the banana, though said numbers were not be visible when pictures were taken for analysis (the side of the banana without this cut was imaged).

Each captured banana image for the provided process was taken in an identical location in identical indoor lighting. Each image was taken on the same location of a homogenous white table, and from the same viewing angle. Identical lighting was guaranteed via each picture being taken with the same amount of artificial light (with every light fixture in the room being turned on) and natural light (with each picture being taken at around midnight when light differences were minimal).

Then, each banana was placed, one at a time, on the white surface, the labelled side facing away from the camera. Each banana was placed in an identical orientation at this point. Every night for ten days, a picture of each of the five bananas at this location was taken, each banana acting as its own trial. Each picture was then added to an external drive to be analyzed in the MATLAB software tool.

Figure 1 shows the daily ripening and/or rotting of two of the five bananas used in the experiment for ten days. It is noted that the banana on the right showed more deterioration since its skin was cracked halfway into the daily experiments.

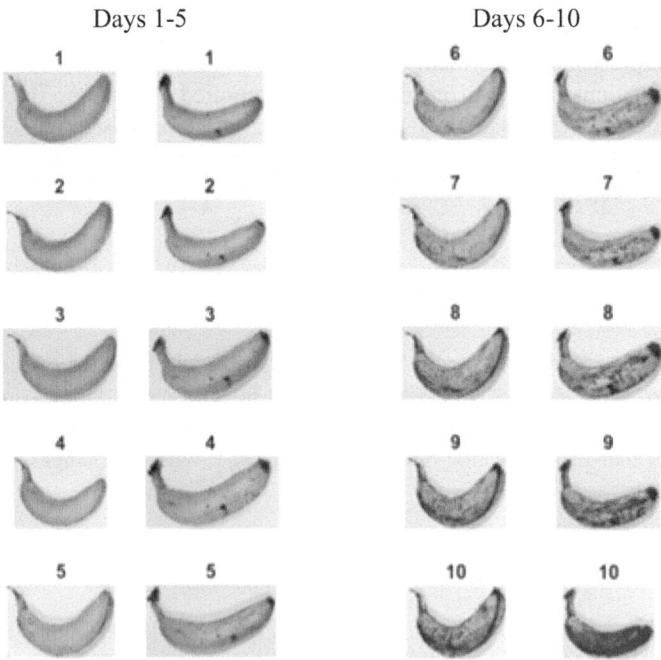

Fig. 1. Process of ripening and/or decaying of two banana samples over ten days.

4   Algorithm Implemented in MATLAB

Figure 2 shows the algorithmic workflow to quantify color brightness for each of the RGB color frames for a single banana image. The process is repeated for each banana image. The single value associated with each banana color frame (red, green, blue) for a given day (Day 1 to Day 10) is computed from the average of associated values obtained from each of the five analyzed banana images' individual color frames.

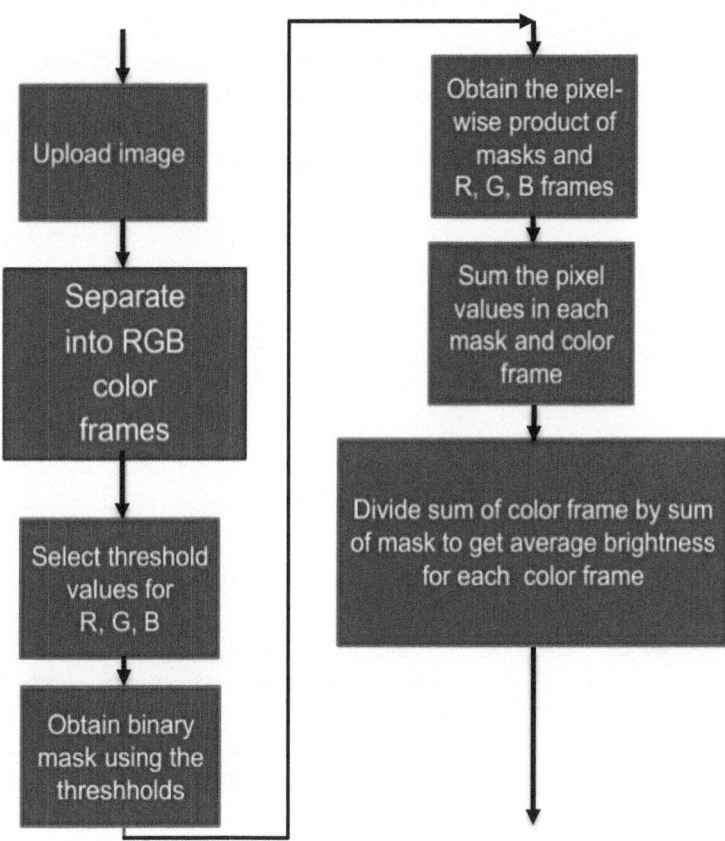

Fig. 2. Workflow diagram to quantify the color representation of a banana.

After the banana images were downloaded to the computer from the cellular telephone with which the images were captured, each image was uploaded into MATLAB 2022b workspace and processed one at a time through batch processing. First, each image was separated into its red, green, and blue frames (Fig. 3). Then, a threshold value was determined heuristically to segment the image into banana and background.

This process was applied separately for each image color frame. The segmented color frames were converted into a binary mask with ones (1s) representing the banana and zeros (0s) representing the background (Fig. 3) using Eq. (1).

$$I_{nc}(i, j) = \begin{cases} 1, & \text{if } I_{oc}(i, j) > T_c \\ 0, & \text{otherwise} \end{cases} \tag{1}$$

where T_c is the threshold value for color frame c (R, G, or B), $I_{oc}(i,j)$ represents the pixel value in the color frame, c, in the original image, I_o, located at pixel index (i,j), $I_{nc}(i,j)$ represents the pixel value of 0 or 1 in the new binary image, and I_n, for the color frame c based on the result of the threshold operation for the color frame c.

As seen in Fig. 3, from top left to bottom right, the images are of a sample banana as it was originally acquired by the digital color phone camera (1a), and the banana as it reflected the color red (1b), the color green (1c), and the color blue (1d), the last three being represented in grayscale. Bright values mean strong presence of the color represented by the color frame. Dark values, on the other hand, suggest weak or no representation of that color in the image.

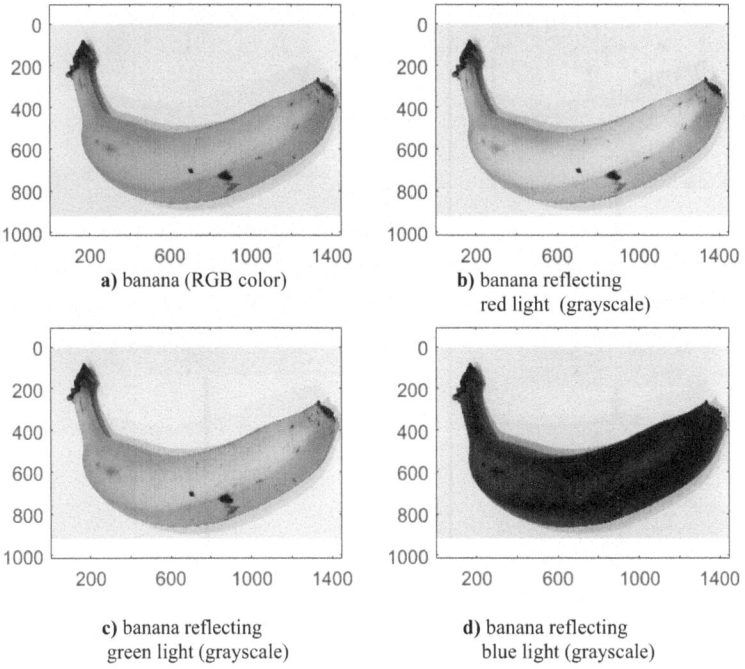

a) banana (RGB color)

b) banana reflecting red light (grayscale)

c) banana reflecting green light (grayscale)

d) banana reflecting blue light (grayscale)

Fig. 3. a) Original digital color image of a banana, b) Red color frame in grayscale, c) Green color frame in grayscale, and d) Blue color frame in grayscale. (Color figure online)

In Fig. 4, from left to right, the columns represent the red, green, and blue color in the banana. The top images represent the discussed binary "banana mask" or the shape of the banana. The middle images represent the color frames R, G, B, with darker images having less of the represented color. The bottom row images show the product of each color frame and its corresponding binary mask which will later be used to quantify the changing color representing the area of each banana.

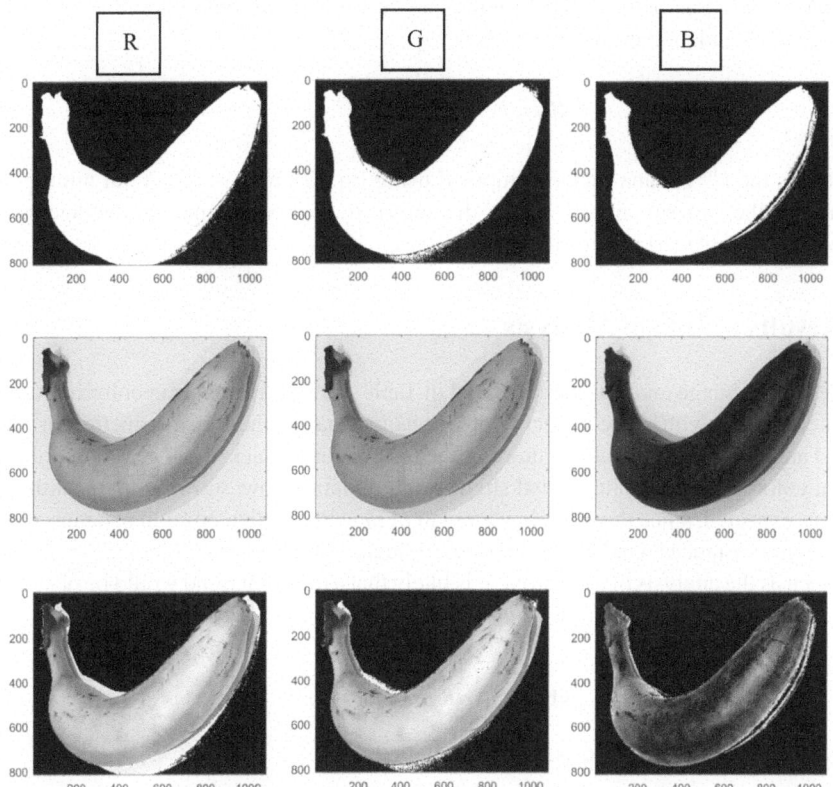

Fig. 4. Top row: Banana masks for Red (R), Green (G) and Blue (B) color frames. Middle row: Red, Green and Blue color frames in grayscale. Bottom row: Product of each mask in the first row with its corresponding color frame in the middle row, representing banana area. (Color figure online)

Since the binary masks ideally represent the banana in pixels whose value is one, as well as the decay and background pixels whose value is zero, taking the product of the mask and color frame will reveal a quantitative brightness representation for the banana. If the product matrix values are summed, the result will reveal the brightness sum for the banana area. By dividing this sum by the total number of white pixels in the corresponding mask, an average banana brightness value is obtained for a single banana image color frame, as in Eq. (2). This value can then be monitored for the same banana over time, exploring trends and correlating the result to banana health, ripeness or rotting state.

$$B_c(i,j) = \frac{1}{MN} \sum_{j=1}^{N} \sum_{i=1}^{m} I_{nc}(i,j) I_{oc}(i,j) \tag{2}$$

where $B_c(i,j)$ represents the brightness value associated with the banana region of a single color image frame, c; M and N are the number of rows and columns in the banana image frame under investigation, and i and j are the pixel index (location of pixel in the image frame) as before. The formula can be extended to obtain the average from multiple independent banana images as in Eq. (3):

$$\overline{B}_c(i,j) = \frac{1}{S} \sum_{k=1}^{S} (i,j) \tag{3}$$

where k is the kth banana image computed using Eq. (2), and S is the total number of bananas in the experiments ($S = 5$ in this case). $\overline{B}_c(i,j)$ represents the average pixel value over multiple (S) images for color frame c.

5   Results of Image Analysis

The results of image analysis are tabulated in Table 1 and show trends in color representation consistent with those expected of a banana. That is, there is a reduction in both the red and green color values as more of the banana turns black, having, at that point, a lack of color. Values for blue varied slightly and remained low, showing no meaningful trend, as expected, since there is a low amount of blue light reflected from bananas under normal circumstances. Under different experimentation where blue light takes a critical role, such as the analysis of blue mold, it is likely that a different trend would be observed for the changes in the blue color frame.

Table 1. Average Color Values

Average Color Values Based on Masked Images			
Day Number	Red Color Value	Green Color Value	Blue Color Value
1.	156.50	145.29	19.75
2.	169.02	147.23	12.05
3.	160.59	136.24	25.57
4.	167.56	139.59	22.97
5.	169.93	139.34	24.65
6.	176.47	143.77	24.64
7.	171.99	133.04	20.96
8.	152.56	121.52	21.20
9.	144.11	109.97	19.14
10.	131.59	100.18	25.58

Such trends can be seen in Figs. 5, 6, and 7 representing the color changes over time, where each point of color intensity is being measured from 0 to 255 (with 255 being the brightest). Graphs of the color values have lines of best fit shown to better represent the trends.

The red frame analysis from Fig. 5 shows a diminishing trend over time as the color of the banana darkens and overall the average pixel brightness goes down. The range of the output is from 131.6 to 176.5, out of 255, arbitrary units, spanning about 45 points. During the first half of the experiment, the average brightness level remained relatively flat. This could be because no significant changes in the color of the banana skin was observable during that time. Slight increasing in average red brightness on the sixth day of the experiment is attributed to the error introduced by the shadows around the banana, which is identified as part of the banana in the mask, thus increasing the average brightness of the represented color. Beginning day 6, the decreasing trend in red brightness becomes apparent, and is attributed to the deterioration of the banana skin.

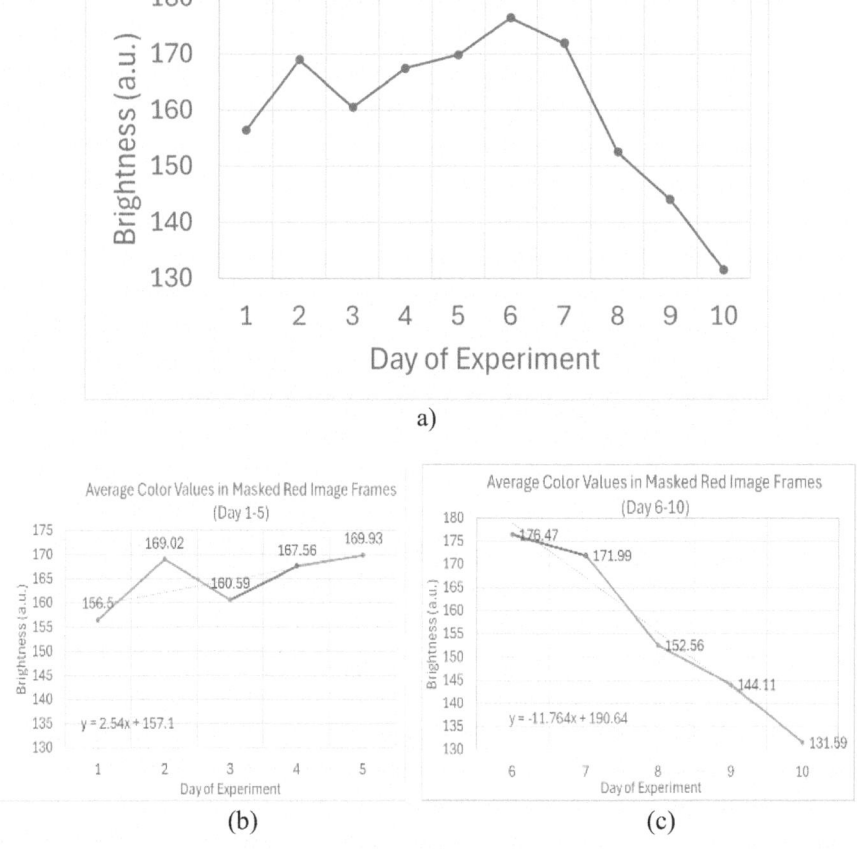

a)

(b)   (c)

Fig. 5. Average Color Values from Masked Image Frames (Red) (a) Full experiment (Days 1–10). (b) First half of the experiment (Days 1–5) with trend line (c) Second half of the experiment (Days 6–10) with trend line

Similar to the red color frame, green also displays a decreasing trend with a negative slope for the best fit linear curve in Fig. 6, as expected. Green also remains relatively flat during the first half of the experiment finally beginning to linearly go down from 6th day of the experiment onwards. The range of values for green was from 100.2 to 147.2 arbitrary units, spanning 40 points.

As can be seen in Fig. 7, blue tells a different story; there is not much blue, if any, represented in the yellow colored banana; therefore, compared to the red and green frames, blue brightness values are in the noise level, ranging from 12.1 to 25.6 with a span of about 13.5 arbitrary units, showing an almost flat response.

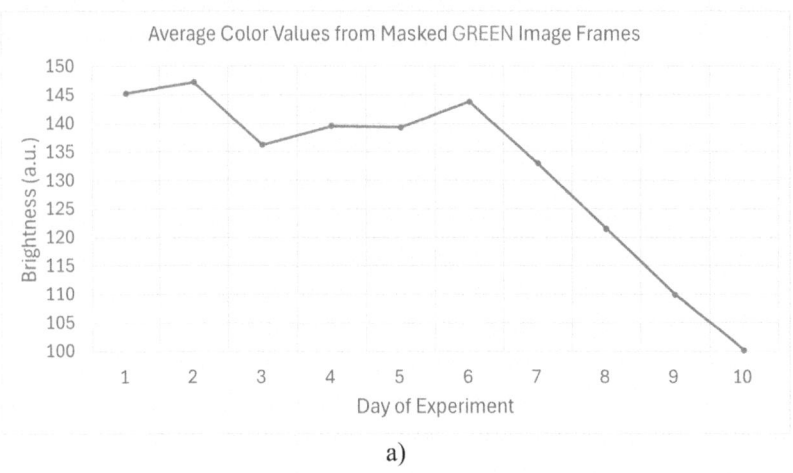

a)

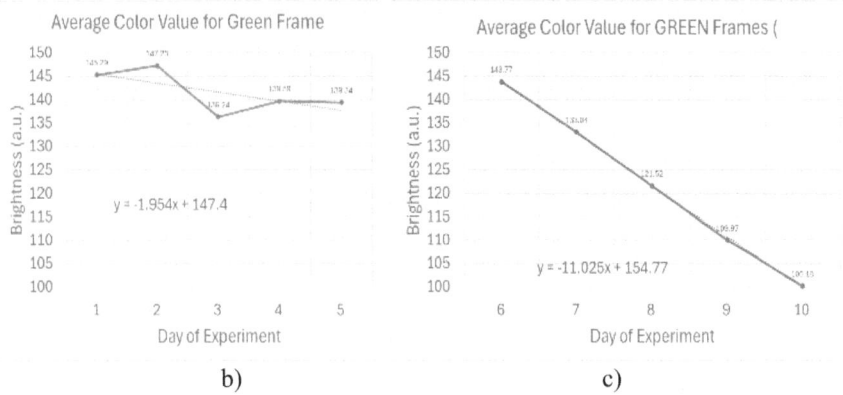

b)   c)

Fig. 6. Average Color Values from Masked Image Frames (Green) (a) Full experiment (Days 1-10) (b) First half of the experiment (Days 1–5) with trend line. (c) Second half of the experiment (Days 6–10) with trend line. (Color figure online)

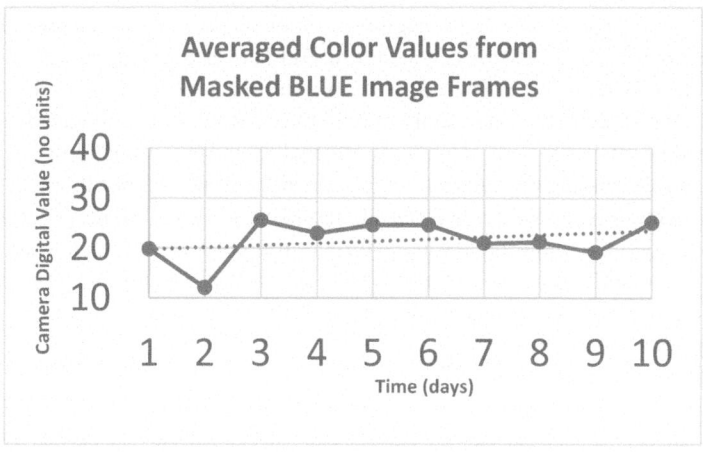

Fig. 7. Average Color Values from Masked Image Frames (Blue) (Color figure online)

6 Conclusions

The results demonstrate that once the banana skin starts darkening, the deterioration occurs linearly. The method used is shown to be conducive to future experimentation. Based on the results, color change values followed expected trends for the studied process (banana decomposition), suggesting that this method was successful in analyzing color data to capture physical changes. After extending the algorithm to correlate color to object's health, this solution could be used on a wider scale.

The application of the described method in other processes is extensive, and the method can technically be applied to study any process or change that is signified by color change. For example, in addition to plant decomposition, the corrosion of metals and certain geothermal events can be studied via this methodology when only considering color changes. As stated in the abstract, this method would serve as an affordable alternative to hyperspectral imaging whose use is much more limited than a smart phone camera. The method, if combined with other programming and physical technologies, such as terrestrial autonomous robots or drones, integrated with artificial intelligence, could be used in additional cases and monitoring applications such as determining whether crops are ready for picking.

It should be noted that future experimentation and work using this methodology would need improvements in the algorithms to reduce the effects of shadows as was observed to contribute to error in this study. Specific considerations would need to be made to extend the methodology to work in separate contexts with different physical processes. The algorithm would also need to be modified to take into consideration different object surroundings and lighting conditions, with adaptive thresholding or other threshold determination schemes.

One advantage of this method is that it is object size and magnification independent, since average values are used to represent the object's color or brightness using a single value. Therefore this approach of color-based quality monitoring would be feasible when the field of view, angle of view and magnification or object distance changes from the camera, such that mobile systems can also be used to cover extended areas.

Similar results could be achieved with artificial intelligence (AI) and associated technologies but such methods currently require massive amounts of image data to train the AI algorithms. It would be simpler, more affordable, and more scalable to employ any camera by simply making the values of colors considered in the algorithm that matches the specific conditions of the studied object, and using classical image processing and pattern recognition techniques that successfully utilize color information to correlate to the object's state without the need for extensive number of training images. This work presented initial studies to correlate color to the rotting of bananas in a limited duration experiment, showing the feasibility of the presented methods for monitoring quality of bananas non-destructively.

References

1. Mehrubeoglu, M., Zimba, P., McLauchlan, L., Teng, M.: Spectral unmixing of three-algae mixtures using hyperspectral images. In: 2013 IEEE Sensors Applications Symposium Proceedings, pp. 98–103. Galveston, TX, USA, 2013. IEEE, Piscataway, New Jersey (2013)
2. Mehrubeoglu, M. et al.: Empirical mode decomposition of hyperspectral images for segmentation of seagrass coverage. In: 2014 IEEE International Conference on Imaging Systems and Techniques (IST) Proceedings, pp. 33–37. Santorini, Greece, 2014. IEEE, Piscataway, New Jersey (2014)
3. Lin, H., Yan, E., Wang, G., Song, R.: Analysis of hyperspectral bands for the health diagnosis of tree species. In: 2014 Third International Workshop on Earth Observation and Remote Sensing Applications (EORSA), pp. 448–451. Changsha (2014)
4. Maimaitiyiming, M. et al.: Modeling Early Indicators of Grapevine Physiology Using Hyperspectral Imaging and Partial Least Squares Regression (PLSR). In: IGARSS 2020 - 2020 IEEE International Geoscience and Remote Sensing Symposium, pp. 1117–1120. Waikoloa, HI, USA, 2020. IEEE, Piscataway, New Jersey (2020)
5. Mehrubeoglu, M., Orlebeck, K., Zemlan, M., Autran, W.: Detecting red blotch disease in grape leaves using hyperspectral imaging. In: Proc. of SPIE, Algorithms and Technologies for Multispectral, Hyperspectral, and Ultraspectral Imagery XXII, pp. 1–8. vol. 9840, 98400D, SPIE, Bellingham, WA (2016). https://doi.org/10.1117/12.2223814
6. Kefauver, S. C., Peñuelas J., Ustin, S. L.: Applications of hyperspectral remote sensing and GIS for assessing forest health and air pollution. In: 2012 IEEE International Geoscience and Remote Sensing Symposium, pp. 3379–3382. Munich, Germany (2012)
7. Qi, Y.-Q., Duan, Z.-Y., Lv, X.: Research of cotton canopy characteristic information by hyperspectral remote sensing data. In: 2013 8th International Conference on Computer Science and Education, pp. 892–896. Colombo, Sri Lanka (2013)
8. Arad, B., Kurtser, P., Barnea, E., Harel, B., Edan, Y., Ben-Shahar, O.: Controlled lighting and illumination-independent target detection for real-time cost-efficient applications. the case study of sweet pepper robotic harvesting. Sensors 19(6), 1–15 (2019)
9. Huang, C., Piñón, C., Mehrubeoglu, M., Cammarata, K.: Image analysis reveals environmental influences on the seagrass-epiphyte dynamic relationship for Thalassia testudinum in the northwestern Gulf of Mexico. Front. Mar. Sci. 9, 1–21 (2023)
10. Yucky, E.D.D., Putrada, A.G., Abdurohman, M.: IoT drone camera for a paddy crop health detector with RGB comparison. In: 2021 9th International Conference on Information and Communication Technology (ICoICT), pp. 155–159. Yogyakarta, Indonesia (2021)

11. Bagha, H., Yavari, A., Georgakopoulos, D.: IoT-based plant health analysis using optical sensors in precision agriculture. In: 2021 Digital Image Computing: Techniques and Applications (DICTA), pp. 01–08. Gold Coast, Australia (2021)

12. Cho, S., Choi, J., Cho, E., Cho, Y.-S., Kim, G.: Water stress evaluation of sweet potato using RGB images with machine learning techniques, poster 13060–48. SPIE Defense and Commercial Sensing, National Harbor, Maryland, USA, 21–25 April 2024. SPIE, Bellingham, WA (2024)

13. Baek, I., Lee, A., Hong, S., Kim, J., Qin, J.J., Kim, M.: Classification of external quality in melon usnig color image coupled with deep-learning method, poster 13060–45. SPIE Defense and Commercial Sensing, National Harbor, Maryland, USA, 21–25 April 2024. SPIE, Bellingham, WA (2024)

14. MathWorks – MATLAB and Simulink: Mathworks.com https://www.mathworks.com Last accessed 28 Dec 2023

Lalitha: A Hand Gesture-Based Computer Control System

Tathagata Bhattacharya, Vinay Alsa$^{(\boxtimes)}$, and Akil Kumar Vujjini

Auburn University at Montgomery, Montgomery, USA
valsa@aum.edu

Abstract. This novel research is dedicated to creating an application called Lalitha that helps disabled people control an entire workstation only with their hand gestures. Lalitha has proved to be a great tool for providing brilliant user interaction and user satisfaction in terms of controlling the computer only with hand gestures. Especially, for people with disability, Lalitha would be an extremely useful tool. We incorporated Arduino, ultrasonic sensors, and software to create Lalitha. We tested our system with almost 300 people and we got positive feedback about our application Lalitha. In a word, we can claim that Lalitha is simple to set up, easy to use and its performance is brilliant. We have provided all the details of this entire application in this paper. In the rapidly evolving field of human-computer interaction (HCI), Many different industries, from gaming and augmented reality to medicine and accessibility, might benefit from this interface, This research proposes using Arduino and infrared sensors to create a system that can be controlled by hand gestures, Here We use ultrasonic sensors to detect the hand gesture and measure the distance of the palm. Ultrasonic sensors work through the time-of-flight principle (ToF), Arduino is an open-source platform that provides an accessible and versatile way to create interactive electronic projects It serves as the brain of the project. Hand gesture control provides novel approaches that increase efficiency and security in several sectors. In our project, we combine the concept of controlling PowerPoint presentations, and multimedia along with tab switching of various applications through various hand gestures. We designed Lalitha, a gesture-based recognition system that will identify gestures efficiently and control the device based on user instructions.

Keywords: Hand gesture · Ultrasonic sensors · Arduino UNO · Python

1 Introduction

Our interaction with computers has accelerated in recent decades [1]. The use of conventional input devices like keyboards and mice has proven useful, but researchers are always looking for new and improved human-computer interaction (HCI) techniques [2]. Since humans use hand gestures so frequently and find them easy to learn, this form of gesture recognition has received a lot of interest. The goal of developing a system for hand gesture control is to enable a computer to recognize and respond to input in the form of human hand gestures. Many different industries, from gaming and

L. Deligiannidis et al. (Eds.): CSCE 2024, CCIS 2262, pp. 138–163, 2025.
https://doi.org/10.1007/978-3-031-85933-5_11

augmented reality to medicine and accessibility, might benefit from this interface [3]. Accurate gesture detection, rapid processing, and an intuitive interface are just a few of the challenges that must be met before such a system can be built [4]. Therefore, it is critical to make use of an appropriate set of tools and technologies to create a robust and effective system. Because of its flexibility, user-friendliness, and compatibility, the hand gesture recognition system has gained massive popularity. A wide range of sensors and open-source electronics platforms like Arduino has become popular for developing gesture- based control systems [4]. Incorporating Arduino and infrared sensors allows us to create a system that can accurately detect and decode human hand gestures [5]. This research proposes using Arduino and infrared sensors to create a system that can be controlled by hand gestures [6]. Ultimately, the system's goal is to facilitate user interaction with computers through the use of predetermined hand gestures to improve usability and accessibility. The research will detail the steps used to create the suggested system, as well as provide an evaluation of how well it performs and where it would be most useful.

1.1 Hand Gesture Control

Humans' interactions with digital systems are becoming more natural, intuitive, and immersive thanks to advancements in hand gesture control technologies [4]. This technology has far-reaching implications, affecting not just traditional sectors but also traffic signal control systems and laboratories, where it is offering new, more convenient, and more efficient ways of working [7]. The origins of hand gesture control systems trace back to the early days of computer vision and image processing [8]. Researchers tried to identify hand movements in order to convert them in software commands, reducing the learning curve of physical input devices such as keyboards and mice [9]. However, early implementations faced challenges due to the limitations of available technology, including the lack of accurate sensors and the computational power required for real-time gesture recognition [10]. As technology progressed, infrared cameras and depth-sensing devices, like the Microsoft Kinect, changed the possibilities in the field [11]. These systems can provide a three-dimensional perspective of the environment, wath enabled new possibilities in the field [12]. Despite the advancements, these systems had limitations in the use as controlling computer systems [13], such as sensitivity to ambient lighting conditions and the data processing required to identify specific movements, greatly increasing the system's latency [14].

1.2 Hand Gesture Recognition System with Ultrasonic Sensors

We use ultrasonic sensors to detect the hand gesture and measure the distance of the palm from our ultrasonic sensors [15]. The use of ultrasonic sensors in hand gesture control systems addresses some of the limitations posed by earlier technologies [16]. Ultrasonic sensors work through the time- of-flight principle (ToF), emitting high-frequency sound waves and measuring the time it takes for the waves to bounce back after hitting an object [17]. This data is then processed to calculate the distance between the sensor and the object, enabling tracking hand positioning without the constraints of lighting or excessive data processing [18]. With this distance value, predetermined movements can be detected to send equivalent keyboard signals and control any computer application. This allows the system to work in different environments and with a faster response [19].

1.3 Hand Gesture Recognition with Arduino Sensors

Arduino is an open-source platform that provides an accessible and versatile way to create interactive electronic projects. It consists of a microcontroller board and a programming environment (IDE) that allows users to develop and control various electronic systems without the difficulty of building a PCB (Printed Circuit Board) [20]. It typically uses a microcontroller from the Atmel AVR family. It serves as the brain of the project, executing code and electrically controlling inputs to get data from sensors, switches, or communication devices and outputs to control relays, motors or send data [21]. An Arduino is an excellent tool for rapid prototyping of electronic projects. Through the use of SHIELDs, it's possible to interface with a wide range of sensors, including temperature, humidity, motion, and distance sensors [22]. This capability makes it possible to collect real-world data for various applications. Arduino's adaptability, ease of use, and extensive community support have democratized electronics and enabled countless individuals to bring their creative ideas to life [23]. From hobbyists and students to professionals and innovators, Arduino serves as a gateway to the world of electronics, fostering exploration, experimentation, and innovation in various domains [24].

1.4 Applications of Ultrasonic and Arduino

In this section, we are going to discuss various applications of using Ultrasonic sensors and Arduino together.

1.4.1 In-House Automation Systems

Controlling smart home systems with a wave of your hand may make them much more accessible and user-friendly [25]. Smart home system uses both Arduino and ultrasonic sensors to achieve its performance. Smart home gadgets like lighting, thermostats, and entertainment systems can all be managed with simple hand gestures [26].

1.4.2 The Automotive Sector

Hand gesture control has the potential to significantly improve both security and usability in automobiles [27]. There is no longer any need for the driver to take their eyes off the road or their hands off the steering wheel in order to adjust the audio level, the navigation system, or the air conditioning [28]; thanks to Arduino and ultrasonic sensors.

1.4.3 Industries

Hand gesture control provides novel approaches that increase efficiency and security in several sectors. In the industrial industry, for instance, workers may operate machines without having to touch them, which is very useful in potentially dangerous settings [29]. The entertainment business is bringing virtual reality to new heights with the use of gesture control technologies, especially in the gaming industry [30].

1.4.4 Management of Traffic Lights

Improving road safety might be as simple as implementing hand gesture control in traffic light systems. In cases when human interaction is required for traffic management, for instance, traffic police can employ pre-defined hand gestures to regulate traffic light systems [31]. In addition, connected cars with gesture recognition technology might decipher signals from law enforcement or other motorists, adding another layer of communication for more secure driving [32].

1.4.5 The Field of Education

Hand gesture control has the potential to radically alter how we educate and what we learn. It may be included into dynamic teaching aids to make lessons more interesting and effective [33]. Teachers might utilized hand gestures to control digital information in class, making it easier for pupils to grasp difficult subjects with the help of interactive visuals [34].

1.4.6 Robotics

Because of its adaptability and user-friendliness, Arduino has found widespread usage in the field of robotics [35]. It can direct the actions of a robot, interact with its sensors, and handle even sophisticated tasks like object identification and route planning [36].

1.4.7 Weather Prediction

Temperature, humidity, light levels, and air quality are just some of the environmental characteristics that may be tracked by systems based on the Arduino platform [37]. Such systems are helpful for urban planning, which requires constant vigilance over environmental factors, and for weather stations [38].

1.5 Novelty of Lalitha

Hand gesture control is a significant product of Computer vision, Augmented, and virtual reality. In the past, several researchers came up with controlling PowerPoint presentations with a hand gesture control system. At the same time, another group of scientists came up with multimedia controlling and tab switching with a gesture control-based approach.

In our novel research, we combine the concept of controlling PowerPoint presentations, and multimedia along with tab switching of various applications through various hand gestures. We designed Lalitha, a gesture-based recognition system that will identify the gestures efficiently and control the device based on user instructions. We incorporated Arduino and ultrasonic sensors that can ease the task of a user, and at the same time, enhance the convenience of a person with a disability. This novel application Lalitha is designed to control any system with high efficiency and convenience. We provide the insight of this application in the following sections.

2 Literature Survey

Within the field of human-computer interaction, one of the most important focuses of study has been the creation of control systems that make use of hand gestures. It is the goal of these systems to let users engage with computer interfaces using natural hand gestures, thus doing away with the need for physical input devices such as keyboards and mice. This literature review investigates previous research in this area, stressing both its contributions and its limits. It then looks into the distinctive characteristics and benefits of the suggested hand gesture control system that economically makes use of ultrasonic sensors.

2.1 Existing Work in Hand Gesture Control Systems

Hand gesture control systems may be traced back to early experiments in computer vision and image processing [39]. These early initiatives laid the groundwork for modern hand gesture control systems. Early computer systems attempted to ease computer use by identifying hand gestures and translating those actions into corresponding software instructions [40]. However, these early implementations had difficulties owing to a lack of processing capabilities, which caused real-time gesture detection to be delayed [41]. The development of infrared cameras and depth-sensing devices, such as the Microsoft Kinect, enabled significant improvements in the capabilities of gesture detection. These developments were made possible by advances in technology [42]. However, these systems had several drawbacks, the most notable of which were their sensitivity to the surrounding illumination conditions and their high computing requirements [39]. Over the course of the last several years, several noteworthy hand gesture control systems have evolved. The Leap Motion Controller is one example of this kind of technology. It employs infrared cameras to provide accurate tracking of the user's hand motions [43]. Even though it provides a high level of precision, it comes at a somewhat expensive cost, which restricts access to it. The Myo armband is another technology that can detect muscle activity and use that information to understand movements made with the hands and arms [44]. The expense of the Myo armband continues to be a barrier to its wider adoption, even though it is revolutionary.

2.2 Comparison with the Proposed Affordable Hand Gesture Control System

The suggested low-cost hand gesture control system differentiates itself from other options by merging low-cost ultrasonic sensors, notably the HC-SR04 ultrasonic sensor, with the Arduino platform. This makes the system stand out from other options that are already available. This strategy has several benefits that set it apart from its rivals in a variety of respects.

- The system that is being presented has one of the most major benefits, and that is the fact that it is quite affordable. Existing solutions often come with large price tags; however, the use of generally accessible and cost-effective components, such as the HC-SR04 sensor and Arduino, dramatically decreases the cost barrier [45]. This is because of the nature of the components. Because of this, a far larger variety of users, such as students, hobbyists, and people from a variety of different backgrounds, will be able to access and use the system.

- Accessibility: In contrast to some current systems, which depend on complex finger motions or specialized hardware, the suggested system makes use of natural hand gestures, making it accessible to people with a wide range of abilities [46]. This inclusiveness extends its potential uses to healthcare settings, where touchless interactions may enhance cleanliness and accessibility for patients who have restricted movement. Specifically, this is because touchless interactions do not need patients to make physical contact [47].

- Ease of Use: Rapid prototyping and development may be accomplished with the Arduino platform because of its user-friendliness and rich library support [48]. Because of how easy it is to use, it encourages research and experimentation, which makes it a desirable option for both novices and seasoned experts.

- Diversity: The capacity of the HC-SR04 ultrasonic sensor to detect distances with accuracy ranging from 2 cm to 400 cm by 3 mm gives diversity in hand gesture identification [49]. The use of several sensors improves the system's capacity to recognize complex and fluid hand motions, which ensures its applicability across a wide range of applications, from gaming to teaching.

In Our System we are mainly designed specifically to control web browsing while the existing system can be used to control a particular applications only. Specific to the task of controlling web browsing, which makes it more efficient and effective. It is easier to understand and modify, as it is written in Python. It is more flexible, as it can be easily customized to support different gestures and actions. The old system only the specialised persons can do the change that to limited one. Overall, our new system is a more robust and user-friendly implementation of a hand gesture controlling system using Arduino.

2.3 Real-Time Hand Gesture Recognition Using Computer Vision

Real-Time Hand Gesture Recognition Employing Computer Vision Several research initiatives have been focused on realtime hand gesture recognition employing computer vision. They make use of cameras to record the motions of the user's hands, and then use machine learning algorithms to identify and understand the gestures [50]. For instance, developed a system for recognizing hand gestures in real time by making use of convolutional neural networks (CNNs). According to Cao et al, their method was successful in recognizing a diverse set of motions to a high degree, which made it appropriate for use in gaming and other interactive applications [51]. Researchers have investigated depth-sensing technologies for hand gesture identification. These studies were conducted as a direct result of the success of the Microsoft Kinect. These systems make use of depth cameras to acquire data in three dimensions, which enables gesture tracking to be performed with greater precision. The research carried out by Wang and colleagues resulted in the development of a depth-sensing hand gesture recognition system [42]. This system was able to exhibit improved accuracy and resilience in a variety of illumination situations. Wearable devices for gesture control Academic research has also concentrated on the development of wearable devices for the recognition of gestures [52]. Wearable sensors such as accelerometers and gyroscopes were investigated in several studies, including the one that was carried out by Lee et al [53]. These sensors were used to detect and analyze hand and arm motions. The results of their study demonstrated the possibility of developing gesture control systems that are both tiny and portable [54].

2.4 Gesture-Based Human-Computer Interaction in Healthcare

Engineers have recognized the relevance of gesture control systems in the medical field. Gesture-based human-computer interaction is used in the medical field [55]. studied the use of gesture-based interaction in healthcare settings, where touch less management of medical equipment and patient monitoring systems may enhance cleanliness and patient care. [42] Studies like the one by Patel et al in 2019 investigated the application of gesture-based interaction in healthcare settings. Applications in the Educational Field Gesture control research has also aided the educational field with its instructional applications. Research conducted in educational settings has investigated the potential for hand gesture control systems to improve both student engagement and the quality of their educational experiences. For example, [56] explored the use of gesture control for interactive educational material. Their findings demonstrated how this kind of control may make learning more immersive and engaging [57].

2.5 Affordable Hand Gesture Control System

These academic works have made major contributions to the subject of hand gesture control systems; nonetheless, they often include sophisticated technology, complicated hardware, and specialized software [58]. On the other hand, the suggested economical hand gesture control system differentiates itself by placing a priority on cost-effectiveness, simplicity, and accessibility. The suggested system overcomes the cost barrier and provides a user-friendly method of gesture control. It does this by merging ultrasonic sensors that are available at a reasonable price with the Arduino platform [44]. This is consistent with the results of several research, including, which emphasize the significance of accessibility and simplicity of use in assuring broad acceptance of a product or service. Additionally, the use of ultrasonic sensors minimizes susceptibility to ambient illumination conditions and decreases computing needs, solving issues that were noted in earlier depth-sensing systems (Wang et al., 2014). This is an advantage over other depth- sensing methods. Because of this, the system that has been presented is suited for a wider variety of applications, including those in the fields of healthcare, education, and work done remotely [40]. Even though academic research has brought significant new insights and technologies to the area of hand gesture control systems, the hand gesture control system that focuses on cost, accessibility, and adaptability is the one that shines out. It provides a solution that is both practical and all-inclusive by combining components that are efficient in terms of cost, and it can make interactive experiences more accessible to a more varied audience. There have been tremendous developments made in the area of hand gesture control systems, and there are a variety of options available today. Existing systems often come with high costs and limited accessibility, even though they provide high levels of accuracy and novel features. These issues are addressed by the suggested economical hand gesture control system, which makes use of cost-effective ultrasonic sensors and Arduino. This solution is not only affordable, but it is also easily accessible and multifunctional. Because it can be used in a variety of contexts, including gaming, healthcare, education, presentation, and remote work, it is a viable option for a wide range of audiences.

3 Hand Gesture Control System

In this section, we are going to discuss the requirements to set up a hand gesture control system and the underlying methodology for developing a gesture-based control environment.

3.1 Software Requirement

We describe the various software requirements to manufacture a hand gesture control system in this subsection.

- The project Arduino-based Hand Gesture Control of Computer is implemented using IDLE (Python 3.9 64- bit) [59].
- Python and pySerial (library for communicating with serial ports) [25].
- To perform actions on our computer we use the Python Pyautogui library.

In this project, We establish serial communication with Arduino through the correct baud rate and then perform some basic keyboard actions. The first step with Python would be to install the Pyautogui module. Later, we need to feed Arduino commands written in C to the Arduino board. Then we need to execute the Python program to establish a communication channel between the Arduino and the computing system (refer Fig. 3).

3.2 Hardware Requirement

We describe the various hardware requirements to manufacture a hand gesture control system in this subsection. We need

- a single Arduino UNO
- 2 Ultrasonic Sensors
- USB Cable to connect Arduino to the computing system
- Jumper Cables for connecting Arduino to sensors
- A Laptop with web connection

Now we will discuss the methodology to implement a hand gesture control system with Arduino and ultrasonic sensors in Sect. 3.3.

3.3 Methodology

In this section, we describe the underlying methodology for implementing a successful hand gesture-based environment control system.

We describe the entire algorithm in this paper to set up Lalitha, a hand gesture-based recognition system. We describe every step diagrammatically in Fig. 5.

- The first task to setup Lalitha is to connect the ultrasonic sensors with the Arduino board through jumper wires.
- Secondly, we connect the Arduino board and the ultrasonic sensors to the workstation using USB cable.
- Thirdly, we write a set of control instructions to the Arduino for detecting the gestures sent by the sensors.
- Fourthly, Arduino will connect to the workstation and instruct the machine to perform a particular action specified in set of instructions written in the Arduino.
- Finally the user can control the entire workstation with his hand gestures using the ultrasonic sensors and Arduino.

We describe each of the previously mentioned steps in detail in the following subsections.

3.3.1 System Architecture

Designing the System architecture is the first step in building Lalitha, the gesture-based control system. Setting up a system to recognize gestures requires specifying both the motions and the appropriate computer responses. In addition, the Arduino board and infrared sensors will be set up so that the motions may be detected and interpreted accurately. We describe the system architecture of our gesture-based recognition system Lalitha in this section. Figure 1 describes the architecture or the framework of our hand gesture based system Lalitha. The 1st image points to the front of the system and the second image points out the rear part of the system. If one notices carefully, he will see that the back of the system is attached to the Arduino, ultrasonic sensors and jumper wires. The ultrasonic sensors and Arduino board will be placed such that they optimally detect the hand motions and the sound waves. Standard jumper wires and a breadboard will be used to connect the workstation to the Arduino board and the sensors. The signals from the sensors will be properly routed to the Arduino board's input pins. Thus whenever a hand gesture is made according to the policy, the workstation will perform the necessary actions. Overall, creating a hand gesture control system, employing an Arduino necessitates a blend of hardware and software skills, as well as knowledge of sensors, Jumper wires, and control systems. However, with the correct methodology and resources, it is feasible to establish a robust and dependable system for controlling hand gestures using an Arduino.

3.3.2 Arduino and Ultrasonic Sensors

Our novel hand gesture based recognition system Lalitha combines two Ultrasonic Sensors and an Arduino UNO board to perform the actions instructed by the user. All of these peripherals like Arduino board and the ultrasonic sensors may be powered directly from the USB port on the laptop. Ultrasonic sensors are used to provide the hand gesture of the user input to the Arduino board. The sensors measure the distance between our hand gestures and the surface of the computer to which we are gesturing. This input is sent to the Arduino board using jumper wires. Now based on the conditions provided to the Arduino board, the Arduino will send an instruction to the computer with the USB

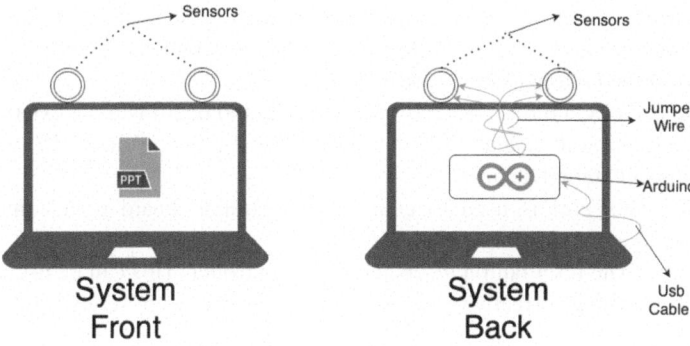

Fig. 1. System Architecture of Lalitha

cable. The circuit diagram of the Arduino board of the system architecture of Lalitha is depicted in Fig. 2.

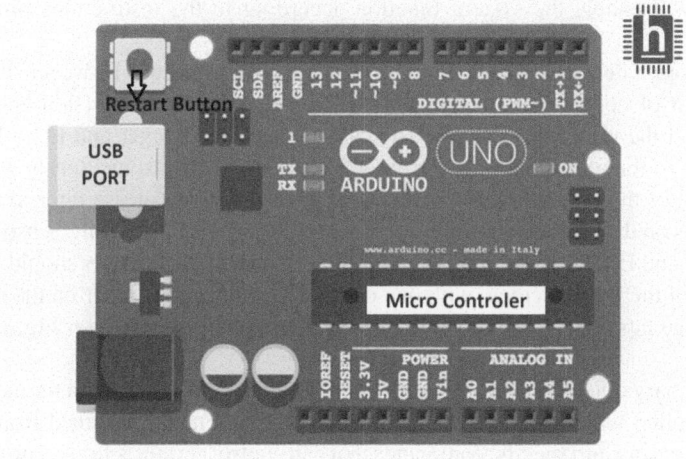

Fig. 2. Circuit Diagram of Arduino Board.

- Microcontroller: The microcontroller is the brain of the Arduino board. In Fig. 2 the black bar above the Power and Analog pins represent the microcontroller. It is responsible for executing the code that we upload on the board.
- Digital I/O pins (0–13): In Fig. 2 we have shown the position of these pins by pointing them out. These pins can be used to read or write digital signals, such as the state of a button or the output to an LED. Some of the digital pins can also be used for pulse width modulation (PWM) output, which can be used to control the speed or brightness of a motor or LED.

- Analog input pins (A0-A5): These pins can be used to read analog voltage signals from sensors, such as a temperature sensor or a potentiometer. Figure 2 represents these pins at the bottom of the board
- Power pins: The Vin pin is used to power the Arduino board with an external power supply, such as a wall adapter or battery (refer Fig. 2). The 5V and 3.3V pins can be used to power external devices.
- USB port: This port is used to connect the Arduino board to a computer for programming and uploading code (refer Fig. 2).
- Reset button: The reset button resets the microcontroller. This can be useful if your code is not working correctly or if you want to start over from scratch (refer Fig. 2).

3.3.3   Connecting the Sensors and Arduino to the Workstation

Once we design the system architecture, we needed to connect our Arduino board, ultrasonic sensors and the jumper wires with the computing system.

The Arduino board will be configured with the Arduino Software Development Kit (IDE). We write Arduino code to specify how sensor data will be interpreted by the Arduino in order to recognize the set of motions. At the same time, we write another code that will enable the system function according to the instructions provided by Arduino.

The project design entails a straightforward circuit design. However, the proper arrangement of components is critical. Figure 3 depicts the connection between the Arduino and the ultrasonic sensors. To start, connect the Trigger and Echo Pins (2nd and 3rd pin of the ultrasonic sensor from left) of the first Ultrasonic Sensor situated on the left side of the diagram to pins 10 and 11 of the Arduino(please refer to Fig. 2 for more details on the Arduino pins). In contrast, for the second Ultrasonic Sensor, connect the Trigger and Echo Pins to pins 5 and 6 of the Arduino. The sensors should be placed on the top of the laptop screen, with one on the left side and the other on the right side. Double-sided tape can be used to hold the sensors in place (please refer Fig. 1 for more insight).

The primary objective of this project Lalitha is to develop a program for the Arduino microcontroller, which can convert the distance measurements obtained from the two ultrasonic sensors into specific commands that can control certain actions. The ultrasonic sensors are strategically placed in front of the user's hand to detect hand gestures, which can be accurately calibrated to perform a variety of tasks on the computer. It is important to note that the specific tasks that can be performed must be defined prior to analyzing the corresponding hand gestures. These are the tasks that we can perform with Lalitha to provide ease and convenience to the user.

- Switch to Next Tab.
- Fast forward/slow motion of Video in VLC Player.
- Play/Pause Video in VLC Player.
- Start and stop the Screen recording.
- Scrolling up and down of web page.

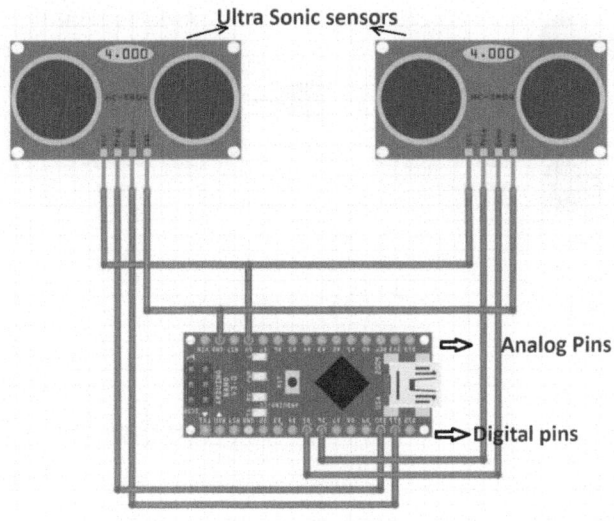

Fig. 3. Circuit Diagram of Arduino connection with two ultrasonic sensors.

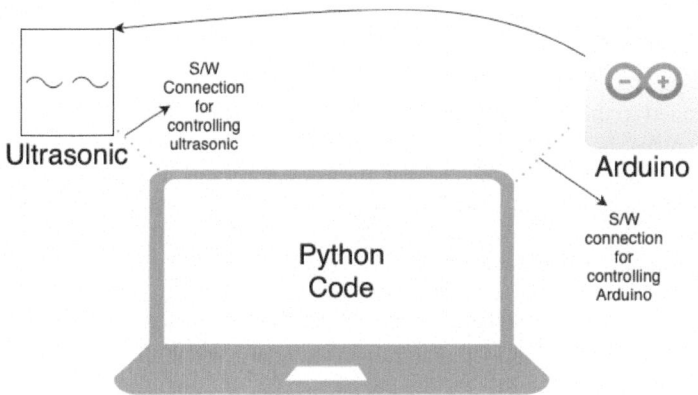

Fig. 4. Connection of Lalitha.

We define each of these tasks and how we can recognize them in Sect. 3.4.

We describe how we connect Arduino Board and ultrasonic sensors to the computer software in Fig. 4.

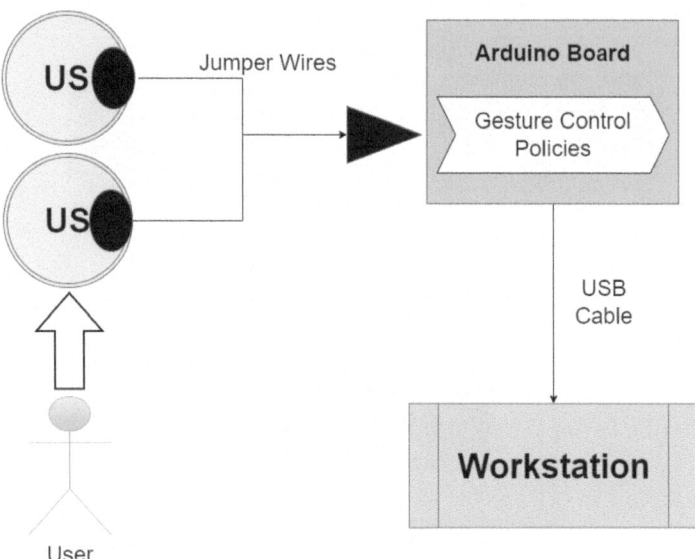

Fig. 5. Flow of control in Lalitha.

3.4 Gesture Recognition Policies in Arduino

Ultrasonic sensors are responsible to capture the gestures made by the user. Now these gestures are fed to the Arduino board for further processing. The processor of Arduino board recognizes these instructions with the help of the complex python code that we embed in the Arduino processor. The accomplishment of this operation necessitates the installation of a specialized Python module known as PyAutoGUI.

The following are the 9 different hand gestures or actions that we have programmed for demonstration purposes:

- Gesture 1: If we place the hand in front of the Right Ultrasonic Sensor at a distance (between 15CM to 35CM) for a small duration and move our hand away from the sensor, then this gesture will Switch the tabs.
- Gesture 2: If we place the hand in front of the Right Ultrasonic Sensor at a distance (between 15CM to 35CM) for a small duration and move our hand towards up to the sensor, then this gesture will Scroll up the Web- page. While moving our hand downwards to the sensor will scroll down the web page.
- Gesture 3: Once we Swipe right hand to the right in front of the Right Ultrasonic Sensor, the gesture will prompt the functionality of right arrow key on the keyboard.
- Gesture 4: Swipe left to the hand in front of the Left Ultrasonic Sensor. This gesture will perform the left arrow task on the keyboard.
- Gesture 5: Controlling of VLC player with our hands, Placing both hands at a distance of 25 cm–30 cm at the same time, This gesture will perform Play/Pause the Video.
- Gesture 6: Placing the Right hand at a distance of less than 20 cm and moving the hand towards the Right sensor will forward a video on a video player.

- Gesture 7: Placing the Left hand at a distance of less than 20 cm and moving the hand towards the Left sensor will perform the Rewind operation on a video that is getting played.
- Gesture 8: Placing both hands at the same distance (25–35 cm) will start the screen recording.
- Gesture 9: Placing both hands at the same distance of less than 20cm will stop the screen recording. Note: Gesture 9 can be executed when Gesture 8 has already been performed.

We mention the pseudocode to implement the hand gesture recognition policies in the Arduino board. Please refer to the following pseudocode.

3.5 Arduino Pseudocode

Step 1 Initilization Define pins and variables - trigger1, echo1, trigger2, echo2 - time taken, dist, distL, distR, duration, r, temp, screen flag, l

Setup: - Initialize Serial communication - Configure pins for ultrasonic sensors

Step 2 Distance Measurment Function(find distance): For each sensor: - Generate ultrasonic pulse - Measure return time - Calculate distance using (3.4 * duration/2)/100.00

Step 3 Distance Calculation Function (calculate Distance) For a given sensor: - Generate ultrasonic pulse - Measure return time - Calculate distance using time taken * 0.034/2

Step 4 Main Loop: Repeat: - Measure distances from both sensors

Step 5 Pause Modes - Hold: - If both distances are between 25 and 50: - Execute "Play/Pause" action - Wait for 500 ms

Step 6 Control Modes:

Lock Left - Control Mode: - If distL is between 13 and 17: - Wait for 100 ms - If distL is still between 13 and 17:

- Lock control for the left hand - While distL is less than or equal to 40: - Monitor hand movement: - If hand moves closer, perform "Volume Up" - If hand moves farther, perform "Volume Down"

Step 7 Lock Right - Control Mode: - If distR is between 13 and 17: - Wait for 100 ms - If distR is still between 13 and 17: -Lock control for the right hand - While distR is less than or equal to 40: - Monitor hand movement: - If hand moves closer, perform "Rewind" - If hand moves farther, perform "Forward"

Step 8 Swipe Next - Control Mode: - If distR is between 0 and 10: - Record current time - Wait for 300 ms - If the hand stays close, execute "Next" action

Step 9 Screen Control: - Detect specific gestures for screen control: - Start screen recording when both hands are at a certain distance - Stop screen recording when both hands are closer - Detect hand movement for "Change" action

Step 10 Direction Control: - If the right hand is closer and very close to the left hand, move in the left direction - If the left hand is closer and very close to the right hand, move in the right direction

Wait for 200 ms

Upon executing each command, the program resets the "incoming" variable to "Sensors Input," signifying its readiness to accept the next instruction from the Arduino. It persists in its loop, anticipating further data from the Arduino and responding to these directives. To encapsulate its functionality concisely, the pseudo code describes a software application that establishes communication with an Arduino device through a serial connection. Subsequently, it emulates keyboard inputs and key combinations in response to specific commands transmitted by the Arduino. The program is tailored to manipulate media playback, volume control, and application switching on a Windows operating system. These actions are achieved through the utilization of the pyautogui library.

4 Results and Observations

In this section, we are going to depict the observations and results after testing Lalitha with almost 600 users.

4.1 System Testing

For testing Lalitha, initially, we need to test Arduino, ultrasonic sensors and the laptop camera. The Arduino UNO can be tested by connecting it to a computer and run a simple program to calculate the distance of the object from the ultrasonic sensors. This will verify that the Arduino UNO is working properly and that it can communicate with the computer (please refer Fig. 2 in Sect. 3.3.2).

Once the system has been tested individually and with each component combined, it is important to test it with the laptop to ensure that it is working properly in a real-world environment. This can be done by connecting the Arduino UNO to the laptop's USB port and running the Python script (please refer to the Algorithm 1.

Algorithm 1: Create Serial port object called Arduino
Serial Data

ArduinoSerial ← serial.Serial('com3',9600)

while *incoming ← str (ArduinoSerial.readline()* **do**
 print (incoming)
 if *'Play/Pause' ∈ incoming* **then**
  | *pyautogui.typewrite(['space'], 0.2)*
 end
 if *Rewind' ∈ incoming* **then**
  | *pyautogui.hotkey('ctrl','left')*
 end
 if *'Forward' ∈ incoming* **then**
  | *pyautogui.hotkey('ctrl','right')*
 end
 if *'Vup' ∈ incoming* **then**
  | *pyautogui.hotkey('ctrl','down')*
 end
 if *'Vdown' ∈ incoming* **then**
  | *pyautogui.hotkey('ctrl','up')*
 end
 if *'next' ∈ incoming* **then**
  | *pyautogui.hotkey('ctrl','x')*
 end
 if *'change' ∈ incoming* **then**
  | if incoming data is 'change'
  | pyautogui.keyDown('alt') performs "alt+tab"
  | operation which switches the tab
  | pyautogui.press('tab') pyautogui.keyUp('alt')
 end
 if *'screenstart' ∈ incoming* **then**
  | *pyautogui.hotkey('winleft','alt','r')*
 end
 if *'screenstop' ∈ incoming* **then**
  | *pyautogui.hotkey('winleft','alt','r')*
 end
 if *'left' ∈ incoming* **then**
  | *pyautogui.hotkey('ctrl','left')*
 end
 if *'right' ∈ incoming* **then**
  | *pyautogui.hotkey('ctrl','right')*
 end
 incoming ← "Sensors Input";
end

The Python script should be able to detect the Arduino UNO and communicate with it to send and receive signals. The hand gesture recognition algorithm should also be able to track the hand gestures in the video stream and recognize the gestures in real-time (refer Sect. 3.3.1).

The system can be tested with a variety of hand gestures and actions to ensure that it is working properly with the laptop.

4.2 User Demographic

In this section we are going to describe various aspects of the users who played with Lalitha and shared their feedback to us for updating Lalitha in the testing phase.

Figure 6 describes the gender of the users. Turns out that 35% female and 65% male took part in this survey.

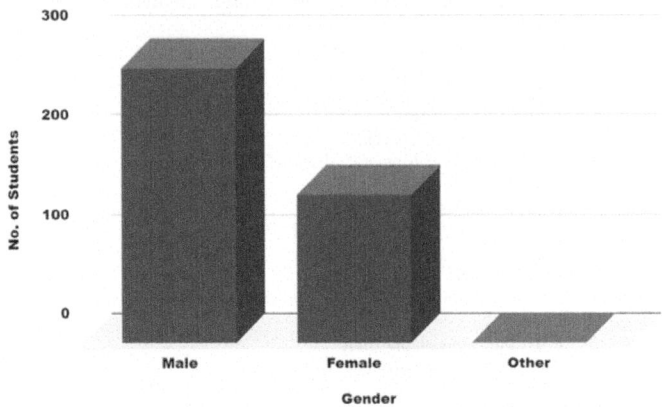

Fig. 6. Gender demographics of the evaluators

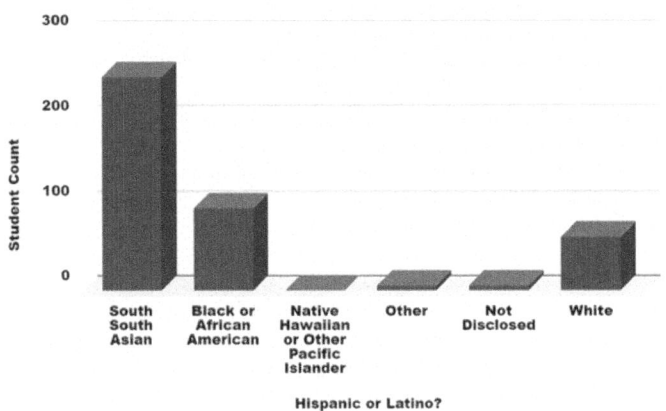

Fig. 7. Race of the evaluators

Figure 7 depicts the race of the users who took part in the survey. Turns out around 170 evaluators identify themselves as South Asian; 100 identify themselves as African American; 55 identify themselves as White and less than 40 evaluators identify themselves as Native Hawaiian.

Figure 8 describes the technical background of the users who tested Lalitha. Figure 8 reveals that most of the users use computers frequently.

4.3 User Experience

In this section, we will discuss various aspects of user experience while testing Lalitha. Based on the survey conducted with 300 users, we get the following evaluations.

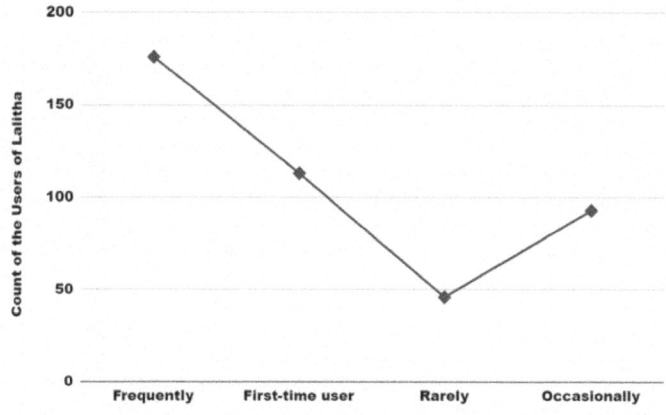

Fig. 8. Technical Backgraound of Lalitha Users

4.3.1 User Interactivity

Figure 9 depicts the feedback from the evaluators on the user interactivity and convenience of use of Lalitha, a novel hand gesture-based recognition system. Around 75% students think that the user interactivity of Lalitha is 5 star. Only 12–15% has rated the user interactivity and user convenience with a 3 star.

Figure 10 describes the user experience on the accuracy and responsiveness of Lalitha while testing. Figure 10 reveals that almost 280 people have given the accuracy and responsiveness of Lalitha a 5 star.

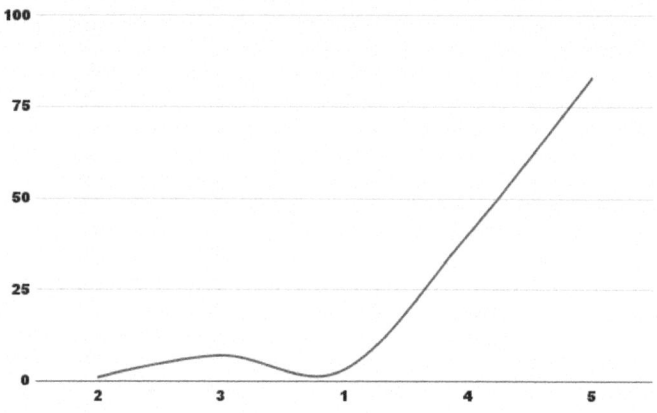

Fig. 9. User Interactivity and convenience of Lalitha

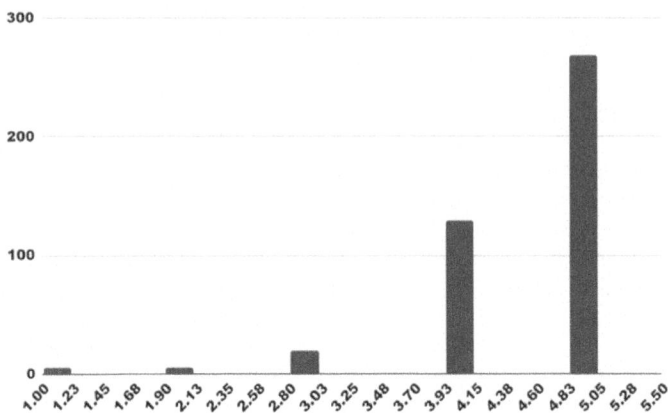

Fig. 10. Accuracy and Responsiveness of Lalitha.

Figure 11 describes the ease of using Lalitha by the users. Figure 11 reveals that almost 250–280 evaluators have given a 5 star rating for Installation and ease of using Lalitha.

4.3.2 Technical Efficiency of Lalitha

In this section, we depict the technical efficiency of Lalitha in terms of gesture detection speed, responsiveness, user satisfaction, and convenience while using Lalitha.

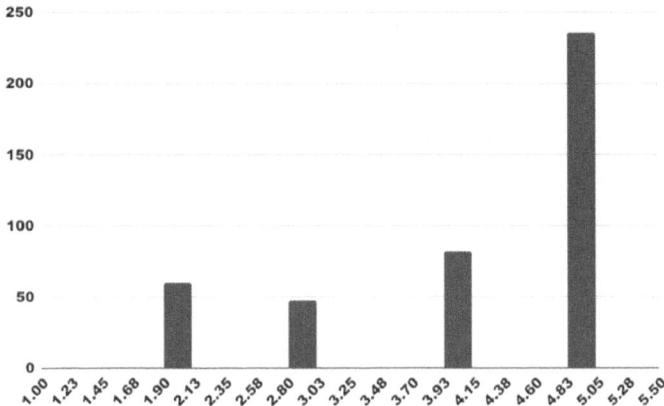

Fig. 11. Ease of Using Lalitha.

Figure 12 describes the speed of gesture detection and command execution with Lalitha. Turns out that 260 of 300 users claim that the response rate is fast.

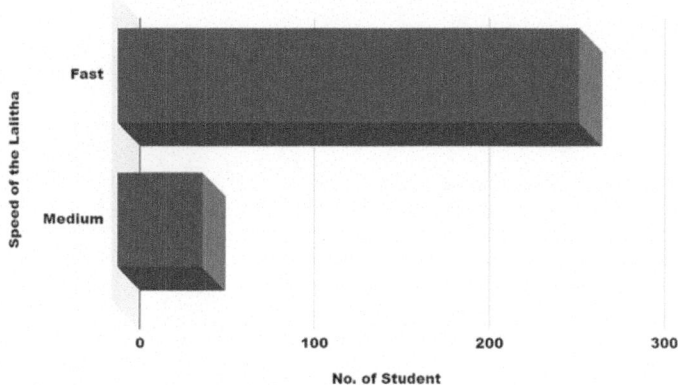

Fig. 12. Speed of lalitha.

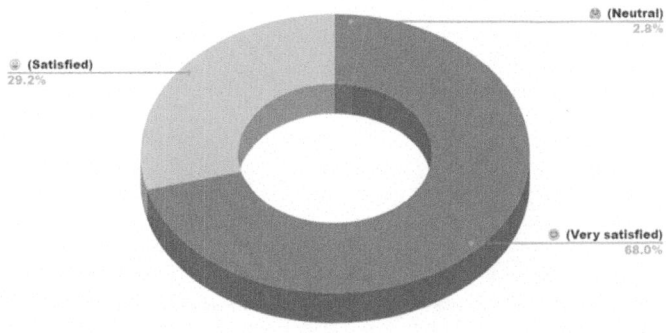

Fig. 13. Use Satisfaction while using Lalitha

Figure 13 describes the user satisfaction with Lalitha in terms of interactivity and responsiveness. Most of the users have exclaimed that they are very satisfied with their interaction with Lalitha Fig. 13.

Figure 14 depicts the convenience of the use of Lalitha. The x-axis symbolizes user rating and the y-axis symbolizes user percentage. Turns out that 80% users expressed that they feel Lalitha is very convenient to use.

4.3.3 User Experience and Suggestions after Using Laitha

In this section, we describe the overall user experience after using Lalitha, a novel hand gesture-based recognition system. At the same time, we also point out user suggestions in terms of making Lalitha better in the future.

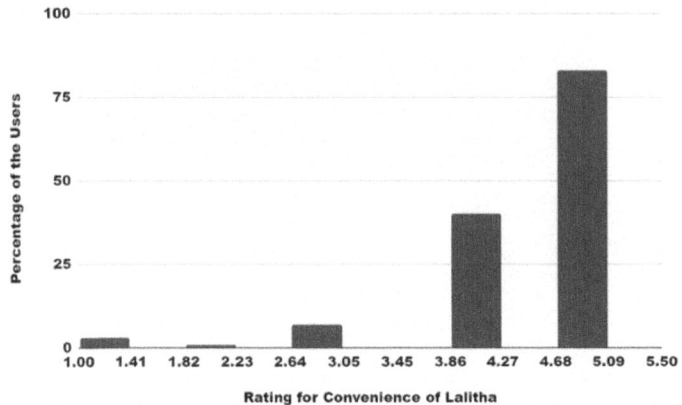

Fig. 14. Convenience of using Lalitha.

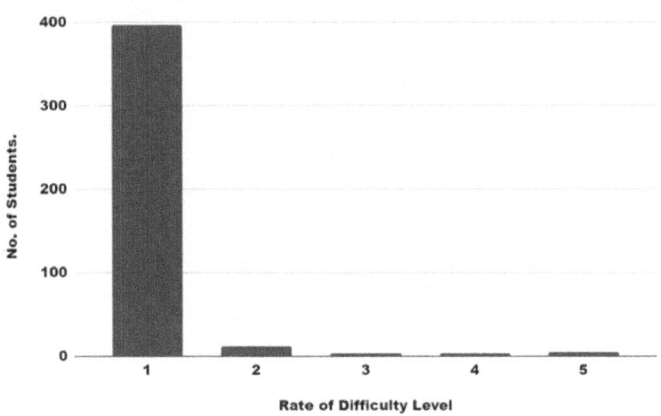

Fig. 15. Difficulties while using Lalitha.

Figure 15 reveals that the users faced the lowest level of challenge while using Lalitha. Here rating 1 suggests that around 90% of people faced almost no technical challenge while using Lalitha. Reveals that almost 250 people are rated as very satisfied with Lalitha interface and working model. Very less like 30 people are neutral with Lalitha. Figure 16 expresses their love for various gestures. Around 150 people loved the swiping right gesture. Around 100 voted for the tab switch gesture.

Figure 17 expresses their Suggestions for Lalitha. Around 90% of people were not given any suggestions.

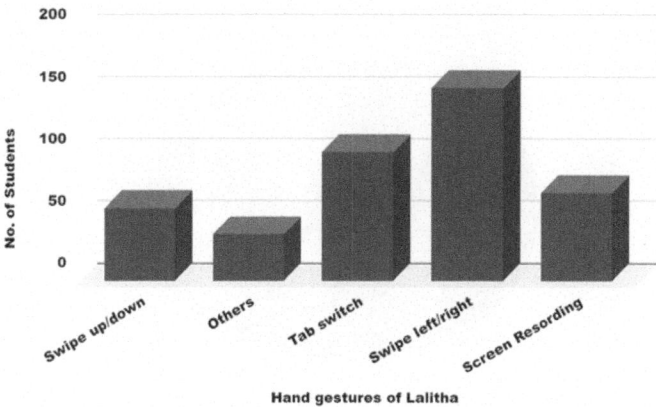

Fig. 16. Popular gesture rating by users

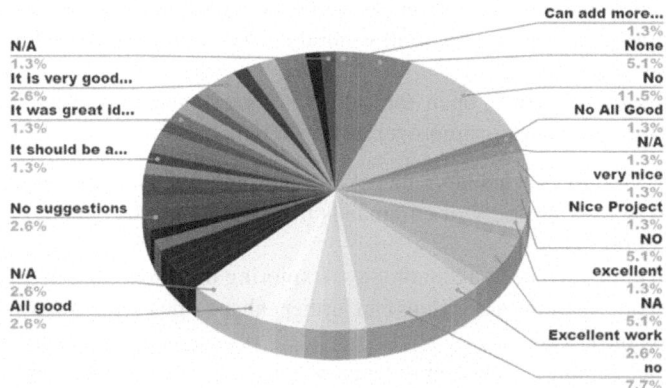

Fig. 17. Flow of control in Lalitha.

5 Conclusion and Future Scope

The proposed system called Lalitha, which uses Arduino and ultrasonic sensors shows promise in improving the way humans interact with computers. By using sensors this system addresses the limitations of technologies, such, as sensitivity to lighting conditions and high data processing requirements. The integration of Arduino, a versatile and open-source platform further enhances the adaptability and user-friendliness of the system. Lalitha offers a variety of nine hand gestures, each assigned to actions like switching tabs, scrolling web pages controlling media playback, and initiating screen recording. The Python code embedded in the Arduino processor along with the PyAutoGUI module enables the recognition and execution of these gestures. The potential applications for Lalitha go beyond the keyboard. Mouse input methods. It finds relevance in industries

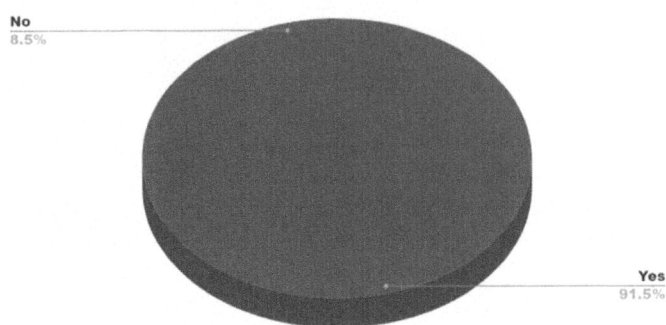

Fig. 18. Future Use of Lalitha

like gaming, augmented reality, medicine, and accessibility. Lalitha's flexibility, accuracy, and fast processing contribute to its usability and effectiveness, in today's IT world (Fig. 18).

The results of this study open the door to advancements, in gesture-controlled computing. There are areas for improvement, which include

- Expanding Gesture Vocabulary; Increasing the range of recognized gestures will provide users with a variety of commands making the interface more versatile and able to meet user needs.
- Integration with Advanced Technologies; Exploring the integration of technologies, such as machine learning algorithms can further enhance the accuracy and adaptability of the recognition system.
- Accessibility Features; Developing features that cater to individuals with abilities is crucial for ensuring inclusivity and usability across a range of users.
- Application in Specific Industries; Investigating how the gesture-controlled system can be applied in industries like healthcare or engineering can tailor the technology to meet their requirements.
- User Interface Customization; Allowing users to customize and personalize gestures to command mappings will provide a user-friendly experience.
- Wearable Integration; Exploring possibilities for reducing hardware size and integrating it into devices will enhance mobility and convenience for users.
- Global Collaboration; Considering opportunities for collaboration and gathering feedback, from users worldwide will help adapt the system to diverse preferences and user habits.

This study lays the groundwork, for progress in gesture- based computing providing a basis for innovation and enhancements, in the field of Human-Computer Interaction. In the future, we want to incorporate all these features to enhance the dimension and usability of Lalitha.

Acknowledgment. Partially supported by a grant from the Auburn University at Montgomery Research Grant-in-Aid Program.

References

1. Bhattacharya, T., et al.: Performance modeling for I/O-intensive applications on virtual machines. Concurr. Comput. Pract. Exp. **34**(10), e6823 (2022)
2. Kaswan, K.S., Singh, S.P., Sagar, S.: Role of arduino in real world applications. Int. J. Sci. Technol. Res. **9**(1), 1113–1116 (2020)
3. Wang, Y., et al.: A novel deep learning method for predictive modeling of microbiome data. Briefings Bioinformatics **22**(3), bbaa073 (2020)
4. Papert, S.: Mindstorms: Children, Computers, and Powerful Ideas, vol. 10, p. 1095592. Basic books, Inc. New York, NY (1980)
5. Omatu, S., Neves, J., Rodrıguez, J.M.C., Santana, J., Gonzalez, S.R.: Distributed computing and artificial intelligence. Springer, 2014
6. Bhattacharya, T., Chatterjee, A.: Evaluating performance of some common filtering techniques for removal of Gaussian noise in images. In: 2017 IEEE International Conference on Power, Control, Signals and Instrumentation Engineering (ICPCSI). IEEE, pp. 1981–1984, 2017
7. Song, S., Yan, D., Xie, Y.: Design of control system based on hand gesture recognition. In: 2018 IEEE 15th International Conference on Networking, Sensing and Control (ICNSC). IEEE, pp. 1–4, 2018
8. Grif, H.-S., Farcas, C.C.: Mouse cursor control system based on hand gesture. Procedia Technol. **22**, 657–661 (2016)
9. Freeman, W.T., Weissman, C.D.: Television control by hand gestures. In: Proceedings of the International Workshop on Automatic Face and Gesture Recognition, pp. 179–183, 1995
10. Kass, M., Witkin, A.: Analyzing oriented patterns. Comput. Vis. Graph. Image Process. **37**(3), 362–385 (1987)
11. Shimada, A., Yamashita, T., Taniguchi, R.-I.: Hand gesture based tv control system—towards both user-& machine-friendly gesture applications. In: The 19th Korea-Japan Joint Workshop on Frontiers of Computer Vision. IEEE, pp. 121–126, 2013
12. Segen, J.: Gest: a learning computer vision system that recognizes gestures. Machine Learning IV. Morgan Kau man, 1992
13. Alon, A.S., Susa, J.A.B.: Wireless hand gesture recognition for an automatic fan speed control system: rule-based approach. In: 2020 16th IEEE International Colloquium on Signal Processing & Its Applications (CSPA). IEEE, pp. 250–254, 2020
14. Fang, Y., Wang, K., Cheng, J., Lu, H.: A real-time hand gesture recognition method. In: 2007 IEEE International Conference on Multimedia and Expo. IEEE, pp. 995–998, 2007
15. Saez, B., Mendez, J., Molina, M., Castillo, E., Pegalajar, M., Morales, D.P.: Gesture recognition with ultrasounds and edge computing. IEEE Access **9**, 38 999–39 008 (2021)
16. Das, A., Tashev, I., Mohammed, S.: Ultrasound based gesture recognition. In: 2017 IEEE International Conference on Acoustics, Speech and Signal Processing (ICASSP). IEEE, pp. 406–410, 2017
17. Kalgaonkar, K., Raj, B.: One-handed gesture recognition using ultrasonic doppler sonar. In: 2009 IEEE International Conference on Acoustics, Speech and Signal Processing. IEEE, pp. 1889–1892, 2009
18. Chen, H., Ballal, T., Saad, M.,. Al-Naffouri, T Y: Angle-of-arrival- based gesture recognition using ultrasonic multi-frequency signals. In: 2017 25th European Signal Processing Conference (EUSIPCO). IEEE, pp. 16–20, 2017

19. Saad, M., Bleakley, C.J., Nigram, V., Kettle, P.: Ultrasonic hand gesture recognition for mobile devices. J. Multimodal User Interfaces **12**, 31–39 (2018)
20. Vimali, J., Srinivasulu, S., Jabez, J., Gowri, S.: Hand gesture recognition control for computers using Arduino. In: Data Intelligence and Cognitive Informatics: Proceedings of ICDICI 2020. Springer, pp. 569–578, 2021
21. Tawde, M., Singh, H., Shaikh, S.: Glove for gesture recognition using flex sensor. Publ. Int. J. Recent Trends Eng. Res. (IJRTER) **3**(03), 35–39 (2017)
22. Panda, A.K., Chakravarty, R., Moulik, S.: Hand gesture recognition using flex sensor and machine learning algorithms. In: 2020 IEEE-EMBS Conference on Biomedical Engineering and Sciences (IECBES). IEEE, pp. 449–453, 2021
23. Harish, N., Poonguzhali, S.: Design and development of hand gesture recognition system for speech impaired people. In: 2015 International Conference on Industrial Instrumentation and Control (ICIC). IEEE, pp. 1129–1133, 2015
24. Duan, F., Ren, X., Yang, Y.: A gesture recognition system based on time domain features and linear discriminant analysis. IEEE Trans. Cogn. Dev. Syst. **13**(1), 200–208 (2018)
25. Manikandan, K., Patidar, A., Walia, P., Roy, A.B.: Hand gesture detection and conversion to speech and text, arXiv preprint arXiv:1811.11997, 2018
26. Mantoro, T., Istiono, W.: Saving water with water level detection in a smart home bathtub using ultrasonic sensor and fuzzy logic. In: 2017 Second International Conference on Informatics and Computing (ICIC). IEEE, pp. 1–5, 2017
27. Francisco, A., Lopes, N.V., Bento, L.C., Ferreira, C.: Arduino based open source electronic control unit for electric utility vehicles. In: 2020 XXIX International Scientific Conference Electronics (ET). IEEE, pp. 1–4, 2020
28. Visconti, P., de Fazio, R., Costantini, P., Miccoli, S., Cafagna, D.: Innovative complete solution for health safety of children unintentionally forgotten in a car: a smart arduino-based system with user app for remote control. IET Sci. Meas. Technol. **14**(6), 665–675 (2020)
29. Kosarev, O.V., et al.: Modeling of industrial iot complex for underground space scanning on the base of arduino platform. In: Topical Issues of Rational Use of Natural Resources: Proceedings of the International Forum-Contest of Young Researchers. CRC, New York, pp. 407–412, 2018
30. Mukherjee, R.P.R., Swethen, P., Rawat, S.S.: Hand gesture controlled laptop using arduino,. Int. J. Manag. Technol. Eng. 1037–1043 (2018)
31. Alaidi, A., Aljazaery, I., Alrikabi, H., Mahmood, I., Abed, F.: Design and implementation of a smart traffic light management system controlled wirelessly by arduino, 2020
32. Zaldıvar-Colado, A., et al.: Management of traffic lights for emergency services. Tehnic̆ki vjesnik **24**(2), 643–648 (2017)
33. Garcıa-Tudela, P.A., Marın-Marın, J.-A.: Use of arduino in primary education: a systematic review. Educ. Sci. **13**(2), 134 (2023)
34. Spillman Jr, W., Sirkis, J., Gardiner, P.: Smart materials and structures: what are they. Smart Mater. Struct. **5**(3), 247 (1996)
35. Sanchez-Nielsen, E., Anton-Canalıs, L., Hernandez-Tejera, M.: Hand gesture recognition for human-machine interaction, 2004
36. Warren, J.-D., Adams, J., Molle, H., Warren, J.-D., Adams, J., Molle, H.: Arduino for robotics. Springer, 2011
37. Parashar, A.: Iot based automated weather report generation and prediction using machine learning. In: 2019 2nd International Conference on Intelligent Communication and Computational Techniques (ICCT). IEEE, pp. 339–344, 2019
38. Wang, P., Liu, H., Wang, L., Gao, R.X.: Deep learning-based human motion recognition for predictive context-aware human-robot collaboration. CIRP Ann. **67**(1), 17–20 (2018)
39. Zlatanov, N.: Arduino and open source computer hardware and software. J. Water, Sanit. Hyg. Dev. **10**(11), 1–8 (2016)

40. Chanda, P., Mukherjee, P.K., Modak, S., Nath, A.: Gesture controlled robot using arduino and android. Int. J. **6**(6) (2016)
41. Jiashan, L., Zhonghua, L.: Dynamic gesture recognition algorithm combining global gesture motion and local finger motion for interactive teaching. IEEE Access (2021)
42. Athavale, S., Deshmukh, M.: Dynamic hand gesture recognition for human computer interaction; a comparative study. Int. J. Eng. Res. Gen. Sci. **2**(2), 38–55 (2014)
43. Sulistyawan, V.N., Salim, N.A., Abas, F.G., Aulia, N.: Parking tracking system using ultrasonic sensor hc-sr04 and nodemcu esp8266 based iot. In: IOP Conference Series: Earth and Environmental Science, vol. 1203, no. 1, p. 012028. IOP Publishing, 2023
44. Jain, U., Kansal, V., Dewangan, R., Dhasmana, G., Kotiyal, A.: Performance comparison of hc-sr04 ultrasonic sensor and tf-luna lidar for obstacle detection. In: Computer Vision and Machine Intelligence: Proceedings of CVMI 2022. Springer, pp. 631–640, 2023
45. Morgan, E.J.: Hc-sr04 ultrasonic sensor, November 2014
46. Abdulkhaleq, N.I., Hasan, I.J., Salih, N.A.J.: Investigating the resolution ability of the hc-sro4 ultrasonic sensor. In: IOP Conference Series: Materials Science and Engineering, vol. 745, no. 1, p. 012043. IOP Publishing, 2020
47. Dimitrov, A., Minchev, D.: Ultrasonic sensor explorer. In: 2016 19th International Symposium on Electrical Apparatus and Technologies (SIELA). IEEE, pp. 1–5, 2016
48. Zhmud, V., Kondratiev, N., Kuznetsov, K., Trubin, V., Dimitrov, L.: Application of ultrasonic sensor for measuring distances in robotics. In: Journal of Physics: Conference Series, vol. 1015, no. 3, p. 032189. IOP Publishing, 2018
49. Hoomod, H.K., Al-Chalabi, S.M.M.: Objects detection and angles effectiveness by ultrasonic sensors hc-sr04. IJSR **6**, 6 (2017)
50. Sudarmanto, A., Khalif, M.A., Huda, A.K.: Detection of building slope and land subsidence using ultrasonic hc-sr04 sensors based arduino uno r3 and blynk. In: AIP Conference Proceedings, vol. 2540, no. 1. AIP Publishing, 2023
51. Yanmida, D.Z., Imam, A.S., Alim, S.A.: Obstacle detection and anti-collision robot using ultrasonic sensor. ELEKTRIKA-J. Electr. Eng. **22**(1), 11–14 (2023)
52. Andreychenko, A.E., Morozov, S.: Automated reporting of medical diagnostic imaging for early disease and aging biomarkers detection. In: Artificial Intelligence for Healthy Longevity. Springer, pp. 15–30, 2023
53. Jaiswal, P., Dhakite, M., Dhule, C., Mungale, N., Wazalwar, S., Deshmukh, A.R..: Smart ai based eye gesture control system. In: 2023 7th International Conference on Intelligent Computing and Control Systems (ICICCS). IEEE, pp. 1873–1876, 2023
54. Kim, E., Shin, J., Kwon, Y., Park, B.: Emg-based dynamic hand gesture recognition using edge ai for human–robot interaction. Electronics **12**(7), 1541 (2023)
55. Solly, E., Aldabbagh, A.: Gesture controlled mobile robot. In: 2023 5th International Congress on Human-Computer Interaction, Optimization and Robotic Applications (HORA). IEEE, pp. 1–6, 2023
56. Kavitha, B., Philip Delapierre, B., Venkata Vikas, P. Thohid, S.: Mid-air gesture for hand control system using leap motion robot. In: Information and Communication Technology for Competitive Strategies (ICTCS 2022) Intelligent Strategies for ICT. Springer, pp. 259–265, 2023
57. Weidner, F., et al.: A systematic review on the visualization of avatars and agents in ar & vr displayed using head mounted displays. IEEE Trans. Vis. Comput. Graph. (2023)
58. Leung, W.K., Chang, M.K., Cheung, M.L., Shi, S.: Vr tourism experiences and tourist behavior intention in covid-19: an experience economy and mood management perspective. Inf. Technol. People **36**(3), 1095–1125 (2023)
59. Colakovic, A., Hadzialic, M.: Internet of things (iot): a review of enabling technologies, challenges, and open research issues. Comput. Netw. **144**, 17–39 (2018)

Dishari: A Novel Gesture-Based Educational Application for Specially Challenged People

Tathagata Bhattacharya$^{(\boxtimes)}$ and Irshad Ali Mohammad

Auburn University, Montgomery, AL, USA
tbhatta1@aum.edu

Abstract. This research explores the integration of advanced technologies, particularly hand gesture detection, and Generative AI, to create an inclusive educational tool called "Dishari" tailored for individuals with hearing and speech impairments. Traditional search engines often fail to address the specific needs of this speech and visually-impaired demographics, leading to a gap in accessibility and inclusivity. Leveraging machine learning algorithms and computer vision technologies, Dishari interprets hand gestures captured via web cameras, translating them into sign language expressions and helping the users search for a particular keyword through the search engine. Furthermore, the incorporation of Generative AI enhances the search functionality, enabling users to input queries through both text and hand gestures. Through a comprehensive literature survey, we highlight the advancements in hand gesture recognition systems and the transformative potential of Generative AI in image and text-based search. Dishari marks a significant milestone in bridging the communication gap and fostering inclusivity by empowering individuals with hearing and speech impairments to navigate the digital landscape effectively.

Keywords: Hand Gesture Recognition · Generative AI · Inclusive Education · Machine Learning · Computer Vision · MediaPipe · Accessibility · Sign Language · Educational Technology

1 Introduction

The usage of computers and IT has evolved exponentially in recent years [1]. From Banking sectors to healthcare; and educational institutes to defense, computers have taken the entire control [2]. In education, computers have given access to unlimited global resources with IoT to the users thereby enhancing the knowledge of the kids thoroughly. Unfortunately, little has been done for people with special abilities.

One of the significant learning tools is to accomplish an effective search online. Over the years, the landscape of text-based search has undergone significant transformations. Early efforts in information retrieval, dating back to 1948 [3],

© The Author(s), under exclusive license to Springer Nature Switzerland AG 2025
L. Deligiannidis et al. (Eds.): CSCE 2024, CCIS 2262, pp. 164–185, 2025.
https://doi.org/10.1007/978-3-031-85933-5_12

laid the foundation for organizing and accessing data stored in databases. Traditional search engines utilized keyword matching techniques, often resulting in irrelevant search queries due to discrepancies in user-inputted keywords and web page content [4]. To address these limitations, researchers explored diverse approaches to improve search results. Multi-layer indexing, introduced to deep crawl methods, is aimed at enhancing the effectiveness of data retrieval [5]. Various methodologies such as metadata-based [6] and semantic search [7] were proposed, each with its set of advantages and constraints.

In the realm of educational image processing engines, the integration of machine learning gained prominence. Pre-trained models were employed to predict search results, offering a more refined and accurate outcome [4]. However, challenges persisted, especially in cases where irrelevant data was uploaded by users, contributing to the need for advanced techniques [4]. Drawing from this historical context, our paper builds on prior research efforts, incorporating advancements in machine learning and Generative AI. We delve into the synergy of hand gesture detection and search functionality, providing an inclusive solution for individuals with hearing and speech impairments. Our approach not only addresses the limitations of traditional search methods but also empowers users with a more intuitive and interactive means of navigating the vast landscape of information on the internet.

We categorize the motivations behind conducting this research in the following subsections (see Sect. 1.1, 1.2 and 1.3). Later in Sect. 1.4 we discuss the novelty of our education tool Dishari.

1.1 Hand Gesture Recognition

Hand gestures, a fundamental form of non-verbal communication, have a rich history deeply intertwined with human expression and cultural diversity [8]. From ancient civilizations to modern societies, gestures have conveyed emotions, commands, and meanings across linguistic barriers. With the advent of the internet, hand gestures have gained a new dimension, playing a pivotal role in human-computer interaction [9]. The integration of gesture-based interfaces, such as touchscreens and motion-sensing devices, has transformed the way we interact with technology. Moreover, the rise of social media platforms and video communication tools has facilitated the widespread use of hand gestures as a means of expression in the digital realm [10]. On the frontier of technological innovation, there is a growing interest in the development of systems capable of detecting and interpreting hand gestures, particularly in the context of sign language. This has profound implications for accessibility, enabling individuals with hearing and speech impairments to communicate effectively through virtual platforms. Advanced machine learning algorithms and computer vision technologies are being employed to create gesture recognition systems that can accurately interpret intricate movements and translate them into meaningful communication [11]. This intersection of hand gestures and the digital landscape not only enhances user experience but also fosters inclusively by breaking down communication barriers. As technology continues to evolve, the synergy between hand gestures and the internet is likely to play an increasingly significant role in shaping the way we communicate, bridging the gap between physical and virtual realms, and fostering a more inclusive and expressive digital environment.

Our web application leverages advanced hand gesture recognition technology by integrating MediaPipe's Gesture Recognizer with machine learning algorithms. MediaPipe's Gesture Recognizer utilizes pre-packaged model bundles to detect hand landmarks and recognize gestures accurately [12]. For training, we used the American Sign Language (ASL) Alphabet Dataset from Kaggle [13], ensuring the model is robust and accurate in interpreting a wide range of gestures. By utilizing this dataset, we have tailored the gesture recognition capabilities specifically for ASL, enhancing the system's effectiveness in real-time communication [14]. The combination of MediaPipe and the ASL dataset allows our application to provide precise and reliable gesture recognition, facilitating seamless interaction for users.

In practical application, our system operates seamlessly, detecting and interpreting hand movements captured by cameras. As users express themselves through sign language, our technology translates their gestures into corresponding sign language expressions, facilitating inclusive communication. By harnessing the synergy of MediaPipe's pre-packaged model bundles, our application "Dishari" not only addresses the communication needs of the deaf and hard-of-hearing community but also demonstrates the transformative potential of technology in fostering inclusivity and accessibility especially for the specially-abled people [15].

1.2 Search Powered by Generative AI

Image and text-based search input powered by Generative AI has revolutionized the way users interact with digital content [16]. Leveraging advanced algorithms, Generative AI enables the generation of relevant textual descriptions or visually similar images based on user queries [17]. This technology finds applications across diverse domains, enhancing user experiences and efficiency [18]. In e-commerce, users can now effortlessly find products by describing them in natural language or uploading images, leading to more accurate search results and increased customer satisfaction [19]. In the realm of content creation, Generative AI facilitates the exploration of creative ideas by suggesting relevant images or generating textual content based on user inputs whether it is an image, voice, or text [20]. Furthermore, in healthcare, this technology assists in medical image analysis, allowing for more precise diagnosis and treatment planning [21]. Overall, the integration of Generative AI in image and text-based search inputs streamlines information retrieval processes and fosters innovation across industries, making it an indispensable tool in the modern digital landscape.

In our smart application "Dishari", we have incorporated Generative AI to make our application stronger, wider, and more convenient for the users(especially for people with special abilities).

1.3   Applications of Image Processing and Analysis Through Generative AI

In this subsection, we will discuss various applications of using Image Processing and Analysis through Generative AI step by step.

1.3.1   Education Enhancement

Sign language detection with hand gestures using MediaPipe's Gesture Recognizer, integrated with Image and text-based search input powered by Generative AI, can significantly enhance educational experiences for individuals with hearing and speech impairments [22]. By translating sign language gestures into text or images, Generative AI enables interactive communication with digital devices, facilitating a more inclusive and effective learning environment [23].

1.3.2   Healthcare Communication

Generative AI has valuable applications in the healthcare sector [24], where effective communication is crucial. Sign language detection enables healthcare providers to understand and respond to patients with hearing and speech impairments. Integrating this information into Generative AI-powered search inputs ensures an accurate and efficient exchange of medical information, improving the overall quality of healthcare communication for patients and doctors [25].

Dishari is a novel hand gesture-based application that has worked with Generative AI to interpret sign language into text and help specially-abled people communicate with each other and the rest of the world through the internet.

1.4   Contributions of Dishari

Dishari is a dedicated and novel application, especially designed for specially-abled people to connect themselves with the world. The primary notion of Dishari is to open a broad spectrum of educational tools to physically challenged people and make them capable of grasping knowledge from the Internet. The main novelty of this research work lies in connecting the world of hand gesture detection with that of generative AI. This is the first application where a physically challenged user can simply use their hand gestures to search for a keyword on the application.

Dishari marks a significant milestone in bridging the gap between human gestures and machine interaction. We discuss the step-by-step processing of our novel gesture-based educational application "Dishari" for specially challenged people as follows.

- Using MediaPipe's Gesture Recognizer, Dishari, a novel gesture-based application, captures hand gesture inputs and processes them to identify hand movements with remarkable accuracy. MediaPipe's advanced technology allows for real-time detection of hand landmarks and gesture recognition, ensuring precise interpretation of user gestures.

- The application integrates a gesture recognition model trained on the American Sign Language (ASL) Alphabet Dataset from Kaggle. This model, fine-tuned specifically for ASL gestures, enables the application to accurately recognize and interpret sign language gestures, providing precise extraction of gesture labels corresponding to the detected hand movements.
- Taking user experience to the next level, the application seamlessly integrates with a search bar, enhanced by Generative AI capabilities. The main novelty of this research lies in this phase. No other researchers earlier have connected gesture detection with generative AI.
- Upon recognizing a sign language gesture, the application automatically populates the search bar with relevant keywords, providing intuitive interaction and accessibility for users.

This innovative fusion of computer vision, machine learning, and Generative AI opens doors to a world where technology empowers communication and accessibility for all.

Next, we discuss the pre-existing research on Hand gesture recognition systems and Generative AI. We also mention how our project has combined both worlds and created a novel application for people with special abilities in Sect. 2.

2   Literature Survey

Hand gesture recognition systems have witnessed significant advancements over the years, driven by the increasing demand for intuitive human-computer interaction interfaces [26]. This section provides an overview of the existing literature on hand gesture recognition systems, highlighting key methodologies, challenges, and applications. Also, we focus on how our novel application "Dishari" is unique from most of the pre-existing research.

2.1   Background of Hand Gesture Recognition Systems

The roots of hand gesture recognition can be traced back to the early developments in computer vision and pattern recognition. Notably, Vicon, a motion capture system introduced in the 1980s, laid the groundwork for capturing and analyzing human movements [26]. However, it wasn't until the late 20th century that research in gesture recognition gained momentum with the emergence of robust algorithms and computational resources [27].

Several methodologies and techniques have been explored in hand gesture recognition, ranging from traditional computer vision approaches to modern deep learning methods. Early systems relied on feature-based approaches, extracting handcrafted features such as shape, texture, and motion to classify gestures [28]. However, these methods often suffer from limited robustness and scalability.

With the advent of deep learning, particularly Convolutional Neural Networks (CNNs), the landscape of hand gesture recognition underwent a paradigm shift. CNN demonstrated superior performance in learning hierarchical features from raw data, enabling more accurate and robust gesture recognition

[27]. Transfer learning techniques have also been leveraged to adapt pre-trained models for gesture recognition tasks, mitigating the need for extensive labeled datasets [29].

Despite significant progress, hand gesture recognition systems still face several challenges. One notable challenge is the variability in gesture appearance and articulation across different users and environments [30]. This variability poses a significant hurdle in designing robust and generalizable recognition algorithms [31]. Additionally, real-time processing requirements impose constraints on computational efficiency and latency, necessitating lightweight models and optimized algorithms [32].

Hand gesture recognition has found diverse applications across various domains. In Human-Computer Interaction (HCI), gesture-based interfaces offer intuitive and immersive interaction experiences, particularly in virtual and augmented reality environments [33]. In robotics, gesture recognition enables natural communication between humans and robots, enhancing collaboration and task execution [34].

We discuss our next focus "Generative AI" in the next subsection(see Sect. 2.2. We discuss how our novel educational application Dishari perfectly blends into the domain of the Gesture recognition system and generative AI in Sect. 2.3.

2.2   Generative AI in Image and Text-Based Search

Generative Artificial Intelligence (GAI) has revolutionized image and text-based search, empowering users with advanced retrieval capabilities and enhancing user experiences [16]. Generative AI has its roots in the field of deep learning and generative modeling, with seminal works such as Generative Adversarial Networks (GANs) and Variational Autoencoders (VAEs) paving the way for realistic data generation [35]. These models enable the synthesis of novel images, texts, and even multimedia content, revolutionizing the landscape of content creation and search.

In image-based search, Generative AI facilitates content-based image retrieval by generating visually similar images based on user queries [36]. Techniques such as Conditional GANs allow for the generation of images conditioned on specific attributes or characteristics, enabling fine-grained search and customization [37]. Similarly, in text-based search, Generative AI models such as Language Models (e.g., GPT series) generate textual descriptions or summaries based on user input, improving search relevance and comprehension [38].

Despite its transformative potential, Generative AI in search is not without challenges. Ethical considerations, such as the potential for bias and misinformation in generated content, require careful attention [39]. Furthermore, ensuring the robustness and reliability of generative models against adversarial attacks and data biases remains an ongoing research endeavor [40]. Future directions in this field include the development of more interpretable and controllable generative models, as well as addressing scalability and efficiency concerns for real-world deployment [41].

We discuss how we incorporate generative AI in our application "Dishari" in Sect. 2.3.

2.3 Dishari and Its Implementation

In comparison to existing hand gesture recognition systems, Dishari offers several unique features and advantages tailored specifically for individuals with hearing and speech impairments. Firstly, Dishari incorporates advanced machine learning algorithms, including CNNs, trained on a diverse dataset of sign language gestures, ensuring robustness and accuracy in interpretation. This specialized training enables Dishari to recognize a wide range of sign language gestures with high precision, making it suitable for practical use in real-world scenarios.

Moreover, Dishari leverages Generative AI technology to enhance the search functionality, enabling users to input queries through both text and hand gestures. By combining hand gesture recognition with Generative AI-powered search, Dishari provides a seamless and intuitive interaction experience for users, enabling them to access information effortlessly.

Furthermore, Dishari is designed with inclusivity in mind, aiming to bridge the communication gap between individuals with hearing and speech impairments and the rest of the world. By providing a platform for interactive communication through sign language interpretation and text-based search, Dishari empowers users to express themselves effectively and access information independently.

In summary, hand gesture recognition has seen significant advancements in recent years, with a shift towards data-driven approaches and the integration of machine learning techniques. Dishari represents a novel approach that combines hand gesture recognition with Generative AI-powered search, offering unique advantages for individuals with hearing and speech impairments.

3 An Insight into Dishari

In this section, we are going to discuss the requirements for using Dishari; the underlying methodology, and the architectural framework for developing it.

3.1 Hardware Requirement

To use Dishari, we require the three fundamental components mentioned below.

- A computer with stable internet connection.
- A web browser (latest version of Google Chrome or Safari or Microsoft Edge or Firefox).
- A webcam (which captures the hand gestures).

Figure 1 depicts the basic prototype of Dishari. Dishari enables users to interact with their computer webcam through hand gestures. These gestures are then processed by a machine learning (ML) model(MediaPipe gesture recognition) embedded within the application. If a recognized gesture is detected, the underlying object detection API (an integration of deep learning algorithms like CNN) analyzes it and provides an output. This output typically includes hand landmarks with colored lines of detected hands along with their name and accuracy. Following this recognition process, the detected gesture information is fed as input for a Generative AI system. Users can initiate searches for desired keywords by pressing the enter button once they are ready. This integration of hand gesture recognition and Generative AI search functionality forms a pivotal aspect of the Dishari, contributing to its goal of providing an inclusive solution for individuals with hearing and speech impairments (refer Fig. 1).

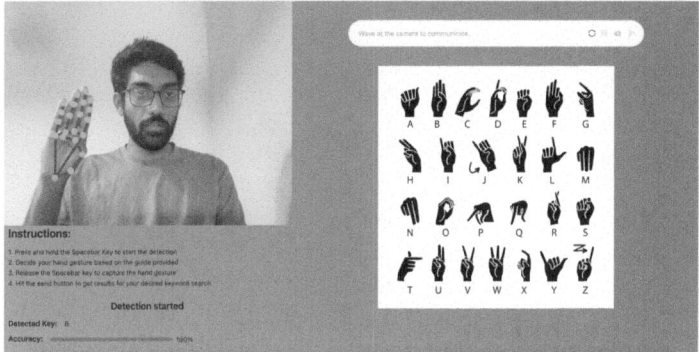

Fig. 1. Dishari prototype

Now we will discuss the underlying methodology implemented in the Dishari in Sect. 3.2.

3.2   Methodology

In this section, we describe the underlying methodology implemented in Dishari.

We describe the entire algorithm in this research to develop Dishari, a hand gesture-based educational application. We describe every step diagrammatically in Fig. 2.

- The first step is to train the MediaPipe's Gesture Recognition task with the chosen American Sign Language dataset and host it on IBM Cloud storage.
- Secondly, we connect the trained model with Dishari and start detecting and recognizing the hand gestures.
- Thirdly, the recognized hand gestures are fed as input to the search bar.
- Finally, we search the keyword generated by the hand gesture using Generative AI and generate the search results.

We describe each of the previously mentioned steps in detail in the following subsections. Initially, we start the next subsection by depicting system architecture(refer to Sect. 3.2.1).

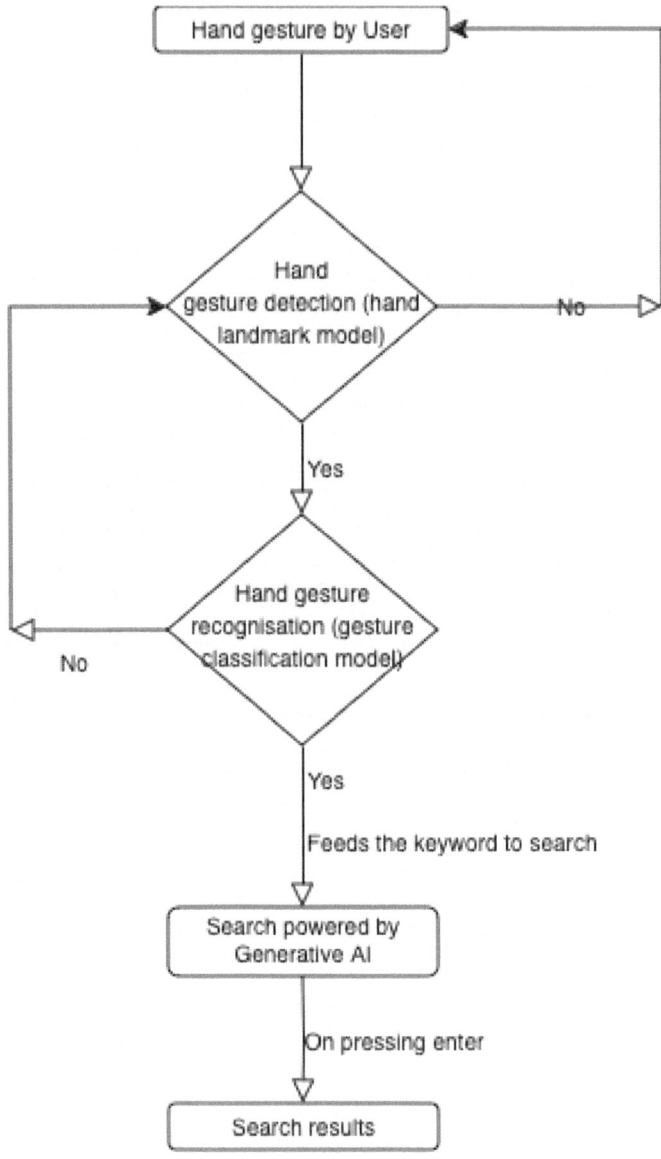

Fig. 2. Dishari flowchart

3.2.1   System Architecture

Dishari is a gesture-based web search application designed to facilitate hand gesture recognition for initiating keyword-based searches. The system architecture of Dishari involves several components working together seamlessly to achieve this functionality. At its core, Dishari utilizes Next.js which is a JavaScript framework for both the front-end user interface and the API for fetching search results.

Additionally, IBM Cloud is employed to store the trained dataset, providing scalability and reliability to the application. (refer Fig. 3)

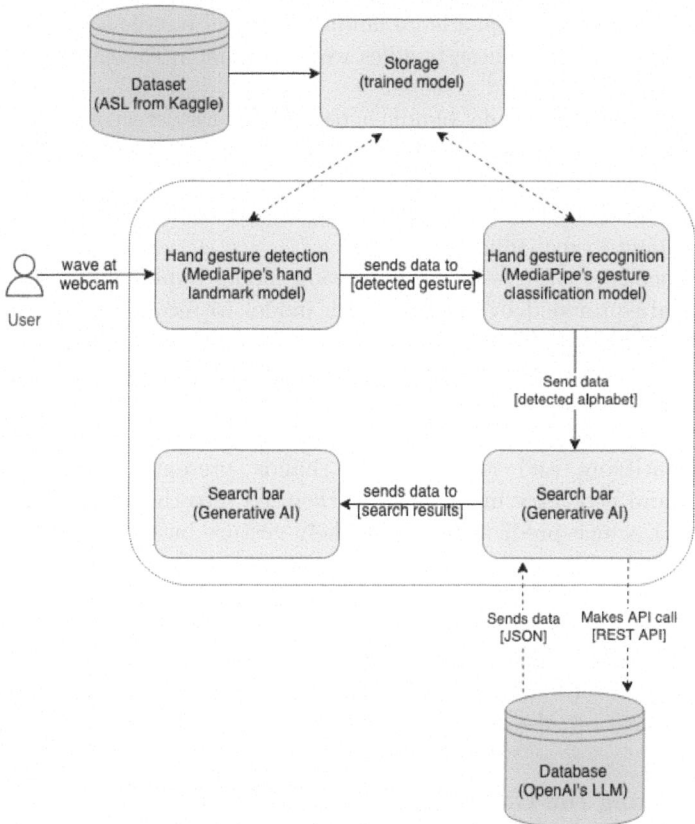

Fig. 3. Dishari system architecure

The front-end interface of Dishari presents users with a simple and intuitive design. Users initiate the gesture recognition process by pressing and holding the space bar key. Once activated, users are guided to perform specific hand gestures based on the provided instructions. Upon releasing the space bar key, Dishari captures the hand gesture and sends it to the back end for processing (refer Sect. 3.2.2).

On the back end, Dishari leverages MediaPipe, a popular open-source framework for building machine learning pipelines, particularly well-suited for tasks such as hand gesture recognition. MediaPipe incorporates Convolutional Neural Networks (CNNs) for efficient and accurate gesture recognition. These CNNs are trained on vast datasets to learn patterns and features essential for recognizing hand gestures accurately (refer Sect. 3.2.3).

3.2.2   Gesture Detection and Recognition Using MediaPipe

Initially, once we press the spacebar, the web camera automatically detects the gestures (ASL) and MediaPipe's Gesture Recognizer module serves as a cornerstone in Dishari's gesture recognition process. This module integrates two crucial pre-packaged model bundles: a hand landmark model bundle and a gesture classification model bundle. These bundles work in tandem to enable accurate and efficient recognition of hand gestures.

The hand landmark model bundle is responsible for detecting the presence of hands within the captured video frames and extracting essential geometric features. By analyzing the hand geometry, including landmarks such as fingertips, joints, and palm contours, this model accurately identifies the spatial configuration of the hand in real-time.

Simultaneously, the gesture classification model bundle leverages the hand geometry data provided by the landmark model to recognize specific gestures performed by the user. This model is trained on a diverse dataset encompassing various hand gestures, enabling it to classify incoming hand configurations with high accuracy.

During inference, the hand landmark model processes the incoming video frames, identifying and localizing the hands present in the frame. The extracted hand geometry information is then fed into the gesture classification model(CNN), which predicts the most likely gesture based on the learned patterns and features.

By utilizing these pre-trained model bundles, Dishari benefits from MediaPipe's robust and efficient gesture recognition capabilities. The integration of the hand landmark and gesture classification models enables Dishari to accurately interpret user hand gestures in real-time, facilitating seamless interaction with the application. We discuss how we train gesture recognition in Sect. 3.2.3.

3.2.3   Training the Gesture Recognition Model

Training the gesture recognition model within Dishari involves fine-tuning the pre-packaged gesture classification model bundle provided by MediaPipe. While the hand landmark model does not require training as it is pre-trained to detect hand geometry, the gesture classification model requires adaptation to specific gesture recognition tasks.

In parallel, the gesture classification model bundle operates on the extracted hand geometry data to recognize specific gestures performed by the user. This model is trained on a diverse dataset, including the American Sign Language dataset sourced from Kaggle. Through extensive training, the gesture classification model learns to associate distinctive hand gestures with corresponding semantic meanings, enabling accurate interpretation of user inputs.

The training dataset encompasses a wide range of hand gestures, providing ample variations and scenarios for training the model effectively. By iteratively optimizing model parameters and training configurations, Dishari ensures that the gesture classification model achieves high accuracy and robustness in recognizing user gestures.

Throughout the training phase, emphasis is placed on generalization and adaptability, enabling the model to perform reliably across diverse environmental conditions and user interactions. Data augmentation techniques may be employed to enhance the model's resilience to variations in lighting, background clutter, and hand orientation, further improving its real-world applicability.

By leveraging the hand landmark and gesture classification model bundles provided by MediaPipe and training them with the ASL dataset from Kaggle, Dishari achieves a sophisticated level of hand gesture recognition capability. This integration of advanced machine learning models with real-time computer vision techniques empowers Dishari to deliver a seamless and intuitive user experience for initiating keyword-based searches through hand gestures.

3.2.4 Connecting Hand Gesture Recognition with Search Powered by Generative AI

Dishari harnesses the power of Generative AI, particularly OpenAI's Generative Pre-trained Transformers (GPT), and Large Language Models (LLMs), for search result generation. Generative AI refers to a class of machine learning algorithms capable of generating new content, such as text or images, based on learned patterns and input prompts.

OpenAI's GPT models, including GPT-3, are among the most advanced LLMs available, pre-trained on vast amounts of text data to understand and generate human-like language. These models excel in tasks such as text completion, summarization, and question answering, making them ideal for generating search results based on user queries.

Within Dishari, the OpenAI completions API serves as the backbone for search result generation. When a user initiates a search query through a hand gesture, Dishari captures the query and sends it to the OpenAI API. The API then leverages the underlying GPT model to generate a list of search results tailored to the user's query.

The beauty of using Generative AI for search result generation lies in its ability to understand and contextualize natural language prompts, enabling it to produce relevant and coherent search results. By tapping into the vast knowledge encoded within the GPT model, Dishari provides users with insightful and informative search outcomes, enhancing their browsing experience.

Moreover, the integration of Generative AI opens up avenues for personalized and adaptive search experiences within Dishari. As users interact with the application and provide feedback on search results, the model can learn and adapt to user preferences over time, delivering increasingly tailored and relevant content.

In summary, by leveraging OpenAI's Generative AI capabilities, Dishari revolutionizes the search experience, offering users a seamless and intuitive way to explore and discover content. As Generative AI continues to evolve, the potential for enhancing search result generation within Dishari remains boundless, promising exciting prospects for the future of human-computer interaction.

We mention the pseudocode to implement Dishari. Please refer to the following pseudocode.

3.3   Pseudocode

This pseudocode outlines the main algorithm for the Dishari web application, including gesture recognition and search functionalities (refer Algorithm 1).

The Algorithm 1 (Dishari Gesture Recognition and Search) orchestrates the entire process of the Dishari web application, taking an input video stream as its parameter. It proceeds by first detecting the hand gesture present in the video using the MediaPipe's DetectGesture subroutine (refer Algorithm 2), then mapping this gesture to a corresponding keyword through MapGestureToKeyword. Subsequently, it utilizes the generated keyword to perform a search operation using the GenerativeSearch subroutine (refer Algorithm 3). Finally, the search results are displayed to the user via the application interface, providing them with relevant information based on the keyword which was formed from the recognized gesture.

Algorithm 1. Dishari Gesture Recognition and Search

1: **procedure** MAIN($input\_video$)
2:     $gesture \leftarrow$ DETECTGESTURE($input\_video$)
3:     $keyword \leftarrow$ MAPGESTURETOKEYWORD($gesture$)
4:     $search\_results \leftarrow$ GENERATIVESEARCH($keyword$)
5:     DISPLAYRESULTS($search\_results$)
6: **end procedure**

The Algorithm 2 (Detect Gesture) is responsible for identifying and classifying hand gestures present in the input video stream. It utilizes the MediaPipe library to extract hand landmarks from the video frames, which are then passed through a gesture classification model to determine the specific gesture being performed. The output of this subroutine is the recognized gesture, which is subsequently used for keyword mapping and search operations (refer Algorithm 2).

Algorithm 2. Detect Gesture

1: **procedure** DETECTGESTURE($input\_video$)
2:     $hand\_landmarks \leftarrow$ MEDIAPIPEHANDLANDMARKS($input\_video$)
3:     $gesture \leftarrow$ CLASSIFYGESTURE($hand\_landmarks$)
4:     **return** $gesture$
5: **end procedure**

The Algorithm 3 (Generative Search) handles the process of retrieving search results based on a given keyword. It interacts with the application's search engine API, passing the keyword as input and receiving relevant search results in return. These results are then returned by the subroutine to be displayed to the user, completing the search functionality of the Dishari web application (refer Algorithm 3).

Algorithm 3. Generative Search

1: **procedure** GENERATIVESEARCH(*keyword*)
2:     *search_results* ← SEARCHENGINEAPI(*keyword*)
3:     **return** *search_results*
4: **end procedure**

This pseudocode provides a comprehensive overview of Dishari's operation, detailing the steps involved in gesture recognition, search query generation, and search functionality. By breaking down the application's processes into functional components, this pseudocode serves as a blueprint for implementing Dishari's functionality in a programming language of choice.

4   Results and Observations

We define the user demographics and their feedback in terms of evaluating Dishari in this section.

4.1   User Demographic

Dishari yields promising results based on both technical performance metrics and user feedback obtained through a survey conducted among 160 participants aged between 20 to 30. Refer to the below charts for the Demographics and Age of the people involved in the survey. (refer Figs. 4, 5).

Figure 4 represents the percentage of the race of the users that are involved in the feedback survey. While Asians are the highest with 95.1%, African Americans are the least with 0.6% and there are 4.3% of Other races.

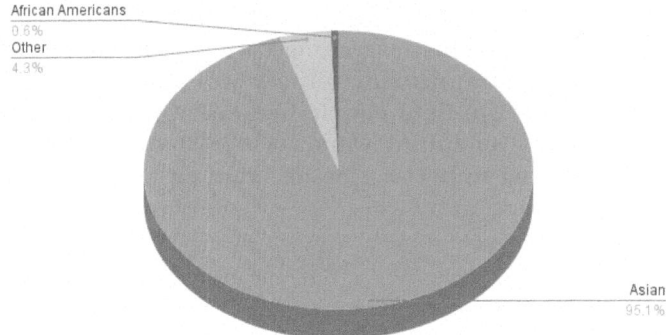

Fig. 4. Demographics

Figure 5 depicts the age of all the users that are involved in the feedback survey which is ranging majorly between 20 to 30.

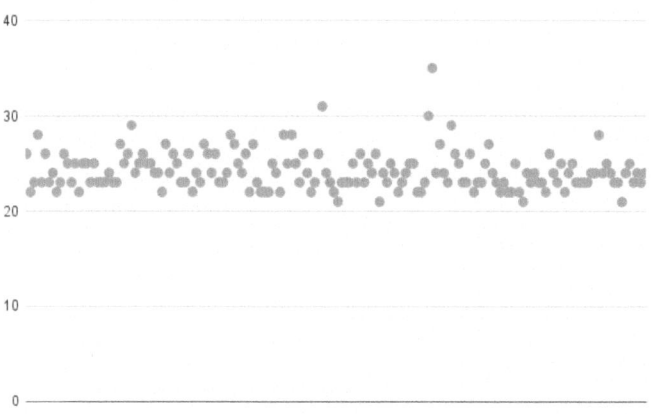

Fig. 5. Age

4.2   Technical Performance

The training of the gesture recognition model within Dishari yielded promising results, as evidenced by the training and validation metrics obtained during the training process. The model architecture, comprising a hand embedding layer, batch normalization, ReLU activation, dropout layer, and a custom gesture recognizer output layer, was trained over 10 epochs using a large dataset of hand gesture samples.

Throughout the training process, the model demonstrated steady improvement in both categorical accuracy and loss metrics. The **categorical accuracy steadily increased from approximately 82.85% during the first epoch to around 86.99% by the final epoch.** Conversely, the **loss metric gradually decreased from an initial value of 0.4893 to 0.3719, indicating that the model learned to better classify hand gestures over successive epochs** (refer Fig. 6).

```
Epoch 1/10
57278/57278 [==============================] - 403s 7ms/step - loss: 0.4893 - categorical_accuracy: 0.8285 - val_loss: 0.0402 - val_categorical_accuracy: 0.9395
Epoch 2/10
57278/57278 [==============================] - 406s 7ms/step - loss: 0.4018 - categorical_accuracy: 0.8597 - val_loss: 0.0658 - val_categorical_accuracy: 0.9380
Epoch 3/10
57278/57278 [==============================] - 391s 7ms/step - loss: 0.3929 - categorical_accuracy: 0.8621 - val_loss: 0.0598 - val_categorical_accuracy: 0.9354
Epoch 4/10
57278/57278 [==============================] - 399s 7ms/step - loss: 0.3851 - categorical_accuracy: 0.8659 - val_loss: 0.0660 - val_categorical_accuracy: 0.9345
Epoch 5/10
57278/57278 [==============================] - 403s 7ms/step - loss: 0.3827 - categorical_accuracy: 0.8657 - val_loss: 0.0652 - val_categorical_accuracy: 0.9365
Epoch 6/10
57278/57278 [==============================] - 412s 7ms/step - loss: 0.3793 - categorical_accuracy: 0.8672 - val_loss: 0.0946 - val_categorical_accuracy: 0.9328
Epoch 7/10
57278/57278 [==============================] - 412s 7ms/step - loss: 0.3784 - categorical_accuracy: 0.8678 - val_loss: 0.1072 - val_categorical_accuracy: 0.9237
Epoch 8/10
57278/57278 [==============================] - 396s 7ms/step - loss: 0.3757 - categorical_accuracy: 0.8691 - val_loss: 0.1110 - val_categorical_accuracy: 0.9279
Epoch 9/10
57278/57278 [==============================] - 401s 7ms/step - loss: 0.3736 - categorical_accuracy: 0.8685 - val_loss: 0.1229 - val_categorical_accuracy: 0.9221
Epoch 10/10
57278/57278 [==============================] - 399s 7ms/step - loss: 0.3719 - categorical_accuracy: 0.8699 - val_loss: 0.1010 - val_categorical_accuracy: 0.9235
```

Fig. 6. Epochs data during the training of the model

In the context of Dishari's model training results, the gradual decrease in loss metrics and increase in categorical accuracy over the 10 epochs suggest that the model is learning from the training data effectively. However, the slight disparity between the performance on the training and validation sets, particularly in the later epochs, could indicate a mild tendency towards overfitting.

Upon completion of training, the trained model was evaluated on a separate test dataset to assess its generalization performance. The test results revealed a **test loss of 0.0973 and a test accuracy of approximately 92.91%** (refer Fig. 7), indicating that the model performs well on unseen data, thereby validating its effectiveness in real-world scenarios.

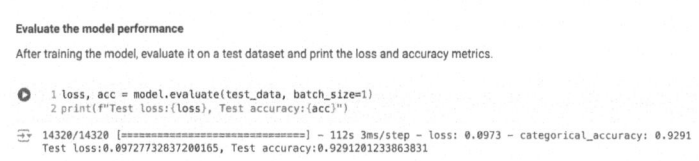

Fig. 7. Model's Loss and Accuracy metrics after evaluating with test data

4.3   User Feedback

The survey results indicated high levels of satisfaction among users regarding various aspects of Dishari's usability and user interface:

- **Convenience of Using Hand Gestures:** Participants rated the convenience of using hand gestures in Dishari very positively, with an average score of 4.53 out of 5 (refer Fig. 8). This suggests that users found hand gestures to be a convenient and intuitive input method for initiating searches.

  Figure 8 depicts the ratings convenience of using hand gestures in Dishari from those involved in the user feedback survey. On the x-axis, numbers are listed as per the rating scale, i.e., 1 to 5. The y-axis shows the total number of users who rated that particular number.

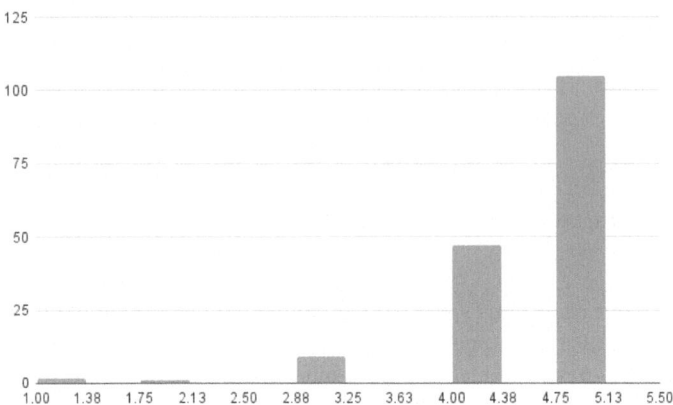

Fig. 8. Convenience of using hand gestures rating

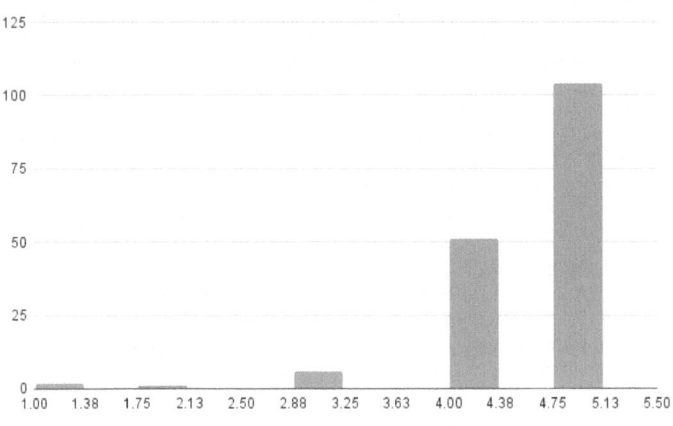

Fig. 9. Ease of use rating

- **Ease of Use:** Dishari received high ratings for ease of use, with an average score of 4.54 out of 5 (refer Fig. 9). This indicates that users found the application easy to navigate and interact with, contributing to a positive user experience.

  Figure 9 depicts the ratings of the ease of use of Dishari from those involved in the user feedback survey. On the x-axis, numbers are listed as per the rating scale, i.e., 1 to 5. The y-axis shows the total number of users who rated that particular number.

- **User Interface (UI) Ratings:** Participants rated various aspects of Dishari's UI highly, with average scores ranging from 4.58 to 4.67 out of 5 (refer Fig. 10). Specifically, the webcam interface, instructions for using

Dishari, search bar, search results display, and hand gesture guide all received favorable ratings. These scores reflect the effectiveness of Dishari's UI design in guiding users through the gesture recognition process and facilitating smooth interactions.

Fig. 10 depicts the average of all the ratings of different User Interface (UI) sections of Dishari from those involved in the user feedback survey. The sections listed on the x-axis are UI-Webcam, UI-Instructions to use Dishari, UI-Search bar, and UI-Hand gestures. The y-axis shows the scale of the rating (1 to 5).

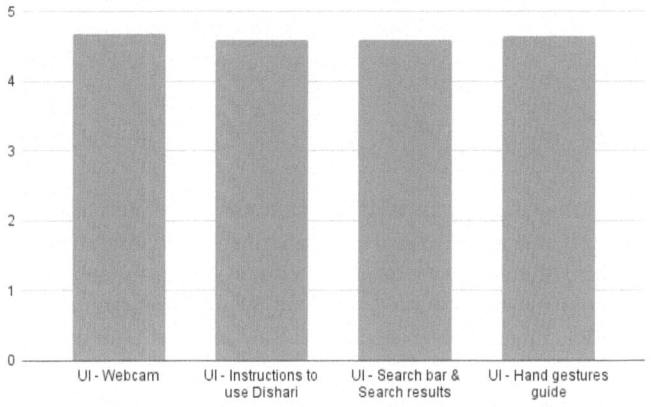

Fig. 10. UI ratings

- **User Experience (UX) Ratings:** Users also provided positive feedback on the interaction aspects of Dishari, with average scores ranging from 4.52 to 4.65 out of 5 (refer Fig. 11). This includes ratings for hand gesture detection, recognition, search bar interaction, and the hand gesture guide. The high scores indicate that users found the interaction with Dishari to be intuitive and responsive, enhancing their overall satisfaction with the application.

Fig. 11 depicts the average of all the ratings of different User Experience (UX) sections of Dishari from those involved in the user feedback survey. The sections listed on the x-axis are UX-Hand gesture detection, UX-Hand gesture recognition, UX-Search bar & Search results, and UX-Hand gestures guide. The y-axis shows the scale of the rating (1 to 5).

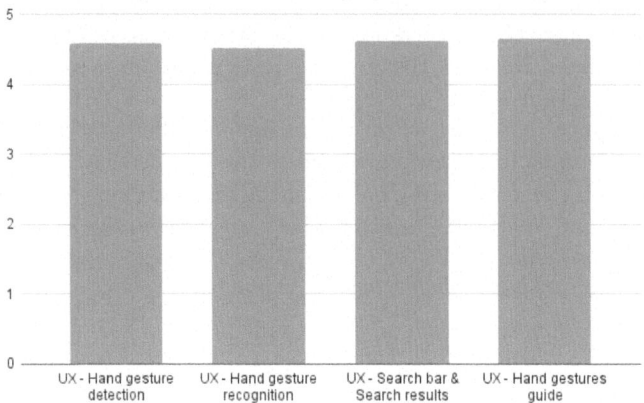

Fig. 11. UX ratings

The results and observations indicate that Dishari effectively bridges the gap between gesture-based interaction and keyword-based search, offering users a convenient and intuitive way to interact with web applications. The high satisfaction levels among users, coupled with the robust performance of the gesture recognition model, underscore the potential of Dishari to enhance user experience and accessibility in digital environments. Moving forward, further refinement and optimization of the application based on user feedback will contribute to its continued success and adoption.

5   Conclusion and Future Scope

In conclusion, Dishari represents a significant advancement in the field of human-computer interaction, leveraging state-of-the-art technologies to enable intuitive gesture-based interactions for initiating keyword-based searches. The integration of MediaPipe's Gesture Recognizer module, coupled with generative AI-powered search, provides users with a novel and efficient means of interacting with web applications.

Through the implementation of Dishari, we have demonstrated the feasibility and effectiveness of using hand gestures as input for initiating search queries, thereby enhancing accessibility and usability for specially-abled people. The robustness and accuracy of the gesture recognition system, coupled with the personalized search results generated by generative AI, contribute to an enhanced user experience.

Looking ahead, there are several avenues for further research and development to enhance the capabilities and functionalities of Dishari. One potential direction is the expansion of gesture vocabulary to encompass a broader range of gestures, including those specific to different sign languages or cultural contexts.

Furthermore, exploring the integration of additional modalities such as facial expressions or body movements could enrich the gesture recognition system, enabling more nuanced and contextually aware interactions. Additionally, ongoing advancements in machine learning and computer vision algorithms may lead to further improvements in gesture recognition accuracy and real-time performance.

Overall, Dishari lays the foundation for future research and innovation in the domain of gesture-based interaction systems, with the potential to revolutionize how users interact with web applications and digital interfaces in the years to come.

References

1. Bhattacharya, T., Qin, X.: Modeling energy efficiency of future green data centers. In: 2020 11th International Green and Sustainable Computing Workshops (IGSC), pp. 1–3. IEEE (2020)
2. Bhattacharya, T., et al.: Capping carbon emission from green data centers. Int. J. Energy Environ. Eng. **14**(4), 627–641 (2023)
3. Mooers, C.N.: Application of random codes to the gathering of statistical information. Ph.D. dissertation, Massachusetts Institute of Technology (1948)
4. El Guemmat, K., Ouahabi, S.: A literature review of indexing and searching techniques implementation in educational search engines. Int. J. Inf. Commun. Technol. Educ. (IJICTE) **14**(2), 72–83 (2018)
5. Guemmat, K.E., Talea, M., et al.: Implementation and evaluation of an indexing model of teaching and learning resources. Procedia. Soc. Behav. Sci. **191**, 1266–1274 (2015)
6. Biletskiy, Y., Baghi, H., Steele, J., Vovk, R.: A rule-based system for hybrid search and delivery of learning objects to learners. Interact. Technol. Smart Educ. **9**(4), 263–279 (2012)
7. Ahmed-Ouamer, R., Hammache, A.: Ontology-based information retrieval for e-learning of computer science. In: 2010 International Conference on Machine and Web Intelligence, pp. 250–257. IEEE (2010)
8. Galvano, F.: Beyond borders: an in-depth analysis of cultural variances in non-verbal communication through gestures and hands (1969)
9. Gota, D.-I., Puscasiu, A., Fanca, A., Valean, H., Miclea, L.: Human-computer interaction using hand gestures. In: 2020 IEEE International Conference on Automation, Quality and Testing, Robotics (AQTR), pp. 1–5. IEEE (2020)
10. Guarino, A., Malandrino, D., Zaccagnino, R., Capo, C., Lettieri, N.: Touchscreen gestures as images. a transfer learning approach for soft biometric traits recognition. Expert Syst. Appl. **219**, 119614 (2023)
11. Núñez-Marcos, A., Perez-de Viñaspre, O., Labaka, G.: A survey on sign language machine translation. Expert Syst. Appl. **213**, 118993 (2023)
12. Obi, Y., Claudio, K.S., Budiman, V.M., Achmad, S., Kurniawan, A.: Sign language recognition system for communicating to people with disabilities. Procedia Comput. Sci. **216**, 13–20 (2023)
13. Sau, D.: ASL(American Sign Language) Alphabet Dataset (2021). Accessed 13 Oct 2021. https://www.kaggle.com/datasets/debashishsau/aslamerican-sign-language-aplhabet-dataset

14. Chatterjee, K., et al.: Hack: Hand gesture classification using a convolutional neural network and generative adversarial network-based data generation model. Information **15**(2), 85 (2024)
15. Rane, N.: Chatgpt and similar generative artificial intelligence (ai) for smart industry: role, challenges and opportunities for industry 4.0, industry 5.0 and society 5.0. Chall. Opport. Ind. **4** (2023)
16. Cao, Y., et al.: A comprehensive survey of ai-generated content (aigc): a history of generative ai from gan to chatgpt. arXiv preprint arXiv:2303.04226 (2023)
17. Oppenlaender, J.: A taxonomy of prompt modifiers for text-to-image generation. Behav. Inf. Technol., 1–14 (2023)
18. Ooi, K.-B., et al.: The potential of generative artificial intelligence across disciplines: Perspectives and future directions. J. Comput. Inf. Syst., 1–32 (2023)
19. Kshetri, N.: Generative artificial intelligence and e-commerce. Computer **57**(2), 125–128 (2024)
20. Liu, G., et al.: Semantic communications for artificial intelligence generated content (aigc) toward effective content creation. IEEE Netw. (2024)
21. Zhang, P., Boulos, M.: Generative ai in medicine and healthcare: promises, opportunities and challenges. Future Internet **15**(9), 286 (2023)
22. Ayoola, O.O., Alenoghena, R., Adeniji, S.: Chatgpt impacts on access-efficiency, employment, education and ethics: the socio-economics of an AI language model. BizEcons Q. **16**, 1–17 (2023)
23. Natarajan, B., et al.: Development of an end-to-end deep learning framework for sign language recognition, translation, and video generation. IEEE Access **10**, 104358–104374 (2022)
24. Kuzlu, M., Xiao, Z., Sarp, S., Catak, F.O., Gurler, N.., Guler, O.: The rise of generative artificial intelligence in healthcare. In: 2023 12th Mediterranean Conference on Embedded Computing (MECO), pp. 1–4. IEEE (2023)
25. Iqbal, J., et al.: Reimagining healthcare: unleashing the power of artificial intelligence in medicine. Cureus **15**(9), 1–14 (2023)
26. Harvey, E., Sandhaus, H., Jacobs, A.Z., Moss, E., Sloane, M.: The cadaver in the machine: The social practices of measurement and validation in motion capture technology. arXiv preprint arXiv:2401.10877 (2024)
27. Eid, A., Schwenker, F.: Visual static hand gesture recognition using convolutional neural network. Algorithms **16**(8), 361 (2023)
28. Bakheet, S., Al-Hamadi, A.: Robust hand gesture recognition using multiple shape-oriented visual cues. EURASIP J. Image Video Process. **2021**(1), 1–18 (2021). https://doi.org/10.1186/s13640-021-00567-1
29. Rong, Y., Gu, G.: Deep transfer learning-based adaptive gesture recognition of a soft e-skin patch with reduced training data and time. Sens. Actuators, A **363**, 114693 (2023)
30. Escalera, S., Athitsos, V., Guyon, I.: Challenges in multi-modal gesture recognition. In: Gesture Recognition, pp. 1–60 (2017)
31. Oudah, M., Al-Naji, A., Chahl, J.: Hand gesture recognition based on computer vision: a review of techniques. J. Imaging **6**(8), 73 (2020)
32. Shuvo, M., Islam, S.K., Cheng, J., Morshed, B.I.: Efficient acceleration of deep learning inference on resource-constrained edge devices: a review. Proc. IEEE **111**, 42–91 (2022)
33. Vatavu, R.-D.: Gesture-based interaction. In: Handbook of Human Computer Interaction, pp. 1–47. Springer, Heidelberg (2023)
34. Fiorini, L., et al.: Daily gesture recognition during human-robot interaction combining vision and wearable systems. IEEE Sensors J. **21**(20), 23568–23577 (2021)

35. Wenzel, M.: Generative adversarial networks and other generative models. In: Machine Learning for Brain Disorders, pp. 139–192 (2023)

36. Sabry, E.S., et al.: Matching evaluation based on image content discriminative features for different image types. Imaging Sci. J. **72**(1), 23–51 (2024)

37. Koh, J.Y., Baldridge, J., Lee, H., Yang, Y.: Text-to-image generation grounded by fine-grained user attention. In: Proceedings of the IEEE/CVF Winter Conference on Applications of Computer Vision, pp. 237–246 (2021)

38. Li, J., Tang, T., Zhao, W.X., Nie, J.-Y., Wen, J.-R.: Pretrained language models for text generation: a survey. arXiv preprint arXiv:2201.05273 (2022)

39. Wach, K., et al.: The dark side of generative artificial intelligence: a critical analysis of controversies and risks of chatgpt. Entrepreneurial Bus. Econ. Rev. **11**(2), 7–30 (2023)

40. Zhang, Y., et al.: Why does little robustness help? a further step towards understanding adversarial transferability. In: Proceedings of the 45th IEEE Symposium on Security and Privacy (S&P'24), vol. 2 (2024)

41. Lim, W., Chek, K., Theng, L.B., Lin, C.: Future of generative adversarial networks (gan) for anomaly detection in network security: a review. Comput. Secur. **139**, 103733 (2024)

Image Processing, Computer Vision, and Pattern Recognition (IPCV) - Detection Methods

Mobility Anomaly Detection with Intelligent Video Surveillance

Fatemeh Ebrahimi[1]($\boxtimes$) (iD), Jacqueline Rousseau[2] (iD), and Jean Meunier[1] (iD)

[1] Department of Computer Science and Operations Research, University of Montreal, Montreal, Canada
fatemeh.ebrahimi@umontreal.ca, meunier@iro.umontreal.ca
[2] School of Rehabilitation, University of Montreal, Montreal, Canada
jacqueline.rousseau@umontreal.ca

Abstract. This paper outlines a study aimed at enhancing elderly care through an intelligent video surveillance system that leverages deep learning for detecting mobility anomalies, specifically near-falls. Identifying near-falls is essential because people who experience frequent near-falls while carrying out their daily activities are at risk of future falls. We successfully developed an autoencoder to detect these anomalies, particularly near-falls, by identifying high reconstruction errors throughout five consecutive frames. To extract a person's skeleton, we utilized MoveNet and narrowed it down to only seven keypoints. We then used a set of 20 features, encompassing joint positions, velocities, accelerations, angles, and angular accelerations, to train the model. Our model was tested on 100 videos of simulated daily activities recorded in an apartment laboratory, where 50 of them contained a near-fall. Results show that our model can successfully detect near-falls with 90% sensitivity, specificity, and accuracy, highlighting its potential to enhance elderly care in their living environments.

Keywords: Video Surveillance · Near-fall · Anomaly Detection · MoveNet · Autoencoder · Skeleton Extraction · Pose Estimation · Human Activity Recognition

1 Introduction

Seniors (aged 65 and over) will constitute 30% of the global population by 2050 [1]. This substantial demographic shift carries significant implications regarding the health, security, and overall quality of life of this population. Notably, accidental falls pose a significant threat to older adults, contributing to 88.6% of injury-related hospitalizations among seniors [2]. Addressing these challenges require the development and implementation of innovative technologies aimed at detecting, preventing, and mitigating the impacts of such incidents.

In this vein, we propose the implementation of intelligent video surveillance (IVS) systems within the homes of older adults (or any other individuals at risk of falling), specifically designed for mobility and fall risk assessment based on near-fall and anomaly detection. Near-falls are incidents where an individual temporarily loses balance, like

L. Deligiannidis et al. (Eds.): CSCE 2024, CCIS 2262, pp. 189–202, 2025.
https://doi.org/10.1007/978-3-031-85933-5_13

slipping or tripping, which could potentially lead to a fall if not corrected through appropriate actions. When near-fall happens, the individual takes two or more actions to prevent the fall. These include unexpected movements in the arms or legs, sudden changes in the speed or length of steps, lowering of the body's center of mass, or a trunk tilt [3]. The rationale for near-fall detection is that individuals who have undergone falls commonly experience frequent near-falls during their routine activities emphasizing the importance of incorporating them into fall risk assessment. Consequently, detecting near-falls during daily activities could help to identify individuals at risk of falling and proactively prevent such incidents [4].

Various technologies can be used for near-fall detection. For instance, wearable sensors (e.g., smart watches), are practical but may be troublesome for seniors, who might also forget to wear them or may be unable to activate them when needed. Moreover, these devices usually lack detailed data, such as body pose, provided by camera-based systems. In addition, video data, captured seconds before and after an event, also provide an understanding of the reasons behind an abnormal event. This, among others, explains why we chose video surveillance for this study. The proposed video surveillance system is based on anomaly detection to identify mobility problems, such as (but not restricted to) near-falls, for assessing fall risk and enabling appropriate interventions before an actual fall occurs. Anomaly detection was preferred to other approaches because abnormal mobility is difficult to characterize explicitly due to its high variability. Notice that in practice, it will uphold privacy by not retaining any records, instead, it would solely dispatch an alert signal (e.g., email or SMS with an image of the detected anomaly or near-fall) to an external authorized resource (e.g., family, or formal caregiver) for documentation purposes.

In the next sections we present a brief review of the literature on anomaly detection with cameras, followed by a description of our methodology using a special kind of deep neural networks: autoencoders. A dataset of simulated normal and abnormal activities in a realistic apartment-laboratory is described and tested with our algorithms in the results section followed by a discussion and conclusion.

2 Literature Review

Human activity recognition (HAR) aims at identifying and labeling activities using artificial intelligence from raw data. It is a crucial component for applications in various domains such as healthcare, surveillance, remote care for the elderly living alone, smart home, and monitoring applications like sports. The extensive utilization of HAR technology has positive impacts on enhancing human safety and improving the quality of life [5]. HAR is supported by different forms of data, especially structured data such as images or video, which are visually or semantically informative. Due to the widespread use of sensors such as cameras and cloud databases, structured data can be easily gathered and shared [6]. HAR and anomalous human activity recognition, in particular, are typically based on appearance, body skeleton, and motion [7, 8].

One of the primary things that video analysts look for is appearance. When there are anomalies in a video, they can be caused by unknown objects that can be identified using appearance-based features. However, anomalies are not always solely defined by appearance. In many cases, it is the motion that defines the anomaly. Motion patterns can be conveyed to a network through motion-based features like optical flow [9] or can be identified by sequence-aware networks such as the RNN family [10]. Skeleton and joint trajectories in human bodies can withstand lighting changes and environmental variations. They can be obtained easily due to the accurate depth sensors or pose estimation algorithms. Consequently, a wide variety of methods are available for recognizing human actions based on body skeleton [7].

One application of anomalous HAR related to our work is fall detection. Such systems can now achieve accuracy as high as 100% in a controlled environment [11]. However, detecting falls does not prevent its serious consequences (e.g., hospitalization), and unfortunately, little attention has been directed towards in-home mobility video monitoring to prevent falls. One group at the University of Missouri used a Kinect depth camera to measure in-home gait speed and stride length to predict possible falls [12, 13]. However, depth cameras are not as flexible (e.g., limited field of view and depth of field) as regular cameras in a real home setting. Moreover, the diversity of abnormal mobility events (i.e. near-falls, abnormal walk, etc.) makes it difficult to characterize all of them explicitly for a conventional computer vision algorithm. Recently, promising experiments with a simple color camera were conducted by Tran et al. [8, 14] for near-fall detection based on features extracted from a skeleton model using one-class classifiers. However, these works were preliminary since they (1) used basic classifiers, (2) were limited to a very simple 3-node skeleton model of the body pose, (3) used only a simple feature (velocity) and (4) were tested on a controlled dataset to reduce perspective distortion (limited range of subject-to-camera distances).

Despite all this progress, additional improvements are thus still needed to further develop IVS to detect 24/7 early signs of mobility decline in older adults, such as near-fall events. In this paper, we present a low-cost video surveillance system using standard cameras that can be used at home to assess the fall risk of older adults. Our work extends previous work [8, 14] with a deep learning approach (autoencoder), a more sophisticated skeleton model, additional features for a more complete representation and is tested on a more challenging dataset.

3 Methodology

We initiate this section by briefly overviewing our utilized dataset. Subsequently, we discuss our methodology to extract the individual's skeleton. Finally, we describe how we utilized the resulting skeleton to generate features to train a near-fall detection model and the specific model we used.

3.1 Dataset

The creation of a new dataset was necessary to develop and test our algorithms with challenging and realistic videos. There are other datasets for fall detection and activity recognition elsewhere, but they are generally too basic and not realistic enough and, above all, not intended for abnormal mobility event detection such as near-falls of seniors at home.

Our dataset was constructed in a realistic experimental apartment with an RGB camera (Intel RealSense Depth Camera D455) under various environmental conditions (e.g., lighting variations, occlusions, nonstationary background). The dataset comprises several videos of an individual (student enrolled in occupational therapy program under the supervision of experts in gerontology) trained to act as a senior to simulate various daily activities (walking, dusting, tying shoelaces, turning on the television with the remote control, opening a door, picking up a book and reading, etc.) in the living room of our apartment laboratory. Some of these videos feature a realistic (simulated) near-fall incident, where the person stumbles while carrying out daily routines, such as tripping over a mat, colliding with a table leg, or losing balance in different parts of the apartment.

Notice that in practice, the training (learning) stage would be performed using the abundance of videos of normal events during a training "observational" phase of the daily living activities of the senior at home for a few weeks (depending on the senior's environment and habits). Each camera will have its own deep learning model specialized for analyzing the specific scene visible by this camera. This will ensure the personalization of the system for each person and each environment, which should result in higher accuracy compared to methods using various scenes and persons for training. Here, in this preliminary study, we only consider one scene and one individual.

We selected 150 videos (with frame size of 1280×720 pixels) from the dataset, each lasting about 15 to 30 s (30 frames per second (fps)), with 50 containing near-fall actions. We employed 50 normal videos to train our model and 100 videos (50 normal and 50 abnormal) to test its performance. To obtain a more versatile system capable of coping with basic and simple two-dimensional RGB data, there was no depth information provided, however we expect that our model will learn to extract some depth cues during training (e.g., a smaller skeleton or a skeleton higher (vertically) in the scene could be farther away).

This dataset will be made available to the scientific community upon request to objectively compare different algorithms.

3.2 Skeleton Extraction

For the task of human skeleton extraction, we used MoveNet Thunder model [15] (see Fig. 1). MoveNet is an ultra-fast and accurate model that detects 17 joints of an individual person. The model is a convolutional neural network that uses RGB images to predict joint locations of a person's body. It is designed specifically for real-time use and is well-suited for movement activities.

The model comes in two versions - Lightning and Thunder- with Lightning being ideal for low latency applications, and Thunder offering better prediction quality while maintaining real-time speed on most modern systems [15, 16].

3.3 Post-processing Skeleton

To minimize the effect of noise and remove some unreliable joints we did the following post-processing of the skeleton without losing significant information for mobility assessment and without impairing anomaly detection. First, we removed the following

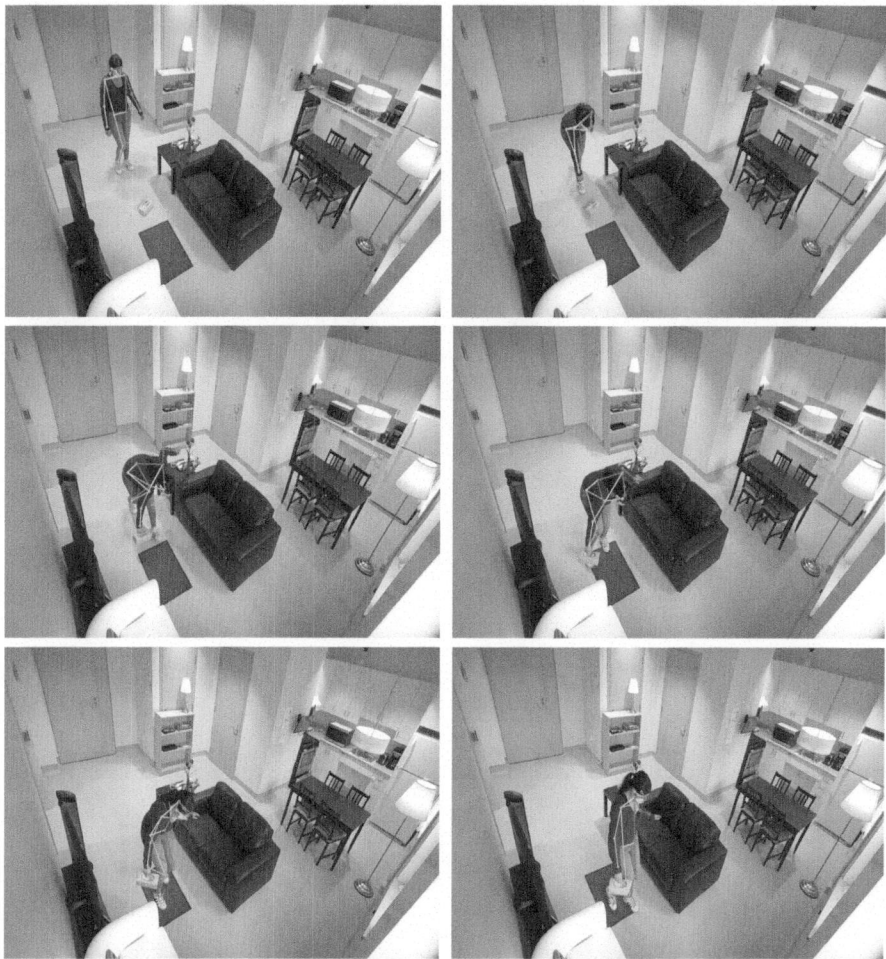

Fig. 1. Extracted skeleton using Movenet Thunder on a few frames of a simulated near-fall. Frames are ordered from left-to-right then top-to-bottom.

joints that were found to be unnecessary for our task, or not reliable enough or not always visible: wrists, ankles, ears, eyes.

Second, frames where MoveNet predicted 4 or more joints with too low confidence score (<0.45) were removed (about 17% of the frames). To further simplify the skeleton and reduce noise, we merged the left and right shoulder joints to obtain a single joint representing the average point of the two. We followed the same procedure for the hip joints, and as a result, we ended up with a total of seven joints: Nose (head), Shoulder, Left elbow, Right elbow, Hip, Left knee, Right knee (see Fig. 2). To further reduce noise more and remove outliers, we computed the median of the positions of each joint within a moving window of 7 frames.

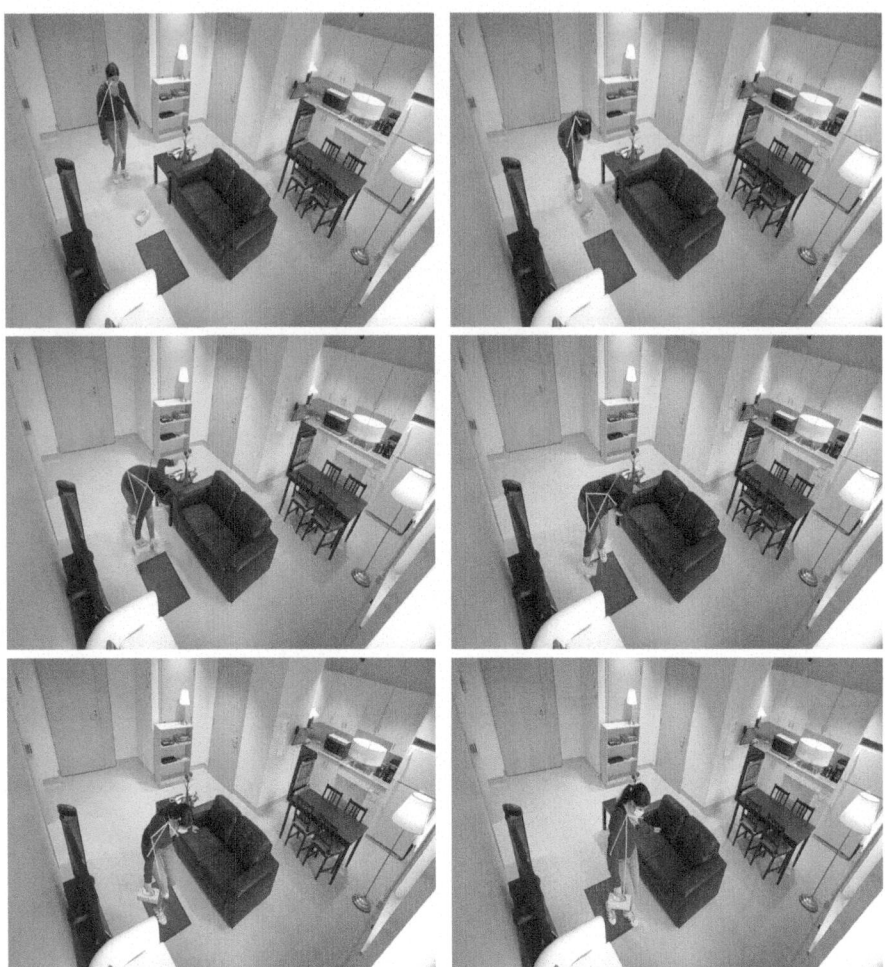

Fig. 2. Result of post-processing skeleton on a few frames of a near-fall (same frames as Fig. 1). Frames are ordered from left-to-right then top-to-bottom.

3.4 Feature Selection

When someone experiences a near-fall, such as tripping or losing balance, their body rapidly adjusts to maintain balance through sudden changes in posture, speed, and hand and leg movements. To account for this, we decided to test specific features such as joint position, velocity, acceleration, angles, angular velocity, and acceleration of the hands and legs. We selected these features as they represented the most logical choices based on the situation and are basic variables of motion in Physics. After testing several subsets of these features, the optimal combination of 20 features (see Table 1) was identified for achieving the best performance which will be individually explored and detailed.

To assess someone's body posture, we need to identify if they are sitting, standing, lying down, bending, or in any other posture. Therefore, our focus is mainly on the relative

Table 1. Summary of the final features used

Feature Type	Shifted Coordinates (x, y)	Actual Coordinates (x, y)	Velocity	Limbs' Angles with Respect to Trunk	Max Absolute Angular Acceleration	Max Absolute Acceleration (Trunk)	Max Absolute Acceleration (Limbs)
Body Parts Applied	Shoulder, Right Elbow, Left Elbow, Nose	Hip	Nose, Shoulder, Hip	Left Arm, Right Arm, Left Thigh, Right Thigh	Left Arm, Right Arm, Left Thigh, Right Thigh	Nose, Shoulder, Hip	Left Elbow, Right Elbow, Left Knee, Right Knee
Number of Features	8	2	3	4	1	1	1

positions of their joints with respect to each other rather than their actual positions in the room. To achieve this, we applied a translation operation on the skeleton so that the Hip point corresponded with the origin (0, 0) of the image. However, this meant that we lost some important information about how far the person was from the camera, which is crucial for addressing the problem of perspective distortion (objects and their motions appear smaller as their distances from the camera increase). To solve this problem, we decided to keep the actual position of the Hip before translation (otherwise it would be (0, 0) for all the samples after translation). This feature is a cue that indicates to a certain degree how far the person is from the camera and helps mitigate the issue of perspective distortion.

We measured velocity using (1) for three joints: Nose, Shoulder, and Hip. These joints were the most stable and provided enough information to determine whether the person was moving fast. Moreover, we needed more features to help us identify any sudden and unexpected movements made by the person. We observed that the limbs generally tend to move more than the trunk, even in normal cases, such as stretching, dusting, or picking up something. So, to better understand sudden movements, we created two features based on acceleration as noted in (2) that allow us to investigate movements of the trunk and limbs separately. The first feature is the maximum absolute acceleration of the trunk, which is the highest absolute acceleration among the nose, shoulder, and hip joints. The second feature is the maximum absolute acceleration among the knee and elbow joints.

$$v_i = \frac{\sqrt{(x_i - x_{i-1})^2 + (y_i - y_{i-1})^2}}{f_i - f_{i-1}} \tag{1}$$

v_i is the velocity of a joint at frame i, x_i and y_i are the positions of the joint, and f_i is the frame number i.

$$acc_i = \left| \frac{v_i - v_{i-1}}{f_i - f_{i-1}} \right| \tag{2}$$

acc_i is the absolute acceleration of a joint at frame i.

To investigate the sudden moves even further, we used angles of the arms and thighs with respect to the trunk as well as the maximum absolute angular acceleration of them as noted in (3) and (3). As the loss of balance starts and the person falls in a direction, their stride length will suddenly change, and their hands will extend and move back and forth to keep balance, causing sudden changes in the angles of their legs and hands with respect to their trunk. Finally, all the features were normalized using min-max normalization.

$$angle\_v_i = \frac{angle_i - angle_{i-1}}{f_i - f_{i-1}} \tag{3}$$

$$angle\_acc_i = \left| \frac{angle\_v_i - angle\_v_{i-1}}{f_i - f_{i-1}} \right| \tag{4}$$

$angle\_v_i$ is the angular velocity of a joint at frame i, $angle_i$ is the angle of the joint with respect to the trunk (the line that connects shoulder joint to hip joint), $angle\_acc_i$ is the absolute angular acceleration of a joint at frame i.

3.5 Model Training

An autoencoder is a neural network consisting of an encoder and a decoder trained to learn reconstructions close to the original input. The difference between the original input and the reconstruction output in the autoencoder is called the reconstruction error [17]. An autoencoder-based anomaly detection system trained with only normal data is expected to recover any given input as close as possible to the learned normal patterns. Therefore, we can classify an input instance as a near-fall if its reconstruction error is larger than a predefined threshold; otherwise, we can classify the input instance as normal.

After conducting several tests on various architectures and tuning the hyper-parameters, we finally identified our autoencoder's best-performing architecture. The autoencoder architecture begins with the encoder's input layer, which contains 20 features. The encoder then undergoes multiple mappings through hidden layers to capture complex features and compress them into smaller sizes until it reaches the code (bottleneck) layer of dimension 8. The decoder then performs the reverse operations to obtain the output vector of 20 features. Table 2 presents a detailed summary of this top-performing model, which was determined through an evaluation process.

Table 2. Summary of the final hyperparameters used to train the model

Hyper-Parameter	Value
Input size	20
Encoder hidden layers sizes	256-64-32
Code size	8
Decoder hidden layers sizes	32-64-256
Output size	20
Activation functions	Relu, Sigmoid
Learning rate	0.005
Training epochs	400
Loss function	MSE
Optimizer	Adam[a]

Adam optimization is a stochastic gradient descent method that adapts the estimation of first-order and second-order moments to improve convergence.

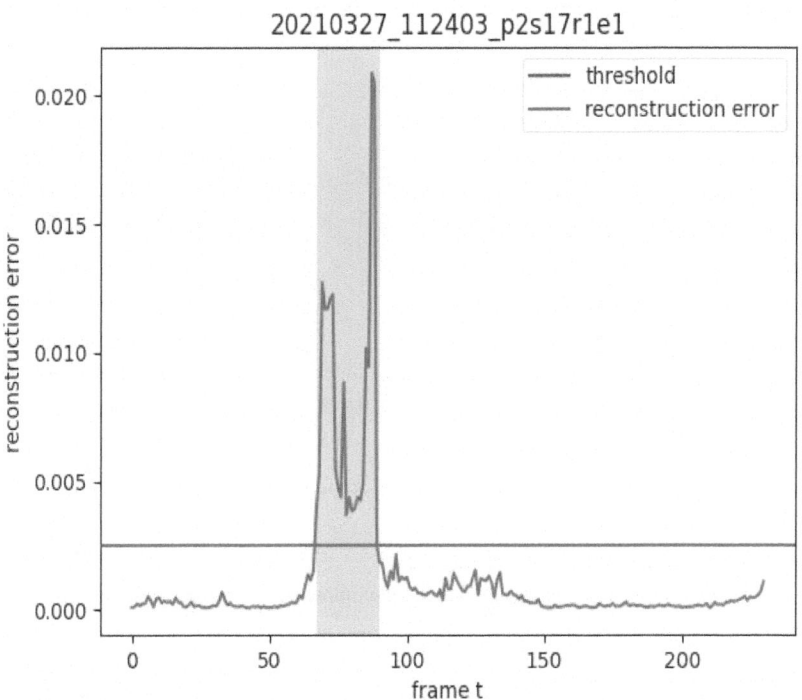

Fig. 3. Reconstruction error of an abnormal video (same video as Figs. 1 and 2). The green area represents the detected near-fall. (Color figure online)

4 Results

The autoencoder was trained on 50 normal videos containing 20515 frames after post-processing (as discussed in Sect. 3.3). The training aimed to enable the model to learn the pattern of the normal videos, and once trained, the model was capable of detecting abnormal videos by measuring their reconstruction error. This was based on a selected threshold value, and if the error remained higher than that for at least five consecutive frames (referred to as the window size, equivalent to a duration of 5/30 s or slightly longer, accounting for any frames removed during postprocessing as detailed in Sect. 3.3), it was marked abnormal (see Fig. 3). We determined the window size of 5 through empirical analysis, considering the AUC results. Similarly, we arrived at the threshold value by examining the ROC-AUC curve presented in Fig. 4. In this particular case, we chose 0.0025 as it allowed us to achieve a good balance between sensitivity and specificity.

Using this threshold and window size, we tested the model with 100 videos (50 normal and 50 abnormal), totaling 37827 frames (after post-processing). It correctly classified 90 videos, 45 normal and 45 abnormal. Performance results on some different thresholds and window sizes are shown in Table 3.

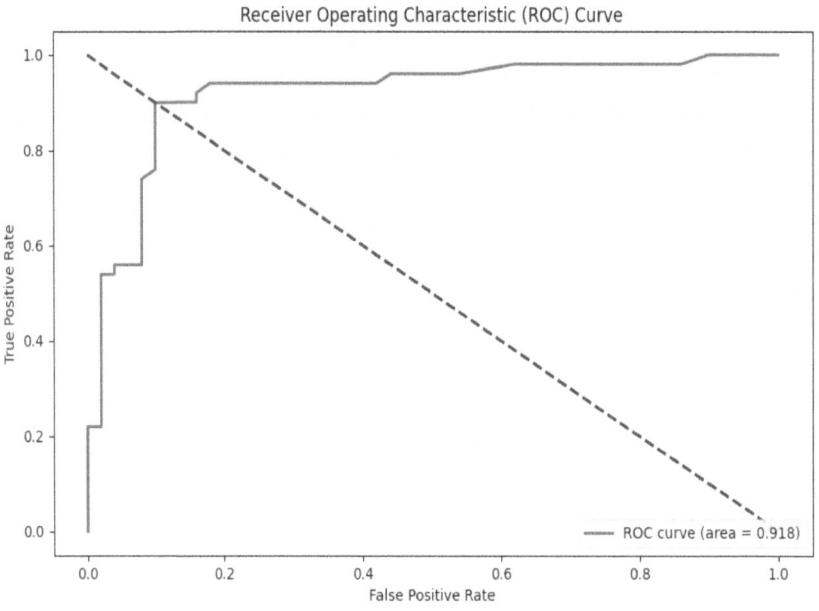

Fig. 4. ROC curve of the model for window size of 5 (best result).

Table 3. Performance results on some different window sizes[a] on test set

Window Size	Threshold	Accuracy	Sensitivity	Specificity	AUC[b]	F1-score	Error Rate	EER[c]
3	2.9×10^{-3}	81	82	80	88.2	81.1	19	19
5	2.5×10^{-3}	90	90	90	91.8	90	10	10
7	2×10^{-3}	89	88	90	91.5	88.8	11	11.2
10	1.8×10^{-3}	87	86	88	91.2	86.8	13	13
15	1.2×10^{-3}	85	86	84	89.8	85.1	15	15.5

a. All the performance metrics are in percentages (%).
b. Area Under Curve.
c. Equal Error Rate.

5 Discussion

In this study, we introduced an advanced intelligent video surveillance system that utilizes cameras and deep learning approaches to enhance the safety and independence of older adults. The system continuously monitors individuals to detect mobility anomalies (near-falls), which can help reduce the likelihood of future falls.

The study findings reveal a promising approach to accurately detect human near-falls using an autoencoder model and a powerful skeleton extraction algorithm like MoveNet. The results have shown an excellent accuracy rate of 90% and an AUC of 91.8%. Out of a total of 100 test videos, 50 were normal and 50 were abnormal, where only 5 videos from each class were incorrectly labeled (5 false positives and five false negatives).

What is noteworthy is that all 5 videos that were falsely identified as normal despite being abnormal (false-negative) had very little near-fall motion, making it difficult to detect the near-fall incident (actually, we can argue about the veracity of these near-falls). In addition, two of them showed a near-fall incident towards or away from the camera and at a far distance from it, making it even harder to identify it in 2D space. A complete system including additional cameras could help in these cases. Conversely, the false-positive cases were mainly attributed to activities that were vastly different from the normal activities the model had been trained on, such as crouching. This could be a result of the limited number of normal motion examples used during the training phase, where only 50 videos were utilized. In addition, it was discovered that two videos of false-positive cases were mislabeled due to excessive movement of one leg. This mistake happened because one (skeleton extracted) leg was moving too much, even though the person was in a stationary position. The reason for this was that the person was in a unique pose where she was lying on a couch with her legs crossed, making it difficult to detect the bottom leg. Additional post-processing or a more robust skeleton extractor could solve this problem.

Table 4 presents a comparison of the performance results of our approach with three previously tested algorithms presented in [8, 14]. The study revealed that the IF (Isolation Forest) algorithm had the best result out of all three algorithms, with a performance score of AUC $\approx$ 92% and EER $\approx$ 10%. Our model (autoencoder) shows a similar result to that of the IF. However, the autoencoder (AE) was tested on a much more challenging dataset that expands the dataset used in [8, 14]. This initial dataset was limited to a training set of 25 normal videos and a testing set of 15 normal activities +15 near-fall situations with the subject constrained to be in a limited range of distances from the camera to simplify the analysis. This is to be compared to the more realistic dataset of 150 videos used here (training set: 50 normal activities, testing set: 50 normal, 50 abnormal) without any specific constraint.

The autoencoder was thus tested on a more challenging dataset, analyzing human behavior through a set of 20 features and a human skeleton model with 7 keypoints. The complexity of this model highlights its robustness and capacity to detect anomalies in more complex scenarios of routine human activities. This is contrary to the IF algorithm, which despite its efficiency in utilizing a minimal feature set of three features and three keypoints, was not tested under similarly challenging conditions.

Table 4. Summary of results: previous study and ours

Model	Skeleton Detection Algorithm	Number of Keypoints	Number of Features	EER (%)	AUC (%)
SVM	Keypoint RCNN	3	3	10	88
GMM	Keypoint RCNN	3	3	20	85
IF	Keypoint RCNN	3	3	10	92
AE[a]	MoveNet	7	20	10	92

a. Results for an expanded and more challenging dataset.

Finally, remember that in a real setup, the training would benefit from much more videos of normal events and additional cameras could be used to cover the whole apartment and avoid blind spots. Nevertheless, this pilot study shows the potential of the personalization of the system for each individual person and each environment.

6 Conclusion

The study underscores the significance of identification and prevention of a potential fall at an early stage. Our research has yielded an advanced IVS system that utilizes standard cameras (for their affordability and widespread availability) and deep learning techniques to promote the safety and autonomy of elderly individuals. By constantly monitoring for mobility irregularities, like near-falls, the system can effectively decrease the risk of falls in the future and enhance elderly care in their living environments with its excellent accuracy in navigating complex situations.

In order to further enhance the system, we can further expand the dataset to include a wider range of daily activities which will help improve the model's ability to learn normality. Other environments and different actors will also improve the dataset for better testing. Additionally, we should enhance the accuracy of the skeleton detection results in difficult scenarios. One way to achieve this is by implementing tracking of the previous positions and applying or learning constraints on sudden, unrealistic changes in position and movement.

Notice that the system will detect any kind of anomaly and is not specific to near-fall events or mobility anomalies. Any significant deviation from normal activities will consequently trigger an anomaly detection. It could be interesting to evaluate how many abnormal events are not related to mobility issues to evaluate their impacts on fall risk assessment and if further improvements are necessary to improve mobility anomaly specificity.

Other works on monocular depth estimation with deep learning could also be investigated in the future to enhance our results if our system is not capable of extracting reliable depth cues from (monocular) RGB image. RGBD cameras that are now cheaper and readily available could also be considered. These improvements could significantly enhance the system's reliability and robustness, which would make it an effective and reliable tool for monitoring and ensuring the safety of elderly individuals in their homes. Longer-term objectives are to build an end-to-end network from raw image data to anomaly detection and deploy it in real-life situations.

Acknowledgments. This work was supported by the NSERC (Natural Sciences and Engineering Research Council of Canada). The authors would like to thank Meryem Gassi and Perla Nehme for their assistance with the dataset construction.

Disclosure of Interests.. The authors have no competing interests to declare that are relevant to the content of this article.

References

1. Organization, W.H.: World report on ageing and health, pp. 1–246. Geneva, Switzerland (2015)
2. Public Health Agency of Canada: Falls among older adults in Canada. Health Infobase of Canada. https://health-infobase.canada.ca/falls-in-older-adults. Accessed 13 Jun 2024
3. Maidan, I., Freedman, T., Tzemah, R., Giladi, N., Mirelman, A., Hausdorff, J.M.: Introducing a new definition of a near fall: Intra-rater and inter-rater reliability. Gait Posture **39**(1), 645–647 (2014). https://doi.org/10.1016/j.gaitpost.2013.07.123
4. Nagai, K., et al.: Near falls predict substantial falls in older adults: a prospective cohort study. Geriatr. Gerontol. Int. **17**(10), 1477–1480 (2017). https://doi.org/10.1111/ggi.12898
5. Gupta, N., Gupta, S.K., Pathak, R.K., Jain, V., Rashidi, P., Suri, J.S.: Human activity recognition in artificial intelligence framework: a narrative review. Artif. Intell. Rev. **55**(6), 4755–4808 (2022). https://doi.org/10.1007/s10462-021-10116-x
6. Feng, M., Meunier, J.: Skeleton graph-neural-network-based human action recognition: a survey. Sensors **22**(6), 2091 (2022). https://doi.org/10.3390/s22062091

7. Yan, S., Xiong, Y., Lin, D.: Spatial temporal graph convolutional networks for skeleton-based action recognition. In: 32nd AAAI Conference on Artificial Intelligence, AAAI 2018, pp. 7444–7452 (2018)

8. Tran, K.C., et al.: Comparison of anomaly detection algorithms for near-fall detection with video surveillance. In: 2022 10th E-Health and Bioengineering Conference, EHB 2022, pp. 01–04 (2022). https://doi.org/10.1109/EHB55594.2022.9991343

9. Mahfouf, Z., Merouani, H.F., Bouchrika, I., Harrati, N.: Investigating the use of motion-based features from optical flow for gait recognition. Neurocomputing **283**, 140–149 (2018). https://doi.org/10.1016/j.neucom.2017.12.040

10. Baradaran, M., Bergevin, R.: A critical study on the recent deep learning based semi-supervised video anomaly detection methods. Multimed Tools Appl. **83**(9), 1–47 (2023). https://doi.org/10.1007/s11042-023-16445-z

11. Vallabh, P., Malekian, R.: Fall detection monitoring systems: a comprehensive review. J. Ambient. Intell. Humaniz. Comput. **9**(6), 1809–1833 (2018). https://doi.org/10.1007/s12652-017-0592-3

12. Stone, E., Skubic, M., Rantz, M., Abbott, C., Miller, S.: Average in-home gait speed: Investigation of a new metric for mobility and fall risk assessment of elders. Gait Posture **41**(1), 57–62 (2015). https://doi.org/10.1016/j.gaitpost.2014.08.019

13. Rantz, M., et al.: Automated in-home fall risk assessment and detection sensor system for elders. Gerontologist **55**, S78-87 (2015). https://doi.org/10.1093/geront/gnv044

14. Tran, K.C., Gassi, M., Nehme, P., Rousseau, J., Meunier, J.: Video surveillance for near-fall detection at home. In: Proceedings - IEEE 22nd International Conference on Bioinformatics and Bioengineering, BIBE 2022, pp. 111–116 (2022). https://doi.org/10.1109/BIBE55377.2022.00031

15. Votel, R., Li, N.: Next-Generation Pose Detection with MoveNet and TensorFlow.js. TensorFlow Blog. Accessed: 13 Jun. 2024. https://blog.tensorflow.org/2021/05/next-generation-pose-detection-with-movenet-and-tensorflowjs.html

16. Google: MoveNet. Kaggle. Accessed: 13 Jun. 2024. https://www.kaggle.com/models/google/movenet

17. Torabi, H., Mirtaheri, S.L., Greco, S.: Practical autoencoder based anomaly detection by using vector reconstruction error. Cybersecurity **6**(1), 1 (2023). https://doi.org/10.1186/s42400-022-00134-9

Weakly-Supervised Video Anomaly Detection Using Modified Anomaly Score Module and Modified BERT

Jun-Xiang Chen and Jin-Jang Leou[✉]

National Chung Cheng University, Chiayi 621, Taiwan, ROC
jjleou@cs.ccu.edu.tw

Abstract. In this study, a weakly-supervised video anomaly detection approach using modified anomaly score module and modified BERT is proposed. The proposed approach consists of four main steps. (1) A video sequence is divided into nonoverlapping video clips and each video clip consists of sixteen adjacent video frames. (2) The video clips are fed into I3D to extract video clip feature vectors, which are fed into the proposed modified anomaly score module and the proposed modified BERT module to obtain the video clip feature vector anomaly scores and the video sequence classification anomaly score, respectively. (3) The video clip feature vector anomaly scores are multiplied by the video sequence classification score to obtain the video clip anomaly scores, which are fed into frame anomaly score production operation to obtain the video frame anomaly scores. (4) Based on the specified threshold, the video frames are determined as abnormal or normal. Based on the experimental results obtained in this study, the performance of the proposed approach is better than those of comparison approaches.

Keywords: Video anomaly detection · Weakly-supervised learning · Video clip feature vector · Video frame anomaly score · modified · BERT

1 Introduction

Recently, cameras are widely installed in various environment to monitor various activities and detect anomaly events. Video anomaly detection has always been an important research topic for computer vision applications.

There are three main difficulties in video anomaly detection [1, 2]. (1) The definition of video anomaly is vague and various from one person or application environment to another. The same behavior may be normal or anomaly. (2) Data imbalance between anomaly/normal samples. (3) There are high deviations in video anomaly samples.

Video anomaly detection approaches can be divided into two main categories: handcrafted feature based [3–5] and deep learning based [6–35]. Handcrafted spatial, temporal, transformed, and spatiotemporal features are used in most traditional approaches to express video normalness. Cui, et al. [3] used the interaction energy potential to find the relationship among the group of people, and used the relationship between the current state of a subject and the corresponding reaction to find the anomaly/normal patterns.

© The Author(s), under exclusive license to Springer Nature Switzerland AG 2025
L. Deligiannidis et al. (Eds.): CSCE 2024, CCIS 2262, pp. 203–215, 2025.
https://doi.org/10.1007/978-3-031-85933-5_14

Cong, Yuan, and Liu [4] proposed a novel sparse reconstruction cost (SRC) approach based on the weighted l1 minimization for both local anomaly event and global anomaly event to quantify the normalness. Lu, Shi, and Jia [5] proposed a sparse combined learning architecture based on three dimensional (3D) gradient features to improve the speed of anomaly detection.

Deep learning based approaches can be divided into three main categories: unsupervised learning based [6–13], supervised learning based [14], and weakly-supervised learning based approaches [15–35]. For unsupervised learning based approaches, Zhang, et al. [6] proposed a modified U-Net as the basic autoencoder (AE), and a memory module is used to store the prototype normal patterns to enhance the ability of remembering normal events. Wang, Yao, and Yao [7] proposed an approach based on the future video frame prediction, in which generative adversarial network (GAN) and attention mechanism are employed and U-Net is modified. Wang, Xie, and Song [8] proposed a deep AE network to learn the appearance and motion features from spatiotemporal dimensions, which is combined with 3D convolutional neural networks (3DCNN) and ConvGRU neural network. Xu, et al. [9] proposed an approach combining a dual discriminator based GAN structure and the future video frame prediction framework. Zhou, Li, and C. Zhao [10] proposed a multi-level attention network, which consists of an object-guided attention module (OGAM) and a motion-refined attention module (MRAM). Le and Kim [11] proposed an approach based on attention-based residual AE, which aims to exploit spatiotemporal features efficiently. Yang, et al. [12] proposed a novel approach, in which each video frame is determined as anomaly or normal by object detection and patch likelihood results. Doshi and Yilmaz [13] combined transfer learning based neural network and statistical clustering to improve performance on anomaly detection in traffic video sequences.

For supervised learning based approaches, for example in Wan, et al. [14], the local spatiotemporal features are extracted by I3D from each video clip, which are fed into a recurrent convolutional architecture to learn global spatiotemporal contextual features. Finally, anomaly scores and anomaly classes are predicted by the fully convolutional layers of two sub-networks.

For weakly-supervised learning based approaches, Sultani, Chen, and Shah [15] proposed a weakly-supervised learning approach using multiple instance learning (MIL). Zhong, et al. [16] proposed a GCN to establish relationships between high-confidence video clips and low-confidence video clips. In the graph, video clips are abstracted into vertices and the abnormal information is propagated through edges. Watanabe, et al. [17] proposed a lightweight and highly accurate approach, in which all video clips in a video sequence are employed to determine whether the video sequence is anomaly or normal. Feng, Hong, and Zheng [18] proposed a multiple instance self-training approach (MIST) for video anomaly detection. Wan, et al. [19] proposed anomaly regression network (AR-Net) for video anomaly detection. Liu, et al. [20] proposed a spatialtemporal attention (STA) approach with MIL ranking module to learn inter- and intra-correlations in video clips. Gong, et al. [21] proposed a multi-scale continuity-aware refinement network (MCR) for weakly-supervised video anomaly detection. Zhang, et al. [22] proposed a two-branch approach, in which the anomalies in seen data and open data can be separately detected. Lv, et al. [23] proposed an unbiased multiple instance learning

(UMIL) approach for video anomaly detection. Tian, et al. [24] proposed robust temporal feature magnitude learning (RTFM) approach for video anomaly detection. Wu, et al. [25] proposed a self-supervised sparse representation (S3R) framework containing two opposite modules for video anomaly detection. Sapkota and Yu [26] proposed a novel Bayesian nonparametric submodularity diversified MIL model for video anomaly detection. Park, et al. [27] proposed a normality guided multiple instance learning (NG-MIL) framework, which will leverage abundant normal video clips to eliminate false positives in the anomaly scores.

Zhang, et al. [28] proposed a novel temporal relation learning approach, in which the temporal relationships between video clips are explored and the separability between anomaly/normal samples are enhanced. Yu, et al. [29] proposed a temporal context alignment network (TCA), in which a sparse continue sampling strategy, a multi-scale attention module, and a topk strategy are employed. Tan, Yao, and Liu [30] combined MIL and bidirectional encoder representations from transformers (BERT) for weakly-supervised video anomaly detection. Deshpande, et al. [31] combined video swin features and RTFM model for video anomaly detection. Liu, et al. [32] proposed a decouple and resolve framework (DAR) for online video anomaly detection. Li, Liu, and Jiao [33] proposed a multi-sequence learning (MSL) approach, in which a video sequence containing multiple instances is treated as an optimization unit. Sun and Gong [34] proposed a long-short temporal co-teaching (LSTC) approach for weakly-supervised video anomaly detection. Rossi, et al. [35] proposed a video anomaly detection approach using a short-term memory module and a video swin transformer.

This paper is organized as follows. The proposed weakly-supervised video anomaly detection approach is described in Sect. 2. Experimental results are addressed in Sect. 3, followed by concluding remarks.

2   Proposed Approach

2.1   System Architecture

In this study, a weakly-supervised video anomaly detection approach using modified anomaly score module and modified BERT is proposed. The proposed approach consists of four main steps. (1) A video sequence is divided into nonoverlapping video clips and each video clip consists of sixteen adjacent video frames. (2) The video clips are fed into I3D to extract video clip feature vectors, which are fed into the proposed modified anomaly score module and the proposed modified BERT module to obtain the video clip feature vector anomaly scores and the video sequence classification anomaly score, respectively. (3) The video clip feature vector anomaly scores are multiplied by the video sequence classification score to obtain the video clip anomaly scores, which are fed into frame anomaly score production operation to obtain the video frame anomaly scores. (4) Based on the specified threshold, the video frames are determined as abnormal or normal.

As shown in Fig. 1, $v_t(x, y)$ denotes video frames, where $v_t(x, y) = (v_{t,R}(x, y), v_{t,G}(x, y), v_{t,B}(x, y))$, $t = 1, 2, ..., T$, $0 \leq v_{t,R}(x, y), v_{t,G}(x, y), v_{t,B}(x, y) \leq 255$, $1 \leq x \leq M$, $1 \leq y \leq N$, T denotes the number of video frames, and $M \times N$ denote size of video frames. By clip production module, the T video frames are divided into J nonoverlapping video clips $c_j, j = 1, 2, ..., J$, where c_j denotes the j-th video clip. The J video clips are fed into I3D feature extraction module to obtain J video clip feature vectors, $f_j, j = 1, 2, ..., J$. The J video clip feature vectors are fed into the proposed modified anomaly score module to obtain J video clip feature vector anomaly scores $s_{clip}^j, j = 1, 2, ..., J$ and the J video clip feature vectors are also fed into the proposed modified BERT module to obtain the video sequence classification score s_{cls}. By multiplication, the J video clip anomaly scores $s_{fin}^j = s_{clip}^j \cdots cls, j = 1, 2, ..., J$ are obtained. The video clip anomaly scores are fed into frame anomaly score production operation to obtain the T video frame anomaly scores $s_t, t = 1, 2, ..., T$. Finally, based on threshold h, the T video frame labels, $label_t$ (normal or abnormal), $t = 1, 2, ..., T$ are obtained.

In the clip production module, sixteen adjacent video frames are sequentially formed as a video clip, i.e., $v_1(x, y) \sim v_{16}(x, y)$ form the first video clip, $v_{17}(x, y) \sim v_{32}(x, y)$ form the second video clip, ..., etc. Using pretrained I3D on Kinetics dataset [36] for feature extraction, the J video clips $c_j, j = 1, 2, ..., J$ are fed into I3D to generate the j-th video

clip feature vectors $f_j = \begin{bmatrix} f_{j,1} \\ f_{j,2} \\ \vdots \\ f_{j,2048} \end{bmatrix}, j = 1, 2, ..., J$, which are fed into the proposed

modified anomaly score module to generate J video clip feature vector anomaly scores $s_{clip}^j, j = 1, 2, ..., J$.

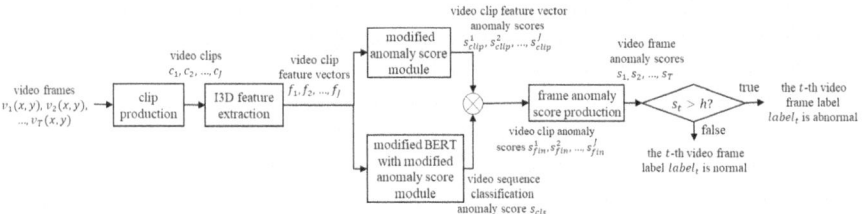

Fig. 1. Framework of the proposed approach.

2.2 Activation Functions

In Tan, Yao, and Liu [30], the activation function, rectified linear unit (*ReLU*) [37], is employed in both anomaly score module and BERT module. Three activation functions, *PReLU* [38, 39], and *GELU* [40], are employed in this study, where *PReLU* and *sigmoid* are employed in both the proposed modified anomaly score module and the proposed modified BERT module, and *GELU* [40] is employed in the proposed modified BERT module. *PReLU* is defined as

$$PReLU(z) = \begin{cases} z, \text{ if } z \geq 0, \\ \beta \times z, \text{ otherwise}, \end{cases} \tag{1}$$

where β denotes learning slope adjusted by training data and $z \in \mathbb{R}$, *sigmoid* is defined as

$$sigmoid(z) = \frac{1}{1 + e^{-z}}, \tag{2}$$

where $z \in \mathbb{R}$, and *GELU* is approximately defined as

$$GELU(z) = 0.5 \times z \times \left(1 + tanh\left[\sqrt{\frac{2}{\pi}} \times \left(z + 0.044715 \times z^3\right)\right]\right), \tag{3}$$

where $z \in \mathbb{R}$ and $tanh(\cdot)$ denotes hyperbolic tangent function.

2.3 Modified BERT Module

BERT is employed in natural language processing (NLP) [41] and video anomaly detection approaches [42]. In this study, one BERT module with modified anomaly score is employed. As shown in Fig. 2, the J video clip feature vectors $\{f_1, f_2, ..., f_J\}$ are together fed into the proposed modified BERT module to obtain video sequence classification feature vector f_{cls}, where $f_{cls} = \begin{bmatrix} f_{cls,1} \\ f_{cls,2} \\ \vdots \\ f_{cls,2048} \end{bmatrix}$. The video sequence classification feature vector f_{cls} is fed into the proposed modified anomaly score module to obtain the video sequence classification score s_{cls}.

As shown in Fig. 3, the proposed modified BERT consists of linear transformation layer, embedding layer (EM), layer normalization (LN) [43], multi-head self-attention mechanism (MSA), element-wise addition operator, position-wise feed forward network (PFFN), and selection operator. The J video clip feature vectors $\{f_1, f_2, ..., f_J\}$ may form a $2048 \times J$ matrix, which is fed into the linear transformation layer to generate the transformation matrix Z_1 ($512 \times J$ in size). The transformation matrix Z_1 is fed into EM to generate the embedding matrix Z_2 ($512 \times (J + 1)$ in size). The embedding matrix Z_2 is defined as

$$Z_2 = Z_1 \copyright x_{cls} + pos, \tag{4}$$

where $\copyright$ denotes concatenation operation, $x_{cls} = \begin{bmatrix} x_{cls,1} \\ x_{cls,2} \\ \vdots \\ x_{cls,512} \end{bmatrix}$ denotes the learnable vector and *pos* denotes the learnable matrix ($512 \times (J + 1)$ in size).

The embedding matrix Z_2 is fed into LN to obtain the normalization matrix Z_3 ($512 \times (J + 1)$ in size), which is fed into MSA to generate the MSA output matrix Z_4 ($512 \times (J + 1)$ in size) defined as

$$SSA_i = V_i \odot softmax\left(Q_i^T \odot K_i\right), \tag{5}$$

$$Z_4 = concate(SSA_1, SSA_2, \ldots, SSA_8), \tag{6}$$

where SSA_i denotes the i-th single-head self attention mechanism output, $i = 1, 2, \ldots, 8$, V_i denotes the i-th value matrix ($64 \times (J + 1)$ in size), $\odot$ denotes matrix multiplication, $softmax(\cdot)$ denotes the probability distribution function [39], Q_i denotes the i-th query matrix ($64 \times (J + 1)$ in size), $\dot{T}$ denotes transpose operation, K_i denotes the i-th key matrix ($64 \times (J + 1)$ in size), and $concate(\cdot)$ denotes concatenation operation. Here, $softmax$ [39] is defined as

$$softmax(z_d) = \frac{e^{z_d}}{\sum_{d=1}^{D} e^{z_d}}, d = 1, 2, \ldots, D, \tag{7}$$

where $z_d \in R$ and D denotes the number of matrix elements.

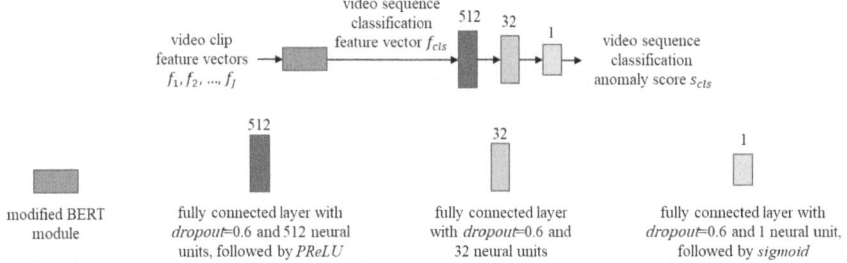

Fig. 2. The proposed modified BERT module with modified anomaly score.

The residual connection matrix Z_5 defined as

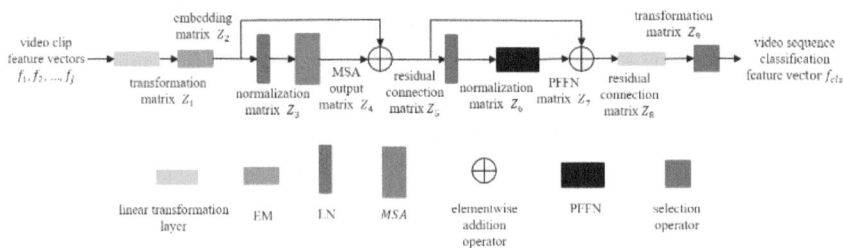

Fig. 3. The proposed modified BERT.

$$Z_5 = Z_2 \oplus Z_4, \tag{8}$$

where $\oplus$ denotes element-wise addition, is fed into LN to generate the normalization matrix Z_6 ($512 \times (J + 1)$ in size). Z_6 is fed into PFFN to generate PFFN matrix Z_7 (512

$\times (J + 1)$ in size) defined as

$$Z_7 = w_2 \times GELU(w_1 \times Z_6 + b_1) + b_2, \tag{9}$$

where w_1 and w_2 denote two model weights of PFFN, $GELU(\cdot)$ is defined in Eq. (3), and b_1 and b_2 denote two bias values of PFFN. The residual connection matrix Z_8 defined as

$$Z_8 = Z_5 \oplus Z_7, \tag{10}$$

is fed into LN to generate the transformation matrix Z_9 ($2048 \times (J + 1)$ in size). Finally, the first column vector of Z_9 will be selected as the video sequence classification feature

vector $f_{cls} = \begin{bmatrix} f_{cls,1} \\ f_{cls,2} \\ \vdots \\ f_{cls,2048} \end{bmatrix}$ by the selection operator.

The J anomaly scores for the J video clips computed as

$$s_{fin}^j = s_{clip}^j s_{cls}, j = 1, 2, \ldots, J, \tag{11}$$

are fed into frame anomaly score production operation to obtain the video frame anomaly scores. Note that the video frame anomaly scores of sixteen video frames within the j-th clip are identically equal to s_{fin}^i. Finally, the t-th video frame v_t, $t = 1, 2, \ldots, T$ is determined as

$$label_t = \begin{cases} abnormal, if\ s_t > h, \\ normal, otherwise. \end{cases} \tag{12}$$

2.4 Loss Functions and Training

In this study, MIL loss function [15] is used, in which there is at least one anomaly video clip in an anomaly video sequence, and there are no anomaly video clips in a normal video sequence. Let $pbag_a = \left\{ s_{anoclip}^{a,j} \right\}$, $nbag_a = \left\{ s_{norclip}^{a,j} \right\}$, where $pbag_a$ denotes the a-th anomaly video sequence, $s_{anoclip}^{a,j}$ denotes the j-th video clip feature vector anomaly score in the a-th anomaly video sequence, $nbag_a$ denotes the a-th normal video sequence, $s_{norclip}^{a,j}$ denotes the j-th video clip feature vector anomaly score in the a-th normal video sequence, $a = 1, 2, \ldots, A$, where A denotes the number of video sequences, and $pbag_a$ and $nbag_a$ represent sets of anomaly/normal video clip feature vector anomaly scores, respectively.

The proposed modified MIL loss function $L_{MIL}(a)$ is defined as

$$
\begin{aligned}
L_{MIL}(a) = \; & max(0, \; 1 - \lambda_1 \times max(pbag_a) + \lambda_2 \\
& \times max(nbag_a) - \lambda_3 \times topk(pbag_a) \\
& + \lambda_4 \times topk(nbag_a)) \\
& + \lambda_5 \times \sum_{j=1}^{J-1} (s_{anoclip}^{a,j} - s_{anoclip}^{a,j+1})^2 \\
& + \lambda_6 \times \sum_{j=1}^{J} s_{anoclip}^{a,j} + \lambda_7 \times ||W||_F,
\end{aligned}
\tag{13}
$$

where $max(\cdot)$ returns the maximum value, $topk(\cdot)$ denotes the average value of the k-highest video clip anomaly scores in the video sequence [24], W denotes the model weights of the proposed modified anomaly score module, and $||\cdot||_F$ denotes Frobenius norm operation. Here, λ_1, λ_2, k, λ_3, λ_4, λ_5, λ_6, and λ_7 are empirically set to 0.5, 0.5, 3, 0.5, 0.5, 0.00004, 0.00004, and 0.01, respectively. The proposed modified MIL total loss function L_{tMIL} is defined as

$$
L_{tMIL} = \sum_{a=1}^{A} L_{MIL}(a).
\tag{14}
$$

Video sequence classification loss function L_{video} is defined as

$$
\begin{aligned}
L_{video} = \; & \sum_{a=1}^{A} \left(-\log\left(s_{anocls}^{a} + \varepsilon_1 \right) \right) \\
& - \sum_{a=1}^{A} \left(\log(1 - s_{norcls}^{a} + \varepsilon_2) \right)
\end{aligned}
\tag{15}
$$

where $log(\cdot)$ denotes natural log operation, s_{anocls}^{a} denotes the a-th anomaly video sequence classification score, s_{norcls}^{a} denotes the a-th normal video sequence classification score, and ε_1 and ε_2 are small positive constants (empirically set to 1×10^{-8} and 1×10^{-8}, respectively) for avoiding ambiguity. Finally, total loss function L_{total} is defined as

$$
L_{total} = L_{tMIL} + L_{video}.
\tag{16}
$$

There are several optimizers used in deep learning, such as stochastic gradient descent (SGD) [44], Adagrad [45], adaptive moment estimation (Adam) [46], etc. In this study, Adam optimizer is employed.

3 Experimental Results

In this study, the proposed approach is implemented on Microsoft Windows 10 platform with AMD Ryzen™ 7 3700X 3.6 GHz (CPU), nvidia geforce RTX 3090 (GPU), 64 GB main memory (RAM), python version 3.7.3, Pytorch version.1.8.0, CUDA version

11.1.0, and cuDNN version 8.0.5. UCF-Crime dataset [15] and ShanghaiTech dataset [16] are employed. UCF-Crime dataset is a dataset containing 1900 indoor and outdoor untrimmed real-world surveillance video sequences with 13 anomaly types. Here, 800 normal and 810 anomaly video sequences are used for training and 150 normal and 140 anomaly video sequences are used for testing. ShanghaiTech dataset is a dataset containing 437 campus surveillance video sequences with 130 anomaly events in 13 scenes. Here, 175 normal and 63 anomaly video sequences are used for training and 155 normal and 44 anomaly video sequences are used for testing.

Two objective video anomaly detection metrics, i.e., area under curve (AUC) [47] and equal error rate (EER) [9] are employed in this study. AUC denotes the area under the receiver operating characteristic (ROC) curve and the larger AUC value responds the better anomaly detection performance. To detect anomalies, different ROC curves are generated by changing threshold h of abnormal scores to determine the "optimal" results. EER denotes the value that the probability of detecting errors for the positive sample and that for the negative sample are equal, i.e., FPR is equal to false negative rate (FNR).

Table 1. In terms of average ACU (%), performance comparisons between seventeen comparison approaches and the proposed approach on UCF-Crime [15] and ShanghaiTech [16] datasets.

datasets and metrics\approaches	UCF-Crime AUC (%)	ShanghaiTech AUC (%)
Zhong, et al.'s approach [16]	82.12	84.44
Watanabe, et al.'s approach [17]	84.91	95.72
Feng, Hong, and Sheng's approach [18]	82.30	94.83
Liu, et al.'s approach [20]	83.00	90.20
Gong, et al.'s approach [21]	81.00	94.92
Zhang, et al.'s approach [22]	85.47	97.48
Lv, et al.'s approach [23]	86.75	96.78
Tian, et al.'s approach [24]	84.30	97.21
Wu, et al.'s approach [25]	85.99	97.48
Sapkota and Yu's approach [26]	83.39	96.00
Park, et al.'s approach [27]	85.63	97.43
Zhang, et al.'s approach [28]	83.17	97.62
Yu, et al.'s approach [29]	83.75	93.60
Tan, Yao, and Liu's approach [30]	86.71	97.54
Liu, et al.'s approach [32]	85.36	97.68
Li, Liu, and Jiao's approach [33]	85.62	97.32
Sun and Gong's approach [34]	85.88	97.92
Proposed	**87.18**	**98.31**

Table 2. In terms of average EER (%), performance comparisons between five comparison approaches and the proposed approach on UCF-Crime dataset [15].

metric\approaches	EER (%)
Sultani, Chen, and Shah's approach [15]	31.80
Lv, et al.'s approach [23]	22.50
Tian, et al.'s approach [24]	28.50
Yu, et al.'s approach [29]	29.10
Tan, Yao, and Liu's approach [30]	22.10
Proposed	**21.18**

Table 3. In terms of average EER (%), performance comparisons between five comparison approaches and the proposed approach on ShanghaiTech dataset [16].

Metric\approaches	EER (%)
Sultani, Chen, and Shah's approach [15]	19.95
Lv, et al.'s approach [23]	19.70
Tian, et al.'s approach [24]	17.10
Yu, et al.'s approach [29]	7.07
Tan, Yao, and Liu's approach [30]	8.50
Proposed	4.94

In this study, in terms of two objective metrics, average AUC (%) and EER (%), performance comparisons between seventeen comparison approaches and the proposed approach on two datasets are listed in Tables 1, 2 and 3, respectively.

4 Concluding Remarks

In this study, a weakly-supervised video anomaly detection approach using modified anomaly score module and modified BERT is proposed. Based on the experimental results obtained in this study, in terms of average AUC (%), the performance of the proposed approach is better than those of seventeen comparison approaches, and in terms of average EER(%), the performance of the proposed approach is better than those of five comparison approaches on UCF-Crime dataset [15] and is better than those of five comparison approaches on ShanghaiTech dataset [16].

Acknowledgements. This work was supported in part by National Science and Technology Council, Taiwan, ROC under Grant NTSC 112-2221-E-194-030.

References

1. Yadav, R.K., Kumar, R.: A survey on video anomaly detection. In: Proceedings of 2022 IEEE Delhi Section Conf., pp. 1–5 (2022)
2. Abbas, Z.K., Al-Ani, A.A.: A comprehensive review for video anomaly detection on videos. In: Proceedings of 2022 International Conf. on Computer Science and Software Engineering, pp. 30–35 (2022)
3. Cui, X., Liu, Q., Gao, M., Metaxas, D. N.: Abnormal detection using interaction energy potentials. In: Proceedings of 2011 IEEE Conf. on Computer Vision and Pattern Recognition, pp. 30–35 (2022)
4. Cong, Y., Yuan, J., Liu, J.: Sparse reconstruction cost for abnormal event detection. In: Proceedings of 2011 IEEE/CVF Conf. on Computer Vision and Pattern Recognition, pp. 3161–3167 (2011)
5. Lu, C., Shi, J., Jia, J.: Abnormal event detection at 150 FPS in MATLAB. In: Proceedings of 2013 IEEE International Conf. on Computer Vision, pp. 2720–2727 (2013)
6. Zhang, L., et al.: A memory-enhanced anomaly detection method for surveillance videos. In: Proceedings of 2021 IEEE International Conf. on Electronic Information Engineering and Computer Science, pp. 1012–1015 (2021)
7. Wang, C., Yao, Y., Yao, H.: Video anomaly detection method based on future frame prediction and attention mechanism. In: Proceedings of 2021 IEEE Annual Computing and Communication Workshop and Conf., pp. 405–407 (2021)
8. Wang, X., Xie, W., Song, J.: Learning spatiotemporal features with 3DCNN and ConvGRU for video anomaly detection. In: Proceedings of 2021 IEEE Annual Computing and Communication Workshop and Conf. on Signal Processing, pp. 474–479 (2018)
9. Xu, J., et al.: Video anomaly detection using dual discriminator based generative adversarial network. In: Proceedings of 2021 20th IEEE International Conf. on Machine Learning and Applications, pp. 1259–1265 (2021)
10. Zhou, W., Li, Y., Zhao, C.: Object-guided and motion-refined attention network for video anomaly detection. In: Proceedings of 2022 IEEE International Conf. on Multimedia and Expo, pp. 1–6 (2022)
11. Le, V.T., Kim, Y.G.: Attention-based residual autoencoder for video anomaly detection. Appl. Intell. **53**, 3240–3254 (2023)
12. Yang, Y., Xian, Y., Fu, Z., Naqvi, S.M.: Video anomaly detection for surveillance based on effective frame area. In: Proceedings of 2021 IEEE 24th International Conf. on Information Fusion, pp. 1–5 (2021)
13. Doshi, K., Yilmaz, Y.: Fast unsupervised anomaly detection in traffic videos. In: Proceedings of 2020 IEEE/CVF Computer Vision and Pattern Recognition Workshops, pp. 2658–2664 (2020)
14. Wan, B., Jiang, W., Fang, Y., Luo, Z., Ding, G.: Anomaly detection in video sequences: a benchmark and computational model. arXiv: 2106.08570 (2021)
15. Sultani, W., Chen, C., Shah, M.: Real-world anomaly detection in surveillance videos. In: Proceedings of 2018 IEEE/CVF Conf. on Computer Vision and Pattern Recognition, pp. 6479–6488 (2018)
16. Zhong, J.X., et al.: Graph convolutional label noise cleaner: train a plug-and-play action classifier for anomaly detection. In: Proceedings of 2019 IEEE/CVF Conf. on Computer Vision and Pattern Recognition, pp. 1237–1246 (2019)

17. Watanabe, Y., Okabe, M., Harada, Y., Kashima, N.: Real-world video anomaly detection by extracting salient features. In: Proceedings of 2022 IEEE International Conf. on Image Processing, pp. 891–895 (2022)

18. Feng, J.C., Hong T., Zheng, W.S.: MIST: multiple instance self-training framework for video anomaly detection. In: Proceedings of 2021 IEEE/CVF Conf. on Computer Vision and Pattern Recognition, pp. 14004–14013 (2021)

19. Wan, B., Fang, Y., Xia, X., Mei, J.: Weakly supervised video anomaly detection via center-guided discriminative learning. In: Proceedings of 2020 IEEE International Conf. on Multimedia and Expo, pp. 1–6 (2021)

20. Liu, Y., et al.: Learning task-specific representation for video anomaly detection with spatial-temporal attention. In: Proceedings of 2022 IEEE International Conf. on Acoustics, Speech and Signal Processing, pp. 2190–2194 (2022)

21. Gong, Y., et al.: Multi-scale continuity-aware refinement network for weakly supervised video anomaly detection. In: Proceedings of 2022 IEEE International Conf. on Multimedia and Expo, pp. 1–6 (2022)

22. Zhang, C., Li, G., Xu, Q., Zhang, X., Su, L., Huang, Q.: Weakly supervised anomaly detection in videos considering the openness of events. IEEE Trans. on Intel. Trans. Sys. **23**, 21687–21699 (2022)

23. Lv, H., et al.: Unbiased multiple instance learning for weakly supervised video anomaly detection. arXiv: 2303.12369 (2023)

24. Tain, Y., Pang, G., Singh, R., Verjans, J.W., Carneiro, G.: Weakly-supervised video anomaly detection with robust temporal feature magnitude learning. In: Proceedings of 2021 IEEE/CVF International Conf. on Computer Vision, pp. 4955–4966 (2021)

25. Wu, J.C., Hsieh, H.Y., Chen, D.J., Fuh, C.S., Liu, T.L.: Self-supervised sparse representation for video anomaly detection. In: Proceedings of 2022 European Conf. on Computer Vision, pp. 1–17 (2022)

26. Sapkota, H., Yu, Q.: Bayesian nonparametric submodular video partition for robust anomaly detection. In: Proceedings of 2022 IEEE/CVF Conf. on Computer Vision and Pattern Recognition, pp. 3202–3211 (2022)

27. Park, S., Kim, H., Kim, M., Kim, D., Sohn, K.: Normality guided multiple instance learning for weakly supervised video anomaly detection. In: Proceedings of 2023 IEEE/CVF Winter Conf. on Applications of Computer Vision, pp. 2664–2673 (2023)

28. Zhang, D., Huang, C., Liu, C., Xu, Y.: Weakly supervised video anomaly detection via transformer-enabled temporal relation learning. IEEE Signal Process. Lett. **29**, 1197–1201 (2022)

29. Yu, S., Wang, C., Xiang, L., Wu, J.: TCA-VAD: temporal context alignment network for weakly supervised video anomly detection. In: Proceedings of 2022 IEEE International Conf. on Multimedia and Expo, pp. 1–6 (2022)

30. Tan, W., Yao, Q., Liu, J.: Overlooked video classification in weakly supervised video anomaly detection. arXiv: 2210.06688 (2022)

31. Deshpande, K., Punn, N.S., Sonbhadra, S.K., Agarwal, S.: Anomaly detection in surveillance videos using transformer based attention model. arXiv: 2206.01524 (2022)

32. Liu, T., Zhang, C., Lam, K.M., Kong, J.: Decouple and resolve: transformer-based models for online anomaly detection from weakly labeled videos. IEEE Trans. on Info. Forensics and Sec. **18**, 15–28 (2023)

33. Li, S., Liu, F., Jiao, L.: Self-training multi-sequence learning with transformer for weakly supervised video anomaly detection. In: Proceedings of 2022 36th AAAI Conf. on Artificial Intelligence, pp. 1395–1403 (2022)

34. Sun, S., Gong, X., Long-short temporal co-teaching for weakly supervised video anomaly detection. arXiv: 2303.18044 (2023)

35. Rossi, L., Bernuzzi, V., Fortanini, T., Bertozzi, M., Prati, A.: Memory-augmented online video anomaly detection. In: Proceedings of 2024 International Conf. on Acoustics, Speech, and Signal Processing, pp. 6590–6594 (2024)
36. Carreira, J., Zisserman, A.: Quo vadis, action recognition? a new model and the Kinetics dataset. In: Proceedings of 2017 IEEE/CVF Conf. on Computer Vision and Pattern Recognition pp. 4724–4733 (2017)
37. Nair, V., Hinton, G.E.: Rectified linear units improve restricted boltzmann machines. In: Proceedings of 2010 27th International Conf. on Machine Learning, pp. 807–814 (2010)
38. He, K., Zhang, X., Ren, S., Sun, J.: Delving deep into rectifiers: surpassing human-level performance on ImageNet classification. arXiv: 1502.01852 (2015)
39. Dubey, S.R., Singh, S.K., Chaudhuri, B.B.: Activation functions in deep learning: a comprehensive survey and benchmark. arXiv: 2109.14545 (2022)
40. Hendrycks, D., Gimpel, K.: GAUSSIAN error linear units (GELUS). arXiv: 1606.08415 (2023)
41. Vaswani, A., et al.: Attention is all you need. arXiv: 2203.13610 (2022)
42. Park, J., Kim, J., Han, B.: Learning to adapt to unseen abnormal activities under weak supervision. arXiv: 2203.13610 (2022)
43. Ba, J.L., Kiros, J.R., Hinton, G.E.: Layer normalization. arXiv: 1607.06450 (2016)
44. Ruder, S.: An overview of gradient descent optimization algorithms. arXiv: 1609.04747 (2017)
45. Duchi, J., Hazan, E., Singer, Y.: Adaptive subgradient methods for online learning and stochastic optimization. J. Machine Learn. Res. **12**, 2121–2159 (2011)
46. Kingma, D., Ba, J.: Adam: a method for stochastic optimization. In: Proceedings of 3rd International Conf. on Learning Representations, pp. 1–15 (2015)
47. Bradley, A.P.: The use of the area under the ROC curve in the evaluation of machine learning algorithms. Pattern Recogn. **30**(7), 1145–1159 (1997)

Contour Detection of Seeds Based on Traditional and Convolutional Neural Network (CNN) Based Algorithms

Kai Zhao and Mitchell L. Neilsen$^{(\boxtimes)}$ 🔟

Department of Computer Science, Kansas State University, Manhattan, KS 66505, USA
{Kzhao,neilsen}@ksu.edu

Abstract. Computer vision algorithms are becoming more widely used in the agricultural domain. Edge detection algorithms are used to detect plant or seed contours. These contours identify regions of interest and delimit the size of plants or seeds from a single perspective. By combining contours from different angles, other plant phenotypes, such as volume, can be computed. This paper delves into the potential of edge detection, specifically contour detection, in the domain of seed phenotyping. Contour detection is significantly influenced by image quality, with color saturation due to ambient light and background color playing important roles. This paper expands traditional contour detection algorithms to address their limitations and improve their accuracy. Images are captured using different physical characteristics and image backgrounds. A consistent background color allows for more contrast with the seeds being analyzed. This paper compares various traditional detection methods with convolutional neural network (CNN) detection methods. The analysis aims to highlight the strengths and weaknesses of each technique, offering valuable insights for seed researchers because contour detection is essential in supporting non-destructive measurement of seed volume. This volume can be used to compute the density of irregularly-shaped seeds.

Keywords: Computer vision · contour detection · convolutional neural network · phenotyping · seed analysis

1 Introduction

Applications in plant breeding programs require precise estimation of morphometric characteristics, often referred to as phenotypes, for various agricultural entities such as seeds, leaves, and fruits. This estimation establishes connections between morphology and plant behavior or traits. Seed volume and density are crucial morphological traits that greatly aid phenotyping endeavors. Accurate seed volume and density estimation significantly contribute to our understanding of plant genetics, breeding, and related research. While seed mass can be easily measured using an accurate scale, the irregular shapes of seeds pose a considerable challenge in accurately estimating their volume. Seed volume is relevant in seed ecology and functional traits studies. In integrating ecological and functional aspects of seed size distributions, especially in soil seed bank studies,

© The Author(s), under exclusive license to Springer Nature Switzerland AG 2025
L. Deligiannidis et al. (Eds.): CSCE 2024, CCIS 2262, pp. 216–227, 2025.
https://doi.org/10.1007/978-3-031-85933-5_15

sorting seeds by size is common. Traditional methods involving sieving, however, have limitations as they sort seeds based on linear dimensions rather than their actual volume. These methods are both labor-intensive and time-consuming, and they can potentially damage the seeds.

Roussel, Geiger, Fischbach, Jahnke, and Scharr [1] presented a methodology for 3D reconstruction of plant seed surfaces, including those with diameters as small as 200 µm. They employed the shape-from-silhouette approach in their study. The automated system has a relatively low throughput as it processes one seed at a time. However, a noteworthy contribution of this work is its effective management of variations in camera pose. Cao and Neilsen [2] expanded Roussel's research by introducing an affordable 3D measurement system for individual seed volumes. Their methodology involved using 3D-printed components to create a framework for mounting the camera. Seeds are placed on a rotating platform against a black background. Cameras capture sequential images of the rotating seed, and volume estimation is performed using silhouette-based sculpting. To validate the system, comparisons are made with a ceramic ball of a known size. The system's estimated volume showed a difference of less than 3% compared to the actual volume. Zhao, Margapuri, and Neilsen [3] further enhanced the hardware and software and conducted experiments with soybean and wheat seeds, comparing different slicing methods. This study reinforced the effectiveness of the 3D reconstruction method and the importance of contour detection, which is essential in supporting non-destructive measuring of the volume of irregularly-shaped seeds. Once contours are computed from known positions, space volume carving algorithms can be used to efficiently compute the volume of the seed as shown by Neilsen and Zhao [4].

Image edge detection has attracted widespread attention from researchers since its inception. Figure 1 outlines the evolution of edge detection algorithms [5]. Contour detection is a type of edge detection and a basic task in the fields of image processing and computer vision. It covers the identification of object boundaries within images, a key process with a wide range of applications, including object recognition, shape analysis, and image segmentation. A large amount of research has focused on image edge detection, especially in the fields of face recognition and autonomous driving. However, in the agricultural domain, especially for seed phenotyping, it has not been extensively explored. This paper aims to fill this gap by providing a brief overview of image contour detection research focusing on seeds in the agricultural domain. Contour detection is significantly influenced by image quality, with color saturation due to ambient light and the background color playing a crucial role. This paper tests various traditional detection methods under different background colors and compares them with CNN detection methods with a consistent background color.

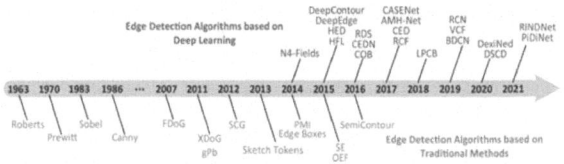

Fig. 1. Evolution of edge detection algorithms [5].

2 Materials and Methods

All experiments use an industrial camera, the ImagingSource IC DFK 37BUX287, a 720 pixel by 540 pixel color camera, to capture images. This camera features a highly sensitive, low-noise Sony Pregius global shutter sensor. Additionally, the setup includes consistent lighting with two 6500 K LEDs supplied by AmScope, a black- or blue-colored background board, and an LED-lighted background.

2.1 Traditional Contour Detection on Single Seed

It is recognized that seeds vary significantly in terms of shapes and colors, even within the same species. This inherent diversity poses a challenge in image analysis. Achieving a clear seed outline necessitates separating each seed from its background environment. When capturing images, a well-adjusted LED with suitable brightness effectively highlights the seed outline while preventing excessive darkness at the bottom where the seed connects to a holder. Striking the right balance in brightness is crucial, as excessive brightness can enlarge the seed's contour and affect contour detection due to surface reflections. On the other hand, very low brightness may make the contour smaller.

Black-Colored Background and Front LED Light

Cao and Neilsen's [2] research utilized the HSV [6] (Hue, Saturation, Value) color space for contour detection, and it required precise control of LED lighting due to the varying reflective effects caused by different seed types and colors. The experiments mainly focused on wheat, corn, and soybean seeds, which have similar yellow-green hues and surface smoothness. In these experiments, a black background is used, and the LED lighting is only positioned in front of the seed. This setup creates a strong contrast between the seeds and the black background, minimizing the impact of weak black reflections in the detection process. Consequently, using fixed HSV values yields satisfactory results, with the difference between the experimental outcomes and the actual volume being less than 3%.

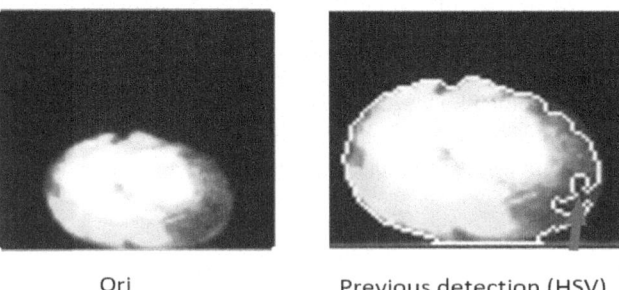

Ori   Previous detection (HSV)

Fig. 2. Original image and HSV contour result.

However, this approach is not suitable for experiments involving other types of seeds, such as milo seeds, which range in size from 3 mm to 6 mm and exhibit colors spanning from white to black, with some light seeds having black regions or spots. Figure 2 provides an illustrative example. In the original image, black spots are visible on the surface of milo seeds. When applying HSV for contour detection within the original black background, challenges arose because the black part of the seed surface merged with the black background, resulting in imperfections in the obtained contour. Even when considering alternative edge detection methods, such as Canny edge detection [7], the distinctive characteristics of milo seeds require a customized approach.

Blue-Colored Background and Front LED Light
The main issue arises from the black spots on the seeds closely resembling the color of the background, prompting the adoption of a blue background. Consequently, we also transition from a fixed HSV color range-based detection method to an automated binary color threshold approach. Unlike a fixed light intensity value, the binary color threshold parameters are automatically computed. This adjustment allows for a more extensive processing range, accommodating seeds of various colors, even when their reflection affects the image.

In contrast to the original method, where contour detection is based on a fixed seed color, the binary color threshold method considers the background color for contour detection. This proves advantageous as it maintains a consistent background color (blue in our case) regardless of the seed color. The binary color threshold method offers a more versatile and standardized approach, especially when dealing with seeds of diverse colors, as shown in Fig. 3. Furthermore, we can extract the color values of the seeds themselves, thereby offering additional research data for seed researchers.

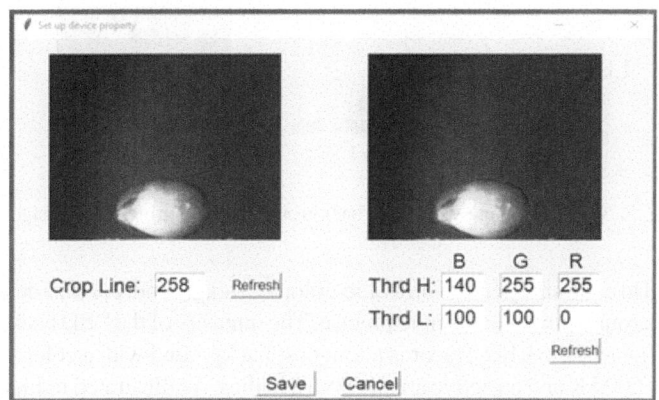

Fig. 3. Contour detected with a binary color threshold.

Figure 4 compares contour detection and the conversion into binary mask images of the same seed under varying color backgrounds. The mask image on the blue background yields more favorable results, although some edge parts will still experience distortion due to the interplay of seed and background colors.

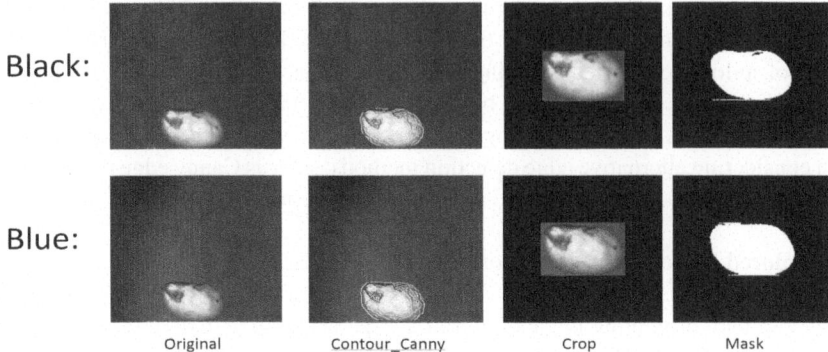

Fig. 4. Comparison of black and blue backgrounds.

LED Background with no Front LED Light

Given our primary objective of obtaining seed outlines rather than focusing on the seed's color, we propose a novel LED background board. This innovative approach involves deactivating the previous two front LED lights and installing an LED background board. The light is directed from behind the seeds towards the camera. Consequently, regardless of the seed color, the black region in the image corresponds to the seed or holder area, while the rest represents the background color. This setup entirely eradicates the impact of the seed's inherent color on contour detection, as shown in Fig. 5.

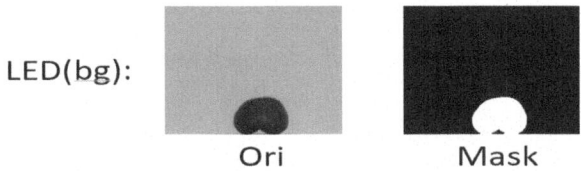

Fig. 5. Original image with LED background and resulting mask image.

Compared to contour detection on a blue-colored background, contour detection with the LED background proves to be more precise. The intensity of the LED background can be adjusted. The ME456 LED Tracer is a low-cost background with a color temperature of 10,000 to 12,000 K and an active area of 9 x 12 inches. As illustrated in Fig. 6, contour detection with a blue-colored background exhibits inaccuracies, particularly evident in the detection indicated by the red arrow.

To validate the testing accuracy of the LED background, multiple tests are conducted on seven reference objects with varying sizes and shapes, as illustrated in Fig. 7. Each reference object underwent testing ten times, and the results are averaged.

The outcome is presented in Table 1, which distinctly reveals that the difference between the test results obtained through the 3D method and the actual volume is less than 3%. Upon closer inspection, we noted that the cylinder and cubes, shown on the right in Fig. 7, have rounded edges. The reference volumes were computed assuming no

Blue(bg):

LED(bg):

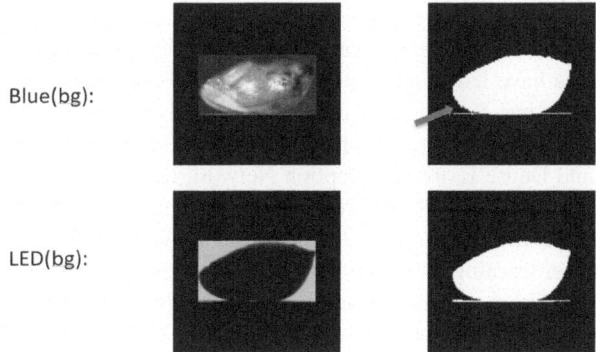

Fig. 6. Comparison between blue-colored background and LED background.

Fig. 7. Steel reference objects.

rounding. So, once we accounted for that, the actual average error was less than 3% -- values computed without considering rounding are shown below in Fig. 8. In all cases, the actual error is less than 3%.

Table 1. Reference test with LED background.

Type	Micrometer (mm^3) Vol	3D (mm^3) Vol	Comparison of Vol (3D VS Micro)			
			Diff	Ave. Error	Min. Error	Max. Error
Ball_sm	32.76	31.95	−0.81	−2.5%	−2.2%	−2.8%
Ball_md	56.12	54.52	−1.59	−2.8%	−2.6%	−3.3%
Ball_lg	65.06	63.08	−1.97	−3.0%	−2.9%	−3.3%
Cone	12.12	11.95	−0.17	−1.4%	−1.3%	−1.6%
Cylinder	112.7	108.8	−3.88	−3.4%	−2.9%	−4.0%
Cube_sm	26.55	25.58	−0.97	−3.7%	−2.7%	−4.7%
Cube_lg	129.4	125.4	−4.08	−3.2%	−2.7%	−4.1%

2.2 CNN Based Contour Detection

In recent years, the integration and advancement of artificial intelligence and machine learning algorithms have led to a proliferation of image edge detection algorithms in digital image processing. Several edge detection methods utilizing deep learning have emerged. This paper primarily focuses on two methods: Holistically-nested Edge Detection (HED) [8] and Dense Extreme Inception Network for Edge Detection (DexiNed) [9], both of which are multi-scale feature fusion-based approaches.

HED was created in 2015, using the state-of-the-art VGG-16 [10] as the backbone network and transfer learning to initialize the network weights. The term "holistically" signifies that the algorithm endeavors to train an image-to-image network, while "nested" underscores the process of iteratively refining the edge prediction map for enhanced accuracy during the output generation. This approach aims to overcome the limitations of Canny edge detectors by leveraging end-to-end deep neural networks. The network receives an RGB image as input and produces an edge map as the output. Notably, the edge maps generated by HED demonstrate superior preservation of object boundaries within the image.

Dense Extreme Inception Network for Edge Detection (DexiNed) represents a significant new deep learning model designed to produce thin edge maps resembling the human eye's perception. This model is versatile and well-suited for various edge detection tasks, requiring no extensive training or fine-tuning. DexiNed is an advancement built upon the foundations of both HED and Xception [11].

To validate the applicability of these models in seed contour detection, this project implements both the HED and DexiNed models. To evaluate the potential impact of lighting conditions on the model, we capture images in both bright and dark environments for comparative analysis. Additionally, to assess the influence of background color on the model, we compare images taken with a blue background to those taken with an LED background. The results, Figs. 9 and 10, clearly demonstrate that both lighting and background color have an almost negligible impact on the performance of the models.

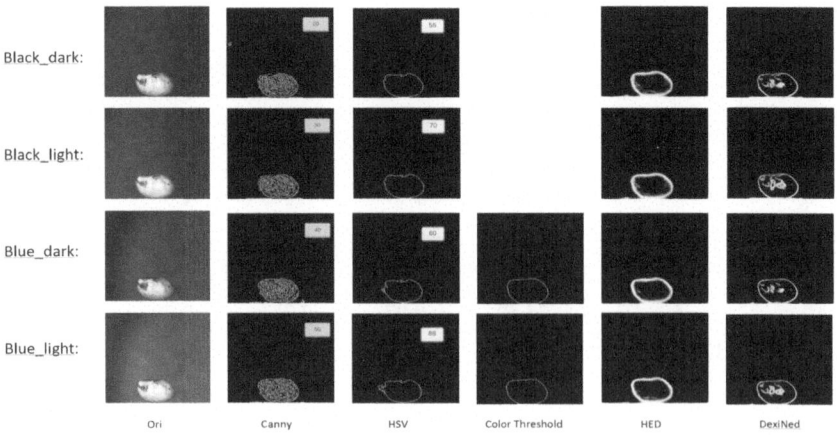

Fig. 9. Original images and results using different methods.

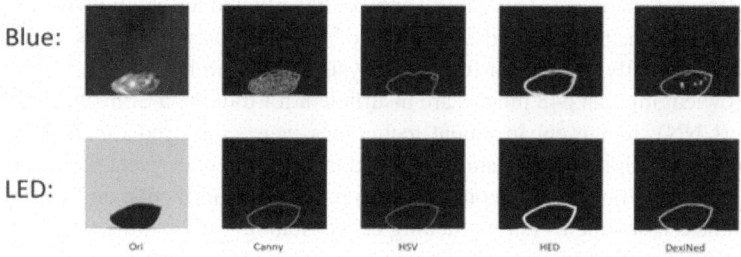

Fig. 10. Results with blue and LED backgrounds.

Both methods are primarily designed for edge detection, and the quality of their results can vary based on the training dataset. Overall, their performance is quite satisfactory. It's worth noting that DexiNed, which utilizes a custom dataset, demonstrates even better results, as shown in Table 2.

To optimize the utilization of DexiNed, we developed an extensive new seed image database, and we use this database to train a custom model tailored to our specific needs. This approach ensures that the model is fine-tuned to meet our requirements and enhances its performance in addressing our unique challenges. By leveraging our proprietary database for training, we aim to maximize the effectiveness and relevance of the DexiNed model in our specific context.

Agricultural seed researchers have categorized milo into four size classifications: small, small-medium, large, and extra-large, and further distinguished them based on color—white and black (specifically, dark green with black spots). To comprehensively capture the size and color variations, a total of sixteen seeds were selected, representing all combinations of sizes and color categories. For each seed, 36 photos were taken, incorporating upside-down flips of each surrounding, resulting in a total of 1152 photos.

Table 2. Comparison of different methods

Dataset	Method	ODS	OIS	AP	Size (MB)	Time (sec.)
MDBD	HED	0.851	0.864	0.890	55	0.46
	DexiNed	0.859	0.864	0.917	138	0.25
BSDS 500	HED	0.790	0.808	0.811	55	0.46
	DexiNed	0.729	0.745	0.689	138	0.25
BIPED	HED	0.829	0.847	0.869	55	0.46
	DexiNed	0.859	0.967	0.905	138	0.25

Contour detection was then applied to these images, which were all set against a blue background plate using the color threshold method. Manual parameter adjustments were meticulously performed to fine-tune the detection process, considering the unique characteristics of each seed. This careful approach facilitated the creation of corresponding ground truth images. Out of the initial set of 1152 photos, 648 images were deemed suitable and carefully curated for further analysis and research.

Acknowledging that 648 images are insufficient for training a Convolutional Neural Network (CNN), image enhancement techniques were employed for image set augmentation. Each original image and its ground truth image underwent various transformations, including random horizontal inversion, rotation, horizontal and vertical shifting, brightness adjustments (strengthening or weakening), and scaling (as illustrated in Fig. 11). This augmentation process resulted in a set of 21 corresponding images for each original image. Consequently, a total of 13,608 image sets were generated. For training purposes, 80% of these sets were randomly selected and designated as the training dataset. This comprehensive methodology ensures a robust dataset for training and enhances the model's ability to generalize across diverse seed variations.

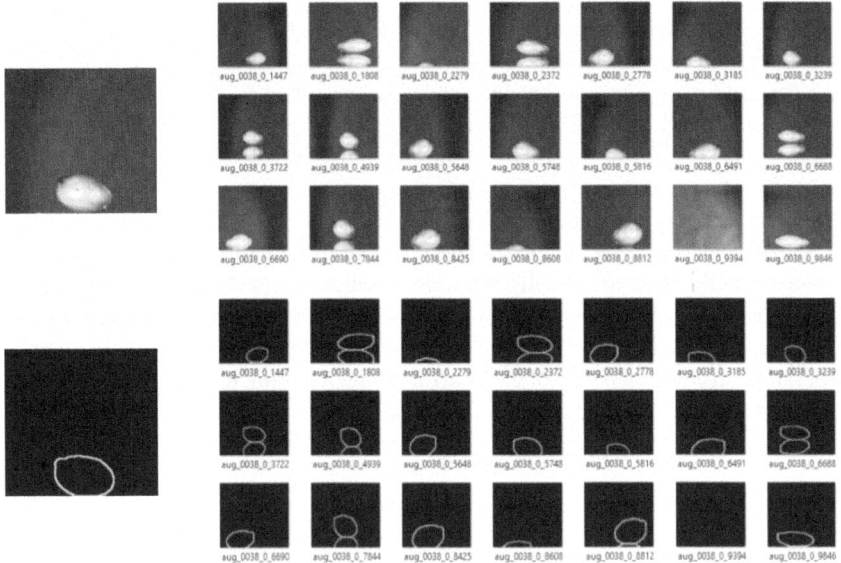

Fig. 11. Single sample and augmented images with ground truth.

After 30 epochs of training, the new model successfully met our expected objective. The output of the model exhibits a desirable outcome, where only the contour lines are retained. Moreover, these contour lines are exceptionally thin and exhibit no disconnections, closely aligning with the characteristics of the ground truth images. As shown in Fig. 12.

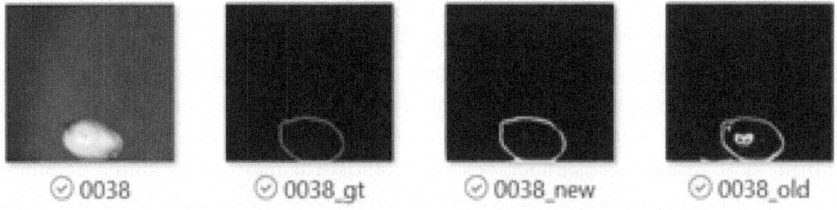

⊘ 0038   ⊘ 0038_gt   ⊘ 0038_new   ⊘ 0038_old

Fig. 12. From left to right: original image, ground truth image, test result using DexiNed with new training dataset, test result using DexiNed with old training dataset.

3 Results and Discussion

Our experiment starts from the basic configuration, improves it step by step, and explores the causes (cons) and effects (accuracy level) of each improvement step as shown in Table 3.

Table 3. Summary of each contour detection approach.

Methods	Disadvantages	RunTime (s)	Note
Sobel Filter	Running time and accuracy	3.686	1
Canny	Accuracy - contour may not be closed	0.003	1
HSV Black	Accuracy – dark parts of seed missed	0.003	1
HSV Blue	Accuracy depends on LED intensity	0.003	1
HSV LED	Color of seed is not accurate	0.003	3
Color Threshold	Time to compute contour	0.013	2
CNN	Time to compute contour	0.46/0.25 HED/DexiNED	3

Note: The accuracy and overhead of contour detection is divided into three levels:

- Level 1: Low-level accuracy and users must adjust some parameters manually.
- Level 2: High-level accuracy, but users must adjust some parameters manually; or median accuracy without adjusting any parameters manually.
- Level 3: High-level accuracy without users adjusting any parameters manually.

For the description of accuracy in each level: If the edge of any image is broken or significantly deviated, it is considered low-level accuracy. At the other extreme, when comparing one image group (36 images per seed), all edge images must be close to the original image, with an error of 1 pixel allowed, which is considered high-level accuracy. When comparing one image group, the probability that the edge image fits the original image does not reach 90%, which is the median level.

The seed contour detection technology utilizing LED as the background provides robust support for 3D reconstruction technology, facilitating the measurement of seed volumes. Although this method is characterized by low throughput, it boasts a rapid detection speed of 0.013 s per image. The 3D reconstruction technology serves as a validation tool for high-throughput measurement methods. Following the assessment of a large batch of seeds, this technology allows for the random selection of dozens of seeds, which are then precisely measured using 3D reconstruction. The acquired data from these sample seeds undergoes a new statistical analysis, including parameters such as variance, difference value, effective interval, etc. Subsequently, a linear relational expression is derived from the analysis results. This expression is then applied to high-throughput measurement methods, contributing to an enhancement in measurement accuracy. Essentially, the 3D reconstruction technology acts as a verification step, allowing for refinement and calibration of high-throughput methods through a targeted analysis of a subset of seeds.

4 Conclusions and Future Work

There is little room for improvement over the traditional method itself, but this project was able to use an extended DexiNed model to achieve some significant improvement with only a small overhead. Further increasing the resolution of the camera only improves the accuracy a small amount. Traditional contour detection is sufficient for most seeds and has high accuracy and fast detection speed, especially with the LED background method. However, if seed researchers also need to know the color of the seeds, then methods that use Convolutional Neural Networks (CNNs) provide an advantage.

While the CNN models, HED and DexiNed, demonstrate impressive capabilities, they still require refinement when applied to a specific seed contour detection task. HED excels in detecting contours with minimal noise inside, but tends to generate overly thick and blurry contours, impacting accuracy. In contrast, DexiNed produces thin and clear contour lines but may result in some discontinuous contours and exhibit higher noise levels within them. These limitations are likely due to the models' training datasets, which are primarily focused on edge detection rather than contour detection. Additionally, both models suffer from large model sizes. Our seed contour images are relatively simple. To address this, we intend to develop a smaller model that retains the essential characteristics of the HED and DexiNed models, but is tailored specifically for seed contour detection. However, the new models described in this paper are very adequate to efficiently compute the contours of single seeds and can be easily incorporated into efficient space carving algorithms to compute seed volume [4].

Acknowledgments. We greatly acknowledge the contributions of seed and discussion with colleagues at the USDA. This work was supported by the United States Department of Agriculture (USDA) National Institute of Food and Agriculture (NIFA), Award Number 2023-67021-40614. Any opinions, findings, and conclusions, or recommendations expressed in this material are those of the author(s) and do not necessarily reflect the views of the USDA NIFA.

References

1. Roussel, J., et al.: 3D surface reconstruction of plant seeds by volume carving: performance and accuracies. Front. Plant Sci. **7**, 745 (2016)

2. Cao, C., Neilsen, M.: Efficient seed volume measurement framework. In: Proc. of the 2020 International Conference on Computational Science and Computational Intelligence (CSCI), pp. 1328–1334 (2020)
3. Zhao, K., Margapuri, V., Neilsen, M.: Automated phenotyping of single seeds using a novel volume sculpting framework. ASABE Annual International Conference. Paper Number 2200403, Houston, TX, July 17–20 (2022)
4. Neilsen, M., Zhao, K.: Multi-threaded space carving for 3-D seed reconstruction. Proceedings of the 29th International Conference on Parallel and Distributed Processing Techniques and Applications, Paper No. 3021, July 23–27 (2023)
5. Sun, R., et al.: Survey of image edge detection. Frontiers in Signal Processing. $9(2)$, 826967 (2022)
6. Hue, S.: Value Color Space. https://en.wikipedia.org/wiki/HSL_and_HSVen
7. Canny, J.: A computational approach to edge detection. IEEE Trans. Pattern Anal. Mach. Intell. $8(6)$, 679–698 (1986)
8. Xie, S., Tu, Z.: Holistically-Nested Edge Detection. ArXiv. /abs/1504.06375 (2015)
9. Soria, X., Sappa, A., Humanante, P., Akbarinia, A.: Dense Extreme Inception Network for Edge Detection. ArXiv (2023). https://doi.org/10.1016/j.patcog.2023.109461
10. Simonyan, K., Zisserman, A.: Very Deep Convolutional Networks for Large-Scale Image Recognition. ArXiv./abs/1409.1556 (2014)
11. Chollet, F.: Xception: Deep Learning with Depthwise Separable Convolutions. ArXiv./abs/1610.02357 (2016)

Early Detection of Lameness in Dairy Cattle Using Activity Data, Image Analysis, AI and ML - An Approach for Improved Animal Welfare and Economic Impact

Chandrasekar Vuppalapati[1]([✉]), Anitha Ilapakurti[2], Sandhya Vissapragada[2], Sriya Vuppalapati[2], Sharat Kedari[2], Santosh Kedari[2], and Jaya Vuppalapati[2]

[1] Computer Engineering (CMPE Department), San Jose State University, San Jose, USA
chandrasekar.vuppalapati@sjsu.edu
[2] Hanumayamma Innovations and Technologies, Inc, Fremont, USA
{ailapakurti,svissapragada,sriya,sharath,skedari,
jaya.vuppalapati}@hanuinnotech.com

Abstract. The economic burden of lameness in dairy cattle is a significant challenge facing the worldwide dairy industry. Studies suggest that it can cost the industry billions of dollars annually, with the exact cost varying by region. In the United States, the cost of lameness is estimated to be approximately \$2 billion per year, while in the United Kingdom, it is around £200 million per year. These costs include lost milk production, decreased fertility, and treatment expenses. The impact of lameness on dairy cattle is far-reaching, posing a significant economic burden on farmers and countries and affecting animal welfare, milk production, and farm profitability. It is particularly concerning for small and marginal farmers, who are vulnerable to economic and financial sustainability concerns.

Early detection and prevention of lameness are crucial to reducing these costs and improving the overall health and productivity of dairy herds. Prevalence rates vary globally, ranging from 17% to 35% in dairy herds, underscoring the urgent need for innovative solutions.

Our proposed paper offers a novel approach to addressing this challenge. By combining activity data captured by Cow Necklace IoT Sensor and image analysis with Computer Vision, alongside expert veterinarian input, we provide a comprehensive and data-driven solution for early lameness detection in dairy cattle. This approach has the potential to significantly improve animal welfare, farm management practices, and overall herd productivity, leading to substantial economic benefits for farmers and the agricultural sector as a whole.

Keywords: Computer Vision · Cow Necklace Sensor · Lameness · Economic and financial sustainability

1 Introduction

Lameness is a serious concern for cattle farmers as it causes significant suffering for the animals, weakening their physical condition and reducing their productivity. From a scientific perspective, the financial impact of lameness cannot be overstated, as it results

L. Deligiannidis et al. (Eds.): CSCE 2024, CCIS 2262, pp. 228–239, 2025.
https://doi.org/10.1007/978-3-031-85933-5_16

in a range of losses including reduced production, increased treatment expenses, longer calving intervals, and the need for extra labor.

In addition to these factors, it's important to consider the impact of pain on milk production. Studies have shown that cows with lameness produce up to 1.7–3 L less milk per day for up to one month before and after treatment. Furthermore, the use of antibiotic therapy during treatment can also result in wasted milk, further exacerbating the financial impact of the condition.

The economic burden of lameness [1] in dairy cattle is a daunting challenge[1] that continues to pose significant obstacles for the worldwide dairy industry. Recent studies have revealed that this issue can cost the industry billions of dollars annually, with the precise figures varying by region. In the United States alone, the cost of lameness is estimated to be a staggering $2 billion per year, while in the United Kingdom, it is around £200 million per year.

These costs are attributed to a variety of factors, including lost milk production, decreased fertility, and the expenses associated with treatment. However, the impact of lameness extends far beyond financial implications. This condition also poses a significant threat to animal welfare, milk production, and farm profitability [2].

Moreover, the impact of lameness is felt around the world[2], with the highest impact on small and marginal farmers who rely on milk production as their primary source of income. For these farmers, the economic and financial sustainability concerns are particularly concerning, as they struggle to maintain their livelihoods in the face of this daunting challenge.

In light of these challenges, it is essential that we continue to prioritize research and development in this area to address the multifaceted effects of lameness. By doing so, we can work towards improving animal welfare, enhancing milk production, and supporting farmers in their efforts to achieve economic sustainability.

With advancements in sensor technologies, we now have the opportunity to approach the issue of lameness in dairy cattle in a more data-driven and comprehensive way. By combining activity data analysis, image analysis with AI and ML, and potentially incorporating lameness scoring systems from veterinarians, we can develop a solution for early lameness detection in dairy cattle that is both efficient and effective.

This approach has the potential to make a significant impact on animal welfare, farm management practices, and overall herd productivity. By detecting lameness at an early stage, we can provide timely treatment and care to the affected animals, leading to improved welfare and health outcomes. Furthermore, by addressing the issue of lameness proactively, we can minimize its impact on milk production and fertility, ultimately leading to potential economic benefits for farmers and the agricultural sector as a whole.

The structure of this paper is presented as: Sect. 2 Data Capture by Sensor, Computer Vision Models, and Ensemble Machine Learning. Section 3 presents our dairy analytics service system by focusing on ML & computer vision models. Section 4 discusses

---

[1] Stop Creating Chronic Lameness – Detecting Lame Cows: Anytime and all the time - https://wcds.ualberta.ca/wcds/wp-content/uploads/sites/57/2018/05/p-321-332-Orsel-WCDS-2018-Chronic-Lameness-Detecting-Lame-Cows.pdf.

[2] Lameness in Dairy Cow Herds: Disease Aetiology, Prevention and Management - https://www.mdpi.com/2624-862X/3/1/16.

its related design and implementation decisions, and Sect. 5 shows a case study. The conclusion and future work are included in Sect. 6.

2 Understanding Computer Vision Models, Sensor Data and Machine Learning Models

2.1 Dairy IoT Edge Sensor

We have collected data from field installed Dairy IoT Sensors. In our case, we have used data from the Dairy IoT Sensor, consisting of Temperature-Humidity record, and Activity record, consisting of sensor movement records (please see Fig. 1 for Printed Circuit Board of the Sensor [5–9]). The use of AI and machine learning to monitor livestock health, including vital signs, daily activity levels, and food intake, is rapidly emerging as a prominent application in the agricultural sector [5]. One notable example of this technology is the Cow Necklace [10, 11], a Class 10 wearable veterinary sensor that captures a cow's vital signs, enabling farmers to monitor milk productivity and improve overall animal health. In this context, innovative companies that leverage AI and machine learning to monitor and optimize livestock health are poised to make a significant contribution to sustainability efforts. It is worth noting that such companies have already gained recognition for their excellence, with some securing Fast Company's Best Designs[3] of 2023 award, alongside other established honorees in this space.

The records are integrated with Clinical parameters to supplement Veterinarian decision processing (please see Fig. 8) [11, 12]. The data collected has following details (please see Fig. 2):

2.2 VGG16 Model

VGG16 is a convolutional neural network (CNN) model that was developed by the Visual Geometry Group (VGG) at the University of Oxford. It is a deep learning model that is widely used for image classification tasks, such as identifying objects in photographs [13].

The VGG16 model consists of 16 layers of convolutional and fully connected neural network layers. The first 13 layers are convolutional layers that extract features from the input image, while the last three layers are fully connected layers that classify the image.

---

[3] Fast Company is the world's leading business media brand, with an editorial focus on innovation in technology, leadership, world changing ideas, creativity, and design. Written for and about the most progressive business leaders, Fast Company inspires readers to think expansively, lead with purpose, embrace change, and shape the future of business.Launched in November 1995 by Alan Webber and Bill Taylor, two former Harvard Business Review editors, Fast Company magazine was founded on a single premise: A global revolution was changing business, and business was changing the world. Discarding the old rules of business, Fast Company set out to chronicle how changing companies create and compete, to highlight new business practices, and to showcase the teams and individuals who are inventing the future and reinventing business. https://www.fastcompany.com/about-us.

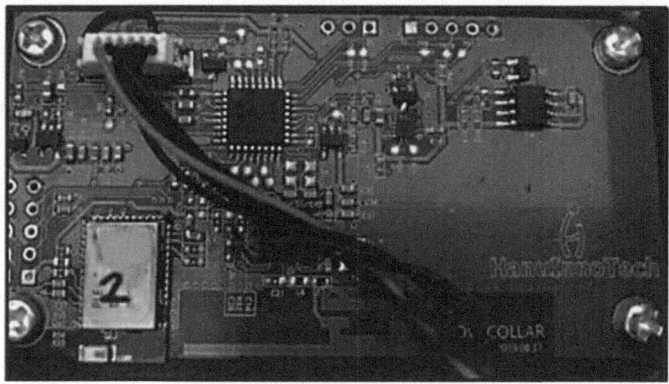

Fig. 1. Dairy Sensor Hardware

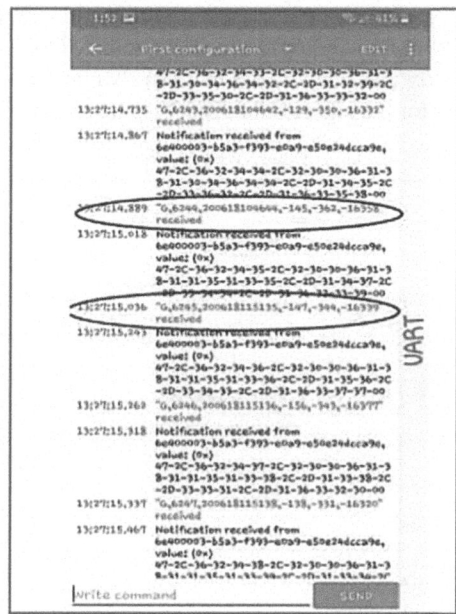

Fig. 2. Dairy Sensor Mobile Data

The convolutional layers in VGG16 have a fixed filter size of 3×3 pixels and use a stride of 1 pixel. The number of filters in each convolutional layer increases from 64 to 512 as we move deeper into the network. The pooling layers in the model use max pooling with a filter size of 2×2 pixels and a stride of 2 pixels.

2.3 Advanced Computer Vision Models

In this section, we will compare different algorithms that are used for various tasks such as image classification, object detection, and more. We will focus on the following algorithms: Mobilenetv2, ResNet18, ResNet34, ResNet50, ResNet101, ResNet152, ResNeSt50, ResNeSt101, SeResNeXt, ViT-S16-R224, ViT-B16-B224, and ViT-L16-B224. We will compare them based on their performance, architecture, and applications [13].

The performance of an algorithm can be measured by various metrics, such as accuracy, speed, memory, and scalability (please see Fig. 3). Accuracy refers to how well the algorithm can predict the correct output for a given input. Speed refers to how fast the algorithm can process the input and produce the output. Memory refers to how much space the algorithm requires to store the parameters and intermediate results. Scalability refers to how well the algorithm can handle large-scale data and complex tasks.

The following table summarizes the performance of the algorithms on the ImageNet dataset, which is a large-scale dataset for image classification with 1000 classes and 1.2 million images. The table shows the top-1 accuracy, which is the percentage of images that the algorithm correctly classified as the most likely class, and the inference time, which is the time it takes for the algorithm to process one image on a single GPU.

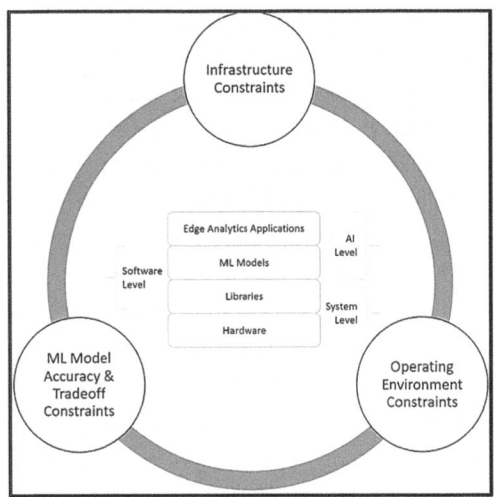

Fig. 3. ML Performance [3]

Algorithm	Top-1 Accuracy	Inference Time
Mobilenetv2	71.8%	2.6 ms
ResNet18	69.8%	5.6 ms
ResNet34	73.3%	8.1 ms

(continued)

(continued)

Algorithm	Top-1 Accuracy	Inference Time
SeResNeXt	80.9%	15.9 ms
ViT-S16-R224	77.9%	8.6 ms

From the table, we can see that the algorithms have different trade-offs between accuracy and speed. Generally, the more complex the algorithm, the higher the accuracy, but the slower [3] the speed (please see Fig. 1). For example, ResNet152 has the highest accuracy among the ResNet variants, but also the slowest inference time. On the other hand, Mobilenetv2 has the lowest accuracy among the algorithms, but also the fastest inference time.

We can also see that the algorithms have different memory requirements. The memory requirement of an algorithm depends on the number of parameters and the size of the input. The following table shows the number of parameters and the input size of the algorithms.

Algorithm	Number of Parameters	Input Size
Mobilenetv2	3.4 M	224 x 224
ResNet18	11.7 M	224 x 224
ResNet34	21.8 M	224 x 224
SeResNeXt	26.5 M	224 x 224
ViT-S16-R224	22.8 M	224 x 224

From the table, we can see that the algorithms have different memory requirements. Generally, the more parameters the algorithm has, the more memory it requires. For example, ViT-S16-R224 has the highest number of parameters among the algorithms, but also the highest memory requirement. On the other hand, Mobilenetv2 has the lowest number of parameters among the algorithms, but also the lowest memory requirement.

We can also see that the algorithms have different scalability. Scalability refers to how well the algorithm can handle large-scale data and complex tasks. Generally, the more scalable the algorithm, the better it can adapt to different domains and scenarios. For example, ViT variants are more scalable than ResNet variants, because they can use larger input sizes and deeper layers. On the other hand, Mobilenetv2 is less scalable than ResNet variants, because it has a fixed input size and a shallow layer.

These performances cannot be made possible in small sensor due to form factors constraints. So, calling service from the Mobile application or Web site would be better alternatives.

3   System Overview

The system calculates the activity of the sensor using Gyroscope and accelerometer data. It will access the drop in movement of activity as the sensor data collection process. The consistent drop of sensor data triggers a process for proactive onset of Lameness, although not confirmed until proven via image analysis that is asked small farmer to upload.

3.1 Sensor Activity Data

In the below Fig. 4, the drop in sensor data could be attributed to early signal of checking the onset of potential lameness unless proven via other datasets – in this case image datasets.

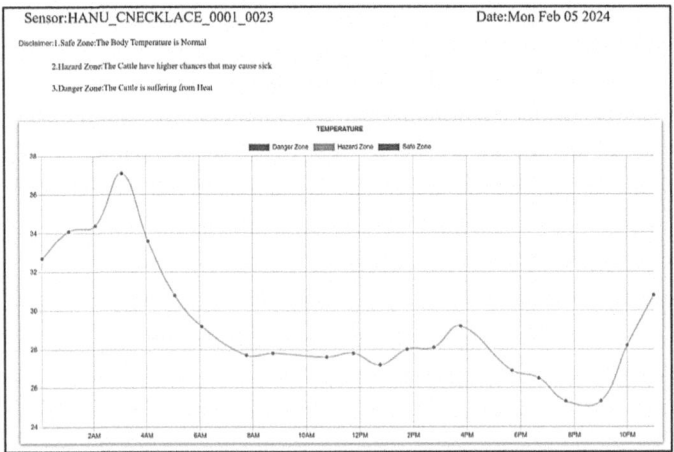

Fig. 4. Sensor Capture

3.2 Lamness Detection

Two ways to detect the drop in activity – via sensor activity as shown above. The second step is to identify the image data analysis. For that we have employed convolutional neural networks (CNN).

We have trained on the image data of cattle to assess the model and constructed neural setwork model.

```
train_batches = ImageDataGenerator(preprocessing_function=
tf.keras.applications.vgg16.preprocess_input)\
.flow_from_directory(directory = train_path, target_size= (224,224), classes =
['Lumpy', 'Normal'], batch_size = 10)
valid_batches = ImageDataGenerator(preprocessing_function=
tf.keras.applications.vgg16.preprocess_input)\
.flow_from_directory(directory = valid_path, target_size=(224,224), classes =
['Lumpy', 'Normal'], batch_size = 10)
test_batches = ImageDataGenerator(preprocessing_function=
tf.keras.applications.vgg16.preprocess_input)\
.flow_from_directory(directory = test_path, target_size= (224,224), classes =
['Lumpy', 'Normal'], batch_size = 10,shuffle= False)
```

We have separated image datasets into three paths: train, validate, and test.
Output: Please see Fig. 5.

Found 2000 images belonging to 2 classes.
Found 300 images belonging to 2 classes.
Found 128 images belonging to 2 classes.

4 System Design and Implementation

As part of the system design, the next step would be binning the budget statements with macroeconomic performance key indicators. Thereafter, apply mathematical model to develop predictability of budget statement & multilabel [6].

4.1 Clipping Input Images

We have implemented image processing that normalize inoput cattle images into the valid range for imsh(please see Fig. 5)ow with RGB data ([0..1] for floats or [0..255] for integers).

```
def graphImages(imageslist):
    fig, axes = plt.subplots(1,10, figsize = (20,20))
    axes = axes.flatten()
    for img , ax in zip(imageslist, axes):
        ax.imshow(img)
        ax.axis('off')
    plt.tight_layout()
    plt.show()
```

Output:
Clipping input data to the valid range for imshow with RGB data ([0..1] for floats or [0..255] for integers).
Clipping input data to the valid range for imshow with RGB data ([0..1] for floats or [0..255] for integers).

4.2 VGG16 Model

The fully connected layers in VGG16 are used for classification and consist of two hidden layers of 4,096 neurons each, followed by an output layer with 1,000 neurons that correspond to the possible classes in the ImageNet dataset.

One of the key features of VGG16 is its simplicity and ease of use, making it a popular choice for image classification tasks. However, it has a large number of parameters, making it relatively slow to train and requiring a lot of computational resources.

```
### VGG16 model

vgg16_model = tf.keras.applications.vgg16.VGG16()
type(vgg16_model)
```

Output: keras.engine.functional.Functional.

```
### VGG16 model

vgg16_model.summary()
```

Fig. 5. Clipped Image

Output:
Model: "vgg16"

Layer (type)	Output Shape	Param #
input_1 (InputLayer)	[(None, 224, 224, 3)]	0
block5_conv2 (Conv2D)	(None, 14, 14, 512)	2359808
block5_conv3 (Conv2D)	(None, 14, 14, 512)	2359808
block5_pool (MaxPooling2D)	(None, 7, 7, 512)	0
flatten (Flatten)	(None, 25088)	0
fc1 (Dense)	(None, 4096)	102764544
fc2 (Dense)	(None, 4096)	16781312
predictions (Dense)	(None, 1000)	4097000

Total params: 138,357,544
Trainable params: 138,357,544
Non-trainable params: 0

4.3 Convert model to Sequential

Next step, convert the code to sequential (Table 1).

The statement layer.trainable = false is used in deep learning models to freeze the weights of a particular layer or set of layers during training.

When we set trainable = false, it means that the weights of that layer will remain fixed and unchanged during the training process. This is useful when we want to use a pre-trained model and fine-tune only a specific set of layers for a new task, while keeping the weights of the other layers fixed.

By freezing the weights of the earlier layers in a pre-trained model, we can prevent the gradients from being backpropagated through those layers during training, which can help to speed up training and reduce the likelihood of overfitting. Additionally, freezing the weights of these layers can help to preserve the learned features that are useful for our new task.

Overall, setting trainable = false is a useful technique for fine-tuning pre-trained models and can help to improve the accuracy and efficiency of deep learning models.

Table 1. Distribution Function Code

```
model = Sequential()

for layer in vgg16_model.layers[:-1]:

        model.add(layer)

model.summary()
```

```
for layer in model.layers:

  layer.trainable = False
```

```
model.add(Dense(units=2, activation = 'softmax'))
```

4.4 Prepare Model

```
model.compile(optimizer=          Adam(learning_rate=
0.0001),   loss  =  'categorical_crossentropy',  metrics=
['accuracy'])))
model.fit(x   =   train_batches,   validation_data   =
valid_batches, epochs = 10 , verbose =2)
```

Now, prepare the model using Adam optimizer.
Output:

```
Epoch 1/10

200/200 - 368s - loss: 0.5553 - accuracy: 0.7405 - val_loss: 0.4345 -
val_accuracy: 0.8300 - 368s/epoch - 2s/step

Epoch 2/10

200/200 - 324s - loss: 0.3359 - accuracy: 0.8545 - val_loss: 0.3830 -
val_accuracy: 0.8567 - 324s/epoch - 2s/step

Epoch 3/10

200/200 - 310s - loss: 0.2851 - accuracy: 0.8805 - val_loss: 0.3639 -
val_accuracy: 0.8533 - 310s/epoch - 2s/step

Epoch 4/10

200/200 - 311s - loss: 0.2556 - accuracy: 0.8930 - val_loss: 0.3531 -
val_accuracy: 0.8633 - 311s/epoch - 2s/step
```

Loss function exhibits a downward trend and accuracies increased on each epoch.

By leveraging the power of modern technology, we now have the ability to combine data from multiple sources to create a more comprehensive view of lameness in dairy cattle. By integrating data from sensors and image data sent from mobile phones, we can gain a more accurate understanding of the onset of this debilitating condition.

While sensor data [14] and image data alone may not provide a complete view of the condition, combining these semi-structured and unstructured datasets can provide a valuable diagnostic aid in the detection of lameness. With this information at their disposal, veterinarians can play a pivotal role in helping to improve the health of cattle and overall outcomes.

By working together with technology, we can help to create a more data-driven and informed approach to managing lameness in dairy cattle. With the potential to improve animal welfare, farm productivity, and economic sustainability, this approach holds immense promise for the future of the dairy industry.

5   A Case Study

We have tested and deployed ML Model for predicting Lameness to serve small farmers around the world on our Hanumayamma[4] Data Analytics Platform. Credits at the company to provide access to sensors and field representatives in Hyderabad, India and Kashmir, India.

6   Conclusion and Future Work

Small farmers are the backbone of the agricultural industry, and it is critical that they have access to the latest data tools to reduce their exposure to risks in farming and dairy production. In this context, this paper presents a novel and radical approach to integrating sensor data and image data to address the onset of lameness in dairy cattle proactively.

We firmly believe that technological innovations, such as computer vision, sensor data, machine learning, and artificial intelligence (AI), are the defenders of the last resort for small farmers. These cutting-edge tools can provide data science advancements that are crucial for improving the livelihood of small farmers in developing countries and across the world.

By embracing these advancements, we can help to empower small farmers with the knowledge and resources they need to make informed decisions about their farming practices and improve their economic sustainability. Ultimately, by working together with technology, we can help to secure the future of the agricultural industry and ensure that small farmers continue to thrive for generations to come.

---

[4] Hanumayamma Innovations and Technologies Inc. is a Delaware based Corporation founded in 2010. We are a U.S. based corporation with leading products in Agriculture Analytics, Dairy Analytics, Specialty Crops Sensors and Analytics, Wearable Veterinary Sensor (CLASS 10) for Animal Husbandry, and Data Analytics (DnA) platform made exclusively for Farmers worldwide. Our Analytics platform and Sensors help farmers around the world with practical suggestions on Yield Analytics, Sustainability, Extreme Weather, and Food Security.- https://www.hanuinnotech.com/.

References

1. Orsel, K.: Stop Creating Chronic Lameness – Detecting Lame Cows: Anytime and all the time (2018). https://wcds.ualberta.ca/wcds/wp-content/uploads/sites/57/2018/05/p-321-332-Orsel-WCDS-2018-Chronic-Lameness-Detecting-Lame-Cows.pdf. Access Date: 15 April 2024
2. Garvey, M.: Lameness in dairy cow herds: disease aetiology. Prevention and Manage. Dairy **3**, 199–210 (2022). https://doi.org/10.3390/dairy3010016
3. Vuppalapati, C.: Democratization of Artificial Intelligence for the Future of Humanity, 1st edition. CRC Press (2021). ISBN-13: 978-0367524098
4. Papastratis, I.: Comparison of Convolutional Neural Networks and Vision Transformers (ViTs) (2023). https://medium.com/@iliaspapastratis/comparison-of-convolutional-neural-networks-and-vision-transformers-vits-a8fc5486c5be. Access Date: 10 January 2024
5. Columbus, L.: 10 Ways AI Has The Potential To Improve Agriculture In 2021 (2021). 12:20pm EST, https://www.forbes.com/sites/louiscolumbus/2021/02/17/10-ways-ai-has-the-potential-to-improve-agriculture-in-2021/?sh=7f611e297f3b. Access Date: 10 March 2021
6. Vuppalapati, C., et al.: Democratization of AI, Albeit Constrained IoT Devices & Tiny ML, for Creating a Sustainable Food Future. In: 2020 3rd International Conference on Information and Computer Technologies (ICICT), pp. 525–530. San Jose, CA, USA (2020). https://doi.org/10.1109/ICICT50521.2020.00089
7. Vuppalapati, C., et al.: The role of combinatorial mathematical optimization and heuristics to improve small farmers to veterinarian access and to create a sustainable food future for the world. In: 2020 Fourth World Conference on Smart Trends in Systems, Security and Sustainability (WorldS4), pp. 214–221. London, UK (2020). https://doi.org/10.1109/WorldS450073.2020.9210339
8. Ilapakurti, A., Vuppalapati, C.: Building an IoT Framework for Connected Dairy. 2015 IEEE First International Conference on Big Data Computing Service and Applications, pp. 275–285. Redwood City, CA, USA (2015). https://doi.org/10.1109/BigDataService.2015.39
9. Ramalingam, A., Kedari, S., Vuppalapati, C.: IEEE FEMH Voice Data Challenge 2018. In: 2018 IEEE International Conference on Big Data (Big Data), pp. 5272–5276. Seattle, WA, USA (2018) https://doi.org/10.1109/BigData.2018.8622164
10. Vuppalapati, C.: Building Enterprise IoT Applications, 1st edition. CRC Press (2019). ISBN-13: 978-0367173852
11. Yang, X.-S., Sherratt, S., Dey, N., Joshi, A. (eds.) ICICT 2019, London, Volume 2, "Fourth International Congress on Information and Communication Technology", eBook ISBN 978-981-329-343-4 and Softcover ISBN 978-981-329-342-7
12. Luedeling, E., Zhang, M., Girvetz, E.H.: Climatic changes lead to declining winter chill for fruit and nut trees in California during 1950–2099 (2009). https://doi.org/10.1371/journal.pone.0006166. Access Date: 06 May 2023
13. Rothman, D.: Transformers for natural language processing and computer vision - third edition: explore generative ai and large language models with hugging face, ChatGPT, GPT-4V, and DALL-E 3, 3rd ed. Packt Publishing (2024). ISBN-13: 978-1805128724
14. Vuppalapati, C.: Building Enterprise IoT Applications, 1st edition. CRC Press (2019). ISBN-13:978-0367173852

Implications for Designing Hawks Detection with Data Augmentation and Network Optimizations

Adam Smith, Judah Small, and Byeong Kil Lee[✉] [iD]

University of Colorado, Colorado Springs (UCCS), Colorado Springs, CO 80918, USA
blee@uccs.edu

Abstract. In the agricultural environment, hawks and other birds of prey that are hunting livestock (e.g., chickens) are critical issues. To address the problems with pasture-raised livestock, the detection mechanism of predators is essential. We focus on hawks as major predators, but the availability of hawks' dataset is very limited. In this paper, we attempt to generate more datasets using data augmentation techniques with several parameters. We also design deep-learning networks that can effectively detect airborne predators to protect livestock. The network has been optimized to improve its performance. We analyze the experimental results and provide implications. The detection scheme can be utilized in the chicken industry to allow corporations to increase animal welfare by raising chickens in an outdoor pasture environment.

Keywords: Deep Learning · Image Classification · Agricultural Hawk Detection · Data Augmentation

1 Introduction

There have been several machine learning models and applications designed to be used in agricultural settings. One major application is pest detection over fields and orchards. Another application is the detection of predators relative to an agricultural livestock living area. Currently, a solution to the predator problem is to hold livestock in an indoor environment year-round. With rising ethical concerns surrounding animal welfare, this solution needs to be reconsidered.

In the agricultural community, it was found that hawks are not only a problem for larger corporations desiring to pasture-raise chickens but also for the common homesteader. One example is a community member who lost 87% of their chicken flock in a single season due to hawks and other airborne predators. For large corporations attempting to profit from the chicken industry, this loss is not acceptable, and as such the transition to pasture raising chickens is difficult. This difficulty presents us with an opportunity to solve the problem at hand and allow companies to have a smoother transition to pasture-raising chickens. However, the availability of hawk's dataset is very limited. In this paper, we attempt to generate more datasets using data augmentation

L. Deligiannidis et al. (Eds.): CSCE 2024, CCIS 2262, pp. 240–248, 2025.
https://doi.org/10.1007/978-3-031-85933-5_17

techniques and use deep learning to create a model that can detect airborne predators (e.g., raptors, and hawks) to protect livestock (e.g., chickens).

The remainder of this paper is structured as follows. Section 2 discusses the dataset including data augmentation and data preprocessing. Section 3 presents the architecture of deep learning networks and optimizations to improve detection performance. Experimental results and analysis are described in Section 4, and Section 5 presents the conclusion and possible future work for further improvement.

2 Data Augmentation and Data Preprocessing

Based on our exploration, we found two major datasets. One of them is the California Institute of Technology's "Caltech-UCSD Birds-200-2011" dataset [1]. This dataset is composed of 11,788 total images split across 200 categories. However, upon further investigation, this dataset was found to lack images related to hawks. As such this data set is not considered for our experiments. Another dataset is Cornell University's "NABirds V1" dataset [2], which is composed of 48,000 images split across 400 categories. Upon investigation, this dataset has 17 categories of hawks totaling 533 images relating to hawks. We decided to utilize this dataset and use every hawk image in the set regardless of species. For the non-hawk images, we randomly picked the same number of non-hawk images from the remaining categories not used (533 images). In total, we acquired 1,066 images to use for the experiments. Due to this randomness, birds that are never in the same environment as hawks were also in the data set which is not ideal.

After extracting images from the dataset and learning that there were only 533 images of hawks, we decided that more data was necessary. Since we could not gather custom data, the approach to acquire more data was to use image augmentation on the images gathered [3, 4]. To continue with this approach, we used the Keras ImageDataGenerator which can be found in the Keras library. This image generator can create several different augmented images from one given original image. The output of the generator depends on the parameters (e.g., rotation, zoom, etc.) set in Table 1. Examples of original images and their augmentations are shown in Figures 1, 2 and 3. The parameters we used to generate unique images that remained realistic. It was found that using high values for the chosen parameters resulted in unrealistic images that would not apply to the problem being attempted to solve in this research. On the other hand, using parameters too small would result in data that was incredibly similar to the data already required. These similarities would essentially cause the same image to be present multiple times in the data set used to train and test the model. The same augmentation was done to the corresponding non-hawk data set. It resulted in a total of 3,198 hawk images and 3,198 non-hawk images totaling 6,396 images.

The images from both the original dataset and image augmentation varied in size. This is due to the nature of the original data set. Based on our observation, the original set was composed of high-quality professional images, but some of these images also include texts relating to the photographer's name, business, time taken, location taken, etc. The images in the data set were also very inconsistent in the zoom level and placement of the object of interest. In some images, the hawk is very far away from the camera, but in others, the hawk is very close to the camera. These inconsistencies are expected to negatively impact the model, but deep learning networks can handle this issue through training.

Since the input layer of a deep learning model must be a set shape, the images in a training data set must be all the same size. All the input images are resized in both the hawk and non-hawk datasets to the smallest image size. We used the image size, 304 × 321.

Table 1. Parameters of Image Generator

Parameters	Value Examples
rotation_range	15
width_shift_range	0.05
height_shift_range	0.05
shear_range	0.1
zoom_range	0.1
horizontal_flip	True
fill_mode	'nearest'
brightness_range	[0.75, 1.25]

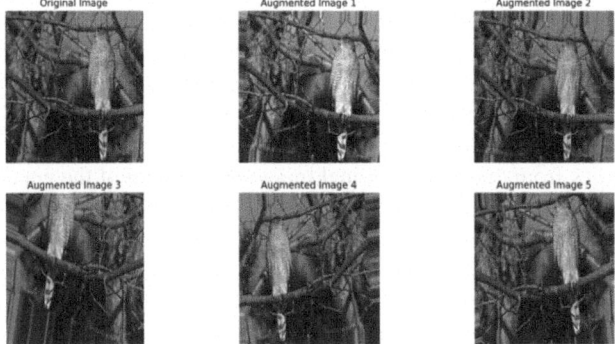

Fig. 1. Example of Hawk Original and Augmented Images

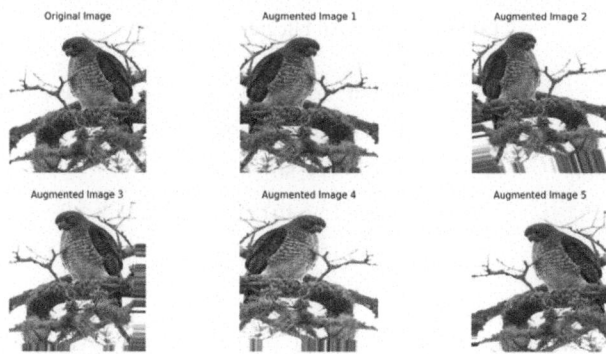

Fig. 2. Example of Hawk Original and Augmented Images

Fig. 3. Example of Non-Hawk Original and Augmented Images

3   Deep Learning Model Optimizations

3.1   Deep Learning Model Design

Since the goal is to determine if an image contains a hawk or not, we identified it as a binominal classification problem. As such, the model design followed the standard design procedure for a binominal classification system using images [5]. We use a series of convolution filters and max pooling layers as shown in Table 2. These layers are designed to extract the most important features from the image and then downscale the result before going into the next layer. The convolution layers can have several parameters designed to improve the model. We use a 'relu' activation function for these layers as this activation function is used to prevent the vanishing gradient problem present in deep learning models. To initialize the weights of these layers the 'he_normal' initializer was used. This initializer allows for the weights of the model to be initialized in a way that allows the model to converge on the ideal weight values more quickly. While we did originally stray away from the L2 regularizer provided by Keras, it was found that adding a small regularization weight of 0.035 impacted the model by positively increasing the accuracy.

Table 2. Model Architecture Summary

Layer	Output Shape	Param #
Conv2d	(None, 319, 302, 128)	3,584
Batch normalization	(None, 319, 302, 128)	512
Max_pooling2d	(None, 159, 151, 128)	0
Conv2d_1	(None, 157, 149, 64)	73,792
Batch normalization_1	(None, 157, 149, 64)	256
Max_pooling2d_1	(None, 78, 74, 64)	0
Dropout	(None, 76, 72, 64)	0
Conv2d_2	(None, 78, 74, 64)	36,928
Batch normalization_2	(None, 38, 36, 64)	0
Dropout_1	(None, 38, 36, 64)	0
Conv2d_3	(None, 36, 34, 32)	18,464
Batch normalization_3	(None, 18, 17, 32)	0
Dropout_2	(None, 18, 17, 32)	0
Flatten	(None, 9792)	0
Dense	(None, 64)	626,752
Dropout_3	(None, 64)	0
Dense_1	(None, 32)	2,080
Dropout_4	(None, 32)	0
Dense_2	(None, 16)	528
Dropout_5	(None, 16)	0
Dense_3	(None, 1)	17

Total params: 762,913 (2.91 MB)
Trainable params: 762,529 (2.91 MB)
Non-trainable params: 384 (1.50 KB)

All the layers used a 'relu' activation function except the last output node. This node used the sigmoid function to output a value of 0 or 1 with 1 corresponding to "hawk" and 0 "not hawk". Since the model was a binary classification problem, the loss function "binary_crossentropy" was used along with the "adam" optimizer during the training process.

3.2 Hardware Limitations for Training

We used "Docker" and "Nvidia CUDA" to access the GPU directly which contained 16 GB of GDDR6 VRAM and 32 GB of DDR5 RAM. We also use a Numpy utility called "memmap" which could save a NumPy array to a local hard drive. The memmap could then be loaded in at a future time and converted back to Numpy arrays, which many deep learning models require the user to use. While opening the images to save as memmaps, the image data was normalized between values of 0 and 1. This normalization is to further prevent the vanishing gradient issue. Before saving the entire data set as a memmaps, the dataset was shuffled to ensure the model did not receive multiple hawk or non-hawk images in a row. Since the code related to the model required Numpy array objects, the memmaps had to be converted back to Numpy arrays once they were loaded in. However, due to memory limitations, the entire dataset could not be converted to one Numpy array. This led us to slice the dataset into 6 different datasets which would then be used on one model. One slice contained 1,066 images to be used for training and testing. Since the kernel needed to be restarted after one program run (to increase RAM space), the model needed to be saved between kernel restarts. This was done using the keras function "model.save()". This function allows a model's state to be preserved on a local hard drive. If desired the model can then be loaded into a program and be used as normal.

3.3 Initial Training Process

Before training with a given slice of data, the slice was split into a training and testing data set. After splitting the data with a 70% training and 30% testing split, the training data had 746 data points while the testing data had 320 data points.

During the training process, we observed that a simple model performed better, considering accuracy, when compared to a more complex model. When running the model on one slice of the data, using a complex model with several convolutional layers caused the model to converge on a 50% accuracy value while the loss function converged on a value and then slowly increased. Despite using early stopping, this increase continued to occur. We remove several convolutional and max pooling layers to just a single layer with 8 filters. This caused the accuracy to converge between 55% and 62% after several training attempts. To increase the accuracy further, we added more dense layers before the final output node. These dense layers cause the model to output an accuracy between 63–70%. The highest accuracy achieved with this architecture was 69.62%. While this accuracy is very low and usually not acceptable, it was deemed reasonable as the slice of data used to train was only 746 images, and as discussed earlier these images varied in their quality.

Several problems occurred during the training process. Upon analyzing the models and training loss vs. validation loss graph (Figure 4), we found that overfitting prevention techniques are necessary. While regularization was already explored, adding in dropout layers was not. As such, dropout layers were added after every pair of convolution and max pooling layers as well as after all the Dense layers except for the final output layer. These dropout layers shared the same dropout weight. This weight value along with other hyperparameters will be discussed in the following section.

3.4 Tuning Hyperparamters

As with any deep learning model, hyperparameters are crucial to the training process. It was found that using 100 epochs was higher than necessary, and computationally inefficient in training the current model so a reduction to 25 epochs was applied. To make sure the model did not overfit, early stopping was used with a patience value of 7. When tuning the batch size, it was found that a larger batch size was not always preferable to a smaller one. With a small batch size, the model was more inclined to converge on the 50% accuracy value when trained with a single slice of data as discussed earlier; however, when using a larger training input set the batch size was reduced to allow for more memory. With these observations, we settled on a value of 32 for the batch size.

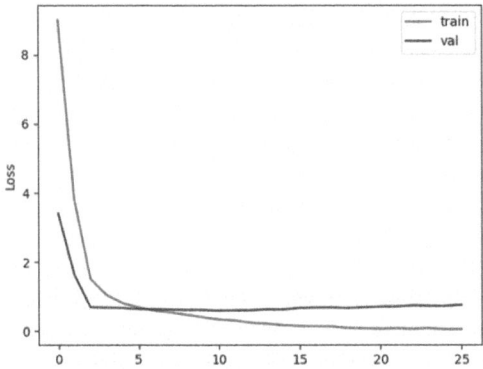

Fig. 4. Training Loss and Validation Loss

The learning rate of the model was fine-tuned to a value of 0.00013. While slight alterations in the learning rate were attempted, they resulted in being less effective. With a higher learning rate, the model learned too quickly, and the validation loss oscillated from the first epoch until early stopping stopped the model training. A lower learning rate would cause the model to converge on similar loss and accuracy values as the learning rate is chosen, only slower.

When choosing a dropout value for the dropout layers, a value of 0.2 was first explored. It caused the model to decrease its accuracy value between 50% and 55%. Several values for dropout were attempted but the most effective value was 0.037. While this value is lower than expected, it did cause the model to have an accuracy of 79.37% for the altered slice of data it was running on.

3.5 Optimizations

After tuning the model architecture and hyperparameters, the model's accuracy was still not good. With only 1/6 of the available data being used the accuracy could be justified. To improve the accuracy, our first solution was to utilize the model.save() function discussed earlier and train 6 models on each slice of data. These 6 models would be then used in an ensemble voting system. However, the performance does not dramatically increase the overall accuracy of a prediction if the models themselves were not producing a more well-established accuracy.

The next avenue we explored was utilizing the model.save() and model.load() functions. Since the model's current state would be preserved, its training process could be continued between kernel restarts. While this method sounded promising, when continuing to train a model on the slices iteratively with a small learning rate, we experienced overfitting with the model which drastically lowered the model's accuracy. The ultimate method used to establish the 79.37% accuracy was making the slice slightly larger, adding more layers to the model, and tuning the regularization for an efficient system.

4   Results and Implications

As shown in Figure 5, a significant number of alternative testing parameters, including the number of epochs and batch sizes used. With several alterations, we were able to find the one that worked best for our model and data.

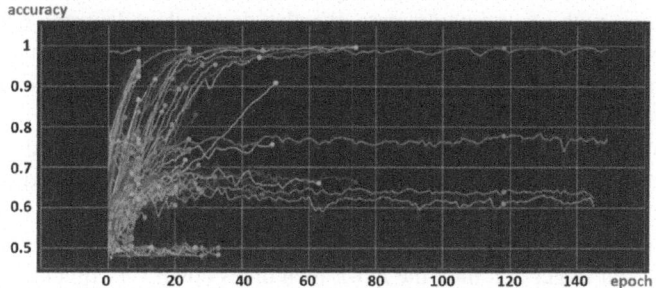

Fig. 5. Tensorboard Graph of Training Runs

When working with the original dataset provided by Cornell University, several observations were made that related to the low accuracy the model converged on. The first of which was the quality of the photos. All the images in the data set were taken with high-quality cameras by professional photographers. This caused the images to have varying dimensions and inconsistent resolution. These inconsistencies perforated during the data preprocessing stage. Since the images varied so drastically when resizing the images to 304×321 the larger images quickly became distorted, and their quality was lost. This distortion made it difficult for the model to determine what images contained hawks and which did not.

In addition to these inconsistencies, some photos also contained information about the photographer and the location as mentioned before. This additional text introduced another layer of complexity that would not be present in a real-world testing environment. In addition, this text varied in size, style, and location on an image. This caused the model to falsify some parameter weights based on information that was only specific to a small number of photos.

Despite the images being resized, we felt the input dimension to the first layer was still far too big. While it was the smallest size we could do with the data set at hand, it caused the model to create a lot of parameters which induced a lot of complexity. Ideally, this complexity would not be found in the first layer but instead throughout the remaining architecture. We estimate this is a reason why a more complex model failed at increasing the accuracy of a model on smaller slices of the data.

When the first layer's input size is smaller, we felt adding more convolution and max pooling layers would greatly increase the accuracy. This would allow the model to extract even more features from a given image. These features can then be used to determine whether an image is a hawk or not based on more effective features. The model would also be able to have more Dense layers which would further fine tune the parameter weights.

5 Conclusion and Future Work

To address the issues with pasture-raised livestock, the detection of predators is critical. We focus on hawks as major predators, but the availability of hawk's dataset is very limited. In this paper, we attempt to generate more datasets using data augmentation techniques with several parameters. We also design deep-learning networks that can detect airborne predators to protect livestock. The network has been optimized to improve its performance. Also, implications are provided from the experiments with optimizations,

To dramatically increase the model's accuracy, we feel that optimized input data is required, particularly data that relates to the problem being solved. After discussing the problem with experts in Ornithology, it was found that hawks hunt ground-based prey by perching in high areas such as dense trees to analyze their prey from an unseen position. Once their chosen target is found, the hawk then dives down very quickly and kills its prey before flying off.

As discussed earlier, the data set chosen did have images of hawks; however, these images varied in their effectiveness in solving the problem. Most images were of hawks flying or perching in open areas, which is contractionary to the expert advice received. These images also varied in size, quality, and overall consistency. As such we would like to create their own data set of relevant images where variables such as size and resolution can be directly controlled. These images would be collected by visiting a hawk conversation center and taking images of hawks when they are analyzing their prey from treetops. This new data would directly solve the proposed problem and allow the model to train on data that is consistent.

References

1. Wah, C., Branson, S., Welinder, P., Peronaand, P., Belongie, S.: The Caltech-UCSD Birds-200-2011 Dataset. In: California Institute of Technology (2011)
2. Cornell Lab of Ornithology: CCUB NABirds 700 dataset competition. In: CCUB NABirds 700 dataset competition. https://dl.allaboutbirds.org/nabirds
3. Wong, S.C., Gatt, A., Stamatescu, V., McDonnell, M.D.: Understanding data augmentation for classification: when to warp? In: International Conference on Digital Image Computing: Techniques and Applications (2016)
4. Shijie, J., Ping, W., Peiyi, J., Siping, H.: Research on data augmentation for image classification based on convolution neural networks. In: Chinese Automation Congress (2017)
5. Zaheer, R., Shaziya, H.: A Study of the Optimization Algorithms in Deep Learning. In: International Conference on Inventive Systems and Control (2019)

A Review of Detecting and Quantification of Cracks Using Convolutional Neural Networks and Image Processing Techniques

Shaikha H. Mokhlis[✉] [iD], Alanoud A. Alhomoud[iD], Reema I. Alshawi[iD], Shatha K. Alhazzani[iD], and Lamees A. Alhazzaa[iD]

College of Computer and Information Sciences, Al-Imam Mohammed ibn Saud Islamic University, Riyadh 11911, Saudi Arabia
shaikhamokhlis7@gmail.com, {442014208,442015230, 442015306,442012765,lahazzaa}@sm.imamu.edu.sa

Abstract. Crack detection plays a crucial role in ensuring the safety and integrity of various structures, including buildings, bridges, and roadways. Convolutional Neural Networks (CNNs) have emerged as powerful tools for automated crack detection, offering the potential for accurate and efficient analysis. In this review paper, we conduct a brief analysis of CNN architectures employed for crack detection, focusing on their comparative performance, application domains, and future research directions. By examining a collection of 20 relevant studies, we identify and evaluate the utilization frequency of popular CNN architectures, namely AlexNet, GoogleNet, ResNet, VGG-16, YOLO v3, and YOLO v4, in the context of crack detection. This review offers valuable insights into the prevalence, usage patterns, and performance of CNN architectures in crack detection. It serves as a guide for researchers and practitioners in developing effective CNN-based crack detection systems.

Keywords: Crack Detection · Convolutional Neural Networks · Image Processing Techniques · Image Classification

1 Introduction

In the past, crack detection and quantification have always been dependent on human inspection, and regardless of the limitations it is still the acceptable method. However with the current advances in the technology fields, researchers have been working toward automating it with digital images. The need for systems rather than relying on human visuals, stems from the fact that the appearance of cracks could be an indicator of structural damage. In order to maintain the integrity of a building, cracks have to be detected at an early stages. Once

S. H. Mokhlis, A. A. Alhomoud, R. I. Alshawi and S. K. Alhazzani—These authors contributed equally to this work.

that has been done a decision has to be made regarding repair of the crack, is it of the utmost importance? Is it costly? Once the crack's depth, and width have been quantified through the image, a wise decision can be made.

Some papers are aimed at detecting cracks in various locations, such as highways, sidewalks, bridges, and surfaces, using different techniques in Machine Learning (ML), Deep Learning (DL), and Image Processing, many of which focus on Neural Networks (NN), such as Convolutional Neural Networks (CNN). Other papers concentrate on investigating detection accuracy and crack feature gathering.

To understand and explore this subject, we present the following research questions.

- **RQ1:** What image processing techniques are most effective for enhancing the visibility for the cracks and their depth in image?
- **RQ2:** How does the architecture of the CNN impact the accuracy of crack detection?
- **RQ3:** How can CNNs be applied to detect and quantify cracks?
- **RQ4:** What specific architectures are utilized in CNNs for crack detection?

Our goal in this paper is to review various techniques that have been used for detecting cracks with high accuracy. We also aim to explore feature extraction methods for cracks, such as identifying their depth. Ultimately, we seek to identify applicable technologies and solutions that can be employed for crack detection in various types of buildings.

2   Background and Related Work

Cracks are extremely important because they are surface deformations that show up as gaps or fractures, causing structural weakness. To reduce potential dangers and maintain the sustainability of buildings, it is imperative to precisely identify and analyze these fractures, necessitating careful detection and investigation [1–3]. Researchers have investigated various approaches to enhance crack visibility and depth perception, ranging from conventional edge detection to advanced deep learning algorithms like U-net and Feature Pyramid Networks (FPN) [4,5]. CNNs have demonstrated the capability to identify fractures at both the patch and pixel levels [6,7]. Techniques such as geometric transformation and image enhancement, including contrast augmentation and filtering, further improve crack visibility [8,9].

3   Methodology

We began our research by using two search engines, Google Scholar and ScienceDirect. Our search phrases were "Analyzing home cracks from images" and "(property OR home OR apartment) AND (damage OR ruin OR leaks) AND (detection OR discovery) AND AI". We focused on publications from 2019 to 2024, specifically those related to detecting and quantifying cracks, as well as evaluating accuracy. Initially, we identified three papers most related to our subject. By employing Litmaps, a specialized tool, we were able to expand our search and ultimately identified an additional 17 papers for further analysis. We formulated four review research questions and addressed them using a range of analytical methods and resources.

4   Results

After collecting 20 papers from peer-reviewed venues, we read and analyzed them. We found many answers to our research questions within these papers. In this section, we will revisit our research questions to summarize and validate the answers provided by the papers we collected.

RQ1: What image processing techniques are most effective for enhancing the visibility for the cracks and their depth in image?

The literature underscores the crucial role of image processing techniques in both preprocessing and post-processing stages for effective crack detection and quantification. Researchers found that by applying a combination of methods, such as contrast enhancement to reveal subtle details, followed by noise reduction and edge detection to emphasize crack boundaries, this approach enhances crack visibility against complex backgrounds. This aids in subsequent threshold segmentation, effectively partitioning images into regions containing cracks and non-cracks. For precise crack quantification, boundary tracking algorithms adeptly define crack contours, facilitating accurate analysis and quantification of crack dimensions. [10].

RQ2: How does the architecture of the CNN impact the accuracy of crack detection?

The accuracy of crack detection is profoundly influenced by the architectural design of neural networks, particularly the depth of the CNN. The Depth crucial in crack detection tasks, as it significantly enhances the network's ability to capture complex features and representations from the input data, potentially increasing accuracy [11].

RQ3: How can CNNs be applied to detect and quantify cracks?

In crack identification and measurement, researchers employ CNNs due to their robust capability to learn and recognize intricate patterns in images. A common approach is patch-based categorization, where images are divided into smaller patches that are individually classified as cracked or uncracked, enhancing local feature detection. Customized loss functions are used to address the issue of imbalanced datasets, ensuring that misclassifications of cracks are penalized more heavily, which improves sensitivity and detection accuracy. Transfer learning from pre-existing architectures like AlexNet, VGG-Net, and ResNet is also utilized to leverage previously acquired knowledge, reducing the need for large, labeled datasets and boosting performance [3,7,12].

To further enhanced detection, decision networks and localization techniques are employed to improve the understanding and pinpointing of the exact location of cracks withing images, thereby increasing the accuracy of detection and assessment processes [3]. Additionally, novel frameworks such as Digital Image Correlation (DIC) displacement fields and Self-Organizing Maps (SOM) contribute significantly to crack detection. DIC uses displacement fields to identify cracks by analyzing deformation patterns in images, while SOMs leverages unsupervised learning to discern patterns without extensive labeled data [8,13].

For quantification, CNNs achieve high accuracy when trained on datasets comprising both cracked and uncracked images. Semantic segmentation methods enable pixel-wise classification to delineate cracks, facilitating precise measurement of crack dimensions. Regression networks predict numerical values for crack width and length directly from images, providing accurate quantification. These advanced methodologies allow CNNs to not only detect but also quantify cracks with remarkable accuracy, making them invaluable in fields such as civil engineering and aerospace, where early detection and precise measurement of structural defects are crucial for maintenance and safety [14].

RQ4: What specific architectures are utilized in CNNs for crack detection?

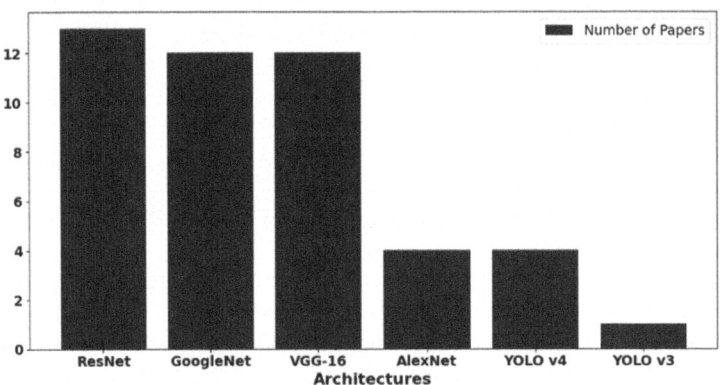

Fig. 1. Frequency of Different CNN Architectures Utilized in the Reviewed Crack Detection Literature

In reviewing relevant literature on CNN architectures for crack detection, various models are employed, including AlexNet, GoogleNet, ResNet, VGG-16, YOLO v3, and YOLO v4. ResNet emerges as the most prevalent, followed by GoogleNet and VGG-16. AlexNet and YOLO v4 are used to a lesser extent, while YOLO v3 shows the lowest frequency of use [9] (see Fig. 1). Factors guiding the choice of architecture include detection accuracy, computational efficiency, and specific application needs [10]. ResNet particularly stands out for its robust performance in crack detection tasks, while YOLO v3, though less common, is still occasionally applied [12,13]. Ultimately, researchers strive to strike a balance between detection performance and computational resources [2–8,11,12,14–17].

5 Discussion

Based on the analysis of 20 papers, various architectures are employed in CNNs for crack detection, including AlexNet, GoogleNet, ResNet, VGG-16, YOLO v3, and YOLO v4. Among these, ResNet emerges as the most prevalent architecture, followed by GoogleNet and VGG-16, both with similar adoption rates. AlexNet and YOLO v4 are utilized to a lesser extent, while YOLO v3 exhibits the lowest frequency of use. The selection of a specific architecture depends on several factors, including detection accuracy, computational efficiency, and specific application requirements. Notably, ResNet is favored for its robust performance in crack detection tasks. Additionally, YOLO v3 is occasional applied, albeit less frequently than other architectures. Ultimately, the choice of the optimal architecture hinges on achieving a balanced trade-off between detection performance and computational resources.

6 Limitations and Gaps

In reviewing relevant articles, significant advances in crack detection techniques are presented, but these studies also have several flaws and limitations. They provide detailed comparisons between various methodologies, discuss constraints or difficulties in deployment and generalization, and highlight possible omissions in investigating scalability and real-world implementation obstacles [3,6–8]. Although the studies demonstrate encouraging outcomes in several areas, including accuracy and efficiency, they may lack thorough analyses of their resilience to varying materials and environmental conditions or their scalability to a range of scenarios [11,16].

7 Conclusion

In conclusion, the review underscores the significance of crack detection in ensuring the safety and integrity of structures. The use of CNNs for automated crack detection offers promising results for accurate and efficient analysis. Through an in-depth examination of 20 relevant studies, the review provides valuable insights into the usage patterns, and performance of CNN architectures, including ResNet, GoogleNet, and VGG-16, in crack detection tasks. Notably, ResNet emerges as the most widespread architecture due to its robust performance, while other architectures, such as YOLO v3, are occasionally applied. The choice of architecture depends on various factors, including detection accuracy, computational efficiency. This review paves the way for the development of effective

CNN-based crack detection systems, contributing to enhanced structural safety and maintenance practices.

Future research should focus on creating diverse datasets, integrating multimodal data, developing lightweight models for real-time detection, and enhancing robustness to noise and environmental variations. Incorporating 3D information, exploring unsupervised learning techniques, establishing standardized benchmarks, and validating models in real-world settings will advance crack detection technology for improved structural safety and maintenance.

References

1. Wang, R., Zhou, X., Liu, Y., Liu, D., Lu, Y., Su, M.: Identification of the surface cracks of concrete based on resnet-18 depth residual network. Appl. Sci. **14**(8), 3142 (2024)
2. Zhang, J., Qian, S., Tan, C.: Automated bridge crack detection method based on lightweight vision models. Complex Intell. Syst. **9**(2), 1639–1652 (2023)
3. Paramanandham, N., Rajendiran, K., Poovathy, J., Premanand, Y.S., Mallichetty, S.R., Kumar, P.: Pixel intensity resemblance measurement and deep learning based computer vision model for crack detection and analysis. Sensors **23**(6), 2954 (2023)
4. Dais, D., Bal, I.E., Smyrou, E., Sarhosis, V.: Automatic crack classification and segmentation on masonry surfaces using convolutional neural networks and transfer learning. Autom. Constr. **125**, 103606 (2021)
5. Zadeh, S.S., Khorshidi, M., Kooban, F., et al.: Concrete surface crack detection with convolutional-based deep learning models. arXiv preprint arXiv:2401.07124 (2024)
6. Yu, G., Dong, J., Wang, Y., Zhou, X.: Ruc-net: a residual-unet-based convolutional neural network for pixel-level pavement crack segmentation. Sensors **23**(1), 53 (2022)
7. Qiao, W., Liu, Q., Wu, X., Ma, B., Li, G.: Automatic pixel-level pavement crack recognition using a deep feature aggregation segmentation network with a scse attention mechanism module. Sensors **21**(9), 2902 (2021)
8. Liu, Y., Yao, J., Lu, X., Xie, R., Li, L.: Deepcrack: a deep hierarchical feature learning architecture for crack segmentation. Neurocomputing **338**, 139–153 (2019)
9. Strohmann, T., Starostin-Penner, D., Breitbarth, E., Requena, G.: Automatic detection of fatigue crack paths using digital image correlation and convolutional neural networks. Fatigue Fract. Eng. Mater. Struct. **44**(5), 1336–1348 (2021)
10. Miao, P., Srimahachota, T.: Cost-effective system for detection and quantification of concrete surface cracks by combination of convolutional neural network and image processing techniques. Constr. Build. Mater. **293**, 123549 (2021)
11. Hamishebahar, Y., Guan, H., So, S., Jo, J.: A comprehensive review of deep learning-based crack detection approaches. Appl. Sci. **12**(3), 1374 (2022)
12. Wang, J., He, X., Faming, S., Lu, G., Cong, H., Jiang, Q.: A real-time bridge crack detection method based on an improved inception-resnet-v2 structure. IEEE Access **9**, 93209–93223 (2021)
13. Zhang, Y., Huang, J., Cai, F.: On bridge surface crack detection based on an improved yolo v3 algorithm. IFAC-PapersOnLine **53**(2), 8205–8210 (2020)
14. Chen, C., Chandra, S., Seo, H.: Automatic pavement defect detection and classification using rgb-thermal images based on hierarchical residual attention network. Sensors **22**(15), 5781 (2022)

15. Chandra, S., AlMansoor, K., Chen, C., Shi, Y., Seo, H.: Deep learning based infrared thermal image analysis of complex pavement defect conditions considering seasonal effect. Sensors **22**(23), 9365 (2022)
16. Xu, L., Lv, S., Deng, Y., Li, X.: A weakly supervised surface defect detection based on convolutional neural network. IEEE Access **8**, 42285–42296 (2020)
17. Guo, Y., Shen, X., Linke, J., Wang, Z., Barati, K.: Quantification of structural defects using pixel level spatial information from photogrammetry. Sensors **23**(13), 5878 (2023)

Information and Knowledge Engineering (IKE)

Using Linkage Context for Automated Correction in Unsupervised Entity Resolution

Fumiko Kobayashi$^{(\boxtimes)}$ ⓘ and John R. Talburt ⓘ

The University of Arkansas at Little Rock, Little Rock, AR, USA
{fxkobayashi,jrtalburt}@ualr.edu

Abstract. Many modern Entity Resolution (ER) systems leverage metadata about the reference data to facilitate processing and making equivalence decisions. This historically has required that each source of input data be pre-processed individually to conform to a common metadata alignment, have data cleansing applied, and the data condensed into a singular dataset to be submitted to an ER process. These are costly processes and require additional passes of the input data prior to ER decisioning. This paper expands on the concept of context within ER to replace the need for metadata alignment and preprocessing that was introduced in previous literature. Leveraging the four (4) points within ER processes for which context can be extracted, and introducing a new n-gram similarity method allows for better more intelligent corrections to be performed to the data during processing without the need for preprocessing or metadata. This paper defines tested methods to enhance the initial context extraction to reduce erroneous automated corrections that thusly impact the final clustering results of the ER system and provides empirical results to support the effectiveness of these methods.

Keywords: Context Token Correction · Unsupervised Entity Resolution · Unsupervised Data Curation · Context-aware

1 Introduction

Entity Resolution (ER) is the process of determining whether two references to real-world objects in an information system are referring to the same object, or to different objects [1, 2]. Real-world objects are identified by their attribute similarity and relationships with other entities. Some examples of attributes for person entities are First Name, Last Name, and Social Security Number (SSN) but in the digital age this has expanded greatly and include things such as IP Address, e-mail address, Device ID, etc. The issue is becoming even more complex recently with the need to adhere to new Privacy laws that govern, sometimes at the international level, how data should be classified as 1st party, 2nd party, 3rd party, personally identifiable information (PII), anonymous, and pseudonymous, what data can be co-mingled, how a real-world entity can be identified, and how this information can be used. These regulations are defined in laws such as the General Data Protection Regulation (GDPR) [3] in the European Union and the California Consumer Privacy Act (CCPA) [4] in the United States with ever more regulations coming into play as they catch up with today's technology and capabilities.

© The Author(s), under exclusive license to Springer Nature Switzerland AG 2025
L. Deligiannidis et al. (Eds.): CSCE 2024, CCIS 2262, pp. 259–272, 2025.
https://doi.org/10.1007/978-3-031-85933-5_19

Regardless of all the regulations, ER is vital in entity management when done in a safe and compliant manner and is a part of a larger process called data curation (DC). DC is the collection of processes applied to data throughout its life cycle from ingestion to disposal [5]. Within DC, ER is important as it provides the processes that allow for deduplication and alignment across data sources, both online and offline. With the evolution of big data technologies coupled with cloud computing, it is becoming increasingly possible to expand the research of DC and ER. This is accomplished through the decoupling of the data storage from the compute that is available to process it and by providing mechanisms to expose this data for easy ingestion across many different types of computing platforms. These advances have opened the field of ER and DC to explore more advanced decisioning systems such as machine learning (ML) [6], deep learning (DL), and other unsupervised techniques. The application of these methods is changing traditional data processing and is allowing for the concept of unsupervised data curation (UDC) [7] and hence unsupervised ER (UER) to be explored.

At its core, all data applications require data that is prepared for the building of information products with a focus on two (2) issues: redundancy and consistent representation. This focus is important and required to provide the most consistent and trustworthy output from the product. In data processing one of the most common causes of redundancy is receiving multiple sources of the same information [8]. This is a very common use case where an organization is receiving information about entities through different channels. The more data an organization can accurately associate with the same customer, patient, product, vendor, or other entity, the better their operational systems will perform their secondary functions such as billing, ordering, and product delivery. The accurate association of data to a real-world entity is the core concept of ER [1] and is what makes it so vital for any organization. With the expansion into the digital age where nearly all companies are necessitated to have an online presence for their customer base and with so many of these discovering that they can capitalize on the exhaust data collected during those interactions, the volume of source data that is available to ingest continues to grow exponentially. This is one of the greatest drivers in the need for a hands-off method of DC in the form of a UDC system.

With the push towards UDC, one approach is to treat data as metadata agnostic and generate a system that can directly ingest and process raw data. A fully fleshed out UDC must consist of methods and techniques to process data from its raw unstructured form and successfully produce information products without human supervision beyond some simple tunning/thresholds. This leads to the concept of a Data Washing Machine (DWM) [9] which is a system that embodies the concepts of a UDC [7].

Many organizations are starting to realize that there is a data ingestion time gap between when data is collected and when final information is produced. They are working towards increasing the level of automation in DC processes [10]. As research progresses into DWM, the need for automated corrections and the removal of human supervision is a vital step. To accomplish this, the replacement of metadata alignment and annotation is an important task and requires systems to become context-aware in order to remove Data Quality (DQ) issues in disjoint data sources. Context-aware is the concept of leveraging all available information that can be extracted from an entity reference to make accurate and informed processing decisions such as corrections to align references [11].

2 Problem Definition

In traditional ER processing, the effort that goes into the initial preparation of the data is no small undertaking as it requires data experts and much time developing business rules to transform the data. This manual process is commonly prone to mistakes that can add additional costs and time to fix. As organizations ingest and process larger amounts and types of data, the time and effort it takes to prepare and integrate data into useful products are also increasing, and many researchers are working to alleviate this bottleneck using several different methods [12, 13]. As mentioned previously, to streamline data processing the concept of a UDC system has been introduced [7] with the goal to take input of any structure and independent of metadata, clean it, and produce a usable output across many domains of information. To support the underlying goals of a UDC, unsupervised ER (UER) processes support that decisioning and functionality of a UDC. To make ER unsupervised the requirement that the data must strictly adhere to a metadata representation, must be removed and instead the characteristics and context of the data itself must drive the UER decisioning. If metadata is provided this should be treated as additional context that can help drive the decisioning within the system.

Previously research has outlined both initial methods for performing automated corrections in UER systems [14] and the four (4) locations within the system that context can be extracted [11]. This paper seeks to expand the research by exploring additional context applications that can be leveraged and how to apply them to avoid "bad" corrections that are ultimately detrimental to the data product of the UER system. The expansion of data context application provides yet another step towards the removal of traditional metadata and provides a new mechanism that supports the UER equivalence decisions by making the systems even more context aware.

3 Proposed Solution

In this section, methods for an expanded data context-aware solution is suggested that can be applied to an UER system. The previous techniques extract context from the data itself, thus reducing the requirement for metadata representation [11]. The enhancements defined in this paper apply findings from the painstaking review process of identifying "good" and "bad" corrections from previous methods and identifying modifications and new methods for context application that enable more accurate and efficient UER operations. During the review, it was also identified that additional methods of context extraction were needed. N-gram extraction was found to be a vital addition and source of context for automated decisioning.

3.1 Data Context Definition

Context, by definition, is the interrelated conditions in which something exists or occurs in a given environment or setting [15]. When applied to data, data context is the information that surrounds a particular piece of data, giving it meaning and relevance. In this domain, this could apply to an individual data element within a group of data elements, a group of data elements within other groups of data elements, or a collection of groups of data elements spanning multiple data sources. The important part is defining the methods of identifying, extracting, and turning these data elements into applicable context within a system that can drive decisions. Theoretically, context at various levels can be extracted and interpolated into data handling rules to allow for more intelligent processing of data. When complex systems are introduced that read and process the data sources, some pieces of their data exhaust byproducts that provide access to additional levels of context. These can be extracted as the system applies processes to the data itself. It is important to understand the level of trust for the context at various levels of processing as the level of the context within the data can dictate the rules that can be applied in the system to be used for decisioning and corrections.

For UER, the defining of the levels and locations within the system that context can be extracted and leveraged for equivalence decisions has already been established [11]. When done correctly, enough context can be extracted to allow the system to leverage it in place of traditional metadata elements or even in addition to traditional metadata where metadata is provided and used as another source of context.

One of the ultimate uses for the extracted context is to apply corrections to data elements to address DQ issues. Corrections are defined for this application as the automated alignment of data elements within data references. Ultimately, the more accurately and consistently the data elements are aligned, the better the equivalence decisions will be from the UER. By understanding the context in which the data exists, we can better infer relationships between different data points, allowing for improved ER.

3.2 N-Gram Application

N-Grams are continuous sequences of words or symbols, or tokens in a document. In technical terms, they can be defined as the neighboring sequences of items in a document. They come into play when dealing with text data in Natural Language Processing (NLP) tasks in textual information systems [16, 17]. In this research N-Grams are leveraged to add another level of context when making correction decisions and are applied at the subsequent character level. These contexts can be broken down into two (2) levels. Reference level and token level.

In this research, 3 levels of n-gram were reviewed, unigrams (1-g), trigrams (3-g) and 4-g. Without expanding here further it was found the most efficient and impactful version was the 3-g and hence all future reference of n-gram will represent a 3-g.

Reference Level. When processing entity data, an entity is represented through a collection of related attributes that are relegated to an entity reference. These references contain tokens that construct each data element. Traditional structured metadata driven systems can break an entity reference into groups of tokens that represent a single type of reference data such as a name or address. When pivoting away from metadata alignment to allow for multiple types of data sources to be processed together, the most that can be assumed is that tokens represent a point of information about the entity. The context is extracted from the surrounding tokens and their relative order in the entity reference.

When performing analysis as discussed in later sections, it was found that a method for determining the overall similarity of two (2) references under review was required as additional context to sway a correction decision by the system. After much testing it was found that n-grams could be leveraged at the method to extract this context.

The method to do this is to apply the following algorithmic approach to each reference in the reference pair.

1. Maintain sort order and all tokens.
2. Remove all whitespace.
3. Break the remaining string into a set of n-grams removing duplication.

Once the set of n-grams is obtained for each of the references, then a similarity calculation between the n-grams in each set is performed as:

1. For the 2 sets of n-grams, get the minimum count of the length of two sets (a count of the set that has the least n-grams)
2. Get the match count of n-grams that exist between both sets
3. Calculate the n-gram match rate as ratio of the match count divided by the min n-gram count

To better understand, consider the following two (2) references.

- Ref1 = "Samantha Johnson 123 West Alpine Street"
- Ref2 = "Samananthaa Johnson 123 West Alpine Street"

The first step is to remove all white space, this gives:

- Ref1 = "SamanthaJohnson123WestAlpineStreet"
- Ref2 = "SamananthaaJohnson123WestAlpineStreet"

Next the n-grams from each string is generated:

- Ref1 = ({Sam}, {ama}, {man}, {ant}, {nth}, {tha}, {haJ}, {aJo}, {Joh}, {ohn}, {hns}, {nso}, {son}, {on1}, {n12}, {123}, {23W}, {3We}, {Wes}, {est}, {stA}, {tAl}, {Alp}, {lpi}, {pin}, {ine}, {neS}, {eSt}, {Str}, {tre}, {ree}, {eet})
- Ref2 = ({Sam}, {ama}, {man}, {ana}, {nan}, {ant}, {nth}, {tha}, {haa}, {aaJ}, {aJo}, {Joh}, {ohn}, {hns}, {nso}, {son}, {on1}, {n12}, {123}, {23W}, {3We}, {Wes}, {est}, {stA}, {tAl}, {Alp}, {lpi}, {pin}, {ine}, {neS}, {eSt}, {Str}, {tre}, {ree}, {eet})

Now the min n-gram count can be captured.

- minCount = min(len(Ref1),len(Ref2)) = min(32,35) = 32

Next, the match count is calculated which upon review is:

- matchCount = 31

Finally, the rate is calculated as:

- Rate = matchCount / minCount = 31/32 = 96.875%

This indicates that there is a 96.875% normalized similarity between the two (2) entity references which when used as context allows the correction algorithms an additional level of confidence that an identified correction is likely to be a good correction.

Token Level Unlike the reference level, the token level n-gram provides another level of context similar to a normalized DLED algorithm that can tell you the edit distance similarity of two (2) tokens. This calculates the similarity rate in terms of extracted n-grams from the tokens under review. The same algorithm for providing the rate is used for the reference for generic application but with the understanding that there will never be any spaces to remove from the tokens. An example of this is as follows.

Assume the two tokens "Houston" and "Hustonn". The first step is to break these down into their set of n-grams:

- Houston:{'{ton}', '{ust}', '{sto}', '{ous}', '{Hou}'}
- Hustonn:{'{ton}', '{ust}', '{Hus}', '{sto}', '{onn}'}

Next the minCount is calculated which in this case the lengths are equal so the minCount is 5.

Next the matchCount is calculated.

- matchCount = 3

Finally, the rate is calculated.

- Rate = 3/5 = 60%

When leveraged as context, the rate can tell the algorithm that the two (2) tokens under review are only 60% similar and allow for that value to be used as context in correction decisions.

3.3 Method Application

In initial iterations of correction testing and research [18], a sliding window approach was taken to select triples on which context was derived and correction decisions were made. This method resulted in many unnecessary token comparisons as it compared every token within every triple extracted from one reference against every token in every triple extracted from a second reference. This resulted in the following equation that represents the number of token equivalence calculations performed leveraging the sliding window method.

$$[(\text{len}(\text{ref1}) - 2) * (\text{len}(\text{ref2}) - 2)] * 3 \tag{1}$$

The most recent approach uses a method referred to as the "Scan" method [14] to only compare key tokens and instantiate deeper investigation when the correct context is identified. The benefit of this method is that it greatly decreases the number of token equivalence calculations which falls somewhere between the above calculation as max and the below as the min:

$$(\text{len}(\text{ref1}) - 2) * (\text{len}(\text{ref2}) - 2) \tag{2}$$

Assume that given two (2) references, where ref1 contains 20 tokens and ref2 contains 14 tokens, their reduces the comparisons from 648 token equivalence calculations to somewhere between 216 and 648 comparisons. With the "Scan" method, the observed average is much closer to the min value which greatly improves performance.

One additional concept that needs to be understood is the frequency of tokens. A token frequency (freq) used in the correction methods is a count of how many times that token occurs within a block (share a token) of references or globally in all blocks of references.

Initially corrections leveraged limited context in the form of the neighboring tokens, the frequency of tokens and DLED similarities of the token under review. With the introduction of the n-gram similarity, additional context is available. A simplified algorithm for applying this as reference level context could be as follows:

• For each block of references

- Build a dictionary where the keys are the unique tokens in the block, and the values are the frequencies of the tokens within the block.
- Generate all pairs of reference: (RefJ, RefK)
- For each pair, for each token (j1) in RefJ

     o For each token (k1) if RefK
       ▪ If j1==k1 and j3==k3
         o If n-gram(j2,k2)>90%
           ▪ If freq(j2)>freq(k2), replace k2 with j2
           ▪ If freq(j2)<freq(k2), replace j2 with k2
         o Else if 50% < n-gram(j2,k2) < 75%
           ▪ If n-gram(RefJ,RefK) > 75%
             • If freq(j2)>freq(k2), replace k2 with j2
             • If freq(j2)<freq(k2), replace j2 with k2
       ▪ Else Continue

Note the additional context added by taking the n-gram of the full reference. This allowed for additional confidence that the replacement should take place. This is further illustrated in Fig. 1.

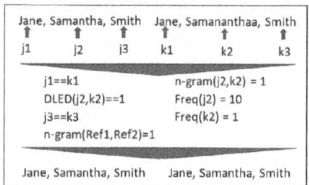

Fig. 1. Example of correction with n-gram

In this, the n-gram calculations provide the additional context needed to for the algorithm to feel confident in the replacement decision. This allows for the misspelled "Samananthaa" to be replaced with the correct spelling "Samantha".

n-grams are leveraged in correction methods outlined in previous papers [11, 14] that: Correct middle tokens; Correct first tokens; Insert missing tokens; Concatenate multiple tokens.

3.4 Drive Towards Better Corrections

Using extracted context, such as the n-gram similarity scores, we can develop a context-aware UER system that makes decisions based on the data's inherent characteristics rather than relying on metadata. Once the context is extracted, they can be leveraged to make corrections to the actual reference tokens. These corrections methods are metadata independent and rely solely on context that can be extracted to make decisions. This has been explored and initial methods have been defined and tested [11, 14, 18]. As introduced through the n-gram method, new methods of correction are being explored and the types of contexts that can be leveraged are also expanding. This is important for enhancing context application and decisioning within UER systems.

4 Practical Application: Discovery, Modification, Testing and Results

This paper has thus far outlined the need for continued enhancements to context aware UER systems by exploring new methods or application of existing methods to expand context types available to the systems. This section discusses the most recent findings on the efficiency of applying these enhanced methods vs relying solely on previous metadata driven options and touches on how the need and approach for the needed context were identified.

4.1 Performance Measures

The final performance statistics for each run include Recall, Precision, and F-Measure. ER outcomes typically fall into one of four categories: True Positive (TP), True Negative (TN), False Positive (FP), and False Negative (FN).

The accuracy in these tests is measured by calculating the F-measure for each result set. To understand this, it is essential to grasp precision and recall. Precision measures the correctness of predicted results compared to the truth set, while recall measures the completeness of predicted coreferences, or the fraction of truths in the result set. Statistically:

$$\text{precision} = \text{TP} / (\text{TP} + \text{FP}), \ \text{recall} = \text{TP} / (\text{TP} + \text{FN}) \tag{3}$$

Here, TP represents true positive count, FP is false positive count, and FN is false negative count. It is important to note the trade-off between precision and recall. For example, if all references are falsely predicted as the same entity, precision is low due to false matches, but recall is high since all true matches are captured.

F-measure is a single measure that combines precision and recall, calculated as:

$$\text{F} - \text{measure} = 2 \times (\text{precision} \times \text{recall}) / (\text{precision} + \text{recall}) \tag{4}$$

4.2 Environment

To evaluate the effectiveness of these correction methods, a refactored version of the Proof-of-Concept (POC) system from previous research [7] served as the core platform. This POC is being developed at the University of Arkansas at Little Rock (UALR) and has been named Data Washing Machine (DWM). The DWM employs frequency-based blocking, a multi-token scoring matrix for ER matching, and entropy-based quality evaluation of clustering [19–22]. Modules were added to implement 18 context-aware correction methods required for this research. Two configurations were applied to each of the test datasets, and performance statistics were collected:

- No Correction – This baseline run is used for comparison to determine any positive shift in results.
- Context-aware Correction – Token corrections based on extracted context are applied. This was ran two times.

  o First to capture the newly added exhaust data for review
  o Secondly to test enhanced context changes.

4.3 Review, Discovery and Modification

The overall testing system used for this research was fundamentally modified to capture and record every single correction decision that was made during reference processing. These corrections were painstakingly reviewed, and each one was classified as "good", "bad" and "valid". A good correction is one that it is completely obvious upon manual inspection that the correction was indeed needed and applied correctly. A bad correction was defined as being a correction that incorrectly modified a token that should not have been modified during the process. A valid correction are corrections that upon manual review are perfectly valid upon human inspection of the reference data but either of the tokens under review could have been corrected to the other as there was no tiebreaking context available to make a better decision. Valid corrections were identified infrequently so were ultimately excluded from further context review in this paper.

Once the classification was completed, the good and valid corrections were ignored, and the bad corrections underwent heavy scrutiny. During this process, an attempt to identify any patterns in the bad corrections was made. Next, we tried to identify any additional information that could be extracted as context that might facilitate a good correction in place of the bad. Finally, if nothing was identifiable, the process was deemed incorrect, and adjustments were needed to be made to avoid these specific corrections.

It was discovered that there were multiple classifications of bad corrections that could be addressed.

1. Some numeric need to be excluded from comparisons overall.
   a. A zip code lookup table was added as a source of context for zip code classification and processing. If one token is a zip code, and the comparing token is a 100% n-gram score match, then make the correction.
   b. Phone number validation rules were coded to identify valid phone numbers. If one token is a phone number and the comparing token is a 100% n-gram score match, then make the corrections.

  c. Exclude all other numeric corrections.
2. Row level context needs to be added in addition to the neighboring token context as there are many bad corrections that are completely different entities upon review.
   a. To address this reference level n-gram match of greater than 75% was introduced.
3. Algorithms are based on point in time frequencies of the tokens under investigation. There are instances where a token is "corrected" in one way on the first pass, but corrected another way in future passes as the token frequencies are updated with each correction.
   a. The system was further modified to capture,
      (1) Initial Token Frequencies
      (2) Final Token Frequencies
      (3) Final Corrected reference data
   b. After more information was collected, it was found that many of these instances are around aliases. Specific logic was embedded for alias type replacement to override the frequency based decisioning that was being performed.
      (1) i.e. "Cali" – >"California"

After reviewing and making all of these modifications, another round of testing was run and the results were further reviewed.

4.4 Data and Tests

To evaluate the correction, 18 sample datasets were taken from four fully annotated reference sources. 16 samples comprise synthetic data and two (2) are from public sources.

The data consists of a mixture of records from single sources, mixed sources and with good and poor levels of DQ. This is described in Table 1.

Table 1. Data Set Description

Sample	Count	Quality	Source	Sample	Count	Quality	Source
S1	51	Good	Single	S10	2,000	Poor	Mixed
S2	101	Good	Single	S11	3,999	Poor	Mixed
S3	868	Good	Single	S12	6,000	Poor	Mixed
S4	1,913	Good	Single	S13	2,000	Good	Mixed
S5	3,004	Good	Single	S14	5,000	Good	Mixed
S6	19,998	Good	Mixed	S15	10,000	Good	Mixed
S7	1,000	Good	Single	S16	2,001	Poor	Mixed
S8	1,000	Poor	Single	S17	5,001	Poor	Mixed
S9	1,000	Poor	Mixed	S18	10,001	Poor	Mixed

Ultimately 3,720 test runs were performed on the 18 data sets, one run with context-aware corrections, one run without the context-aware corrections, and a final run with enhanced context-aware correction. By testing combinations of different correction rules in an effort to capture every potential correction for a data set, this necessitated 36 runs per data set including the run with no corrections. The resulting 53,604 corrections were captured by aggregating all the corrections from each dataset for each rule from the first corrections run and good/bad analysis was performed. The results are shown Table 2.

Table 2. Initial Correction: Good/Bad Analysis

Method	Good	Bad	Total	Good %	Bad %
M1	2,592	72	2,664	97.30%	2.70%
M2	1,620	504	2,124	76.27%	23.73%
M3	13,860	3,276	17,136	80.88%	19.12%
M4	2,988	2,268	5,256	56.85%	43.15%
M5	756	360	1,116	67.74%	32.26%
M6	1,008	576	1,584	63.64%	36.36%
M7	180	180	360	50.00%	50.00%
M8	8,964	720	9,684	92.57%	7.43%
M9	10,476	504	10,980	95.41%	4.59%
M10	36	-	36	100.00%	0.00%
M11	612	-	612	100.00%	0.00%
M12	252	324	576	43.75%	56.25%
M13	144	108	252	57.14%	42.86%
M14	180	-	180	100.00%	0.00%
M15	144	-	144	100.00%	0.00%
M16	72	-	72	100.00%	0.00%
M17	432	-	432	100.00%	0.00%
M18	396	-	396	100.00%	0.00%
Total	44,712	8,892	53,604	83.41%	16.59%

Once these were captured, and the findings from earlier were identified, the enhanced context methods were rerun and the same results were captured and that good/bad analysis results are shown in Table 3.

Surprisingly on the same dataset the enhanced correction methods created 1,651 new corrections but decreased the bad corrections by 5,998. This is a vast improvement in the correction methods across the board as shown in Tables 2 and 3.

Lastly to validate, the F-measures for all the runs were captured for both the original and the enhanced correction methods and were compared to see how many had a positive, negative, or no shift result. As there are over 1,000 of these, only the aggregate is presented here, and these results are shown in Fig. 2.

Table 3. Initial Correction: Good/Bad Analysis

Method	Good	Bad	Total	Good %	Bad %
M1	2,664	-	2,664	100.00%	0.00%
M2	2,244	139	2,383	94.17%	5.83%
M3	16,377	929	17,306	94.63%	5.37%
M4	4,943	728	5,671	87.16%	12.84%
M5	1,070	108	1,178	90.83%	9.17%
M6	1,484	232	1,716	86.48%	13.52%
M7	327	77	404	80.94%	19.06%
M8	9,731	310	10,041	96.91%	3.09%
M9	10,887	217	11,104	98.05%	1.95%
M10	36	-	36	100.00%	0.00%
M11	612	-	612	100.00%	0.00%
M12	530	108	638	83.07%	16.93%
M13	232	46	278	83.45%	16.55%
M14	180	-	180	100.00%	0.00%
M15	144	-	144	100.00%	0.00%
M16	72	-	72	100.00%	0.00%
M17	432	-	432	100.00%	0.00%
M18	396	-	396	100.00%	0.00%
Total	52,361	2,894	55,255	94.76%	5.24%

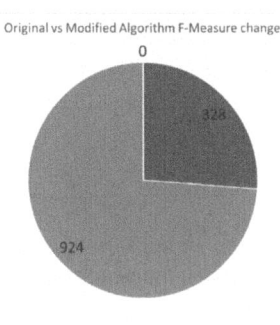

Original vs Modified Algorithm F-Measure change

■ Improved F measure   ■ No Change   ■ Worse F Measure

Fig. 2. F-measure comparison original vs enhanced methods

This shows that 26.2% of all runs had an improvement in overall ER decisioning through the enhancement of the context-aware correction algorithms. This is a massive improvement to the equivalence decisions and the final product of the UER and shows that there are still avenues for improvement within the unsupervised corrections.

5   Summary and Conclusion

Reference data can come from any different entity domains. It also often comes from different sources with different metadata descriptions and varying levels of data quality errors. Most previous systems require metadata to be aligned across all sources and that preprocessing to address data quality errors happens before ER can be performed.

This research expanded upon methods that previously were defined for both extracting context and applying unsupervised corrections in UER systems. Through the introduction of both algorithms to perform limited classification on certain numeric types such as zip codes and phone numbers, and the addition of a new similarity score through the use of n-grams it was found that the existing correction mechanisms can be enhanced to reduce invalid corrections. In turn this has a positive impact on the resulting F-measures generated by the UER system which are a direct representation of the linking results of the system. This also has implications in being able to provide better, more accurate automated standardizations for the final data product of future DWMs. This is further demonstrated in the previous sections with the promising results obtained during testing.

6   Future Work

This work expands upon some fundamental ideas recognized but not fully defined in current research into unsupervised data curation systems [14, 18]. The next step is to continue with the review and automation of the correction methods currently under review. To accomplish this, new ways to leverage and extract context must be identified and tested. These new types of context and correction methods need to be formally defined.

Acknowledgment. This material is based upon work supported by the National Science Foundation Program under Award No. OIA-1946391. Any opinions, findings, and conclusions or recommendations expressed in this material are those of the author(s) and do not necessarily reflect the views of the National Science Foundation.

References

1. Talburt, J.R.: Entity resolution and information quality, Burlington. Morgan Kaufmann, MA (2011)
2. Alsarkhi, A., Talburt, J.R.: A method for implementing probabilistic entity resolution. Int. J. Adv. Comput. Sci. Appl. (2018). https://doi.org/10.14569/IJACSA.2018.091102
3. Intersoft consulting: general data protection regulation (GDPR) – legal text, 22 4 2024. https://gdpr-info.eu/. [Accessed 8 May 2024]
4. State of California – Department of Justice – Office of the Attorney General, California Consumer Privacy Act (CCPA), 13 03 2024. https://oag.ca.gov/privacy/ccpa. Accessed 8 May 2024

5. McGilvray, D.: Executing data quality projects: ten steps fo quality data and trusted information, morgan kaufmann (2008)
6. Kunal, S., Meenakshi, K.: Automated metadata harmonization using entity resolution and contextual embedding. In: Intelligent Computing. Lecture Notes in Networks and Systems, Cham (2021)
7. Talburt, J.R., Al Sarkhi, A.K., Pullen, D., Claassens, L., Wang, R.: An Iterative, self-assessing entity resolution system: first steps toward a data washing machine. Int. J. Adv. Comput. Sci. Appl. (2020). https://doi.org/10.14569/IJACSA.2020.0111279
8. Lee, Y., Pipino, L., Funk, J., Wang, R.: Journey to data quality. Cambridge, MA, MIT Press (2006)
9. Wang, R.Y., Talburt, J.R., Lee, Y.W.: A framework for analysis of data washing machines. Cambridge, MA (2020)
10. Polyzotis, N., Roy, S., Whang, S.E., Zinkevich, M.: Data lifecycle challenges in production machine learning: a survey. SIGMOD Rec. **47**(2), 17–28 (2018)
11. Kobayashi, F., Talburt, J.R.: Context Extraction in unsupervised entity resolution. In: IKE'23 - The 22nd Int'l Conference on Information and Knowledge Engineering, Las Vegas, NV July 2023
12. Saeedi, A., Peukert, E., Rahm, E.: Incremental multi-source entity resolution for knowledge graph completion, pp. 393–408. Springer International Publishing, Cham (2020)
13. Stonebraker, M., Ilyas, I.: Data integration: the current status and the way forward. IEEE Data Eng. Bull. **41**, 3–9 (2018)
14. Kobayashi, F., Talburt, J.R.: Unsupervised reference correction methods for a data washing machine. In: The 21st International Conference on Information and Knowledge Engineering (IKE'22), Las Vegas (2022)
15. Merriam-Webster.com: Context definition and meaning – merriam-webster. Merriam-Webster https://www.merriam-webster.com/dictionary/context. Accessed 5 Aug 2022
16. Robertson, A.M., Willett, P.: Applications of n-grams in textual information systems. J. Documentation **54**(1), 48–67 (1998)
17. Khem, D., Panchal, S., Bhatt, C.: An overview of context capturing techniques in NLP. Int. J. Recent Innovation Trends Comput. Commun. **11**, 193–798 (2023)
18. Kobayashi, F., Talburt, J.R., Al Sarkhi, A.K.: Token correction for the data washing machine: types and comparisons. In: The 20th International Conference on Information and Knowledge Engineering (IKE'21), Las Vegas, Nevada (2021)
19. Draisbach, U., Christen, P., Naumann, F.: Transforming pairwise duplicates to entity clusters for high-quality duplicate detection. J. Data Inf. Qual. (JDIQ) **12**(1), 1–30 (2019)
20. Christen, P.: A survey of indexing techniques for scalable record linkage and deduplication. IEEE Trans. Knowl. Data Eng. **24**(9), 1537–1555 (2012)
21. Ardalan, P.S.G.C.A., Doan, A., Akella, A.: Smurf: self-service string matching using random forests. Proc. VLDB Endow. **12**(3), 278–291 (2018). https://doi.org/10.14778/3291264.329 1272
22. Mazeika, A., Böhlen, M.H., Koudas, N., Srivastava, D.: Estimating the selectivity of approximate string queries. ACM Trans. Database Syst. **32**(2), 12 (2007). https://doi.org/10.1145/1242524.1242529

The Rising Threat Against Modern Technology in Cybersecurity

Rashel Dibi and Samuel Olatunbosun[✉]

Norfolk State University, Norfolk, VA, USA
r.s.dibi@spartans.nsu.edu, sbolatunbosun@nsu.edu

Abstract. Over the past decade, businesses and corporations have shifted more to using automated services as their data collection of storing sensitive information for their clients has expanded. The most popular way to access these applications that hold and maintain this information is through the internet. The internet has become vital in our society that includes our federal and state governments, bank institutions, and numerous corporations throughout the world. Utilizing the internet has transitioned into the category that holds major security issues that could cause national degradation within our economy. The internet has become the number one platform for cyber criminals to conduct their attacks for profit or exercise their newly designed tools on targeted organizations to track the effectiveness of their tools to better improve their tactics. This paper explores types of malwares throughout the past years that have evolved with technology, the techniques that were, or are currently being used with the malware, vulnerabilities within the hardware, software used by organizations, and mitigations on devices that can better protect end user devices.

Keywords: Automated services · Data collection · Internet security · Malware evolution · Cyber attacks

1 Introduction

The threat to modern technology has significantly grown in the past decade. As technology advanced in critical infrastructures, so did the evolution of malware to match these security measures. Malware has transformed over time and now poses a direct threat to current technology. Techniques for breaching devices have become more strategic, aiming to disrupt services that support the economy and create chaos [1]. Staying ahead of these evolving malwares is crucial, involving proactive measures like regular scanning, patch updates, and user training on emerging threats.

This paper explores past and present malware types and techniques. It highlights the reasons behind the effectiveness of certain malwares, outlines mitigation strategies against them, and delves into the history of successful malware attacks on critical infrastructures.

© The Author(s), under exclusive license to Springer Nature Switzerland AG 2025
L. Deligiannidis et al. (Eds.): CSCE 2024, CCIS 2262, pp. 273–283, 2025.
https://doi.org/10.1007/978-3-031-85933-5_20

1.1 Cybercrime

Malware attacks are on the rise and stand as a top security risk for the economy, confronting both governments and corporations [1]. The primary focus is infiltrating networks to severely disrupt internal systems, leading to crippling effects that jeopardize brands and client services. While malware remains the preferred tool for malicious acts against these entities, the surge in advanced mitigations has become essential in cybersecurity. This need has intensified due to the growing reliance on computer networks and information technology in critical infrastructures and society.

Cyber-attacks alone incur a cost of over one hundred billion dollars annually for the economy, not including the recovery expenses [2]. Cyber criminals favor cyber-attacks over physical ones due to lower risks, cost-effectiveness, and the ability to operate remotely, staying hidden [1]. The required technology varies, and multiple malware types are available to breach networks. Depending on the chosen malware, it can infiltrate networks surreptitiously and without user consent.

Malware employs tactics like tricking users into accessing false websites via malicious links, automatically downloading viruses onto workstations, and subsequently spreading across networks [1]. These actions compromise the network's confidentiality, integrity, and availability. Urgent measures are necessary to prevent further harm to both the network and its users. Confidentiality prevents unauthorized disclosure, integrity guards against data tampering, and availability ensures constant access to sensitive information by authorized personnel.

1.2 Purpose of Study

In our modern society, various factors have shaped the significance of global cyber security, given the interconnectivity via multiple communication channels. The urgency to defend and maintain the integrity of cyberspace against cyber-attacks has markedly increased [1]. Safeguarding critical infrastructures and personal and work emails involves grappling with numerous security challenges.

These challenges are now ingrained in daily routines and the technology used in both workplaces and homes. The prevalence of wireless devices connects individuals to the internet for tasks like bill payment, socializing, and remote work, consequently exposing them to a higher risk of cyber-attacks. The internet's inception decades ago aimed to facilitate government information sharing, utilizing large, immobile computers. Information storage and exchange were manual, often involving tapes or physical transfer.

Jumping to the present day, operations are user-friendly, with information seamlessly stored and sent via the cloud or email at the click of a button [1]. However, as data transfer methods advanced, cyber criminals targeted these routes to compromise data, impacting its confidentiality, integrity, and availability.

1.3 Research Questions

This research is focused on eight questions:

1) What are the various malware and malware types that are in existence to date?

2) What are the various techniques of using the various malware in computer networks and related attacks?
3) What are the most used ones and why have they been effective weapons?
4) What are the various defense mechanisms (mitigation tools) in use against the various malware?
5) How effective have these malware defense mechanisms been over the years?
6) What are the most exploited vulnerabilities in existing hardware, software, and network layers?
7) In social media, what are the new attack patterns in emerging technologies such as social media, cloud computing, smartphone technology, etc.?
8) What are the new attack patterns in use and directed towards US critical infrastructures: e.g., pipeline, power grid, nuclear power stations, water resources, agricultural farms etc.?

Information and answers to the questions above will be discussed further in this research.

2   Literature Review

The history of malware is a longstanding debate, lacking clear evidence of its actual invention. However, recorded instances shed light on its emergence. Initially developed for assessment, malware's purpose shifted towards criminal intent – stealing sensitive information for profit and manipulating unauthorized networks to induce chaos [3]. In 1949, John Von Neumann proposed the concept of a self-duplicating virus, initiating the idea of automatic replication between programs [3]. The first virus, "Creeper Worm," emerged in 1971, displaying the message "I'm the Creeper: Catch me if you can" [4]. A subsequent version with self-replication capabilities was created by Ray Thomlinson [4].

The term "virus" was coined by Fred Cohen in the mid-1980s, who also developed defense techniques against viruses [4]. Notable viruses post-Creeper include Wabbit 1974, Elk Cloner 1982, Brain Boot Sector Virus, PC-Write Trojan 1986, Morris Worm 1988, Michelangelo Virus 1991, and Melissa Virus 1999 [4].

2.1   Types of Malwares

Over time, various malwares have targeted critical infrastructures and major corporations. This paper examines eleven types: Ransomware, File-less malware, Spyware, Adware, Trojans, Worms, Virus, Rootkits, Key-loggers, Bots, and Mobile malware [3]. Ransomware locks systems until a ransom is paid, even after payment, network functionality may not fully restore, as seen in Baltimore's case [5]. File-less malware modifies OS files like PowerShell, evading antivirus detection, allowing hackers to navigate and extract sensitive data [5]. Spyware covertly collects information without consent, like DarkHotel targeting hotel guests [5]. Adware monitors online activity to tailor ads, infringing on privacy, as seen with Fireball impacting millions [5]. Trojans masquerade as OS components, Emotet being a well-known example [5]. Worms exploit vulnerabilities to penetrate systems, entering through software and backdoors [5]. Viruses replicate within programs, needing them to be active for execution [5].

Rootkits can be activated via phishing emails, granting unauthorized remote access [5]. Key-loggers, a type of Spyware, record keystrokes for unauthorized access, like Olympic Vision [5]. Bots form botnets to initiate distributed denial of service attacks, overwhelming networks [5]. Lastly, Mobile malware targets devices via phishing emails and harmful downloads, such as Triada pre-embedded in Android devices [5].

2.2 Vulnerabilities in Modern Technology

Technology has significantly advanced over the decades, bringing automated and user-friendly devices. Despite the benefits, vulnerabilities persist in today's technology. Weak passwords remain a key vulnerability, often due to default settings left unchanged, enabling unauthorized access [6]. Strengthening authentication can enhance network security.

Another concern is end-to-end security, ensuring secure data transfer through encryption and decryption [6]. Not all technology employs this practice, potentially due to incomplete network hardware and software security. Securing a corporation also involves fortifying its firewall with multiple layers of protection, including training remote workers [6].

Operating vulnerable systems makes corporations easy targets for hackers [6]. System hardening prevents malware installation, while eliminating outdated technology is vital to prevent attacks due to the absence of software patches [6].

2.3 Current Mitigations

Working with today's technology demands continuous implementation of mitigations to ensure robust security for network operating systems. Ensuring daily back-ups of the operating system is crucial, including full, differential, and incremental types [6]. Administrators should also be adept at restoring servers from these back-ups [6]. Storing back-ups offsite adds another layer of protection against malware attacks and aids in recovery.

Implementing file type filters blocks unauthorized formats from entering the network, while blocking non-work-related websites reduces the risk of malware attacks and data transfer monitoring [6]. Authorizing specific applications for employee devices prevents unauthorized downloads and enhances security [6]. The network team's role extends to training on identifying phishing emails, workplace best practices, and timely security updates execution [6]. Collectively, these measures prepare major corporations and governments to effectively counter malware threats.

The origin of malware was discussed in this section providing a clear picture of when the first virus was recorded. The most common different types of malwares along with the different types of vulnerabilities that are presented within major corporations were also discussed. Implementing mitigations and remaining vigilant to prevent any future attacks on any network to ensure the corporation's finances and reputation are protected is vital today.

3   Methodology

The overall research is concerned with the rising threat against modern technology in cybersecurity. Cybersecurity is another world itself, but this research focused on the malware that is used within the cyber world by cyber criminals and how it impacted many corporations and businesses to include the sectors that lay within the critical infrastructure.

A qualitative approach was chosen in this research. It was chosen over quantitative because this approach provided valuable data and added the important details to include concepts, ideas, and experiences. This approach focuses more on meanings and behavioral science which includes textual data [7]. Labs were not conducted, and all the information was secondary data that was already previously researched, and the information contained through studies and current events that took place [7]. Qualitative research contains many different methods. This research falls under the grounded theory and the survey method where both methods were conducted online [7]. Both methods involved the collection and analysis of information which is an important factor in utilizing secondary data and by this research being of a particular area in cybersecurity the process in which the data was collected was important [7]. There are so many different types of malware that cyber criminals utilize and many of the references used in this research to identify those malware overlapped with one another.

This research was carried out by accomplishing the following tasks:

1) The various malware and malware types that are in existence to date were researched.
2) The various techniques of using the various malware in computer networks and related attacks were identified.
3) The most used malware and why it was effective was identified.
4) The various defense mechanisms in use against various malware were identified.
5) The effectiveness of malware defense mechanisms have been over the years was explained.
6) The most exploited vulnerabilities in existing hardware, software, and network layers were explained.
7) New attack patterns in emerging technologies such as social media, cloud computing, smartphone technology was explained.
8) New attack patterns in use and directed towards US critical infrastructures were identified.

The qualitative approach allowed the use of secondary data to complete the above tasks. The secondary data fell under the ground theory and survey methods and below is a breakdown of the material collected to complete this research [7].

Reviewing the data collection graph, the areas of discussion for this research are presented along the left side of the graph. The numbers at the bottom of the graph represent the quantity of references used for each discussion area. More information was collected concerning cyber-attacks. Given the rising prevalence of cyber-attacks, comprehending malware types and their associated behaviors becomes crucial. This is where malware analysis comes into play to carry out the necessary procedures. The realm of malware analysis encompasses Static Analysis and Dynamic Analysis.

Static Analysis can analyze malware files without executing the program [8]. This type of analysis doesn't require code examination, acting as a protective measure against harmful files. During this analysis, Static gathers details like file name, type, and size to formulate a comprehensive understanding of potential malware [8]. Additionally, this analysis involves cross-referencing databases to identify whether the malware is known elsewhere in the cyber world. Virus detection software is also utilized to determine the type of malware [8].

As malware evolves into more sophisticated forms, Dynamic Analysis comes into play. This approach involves executing malware in a controlled network environment [8]. This environment, also known as a sandbox, is isolated and virtual to prevent network damage. Dynamic Analysis focuses on the malware's actions to ascertain its type [8]. This analysis, conducted within the sandbox, delves into modifications made by the malware, spanning from IP addresses to updated registry keys.

Although cyber criminals have devised ways to bypass these methodologies, combining both Static and Dynamic Analysis remains highly effective in countering malware infiltration within current network systems [8].

In summary, the research methodology was presented to address the research questions. The approach and data type were outlined. A summary chart illustrated collected data and introduced the two malware analysis methodologies. Understanding these techniques is vital for network administrators to effectively manage threats, safeguard company reputation, and protect clients. Both methodologies provide the advantage of being ahead in comprehending detected malware types, behaviors, and strategies to counter the threat.

4 Results

Malware attacks can be quite expensive for the targeted audience when restoring the aftermath of the attack but is a financial gain for cyber criminals carrying out the attack. There are five areas that are impacted when cyber criminals are successful when carrying out their attack [9]. Those five areas are discussed regarding the impact it caused on corporations and the reasoning why cyber criminals chose that route. The different sectors impacted by malware attacks in 2021 were also identified along with the disruptions caused from cyber-attacks.

4.1 Findings

When cyber criminals initially plan their attacks, there are five areas that are impacted with potential to cause mayhem. They are interference of business operations, loss of property, loss of sensitive information, the company's reputation and brand, and loss of finances [9]. Interference of business operations causes a domino effect. Depending on what services were offered through the corporation or business, the interference would impact the headquarters initially, then the domino effect will take place all the way down to the clients who are unable to complete their day-to-day operations to provide services to their every-day users.

The second area impacted is loss of property. For loss of property, the cyber-criminal targeted an item that is owned by the corporation or business that has caught their attention [9]. The next area that can be impacted is the loss of sensitive information. Loss of sensitive information includes the corporations or business information on their personnel, business records, and the customer's personal identifiable information [9]. When cyber criminals are successful in stealing this kind of information, it leads to identity fraud and depending on how sensitive the information is, they can blackmail the person who the information belongs to for profit gain. The fourth area impacted is the corporation's reputation and brand [9]. Cyber-attacks can show that the corporation's network information assurance is not on the level of security the company promised and could lead the corporation to lose their clientele and services. Any cyber-attack can impact the corporation's reputation and brand. What is vital are the steps taken, following, and enforced to ensure no future attacks occur. The last area impacted is the corporation's finances [9].

Ransomware attacks can cause corporations to spend thousands or even millions of dollars to regain access to their network. It is the aftermath that causes corporations millions of dollars on recovering efforts from ransomware attacks to ensure their network system is back to its normal state to run daily operations without future attacks re-occurring [10].

In 2021 and 2020, the top three malware attacks were ransomware attacks. Ransomware attacks have been on the rise as the focus of cyber criminals has shifted to make a profit for personal gain. The first sector impacted was the Education Facilities that fell under the Government Facilities Sector as a subsector [10]. Buffalo Public Schools were targeted, the attack took them completely off-line for ten days. The ransomware impacted the entire school system that serviced 34,000 students [10]. The school system was not able to operate remotely or conduct in-person classroom instruction. Sensitive information was also compromised and if it was sold on the black market, that question remains. The second sector was the Information Technology Sector.

The targeted company was Acer, a personal computer manufacturer [10]. This attack was the highest ransomware attack in 2021 that requested $50 million dollars for the corporation to regain access back to their network [10]. This attack happened on March 18, 2021, and is still unknown if the ransomware was ever paid. The third sector that was impacted by malware ransomware attack is the Financial Services Sector. The targeted company was CNA Financial, who is considered one of the largest insurance carriers in the United States [10].

It took the company two months to fully restore its network back to normal operation status. One quick action that was taken by CNA to prevent further sensitive information from being compromised was isolating the affected system from the actual CNA network.

The corporation did agree to pay the requested $40 million dollars to regain access to the affected system, but it was not fully verified if the demand was satisfied [10]. Even though there are companies that help in recovering from brutal ransomware attacks, they can still be quite costly and cost future problems within the corporations when trying to regain the confidence of their clients. The corporation will spend more funds in hardening their networks and ensuring mitigations are in place to prevent and detect any future attacks.

Five areas that were impacted when malware attacks were conducted within corporations and businesses were discussed. Identifying the areas impacted showed the domino effect it had on their employees, clients, and services the clients provided to their users. Malware attacks that heavily impacted the top three sectors were also discussed. Malware attacks created distrust within corporations and clients due to the inability of fully securing the corporation's network.

5 Discussions

5.1 Addressing the Research Questions

What are the various malware and malware types that are in existence to date?
Various malware types exist, including Spyware, Adware, Trojans, Key-loggers, Bots, Mobile malware, Rootkits, File-less malware, and Ransomware [11]. They collect sensitive data, monitor user activity, camouflage as system components, and more [11].

What are the various techniques of using the various malware in computer networks and related attacks?
Techniques for using malware in attacks involve environmental awareness, user interaction, domain/IP identification, stegosploit, timing-based execution, code-obfuscation, code encryption, and code compression [18]. They manipulate configurations, surveil users, and hide code in images [18].

What are the most used ones and why have they been effective weapons?
Commonly used malware includes crypto-mining, mobile malware, botnets, and trojans [19]. They exploit trends like remote work and offer effective ways to mine cryptocurrencies, compromise mobile devices, perform DDoS attacks, and deceive users [19].

What are the various defense mechanisms (mitigation tools) in use against the various malware?
Defense mechanisms include prompt updates, privilege account management, network scans, security policies, recovery plans, and two-factor authentication [20].

How effective have these malware defense mechanisms been over the years?
Combining multiple mitigation tools is essential for effective defense against malware attacks. Documenting security steps ensures accountability.

What are the most exploited vulnerabilities in existing hardware, software, and network layers?
Exploited vulnerabilities include updateable firmware, vulnerabilities in billing software, and compromised TCP/IP stacks [22]. They allow unauthorized access and compromise [24].

In Social-Media, what are the new attack patterns in emerging technologies such as social media, cloud computing, smartphone technology, etc.?
Emerging attack patterns involve command and control tools, living off the land binaries and scripts, wire-embedded malware, Checkm8 and Checkra1n, and DNS over

HTTPS malware. They manipulate networks, hide as operating systems, exploit USB connections, and encrypt DNS requests [17].

What are the new attack patterns in use and directed towards US critical infrastructures: e.g., pipeline, power grid, nuclear power stations, water resources, agricultural farms etc.?

In 2021, cyber criminals targeted IoT, exploiting vulnerabilities in remote work setups. Ransomware attacks surged, impacting healthcare, manufacturing, and utilities sectors. Industrial Control Systems faced threats, potentially leading to man-in-the-middle attacks and disruptions [25].

5.2 Limitations of the Study

The time allotted for selecting this topic, performing the research, and applying an approach to generate the results was a period of 12 weeks. This timeframe allowed us to produce focused information gathered from research questions concerning malware and its impact on critical infrastructure. The study provided valuable insights into the history and types of malware, as well as the vulnerabilities that persist today. However, it was limited in terms of demonstrating the actual damage that malware can cause to a network due to the absence of laboratory investigations [7].

This limitation arises from the fact that the same information has been shared across agencies for many decades [7]. While some information might have evolved due to different configuration styles, the overall results remain consistent. In the United States Navy, the practice is to avoid reinventing the wheel, as the groundwork has already been laid. Current networks are configured or tailored to operate effectively with established mitigations and practices. This approach, while practical, may not always be optimal if system administrators lack the necessary knowledge. Many sites follow this approach due to limited timeframes for re-certifications. Conducting labs in a controlled environment with various types of malware prevalent today would yield more precise results and offer better insights into malware behavior.

5.3 Future Directions

The rising threat in today's modern technology in cybersecurity will always remain a significant concern. Cybercriminals will continue to develop advanced malware with the primary goal of remaining undetectable while compromising sensitive information and pursuing profitable gains [26]. Ransomware has been a common factor behind many attacks within critical infrastructure sectors.

This study can be used to gain a better understanding of the different types of malware currently employed by cybercriminals. It serves as a starting point for tracing the origins of the first reported malware and its original purpose. With the continuous production of new malware, this study can provide insights into where to begin enforcing mitigation tools for enhancing network system security. Staying ahead of cybercriminals is crucial in combating today's malware threats [26].

6 Conclusion

In conclusion, the rising threats to modern technology encompass unauthorized access to network systems, misuse of stolen data to harm corporations and governments, and malware attacks that exploit network systems for financial gains [26]. It's imperative for corporations and governments to uphold the mitigation strategies discussed in chapter two to safeguard sensitive information and network systems. Additional layers such as monitoring tools can provide 24/7 scanning and aid in detecting data breaches.

As technology advances and automation becomes more prevalent, implementing tailored measures to combat various types of malware becomes critical for safeguarding systems in finance, healthcare, education, and communication [26]. Defending the modern technology integrated across the economy's network systems will always be a prime target for cybercriminals. It's the responsibility of information technology teams to ensure the confidentiality, integrity, and availability of connected devices, thereby maintaining societal trust. The ongoing cyber war involves all stakeholders, from governments to end users, to ensure uninterrupted operations within the economy [26].

References

1. KPMG: The risk of cybercrime and emerging technologies (2020). https://home.kpmg/ae/en/home/insights/2020/05/the-risk-of-cybercrime-and-emerging-technologies.html. Accessed 12 Sept 2021
2. Karafiloski, D.: Cost of cyber-attacks vs. cost of cybersecurity in 2021 (2021). https://www.sumologic.com/blog/cost-of-cyber-attacks-vs-cost-of-cyber-security-in-2021/. Accessed 12 Sept 2021
3. Martindale, J.: From pranks to nuclear sabotage this is the history of malware (2018). https://www.digitaltrends.com/computing/history-of-malware/. Accessed 12 Sept 2021
4. Love, J.: A brief history of Malware-its evolution and impact (2018). https://www.lastline.com/blog/history-of-malware-its-evolution-and-impact/. Accessed 13 Sept 2021
5. Baker, K.: The 11 most common types of malware (2021). https://www.crowdstrike.com/cybersecurity-101/malware/types-of-malware/. Accessed 13 Sept 2021
6. Forbes Technology Council: 13 troubling tech vulnerabilities the industry needs to address (2021). https://www.forbes.com/sites/forbestechcouncil/2021/09/10/13-troubling-tech-vulnerabilities-the-industry-needs-to-address/?sh=52f088d10498. Accessed 15 Sept 2021
7. National Cyber Security Centre: Mitigating malware and ransomware attacks (2020). https://www.ncsc.gov.uk/guidance/mitigating-malware-and-ransomware-attacks. Accessed 15 Sept 2021
8. Fullstory: Qualitative vs. quantitative data: what's the difference? (2021). https://www.fullstory.com/blog/qualitative-vs-quantitative-data/. Accessed 15 Oct 2021
9. Khillar, S.: Difference between static malware analysis and dynamic malware analysis (2018). http://www.differencebetween.net/technology/difference-between-static-malware-analysis-and-dynamic-malware-analysis/. Accessed 31 Oct 2021
10. Trend Micro: Understanding targeted attacks: the impact of targeted attacks (2015). https://www.trendmicro.com/vinfo/de/security/news/cyber-attacks/the-impact-of-targeted-attacks. Accessed 31 Oct 20121
11. Waldman, A.: 10 of the biggest ransomware attacks of 2021 – so far (2021). https://searchsecurity.techtarget.com/feature/The-biggest-ransomware-attacks-this-year. Accessed 30 Oct 2021

12. Tunggal, A.T.: 22 Types of malware and how to recognize them in 2021 (2021). https://www. upguard.com/blog/types-of-malware. Accessed 17 Sep 2021
13. Sowells, J.: 8 different types of malware (2021). https://www.uscybersecurity.net/malware/. Accessed 17 Sep 2021
14. Wikipedia: Malware (2021). https://en.wikipedia.org/wiki/Malware. Accessed 17 Sep 2021
15. Milosevic, N.: History of malware (2013). https://www.researchgate.net/publication/235666 537_History_of_malware. Accessed 17 Sep 2021
16. Melnick, J.: Top 10 most common types of cyber attacks (2021). https://blog.netwrix.com/ 2018/05/15/top-10-most-common-types-of-cyber-attacks/. Accessed 17 Sep 2021
17. Multi-State Information Sharing and Analysis Center and United States Computer Emergency Readiness Team: Malware threats and mitigation strategies (2005). https://uscert.cisa.gov/ sites/default/files/publications/malware-threats-mitigation.pdf. Accessed 17 Sep 2021
18. Echosec Systems LTD: 5 current cyber attack techniques and how to stay threat-informed (2021). https://www.echosec.net/blog/5-current-cyber-attack-techniques-and-how-to-stay-threat-informed. Accessed 31 Oct 2021
19. Gatefy: 8 most common malware evasion techniques (2021). https://gatefy.com/blog/com mon-malware-evasion-techniques/. Accessed 31 Oct 2021
20. Check Point: The 5 most common types of malware (2021). https://www.checkpoint. com/cyber-hub/threat-prevention/what-is-malware/the-5-most-common-types-of-malware/. Accessed 31 Oct 2021
21. Google Ads Help: Protect yourself from malware (2021). https://support.google.com/google-ads/answer/2375413?hl=en. Accessed 29 Oct 2021
22. National Security Agency Cybersecurity Information: NSA's top ten cybersecurity mitigation strategies (2018). https://www.nsa.gov/portals/75/documents/what-we-do/cybersecurity/pro fessional-resources/csi-nsas-top10-cybersecurity-mitigation-strategies.pdf. Accessed 31 Oct 2021
23. Heimdal Security: Most dangerous hardware vulnerabilities in 2021 (2021). https://heimdalse curity.com/blog/most-dangerous-hardware-vulnerabilities-in-2021/. Accessed 10 Nov 2021
24. Stewart, C.: Threat advisory: hackers are exploiting a vulnerability in popular billing soft-ware to deploy ransomware (2021). https://www.huntress.com/blog/threat-advisory-hackers-are-exploiting-a-vulnerability-in-popular-billing-software-to-deploy-ransomware. Accessed 31 Oct 2021
25. Forescout: New critical vulnerabilities found on nucleus TCP/IP stack (2021). https://www.for escout.com/blog/new-critical-vulnerabilities-found-on-nucleus-tcp-ip-stack/. Accessed 15 Nov 2021
26. Kaye, J.: Protecting critical infrastructure from a cyber pandemic (2021). https://www. weforum.org/agenda/2021/10/protecting-critical-infrastructure-from-cyber-pandemic/. Accessed 31 Oct 2021
27. M.L.: What is cybersecurity: learning about the network security. https://www.bitdegree.org/ tutorials/what-is-cyber-security/#:~:text=you%20could%20earn.-,Conclusion,how%20to% 20do%20it%20too. Accessed 31 Oct 2021

An Online Bookstore Design and Implementation

Jacob Wilson and Zizhong John Wang$^{(\boxtimes)}$

Virginia Wesleyan University, Virginia Beach, VA 23455, USA
zwang@vwu.edu

Abstract. This paper presents an online Amazon-like bookstore that weighs more on customers' experiences and providing a straight way to buy and rate books. The website will have a user-friendly layout and a substantial and varied book library. Users will be able to sign up, establish profiles, browse books with ease, add them to carts, and make purchases directly from their Amazon carts. The website will also offer readers a special chance to post comments, express their ideas, and rate the books they have read. The system ensures high responsiveness, security, and scalability through the use of cutting-edge web technologies, leading to an effective and secure online buying experience for book enthusiasts. The system is implemented with the use of HTML, CSS, PHP, and MYSQL.

Keywords: Bookstore · Online Database · PHP/MySQL · User-friendly Website

1 Introduction

Online shopping could be challenging since there are so many "stores" especially for shopping books. Reading users' comments can be a headache for many. Therefore, people are more likely to go to physical stores for more experiences [1]. To overcome the challenge, the revolutionary concept we are bringing to the table allows customers to easily browse and purchase books online from a vast array of categories. With the option to register for an account or use the general user account to login, users can seamlessly add their desired books to their basket and submit personalized reviews and ratings. Our ultimate objective is to provide avid book enthusiasts with a practical and straightforward platform for all their book purchases and reviewing needs.

The paper is organized as follows. In the next section, we introduce the system design including the flow chart and database tables. Case study is presented in Sect. 3, followed by conclusion.

2 System Design

In order to accomplish the goals proposed in the abstract, the first step was to focus on a secure login feature. The other significant result from research was the creation of a dynamic page which allowed users to add books to their cart and wish lists, and be able to review books. This website was coded with HTML, CSS, JavaScript, PHP, and MySQL [2]. The bootstrap library was used in order to create a responsive website that could be used from a mobile device with good usability. The online bookstores are functioned based on its user-friendly website. The goal of the project is to combine the great aspects from many different online books related websites. These things were done by creating many different MySQL tables to be used throughout the site in many different ways. From a user's cart and wish list to being able to add books from the open library API with a search engine inside the website itself. Finally, a logout feature was incorporated to ensure that no session variables were vulnerable when a user was done.

2.1 Bootstrap

This website (https://zeus.vwu.edu/~jawilson/) uses the CSS and JavaScript library to beautify the website and make the website responsive [3]. According to Brett Gardner in his article talking about responsive web design [4], he says, "In a blog entry, Marc Otte outlined a method for creating fluid layouts … he described responsive design as having three parts[,] a fluid layout that uses a flexible grid …[,] images that work in a flexible context … [, and] media queries, which optimize the design for different viewing contexts and spot-fix bugs that occur at different resolution ranges." (Gardner 14) This type of design is essential on today's web and what all websites should strive to achieve. To achieve responsive web design on this site the use of bootstrap was implemented as it makes predefined CSS and JavaScript to make responsive web design easier to implement. Bootstrap works off a grid system that is 12 columns in each row [5]. There are five grid tiers, one for each range of devices supported. The five tiers are small, medium, large, extra large, extra extra large, each tier has their own abbreviations they use and they go like this, sm, md, lg, xl, xxl. There is also a final tier that is extra small but this is default.

2.2 Website Flow

Figure 1 shows the flowchart of the whole platform. When users visit the website, they are initially sent to the login page where they can login if they have an account. If they don't have an account, they can make their way over to the registration page where they can register for an account and after registering, they can login in. After login in they are greeted with a welcome message on our main page where they will see the top books on our site and a navigation to get access to the rest of the website.

This above flowchart shows how the website flows together. Each page is connected to a template navigate bar that when on each page will use JavaScript to add a class to show which page is active.

2.3 Database Tables

The initial table (see Fig. 2) created via MySQL contains important information regarding user login credentials. Upon registration, each user's password is encrypted using the md5 format to guarantee that their accounts remain secure from any unauthorized access, such as hacking.

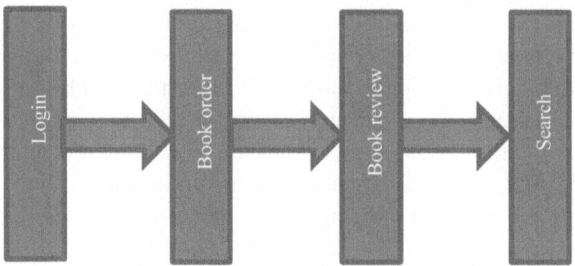

Fig. 1. Flow chart shown the system design.

```
mysql> desc users;
+--------------+-------------+------+-----+-------------------+-----------------------------+
| Field        | Type        | Null | Key | Default           | Extra                       |
+--------------+-------------+------+-----+-------------------+-----------------------------+
| id           | int(11)     | NO   | PRI | NULL              | auto_increment              |
| username     | varchar(50) | NO   |     | NULL              |                             |
| password     | varchar(50) | NO   |     | NULL              |                             |
| firstName    | varchar(50) | NO   |     | NULL              |                             |
| lastName     | varchar(50) | NO   |     | NULL              |                             |
| type         | varchar(50) | NO   |     | NULL              |                             |
| loginAttemps | int(11)     | YES  |     | NULL              |                             |
| lastLoginTime| timestamp   | NO   |     | CURRENT_TIMESTAMP |                             |
| created_at   | timestamp   | NO   |     | CURRENT_TIMESTAMP |                             |
| updated_at   | timestamp   | NO   |     | CURRENT_TIMESTAMP | on update CURRENT_TIMESTAMP |
+--------------+-------------+------+-----+-------------------+-----------------------------+
10 rows in set (0.00 sec)
```

Fig. 2. The user table.

The table is named "users," and we refer to it each time we access the user data. Within this table, each user account is assigned a unique ID number, a display name or username, a password, a first and last name, a login count, and the date and time of their most recent login. The next table, booklist (see Fig. 3) stores all of the relevant information pertaining to books. This table is the home to a comprehensive list of each book's details, including a unique record number and works ID, the book's title, author's name, initial publication year, edition number, rating score, and total number of ratings received.

```
mysql> desc bookList;
+---------------------+--------------+------+-----+---------+----------------+
| Field               | Type         | Null | Key | Default | Extra          |
+---------------------+--------------+------+-----+---------+----------------+
| _record_number      | int(11)      | NO   | PRI | NULL    | auto_increment |
| Work_ID             | varchar(50)  | YES  |     | NULL    |                |
| Title               | varchar(500) | YES  |     | NULL    |                |
| Authors             | varchar(500) | YES  |     | NULL    |                |
| First_Publish_Year  | varchar(10)  | YES  |     | NULL    |                |
| Edition_ID          | varchar(50)  | YES  |     | NULL    |                |
| Rating              | decimal(4,2) | YES  |     | NULL    |                |
| Total               | int(11)      | YES  |     | NULL    |                |
+---------------------+--------------+------+-----+---------+----------------+
8 rows in set (0.00 sec)
```

Fig. 3. The bookList table.

The third table is dedicated to storing information about each user's cart. Aptly named "cart," this table is where we keep track of the user's username, the title and author's name of each book added to the cart, and the corresponding quantity of each book (Figs. 4 and 5).

```
mysql> desc cart;
+------------+---------------+------+-----+-------------------+-----------------------------+
| Field      | Type          | Null | Key | Default           | Extra                       |
+------------+---------------+------+-----+-------------------+-----------------------------+
| username   | varchar(50)   | NO   |     | NULL              |                             |
| edition_id | varchar(50)   | NO   |     | NULL              |                             |
| title      | varchar(500)  | NO   |     | NULL              |                             |
| authors    | varchar(500)  | NO   |     | NULL              |                             |
| quantity   | int(11)       | NO   |     | NULL              |                             |
| created_at | timestamp     | NO   |     | CURRENT_TIMESTAMP |                             |
| updated_at | timestamp     | NO   |     | CURRENT_TIMESTAMP | on update CURRENT_TIMESTAMP |
+------------+---------------+------+-----+-------------------+-----------------------------+
7 rows in set (0.00 sec)
```

Fig. 4. The cart table.

The Fourth table is dedicated to storing each user's personal book wish list. Appropriately named "wishList," this table contains columns for the user's username, the title and author's name of each book added to the wish list, and the corresponding quantity of each book.

```
mysql> desc wishList;
+------------+---------------+------+-----+-------------------+-----------------------------+
| Field      | Type          | Null | Key | Default           | Extra                       |
+------------+---------------+------+-----+-------------------+-----------------------------+
| id         | int(11)       | NO   | PRI | NULL              | auto_increment              |
| username   | varchar(50)   | NO   |     | NULL              |                             |
| edition_id | varchar(50)   | NO   |     | NULL              |                             |
| title      | varchar(500)  | NO   |     | NULL              |                             |
| authors    | varchar(500)  | NO   |     | NULL              |                             |
| created_at | timestamp     | NO   |     | CURRENT_TIMESTAMP |                             |
| updated_at | timestamp     | NO   |     | CURRENT_TIMESTAMP | on update CURRENT_TIMESTAMP |
+------------+---------------+------+-----+-------------------+-----------------------------+
7 rows in set (0.00 sec)
```

Fig. 5. The wishList table.

3   Case Study

In this section, we briefly introduce some of the main functional components of the database system. When you visit our Online Bookstore for the first time, you will be greeted by the login page. Here, you can either log in to your existing account or create a new one by clicking the click to register link (see Fig. 6). To log in, simply provide your username and password in the form provided on the page.

After entering your login details, our system will validate the information you have provided. If you have forgotten to enter either your username or password, we will notify you that both are required. If the username you have entered does not match what we have in our database, we will inform you that your username is incorrect. Similarly, if the password you have entered does not match what we have on record, we will notify you that your password is incorrect. In the event that any of these errors occur, we will give you the opportunity to re-enter your login details so that you can access your account.

On the Registration page users will be able to register for an account on the site they will need to enter a username, password, and first and last name. When they click the registration button, they will either receive an error message stating that information was not entered correctly or that their account has been registered correctly and redirect them to the login page.

The image in Fig. 7 shows information about upon successfully logging in, the user will be directed to the website's main page, which features an eye-catching cover

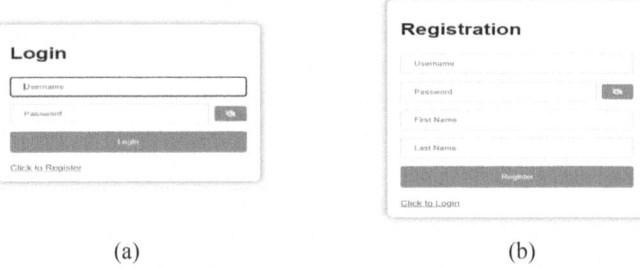

(a)   (b)

Fig. 6. (a) The login page. (b) The registration page.

image and a personalized welcome message using the first and last name provided during registration. As the user navigates down the page, they will come across the site's navigation bar, which we will discuss in more detail later on. In addition to this, the main page displays the top 16 highest-rated books from our extensive collection, allowing users to quickly and easily discover new reads. Overall, the main page serves as a welcoming and user-friendly hub that provides a glimpse into the website's vast offerings, encouraging users to further explore the site.

Fig. 7. The main page and the top book layout.

The site's navigation is a crucial component of the site access, included on every page (see Fig. 8). It enables users to navigate the site quickly and easily, with the active pages highlighted to show which page they are currently on. Whether browsing on a larger display or a smaller one, the site's navigation bar remains accessible, adapting to display a hamburger menu on smaller screens. For those with admin user account type, a drop-down menu appears, giving them access to additional features. This admin drop-down menu provides an efficient way for admins to manage the site's content and user accounts, improving their workflow and ensuring that the site runs smoothly (see Fig. 8b).

The cart page (see Fig. 9a) on this e-commerce website displays the cart information of the user's selected items before proceeding to checkout. It includes the book cover, title, author, and the quantity of each book in the cart. In addition, there are three buttons for each book in the cart. The first button increases the quantity of that book, the second button decreases the quantity of that book until zero, where the book will be removed from the cart. Finally, there is a button to remove all of that book from the cart. Along

(a) Hamburger Menu Dropdown

(b) Admin Site Navigation

Fig. 8. The navigation menus.

with the product information, the cart page also displays the total number of books within the cart. The cart page has a clear call to action button that prompts users to proceed to checkout and complete their purchase. When this button is clicked it moves the users to an amazon cart with their desired books. It is important for the cart page to be user-friendly and intuitive to ensure that customers have a seamless and hassle-free shopping experience.

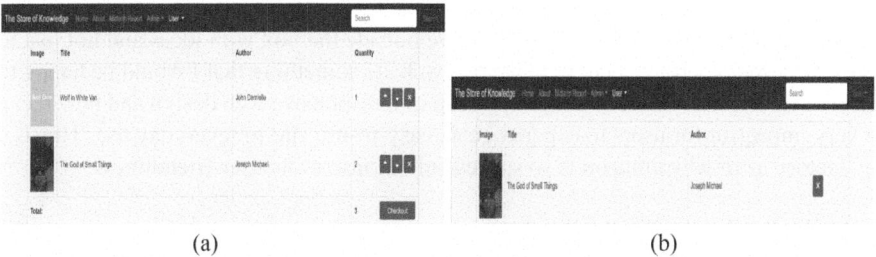

(a)　　　　　　　　　　　　　　　　　(b)

Fig. 9. The navigation menus (a) and the wishList page (b).

The wishList page is a useful feature that enables users to keep track of the books they want to read (see Fig. 9b). It displays the cover of the book, the title of the book, and the author's name for each book in the user's wish list. Additionally, users can remove a book from their wish list by clicking the delete button, which is available for each book displayed. The book request page is a vital feature that manages all book-related requests, including adding a new book to our database when one of the three buttons on the search API output page is clicked (Fig. 10a). These three buttons are Add to Cart, Add to List, and Review Book.

When a user clicks the Add to Cart button, the book is added to our database and subsequently added to the cart. Alternatively, if the book is already in our database, it will be directly added to the cart. Similarly, when the Add to List button is clicked, the book is either first added to our database and then added to the wishList or directly added to the wishList if it's already in our database. Finally, when the Review Book button is clicked, the book is either first added to our database and then the user is redirected to the book review page, or the user is directly redirected to the book review page if the book is already in our database. If a user wants to give a particular book a rating, they can click

Fig. 10. The three buttons page (a) and the bookReview page (b).

the "review book" button, which will redirect them to a dedicated page (Fig. 10b). On this page, they can rate the book on a scale of 0.5 to 5 stars. Once they have given the book a rating, they can click the "submit" button, which will take them to the action page. On the action page, the system will update the book's rating and total number of ratings in the bookList table, reflecting the user's review. After the update is complete, the user will be redirected back to the home page. This process is straightforward and efficient, allowing users to give books a rating and share their thoughts quickly and easily.

4 Conclusion

The paper presents a user-friendly way for book lovers to find and rate books and this project was a great way for me to think more outside the box with ideas and not just to go for easy robust projects but to make this website something that I would be happy to put on my portfolio. This project jumps deep into responsive web design and how it can be very impactful for users to experience an easy-to-use site for everyday use. This is a key factory as to why amazon is so successful because of its user-friendliness.

References

1. Stevenson, T.: The joys of the bookstore – the online experience doesn't compare to the real world. Books Are Our Superpower (2020). https://baos.pub/, Last accessed Jan 2024
2. Wang, Z.: Web programming with PHP/MySQL, VWU online bookstore (2023)
3. Murach, J., Harris, R.: Murach's PHP and MySQL, 3rd edn. Mike Murach & Associates, Inc., Freshno, CA (2021)
4. Gardner, B.S.: Responsive web design: enriching the user experience. Sigma J. Inside Digital Ecosys. 11.1: 13–19 (2011)
5. Jacob, T., Otto, M.: Bootstrap. Bootstrap The Most Popular HTML, CSS, and JS Library in the World. https://getbootstrap.com Last accessed 25 Jan 2024

Cybersecurity: Sight and Foresight

Kevin Brodie and Samuel Olatunbosun[✉]

Norfolk State University, Norfolk, VA, USA
k.d.brodie@spartans.nsu.edu, sbolatunbosun@nsu.edu

Abstract. This paper's focus is on information systems (IS), emerging threats, and advancement of information technology, (IT). Many of the modern-day cybersecurity threats are targeting the newer technology used in IS. These include smartphones and other portable hand-held devices. Social media has also become a target in the hands of cybercriminals where perpetrators are increasingly exploiting the vulnerabilities within the general computer systems critical hardware. The paper highlights common attacks that are used in malware attacks. Stationary hardware is no longer the focal target, but attackers are now exploiting whatever means are possible to attain private and confidential information of users [9]. The growth of global Internet connectivity and the technological advancement of business concerns have greatly increased the attack vectors available to cybercriminals and without the proper countermeasures and security control implementation, IS are susceptible to compromise at all levels [9]. There have been many malicious exploits over the world wide web of computer interconnections with known cybercriminal attack patterns, and this paper also examine the mitigating capabilities of existing security mechanisms and countermeasures that are used to prevent cybercriminal threats [9].

Keywords: Vulnerabilities · malware attacks · Technological advancements · countermeasures · system security

1 Introduction

Security is a broad subject with various aspects, including platform, network, physical, and application security. Each aspect has its own threats, risks, and mitigation solutions. Information security often recalls hackers and system vulnerabilities. To truly understand the intricacies and interdependencies of information system security, action and awareness are essential. Over time, computing systems have evolved from closed mainframes to individual computers, introducing new challenges. While computers are valuable tools, they can also cause harm when misused. The growing dependency on technology has led to an increase in malicious attacks, requiring continuous efforts to overcome such threats. Information systems security is crucial for financial, professional, and personal growth, and it remains an ongoing task in the face of evolving attack methods.

L. Deligiannidis et al. (Eds.): CSCE 2024, CCIS 2262, pp. 291–303, 2025.
https://doi.org/10.1007/978-3-031-85933-5_22

a) Problem statement

The world is moving in the direction of the internet of things (IoT), and security attacks keep rising in the form of malware, viruses, network compromise, theft of assets/technology, and other resources. These attacks are a big concern for any organization or business [2]. Loss within an organization is an enormous factor, and we have observed several cyber-attacks on companies and organizations in the world. Companies and organizations have experienced data breaches due to malware, social engineering, and other cybercrime exploits. Some organizations have the tools and expertise to protect their company's resources from these attacks by devoting massive amounts of capital to human resources and security tools. With the rise of new technology also comes a growth in attack vectors that need be addressed. A threat and instance where a potential activity could result in an unwanted outcome [2]. A vulnerability is defined as any kind of weakness. Exploitation is when a threat successfully carries out an unwanted outcome via vulnerability. When a vulnerability is present, there is an absence of an information system security control and/or a fallacy within an information system resource. It is essential that an organization employs information system security practitioners to perform risk management endeavors that will work diligently to eradicate vulnerabilities and minimize potential impact of threats.

b) Historical perspectives of cybersecurity

Albert Einstein once said that the measurement of intellect is defined by the ability to change and adapt [26]. From agrarianism to industrialized marketing on a global scale, change remains constant today and forevermore. Humans have optimized their resources throughout history to efficiently occupy and operate within their domains. Transactions are inherent in any occupation, whether involving information, agreements, or assets. Attaining and disseminating within business, both internally and externally, is essential, considering the principle of supply and demand. Telecommunications, wide area networks, internet, and electronic mail have simplified outsourcing, correspondence, and association worldwide. In the past, a network consisted of devices connecting to servers within a defined and secured perimeter. Nowadays, remote servicing and constant connectivity to email, data, and personal devices make it challenging to define where a network begins. High mobility and remote connectivity have been embraced, allowing access to various services and applications, including cloud-based servers [1]. However, this also presents security risks, as personally owned devices can introduce malware and jeopardize sensitive information.

The increase in network complexity leads to an increase in network vulnerability [5], overwhelming security personnel with a load of potential attack vectors. Device hardening, such as proper security configuration, full device encryption, remote wiping, screen locks, and lockouts, can mitigate risks in case of device theft or unauthorized access. Resource tracking, whether active or passive, is essential to ensure oversight of valuable assets within an organization. Active asset tracking uses relays to communicate with devices and verify their authorized user's care [3], while passive asset tracking relies on periodic check-ins with an information system inventory management database, which contains metadata for detailed monitoring and review during security audits.

A comprehensive information system requires security assessments and audits. Security testing, including scans, penetration tests, and thorough evaluations of information system controls, is crucial to address information confidentiality, data integrity, and resource availability. Security assessment outcomes are provided to senior management, and security hardening techniques are applied to ensure a high level of assurance for the organization.

c) Contextualizing the problem

Computer crimes encompass illegal offenses carried out with a computer [5]. The Department of Justice defines them as violations of criminal law using information technology [9]. In 2019, over 1 billion data breaches exposed 165 million records due to inadequate security controls [9]. Attackers range from small-time script kiddies to terrorists, each with diverse motivations. Common attack types include business, financial, military, intelligence, thrill, and terrorist attacks.

Business attacks target organizations' confidential information [9]. Financial attacks aim to attain money illegally, while thrill attacks are often for fun. Military and intelligence attacks seek sensitive information for national security threats. Terrorism targets information systems to cause chaos. Continuous monitoring is vital to detect and prevent such attacks. Malicious insiders pose significant risks to information system assets. Understanding attackers' goals helps categorize attacks. Computer crimes share motivations with regular crimes but differ in methodology.

d) Description of the case

At the rise of technology and information security, malicious code (also known as malicious software or malware) was written by selective computer software developers who found value in crafting coding techniques that exposed holes in popular software packages, computing processes, and operating systems. The infamous computer virus is now prevalent due to the reporting of computer security events and compromises of system assurance from mass media outlets. In 2012, Symantec published that a whopping 17 million separate signatures for computer viruses existed and suggested that the number of defined virus files for antivirus programs would grow by a hundred thousand or more within a span of days [7]. This means that each day, information systems are targeted by existing and newly created viruses that focus on propagation and destruction. Although the focus is propagation, the true goal seems to be escaping detection, ensuring repudiation, and overcoming prevention mechanisms within any entity's security controls. For the antivirus technician, the battle lies between the malware creator and the antivirus practitioner – both performing at a high level with the ideals of advancing past the other in the dichotic realm of action and countermeasures.

e) Purpose of study

One focus of this research was to discover the changes within the Cybersecurity space in recent years, as well as identify new attack vectors, understand various types of attack, and examine mitigation methodologies. With this focus, the research questions below are addressed:

- Is increased usability of technology connected with security breach trends, up or down?
- Does system complexity correlate with instances of vulnerabilities?
- Is data privacy limited or leveraged within information system services?

2 Literature Review

2.1 Cyber Warfare

International cyber warfare is increasing as society continues to be more dependent on technology. Instances of espionage are trending within organizations in efforts to gain trading secrets. Some countries are participating in cyber warfare with desires of destroying economic functionality of their enemies. There are many mediums of attack that are enabled and used by malicious personnel. Viruses have become a growing concern for all systems, networks, and connections throughout the world. The virus technology enables it to travel from system to system, aided by users sharing data by exchanging disks, mediums for communication, and networked resources. Once the virus has contacted a new system, many sophisticated propagation techniques are activated to ensure infection and continuous expansion of the virus [18].

Common virus propagation techniques include master boot record infection, file infection, macro infection, and service injection [18]. Master boot record infections load the virus during the boot process, activating its malicious payload. File infections alter executable files to replicate and destroy the system. Macro viruses exploit scripting and automation in applications like Microsoft Word [4]. Service injection viruses hide within trusted runtime processes to evade detection [11]. Protecting against viruses requires up-to-date patching and upgrades for systems processes viewing web content [11].

2.2 Virus Attacks and Strategies

Virus detection and eradication endeavors continued to rise as new virus threats are created by malicious programmers. Malicious developers' products escape detection by implementing various techniques such as multipartite viruses, stealth viruses, poly-morphic viruses, and encrypted viruses [5]. Multipartite viruses typically use multiple propagation techniques in an attempt to penetrate systems with a single methodology of protection. For example, the Marzia virus emerged in the 1990's as a malware compound that infected.com and.exe files [5]. Initially the virus propagates just as a file infector virus, but uniquely writes malicious instructions within the systems master boot record shortly after. So, if the target system is solely focused on protecting against master boot record viruses, the portion of the virus that activates the file infector malware will con-tinue to propagate and remains to have probable success of propagation and destruction of the target system [2].

Stealth viruses hide by fooling antivirus components, overwriting the master boot record, and modifying access control functionality [5]. During automatic scanning, the antivirus software fails to detect virus signatures, allowing the malicious code to be loaded into memory upon system boot-up. Polymorphic viruses constantly modify their code to evade signature-based detection, rendering such detection packages ineffective [2]. Encrypted viruses also avoid detection by altering their signatures through encryption [2]. Each infection has a unique cryptographic key, making the virus signature unique in every instance. Patching information systems can help antivirus packages detect and prevent infections from these types of viruses [2].

2.3 Trust vs Trojan Horse

No matter the attack, the most important goal of the exploit is access. Sometimes the attack vector is not always in the organization's resources and technical controls but can be exposed in administrative controls and judgement/trust of the user. Information security practitioners implore users to not download random content off the world wide web, unless they are very sure that the source is a trusted source. Even if the user is trustworthy of such, organizations with tighter security controls will disallow the downloading of foreign content that has not been prescreened by the information security practitioners within the company. Policies like such guarantee that the risk of an organization being compromised by trojan horse is far smaller than the organization that allows any form of activity to take place within a network. Trojan horses today seem to be ordinary packages, but house detrimental malware that cripple an unsuspecting system and network [8]. There are instances where Trojan makes an impact on organizations – as it pretends to act as an antivirus program. The software will deceive users into installing it by claims of being a legitimate security software, but once the user installs the software – the malware steals personal private information or prompts user for pay to "patch/upgrade" the rogue malware prevention software. Like a trojan horse, there is another instance of malware called "ransomware" that infects a target machine, and then uses encryption to cause a direct disruption within a user system – prompting immediate pay or threatening loss of sensitive information [18].

Trojan horses can cause network speed issues, acting as a catalyst for slower connections. They can also infect systems to form botnets controlled by a "botmaster" for distributed denial of service attacks [2]. Antivirus and intrusion prevention systems are crucial for detection and protection. Spyware and adware are additional unwanted malware types used for monitoring and displaying ads on infected systems [2]. They can be used to capture sensitive information, like login credentials for banks and social networks.

2.4 Application Exploits

Unfortunately, there is an extensive variety of application vulnerabilities within web-based information systems. Some of such are vulnerabilities related to extensible markup language (XML) and security association markup language (SAML) [22]. Luckily these and many other concerns for web applications are mentioned in open discussion for the world's interest by the Open Web Application Security Project (OWASP). OWASP isn't just any organization, but it is a community that works together to enlighten each other of tools, techniques, and methods to effectively protect from past, common, and new cyber threats [22]. They establish open forums that shed light on how information system security practitioners can evaluate technologies, properly configure resources, authenticate personnel, web session access, and validate all information exchanged in the process.

XML is used in dynamic web applications to transform static webpages into on-demand content providers, aiding commerce and tracking. However, it can also be exploited by malicious attackers to gain unauthorized access to stored data. SAML is used for authentication, enabling single sign-on functionality. If SAML communications are interrupted by a 'man in the middle' attack, login credentials can be compromised. OWASP highlights malware injection attacks like cross-site scripting, enabling attackers to inject malware into web systems and visitors, potentially leading to criminal offenses such as identity theft and financial gain. Vigilance and proper security measures are crucial to protect against these threats.

2.5   Social Engineering

Social engineering is a prominent tool used for compromising information system access controls. It encompasses various attack methods, such as phishing via emails and phone calls, targeting finance and information services. Spear phishing and whaling focus on personalized attacks on specific individuals or high-profile targets [12]. Vishing employs voice communication mediums for phishing. Attackers also gather information from social media platforms and mutual connections to strengthen their attacks. Dumpster diving is another variant of social engineering, involving searching through discarded materials for sensitive information. Proper precautions, like paper shredding and secure media disposal, can help protect against such attacks [2].

2.6   Cyber Warfare Prevention

The foundation of information security lies in awareness and education. Security practitioners should promote secure password practices and provide regular security awareness training to prevent unauthorized access. Efficient software engineering processes help prevent vulnerabilities like buffer overflows and time of check to time of use attacks. Proper parameter checks are crucial for developers to mitigate the risk of buffer overflow exploits.

"Due care" and "due diligence" principles involve giving continuous attention to protecting an organization's assets. Implementing security concepts based on these principles reduces vulnerabilities and potential loss. The time of check to time of use issue is a vulnerability where access permissions are checked too early, allowing users to retain revoked permissions until the next login. To address this, session timeouts or reauthentication during periods of idleness are necessary. Users should have the least privilege necessary for their roles to prevent insider threats and escalation of privileges. Privileges should be segregated with policies to ensure specific rights within domains. To avoid escalating privilege attacks, strong policies, regular updates, and reviews of accounts are essential for maintaining least privilege principles.

Malware compositions can be multifaceted, with remote systems initiating command sequences through backdoors or covert channels [2]. Backdoors bypass access restrictions and provide unauthorized access to critical infrastructure, allowing data access and monitoring. Lack of proper maintenance and secure patching can leave the target vulnerable to these attacks. Organizations should protect both hardware and software assets using various resource protection techniques. Techniques such as desktop imaging, change management, and patch management keep systems up to date. Virtualization can be applied to save space and resources. Virtual assets, including virtual machines, desktop infrastructures, networks, and storage, must be individually hardened and backed up regularly to ensure security and continuity [23].

With regards to prevention, cloud computing offers real-time access to scalable computer resources without location restrictions [23]. It can be on-site or off-site, but organizations must ensure security controls are in place to prevent unauthorized access. Service level agreements should be established to define expectations and responsibilities between organizations and cloud service providers. Privacy in information systems requires striking a delicate balance between personnel rights and organizational permissions. Legislative and regulatory compliance laws at both federal and state levels address these issues. Information security practitioners and users must understand government regulations to ensure compliance. The information system security policy should encompass all aspects related to online privacy, irrespective of personal or organizational perspectives.[14].

3   Methodology

This explorative study brings forth the evaluation of secondary data using quantitative and qualitative analysis. There were two general approaches involved in this study, the first was to gather quantified variables expressed in a graphical format and to examine the linear association of distinct data sets, and secondly research was done to interpret implications of secondary data sets using qualitative analysis while contrasting variableness of perspectives.

3.1   Using Secondary Data

Secondary analysis involves examining existing studies on primary data, proposing new questions, and establishing alternative perspectives. It is a valuable option for research due to time and resource limitations, especially in rapidly evolving fields like cybersecurity and information technology. Leveraging secondary data allows for quicker methodologies and rapid results to contribute to increased understanding in the field [27]. Secondary analysis was a fruitful option of study over primary data collection because of the benefits involved. For this study, was no trouble involved in the overall data collection of preexisting data due to the vast provisioning of information offered via the world wide web of interconnections and information. Also, there was no monetary cost involved in the gathering of this secondary data. This research focused on refining various implications and establishing answers to the proposed research questions in the introduction. There were various secondary sets used within this research to address different components within Cybersecurity.

This research used secondary data sets from the information technology industry to collect statistics, make inferences, and answer research questions. Sampling involved gathering subjects from a population to observe, with the actual population being the target. Findings from accessible subsets of the information technology industry were used to infer conclusions about the industry.

3.2   Relationship Between Usability and Security Breaches

One of the initial secondary data sets, which was attained from McKinsey & Company – documented metrics related to the market revenue for platform to consumer services, specifically that of the U. S. Online Food Delivery Market. In just 5 years, the revenue for online food delivery tripled. See Fig. 1 below.

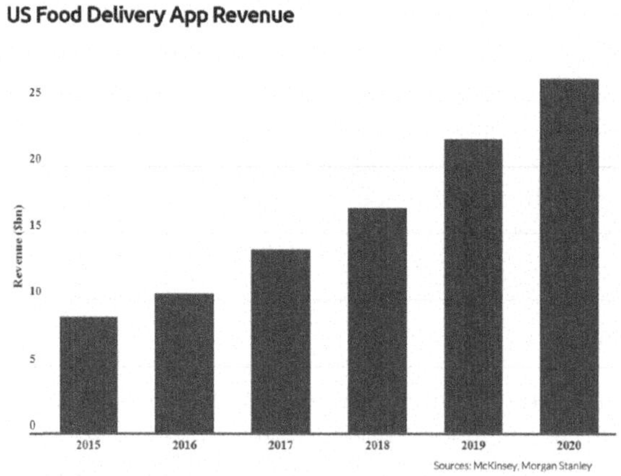

US Food Delivery App Revenue

Fig. 1. U. S. Food Delivery Application Revenue

An additional secondary data set was also attained from McKinsey & Company that described the increase in usage of the platform to consumer services from 2015, specifically the U. S. Online Food Delivery Market. See Fig. 2 below.

Since 2015, there has been a significant increase in security breaches in U.S. food delivery applications. Approximately 4.8 million DoorDash customers were affected by a security compromise. Analysis was conducted to assess if the rise in usage shown in Figs. 1 and 2 correlates with the occurrence of security breaches. A media outlet also engaged in dialogue with DoorDash's Communications Manager to understand the cause and effects of the security compromise.

3.3   Relationship of System Complexity and Vulnerabilities

Secondary data was collected from a NASA GSFC System Engineering Seminar on complexity and systems. The presentation included a question and answer from primary research by Arthur D. Hall III in 1962, discussing the factors contributing to the emergence of systems engineering as a separate function in organized technology due to increasing system complexity. The qualitative variables proposed in the seminar included adaptive systems, system dynamics, requirements, architecture, hierarchy, and socio-political perspective, providing a foundation for evaluating complexity in information technology. Summary:

US Food Delivery App Users

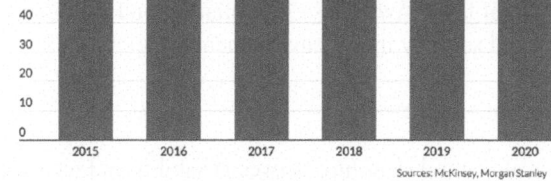

Fig. 2. U. S. Food Delivery Application Users

An additional secondary data set was collected from Claroty, an Industrial Cybersecurity Company. The report highlighted an increase in critical vulnerabilities in Industrial Control Systems during the first 6 months of 2021, affecting numerous systems and vendors worldwide. Claroty identified challenges in efficiently securing Industrial Control Systems due to complexities in management and the design of information and operational technology. Service level agreements, performance requirements, and platform-to-consumer expectations were also cited as challenges in implementing security measures. The data from the NASA GSFC System Engineering Seminar and Claroty's Report were used for qualitative analysis and to create an inferential generalization applicable to the research questions.

Secondary data was gathered from a CBSN interview with TechRepublic Senior Writer Dan Patterson on Facebook data privacy scandals. The data highlighted users' unawareness of their personally identifiable information being gathered and the problem of inadequate safeguards, limited oversight of developers, API abuse, and vague terms and conditions. The focus is on data privacy, and an additional data set with regulatory guidelines will be used to address research.

3.4 Usability Correlation with Security Breaches

The popularity of food delivery apps has led to an increase in security breaches, as seen in the case of DoorDash, where 5 million users' data was potentially compromised. DoorDash responded by conducting a thorough investigation, implementing two-factor authentication, and prioritizing security to protect their platform from unauthorized access [6]. According to NASA's Goddard Space Flight Center, complexity in systems is influenced by structure, dynamics, and socio-political factors, leading to vulnerabilities [15]. Integrated systems increase complexity and require secure programming and layered security to mitigate vulnerabilities. Claroty, an industrial cybersecurity company, reports a significant increase in vulnerabilities in the industrial control system sector in 2021. These vulnerabilities are found in applications involving complex artificial intelligence and decentralized control, making security challenging for practitioners [21].

In 2018, Facebook experienced a breach that compromised approximately fifty million user accounts. Access tokens were stolen, granting unauthorized access to users' personal information. Social networking sites are potential targets for cybercriminals, making privacy awareness crucial. Unlike the European Union, the United States lacks a single overarching regulation for information security and privacy, but there are industry-specific state and federal laws. Awareness, compliance, and user consent are essential for ensuring privacy and security in any environment [10].

4   Results

The results section evaluates relationships between usability and security breaches, complexity correlating with vulnerability, and deducing whether data privacy is limited or leveraged for information system services.

4.1   Usability and Security Breaches

The secondary data collected on U.S. Online Food Delivery Application statistics represents the entire information technology industry and shows a consistent increase in usage over the last 5 years. While one instance of a security breach was reported during this period, the overall growth and revenue of food delivery applications do not seem significantly impacted by this single breach.

4.2   Relationship of Complexity and Vulnerability

The research based on secondary data sets linked system complexity and vulnerability in the information technology industry. One data set from NASA GSFC System Seminar provided evidence of interdependence between parameters, while the other data set from Claroty's Industrial Control System Risk & Vulnerability Report showed an increase in critical vulnerabilities within Industrial Control Systems. Both data sets offered applicable qualitative variables for the entire industry.

4.3   Privacy: Limited or Leveraged?

The research conducted on this secondary data served as evidence to infer generalizations that answer whether data privacy is limited or leveraged within information system services. Part of this study investigated Facebook users' information. The conducted study yields qualitative variables, such as: inadequate safeguards for companies engaging in data retrieval, limited oversight of Facebook developers, developer abuse of Facebook's application programming interface, and users agreeing to vague understanding of terms and conditions. Also, an additional secondary data set was studied to collect qualitative variables that will aid in establishing a generalized inference for the sampled secondary data sets that will apply to the information technology industry. This additional data set yielded guidelines and existing jurisdictional expectations of laws pertaining to data privacy.

5 Discussions

This section discusses the research questions as proposed.

RQ1. Is increased usability of technology connected with security breach trends, up or down?

The study utilized secondary data and sampling, revealing weak links between security breach trends and technology usage. The target was the IT industry, assessing U.S. Food Delivery Application data. Despite noting increased app usage, no consistent link emerged between usability and breaches. While breaches occurred, their limited frequency in the sample doesn't prove a direct correlation between technology usability and breaches.

RQ2. Does system complexity correlate with instances of vulnerabilities?

Based on gathered secondary data, technological advancements bring intricate challenges. The vast complexity, spanning performance, socio-political aspects, and implementation, can lead to vulnerabilities. All systems, regardless of complexity, hold value, threats, and enactable probabilities. Countermeasures don't negate vulnerability entirely. Thus, the research question's answer is affirmative: system complexity correlates with vulnerability instances as no system is entirely impermeable.

RQ3. Is data privacy limited or leveraged within information system services?

Sampled secondary data underwent qualitative analysis to address the question. Violated trust and assurance disturb both companies and users. Privacy exists until observed, knowingly or unknowingly. Facebook's case exemplifies this, as a third-party misused user data. Users agreed, via terms, to potential misuse of their data. Data was possibly used for elections, ads, and profiling. Privacy within information systems is limited and negotiable. It's restricted by terms, laws, and regulations. Privacy can also be traded for compensation or incentives. Ultimately, what's observed or manipulated can't remain private.

6 Future Work

The internet will keep growing in complexity, but misuse consequences might be overlooked. More data means more compromise risks. Security tech could rise to safeguard user info. Cybersecurity uses incremental patching [9]. Anonymity for cyberattacks shrinks [9]. Research needs to focus on tracing identities and mobile-based systems [9]. Collaborative global efforts are key [9]. Identity tracking should cover small data packets using AI [9].

JP Morgan's $963B e-commerce sales show comfort with online finance, attracting cybercriminals [12]. Monitoring matters, especially for unaware users [12]. Internet growth affects communication, business, and security. Packet routing shifts to compliance [19]. Research aims for a secure internet with better content delivery [19].

7 Summary

Modern systems often rest on outdated infrastructures lacking robust security. Trusted bases of older systems aim to protect, but new cyber threats demand diverse approaches. Research must advance against evolving cyberattacks. Long-term security is crucial for reliability, error handling, and resilience. Resources for separation and isolation are vital. Security awareness fosters usability and readiness. Future research should address various users and systems, focusing on privacy, secure internet, reliability, and usability against malicious attacks.

Security hinges on core principles: confidentiality, integrity, and availability. Controls align with these in a complete security policy. Confidentiality restricts unauthorized access, integrity ensures data reliability, and availability supports operations. True readiness involves resource identification, protection, careful implementation, and ongoing monitoring for business optimization [10].

References

1. Ahmed, Latif, R., Latif, S., Abbas, H., Khan, F.: Malicious insiders attack in IoT based Multi-Cloud e-Healthcare environment: A Systematic Literature Review
2. A Brief History of Computer Viruses & What the Future Holds (2021). www.kaspersky. com. [Online]. Available: https://www.kaspersky.com/resourcecenter/threats/a-brief-history-of-computer-viruses-and-what-the-future-holds. Accessed 01 Oct 2021
3. Choosing Between Passive or Active Asset Discovery. Automation World (2021). [Online]. Available: https://www.automationworld.com/products/data/blog/13319123/choosing-between-passive-or-active-asset-discovery. Accessed 01 Oct. 2021
4. Cybersecurity and Privacy Laws Directory (2021). Itgovernanceusa.com. [Online]. Available: https://www.itgovernanceusa.com/federal-cybersecurity-and-privacy-laws. Accessed 20 Oct 2021
5. Sutton, D.: Business Continuity in a Cyber World. Business Expert Press, New York (2018)
6. DoorDash confirms hack affecting nearly 5 million people — here's what you need to know (2021). TODAY.com. [Online]. Available: https://www.today.com/food/doordash-announced-data-breach-affected-4-9-million-customers-t163531. Accessed 20 Oct 2021
7. Facebook Data Breach 2018 – 3 Simple Steps To Prevent Privacy (2021). *CloudCodes Blog*. [Online]. Accessed: 20 Oct 2021
8. Food Delivery App Revenue and Usage Statistics (2021). *Business of Apps*, 2021. [Online]. Available: https://www.businessofapps.com/data/food-delivery-app-market/. Accessed 20 Oct 2021
9. https://www.semanticscholar.org/paper/A-survey-of-emerging-threats-in-cybersecurity-Jang-Nepal/20744c35e90068e0102101bd724513aa f816afda. Accessed 20 Oct 2021
10. ICS vulnerability reports are increasing in number and severity, and exploit complexity is dropping (2021). *TechRepublic*. [Online]. Available: https://www.techrepublic.com/article/ics-vulnerability-reports-are-increasing-in-number-and-severity-and-exploit-complexity-is-dropping/. Accessed 20 Oct 2021
11. Macro malware Windows security (2021). Docs.microsoft.com. [Online]. Available: https://docs.microsoft.com/en-us/windows/security/threat-protection/intelligence/macro-malware. Accessed 01 Oct 2021
12. Kunz, M., Wilson, P.: Computer Crime and Computer Fraud, pp. 6–12. University of Maryland, Department of Criminology and Criminal Justice (2004)
13. Onlinelibrary (2021). wiley.com. [Online]. Available: https://onlinelibrary.wiley.com/pb-assets/assets/1098111X/Complex%20Industrial%20Intelligent%20Systems%20SI-1599226479497.pdf. Accessed 20 Oct 2021
14. Privacy and Cybersecurity Are Converging. Here's Why That Matters for People and for Companies. Harvard Business Review (2021). [Online]. Available: https://hbr.org/2019/01/privacy-and-cybersecurity-are-converging-heres-why-that-matters-for-people-and-for-companies. Accessed 20 Oct 2021

15. Ses.*gsfc.nasa.gov* (2021). [Online]. Available: https://ses.gsfc.nasa.gov/ses_data_2011/110 405_Sheard.pdf. Accessed 20 Oct 2021
16. Symantec Cyber Security (2021). Broadcom.com. [Online]. Available: https://www.bro adcom.com/products/cyber-security. Accessed 01 Oct 2021
17. Tips for protecting your social media privacy (2021). Us.norton.com. [Online]. Available: https://us.norton.com/blog/privacy/protecting-privacy-social-media#:~:text=Tips%20for% 20protecting%20your%20social%20media%20privacy%201,provide%20in%20your%20p rofile.%20...%20M%20ore%20items...%20. Accessed 20 Oct 2021
18. Trojan Horse Virus | Trojan Horse Malware | What is a Trojan Virus (2021). Malware-bytes.com. [Online]. Available: https://www.malwarebytes.com/trojan. Accessed 01 Oct 2021
19. Usability vs Security - The myth that keeps CISOs up at night | Cybersecurity Tech Accord. Cybersecurity Tech Accord (2021). [Online]. Available: https://cybertechaccord.org/usabil ity-vs-security-the-myth-that-keeps-cisos-up-at-night/. Accessed 20 Oct 2021
20. Bureau, U.: Computer Crime Questions for 2001 National Crime Victimization Survey. The United States Census Bureau (2021). [Online]. Available: https://www.census.gov/library/ working-papers/2003/adrm/ssm2003-02.html. Accessed 01 Oct 2021. Us-*cert.cisa.gov*, 2021. [Online]. Available: https://us-cert.cisa.gov/sites/default/files/documents/Metrics_Primer_7-13-09_FINAL.pdf. Accessed 20 Oct 2021
21. Us-cert.cisa.gov (2021). [Online]. Available: https://us-cert.cisa.gov/sites/default/files/doc uments/Metrics_Primer_7-13-09_FINAL.pdf. Accessed 20 Oct 2021
22. Vulnerabilities Related to SAML [Security Assertion Markup Language] – Part 1 – Varu-tra (2021). [Online]. Available: https://www.varutra.com/vulnerabilities-related-to-saml-sec urity-assertion-markup-language-part-1/. Accessed 01 Oct 2021
23. What Is Cloud Computing Security? | McAfee (2021). Mcafee.com. [Online]. Available: https://www.mcafee.com/enterprise/en-us/security-awareness/cloud/what-is-cloud-comput ing-security.html. Accessed 01 Oct 2021
24. What is Social Engineering | Attack Techniques & Prevention Methods | Imperva. Learning Center (2021). [Online]. Available: https://www.imperva.com/learn/application-security/soc ial-engineering-attack/. Accessed 01 Oct 2021
25. Facebook data privacy scandal: A Cheat Sheet. TechRepublic, TechRepublic.com2020. [Online]. Available: https://www.techrepublic.com/article/facebo ok-data-privacy-scandal-a-cheat-sheet/. Accessed 01 Oct 2021
26. 100 Best Albert Einstein Quotes, Advice and Thoughts | BrilliantRead Media. Brilliant Read Media (2021)
27. Cheng, H.G., Phillips, M.R.: Secondary analysis of existing data: Opportunities and Implementation (371–375). Shanghai Arch Psychiatry (2014)

The Application of Blockchain Technology in the Transmission of Semiconductor Process Recipes

Iuon-Chang Lin[1] , Mao-Hsiu Hsu[2]([✉]) , and Hung-Kai Wan[1]

[1] National Chung Hsing University, Taichung, Taiwan
[2] Department of Electro-Optical Engineering, National Formosa University, Yunlin, Taiwan
`mh.hsu@nfu.edu.tw`

Abstract. In contemporary society, semiconductors have become an indispensable part of daily life. From traffic lights, electric vehicles, computers, and smartphones to aerospace and military applications, most instruments requiring precise control feature semiconductors. However, the semiconductor manufacturing process is extremely complex and challenging, leading to the development of various semiconductor-related management systems, such as automated transport systems and production scheduling systems. Among these, the recipe management system, which controls production parameters, is particularly important.Against this backdrop, the main objective of this thesis is to address the semiconductor production process by utilizing blockchain technology to design a secure and immutable recipe transmission process. This ensures that the recipe remains consistent with the experimental results after being verified and uploaded by process engineers, thereby reducing errors due to manual modifications that could lead to production mistakes. This thesis proposes integrating a secure hashing algorithm with blockchain into the recipe management system. When recipes are uploaded, the blockchain data is simultaneously updated, and computations are performed during the download process. By comparing the current recipe with the records in the blockchain using a binary tree algorithm, a list of differing files is obtained. This allows for differential downloads, thereby reducing file transmission time and accelerating the production process.

Keywords: Semiconductor · Blockchain · Recipe · SHA · MD5

1 Introduction

1.1 Research Background and Motivation

The advancement of semiconductor technology, driven by Moore's Law, has led to the miniaturization and refinement of wafer processes, evolving from manual operations with 8-inch wafers to automated production with 12-inch wafers. The manufacturing process has grown more complex, now involving over a thousand steps and taking months to produce a single wafer. As a result, defects are intolerable, making strict control over the production environment crucial.

L. Deligiannidis et al. (Eds.): CSCE 2024, CCIS 2262, pp. 304–319, 2025.
https://doi.org/10.1007/978-3-031-85933-5_23

The Manufacturing Execution System (MES) is central to this control, managing production parameters, process recipes, quality control, equipment management, and inventory. The Automated Material Handling System (AMHS) was developed due to the increased wafer size, automating the transport of materials according to MES instructions. The Equipment Automatic Program (EAP) facilitates communication between MES and equipment using SECS/GEM protocols [4, 5], translating production information into machine-readable commands. The Recipe Management System (RMS), a key MES subsystem, controls production recipes and parameters, which are either manually entered or automatically matched by the system and then downloaded by EAP to the equipment for production.

1.2 Research Framework

This study aims to enhance the immutability and security of semiconductor process recipes during transmission, focusing on Taiwan's mainstream recipe download process.

As shown in Fig. 1, a typical automated semiconductor process involves the scheduling system managing material reservations and discharges. When a discharge notification is received, the automated transport system moves materials to the designated equipment. The equipment then verifies the material, downloads the recipe, and begins processing. Afterward, the material is transported to the next equipment for further processing, continuing in a cyclical manner [3].

The common recipe structure in the semiconductor industry is illustrated in Fig. 2. Recipes can be single-level, containing all process control parameters, or hierarchical, where the main recipe references sub-recipes and includes some critical parameters.

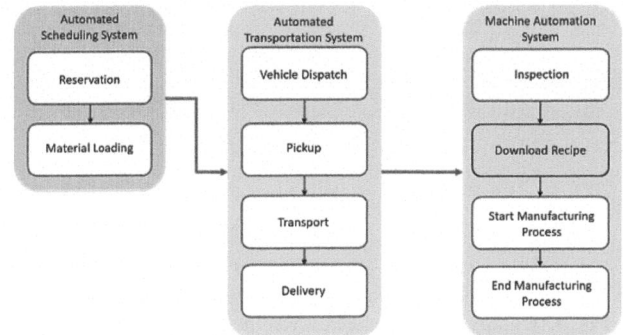

Fig. 1. Semiconductor Automation Process Flowchart

Fig. 2. Recipe Composition Framework Diagram

The file size of a single-level recipe varies by equipment process, while hierarchical recipes typically have smaller main files that reference sub-recipes of varying sizes.

As shown in Fig. 3, the common recipe upload process in the semiconductor industry involves personnel modifying and testing the recipe at the equipment. If it's a new recipe, a record is created; if not, the existing file is overwritten. For hierarchical recipes, each sub-recipe is verified individually before the upload is complete.

The common recipe download process, illustrated in Fig. 4, uses either a shared folder or SECS/GEM protocol [6], depending on the equipment. In the shared folder method, the system compares the recipe's MD5 checksum between the equipment and the RMS [8]. If they differ, the recipe is downloaded and verified. In the SECS/GEM method, the recipe is uploaded to the RMS, checksums are compared, and if they differ, the recipe is downloaded and verified. Any issues during the download trigger alerts for personnel to resolve.

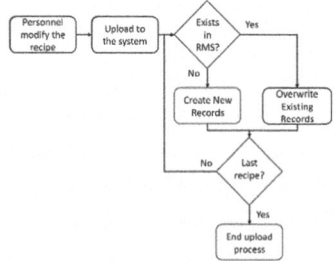

Fig. 3. Common Semiconductor Recipe Upload Flowchart

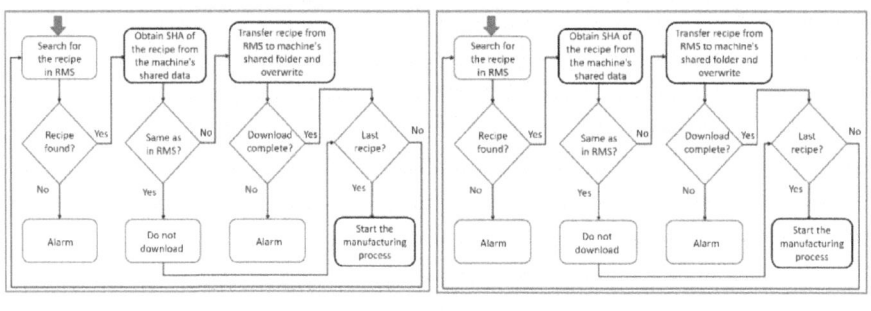

(a) Shared Folder (b) SECS/GEM

Fig. 4. Common Semiconductor Recipe Download Flowchart

1.3 Research Objectives

Currently, the RMS recipe download process encounters the following issues:

For some equipment, the last modified time of the recipe changes after use, causing discrepancies in the MD5 checksum results between the equipment and the server.

Due to internal factory recipe management, some external factories or subcontractors need to download recipes remotely. If the recipes are large, the download process can be time-consuming.

Therefore, the research objectives are as follows:

1. Utilize blockchain technology by applying SHA (Secure Hash Algorithm) in the computation of semiconductor recipes and upload the computed results to the blockchain.
2. Use the SHA results stored on the blockchain to perform file difference comparisons and execute differential downloads, thereby reducing the time required to download identical files.

2   Literature Review

This chapter will provide a brief introduction to the systems used for semiconductor recipe download processes, followed by an explanation of the download process utilized in this study.

2.1   Semiconductor Equipment Communication Standard (SECS)

SECS/GEM (SEMI Equipment Communication Standard/Generic Equipment Model) is a protocol for communication between semiconductor equipment and control systems [1, 7]. Here's a simplified breakdown:

- SECS I: Defines electrical specs, transmission speed, and communication protocol, using RS232 with speeds of 9600 bps or 19200 bps.
- HSMS: Replaces SECS I with faster Ethernet-based TCP/IP communication.
- SECS II: Standardizes data transmission in messages categorized into streams (e.g., equipment status, data collection) with each stream containing specific messages or functions [12].
- GEM: Provides a guideline for implementing SECS II in equipment [12], specifying which SECS II messages to use and under what conditions, helping to reduce development costs [5] (Figs. 5and 6).

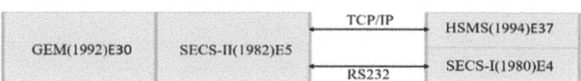

Fig. 5. The SECS/GEM Protocol Communication Standard (The source of information: ITRI)

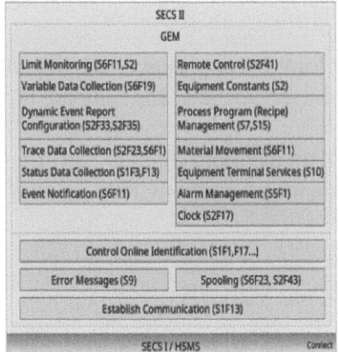

Fig. 6. GEM Main Functions and Hierarchical Diagram (The source of information: ITRI)

2.2 MD5 Hash Algorithm

The MD5 Message-Digest Algorithm (MD5) is currently one of the most widely used one-way hash functions [8]. It was designed and introduced by American cryptographer Ronald Linn Rivest in 1992 as a replacement for the earlier MD4 hash algorithm. The MD5 algorithm's code is defined in RFC 1321.The basic principle of hash computation is to transform [9].

Data of variable length into a fixed-length hash value. MD5 achieves this by producing a fixed-length hash value of 128 bits from data of variable length. During the MD5 computation process, four 32-bit data blocks are generated, which are then combined to obtain a 128-bit hash value.

Known weaknesses of MD5 include:

1. In 2004, Professor Wang Xiaoyun of Shandong University, China, presented collision attacks on MD5 at an international cryptography conference, creating collisions in MD5 in a short period.
2. In 2008, a group of researchers in the Netherlands successfully created forged SSL certificates through MD5 collisions (Figs. 7and 8).

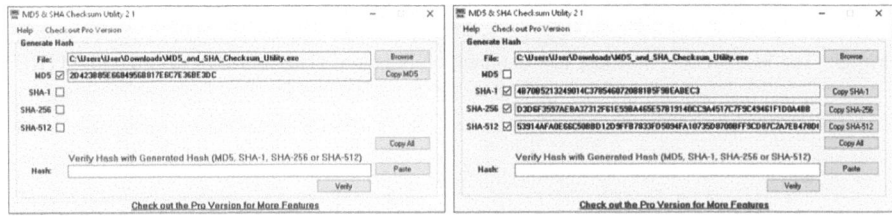

Fig. 7. MD5 Algorithm Result Illustration   **Fig. 8.** SHA Algorithm Result Illustration

2.3 SHA Secure Hash Algorithm

The Secure Hash Algorithm (SHA) generates a fixed-length string from an input message [9], with even a single-bit change resulting in a different output. SHA, certified by FIPS and designed by the NSA, includes five variants: SHA-1, SHA-224, SHA-256, SHA-384, and SHA-512. These algorithms, along with MD5 [2], are defined in Chapter 27 of the UEFI specification and are widely used in data transmission to ensure integrity. By comparing hash values before and after transmission, the integrity of the data can be verified.

3   System Design

This research primarily focuses on improving the current semiconductor recipe download process. The following chapters will sequentially explain the following contents:

- System Planning
- Integration of SHA-based Recipe Comparison Framework
- Design of Recipe Upload Process Integrated with Blockchain
- Design of Recipe Download Process Integrated with Blockchain

3.1   System Planning

The designed process of this research mainly includes the following systems:

- Recipe Management System (RMS):

Used to store recipe-related information and recipe files.

- Manufacturing Execution System (MES):

Acts as the central hub in factory production, managing various production information.

- Equipment Automatic Program (EAP):

Integrated with MES, directly communicates with the equipment, verifies product information, and collects process results.

- Blockchain:

Integrated with the recipe management system, stores the computed SHA values in the blockchain as the basis for subsequent equipment verification of recipe comparisons [10].

3.2   Integrating SHA-Based Recipe Comparison Framework

Based on the different structures of recipe compositions, they are categorized into: Single Recipe and Hierarchical Recipe. This section will explain their architectural designs sequentially.

Single Recipe
The single recipe type contains only one file, so comparison is only necessary for that file. In the architecture designed in this paper, as shown in Fig. 9, the SHA hash of the recipe on the equipment is obtained, and compared with the SHA hash value of the same recipe recorded in the RMS system on the blockchain [9]. Based on the comparison

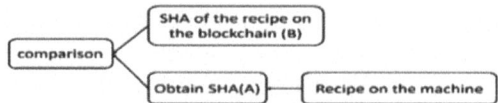

Fig. 9. The Architecture Diagram for SHA Comparison of Single Recipe

result, subsequent programs determine whether to proceed with the download of this recipe [13].

Hierarchical Recipe

The hierarchical recipe type mostly consists of one main recipe and several sub-recipes [13]. According to the architecture designed in this paper, as shown in Fig. 10, the SHA hash values of the files covered by the hierarchical recipe on the equipment are individually obtained, combined layer by layer upwards [9], and computed to produce a combined SHA hash value until all recipe files are processed. Similarly, in the blockchain, the recipe records contain the same files, and the SHA hash values are computed layer by layer upwards until all files are processed. After both computations are completed, a comparison is made by traversing each node one by one to identify the differences in SHA hash values. These differences are then recorded in a list, which serves as the basis for subsequent programs to determine whether the file should be downloaded."

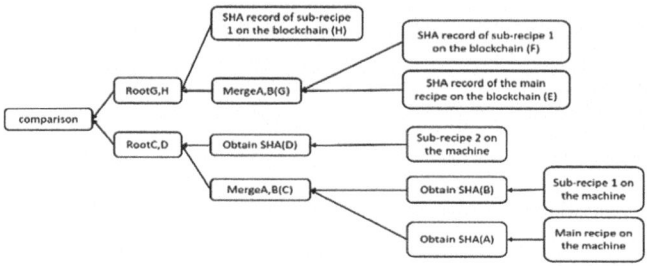

Fig. 10. The Architecture Diagram for SHA Comparison of Hierarchical Recipe

When comparing each node one by one, the algorithm used in this paper is the preorder binary tree traversal. The traversal rule is to visit from top to bottom, from left to right, sequentially visiting the nodes composed of SHA hashes. In this algorithm comparison, differences in SHA hash values are identified. If the differing node is a combined SHA hash value [9], it indicates that one of the nodes in its combination has been changed. Therefore, by continuing to search from this node downwards, the files that need to be re-downloaded can be determined. Conversely, if the upper-level nodes are the same, it indicates that the lower-level nodes have not been changed, and none of the files below need to be re-downloaded.

Algorithm 1: Preorder Binary Tree Traversal

```
1.    public static List<T> PreOrder<T>(BinaryTree<T> tree)
2.    {
3.        List<T> list = new List<T>(tree.Count);
4.        PreOrder(tree, list);
5.        return list;
6.    }
7.
8.    private static void PreOrder<T>(BinaryTree<T> tree, List<T> list)
9.    {
10.       list.Add(tree.Value);
11.       if (tree.Left != null)
12.       {
13.           PreOrder(tree.Left, list);
14.       }
15.       if (tree.Right != null)
16.       {
17.           PreOrder(tree.Right, list);
18.       }
19.   }
```

3.3 Design of Recipe Upload Process Integrated with Blockchain

According to the design of this research as depicted in Fig. 11, in the recipe upload process, personnel at the equipment end will perform the upload action after modifying the test recipe. If it is the first time uploading the recipe and requires creating a new record, the RMS will compute the SHA hash of the uploaded files and upload them to the blockchain. This SHA hash will be used for recipe comparison in subsequent program downloads. If it is not the first time uploading the recipe, the system will directly overwrite the current record of the recipe with the updated SHA hash after recomputing it, and then upload it to the blockchain. After uploading the recipe, each recipe will need to be confirmed one by one until all recipes have been edited before ending the upload process [11].

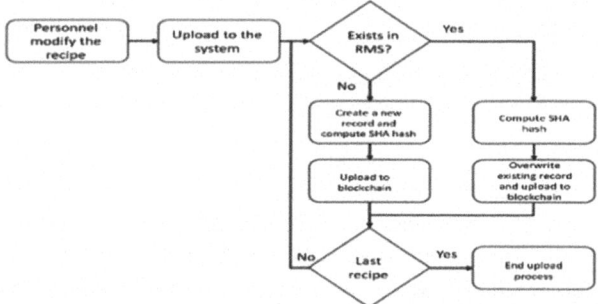

Fig. 11. Architecture Diagram for Recipe Upload Process Integrated with Blockchain

3.4   Utilizing Blockchain in the Recipe Download Process

According to the design of this research, as shown in Fig. 12, the comparison method is changed from comparing MD5 transformations by the RMS system to comparing SHA differences in the blockchain [11]. If there are differences [9], the differing files are identified using a binary tree for downloading, aiming to reduce the time required for complete downloading and overwriting.

For machines using shared folders, the RMS system checks for the recipe, retrieves its SHA hash, and compares it with the blockchain record. Differences are identified through preorder binary tree traversal. If discrepancies are found, the affected files are downloaded, copied to the machine's shared folder, and overwritten. The system then verifies file completeness; if all files are correct and no further recipes are pending, manufacturing begins. Issues such as missing recipes or incomplete downloads are flagged for attention.

For machines using the SECS/GEM protocol, the RMS system uploads the recipe from the machine, computes its SHA hash, and compares it with the blockchain. Differences are noted through preorder binary tree traversal. If discrepancies exist, files are downloaded from the RMS to the machine via SECS/GEM. The system then checks file completeness and, if all files are correct and no further recipes are pending, starts the manufacturing process. Issues are flagged for resolution.

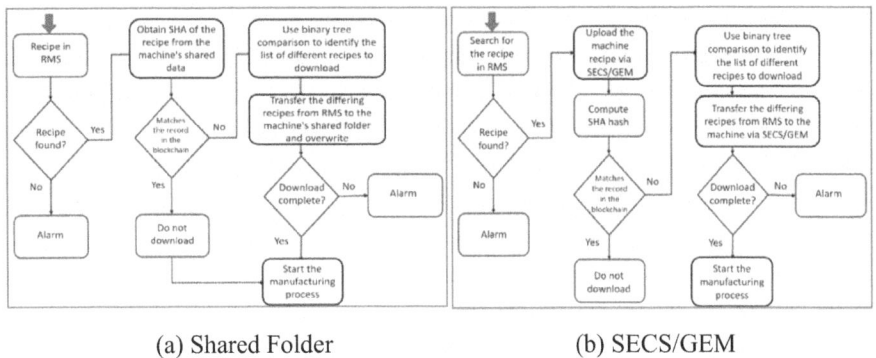

(a) Shared Folder   (b) SECS/GEM

Fig. 12. Architecture Diagram for Recipe Download Process Integrated with Blockchain

During the process of obtaining the differential download list, SHA hash value comparison is performed. In the comparison process, a SHA256 Managed object is used and created. The file is then loaded into a FileStream, and ComputeHash function is used for computation. The resulting byte data is converted into the appropriate type and compared with the SHA hash value of the corresponding node in the blockchain. If they match, True is returned; otherwise, False is returned.

Algorithm 2: Obtaining SHA Comparison Results
1.   private static boolean IsSHASame(string FilePath, int Index)
2.   {
3.   FileStream oFileStream;
4.   SHA256 oSHA256 = SHA256Managed.Create();
5.   oFileStream = new FileStream(FilePath, FileMode.Open);
6.   oFileStream.Position = 0;
7.   byte[] bHashValue = oSHA256.ComputeHash(oFileStream);
8.   sFileSHA = BitConverter.ToString(bHashValue).Replace("-", String.Empty);
9.   oFileStream.Close();
10.
11.   if (sFileSHA != blockchainshalist[Index])
12.   {
13.   return false;
14.   } else {
15.   return true;
16.   }
17.   }

4 Expected Benefits

4.1 Test Scenario Description

This test will involve two different types of recipes: single recipe and hierarchical recipe. The composition of recipe files is described in Table 1 below, respectively. The tests will be conducted in two common network environments, as described in Table 2.

A single recipe file is typically used for single-module machine usage, consisting of only one file. The process is relatively simple with fewer parameter entries, hence the file size is relatively small. For testing purposes, a file size of 200 KB will be used as the condition.

Hierarchical recipe files are typically used for machines with multiple modules, with most machines composed of multiple files. The process is relatively complex, with more parameter entries, and some machine types may include image files for identification. As a result, file sizes are relatively large. For testing purposes, a file count of 3 and a total file size of 4.2 GB will be used as conditions.

Network Environment A assumes a common small-scale factory background. In small-scale factories, due to budget constraints and fewer machines, the upgrading speed of network equipment is relatively slow. The download and upload bandwidths commonly used are both 100 Mbps.

Network Environment B is assumed to be based on common medium to large-scale factories. In such environments, budgets are relatively abundant, and there are more machines. Whenever new network equipment is released, it is typically upgraded or replaced. Therefore, for this scenario, we assume a download bandwidth of 1000 Mbps and an upload bandwidth of 600 Mbps.

Table 1. Composition of Single/Hierarchical Recipe File

Item	Single Recipe File	Hierarchical Recipe File
Main Recipe File Size	200 KB	50 KB
Sub-Recipe 1 File Size		150 KB
Sub-Recipe 2 File Size		4 GB
Total File Size	200 KB	4.2 GB
Number of Files	1	3

Table 2. Network Environment A/B Specifications

Item	Network Environment A	Network Environment B
Download Bandwidth	100 Mbps	1000 Mbps
Upload Bandwidth	100 Mbps	600 Mbps
Download Speed	12.5 MB/s	125 MB/s
Upload Speed	12.5 MB/s	75 MB/s

4.2 Expected Benefits of Single Recipe in Testing Scenarios

In the single recipe scenario, only the main recipe file needs to be downloaded. According to the design of this study, if the recipe matches, there is no need to download the recipe file. Therefore, this section only calculates the time saved from file downloads.

In the scenario of Network Environment A, the main recipe file size is 200 KB, with a download bandwidth of 100 Mbps, which translates to a download speed of 12.5 MB/s. The original and the proposed download methods are shown in Table 3, respectively.

Table 3. Download Results in Network Environment A

Download File	Item	Original Single Recipe Method	Proposed Single Recipe Method
Main Recipe	Download Time (s)	0.0156	(No Download)

In the scenario of Network Environment B, the file size is 200 KB, with a download bandwidth of 1000 Mbps, which translates to a download speed of 125 MB/s. The original and the proposed download methods are shown in Table 4, respectively.

Table 4. Download Results in Network Environment B

Download File	Item	Original Single Recipe Method	Proposed Single Recipe Method
Main Recipe	Download Time (s)	0.0016	(No Download)

4.3 Expected Benefits of Hierarchical Recipe in Testing Scenarios

In the hierarchical recipe scenario, multiple recipe files need to be downloaded. According to the design of this study, if the recipe files match, there is no need to download the files. Therefore, this section calculates the time saved if the files do not need to be downloaded.

In Network Environment A, with a total file size of 4.2 GB across three files and a download bandwidth of 100 Mbps (12.5 MB/s), the estimated download time using the original method is shown in Table 5. In contrast, the method proposed in this study requires downloading only one file in the hierarchical recipe scenario, with estimated download times for the main recipe, sub-recipe 1, and sub-recipe 2 also shown in Table 5.

Table 5. Download Results of Hierarchical Recipe Method in Network Environment A

Method	Download File	Item	Value	Time Saved Percentage
Original Hierarchical Recipe Method	–	Download Time (s)	344.064	–
Proposed Hierarchical Recipe Method	Main Recipe	Download Time (s)	0.0039	99.9989%
	Sub-recipe1	Download Time (s)	0.0117	99.9966%
	Sub-recipe2	Download Time (s)	327.68	4.7619%

Under network environment B, with a file size of 4.2 GB across 3 files and a download bandwidth of 1000 Mbps (125 MB/s), the estimated download times using the original method are shown in Table 6. For the method designed in this study, assuming only one file is downloaded in the hierarchical recipe, the estimated download times for the main recipe, sub-recipe 1, and sub-recipe 2 are also shown in Table 6.

Table 6. Download Results of Hierarchical Recipe Method in Network Environment B

Method	Download File	Item	Value	Time Saved Percentage
Original Hierarchical Recipe Method	–	Download Time (s)	34.4064	–
Proposed Hierarchical Recipe Method	Main Recipe	Download Time (s)	0.0004	99.9989%
	Sub-recipe1	Download Time (s)	0.0012	99.9965%
	Sub-recipe2	Download Time (s)	32.768	4.7619%

4.4 Overall Benefits

In a typical semiconductor company with hundreds to thousands of processing machines, some of which contain larger processing recipes, this section estimates the overall benefits using 200 machines to calculate the impact on the overall production environment when a process engineer changes a recipe.

When a file change is made in network environments A and B, modifying only part of a smaller recipe file can yield significant benefits for the production environment, as shown in Tables 7 and 8.

In network environment A, downloading a single recipe over 200 machines saves just 3.12 s, while downloading a hierarchical recipe saves 65,616.34 s (about 18.23 h), significantly reducing processing time after the update.

In network environment B, downloading a single recipe over 200 machines saves only 0.32 s, offering minimal time savings, while downloading a hierarchical recipe saves 6,553.92 s (about 1.82 h), significantly reducing processing time after the update.

Table 7. Results of Downloading Single/Hierarchical Recipe Using This Study's Method in Network Environment A for 200 Machines

Download File	Item	Single Recipe	Hierarchical Recipe
Main Recipe	Download Time (s)	3.12	78
Sub-recipe1	Download Time (s)	–	2.34
Sub-recipe2	Download Time (s)	–	65536
Total	Download Time (s)	–	65616.34

Table 8. Results of Downloading Single/Hierarchical Recipe Using This Study's Method in Network Environment B for 200 Machines

Download File	Item	Single Recipe	Hierarchical Recipe
Main Recipe	Download Time (s)	0.32	0.08
Sub-recipe1	Download Time (s)	–	0.24
Sub-recipe2	Download Time (s)	–	6553.6
Total	Download Time (s)	–	6553.92

5 Conclusion and Future Prospects

5.1 Conclusion

Through the design proposed in this thesis, the use of pre-order binary tree traversal helps identify recipe files with differing SHA hash values between the machine and the RMS system, enabling differential downloads. By incorporating blockchain concepts, data integrity is ensured. According to the estimated benefits, implementing this design architecture for single recipes yields varying benefits based on the size of the main recipe file. For hierarchical recipes, the architecture significantly improves download time savings as not all recipe files need to be downloaded.

This thesis effectively addresses the following issues:

1. The last modified time of recipes changes after being used by some machines, causing discrepancies in MD5 calculations between the machine and the server.

   Solution provided by this thesis:
   By using the design proposed in this thesis, each recipe file is traversed individually. Commonly, the main recipe, which is frequently modified by the machine, is identified and re-downloaded through differential downloading. This approach saves the download time for the remaining sub-recipes.

2. Managing recipes within internal factory areas and the need for remote downloading by external factories or subcontractors can be time-consuming if the recipes are large.

   Solution provided by this thesis:
   By using the design proposed in this thesis, each recipe file is traversed individually, identifying the modified files through comparison. Only the files listed in the difference list are re-downloaded during the differential download process, saving the download time for the remaining recipe files.

   In the factory setting, after modifying the recipe at the machine end, process engineers need to deploy the modified recipe to production machines of the same model on the production line. Deploying to other machines of the same model using the downloading method designed in this thesis helps reduce the time required for recipe deployment, thereby maximizing production efficiency. The comparative results are presented in Table 9 below.

In the scenario of a single recipe, as simulated in the expected benefits of the test scenario, it is observed that the reduction in download time mainly originates from the main recipe itself. Therefore, the benefits of a single recipe depend on the size of the recipe file. If the recipe file is larger, more time can be saved, whereas smaller files result in limited space savings.

In the hierarchical recipe scenario, as simulated in the expected benefits of the test scenario, it is observed that through differential downloading, significant benefits can be achieved when the saved file sizes are relatively large.

Table 9. Comparative Results for Single/Hierarchical Recipe

Recipe Type	Network Environment	Original Environment Download Time (seconds)	Design in this Thesis Download Time (seconds)
Single Recipe	100 Mbps/100 Mbps	0.0156	(No download required)
	1000 Mbps/600 Mbps	0.0016	(No download required)
Hierarchical Recipe	100 Mbps/100 Mbps	344.064	Main Recipe - 0.0039 Sub Recipe 1 - 0.0117 Sub Recipe 2 - 327.68
	1000 Mbps/600 Mbps	34.4064	Main Recipe- 0.0004 Sub Recipe 1 - 0.0012 Sub Recipe 2 - 32.768

5.2 Future Prospects

Regarding this thesis, several directions can be proposed for future research:

1. This thesis design focuses only on solving the efficiency issues of recipe transmission in manufacturing. There is relatively less emphasis on the blockchain design aspect. Future research could delve into the data format stored within blockchain blocks and explore more detailed designs for application across various types of machines.
2. While this thesis design uses the SHA hashing algorithm, there are still many algorithms that can be applied to such designs. With technological advancements, more advanced algorithms may be proposed. If other types of algorithmic modules can be integrated, it may provide for more customized service requirements.
3. By combining the above two research directions and applying them in a mutually complementary manner, it is believed that a more diverse range of services and applications can be provided.

References

1. Chen,W.C.: Design and Development of Communication Modules for CD Rotating Coating Equipment Using Embedded Controllers. National Chiao Tung University (2007). Retrieved from https://hdl.handle.net/11296/a98tbc
2. Chen, C.H.: Application of SHA-256 and RSA Algorithms in System Boot Programs to Enhance System Security. National Taiwan Ocean University (2014). Retrieved from http://hdl.handl.net/1129/9634x4
3. Chen, C.H.: Research on Semiconductor Equipment Automation Extended to Whole Factory Equipment Performance Analysis. Yuan Ze University (2005). Retrieved from https://hdl.handle.net/11296/9jagj2
4. SEMI E4-0301: SEMI Equipment Communications Standard 1 Message Transfer(SECS-I). Semiconductor Equipment and Materials International (2002)
5. SEMI E5-0301: SEMI Equipment Communications Standard 2 Message Conten t (SECS-II). Semiconductor Equipment and Materials International (2002)
6. SEMI E30: Generic Model for Communications and Control of Manufacturing Equipment (GEM). Semiconductor Equipment and Materials International, (2001)
7. SEMI E37: High-Speed SECS Message Services (HSMS) Generic Services.Semiconductor Equipment and Materials International (2002)
8. MD5 - Wikipedia, the free encyclopedia
9. Secure Hash Algorithms – Wikipedia
10. Khalid, A., Iftikhar, M.S., Almogren, A., Khalid, R., Afzal, M.K., Javaid, N.: A blockchain based incentive provisioning scheme for traffic event validation and information storage in VANETs. Inf. Process. Manag. **58**(2), 102464 (2021)
11. Lu, Y., Huang, X., Zhang, K., Maharjan, S., Zhang, Y.: Communication-efficient federated learning and permissioned blockchain for digital twin edge networks. IEEE Internet Things J. pp. 1–1 (2020)
12. HUME: SECS-II Automated Code Generation Tool (1992). Retrieved from http://www.hume.com/secs/
13. Yu, J.-H.: Factory Automation Series IV: How to Achieve Factory Automation with "Automation System Integration Architecture"?(2022) (Continued). Retrieved from https://marketing.ares.com.tw/newsletter/2021-06-financial-reporting/mes-factory-automation-4

The Use of Social Media and the Internet for the Facilitation of Human Trafficking

Maria Paulina Ramirez and Samuel Olatunbosun[✉]

Norfolk State University, Norfolk, VA, USA
m.ramirez97723@spartans.nsu.edu, sbolatunbosun@nsu.edu

Abstract. Networked technologies such as social media, smartphones, and the Internet have dramatically changed how information is exchanged and how people communicate these days. These media also have been recognized as facilitators of various cybercrime activities, one of which is human trafficking. The Internet has become like a one-stop-shop for traffickers, who use its anonymizing capabilities to evade detection as they recruit, market, monitor, sell, and exploit individuals. This project explored how human traffickers are finding ways to adopt new social media platforms to operate human trafficking rings; the vulnerabilities they exploit in people, processes and technologies while doing so; and how law enforcement and citizen advocates are turning the tables to use social media to monitor and undo these criminal operations. A primary finding is that while progress is being made in understanding the destructive and constructive roles of social platforms in trafficking, there are still many knowledge gaps and missed opportunities, offering ample directions for further work.

Keywords: human trafficking · social media platforms · technology · internet

1 Introduction

1.1 Technology and Human Trafficking

Human trafficking is a troubling undercurrent today. These crimes involve the unlawful coercion of people by others who benefit from their work or service, typically in the form of forced labor or sexual exploitation and may not immediately seem to have a cyber element. But in fact, the evolution of technology has had transformative impacts on trafficking in persons, presenting both challenges and opportunities.

The use of technology takes many forms, including text messaging, social media, the Internet, smartphones, and tablets. According to the United States (U.S.) Department of State's 2020 report on combatting human trafficking, the use of the Internet and online networks to facilitate human trafficking is now a paramount concern. The cumulative accessibility and developing technologies of the Internet and digital networks enable traffickers to operate with increased efficiency and anonymity [1]. According to researcher Dr. Mark Laterno, social networking, online classified, and dating websites facilitate recruiting people into trafficking and – once indentured – advertising their labor [2].

L. Deligiannidis et al. (Eds.): CSCE 2024, CCIS 2262, pp. 320–335, 2025.
https://doi.org/10.1007/978-3-031-85933-5_24

As technology evolved, the trafficking industry followed suit. While human trafficking is not a new problem, the onset of globalization has proven to facilitate traffickers' means. In short, the prevalence of social media and technological devices is helping to increase the instances of human trafficking. The Internet provides predators an extensive potential customer base, which now crosses not just U.S. state lines but also international borders. It has given them unprecedented access to a staggering number of potential victims on a global scale. Traffickers use social media platforms such as Facebook to hunt potential victims. The methods used to lure the victims range from promises of employment, love, and admiration of the victim to a promise of a better life. Lisa Nicely, a news reporter for *Crescent News*, has stated that social media plays a significant role in what we see most; girls caught in sex trafficking who have met their exploiters online [4].

Just as traffickers are using social media and technology to facilitate their operations, law enforcement agencies and the public are seeking ways to use social media and technology to stop the epidemic of human trafficking. At the same time, digital networks have lowered the barriers to citizen participation by allowing individuals and activist groups to transcend geographical boundaries and to organize around global causes, including human trafficking.

1.2 Problem Statement

Social media platforms, networking websites, and online classifieds have fundamentally expanded the reach and reinvented the means for human trafficking. Understanding the relationship between technology and human trafficking is a critical element in advocating for further research on this illegal industry and strategizing the best ways to mitigate or eliminate these activities. This project focused on gaining a better understanding of how human traffickers are exploiting social media for their illegal ends, and uncovering ways online networks can be made less hospitable to practitioners in this illegal industry. The remainder of this report is organized as follows: Sect. 2 provides background on human trafficking as a cybercrime. Section 3 explains the methodology followed to conduct the project. Findings and analysis are detailed in Sect. 4. Section 5 presents conclusions and recommendations, while Sect. 6 summarizes and suggests some ways to build upon this work.

1.3 Research Questions

The research questions for this project focused on social media, and what online human traffickers look for in a victim.

1. How do traffickers use social media, the internet, or technology to facilitate human trafficking?
2. What do online human traffickers look for in a victim?

2 Literature Review

The rise of human trafficking has become an increasingly alarming issue. Not only does it continue to occur, but it thrives in the presence of globalization. It is an industry that has quickly adapted to the technological advancements of the twenty-first century.

From harmless communication to sexual exploitation, the Internet provides countless services for users. However, traffickers are using the Internet in general – and social media platforms in particular – to enable and expand their illicit activities.

Table 1. Pew Research Survey on U.S. adults (2012–2021) [18]

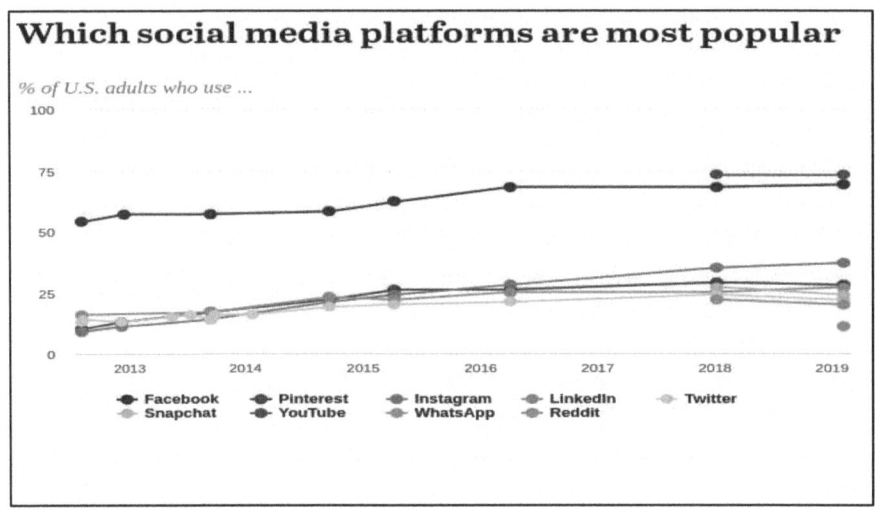

2.1 Prevalence of Social Media Use

Presently, hundreds of millions of users regularly use social media platforms, networking websites, and online classifieds to communicate and engage with other users. These sites range from social media platforms such as Facebook, Twitter, Instagram, and Snapchat to online classifieds like Craigslist and Backpage. Mark Later, author and researcher on communication technology, stated that 79 percent of the population uses the Internet, and almost half use at least one social networking site [8]. According to Anderson & Jiang from the Pew Research Center, the sudden change in youth social media use is an example of how the technology landscape for young people has evolved since the last survey of teens and technology use was conducted in 2014–2015 [17].

According to a Pew Research survey covering 2005 to 2019, more Americans are utilizing social media; the social media user base has also grown more representative of the broader population. Young adults are among the earliest social media adopters and continue to use these sites at high levels; but usage by older adults also has increased in recent years [18]. The survey report collected by the Pew Research Center stated that Facebook and YouTube are the most widely used online platforms, and its user base is broadly representative of the population. Smaller shares of Americans use Twitter, Pinterest, Instagram, and LinkedIn [18]. These overall findings are summarized in Tables 1 and 2.

Table 2. Pew Research Survey on Social Media Use (2006 – 2018) [18]

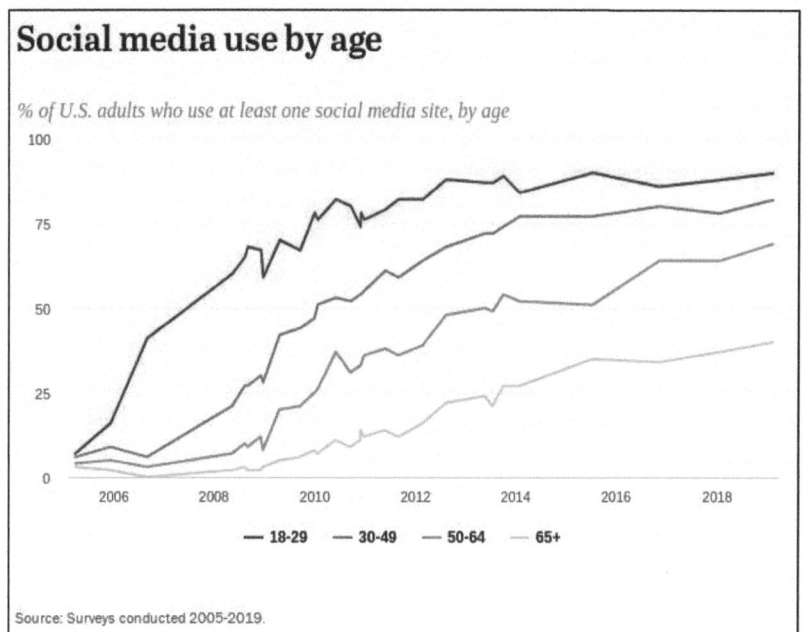

Social media use by age

% of U.S. adults who use at least one social media site, by age

Source: Surveys conducted 2005-2019.

2.2 Human Trafficking as Cybercrime

Cybercrime is popularly associated with technology-related incidents such as hacking confidential data, ransomware, and identity theft. In fact, technology is fueling a digital underground economy while at the same time providing new means for the commission of traditional crimes and enabling new technology-driven crimes. But cybercrime can additionally be linked to other forms of transnational organized crime such as terrorism, child pornography, and trafficking in drugs, arms, wildlife, and human beings.

Table 3 depicts the basis for definitions given in the *Trafficking in Persons Protocol*, which shows that trafficking has three major elements:

(1) The Purpose (why it is done),

(2) The Means (how it is done), and (3) The Act (what is done). [21] The protocol likewise reveals how social media is playing a central role in the evolution of trafficking to unveil new avenues of exploitation. That is, the prevalence of social media and technological devices is helping to increase the incidence of human trafficking.

2.3 Online Social Networks Enable Trafficking

The Internet is known for its facilitation in several cybercrime activities, one of which is human trafficking. Its role in this cybercrime has resulted in increased attention by policy-makers, media outlets, and the public by highlighting how traffickers utilize technological platforms to recruit and control victims. The Internet is like a one- stop-shop for human

Table 3. Elements of Social Networking and Human Trafficking

Vulnerability	Act of Trafficking	Means of Trafficking	Purpose of Trafficking	Social Media Platforms
Low esteem self Esteem	Recruitment	Vulnerability	Modern Slavery	Facebook
	Transport	Abduction	Forced Labor/Services	Instagram
Problems at home	Transfer	Threat/use offorce	Sexual Exploitation	Twitter
Loneliness	Receipt of Persons		Prostitution	TikTok
		Coercion		
			Servitude	Snapchat
		Abuse of Power		
			Removal of Organs	YouTube
		Fraud		

traffickers; it is a way to market, recruit, sell, and exploit individuals. Online recruitment has occurred for as long as there has been prevalent access to internet platforms. Sex trafficking survivors attending a Polaris focus group – and who were entrapped in situations including escort services, outdoor solicitation, remote interactive sexual acts, pornography, strip clubs and bars – discussed their shared experience of being recruited MySpace in the early-to-mid 2000s [6].

Dr. Jonathan Mendel & Dr. Kiril Shaparov compiled a policy briefing titled *Human Trafficking and Online Networks*. In the briefing, Mendel indicated that using the Internet and online networks to facilitate human trafficking has been identified as an emerging concern, with the increasing accessibility and developing technologies of the Internet and digital networks enabling traffickers to operate with increased efficiency and anonymity [3].

According to Polaris, The National Human Trafficking Hotline has recorded recruitment in all types of both sex and labor trafficking on mainstream social media platforms and apps including, but not limited to, Instagram, Facebook, Snapchat, Kik, Meetme.com, WhatsApp, and dating sites/apps like Plenty of Fish, Tinder, and Grindr [5]. Traffickers have used social media to recruit victims, proliferate their trafficking operations, and regulate their victims through impersonating the victim, restricting their social media access, or spreading lies and rumors online. The increased mobility and development of social networking technologies have played unique roles in the ways traffickers target individuals. The Internet's advanced capabilities allow for these platforms to be utilized in several different capacities.

2.4   How Human Traffickers Use Social Media

Perpetrators lure human trafficking victims in various ways, and many victims deny help for multiple reasons. Kendra Martin, a technology columnist for *Dressember*, stated that traffickers around the world are expanding their use of social media to interact with vulnerable teenagers to sell them into sex work, quick to adopt the latest online platforms popular with young people. Traffickers lurk through apps like Facebook, Instagram, Snapchat, and TikTok, looking for vulnerable children and girls. Once they have found a potential target, grooming begins by establishing a connection through a friend request, liking, or commenting on a post. [10].

Technology has many purposes worldwide and in our present culture: communication, tracking payment services, and collaboration. While those purposes are not criminal in and of themselves, a trafficker's use of technology is typically criminal in nature and exploitive. Traffickers prey on victims who share some of the same characteristics, whether it be a psychological or emotional vulnerability, economic hardship, lack of social safety net, natural disasters, and sometimes political instability. Fight The New Drug Organization stated that according to experts from the University of Toledo study, traffickers are drawn to children who post an expression of fear, emptiness, and disappointment, such as "my life sucks," "nobody gets me," or "I need to get out of here." Traffickers also look for indicators of home instability, runaway activity, and substance abuse [11].

Furthermore, the offenders find impressionable young adults that display a feeling of disdain towards their parents, then use sympathy and mutual feelings to further drive a wedge between the two. This type of persuasion works in offenders disguising themselves as individuals closer to the victim's age or as an older, more understanding adult. Nevertheless, vulnerable populations are often targeted.

The recruitment process takes years of grooming. Danah Boyd, Heather Casteel, Mitali Thakor, and Rane Johnson are the authors of Human Trafficking and Technology: A Framework for understanding the role of technology in the commercial sexual exploitation of children U.S from Microsoft Research. Boyd, Casteel, Thakor, and Rane stated, evidence suggests that perpetrators sometimes use social media to identify potential victims. Communication platforms can be used for grooming, coercion, and other forms of deceit [12].

Technology can be used to exploit, particularly sexual, either by individuals for their sequestered use, by organized cybercriminal groups, or other entities using the Internet as a commercial tool to general profit by selling images or services [12]. As mentioned by the United Nations [12], the types of online social technologies that can be exploited for such purposes include the following:

- **Newsgroups**: These sites for exchanging information can be misused to find women and children for exploitation and upload and download illegal pornography.
- **Web message and bulletin boards**: Such venues are misused sexual perpetrators for information exchange. They are similar to newsgroups but can be private and password protected.
- **Websites**: can be misused as venues for distribution of pornography, maintained recreationally, or for profit. These venues may now offer streaming videos as well.

- **Chat rooms**: Predators can misuse real-time communication platforms to abuse children or recruit potential victims. No messages are archived or stored, and no log files are maintained.

3 Methodology

3.1 Rationale and Key Questions

The skyrocketing amount of research effort government and non-profit agencies are investing in understanding and combating human trafficking continually circles back to focus on the role of social media in these criminal activities. Even the limited background material presented in this report into the nature and scope of human trafficking in relation to internet services immediately raises many concerning questions, including the following:

- What do online traffickers look for in their victims?
- How do traffickers use social media, the internet, or technology to facilitate human trafficking?
- What role does the Internet at large play?
- What methods can social media platforms use to help deter online human trafficking?
- What are the best mitigations available to social media users and the general public?
- How can proponents bring awareness to human trafficking facilitated by social media?

This project aimed to gain insights from published research and ongoing initiatives to start to answer these questions. An additional goal was to propose some ways the platforms, tools, tactics, and techniques now being used by human traffickers to exploit victims can be used instead to uncover and prosecute the criminals themselves.

3.2 Research Approach

The U.S. Department of State (DOS) and other humanitarian agencies have a vested interest in assessing and preventing online human trafficking in its many forms.

U.S. domestic agencies and academic studies report on the facilitation of human trafficking through social media platforms, and on governmental actions underway to fight trafficking. These efforts are based on thorough research that includes journalists, academics, victims/survivors, local non-profit organizations, and official governmental studies and advocacy.

This study is archival in nature. It was prepared using secondary data analysis via mixed methods on historical and contemporary information from the copious sources described above, including the U.S. Department of Homeland Security (DHS), international organizations, published reports, news articles, academic studies, U.S. government officials, and non-governmental organizations (NGOs).

The following steps were followed to arrive at the conclusions and recommendations presented later in this report:

1. Collect general background information about technology enablement of human trafficking.

2. Do deeper investigation of specific relevant uses of social media and internet capabilities in the commission of human trafficking crimes.
3. Draw generalizations by analyzing factual and speculative information gathered.
4. Make recommendations for undermining exploitative uses of social media, and for expanding is positive applications to thwart human trafficking uses.
5. Summarize conclusions and propose remaining areas for further research.

3.3 Limitations

Due to time and resource constraints, this study focused on gathering and analyzing information published in research literature including use-cases and exploits attributed to traffickers, all of which is freely available in the open media. There may be additional relevant information beyond the scope of this project, such as or findings that are part of ongoing criminal investigations or sting operations. Similarly, analysis was accomplished "on paper" versus by conducting direct interviews, hands-on experiments or surreptitious infiltration of trafficking venues on the "dark web," involving any victims, criminals or law enforcement personnel.

4   Findings and Analysis

Social media platforms and the Internet can be excellent resources for communication if used wisely. But they can be a dangerous dead end for users, especially teens, who do not know or understand the risks. Youth need to be protected while online; they need to protect themselves when offline in the physical world. Their reputations, personal information, and lives are at stake. After collecting and analyzing available materials regarding the status quo, a primary of finding of this research is that while progress is being made in understanding the role of social platforms in trafficking, there are still many missing pieces and missed opportunities.

4.1   Vulnerabilities in Humans

The increased mobility and development of online social networking technologies have played a unique role in the way traffickers target individuals. Ideally, social media is meant to connect people, but it also allows easy access for predators to communicate with naive and vulnerable users. A particularly challenging problem is that – in many cases – cybercriminals are not stealing information about potential victims; rather, potential victims are furnishing all this information voluntarily and unwittingly. Young adults use their cell phones and publicly post where they go to school, their interests, their place of residence, email address, cell phone number, and the city they reside in. Gullibility on the part of users means hackers do not even have to break through a site's defenses; phishing schemes, spoofed accounts, and other ways to trick users into giving up their credentials are a constant threat, targeting users who may not be ready or educated to spot when they are being fooled.

Lenhart indicated that according to a study done by Pew Research Internet Project, more than half (56 percent) of teens ages 13 to 17 go online several times a day, and 12 percent report once-a-day use. Just 6 percent of teens report going online weekly, and 2 percent go online less often [19]. So teenagers are spending much time online, and their lack of worldliness and caution makes them easy victims. For example, teenagers often can be persuaded to provide strangers provocative pictures of themselves, under the belief that once they delete their photo, it is gone forever. Similarly, female users with a history of abuse are more likely to exhibit risky online behavior. These young women are more likely to meet people offline, respond to sexual advances, and post explicit photos.

As another example, consider sextortion, which occurs when someone threatens to distribute confidential and sensitive material if they are not provided with something in return, such as images of a sexual nature, sexual favors, or money. In the U.S., 78 percent of child victims are females, and many of them had engaged in- person with their perpetrators before the online threats [14]. Still, how many of these victims are exploited further in social media or ultimately sex-trafficked is unknown, despite this being a recognized form of online coercion [15].

Human trafficking is not limited to adults victimizing children either. There have been multiple cases of teenagers in America trafficking other teenagers, sometimes even younger children. In these cases, the trafficker will sometimes attend school with the victim, use instant messaging to arrange for various appointments for the victims, then drive them to the meetings and return to school. Identifying these types of victims becomes more difficult as they are still attending school on a somewhat regular basis [15].

Another human vulnerability that creates risk for social media use is the lack of parental guidance. Some caregivers provide their children with a smart device as early as they enter elementary school "in case of emergencies" and make sure they have a direct line. With inadequate monitoring, children and teens tend to mismanage social media, leading them to suffer psychological disorders and risk committing suicide or falling prey to predators.

Clearly, it is imperative for adult caregivers to become knowledgeable about their children's technology devices, especially the "parental control" features.

4.2 Vulnerabilities in Platforms

Mainstream social media platforms and apps are commonly mentioned in reports to the National Hotline, including Facebook, Instagram, Snapchat, Kik, Plenty of Fish, OkCupid, and Tinder [7]. According to Polaris, in 2017, nearly 8 percent of active federal online sex trafficking cases prosecuted in the United States involved advertisements for sex on Facebook [5]. This calls into question the extent and effectiveness of any monitoring or auditing that may be conducted on these platforms for inappropriate behaviors, fake profiles, and suggestive material, whether by law enforcement officials or the platforms themselves.

Data breaches have demonstrated the presence of weaknesses in social networks that hackers can easily slip through. MacAfee's recent Stratecast study states that 22 percent of social media users have fallen victim to a security-related incident, and recent documented attacks support the numbers. The Pony botnet affected Facebook, Google,

Yahoo, and other social media users, stealing more than 2 million user passwords. These breaches stem from the fact that users rarely embrace even basic security guidelines.

Any technical vulnerabilities are further magnified by the vast quantity of data that has been collected and leaked on the Dark Web about social media users. Taken together, this can spell trouble for data security overall. According to Kevin Lancaster, a technology columnist for Idagent.com, stated that in one 2020 breach, a social media data broker exposed the public-facing profiles of 235 million users; 92 million profiles were scraped from Instagram, 42 million from TikTok, and four million from YouTube via a misconfigured online database. That data almost inevitably ends up on the Dark Web, powering cybercrime like password cracking, credential stuffing, and phishing [16] that may serve as a "steppingstones" to traffickers on the breached platforms.

Common ploys social media users need to watch out for include [17]:

- **Phishing attempts**: Phishing is one of the most common ways criminals attempt to access sensitive personal information. Often in the form of an email, a text message, or a phone call, a phishing attack presents itself as a message from a legitimate organization [17].
- **Data Mining**: Every user leaves a data trail behind on the Internet. Every time someone creates a new social media account, they provide personal information that can include their name, birth date, geographic location, and personal interests. All the data is stored and leveraged by companies to advertise their users [17].
- **Malware sharing**: Malicious software is designed to gain access to computers and the data they contain. Once the malware has penetrated a user's computer, it can utilize delicate information (spyware), extort money (ransomware), or profit from forced advertising. Social media platforms are a perfect delivery system for malware distributors. Once an account has been compromised, cybercriminals can take over that account to distribute malware to all user's friends [17].
- **Botnet Attacks**: Social media bots are automated accounts that generate posts or automatically follow new people whenever a particular term is mentioned. Botnets and bots are prevalent on social media. They are utilized to send spam, steal data, and execute distributed denial-of-service (DDoS) attacks that help cybercriminals gain access to people's devices and networks [17].

4.3 Technology Misuse by Traffickers

As the Inter-Agency Coordination Group Against Trafficking in Persons (ICAT) indicated in a 2019 study, research and data collection on the misuse of technology to enable human trafficking is lacking and needs to be remarkably expanded. A deeper understanding of the scope of the problem is an important step, and not enough is known currently [13]. Still, some problems and consequences of misuse are obvious.

Cybercriminals control technology as a fundamental tool to recruit for and operate human trafficking rings. One factor is the extent to which a trafficker's level of expertise regarding how a forum works or what it is used for can help reinforce the trafficker's online prowess and success. According to Amanda Lenhart, Pew Research Center, such expertise plays a considerable role in establishing and maintaining their online identity. It logically follows, then, that law enforcement officials and concerned citizen advocates will have to match or exceed such criminals in their prowess if they are to undermine them.

4.4 Privacy Violations Enable Traffickers

Understanding the potential role of social and digital media in exploitative activities such as human trafficking obviously is critical, given how deeply enmeshed these technology tools are in the lives of American youth and how rapidly these platforms and devices change. It is likewise imperative to consider social media privacy issues because they cannot be underestimated. Social media is so easy to utilize; most people let their guard down when it comes to cybersecurity, not realizing it can haunt them at some point in the future in several different ways.

What has become normal daily activities – such as tweeting, updating a Facebook status, or using an app or smart device GPS to find local restaurants – can all be misused by predators to harass, surveil, and control victims. The digital world has become a lucrative playground for cybercriminals who can launch attacks on vulnerable youth online in multiple countries and jurisdictions with little to no fear of being caught.

Social media allows traffickers to ascertain what a youth's vulnerabilities are more accessible, whereas pre- social media, learning and understanding these vulnerabilities was a process that took more time. Social media also aids to mask traditional cues that alert individual to a potentially dangerous person and enables rapid relationships. There is no doubt that the human aspect of cybersecurity plays a significant role in cybersecurity and social media platforms because the risks people pose when interacting with technology are significant. The framework against which this exploration is framed is related to the insider threat, in this case, the trafficker with malicious intent.

4.5 Cybersecurity Approaches to Combating Human Trafficking

Ironically, the same technology used to facilitate human trafficking can also be used to fight it. There are some incredible advances in tools to fight human trafficking on the surface web, the dark web, and social media platforms. Digital activism and advocacy are transforming individual and group participation in social causes. Social media serves as a hub for activism around human trafficking issues. Twitter hosts dozens of influential individuals and organizations focused on human trafficking and appears to be a central venue for information sharing among users. Facebook is another social media platform used as a natural hub for socially conscious networking. Many anti-trafficking organizations have created Facebook groups or pages to expand their audience.

According to Polaris, The National Hotline has received countless calls from family members who have had their trafficked loved ones reach out to them via social media platforms, including but not limited to Facebook Messenger, direct message on Instagram, or through Kik [17]. Facebook the number one platform used by 37 percent of victims. Instagram ranked second most common with 22 percent, and 15 percent of survivors said using Google Hangouts / GChat / Google Voice and dating sites or apps [5]. Furthermore, Polaris elaborated that different organizations have developed several initiatives that have been executed worldwide to use technology to fight human trafficking. Some extreme categories of technology currently being used by law enforcement to combat trafficking include [5]:

- Data aggregation and analysis
- Blockchain for traceability and provenance
- Artificial Intelligence
- Facial recognition
- Technology for victims and survivors.

More criminal cases are being solved based on digital evidence than any other type of evidence today. Technology also is enhancing victim identification and referrals for service. The United States has sought to modernize our national human trafficking hotline, operated by Polaris Project, which refers tips to law enforcement, provides victims and survivors with access to critical support services anywhere in the U.S., and equips the anti-trafficking community with tools to combat all forms of human trafficking effectively. [5] Technological advancements provide unprecedented opportunities for law enforcement and service providers to monitor illicit activity, locate and rescue victims, collect, and analyze data leading to the prosecution of traffickers, and streamline communication between anti-trafficking actors and agencies.

5 Conclusions and Recommendations

This project began by raising some *"how to"* questions related to the role of the internet and social media in human trafficking, particularly how to raise awareness of the problem, how the internet and social media can both contribute to the problem and be used to contribute to solutions, and practical self-protection measures for social media users. This chapter synopsizes the key information relevant to these focus areas and discussed in this report, as gleaned from authoritative sources during the research process. In addition, some recommendations are offered for ways to make social media a less hospitable environment for trafficking activities.

5.1 Raising Awareness

This research revealed a general need for raising awareness of the evolution in the emergence of human trafficking facilitated by social media. A coordinated effort between the government taskforces and the private sector in detecting and stopping online human trafficking is warranted. The federal government is responsible for establishing a national-level task force that trains experts in the human trafficking field. As one example, in Southeastern Virginia a Hampton Roads Human Trafficking Task Force has been established with programs for Victims of Crime, Office of Justice Programs, and the U.S. Department of Justice. The Task Force takes a comprehensive approach to human trafficking that meets the personal needs of victims and the community's public safety goals. To date, the Hampton Roads Human Trafficking Task Force has opened 337 investigations, made 135 arrests identified 227 confirmed victims, and prosecuted 38 cases [20].

5.2 Deterring Social Media as a Trafficking Means

This research revealed that social media platforms – like any other technology – can be used for nefarious or noble purposes; it all depends on who is in control. Social media is being used by skillful predators to recruit and exploit others. Law enforcement and private citizens are now "bringing up the rear" and learning how to turn these same tools against the criminals to uncover them and put them out of business.

Social media platforms likewise should accept their share of responsibility to ensure their venues are safe for all users. Facebook estimates that anywhere from 50 million to 100 million of its monthly active user accounts are fake duplicates, and as many as 14 million of those are "undesirable" on the site [17]. Social media providers should be policing profiles *voluntarily* by requiring background checks for users who join their platform to verify the person's identity is truthful. Known predators or those who have attempted suspicious interactions should be barred from membership. Participation on the site should incur an implicit "consent to monitor." Sites could then legally trawl traffic for the appearance of trigger keywords in conversations that indicate potential grooming, kidnapping or other signs of potential exploitative interactions so they can be investigated and pre-empted as appropriate. Big data analytics should be running in the background to identify and take down falsified profiles.

An educated parent, guardian or adult caregiver is the best "human firewall" against a trafficker. Adults who are educated can wage a notable defense against the potential recruitment of their teenagers online. Parents who work to build healthy, open, and communicative relationships are more likely to have teenagers who share information about where they go and whom they interact with online. Parents and guardians must understand the variations within developmental age for teenagers and different strategies for different ages. The younger the child, the more parents should monitor where the child may go on the Internet and talk to them. They must be savvy and enact all age-appropriate parental controls on the apps used by the youth in their care. The older the child, the more adult caregivers will need to educate and partner with youth to empower them to practice common sense and safety while online.

5.3 Other Key Recommendations

- Federal, State, and local agencies and private/public schools and universities should join forces to educate the community and their students about the dangers of social media. From a cybersecurity perspective, curriculums should address the dangers of social media facilitating human trafficking.
- National Helpline advertisements should be placed on search engine results and as ads on social media and apps rather than on bulletin boards. Since traffickers use these venues to recruit and advertise victims online, these methods will alert victims how to get help.
- To succeed against human trafficking, social networking, and classified advertising websites should be held liable and prosecuted for any trafficking that takes place on their sites. This may require new legislation since laws, in general, have not kept pace with technology.

5.4 Conclusion

This research aimed not only to bring awareness to the dangers of social media, but also to find links between technology and human trafficking so they can be understood. Traffickers use different platforms and media to recruit victims and to operate trafficking rings. Although traffickers are using technology for evil ends, technology still can be a powerful, beneficial tool to combat human trafficking. The perceived anonymity of technology-driven human trafficking provides can also be used to catch and prosecute offenders. If social media assists predators in reaching out to both active and potential victims, law enforcement too can harness the same technology that traffickers use to catch and prosecute them.

Allowing youth, the use of technology without supervision and proper training is like giving them a loaded weapon. Every click potentially is a virtual step on a dead-end street. Education is imperative and necessary to protect the naïve and innocent from trafficking predators. All adults in positions of trust involving youth need to educate themselves to become more familiar with popular social media platforms and apps, and how to enable appropriate privacy settings. Raising children to become responsible digital citizens is necessary to limit the dangers of social media for all involved.

5.5 Future Directions

Research and data collection on the misuse of technology to enable human trafficking needs to be significantly expanded to better understand the complex relationships between technology and cybercrime in general – and human trafficking in particular – and how to combat this insidious dark economy. Little research exists on online classified and social networking sites and their relation to human trafficking, so there is considerable room for making contributions in that area. The reported incidence of all types of sex and labor trafficking on mainstream social media platforms and apps is particularly troubling, and merits further investigation to determine the best ways to undermine and thwart such activities. A better understanding of law enforcement opportunities to use social media "for the good" – that is, for tracking and apprehending traffickers, and for locating and recovering victims – is another much needed avenue for future work. Educational material can be developed to guide adults in setting appropriate privacy controls in apps used by the children in their care, and ways to monitor online activities for signs of trouble. "Plug-in modules" for current cybersecurity curriculums are needed to further students' knowledge on technology-driven trafficking. This should cover both manual and automated methods, how investigations must be balanced against fundamental human rights of privacy, speech, and self-expression, and address the important legal implications of cybersecurity measures.

References

1. 2020 Report on U.S. Government Efforts to Combat Trafficking in Persons - United States Department of State. U.S. Department of State (2021). https://www.state.gov/2020-report-on-u-s-government-efforts-to-combat-trafficking-in-persons/. Accessed: 26 Apr 2021

2. Latonero, M.: The Rise of Mobile and Diffusion of Technology-Facilitated Trafficking (2012). https://technologyandtrafficking.usc.edu/files/2011/09/HumanTrafficking_FINAL.pdf. Accessed: 23 Dec 2020

3. Mendel, J., Sharapov, K.: Human Trafficking and Online Networks (2014). http://publicservicesalliance.org/wp-content/uploads/2018/06/Teens-Social-Media-Technology-2018-PEW.pdf. Accessed: 20 Feb 2021

4. L.I.S.A.NICELY@cnLisaNicelylnicely@crescent-news.com. Human traffickers lurking on social media. News (2018). https://www.crescent-news.com/news/local_news/human-traffickers-lurking-on-social-media/article_9fd7acf0-bf1f-59ef-852f-53cfcf4f9e3b.html. Accessed: 10 Apr 2021

5. Human Trafficking and Social Media. Polaris (2020). https://polarisproject.org/human-trafficking-and-social-media/. Accessed: 10 Oct 2020

6. Social Media/Online. Polaris Social MediaOnline Category. https://polarisproject.org/category/social-media-online/. Accessed: 23 Dec 2020

7. Lenhart, A.: Teens, Social Media & Technology Overview 2015. Pew Research Center: Internet, Science & Tech (2020). https://www.pewresearch.org/internet/2015/04/09/teens-social-media-technology-2015/. Accessed: 20 Feb 2021

8. Latonero, M.: The Rise of Mobile and Diffusion of Technology-Facilitated Trafficking. (2012). https://technologyandtrafficking.usc.edu/files/2011/09/HumanTrafficking_FINAL.pdf. Accessed: 23 Dec 2020. https://www.idagent.com/blog/3-ways-that-social-media-is-a-data-breach-risk. Accessed: 04 Feb 2021

9. Anderson, M., Jiang, J.: Teens' Social Media Habits and Experiences. Pew Research Center: Internet, Science & Tech (2020). https://www.pewrerch.org/inteet/2018/11/28/teens-social-media-habits-and-experiences/. Accessed: 20 Feb 2021

10. December. Social Media: Making Targeting Easier for Human Traffickers. Dressember (2019). https://www.dressember.org/blog/social-media-making-targeting-easier-for-human-traffickers. Accessed: 10 Oct 2020

11. How Sex Traffickers Use Social Media to Contact, Recruit, and Sell Children for Sex. Fight the New Drug (2020). https://fightthenewdrug.org/how-sex-traffickers-use-social-media-to-contact-recruit-and-sell-children-for-sex. Accessed: 10 Oct 2020

12. Human Trafficking and Technology. A framework for understanding the role of technology in commercial sexual exploitation children the U.S. - Together Against Trafficking in Human Beings - European Commission (2014). https://ec.europa.eu/anti-trafficking/publications/human-trafficking-and-technology-framework-understanding-role-technology-commercial_en. Accessed: 20 Apr 2021

13. Technology and Trafficking. Equality Now. https://www.equalitynow.org/technology_and_trafficking_the_need_for_a_stronger_gendered_and_cooperative_response. Accessed: 29 Apr 2021

14. 3 Ways That Social Media is a Data Breach Risk – and How to Fight Back. ID Agent (2020). Accessed: 21 May 2021

15. Technology and Trafficking. Equality Now. https://www.equalitynow.org/technology_and_trafficking_the_need_for_a_stronger_gendered_and_cooperative_response. Accessed: 03 Apr 2021

16. 3 Ways That Social Media is a Data Breach Risk – and How to Fight Back. ID Agent (2020). https://www.idagent.com/blog/3-ways-that-social-media-is-a-data-breach-risk. Accessed: 20 Feb 2021

17. Business Home. McAfee. https://www.mcafee.com/enterprise/en-us/security-awareness/cybersecurity/cybercriminal-social-media.html. Accessed: 14 Jan 2021

18. Demographics of Social Media Users and Adoption in the United States. Pew Research Center: Internet, Science & Tech (2021). https://www.pewresearch.org/internet/fact-sheet/social-media/. Accessed: 26 Apr 2021

19. Lenhart, A.: Teens & Tech Introduction. Pew Research Center: Internet, Science & Tech (2019). https://www.pewresearch.org/internet/2015/04/09/introduction-teens-tech/. Accessed: 21 Dec 2020
20. Attorney General of Virginia. https://www.oag.state.va.us/media-center/news-releases/1898-december-15-2020-herring-expands-work-to-combat-human-trafficking-in-Hampton-roads. Accessed: 14 Jan 2021
21. An Introduction to Human Trafficking: Vulnerability, Impact and Action. https://www.unodc.org/documents/human-trafficking/AnIntroduction_to_Human_Trafficking_-_Background_Paper.pdf

Cybersecurity Techniques, Emerging Threats, and Industry Responses

Momo A. Tulay and Samuel Olatunbosun[✉]

Norfolk State University, Norfolk, VA, USA
m.tulay@spartans.nsu.edu, sbolatunbosun@nsu.edu

Abstract. Data security has become increasingly important in today's world of information technology. A modern lifestyle, made possible by advances in technology, is driving people to use their portable devices for shopping and financial transactions in cyberspace. Simultaneously, cybercrime has increased due to the heavy use of social media. Information security has become a major issue today. Cyber-attack incidents have increased significantly with the massive growth of Internet interconnection, often resulting in devastating and grievous consequences. Cyberspace is dominated by malware, which frequently exploits existing vulnerabilities or advances in technology to carry out malicious goals. Security experts have long considered it imperative to develop more innovative and effective mechanisms to defend against malware. Businesses and governments adopt varied measures against cybercrime. Despite ongoing initiatives, cybersecurity remains vital to many. This report outlines common vulnerabilities in software, hardware, and networks. It focuses on new technology-related cybersecurity issues and includes an analysis of ethical and developmental aspects, alongside a review of the latest technological advancements.

Keywords: Data security · information technology · cybercrime · social media · malware · vulnerabilities · innovative mechanisms

1 Introduction

Cybersecurity evaluates threats, vulnerabilities, exposures, and impacts on stability and survival. It deploys technologies, processes, and controls to defend networks, programs, and devices. Cyber-attacks involve unauthorized system access, affecting single elements or entire networks [18].

Malware, a broad term, encompasses software used by threat actors to breach systems and access sensitive data, posing a major cybersecurity concern. Viruses, a malware form, inject code into software, disrupting systems and causing data loss when activated. Worms, distinct from viruses, independently self-replicate and perform destructive tasks on computers. Ransomware, another malware variant, encrypts victim data and demands payment, often in cryptocurrencies, for data restoration. Malware spreads via email, web, social media, malvertising, exploit kits, networking, removable media, and infected email attachments [1–3].

© The Author(s), under exclusive license to Springer Nature Switzerland AG 2025
L. Deligiannidis et al. (Eds.): CSCE 2024, CCIS 2262, pp. 336–353, 2025.
https://doi.org/10.1007/978-3-031-85933-5_25

1.1 Problem Statement

In 2020 and 2021, cyber-attacks surged, including ransomware, data breaches, and nation-state actions, as per NCC Group's 2021 Annual Threat Monitor [91]. Ransomware attacks spiked by 92.7% in 2021 compared to 2020 [91]. Notably, the COVID-19 pandemic sparked a consistent rise in ransomware attacks, constituting 64% of 2021's cyber incidents investigated by the global CIRT. North America and Europe, targeted due to wealth and population density, suffered 53% and 30% of attacks [91].

This trend, predicted to continue into 2022, posed India's significant cybersecurity challenge in 2020 [4]. Ransomware affected 82% of Indian organizations in six months, hindering data access until ransoms are paid. Businesses are hit harder, often without data restoration post-payment. Cloud computing's necessity led to concerns over data theft and breaches [5]. Infamous iCloud-like attacks on enterprises risk data exposure and organizational collapse. Cyberattacks spread via networks, accessing multiple devices. Over 1,000 breaches last year impacted governments and businesses, fueled by malware. Malware, particularly spyware or Trojans, facilitates data theft, compromising personal and company information [6, 7].

1.2 Historical Perspective on Malware

The existence of malware dates to the invention of computers, so it has been around for millennia. A computer virus has been in existence since 1949 when computer scientist John von Neumann published his book "The Computer and the Brain," which explains how a computer program can replicate itself [13]. In the 1950s, Bell Labs employees created a computer game known as "Core Wars," where software systems competed for control over a system. It was not until the early 1970s that viruses became documented [14]. The following paragraph showcases some of the most well-known and prominent viruses.

1.2.1 Viruses that Have Become Famous in the Digital Era

In 1991, Australia discovered the "Michelangelo" virus [8]. It stayed inactive until March 6th, when it wiped the initial 100 memory sectors with zeros, rendering computers unbootable. The infection count was low at 20,000, around the time of CIH's emergence. The CIH virus, overwriting vital files, infected 60 million computers, causing extensive harm and attributed to Taiwanese students. Named Melissa, it was the first global virus [9]. Utilizing Outlook addresses, Melissa self-propagated, sending to the first 50 contacts, causing email server crashes. "I love you" spread widely in 2000 via email, damaging audio and image files, infecting 50 million computers in days from the Philippines. Amid the influx of new viruses after 2000, notable examples include Code Red, Nimba, Beast, SQL Slammer, Blaster, Sobig, Sober, My Doom, NetSky, Zeus, Conficker, Stuxnet, CryptoLocker, Locky, Mirai, and WannaCry [10].

1.2.2 Ransomware's Most Dangerous Threats and the Threat's Future

Since the mid-2000s, ransomware emerged as a major threat across enterprises, small businesses, and individuals. In 2017, the FBI's IC3 reported ransomware causing over

$2.3 million in losses [11]. However, this underestimates its prevalence and cost. Estimated at 184 million attacks last year, individuals remain primary targets. Ransomware debuted in healthcare in 1989, enduring as a prime target [12]. Dr. Joseph Popp initiated the first known ransomware assault, deploying malicious software via 20,000 disks that activated after 90 starts, demanding $189 and $378 for software use. Named AIDS Trojan or PC Cyborg, this marked the inception of ransomware attacks [12].

1.3 Contextualizing the Problem

Previously, businesses operated isolated networks, but Internet adoption for its features has reduced this separation. Recent advancements, like real-time monitoring, peer-to-peer, concurrent communications, maintenance, and redundancy, have enhanced services. Smart grids and IoT have increased utility interconnectedness, exposing once-isolated systems to rising threats [15].

Zou et al. (2010) [5] argues holistic defense, combining computer, communication, control, and physical monitoring, to counter daily vulnerabilities [16]. IP-based shifts render traditional protection less effective. A survey of 268 companies revealed reliance on staff, not software, for issue detection [17].

1.4 Research Questions

This paper sought to answer the following questions:

1) What are the most frequently attacked industries and what are the motivations for attacking them?
2) What are the most common methods for deploying malware in computers and the consequences of those respective attacks.
3) What cybersecurity preventive measures are available to counter the most prevalent cyber-attacks?
4) What mitigation strategies appear to be effective and which ones have not?

2 Literature Review

2.1 Cybersecurity and Critical Infrastructure

Researchers' varied perspectives have shaped cybersecurity's definition over time. Beyond safeguarding data and systems, cybersecurity ensures stability and sustainability, in contrast to prior definitions. This new view links cybersecurity to potential company impact from breaches [19]. Understanding cybersecurity involves adapting critical infrastructure amidst evolving technology, reflecting security levels within organizations and countries [20].

Critical infrastructure (CI) is vital for public safety and economies. Uninterrupted CI operation is crucial, necessitating continuous security reinforcement [21]. U.S. CI, ranging from agriculture to nuclear plants, relies on operational reliability [22]. Growing cyber threats exploit complex, connected CI systems, endangering security, economy, and safety. This issue's gravity in a major economy suggests global vulnerability [21].

Organizing American Standards highlights digital hacking's increasing capacity, including cyberbullying, terrorism, and data breaches, posing disaster potential. Socioeconomic factors, laws, governance, and security strategies require addressing for effective change [23]. The myriad options attackers have underscored the need for comprehensive approaches to counter cyber threats.

2.2 Cybercrimes and Their Impact

Cybercrimes encompass illegal activities in cyberspace, ranging from data theft to breaches. In cyberspace, connected through the web, threats evolve incessantly, rendering full protection challenging [24]. Internet threats evolve swiftly, surpassing traditional military and terrorism changes [75]. Law enforcement difficulties arise in locating criminals, often due to their masking techniques or attacks outside jurisdiction [25].

Internal actors caused 23% of 2016's cybercrimes, surprising given external concerns [26]. Attack frequency varies, with evolving complexity, posing infrastructure risks [27]. User community remains a vulnerability, necessitating combined power and precision [27]. Over the past decade, cybercrime incurred substantial global losses, 0.70% of GDP in 2016 [28]. In Latin America and the Caribbean, costs reached billions [28]. Personal data exploitation also occurred, as in a South African breach exposing 31 million people's data, risking identity theft [28].

Addressing these issues requires grasping their roots. Culture and accountability gaps top concerns, with available encryption methods often underused [29–32]. Robust cybersecurity laws and individual responsibility are essential [28].

2.3 Components of Cybersecurity

Tiers are the building blocks that makeup cybersecurity, and this section provides a foundational understanding of them. The remainder of the section discusses additional aspects of strengthening this framework.

2.3.1 Cybersecurity Governance and Risk Management

Cybersecurity governance employs tools like Frameworks to assess and mitigate risks. Standards of varying complexity are useful, with Siemens (2018) emphasizing cybersecurity integration into an organization's DNA and strategy [33]. Government regulation enforces standards when market incentives fall short.

Frameworks are vital for cybersecurity, ensuring security's foundation. Risk management frameworks are key for reliable governance, consisting of 4 tiers for organization-wide security [34]. On a global scale, cybersecurity frameworks prioritize risk management over compliance, enhancing NIST CSF with real-world Intel-based factors. Governance and risk management are pivotal for effective cybersecurity implementation [35].

2.3.2 Culture and Awareness

Embedding cybersecurity in corporate culture is essential. Often, user disregard for cybersecurity's importance causes problems. Ordinary users, with system access, must understand security's significance. Risks arise when known security rules are ignored, aiding attackers. Users' unawareness and lax enforcement of policies create vulnerabilities and losses [36].

Effective cybersecurity governance depends on frameworks, risk management, culture, and awareness. Neglecting it can lead to irreparable harm. OAS survey in Latin America and the Caribbean identified top reasons for cyber incidents:

- Insufficient employee awareness
- Security knowledge gaps
- Patch mismanagement
- Inadequate access control
- Weak support for application and internal security

Cultural and awareness issues prevail in these causes [37]. Addressing these challenges is complex [37].

2.3.3 Adequate Cybersecurity Governance

Cybersecurity governance safeguards organizations, but implementation complexity arises due to numerous variables [38]. Inadequate governance stems from issues like enforcement gaps, internal disarray, reporting inaccuracies, and infrastructure deficiencies, creating exploitable vulnerabilities.

2.3.4 Proper Risk Management

Risk management should be consistent and should be a top priority. There are most likely no adequate risk management policies in place due to undermining the potential dangers that these policies could cause.

2.3.5 Instilling Culture and Awareness

In the cultural domain, there are many issues that persist, such as skepticism, disregard, ignorance, and too much trust [39]. The cybercriminal exploits these human factors or is the root cause for vulnerabilities to exist. Trusting people can be risky.

2.3.6 Emerging Threats

One worrisome aspect of cybersecurity is the integration of trends like IoT, Cloud Computing, Smartphones, social media, and Big Data into the digital realm. Cybercriminals exploit these trends to magnify vulnerabilities due to their substantial impact on the digital world [40].

2.3.7 The Need for a Change in Perception

Comprehending challenges and resolutions is vital, especially in cybersecurity. Real-world instances illustrate this [41]. Traditional governance enforces security collectively, including risk, culture, and awareness. Emerging threats intertwine these aspects. When organizations handle data extensively, expand globally, and employ many, unified cyber-security governance is crucial. It secures data flows, prevents breaches compromising infrastructure, often due to weak governance. Poor awareness and culture exacerbate this issue. Emerging threats exploit trends [42].

As technology integrates further, impacting progress and security, user vigilance is pivotal [43].

3 Methodology

The research began with a review of the emerging threat of cyber-crimes around the world. Literature review of cases, including legal aspects, and analysis of major events were examined. The research was based on information gathered from data regarding attacks detected and traced, as well as from global reports and surveys. The goals were three-fold:

1) establish a general overview of cyber-attacks from across the globe.
2) understand the potential impact of cyber-crimes on businesses and individuals; and
3) inventory existing and propose new countermeasures address the risks.

Narrative analysis was used in the research as a means of extracting information about various studies and to conduct an analysis in a manner consistent with the review question. A comparative analysis was used to highlight similarities and differences between the study outcomes.

3.1 Limitations

Despite many cyber-attacks occurring daily around the world, businesses provide limited information when they are victimized by cyber-crime. In addition, the origins of some attacks are difficult to trace. For these reasons it was impossible to gain a complete set of data for analysis purposes (Fig. 1).

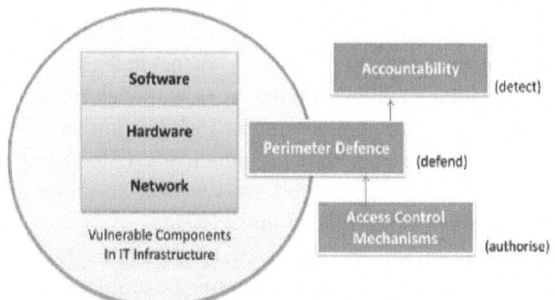

Fig. 1. Vulnerabilities and Defense Strategies in existing systems

4 Findings

This research aimed to identify enterprise data leak risks, detect prevention systems, and suggest future research. It emphasizes corporate data breach risks, reviews recent cases, and summarizes lessons learned. The prior section outlines effective leak prevention and detection methods, addressing some flaws [20]. A privacy-preserving data leak detection system in our case study addresses modern concerns.

Artificial intelligence makes information theft increasingly secure, especially in the digital age. Because data is one of the most valuable components of a market, it can help companies achieve a major competitive advantage (for example, business intelligence or providing personalized services). However, businesses face significant security risks because of exposing sensitive and confidential enterprise data to theft or fraud.

The private sector and government agencies will both suffer a data breach at some point in their lives. This fate is inevitable for some people and the only way forward is to trust in the company's cybersecurity measures [62]. The organization can better establish trust if it informs the community about the challenges and risks it faces internally and externally from cyberspace. Being a competent cyber-threat manager necessitates a deep understanding of how to defend networks, operating systems, and infrastructure against internal and external attacks (Kaspersky, n.d.). The purpose of data management is to protect computers from disruptions and unwanted behavior (Kaspersky, n.d.). It is also concerned with making sure sensitive data isn't exposed to the wrong hands by preventing cyber-attacks.

Cybercriminals are pushing boundaries, evolving in data collection methods. Recent breaches underscore the need for businesses to prioritize data protection, involving CEOs and security experts for effective change [63]. Employing skilled staff and maintaining security processes is crucial [63]. Network breaches expose confidential data, necessitating vigilant vulnerability management. Policies and investments grow, responding to violations promptly [64]. Companies like Facebook, Yahoo, and Marriott must secure sensitive data for clients and employees [64]. Data leaks carry grave risks, allowing malicious activities and threatening millions. Learning from breaches is crucial for long-term security [64] (Fig. 2).

Businesses gain from AI but face rising data leakage costs due to sensitive information storage. Shared data among partners and clients heightens risks, especially in cloud sharing [65]. Watermarking can prevent and detect leakage, labeling data of interest as it enters or exits systems. Outbound messages with watermarks suggest potential compromise. Continuous commitment is vital for leak prevention [66].

The report outlines techniques and risks of data leakage, focusing on the AI context [66]. New approaches, like AI-based cloud service leak detection and deep learning anomaly detection for insider risks, hold promise [67].

Upon reviewing the findings, it was discovered that various studies on cybersecurity had been undertaken. Past studies aimed to determine the problems associated with spam and spam filtering systems. Furthermore, more research has been conducted with the goal of developing an effective, accurate, and dependable spam detection method among the existing spam detection approaches. When using a personal firewall system, the act of applying cognitive analysis to determine design features that contradict usability criteria is referred to.

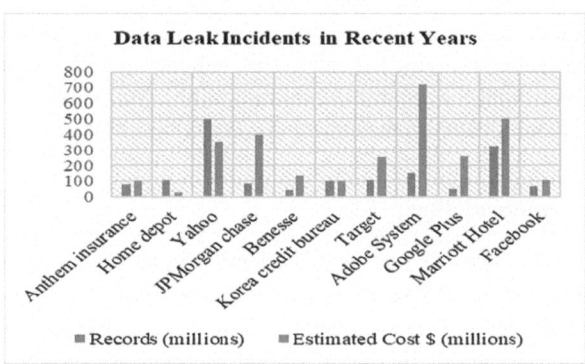

Fig. 2. Significant Corporate Data Breach Events in Recent Years (Source of Data: The World's Largest Data Breach Dataset)

To accomplish the intended outcome of limiting the maximum firewall ruleset, it is required to consider how to organize the topology of firewalls within a network design and how to frame the routing tables. When more security is necessary, attribute-based methods might be used. Only technological measures can decide cybercrime in next-generation safety digital environments; capacity building, organizational structure, and worldwide collaboration, as well as legislative initiatives, are also required.

5 Discussion and Recommendation

Cybercriminals exploit vulnerable users in digital spaces, including businesses and new-comers. Large corporations face higher risks due to potential gains from successful hacks [68]. The elderly and young adults are most vulnerable, with young adults often having a false sense of security [68]. Global transaction volume growth, primarily in e-commerce and financial services, drove a 29% rise in cybercrime [68]. E-commerce suffered bot attacks during the pandemic [68].

2020 marked a record-breaking year for cyberattacks, particularly targeting six industries:

1) Small businesses, lacking cybersecurity resources, made up 43% of cyberattack targets [68].
2) Healthcare faced increasing cyberattacks, with over 90% of organizations reporting breaches [68].
3) Government agencies' sophisticated security attracted hackers seeking sensitive data [68].
4) Financial institutions were at risk due to server attacks and data theft [68].
5) Education's tech integration led to a vulnerability increase, accounting for 62% of reported malware cases [68].
6) Energy and utility firms, like Colonial Pipeline, experienced disruptive cyberattacks [68].

Cybercrime affects national and economic security, requiring comprehensive strategies [68]. Defense against evolving cybercrime is challenging [68]. Encouraging cybersecurity innovation is vital for a stable digital future [68]. Monitoring opponents in the growing field of global identity management is a future concern [68].

5.1 Existing Recommendations

Three essential cybersecurity factors include identifying methods to protect IT, ensuring data integrity, and securing data processing and transmission [45]. A cybersecurity strategy combines actions, risk management, technology, processes, and skills to safeguard organizations and assets. Research highlights significant threats to systems and data [46].

To enhance cybersecurity, organizations across industries should:

1) Restrict information access to minimize human errors and risks.
2) Conduct vulnerability assessments to identify and rectify weaknesses.
3) Employ and update firewalls to prevent cyber-attacks.
4) Secure Wi-Fi using WPA2, changing passwords, and separating networks.
5) Utilize AI for enhanced protection.
6) Train employees according to cybersecurity policies for safe data usage and sharing.

5.2 Proposed Recommendations

Previous research proposed effective mitigation strategies to defend against known attacks, yet the threat landscape remains dynamic with hackers constantly inventing new forms of attacks, targeting organizations of all sizes. To delve into system protection against hackers, an alternative method involves securing data through RSA and Hash functions using mobile cloud computing. This service allows resource-constrained mobile users to offload computationally intensive tasks to traditional cloud resources, enhancing processing and storage capabilities [59].

Mobile applications have shifted to more powerful cloud platforms, raising concerns about data security. Unauthorized access to user data by hackers could result in severe damage. A survey showed that 74 percent of IT executives and Chief Information Officers are reluctant to adopt cloud services due to security risks [59]. To address these concerns, cloud service providers introduced RSA, Hash functions, and DES algorithms to protect mobile users' information.

5.2.1 RSA Algorithm

RSA, a prevalent public key cryptography algorithm, serves multiple purposes such as key exchange, digital signatures, and encryption of small data blocks. It employs variable-sized encryption blocks and keys, finding extensive application in secure communication channels, service provider authentication, and identity verification across insecure mediums. Through public key authentication, servers establish trust by signing unique client messages with their private key, generating digital signatures [88].

5.2.2 Hashing Function

A cryptographic hash function processes messages of varying lengths to generate fixed-length message digests. These digests are unique for each message and possess security requirements like being one-way and collision-resistant [89].

5.2.3 DES Algorithm

The Data Encryption Standard (DES) is a symmetric-key block cipher with a 64-bit block size and a 56-bit key. It transforms a 64-bit plaintext into 64-bit ciphertext during encryption and reverses the process during decryption, using the same 56-bit cipher key for both actions.

In ensuring secure data storage, three key participants are involved: Data owner (DO), Third Party Auditor (TPA), and Cloud Service Provider (CSP). Each participant has distinct roles. The DO uses storage services from the CSP, the TPA verifies data integrity on the mobile cloud, and the CSP offers storage services to mobile users [90].

5.2.4 Proposed Scheme

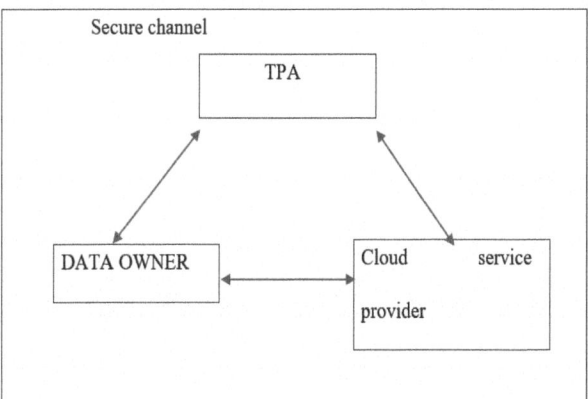

This scheme or figure suggests a secure data storage approach in Mobile Cloud Computing that employs Hash functions and cryptographic tools for enhanced data security. A Trusted Third-Party Auditor (TPA) plays a vital role in this proposal, verifying data integrity on the mobile cloud for the data owner. By verifying hash and message content, TPA ensures data integrity, lessening the workload for mobile users and providing efficient Integrity Verification [90].

- Key Generation: Data Owner uses RSA algorithm for generation of combination of public and private key for himself. TPA also uses RSA algorithm for generating key pair for its own. The private key of TPA is pkl and of Data Owner is pk2, while public key of TP A is dl and public key of data owner is d2.
- Key Sharing: Key set of TPA: {pkl, dl} at TPA Key set of DO: {pk2, d2} at Mobile device Here only public key of TP A is exchanged between DO and TP A using secure channel.

- Encryption: At first, the owner of data encrypts the message/ file (F) using his public key (d2) E(F,d2) and then generates the hash of encrypted message H(E(F,d2)). Now, the encrypted file is re-encrypted with public key (dl) of TPA E(E(F,d2),dl).

After re-encrypting the hash with TPA's public key (dl) as E(H(E(F,d2)),dl), the two packages are combined as E(E(F,d2),dl) II E(H(E(F,d2)),dl) and sent to TPA. TPA securely stores the encrypted hash to ensure data integrity. TPA then decrypts the received package E(E(F,d2),dl) using its private key. TPA generates a random key for encrypting the message E(F,d2) produced after encryption. For enhanced security, TPA employs the Data Encryption Standard (DES) for encryption. The generated random key is retained by TPA for future decryption purposes. Finally, the encrypted result is transmitted to the cloud for storage.

ALGORITHM   1:

Set Up

TPA: pkl,   dl= GenKeyO

Client: Pk2, d2= GenKeyO

TPA ---+ Client: d 1

Client: F'= (E (F, d2)), H(F') = H(E (F, d2)) F"= E (F', dl), H'(F') =E (H(F'), dl)

Client ---+ TP A: F"II H'(F')

TPA: Store(H'(F')), k=RandomO,   F'= D(F",pkl),

F"= Encrypt (F' ,k)

TPA ---+ CSP: F"

CSP:

Store(F")

ALGORITHM   2:

Verification

CSP ---+ TP A: F"

TPA: F'= D (F", k), newH'(F')=H(F'), retrieve(H'(F')), H(F')=D(H'(F'),pkl), Result= Compare (H(F'), newH'(F'))

TPA   ---+   Client: Send (Result)

ALGORITHM   3:

Message Retrieval

Client --TPA : Re- quest (F)

TPA--- CSP: Re- quest (F")

CSP ---+ TP A: Send (F")

TPA: Verification (F"), F'=E (F, d2)

            TPA   ___

Client: Send (F')

In conclusion, his section outlines preventive measures against prevalent cyber-attacks and introduces a proposed mechanism. The mechanism utilizes RSA algorithm alongside encryption/decryption processes like hashing to enhance data security on the cloud and during transit. By ensuring that only encrypted files are transmitted, users gain confidence in data security. This approach is applicable to mobile users and other digital platforms, offering effectiveness and efficiency.

6 Conclusion

With organizations increasingly relying on the internet for services, hackers continually devise new ways to target them. During the Covid-19 pandemic, with in-person shopping restricted, hackers exploited the web for ransomware attacks. This prevalent attack vector sought financial gain from victims. In response, organizations implemented countermeasures to prevent such breaches. Cybersecurity requires a holistic approach, addressing challenges, emerging threats, and societal perceptions that influence cybersecurity.

Amid the surge in information due to technology and media, individuals and businesses remain vulnerable to cybercriminals. Thus, innovative preventive strategies are crucial. As industries shift online, malware attacks on businesses rise. Safeguarding customers, particularly the vulnerable, becomes paramount. Measures like scrutinizing emails, updating anti-virus software, and scanning attachments help mitigate threats.

Notably, ransomware stands as a significant hacker tactic, demanding ransom for victims' data. To counter cyber threats, organizations must enhance existing measures. This research delved into cloud computing security, outlining safeguards for consumer data. A proposed mechanism bolstered data integrity and confidentiality within mobile cloud using the RSA algorithm and encryption methods.

Larger companies favor cloud storage due to its security potential. However, users must understand associated risks. Businesses should invest in research for innovative threat mitigation, educate customers about fraud attacks, and improve transaction security. Governments should ensure tech companies adhere to cyber-safety standards.

6.1 Future Work

Predictions and speculations emerging from this research include:

- The escalating influx of personal data into the online realm will intensify concerns about its security.
- A new generation of secure Internet must be constructed, contrasting with the previous unattended growth.
- Security systems will evolve with distinct architectures to combat evolving malware [85].
- Resources will be allocated to track attack origins via global identity management and trace-back techniques [86].

Central to this commitment is upholding confidentiality, trustworthiness, and accessibility of computing systems and components. Hardware, software, and data vulnerabilities render computer systems susceptible to attacks. Cybersecurity vulnerabilities exist within these components and their interactions [87]. Cyber-attacks are typically the work of hackers, groups, or criminals for financial gain, while some pose national security threats. Responding to cyber-attacks today prepares us for future security challenges.

Notably, many research articles didn't detail defense mechanisms against cyber-attacks. Continued studies on mitigation and defense strategies are vital, especially in anticipating and preventing early-stage attacks. A proposed encryption scheme offers transit data security, particularly for mobile cloud use. Further work is needed to minimize computational overhead and thwart imminent RSA cracking threatened by quantum computing.

As identified, human behavior lapses contribute to cybersecurity incidents. Altering cybersecurity hygiene habits remains challenging. Focusing on motivating human involvement and limiting their mistakes' impact on cybersecurity posture is a promising research avenue.

References

1. Mohurle, S., Patil, M.: A brief study of wannacry threat: Ransomware attack 2017. Int. J. Adv. Res. Comput. Sci. **8**(5), 1938–1940 (2017)
2. Richardson, R., North, M.M.: Ransomware: Evolution, mitigation and prevention. Int. Manage. Rev. **13**(1), 10 (2017)
3. Dobrygowski, D.: Why Companies Are Forming Cybersecurity Alliances. Harvard Business School Publishing, Harvard Business Review (2019)
4. Kshetri, N.: Cybercrime and cyber-security issues associated with China: some economic and institutional considerations. Electron. Commer. Res. **13**(1), 41–69 (2013)
5. Zou, T., et al. : Smart grids cyber–physical security: Parameter correction model against unbalanced false data injection attacks Electr. Power Syst. Res. **187**, Article 106490 (2020)
6. CESG: Common Cyber Attacks: Reducing the Impact. CESG (The Information Security Arm of GCHQ) with CERT-UK (2015)
7. Boiko, A., Shendryk, V., Boiko, O.: Information systems for supply chain management: uncertainties, risks and cyber security. Procedia Computer Science **149**, 65–70 (2019)
8. Kephart, J.O., White, S.R.: Measuring and modeling computer virus prevalence. In: Proceedings 1993 IEEE Computer Society Symposium on Research in Security and Privacy, pp. 2–15. IEEE (1993)
9. Best, K., Lewis, J.: Hacking the democratic mainframe: the Melissa virus and transgressive computing. Media International Australia **95**(1), 207–226 (2000)
10. Mansfield-Devine, S.: Ransomware: taking businesses hostage. Netw. Secur. **10**, 8–17 (2016)
11. Mohamed, A., Køien, G.M.: Cyber security and the Internet of things: vulnerabilities, threats, intruders and attacks. J. Cyber Secu. **4**, 65–88 (2015)
12. Gopika, B., Rashi, Y.: Predicting the Spread of Malware Outbreaks Using Autoencoder Based Neutral Networks. In: MENDEL, Vol. 25, No. 1, pp. 157–164 (2019)
13. Von Neumann, J.: The computer and the brain. Yale University Press (2012)
14. Coleman, R.C.: 2015 IC3 Annual Internet Crime Report. Annual Report, Annual Report, Washington DC, USA: FBI Internet Crime Complaint Center, 1–236 (2015)
15. Roa, R.E.E.: Ransomware Attacks on the Healthcare Industry, Doctoral dissertation, Utica College (2017)
16. Reka, S.S., Dragicevic, T.: Future effectual role of energy delivery: A comprehensive review of Internet of Things and smart grid. Renew. Sustain. Energy Rev. **91**, 90–108 (2018)

17. Corno, F., Sánchez, E., Squillero, G.: Evolving assembly programs: how games help microprocessor validation. IEEE Trans. Evol. Comput. **9**(6), 695–706 (2005)
18. Okoye, E.I., Gbegi, D.O.: Forensic accounting: a tool for fraud detection and prevention in the public sector. (A study of selected ministries in Kogi state). Int. J. Acad. Res. Bus. Soc. Sci. **3**(3), 1–19 (2013)
19. Abouzakhar, N.: Critical infrastructure cybersecurity: A review of recent threats and violations (2013)
20. Bada, M., Sasse, A.M., Nurse, J.R.: Cyber security awareness campaigns: Why do they fail to change behavior? arXiv preprint arXiv:1901.02672 (2019)
21. Haber, E., Zarsky, T.: Cybersecurity for Infrastructure: A Critical Analysis. Fla (2016)
22. Homeland Security: State Cybersecurity Governance Case Studies: Cross Site Report. US Department of Homeland Security (2017)
23. Ibrahim, A., Valli, C., McAteer, I., Chaudhry, J.: A security review of local government using NIST CSF: a case study. J. Supercomput. **74**(10), 5171–5186 (2018)
24. Jang-Jaccard, J., Nepal, S.: A survey of emerging threats in cybersecurity. J. Comput. Syst. Sci. **80**(5), 973–993 (2014)
25. Mylrea, M., Gourisetti, S.N.G., Larimer, C., Noonan, C.: Insider threat cybersecurity framework webtool & methodology: Defending against complex. cyber-physical threats. In: 2018 IEEE Security and Privacy Workshops (SPW), pp. 207–216. IEEE (2018)
26. OAS: Critical Infrastructure Protection Report Latin America and the Caribbean 2018. Organization of American States (2018)
27. Ramon, M.C., Zajac, D.A.: Cybersecurity Literature Review and Efforts Report. Prepared for NCHRP Project, 03–127 (2018)
28. Rao, V.M., Francis, R.A.: Critical review of cybersecurity protection procedures and practice in water distribution systems. In: Proceedings of the 2015 Industrial and Systems Engineering Research Conference (2015)
29. Siemens: Cybersecurity in the Modern Industrial World. Harvard Business School Publishing, Harvard Business Review (2018)
30. Tonge, A.M., Kasture, S.S., Chaudhari, S.R.: Cyber security: challenges for society-literature review. IOSR J. Comp. Eng. **2**(12), 67–75 (2013)
31. Gelles, M.G.: Insider threat: Prevention, detection, mitigation, and deterrence. Butterworth-Heinemann (2016)
32. Sadeghi, A.R.: Trusted computing—special aspects and challenges. In: International Conference on Current Trends in Theory and Practice of Computer Science, pp. 98–117. Springer, Berlin, Heidelberg (2008)
33. Ahrendt, W., Beckert, B., Hähnle, R., Rümmer, P., Schmitt, P.H.: Verifying object-oriented programs with Key: A tutorial. In: International Symposium on Formal Methods for Components and Objects, pp. 70–101. Springer, Berlin, Heidelberg (2006)
34. Chaithanya, B.N., Veena, R.: Emerging trends and challenges in advanced technologies on cyber security. IJO-International J. Comp. Sci. Eng. **2**(1), 01–16 (2019)
35. Chitneni, A.: Study of emerging trends on latest technologies and its cybersecurity challenges. J. Innov. Develop. Pharmaceut. Techn. Sci. (JIDPTS) **3**(11) (2020)
36. Corrons, L.: A look back at cyber-security in 2012. Panda Labs (2013)
37. Potlapally, N.: Hardware security in practice: challenges and opportunities. In: 2011 IEEE International Symposium on Hardware-Oriented Security and Trust, pp. 93–98. IEEE (2011)
38. Li, Q., Gao, H., Xu, B., Jiao, Z.: Hardware threat: the challenge of information security. In: 2008 International Symposium on Computer Science and Computational Technology, Vol. 1, pp. 517–520. IEEE (2008)
39. Karri, R., Rajendran, J., Rosenfeld, K., Tehranipoor, M.: Trustworthy hardware: Identifying and classifying hardware trojans. Computer **43**(10), 39–46 (2010)

40. Chakraborty, R.S., Narasimhan, S., Bhunia, S.: Hardware Trojan: Threats and emerging solutions. In: 2009 IEEE International high level design validation and test workshop, pp. 166–171. IEEE (2009)
41. Reddy, G.N., Reddy, G.J.: A study of cyber security challenges and emerging trends on latest technologies. arXiv preprint arXiv:1402.1842 (2014)
42. Singh, N.: A Study of Cyber Security Trends and Its Challenges: A Conceptual Framework. Trusted Computing Group TPM Main, Part 1 (2006), Design Principles Specification version 1.2. Revision 94
43. Trusted Computing Group TPM Main, Part 2 (2006), TPM Structures Specification version 1.2. Revision 94
44. Trusted Computing Group TPM Main, Part 3 (2006), Design Principles Specification version 1.2. Revision 94
45. Vidhya, P.M.: Cyber security-trends and challenges. Int. J. Comput. Sci. Mob. Comput. **3**(2), 586–590 (2014)
46. Qamar, S., Anwar, Z., Rahman, M.A., Al-Shaer, E., Chu, B.T.: Data-driven analytics for cyber-threat intelligence and information sharing. Comput. Secur. **67**, 35–58 (2017)
47. Meier, R., Scherrer, C., Gugelmann, D., Lenders, V., Vanbever, L.: FeedRank: a tamper-resistant method for the ranking of cyber threat intelligence feeds. In: 2018 10th International Conference on Cyber Conflict (CyCon), pp. 321–344. IEEE (2018)
48. Sauerwein, C., Pekaric, I., Felderer, M., Breu, R.: An analysis and classification of public information security data sources used in research and practice. Comput. Secur. **82**, 140–155 (2019)
49. Pitropakis, N., et al.: An enhanced cyber-attack attribution framework. In: International Conference on Trust and Privacy in Digital Business, pp. 213–228. Springer, Cham (2018)
50. Singhal, A., Ou, X.: Security risk analysis of enterprise networks using probabilistic attack graphs. In: Network Security Metrics, pp. 53–73. Springer, Cham (2017)
51. Kaloudi, N., Li, J.: The ai-based cyber threat landscape: A survey. ACM Computing Surveys (CSUR) **53**(1), 1–34 (2020)
52. Razzaq, A., Latif, K., Ahmad, H.F., Hur, A., Anwar, Z., Bloodsworth, P.C.: Semantic security against web application attacks. Inf. Sci. **254**, 19–38 (2014)
53. Oltramari, A., Cranor, L.F., Walls, R.J., McDaniel, P.D.: Building an Ontology of Cyber Security. In: STIDS, pp. 54–61 (2014)
54. Geramiparvar, M.S., Modiri, N.: An approach to counteracting common cyber-attacks according to the metric-based model. Int. J. Comp. Sci. Netw. Sec. (IJCSNS) **16**(1), 81 (2016)
55. Yeboah-Ofori, A., Brimicombe, A.: Cyber intelligence and OSINT: developing mitigation techniques against cybercrime threats on social media. Int. J. Cyber-Sec. Digi. Forensics (IJCSDF) **7**(1), 87–98 (2018)
56. Anwar, Z., Montanari, M., Gutierrez, A., Campbell, R.H.: Budget constrained optimal security hardening of control networks for critical cyber-infrastructures. Int. J. Crit. Infrastruct. Prot. **2**(1–2), 13–25 (2009)
57. Dehue, F., Bolman, C., Vollink, T., Pouwelse, M.: Cyberbullying and traditional bullying in relation to adolescents' perception of parenting. J. Cyber Therapy and Rehabilit. **5**(1), 25–34 (2012)
58. Stancu, A.I.: Evolution of the international regulations regarding cybercrime. Public Administ. Region. Stud. **18**(2), 72–79 (2016)
59. Rege-Patwardhan, A.: Cybercrimes against critical infrastructures: a study of online criminal organization and techniques. Crim. Justice Stud. **22**(3), 261–271 (2009)
60. Alkaabi, A., Mohay, G., McCullagh, A., Chantler, N.: Dealing with the problem of cybercrime. In: International Conference on Digital Forensics and Cyber Crime, pp. 1–18. Springer, Berlin, Heidelberg (2010)

61. Banday, M.T.: Emerging Challenges of Cyber Crimes to Cyber Security (2011)
62. Nurse, J.: Cyber Security Awareness Campaigns: Why do they fail to change behavior? (2015)
63. Ahamad, M., et al.: Emerging cyber threats report for 2009 (2008)
64. Van Eeten, M., Bauer, J.M.: Emerging threats to internet security: incentives, externalities, and policy implications. J. Conting. Crisis Manage. **17**(4), 221–232 (2009)
65. Raban, Y., Hauptman, A.: Foresight of cyber security threat drivers and affecting technologies. foresight (2018)
66. Abomhara, M., Køien, G.M.: Cyber security and the internet of things: vulnerabilities, threats, intruders and attacks. J. Cyber Sec. Mobi. 65–88 (2015)
67. AlDairi, A.: Cyber security attacks on smart cities and associated mobile technologies. Procedia Comp. Sci. **109**, 1086–1091 (2017)
68. Pan, L., Zheng, X., Chen, H.X., Luan, T., Bootwala, H., Batten, L.: Cyber security attacks to modern vehicular systems. J. Info. Sec. Appl. **36**, 90–100 (2017)
69. Middleton, B.: A history of cyber security attacks: 1980 to present. Auerbach Publications (2017)
70. Chowdhury, A.: Recent cyber security attacks and their mitigation approaches–an overview. In: International conference on applications and techniques in information security, pp. 54–65. Springer, Singapore (2016)
71. Conteh, N.Y., Schmick, P.J.: Cybersecurity: risks, vulnerabilities, and countermeasures to prevent social engineering attacks. Int. J. Adv. Comp. Res. **6**(23), 31 (2016)
72. Lallie, H.S., et al.: Cyber security in the age of covid-19: A timeline and analysis of cyber-crime and cyber-attacks during the pandemic. Comput. Secur. **105**, 102248 (2021)
73. Choo, K.K.R.: The cyber threat landscape: challenges and future research directions. Comput. Secur. **30**(8), 719–731 (2011)
74. Farahmand, F., Navathe, S.B., Sharp, G.P., Enslow, P.H.: A management perspective on risk of security threats to information systems. Inf. Technol. Manage. **6**(2), 203–225 (2005)
75. Baldwin, A., Gheyas, I., Ioannidis, C., Pym, D., Williams, J.: Contagion in cyber security attacks. J. Operat. Res. Soc. **68**(7), 780–791 (2017)
76. Abu, M.S., Selamat, S.R., Ariffin, A., Yusof, R.: Cyber threat intelligence–issue and challenges. Indonesian J. Electr. Eng. Comp. Sci. **10**(1), 371–379 (2018)
77. Carlton, M., Levy, Y., Ramim, M.: Mitigating cyber-attacks through the measurement of non-IT professionals' cybersecurity skills. Info. Comp. Sec. (2019)
78. Semerci, M., Cemgil, A.T., Sankur, B.: An intelligent cyber security system against DDoS attacks in SIP networks. Comput. Netw. **136**, 137–154 (2018)
79. Teixeira, A., Dán, G., Sandberg, H., Johansson, K.H.: A cyber security study of a SCADA energy management system: Stealthy deception attacks on the state estimator. IFAC Proceedings Volumes **44**(1), 11271–11277 (2011)
80. Dagoumas, A.: Assessing the impact of cybersecurity attacks on power systems. Energies **12**(4), 725 (2019)
81. He, Q., Meng, X., Qu, R., Xi, R.: Machine learning-based detection for cyber security attacks on connected and autonomous vehicles. Mathematics **8**(8), 1311 (2020)
82. Keller, S., Powell, A., Horstmann, B., Predmore, C., Crawford, M.: Information security threats and practices in small businesses. Inf. Syst. Manag. **22**(2), 7 (2005)
83. Loch, K.D., Carr, H.H., Warkentin, M.E.: Threats to information systems: today's reality, yesterday's understanding. Mis Quarterly, 173–186 (1992)
84. Dokuchaev, V.A., Maklachkova, V.V., Statev, V.Y.: Classification of personal data security threats in information systems. T-Comm-Телекоммуникации и Транспорт **14**(1), 56–60 (2020)
85. Wall, D.S.: Crime, security and information communication technologies: the changing cyber-security threat landscape and its implications for regulation and policing. Security and Information Communication Technologies: The Changing Cybersecurity Threat Landscape and Its Implications for Regulation and Policing (July 20, 2017) (2017)

86. Wang, L., Jones, R.: Big data analytics in cyber security: network traffic and attacks. J. Comp. Info. Sys. **61**(5), 410–417 (2021)
87. Shaukat, K., Luo, S., Varadharajan, V., Hameed, I.A., Xu, M.: A survey on machine learning techniques for cyber security in the last decade. IEEE Access **8**, 222310–222354 (2020)
88. Seth, S.M., Mishra, R.: Comparative analysis of encryption algorithms for data communication. IJCST **2**(2) (2011)
89. Amini, A.: Secure Storage in Cloud Computing (2012)
90. Forouzan, B.A.: Cryptography and Network Security, special Indian edition. The McGraw-Hill Companies
91. https://www.securitymagazine.com/articles/971

Models for Security Management

Christopher Spruill, Md Khalil, and Samuel Olatunbosun[✉]

Norfolk State University, Norfolk, VA, USA
{c.m.spruill126278,m.i.khalil}@spartans.nsu.edu,
sbolatunbosun@nsu.edu

Abstract. In today's face-paced world access to information is crucial to the success of organizations from both private, public, and government sectors. With the ever-growing demand for information to be readily available in today's world, growing organizations may be at a point where the implementation of an information security management plan has become a necessity. One of the primary reasons for hesitation may be the lack of knowledge of where to begin or the cost of implementing such a plan in the organization. We investigate popular information management frameworks such as the ISO 27000 and National Institute of Standards and Technology (NIST) publications along with their ability to meet the needs of a growing organization. [1]

Keywords: Information Management Framework · Infosec Models · Cybersecurity · ISO 27000 Standard series · Infosec Technology Infrastructure

1 Introduction

1.1 Models vs. Methodologies vs. Frameworks

- **InfoSec Models:** These serve as high-level blueprints or architectural references for information security. They outline the components and their relationships within a secure system, without specific implementation details.
- **Methodologies:** These represent a prescribed approach or process for achieving
- a specific InfoSec objective. They detail the steps and activities required to accomplish a security task, often including best practices.
- **Frameworks:** Frameworks provide a structured collection of principles, guidelines, and practices for approaching information security. They offer a flexible structure that organizations can adapt to their specific needs. One may think of them as pre-built toolkits for security management.

1.2 Choosing an InfoSec Approach

Organizations should consider a combination of models, methodologies, and frameworks when designing their security plan. Existing options can be adapted or merged to create a custom solution. Popular resources include publications from governments and standards organizations (e.g., NIST CSF, ISO 27001).

L. Deligiannidis et al. (Eds.): CSCE 2024, CCIS 2262, pp. 354–361, 2025.
https://doi.org/10.1007/978-3-031-85933-5_26

1.3 Developing a Security Blueprint

- **Security Framework/Model as Foundation:** This initial stage involves selecting a high-level framework or model that aligns with the organization's security goals. It defines the overall structure and scope of the security program.
- **InfoSec Blueprint for Implementation:** This detailed document builds upon the chosen framework and adds specific implementation details. It identifies existing security controls, pinpoints any gaps, and outlines the steps for implementing necessary controls. Here, the blueprint translates the "what" (framework) into the "how" (specific actions).

1.4 Blueprint vs. Framework/Model

The key difference lies in the level of detail. Frameworks and models offer a generalized overview, while blueprints provide a specific action plan tailored to the organization's environment.

1.5 Selecting Resources

A variety of free and paid resources are available for building an InfoSec blueprint. Popular free options include frameworks from NIST and other organizations. Paid models may offer additional features or customization options. Key considerations include flexibility, scalability, robustness, and the level of detail provided.

1.6 Benchmarking for Improvement

Benchmarking involves comparing an organization's security posture against industry standards or best practices. It provides insights into areas for improvement and helps identify effective control strategies.

Two types exist:

- **Internal Benchmarking (Baselining):** This compares the organization's current security posture against historical data to measure progress.
- **External Benchmarking:** This compares the organization's security performance against similar organizations to identify strengths and weaknesses.

Benchmarking can inform the selection or modification of controls within the InfoSec blueprint, but it doesn't provide specific implementation steps.

2 Literature Review

2.1 The ISO 27000 Series

The ISO 27000 series is a prominent framework for managing information security (InfoSec). It has its roots in the British Standard BS7799, which later became ISO/IEC 17799 in 2000. This standard served as a guide for organizations to establish and maintain effective information security practices.

ISO/IEC 27002, the successor to 17799, provides a comprehensive overview of various security areas. It outlines over 110 individual controls categorized under 14 security control clauses, addressing 35 control objectives. This standard offers a broad understanding of information security best practices.

However, implementing these controls requires a structured approach. This is where ISO/IEC 27001 comes in. It outlines how to implement the security controls suggested in ISO/IEC 27002 and establish an Information Security Management System (ISMS). Unlike ISO 27002, ISO 27001 is designed for certification purposes, allowing organizations to demonstrate their adherence to information security best practices.

The ISO 27000 series is rapidly gaining traction, particularly for large organizations in the United States. Compliance can be crucial for businesses operating in the European Union or adhering to industry standards that leverage the ISO 27000 framework. While not mandatory for most US organizations, it demonstrates a commitment to robust information security practices.

The adoption of ISO 27000 initially faced some criticism. Some countries, including the US, questioned the justification for a code of practice and the lack of precise measurement standards. However, the series has undergone revisions and continues to evolve as a valuable resource for organizations seeking to establish a comprehensive information security posture.

2.2   NIST Security Publications

NIST Special Publications (SPs) offer a comprehensive set of publicly available resources for information security (InfoSec) management. These SPs cover a wide range of topics, from foundational concepts to specific practices like risk management and incident response.

Central to NIST's approach are the 20 NIST Security Control Families, a categorization scheme for various security controls. SPs like 800-53 detail these controls, while others like 800-14 and 800-30 provide guidance on implementing them within the context of risk management and secure system design principles. NIST SPs also address critical areas like security planning (SP 800-18), contingency planning (SP 800-34), and security assessment (SP 800-53A). By leveraging these SPs, organizations can develop a robust InfoSec program that effectively manages risks and safeguards sensitive information.

2.3   Control Objectives for Information and Related Technology

COBIT 5 by ISACA offers a business framework for IT governance and management. It incorporates best practices and provides a structured approach through five principles (meeting stakeholder needs, covering the enterprise, etc.) and seven enablers (policies, processes, etc.). While COBIT focuses on broader IT governance, it also includes a framework to assess InfoSec requirements and helps organizations with general InfoSec risk management.

2.4   Key Points for InfoSec Professionals

- COBIT provides a structured approach to IT governance, which can indirectly benefit InfoSec.

- The framework includes considerations for InfoSec assessments.
- Organizations using COBIT assessments are better prepared for InfoSec risk management.

2.5 Information Technology Infrastructure Library

This paper further explores two frameworks for managing information security (InfoSec): the National Information Security Governance Framework (**NISGF**) and the FISMA Risk Management Framework (**RMF**).

NISGF: Targets state governments, emphasizing alignment with existing regulations and a uniform security model for efficient resource allocation.

FISMA RMF: A US federal framework, adaptable and focused on understanding system-specific risks for ongoing governance decisions.

2.6 Choosing the Right Framework

- **Governance Structure:** Distributed structures (like state governments) might prefer NISGF's uniformity.
- **Compliance Needs:** FISMA RMF simplifies compliance with federal regulations.
- **Adaptability:** Both offer adaptability, but FISMA RMF's focus on system-specific risks may be better for dynamic environments.

The choice depends on the organization's structure, compliance needs, and desired level of adaptability.

3 Methodology

Prioritizing an information security management plan that was optimized for a smaller organization up to a medium sized organization was our focus. The NISP Cybersecurity Framework 2.0 was the framework chosen as it is easily scaled to fit a small to medium sized business. To measure how effective and easy to implement for a small business we consider some of the main differences between a larger organization versus that of a smaller one. Two major differences were selected as our focus to determine how effective this framework would be for a smaller organization including available budget, and personnel. The U.S. Small Business Administration defines a small business as having a revenue ranging from 1 million to over 40 million and employment from 100 to 1500 employees. [2]

According to a report from Netwrix Research Lab, 68% of all organizations experienced a data breach in 2023 with 43% involving small businesses. [3] Data breaches like these are reasons each organization must take the necessary steps to implement and or improve their information security plans. Results from 2023 data breaches shown in Table 1, we were able to see how employees were a major part of the root cause in organizations data breaches.

Using these results for data breaches and its cost per head count [4] for the average small business of a size 1000 we can determine an acceptable budget needed to implement an InfoSec plan with 12% being the average percentage spent on cybersecurity for

Table 1 .

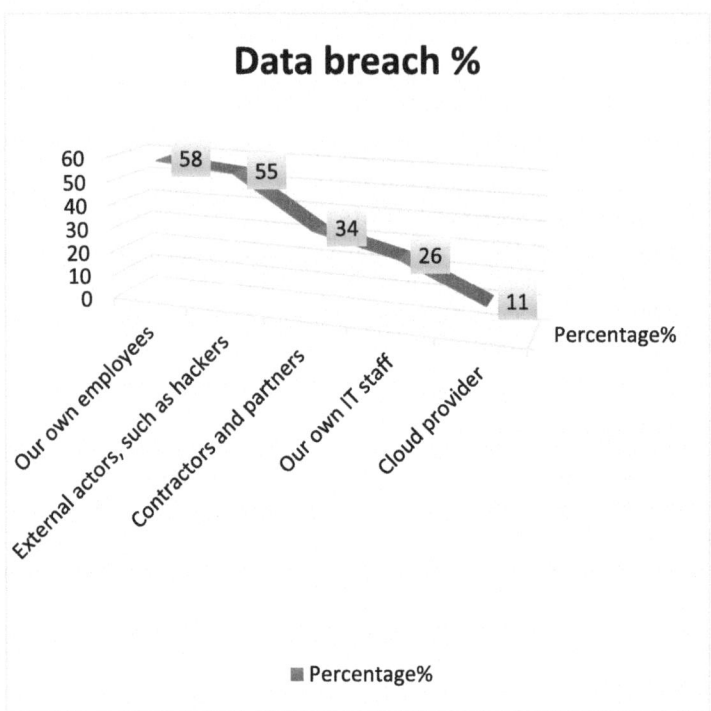

businesses worldwide [3]. We use the Gordon-Loeb Model to weigh the cost-benefits for a small business of revenue of that fall into the lower, mid, and higher end of the spectrum in revenue.

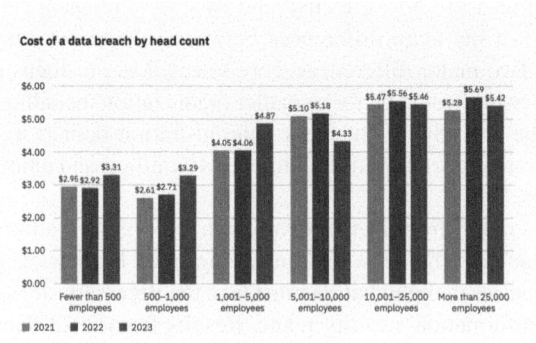

4   Results

The NISP framework 2.0 has six high-level functions: *Govern, Identify, Protect, Detect, Respond, and Recover.* Using this simple guide, small organizations can implement a new InfoSec plan within an acceptable budget based on the 4-tiers. The NIST framework recommends organizations use a cost to benefits process to determine the level of rigor needed to serve them. Using the 4 tiers of the NIST framework in conjunction with the Gordon-Loeb Model organizations will be able to scale their plan to the most cost-effective level needed.

Tier 1 (partial) organizations will not have a formalized integrated infosec process in place. These organizations tend to be more reactive than proactive. Organizations at the lower level of the spectrum in terms of number of employees and revenue should aim to tailor their plan with the rigor of this Tier.

Tier 2 (Risk Informed), these organizations have a more formal approach than Tier 1 but tend to lack enforcement. Small businesses that have a mid to large employee size but are on the higher side in terms of revenue should consider this tier for their InfoSec plan.

Tier 3 (Repeatable) organizations have a formal process and are proactive toward events rather than reactive.

Tier 4 (Adaptive) is the most formal of the four. These organizations have formal processes in place and are proactive and reactive in terms of their management of risks.

Tiers 3 and 4 are not recommended for small businesses, however growth into this later tier can happen as revenue and potential loss increases.

5   Discussion

NIST Special Publications (SPs) serve as a comprehensive collection of resources available to the public for managing information security (InfoSec). These publications cover a wide array of topics, ranging from fundamental concepts to specific practices such as risk management and incident response.

At the core of NIST's methodology are the twenty NIST Security Control Families, which categorize different security controls. Publications like 800-53 elaborate on these controls, while others like 800-14 and 800-30 offer guidance on how to implement them in the context of risk management and secure system design principles. NIST SPs also tackle crucial areas like security planning (SP 800-18), contingency planning (SP 800-34), and security assessment (SP 800-53A). By utilizing these SPs, organizations can establish a strong InfoSec program that efficiently handles risks and protects sensitive information.

6   Summary

A framework serves as the skeleton of a comprehensive plan utilized in establishing the InfoSec landscape. Meanwhile, a security model represents a general plan provided by a service entity.

One of the most cited security models is the "ISO/IEC 27001: 2005 Information Technology—Code of Practice for InfoSec Management," which aims to provide guidance for InfoSec management. Alternative methods for organizing InfoSec management can be discovered in the various resources offered by NIST's Computer Security Resource Center.

COBIT offers guidance on implementing effective controls and objectives for information security.

Version 1: COBIT offers suggestions on how to enforce strong controls and objectives for information security.

The Information Security Governance Framework, developed by an industry working group, serves as a managerial model offering direction for establishing and executing an organizational InfoSec governance structure.

Security architecture models establish InfoSec implementations and facilitate organizations in making rapid enhancements through adjustment. One usual model is the Trusted Computer System Evaluation Criteria (TCSEC).

Seizure controls are responsible for supervising the entry of users into secure sections of the company. The foundation of access control consists of four components: *identification, authentication, authorization, and accountability*.

Access control is established based on the principles of least privilege, need-to-know, and separation of duties.

Various approaches to access control include directive, deterrent, preventative, detective, corrective, recovery, and compensating measures. Access controls can be categorized as management, operational (or administrative), or technical.

Mandatory access controls (MACs) are controls mandated by the system, which operate within a data classification and personnel clearance framework.

A central authority within the organization determines nondiscretionary controls, which can be established according to roles or a specific set of tasks.

Data users have the option to implement discretionary access controls (DACs) based on their own discretion.

Prominent academic access control models encompass the Bell-LaPadula (BLP) confidentiality model, the Biba integrity model, the Clark-Wilson integrity model, the Graham-Denning access control model, the Harrison-Ruzzo-Ullman (HRU) model for access rights, and the Brewer-Nash model.

7   Recommendation

Every company should have some info sec plan. It should be synchronized with the company budget and business strategy. This involves Risk Management, policy development and enforcement, access control, security awareness and training, incident response and management, security monitoring and surveillance, vulnerability management, security governance, compliance management, security culture and communication.

8 Conclusion

For organizations today, there are several reputable information security models to choose from, but cost-benefit analysis should be a priority. We recommend that every organization implements an information management plan to safeguard their customers and the organization's information in which ISO 27000 and the NIST framework are great starting points. For small businesses, the NIST framework using Tiers 1 and 2 as their guide will be the most beneficial. The implementation of the NIST framework using Tiers 3 & 4 would be recommended for larger organizations only. Only by continuously evolving, and by throwing out concepts that are no longer relevant and modifying others to consider added information, can security be attained.

References

1. Petrosyan, A.: (2024). https://www.statista.com/statistics/273550/data-breaches-recorded-in-the-united-states-by-number-of-breaches-and-records-exposed/. Accessed 29 Feb 2024
2. Hait, A.W.: What is a Small Business? (2021). https://www.census.gov/library/stories/2021/01/what-is-a-small-business.html. Accessed 29 February 2024
3. Rinaldi, A.: The Cost of Cybersecurity and How to Budget for It (2024). https://www.business.com/articles/smb-budget-for-cybersecurity/. Accessed 29 February 2023
4. Cost of a Data Breach Report 2023. IBM Security, Armonk, NY (2023)
5. Gordon, L.A., Loeb, M.P.: Integrating cost-benefit analysis into the NIST Cybersecurity Framework via the Gordon-Loeb Model. Journal of Cybersecurity 6(1) (2020)
6. visit www.sans.org/score/ or download their ISO/IEC 17799:2005 checklist at www.sans.org/score/ checklists/iso-17799-2005
7. A complete guide to ISO 27001, download the ISO 27001 Tool Kit: http://www.iso27001security.com/html/toolkit.html
8. Information on TCSEC, the DoD Standard publication at http://csrc.nist.gov/publications/history/dod85.pdf
9. Information on the Common Criteria, at the Common Criteria Portal: www.commoncriteriaportal.org
10. Information on governmental security classifications, Executive Order 13526 (For NSI) at https://www.archives.gov/isoo/policy-documents/cnsi-eo.html or Executive Order 13556 for Non-NSI (https://www.gpo.gov/fdsys/pkg/FR-2010-11-09/pdf/2010-28360.pdf)

A Comprehensive Analysis of Information Security Policy and Security Program Development

Salim Jackson, Willis Dunn, and Samuel Olatunbosun[✉]

Norfolk State University, Norfolk, VA, USA
{s.a.jackson97642,w.n.dunn18268}@spartans.nsu.edu,
sbolatunbosun@nsu.edu

Abstract. This study examines in-depth the intricate realm of privacy-preserving technologies in the corporate sector, drawing inspiration from the fundamental tenets of Information Security policy and Security Program Development. It incorporates information from various sources to offer a thorough grasp of the effective implementation of information security policies and the strategic development of security programs. The findings underscore the significance of adherence to the ISO/IEC 27001 standard, which offers a consistent and internationally recognized framework for strengthening policy development and safeguarding sensitive data globally. Furthermore, the study emphasizes the importance of cultivating a cybersecurity mindset, particularly in remote work environments, and the necessity for employees to comply with policies to mitigate emerging cyber risks. Despite notable achievements, ongoing challenges persist in policy implementation and security program development. Continuous innovation and adaptation are required to effectively address the evolving cybersecurity threat landscape. The research offers practical recommendations that empower businesses in strengthening their security postures. These recommendations encompass adherence to international standards, fostering a robust cybersecurity culture, conducting regular assessments, encouraging innovation, and establishing Security Operations Centers. This research significantly enhances the understanding of privacy-preserving technologies and provides practical guidance for businesses in navigating the multifaceted challenges in managing information security.

Keywords: Information security policy · Cybersecurity · Management information security

1 Introduction

In the contemporary digital era, the necessity for privacy-preserving solutions has emerged as a fundamental component of efficacious business operations. Enterprises increasingly rely on interconnected platforms for the management of sensitive information, escalating the risk of unauthorized data access and privacy breaches. Stringent data protection regulations and the progressive sophistication of cyber threats intensify this

© The Author(s), under exclusive license to Springer Nature Switzerland AG 2025
L. Deligiannidis et al. (Eds.): CSCE 2024, CCIS 2262, pp. 362–369, 2025.
https://doi.org/10.1007/978-3-031-85933-5_27

concern. The adoption of privacy-preserving technologies, such as enhanced encryption algorithms and secure data anonymization techniques, is paramount in safe- guarding sensitive data and minimizing the risk of security breaches.

The proliferation of remote work and the widespread adoption of cloud-based services further underscore the exigency for robust privacy controls. Remote employees, often accessing company networks from diverse locations, pose a unique set of security challenges. Cloud-based services, while offering convenience and scalability, introduce additional data privacy considerations. Enterprises must prioritize the implementation of privacy-preserving technologies to address the evolving threat landscape and maintain the trust of their clientele, partners, and employees. Investing in these technologies demonstrates a commitment to data protection and compliance with privacy regulations. Failure to adopt adequate privacy measures could result in reputational damage, loss of customer trust, and potential legal ramifications.

Moreover, privacy-preserving solutions contribute to the long-term sustainability and growth of enterprises. By safeguarding sensitive information, companies can foster a culture of trust, enhance customer loyalty, and attract top talent seeking employers that prioritize data privacy. In a business environment where data is a key asset, the adoption of privacy- preserving technologies is not merely a compliance requirement but also a strategic imperative.

This report is based on the framework provided by Chapters 4 and 5 of Whitman and Mattord's *"Management of Information Security"* [1]. These chapters focus on the creation of security programs and information security policies, respectively. As the cornerstone of an organization's protection against cyber threats, the textbook chapter 4, on Information Security Policy, discusses methods of creating and applying information security policies [1]. The chapter further highlights the strategic importance of policies in establishing a comprehensive infrastructure for safeguarding sensitive data within an organization. Meanwhile, Chapter 5 of the same textbook: *Developing the Security Program,* outlines the methodical steps necessary for strong cybersecurity defenses and presents a pragmatic approach to security program creation [1]. When these two chapters are combined, a synergistic viewpoint is presented in which the creation of information security policies are inextricably related to the ensuing creation of a robust security program as described in Chapter 5. The insights gleaned from the textbook's fundamental chapters have therefore guided our inquiry into the practical implications and challenges of implementing enhanced privacy safeguards within the organizational structure. This study therefore culminates in this report about the applications of shielded technology in the business context.

2 Literature Review

2.1 Information Security Policy

Enterprises place significant reliance on information security policies as they constitute a systematic structure for elucidating the policies, processes, and standards pertinent to safe- guarding classified data. An understanding of the critical role of information security policies in shielding sensitive data is the fundamental premise of Chapter 4. Culot et al. **advance** this knowledge by highlighting the ISO/IEC 27001 standard and its significance in creating and using successful information security policies [2]. Masilela and Nel stress the significance of governance in public sector data protection even more, reiterating that strict rules are necessary to secure sensitive assets [3]. Szczepaniuk et al. showcase the usefulness of policies in assessing and improving data protection measures, offering insights into information security evaluations in public administration [4]. Combining these sources emphasizes how vital information security policies are used as the basis to build a proactive and robust defense against possible attacks on sensitive data in various corporate contexts.

Extant literature offers valuable insights into the considerations surrounding the successful and complex endeavor of establishing information security policies in organizations. Culot et al.'s comprehensive study of ISO/IEC 27001 underscores its position as a widely accepted global framework, thus laying the foundation for effective policy implementation. Conversely, Georgiadou et al. contribute to the discourse by assessing cybersecurity culture within remote work settings, bringing to light potential challenges associated with policy adherence. Szczepaniuk et al. provide helpful insights into public administration challenges by highlighting the obstacles organizations may encounter while implementing policies [4]. In their discussion of governance issues in the public sector, Masilela and Nel draw attention to the complications that can occur when coordinating policies with governmental frame- works [3]. This literature synthesis highlights the complex terrain of information safety policy implementation, recognizing the need for international standards and the unique contextual difficulties that arise in organizational settings. As a result, it offers a comprehensive view of policy implementation in various business environments.

2.2 Security Program Development

Developing the Security Program examines the essential phase of developing a comprehensive security plan, a field further enriched by insights derived from various sources. The systematic study on Security Operations Centers contributes by describing the essential elements and difficulties in implementing such programs [5, 6]. Szczepaniuk et al. contribute to the discussion by analyzing information security assessment techniques, which facilitates the comprehension of the significance of assessments in creating successful security initiatives [7]. In line with Mazzucato et al., who support challenge-driven innovation policies to guide the strategic development of security programs, Whitman and Mattord underscore the significance of matching organizational goals with the security program [1, 8]. This report thus investigates the various facets of developing security programs by integrating ideas from various sources. It also addresses obstacles and highlights optimal approaches to assist enterprises in developing resilient and flexible security infrastructures.

Developing a security program is a complex and evolving procedure incorporating industry standards, difficulties, and advancements. Vielberth et al. conducted a thorough study on Security Operations Centers, focusing on best practices, stressing the importance of a structured approach, and identifying critical components [6]. Szczepaniuk et al. studied information security assessment approaches, providing valuable insights into evaluation procedures for security program creation [4]. Mazzucato et al. proposes innovation policies focusing on a challenge-driven approach to stimulate innovative ideas in security program development [8]. Georgiadou et al. identified issues in cyber-security culture during remote work, offering a detailed insight into such obstacles [4]. This report highlights the complex nature of developing security programs, providing a thorough viewpoint that combines best practices, tackles obstacles, and welcomes novel methods to establish strong and flexible security frameworks.

3 Methodology

3.1 Research Design

This study utilizes an extensive literature review as the research methodology, gathering information from multiple sources to investigate discreet technology in the business sector. This design is based on its capacity to combine many viewpoints and research results to comprehensively comprehend the intricate relationship among information security policy, security program development, and the integration of secured technology. Culot et al. provide theoretical foundations in their ISO/IEC 27001 literature survey, while Georgiadou et al., Szczepaniuk et al., and Masilela and Nel offer insights into real-world applications and problems [2, 3, 7]. Mazzucato et al. provide strategic insights through their policies [8]. This methodology aligns with the research goal of providing a thorough overview and enabling a detailed examination of successful implementations and issues in anonymity-promoting technology in the business sector. By incorporating data from several sources, a nuanced analysis is achieved, enhancing the research's credibility and depth.

3.2 Data Collection

The research draws upon various sources, including academic journals, case studies, and industry reports, to gain comprehensive insights into privacy-preserving technologies in a business context. This approach ensures a rigorous and in-depth examination of the subject matter. Scholars such as Georgiadou et al., Shaikh and Siponen, Szczepaniuk et al., and Li and Liu provide valuable scientific perspectives [4, 7, 9, 10]. Case studies, such as the one conducted by Masilela and Nel, offer practical insights into real-world challenges and solutions in the context of data and information security governance in the public sector [3]. Industry publications, exemplified by Vielberth et al.'s systematic analysis of Security Operations Centers, provide a strategic overview of advancements in security programs [6]. The selection criteria for the sources employed in this research include relevance to the study of privacy-preserving technologies, recentness of publication, and legitimacy of the source. This approach aims to strike a balance between theoretical foundations and practical implementations across a spectrum of organizational settings.

4   Results

4.1   Information Security Policy Implementation

The efficacious implementation of an information security policy is paramount in augmenting an organization's resilience against cyber threats. Culot et al. stress the importance of the ISO/IEC 27001 standard as a fundamental tool for implementing policies effectively, emphasizing its contribution to establishing a solid information security framework [2]. Georgiadou et al. examined cybersecurity culture during remote work, emphasizing the significance of employee awareness and compliance with policies [7]. Szczepaniuk et al. offer practical perspectives on information security assessments in public administration, highlighting the importance of continuous evaluations to guarantee policy success [4]. Nevertheless, common difficulties remain. Masilela and Nel discussed governance challenges, highlighting the challenge of integrating policies with governmental structures [3]. Georgiadou et al.'s study highlights the difficulties in distant work settings, particularly in maintaining policy adherence [7]. Effective policy implementation necessitates compliance with established standards and the judicious navigation of unique challenges posed by diverse organizational and operational contexts.

4.1.1   Security Program Development Outcomes

Whitman and Mattord textbook Chapter 5 emphasizes the significance of effectively developing a robust security program, supported by insights from various sources. The report by Vielberth et al. focuses on Security Operations Centers and highlights practical strategic efforts, including essential elements and operational effectiveness [6]. Szczepaniuk et al. examine information security evaluations, demonstrating effective evaluation methodologies for successful program creation [4]. While the achievement is evident, there are certain domains that necessitate further development. Mazzucato et al. support using challenge-driven policies to encourage creative solutions, proposing that innovative methods can improve program development [8]. Vielberth et al. recognize existing difficulties in Security Operations Centers and stress the importance of continuous adjustment [6]. This analytical report highlights the paramount importance of ongoing innovation and adaptability in effectively countering emerging threats and upholding robust security protocols in the dynamic and evolving cyber security landscape.

5   Discussion, Summary, and Recommendations

5.1   Integration of Findings

The integration of the findings presented in Chapters 4 and 5 of Whitman and Mattord textbook, which focus on information security policy and security program development, facilitates a holistic understanding of privacy-preserving technologies within business contexts. The ISO/IEC 27001 standard, emphasized by Culot et al., pro- vides a basis for implementing information security policies, offering a thorough framework for protecting sensitive data [2]. Georgiadou et al. highlights the importance of cybersecurity culture in remote work, focusing on human-centric components essential for policy compliance [7]. Szczepaniuk et al. offer valuable perspectives on information security assessments that connect policy creation with program establishment [4]. The study by Vielberth et al. highlights the importance of program creation in Security Operations Centers, demonstrating successful efforts and stressing the necessity for continuous adaptation [6]. Mazzucato et al. emphasize the significance of challenge-driven innovation strategies, highlighting the dynamic character of program creation [8]. This synthesis presents a comprehensive analysis that integrates the organizational, cultural, and strategic elements essential for the effective integration of privacy-preserving technologies into intricate contemporary business environments.

5.2 Implications

The implications of this report have profound consequences for various stakeholders, including businesses, policymakers, and security professionals. Businesses benefit from the lessons learned in successful security program development and effective information security policy implementation, emphasizing the crucial need for a thorough strategy in privacy-preserving technologies [5, 10]. Adaptable rules are needed to protect data in changing work contexts [7]. Policymakers can use the ISO/IEC 27001 standard as a benchmark for regulatory frameworks to promote a uniform and internationally acknowledged method for information security. Mazzucato et al. propose challenge-driven innovation regulations to encourage creative solutions in the always changing cybersecurity environment [8]. Security professionals' benefit from the practical insights provided by Szczepaniuk et al.'s evaluation methodology, which helps create strong security measures [4]. The repercussions facilitate the adoption of a collaborative and adaptable approach among stakeholders in managing the intricate challenges of privacy protection within modern business landscapes.

5.3 Recommendations

For the enhancement of privacy, organizations should adopt a multifaceted strategy that encompasses insights from various sources during the formulation and implementation of information security policies and programs. Adhering to the ISO/IEC 27001 standard is an essential initial step [2]. Organizations can leverage this globally recognized standard as a guiding framework in the formulation and implementation of robust information security strategies, ensuring a comprehensive and consistent approach to securing sensitive data. Adhering to industry accepted standards enhances regulatory compliance and establishes a structured foundation for proactive data protection.

Furthermore, it is imperative to integrate a cybersecurity-centric mindset into remote work protocols. Businesses allocate resources toward awareness initiatives, training, and communication techniques to cultivate a security-conscious culture among employees [7]. Security professionals play a pivotal role in the design and implementation of these projects, ensuring that remote employees grasp and adhere to information security protocols. Organizations must also perform routine information security evaluations [4].

Organizations can employ continuous evaluation methodologies to identify vulnerabilities, adapt policies, and enhance security protocols effectively. This iterative process addresses current concerns and equips the organization to respond proactively to emerging threats.

Implementing challenge-driven innovation policies can enhance the development of security programs. Organizations should promote an innovative culture and foster collaboration among their personnel to facilitate creative problem-solving in security endeavors. Policymakers can facilitate this by creating frameworks that incentivize firms for their creative security strategies. Establishing Security Operations Centers is crucial for maintaining a proactive security stance [6]. Businesses should allocate resources to these centers to swiftly identify and address security events, ensuring the ongoing development of security protocols. These ideas provide a comprehensive approach for enterprises to strengthen privacy-preserving technologies by integrating standards, culture, innovation, and ongoing evaluation to establish a robust and flexible security environment.

6 Conclusion

In the contemporary digital landscape characterized by heightened interconnectedness, safeguarding privacy and sensitive information within the corporate sphere assumes paramount significance. This report delved into the realm of privacy-preserving technologies, scrutinizing the efficacy of organizational implementation of information security policies, and charting the challenges encountered in maintaining privacy.

The report underscores the imperative of adherence to internationally recognized standards such as ISO/IEC 27001, which offers a comprehensive framework for information security management. It emphasizes the necessity for businesses to foster a cybersecurity culture that permeates all organizational strata, especially considering the proliferation of remote work arrangements. Employee comprehension and compliance with security policies are pivotal elements in achieving a robust security posture. Several impediments are identified confronting organizations in implementing security policies and developing effective security programs. These include the perpetually evolving threat landscape, the intricate nature of IT systems, and the inexorable need for continuous innovation to stay ahead of potential vulnerabilities. The study accentuates the significance of ongoing assessment, adaptation, and collaboration among stakeholders to effectively address these challenges. Furthermore, the report offers practical counsel for security professionals, emphasizing the benefits of continuous evaluation and innovation. By implementing these measures, organizations can foster a flexible and resilient security environment capable of adapting to evolving threats and safe- guarding the confidentiality, integrity, and availability of their sensitive information. This report bridges the chasm between theoretical principles and practical applications, presenting a holistic understanding of privacy-preserving technologies in the burgeoning field of management information security. It provides valuable insights for organizations, policymakers, and security practitioners seeking to enhance their privacy protection strategies and maintain a competitive advantage in the digital age.

References

1. Whitman, E., Mattord, H.J.: Management of Information Security. Cengage (2019)
2. Culot, G., Nassimbeni, G., Podrecca, M., Sartor, M.: The ISO/IEC 27001 information security management standard: literature review and theory-based research agenda. The TQM Journal **33**(7), 76–105 (2021)
3. Masilela, D., Nel: The role of data and information security governance in protecting public sector data and information assets in National Government in South Africa. Public Service Delivery and Performance Review **9**(1), 1–10 (2021)
4. Szczepaniuk, E.K., Szczepaniuk, H., Rokicki, T., Klepacki, B.: Information security assessment in public administration. Computers & Security 90, 101 709–101 709 (2020)
5. ˙ Żywiołek, J.Z., Rosak-Szyrocka, J., Jereb, B.: Barriers to knowledge sharing in the field of information security. Manage. Sys. Prod. Eng. **29**(2), 114–119 (2021)
6. Vielberth, F., Bohm, I., Fichtinger, G., Pernul: Security operations center: a systematic study and open challenges. IEEE Access **8**, 227 756–227 779 (2020)
7. Georgiadou, S., Mouzakitis, D., Askounis: Working from home during COVID-19 crisis: A cyber security culture assessment survey. Security Journal **35**(2), 486–505 (2021)
8. Mazzucato, R., Kattel, J., Ryan-Collins: Challenge-driven innovation policy: Towards a new policy toolkit. Journal of Industry, Competition and Trade **20**(2), 421–437 (2019)
9. Shaikh, F.A., Siponen, M.: Information security risk assessments following cybersecurity breaches: The mediating role of top management attention to cybersecurity. Computers & Security **124**, 102 974–102 974 (2023)
10. Li, Y., Liu, Q.: A comprehensive review study of cyber-attacks and cyber security; emerging trends and recent developments. Energy Rep. **7**, 8176–8186 (2021)

Review of Emerging Threats in Cyberspace: A Replicated Study Based on a Year 2022 Research

Devonte W. Bethea and Samuel B. O. Olatunbosun$^{(\boxtimes)}$

Department of Computer Science, Norfolk State University Norfolk, Norfolk, VA, USA
d.w.bethea@spartans.nsu.edu, sbolatunbosun@nsu.edu

Abstract. The rapid explosion of the Internet and computer interconnections has led to a progressive incident of cybersecurity attacks. The news media have reported several attacks that have resulted in devastating and grievous consequences for the victims. Malware has been the primary weapon of choice that perpetrators have used repeatedly to carry out many of these malicious cyber-attacks. Perpetrators either have exploited loopholes in existing network systems to attack or have used the weaknesses discovered in several emerging technologies to facilitate these malware related crimes. There is therefore the necessity to keep developing more effective and innovative malware defense mechanisms to meet head-on, the existing cybersecurity challenges. A study and an article published in 2022 titled **"A Survey of Emerging Threats in Cybersecurity"** provided updated information that include statistical data, figures, and tables to report incidents of malware attack cases. In this replicated study, we investigated and provided further information on the latest trends in the Cyber Malware war. An overview of the most exploited vulnerabilities in existing hardware, software, and network layers are discussed, followed by critiques of the existing mitigation techniques, in terms of why some have proven effective and why some have not. New attack patterns evolving in the use of technologies such as social media, cloud computing, smartphones, and other critical infrastructure are also discussed. Finally, this report compares today's current situation with the earlier year 2012 study to make recommendations for future research on the subject.

Keywords: Cybersecurity · malware · cyber-attacks · emerging threats · countermeasures · emerging technology trends

1 Introduction

In this study, we carried out a review of emerging threats in Malware cybersecurity and provide an updated report, similar to a previous study carried out in the year 2022 titled: "*A Survey of Emerging Threats in Cybersecurity (2012):* This new study builds upon the 2022 research project from the that explored malware characteristics and trends. As IT usage rises, so does the potential for cyber-attacks, which have become more attractive and devastating due to the proliferation of sophisticated malware. The cost of cyber-attacks is staggering, reaching billions of dollars annually [1]. According to Symantec

Cybercrime, an article that was published in April 2012, states "Cyber- attacks cost $114 billion (about $350 per person in the US) dollars each year. If the time lost by companies trying to recover from Cyber-attacks is counted, the total cost of cyber-attacks would reach a staggering $385 billion (about $1,200 per person in the US) dollars" [1]. In 2019, Cybercrime has increased the cost of data breaches globally with a total of $2.1 billion (about $7 per person in the US) dollars [20]. There are many victims, who have gone through and are still facing cyber-attacks. With the increase of IT solutions, it is expected that cyber-attacks will keep expanding in size [1]. With the surge in IT solutions, cyber-attacks are expected to expand further.

Cybersecurity is defined as "the practice of protecting critical systems and sensitive information from virtual attacks" [1]. It involves preserving the confidentiality, integrity, and availability of digital technologies. Confidentiality prevents unauthorized information disclosure, integrity prevents unauthorized modification/deletion, and availability ensures accessibility to authorized users [1].

This paper further highlights various historical perspectives on malware, identifying seven types: Trojan Horses, Worms, Spyware, Adware, Ransomware, Key-Loggers, and Rootkits [4]. Malware infects systems through various means, including infected machines, tainted emails, and malware-infected websites. The sophistication of malware indicates that cyber-attacks will continue to rise [1].

1.1 Historical Perspective on Malwares

Malware is considered as the primary choice of weapon by cybersecurity experts to breach network infrastructures maliciously [1]. The term "Malware" stands for malicious software and refers to software specifically designed to disrupt, damage, or gain unauthorized access to computer systems [3]. There are seven notorious types of malwares known to cause system corruption. These include Trojan horses, Worms, Spyware, Adware, Ransomware, Key-loggers, and Rootkits [4].

Each type of malware serves different purposes. Trojan horses, for instance, breach system security while appearing innocuous [5]. Spyware, on the other hand, will covertly gather information from a user's computer and transmit it to attackers [6]. Adware automatically displays or downloads advertising materials while the user is online [7]. Ransomware blocks access to a computer system until a ransom is paid [8]. Key-loggers record keystrokes to fraudulently access passwords and confidential data [9]. Rootkits enable unauthorized control of a computer system without detection [10].

Malware infects systems through various means, such as propagation from infected machines, tainted emails, or enticing users to visit infected websites. Additionally, malware can spread from devices with embedded systems and computational logic [1]. The increasing sophistication of malware on the internet has led users to expect a continued rise in cyber-attacks [1].

1.2   Contextualizing the Problems

One needs to understand the origin of the problem that emphasizes the rise of hardware-based attacks and software vulnerabilities. Hardware attacks exploit compromised hardware, making detection challenging. Software vulnerabilities, such as bugs and design flaws, remain a common target for cyber-attacks [1] (Fig. 1).

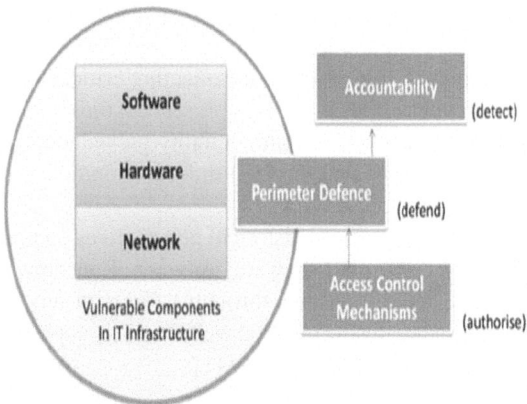

Fig. 1. Vulnerabilities and Defense Strategies in Existing Systems [1]

Out of eleven malware attack cases, here are five current real-world malware attack cases: **CovidLock ransomware 2020**, **LockerGoga ransomware 2019**, **Emotet Trojan 2018**, **WannaCry ransomware 2017**, and **Petya ransomware 2016** [13]. These cases exemplify how cybercriminals exploit fear, use phishing emails, and target specific industries, causing substantial financial losses.

The purpose of the study is to analyze data from the 2014 research project and provide updated research on each discussed topic, focusing on malware attacks. The research questions explore ways to empower users, develop secure computing systems, implement global- scale identity management, and create user-friendly security systems. Overall, the article emphasizes the pressing need for robust cybersecurity measures and the understanding that malware attacks are a persistent threat. It aims to contribute to the knowledge base surrounding malware attacks and proposes potential solutions to address this critical issue.

1.3   Research Questions

R1. How can users of the Internet better protect their confidential information?

R2. Is it possible to design the current Internet system from scratch without being restrained by the existing system?

R3. How can a computing system be developed that is inherently secure, available, and reliable despite disruptions, errors, and attacks?

R4. What are approaches to developing global- scale identity management for accessing critical information systems?

R5. Could a security system be developed that can be managed by users with all levels of computer skills?

2 Literature Review

This chapter provides a literature overview of the background of cybersecurity, several types of malicious software attacks affecting devices, state-of-the-art mitigation tools and techniques, exploiting vulnerabilities, and the effects of social media.

2.1 Background of Cybersecurity

In the research article, *A Study of Cybersecurity Education Using a Present-Test-Practice-Assess Model 2021*, cybersecurity capabilities in organizations lag the threats; discusses cybersecurity education and its importance in organizations to address the growing threats. Despite the emphasis on education, it has not fully reached its potential in many settings. Empirical studies on training methods are limited and yield inconsistent results. The article explores the use of gamified simulations and live activities like hack-a-thons to enhance cybersecurity behaviors. The study systematically investigates these methods by randomly assigning computer science students to different modalities. Pretest and post-test scores were used to measure learning performance. The findings indicate that simulations outperformed traditional instruction, and the most effective approach involved combining structured cybersecurity simulated environments with live competitive activities.

2.2 Malicious Software Attacks

In the research article "Spyware Injection in Android using Fake Application" [15], the researchers aimed to analyze the behavior of venomous Android spyware. They developed a complete Spyware system concealed within a fake application on an Android phone. This spyware system was designed to obtain sensitive information about the victim, including contacts, messages, calls, accounts, geographical location, and other personal data. The presence of such spyware poses significant challenges for protection companies and software developers, as it is often hidden within the system or disguised as fake applications.

Another research article, "Cyber Threat Intelligence Model: An Evaluation of Taxonomies, Sharing Standards, and Ontologies within Cyber Threat Intelligence" [19], introduces the Cyber Threat Intelligence (CTI) model. The CTI model enables cyber defenders to explore their threat intelligence capabilities and understand their position against the ever-changing cyber threat landscape. The study evaluates existing taxonomies, sharing standards, and ontologies relevant to cyber threat intelligence. The findings highlight the need for a multi-layered cyber threat intelligence ontology to cover the complete spectrum of threat intelligence. Additionally, the research paper "Comprehensive Survey on Petya Ransomware Attack, 2017, as well as Awareness and Mitigation" [22], emphasizes the exponential increase in ransomware attacks, with a focus on the Petya ransomware attack. The paper outlines the methodology and threats associated with Petya ransomware, emphasizing the need for awareness and mitigation techniques to combat such attacks effectively. Different types of ransomwares and the encryption algorithms they employ for data corruption are also explored. The paper suggests implementing prevention techniques and patches to protect systems and prevent data encryption in the event of a ransomware attack.

2.3 Exploiting Vulnerabilities

The research paper titled "MALPITY: Automatic Identification and Exploitation of Tarpit Vulnerabilities in Malware" [17] proposes the use of malware tarpits as a defense against global malware operations. Instead of seizing botnet infrastructures, the researchers suggest employing tarpits, which are network services that keep malware clients engaged in busy network operations, slowing down, or stopping their spreading and monetization techniques. The researchers automatically identify network operations used by malware and exploit tarpit vulnerabilities to block malware effectively.

Using dynamic malware analysis, the researcher's study how malware interacts with network APIs to infer operations that would have been blocked with certain inputs. The paper demonstrates the effectiveness of their approach by halting specific malware activities, such as DGAbased C2 communication in Pushdo, hindering SalityP2P peers' commands or updates, and stopping Bashlite's spreading engine.

The paper also highlights the threat posed by banking botnets, such as the Zeus banking botnet, which caused significant financial damage. The researchers propose an approach to combat banking botnets by exploiting inherent vulnerabilities in their Command and Control (C&C) systems. Their focus is on interrogating the C&C rather than the compromised clients, offering organizations an active defense option alongside traditional malware removal and clean-up processes. The researchers validate their approach using the leaked Zeus 2.0.8.9 toolkit and identify security flaws in its C&C web application, including lack of authentication between the client-side malware and C&C, inadequate access control in web application folders, and clear text authentication between C&C and the remote bot-herder. These vulnerabilities make a range of offensive measures, such as Buffer-Overflow, Denial-of-Service, and Dictionary or Brute Force Attacks, viable against the Zeus C&C. [21].

2.4 The Effects of Malware Attacks on Social Media

The research article "The Role of Artificial Intelligence and Cyber Security for Social Media" [18] discusses the significant impact of social media applications like Facebook, Instagram, and Twitter in connecting billions of people worldwide and facilitating communication and information sharing. Social media platforms have the potential to benefit humanity by spreading information about infectious diseases and fostering discussions to address various societal challenges, including child trafficking and violence against women. However, the article also acknowledges the negative aspects of social media, such as the spread of false information or fake news and violations of individual privacy. The proliferation of Artificial Intelligence (AI) systems and powerful machine learning techniques, coupled with cyber-attacks on information systems, are transforming the way social media is used by users. Malicious software poses a threat to social media platforms by potentially altering the contents of posted messages, creating fake profiles to disseminate false information, and subjecting images and videos to attacks. Additionally, users' machines and mobile phones are susceptible to attacks that can further infect the social media system.

3   Methodology

3.1   Using Secondary Data

Secondary analysis refers to the re-analysis of previously collected qualitative or quantitative data from a prior study [23]. Researchers use this method to explore new research interests, distinct from the original study, or gain additional perspectives on the original research question. It offers a viable option for researchers with limited time to conduct new experiments. Additionally, it allows researchers to expand on existing work by testing new ideas, frameworks, models, and theories. In rapidly changing fields like information technology, utilizing existing data enables faster completion of projects and the generation of findings before they become outdated due to new developments in the field. [24].

3.2   Using Mixed Methodology

This research paper utilizes secondary analysis to explore relatively unexplored research questions and leverage variables defined in previous studies. The aim is to analyze data from the 2014 study, "A Survey of Emerging Threats in Cybersecurity," and provide updated extensive research on topics like Exploiting Vulnerabilities, Malicious Software Attacks, Effects of Cyber-Attacks on social media, and State-of-the-Art Mitigation Tools and Techniques. The chosen approach is mixed methodology, incorporating both qualitative and quantitative data from various sources, including open-ended communication and computational techniques. A potential weakness is the lack of experimental research. The discussion section includes a comparative analysis between the 2014 study's data and the data collected in this paper.

In summary, this is an overview of secondary data and the various data collection methods used in both the 2014 study and the current research paper. Mixed Methodology, combining qualitative data obtained through open-ended communication and quantitative data involving numerical analysis, is chosen as an effective approach. The next chapter presents the results, including findings from the literature review, Cybersecurity trends, and tips for companies. Extensive research is also conducted on other topics like cloud computing, critical infrastructure, smartphone technology, and privacy, mentioned in the previous study.

4 Results

Below are the results and findings of the extensive research implemented using secondary data gathered from the 2014 study and various websites displayed in the methodology. There are emerging cybersecurity trends and tips for users to protect and prevent malicious software attacks.

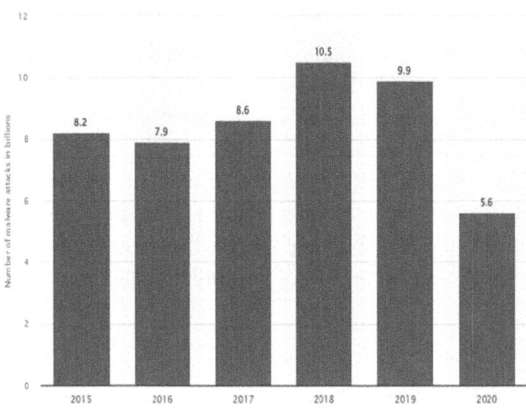

Fig. 2. Annual Number of Malware Attacks Worldwide from 2015 to 2020 (in Billions) [25]

According to statista.com, SonicWall Capture Labs conducted an annual worldwide survey to gather malware attacks annually from 2015 to 2020. Each year, the number of malware attacks reached in the billions and the highest years were in 2018 and 2019. In 2018, there were over ten and a half (10.5) billion malware attacks and there was nearly the same amount in 2019, which was 9.9 billion. The information in this graph, shown in Fig. 2 displays research evidence for this paper [25].

Table 1. Eight (8) New Known Exploited Vulnerabilities Catalog [26].

CVE Number	CVE Title	Required Action Due Date
CVE-2022-22587	Apple IOMobileFrameBuffer Memory Corruption Vulnerability	2/11/2022
CVE-2021-20038	SonicWall SMA 100 Appliances Stack-Based Buffer Overflow Vulnerability	2/11/2022
CVE-2014-7169	GNU Bourne-Again Shell (Bash) Arbitrary Code Execution Vulnerability	7/28/2022
CVE-2014-6271	GNU Bourne-Again Shell (Bash) Arbitrary Code Execution Vulnerability	7/28/2022
CVE-2020-0787	Microsoft Windows Background Intelligent Transfer Service (BITS) Improper Privilege Management Vulnerability	7/28/2022
CVE-2014-1776	Microsoft Internet Explorer Use-After-Free Vulnerability	7/28/2022
CVE-2020-5722	Grandstream Networks UCM6200 Series SQL Injection Vulnerability	7/28/2022
CVE-2017-5689	Intel Active Management Technology (AMT), Small Business Technology (SBT), and Standard Manageability Privilege Escalation Vulnerability	7/28/2022

The Cybersecurity Infrastructure and Security Agency (CISA) has identified eight (8) new vulnerabilities that are actively being exploited by cyber threat actors. These vulnerabilities are considered significant risk factors for the federal enterprise. The list of known Common Vulnerabilities and Exposures (CVE) is maintained through the Binding Operational Directive (BOD) 22–01, which requires Federal Civilian Executive Branch (FCEB) agencies to address these vulnerabilities by specific deadlines to safeguard their networks against active threats. Although BOD 22–01 applies to FCEB agencies, CISA strongly advises all organizations to prioritize timely remediation of vulnerabilities from the catalog to reduce exposure to cyberattacks. Table 1 displays the list of the 8 new exploited vulnerabilities [26].

Figure 3 shows a graph displaying the monthly social media attacks per target from January to September 2021. According to the PhishLabs Quarterly Threat Trends and Intelligence Report, attacks on enterprises through social media have increased by 82 percent since January 2021. Threat actors are exploiting social media platforms due to the lack of security vigilance among users and the critical brand presence of organizations, making them attractive targets for malicious activities and impersonating legitimate businesses. PhishLabs regularly analyzes numerous phishing and social media attacks on brands and their employees. The figure also presents the percentages of trending social media threats and the targeted industries [27].

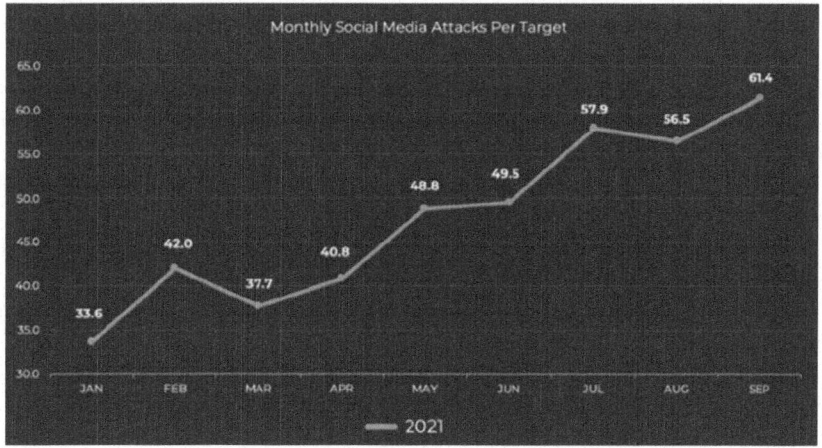

Fig. 3. Monthly Social Media Attacks Per Target [27]

Social media attacks on enterprises have increased significantly, with the average organization facing around 34 attacks per month at the beginning of the year, rising to 61 attacks per month between July and September [27]. Security teams should closely monitor social media activity and prioritize actions to detect and remediate threats [27].

Identity theft is a significant cybersecurity concern for cybercriminals, especially in the US. The transition to remote and at-home work during the COVID-19 pandemic has led to higher data security risks [28]. Figure 4 shows that data breach and identity theft reports doubled between 2014 and 2019, indicating the heightened security risks associated with remote work [28].

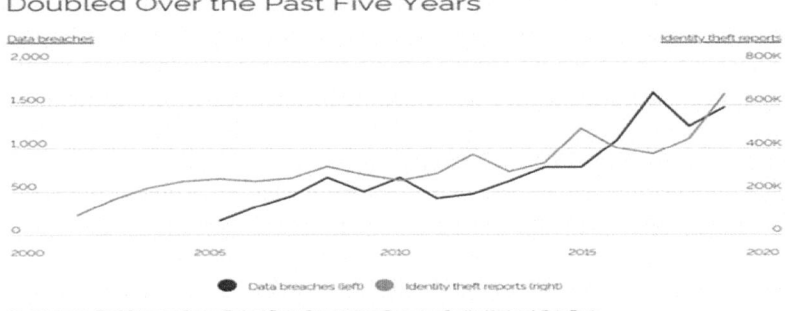

Fig. 4. Data Breaches and Identity Theft Reports Have Doubled Over the Past Five Years [28]

In 2019, the business and healthcare industries experienced the highest number of data breaches, with over 500 and 650 breaches, respectively. The business industry's vulnerability to data breaches increased by 150 percent during that five-year period. However, data security remained strong in the banking and government sectors, both of which saw a decline in total data breaches between 2018 and 2019 [28] in 2021 an article from the Panda Security website informs users about eleven (11) tips and trends that analyze the emerging threat landscape that comes as a result, and what cybersecurity trends pose the most risk and beyond.

Trend 1: Remote-work impact and new threats call for long-term security assessment and vulnerability identification [29].

Trend 2: Ransomware attacks continue to increase; transitioning from VPNs to ZTNAs can enhance security [29].

Trend 3: MFA adoption rises, but phone-based MFA is criticized for weak security; application-based MFA should be considered [29].

Trend 4: AI and ML play crucial roles in threat detection and attacks; implementing AI-powered security systems can save millions [29].

Trend 5: Cloud services are prime targets; companies should assess security implications before migration [29].

Trend 6: Data privacy becomes a standalone program; organizations must strengthen privacy efforts [29].

Trend 7: COVID-19 vaccine-related phishing attacks surge; identity management strategies are vital for securing remote workforce [29].

Trend 8: Increasing demand for cybersecurity professionals; company-wide training and executive involvement are essential [29].

Trend 9: Insider threats on the rise; organizations need tools to detect internal data breaches [29].

Trend 10: Increased need for Chief Security Officers; aligning security operations with business strategy is crucial [29].

Trend 11: Real-time data visibility critical for comprehensive risk assessment; security automation and cloud-native solutions recommended [29].

4.1 Focus on Privacy

1) Focus on Privacy: Privacy has become a critical concern in the development of IT systems due to the increasing volume of personal information entered online. The Privacy Engineering Program (PEP) offers trusted tools and resources to support privacy in various categories [1].
2) Cloud Computing: Cloud computing offers efficiency and agility, attracting consumers and businesses alike. It provides on-demand self- service, resource pooling, elasticity, and measured service. Different service models - SaaS, PaaS, and IaaS - pose unique security and privacy challenges [1].
3) Critical Infrastructure: The reliable and secure operation of critical infrastructure is vital for national security and economic vitality. Cybersecurity seeks to protect critical infrastructures from terrorism, sabotage, information warfare, and natural disasters. Researchers continue to understand and address complexities in critical infrastructure systems [1].
4) Smartphone Technology: Smartphones have become powerful and personalized devices, widely used in daily life. However, they also present significant security threats, including data leaks, phishing attacks, and identity theft [35, 36].

5 Discussions

5.1 Addressing the Research Questions

R1. How can users of the Internet better protect their confidential information?

The research focuses on empowering users to protect their confidential information on the internet. Various directions were explored, including selective data disclosure, privacy policy, and data sanitization. Ten tips to improve internet privacy were presented, including checking social privacy settings, using secure passwords, and employing messaging apps with end-to-end encryption.

R2. Is it possible to design the current Internet system from scratch without being constrained by the existing system?

The study investigates the concept of a Next Generation Secure Web Gateway (SWG) as an evolution of traditional web proxies. It deals with both cloud and web traffic, addressing cloud-enabled threats, shadow IT apps, and data risks. Next Gen SWGs offer various capabilities such as monitoring individual actions, granular application control, and protection against threats.

R3. Can a computing system be developed that is inherently secure, available, and reliable despite disruptions, errors, and attacks?

The research explores trustworthy systems and addresses seven approaches, including secure hardware and software, architecture design, self-testing, and automated remediation. These approaches remain relevant in addressing challenges related to system trustworthiness.

R4. What are approaches to developing global-scale identity management for accessing critical information systems?

Global-scale identity management aims to identify and authenticate entities accessing critical IT systems from anywhere. It involves managing digital identities and log-in credentials, using protocols like SAML, OpenID, OAuth, and TACACS. Approaches discussed include federated identity, attack attributes, and data provenance.

R5. Could a security system be developed that can be managed by users with all levels of computer skills?

The study focuses on usable security, and approaches include integration with human-computer interaction, security interface design, and evaluating usable security. For secure user access, implementing individual accounts, limiting access to necessary files, and monitoring account activities are suggested. Authentication options range from passwords to biometrics.

6   Conclusion

The difference between the data collected in the 2012 study and this new study is that, even though this new study focuses more on mixed methodology, the prior study gravitated more towards qualitative research data. One of the reasons for this is that the data collected was used for Survey Research. Additionally, the approach for this new study is similar because of the qualitative research data collected. The reason why the new study uses mixed methodology is because of the non-numerical and measurement analysis collected from the extensive research conducted. For example, in Chapter 4, there were figures and tables that analyze both qualitative and quantitative data from other sources.

The findings from the results chapter and the research questions answered in this chapter indicate that there are threats still occurring in the present day. Even with technology expanding, there are tools developing to prevent cyber-attacks on systems as well as to harm them. The data collected from this new study provides tips for privacy usage on the internet, displays cybersecurity trends for topics such as COVID-19, and even introduces new ways to access the internet without restrictions, such as the Next Generation Secure Web Gateway (Next Gen SWG). The information collected for this paper highlights current issues addressed in the 2014 study and more to come in the near future.

6.1   Future Work

The growth in Internet availability and Internet-enabled devices has led to increased use of the Internet, resulting in the exposure of sensitive personal information without understanding the risks of data misuse. Virtual machines like Oracle VirtualBox and VMWare allow users to practice ethical hacking and penetration testing with Kali Linux tools, which can be valuable for a thesis. Conducting extensive research on emerging cybersecurity threats is essential due to the constant rise in online attacks across various areas, including social media, cloud computing, smartphones, and critical infrastructure. The project draws from a 2014 study, with 60 percent of the data referenced from it, and 40 percent from other sources like research articles and websites. The study highlights the worsening of malware attacks and cyber threats since 2014, with a focus on topics such as malicious software attacks, exploiting vulnerabilities, state-of-the-art mitigation tools, techniques, and social media attacks. The research questions from the previous study were instrumental in comparing the findings to the current study, showing advancements like the Next Generation Web Secure Gateway for protecting against cyber- attacks.

References

1. Jang-Jaccard, J., Nepal, S.: A survey of emerging threats in cybersecurity. J. Comput. Syst. Sci. **80**(5), 973–993 (2014)
2. What is cybersecurity? IBM. https://www.ibm.com/topics/cybersecurity. Accessed: 31 Oct 2021
3. Oxford Languages: Definition of Malware. Google search. https://www.google.com/search?q=malware%2Bdefinition&rlz=1C1GCEA_enUS915US916&oq=malware%2Bdef&aqs=chrome.0.69i59i433i512j69i57j0i20i263i512j0i512l7.4192j0j4&sourceid=chrome&ie=UTF-8. Accessed: 31 Oct 2021
4. Malware and its types. GeeksforGeeks (2019). https://www.geeksforgeeks.org/malware-and-its-types/. Accessed: 31 Oct 2021
5. Oxford Languages: The Definition of Trojan Horse, Google search. [Online]. Available: https://www.google.com/search?q=trojan%2Bhorse%2Bdefinition&rlz=1C1GCEA_enUS915US916&oq=trojan%2Bhorse%2Bde&aqs=chrome.1.69i57j0i433i512j0i512l8.5578j0j4&sourceid=chrome&ie=UTF-8. Accessed: 31 Oct 2021
6. Oxford Languages: The Definition of Spyware, Google search. https://www.google.com/search?q=spyware%2Bdefinition&rlz=1C1GCEA_enUS915US916&sxsrf=AOaemvLqy2AErkhJuHEzpqx21r4OdkY1K3A1635528706408&ei=AjB8YduiGMiLxc8P15Od-A0&oq=Spyware&gs_lcp=Cgdnd3Mtd2l6EAEYADIHCAAQsQMMQQzIECAAQQzIHCAAQsQMQQzIECAAQQzIECAAQQzIFCAAQgAQyBAgAEEMyBAgAEEMyBQgAEIAEMgUIABCABDoHCCMQ6gIQJzoECCMQJzoECC4QQzoKCAAQsQMMQgwEQQQ0oECEEYAFDYsglYwr8JYJrKCWgBcAJ4AIAB6gGIAf8HkgEFMS40LjYlKYAQCgAQGwAQrAAQE&sclient=gws-wiz. Accessed: 31 Oct 2021
7. Oxford Languages: The Definition of Adware, Google search. https://www.google.com/search?q=adware%2Bdefinition&rlz=1C1GCEA_enUS915US916&sxsrf=AOaemvIk1uqqD9LpWjCjwFSlvMrDvh9BuQ%3A1635529052863&ei=XDF8Yfv0M5ePtAbs5IgCw&oq=adware%2Bdefinition&gs_lcp=Cgdnd3Mtd2l6EAMyBQgAEMQCMgYIABAHEB4yBggAEAcQHjIGCAAQBxAeMggIABAHEAoQHjIGCAAQBxAeMgYIABAHEB4yBggAEAcQHjIICAAQBxAKEB4yBggAEAcQHjoHCCMQsAMQJzoHCAAQRxCwAzoHCAAQsAMQQzoHCAAQgAQQCjoECAAQDToHCAAQsQMQCjoECAAQCkoECEEYAFDSI1isL2D9N2gBcAJ4AIA10.BvQGIAYcIkgEDMC43mAEAoAEByAEKwAEB&sclient=gwswiz&ved=0ahUKEwj7ktzBlPDzAhWXB80KHWzyA7QQ4dUDCA4&uact=5. Accessed: 31 Oct 2021
8. Oxford Languages: The Definition of Ransomware, Google search. https://www.google.com/search?q=ransomware%2Bdefinition&rlz=1C1GCEA_enUS915US916&sxsrf=AOaemvKr5rk0dzM2rez7YWc6cNqGEBz8qA%3A1635708460890&ei=LO512.Ye3pNbKKwbkPkaeriAQ&oq=rans%2Bdefinition&gs_lcp=Cgdnd3Mtd2l6EAEYADIGCAAQBxAeMgYIABAHEB4yBggAEAcQHjIGCAAQBxAeMgYIABAHEB4yBggAEAcQHjIGCAAQBxAeMggIABAHEAoQHjoECEEYAFCAggxYhogMYIOSDGgAcAJ4AIABaIgB_QKSAQMzLjGYAQCgAQHAAQE&sclient=gws-wiz. Accessed: 31 Oct 2021

9. Oxford Languages: The Definition of Keylogger, Google search. [Online]. Available: https://www.google.com/search?q=keylogger%2Bdefinition&rlz=1C1GCEA_enUS915US916&sxsrf=AOaemvKylctXs7wtjfOsDMFFbbXO78zZQQ%3A1635529536069&ei=QDN8Yf bVA8SntQaO75uoDA&oq=keylogdefinition&gs_lcp=Cgdnd3Mtd2l6EAEYADIECAAQ DTIECAAQDTIGCAAQBxAeMgYIABAHEB4yBggAEAcQHjIGCAAQBxAeMgYIA BAHEB4yBggEAcQHjIGCAAQBxAeMgYIABAHEB46BwgAEEcQsAM6BwgAELA DEEM6CwgAEAcQHhBGEPkBOgkIABANEEYYQQE6CAgAEAcQChAeSgQIQRgAU OvbBljn5gZgIGaAFwAngAgAGAogBgQiSAQczLjIuMS4xmAEAoAEByAEKwAEB& sclient=gws-wiz. Accessed: 31 Oct 2021
10. Oxford Languages: The Definition of Rootkits, Google search. [Online]. Available: https://www.google.com/search?q=rootkits%2Bdefinition&rlz=1C1GCEA_enUS915US916&sxsrf=AOaemvJzLKsiiW_O7aLX6VOlzwMAEFQ%3A1635529650286&ei=sjN8YZbxE PDMytMP9qSr8Ao&oq=rootkits%2Bdefinition&gs_lcp=Cgdnd3Mtd2l6EAMyBQgAE IAEMgYIABAHEB46CAgAEAcQChAeOhAIABCxAxCDARCRAhBGEPkBOgQIAB ANSgQIQRgAUMOwBVjJuwVgvL0FaABwAngAgAFiAHdBZIBAzcuMZgBAKABAcA BAQ&sclient=gws-wiz&ved=0ahUKEwiWkszelvDzAhVwpnIEHXbSCq4Q4dUDCA4& uact=5. Accessed: 31 Oct 2021
11. Bedell, P.L., Hanna, K.T.: What is a computer worm and how does it work?, Search Security (2021). https://searchsecurity.techtarget.com/definition/worm. Accessed: 31 Oct 2021
12. Software, Encyclopædia Britannica. https://www.britannica.com/technology/software. Accessed: 31 Oct 2021
13. Gatefy: 11 real and famous cases of malware attacks. Gatefy (2021). https://gatefy.com/blog/real-and-famous-cases-malware-attacks/. Accessed: 31 Oct 2021
14. Workman, M.D., Luevanos, J.A., Mai, B.: A study of cybersecurity education using a present-test-practice-assess model. IEEE (Institute of Electrical and Electronics Engineers) Transactions on Education, pp. 1–6 (2021)
15. Salih, H.M., Mohammed, M.S.: Spyware injection in Android using fake application. 2020 International Conference on Computer Science and Software Engineering (CSASE), pp. 100–105 (2020)
16. Farooq, M.J., Zhu, Q.: Modeling, analysis, and mitigation of Dynamic Botnet Formation in wireless IOT Networks. IEEE Trans. Inf. Forensics Secur. 14(9), 2412–2426 (2019)
17. Walla, S., Rossow, C.: Malpity: Automatic identification and exploitation of Tarpit vulnerabilities in malware. 2019 IEEE European Symposium on Security and Privacy (EuroS&P), pp. 590–605 (2019)
18. Thuraisingham: The role of Artificial Intelligence and cyber security for social media. 2020 IEEE International Parallel and Distributed Processing Symposium Workshops (IPDPSW), pp. 1116–1118 (2020)
19. Mavroeidis, V., Bromander, S.: Cyber Threat Intelligence Model: An evaluation of taxonomies, sharing standards, and ontologies within Cyber Threat Intelligence. In: 2017 European Intelligence and Security Informatics Conference (EISIC), pp. 91–98 (2017)
20. Cybercrime will cost businesses over $2 trillion by 2019: Cybercrime will Cost Businesses Over $2.1 Trillion by 2019 (2021). https://www.juniperresearch.com/press/cybercrime-cost-businesses-over-2trillion-by-2019. Accessed: 10 Nov 2021
21. Watkins, L., Kawka, C., Corbett, C., Robinson, W.H.: Fighting banking botnets by exploiting inherent command and control vulnerabilities. 2014 9th International Conference on Malicious and Unwanted Software: The Americas (MALWARE), pp. 93–100 (2014)
22. Aidan, J.S., Verma, H.K., Awasthi, L.K.: Comprehensive survey on Petya Ransomware attack. In: 2017 International Conference on Next Generation Computing and Information Systems (ICNGCIS), 31. pp. 122–125 (2017)
23. G., Payne, J.: Secondary analysis. Sage Research Methods (2004). https://methods.sagepub.com/book/key-concepts-in-social-research/n45.xml. Accessed: 01 Dec 2021

24. Johnston, M.P.: Secondary data analysis: a method of which time has come. Qualitative and Quantitative Methods in Libraries **3**(1), 619–626 (2014)

25. Johnson, J.: Number of malware attacks per year 2020. Statista (2021). https://www.statista.com/statistics/873097/malware-attacks-per-year-worldwide/. Accessed: 31 Jan 2022

26. Cisa adds eight known exploited vulnerabilities to catalog. CISA (2022). https://www.cisa.gov/uscert/ncas/current-activity/2022/01/28/cisa-adds-eight-known-exploited-vulnerabilit ies-catalog. Accessed: 31 Jan 2022

27. Social media attacks increase 82%. PhishLabs (2021). https://www.phishlabs.com/blog/soc ial-media-attacks-increase-82/. Accessed: 31 Jan 2022

28. The largest data breaches in U.S. history. Spanning (2020). https://spanning.com/resources/industry-research/largest-data-breaches-us-history/. Accessed: 31 Jan 2022

29. P.S. Panda Security specializes in the development of endpoint security products and is part of the WatchGuard portfolio of IT security solutions. Initially focused on the development of antivirus software, "11 emerging cybersecurity trends in 2021 - Panda Security," Panda Security Mediacenter (2021). https://www.pandasecurity.com/en/mediacenter/tips/cybersecu rity-trends/. Accessed: 01 Mar 2022

30. O'Reilly, P., Rigopoulos, K., Feldman, L., Witte, G.: 2020 cybersecurity and privacy annual ... - nvlpubs.nist.gov. National Institute of Standards and Technology (2021). https://nvlpubs.nist.gov/nistpubs/SpecialPublications/NIST.SP.800-214.pdf. Accessed: 01 Mar 2022

31. Perekalin, L.G., Aver, H., the Robot, M., Ferapontov, A.: How to improve privacy online in 10 easy steps. Daily English India wwwkasperskycoinblog (2019). https://www.kaspersky.co.in/blog/privacy-ten-tips-2018/13653/. Accessed: 07 Mar 2022

32. Security, N.: What is a next generation secure web gateway (SWG)? Netskope (2022). https://www.netskope.com/security-defined/next-gen-secure-web-gateway. Accessed: 07 Mar 2022

33. Bhatia, G.: Follow CEH |CPEH |RHEL 6 |OWASP |Cryptography |Cyber Law |Docker |Cloud Security |OpenStack |AWS |AWS S3 |Python, Global Scale Identity Manage-ment, SlideShare (2017). https://www.slideshare.net/Gauravhatia/global-scale-identity-man agement. Accessed: 07 Mar 2022

34. N. C. for Education Statistics, Chapter 8-Protecting Your System: User Access Security, from safeguarding your technology, NCES publication 98–297 (National Center for Education Statistics). https://nces.ed.gov/pubs98/safetech/chapter8.asp. Accessed: 07 Mar 2022

35. Demographics of mobile device ownership and adoption in the United States. Pew Research Center: Internet, Science & Tech (2021). https://www.pewresearch.org/internet/fact-sheet/mobile/. Accessed: 07 Mar 2022

36. Nelson: Top security threats of smartphones (2022). Reader's Digest (2022). https://www.rd.com/article/mobile-security-threats/. Accessed: 07 Mar 2022

37. Kali tools: Kali linux tools: Kali Linux (2022). https://www.kali.org/tools/. Accessed: 07 Mar 2022

38. What is a VM? why use a virtual machine?, DNSstuff (2020). https://www.dnsstuff.com/what-is-vm-virtual-machine#:~:text=The%20main%20purpose%20of%20VMs,require%20two%20separate%20physical%20units. Accessed: 07 Mar 2022

39. What is IoT?, Aeris (2020). https://www.aeris.com/in/what-is-iot/. Accessed: 17 Mar 2022

40. Qualitative research: Definition, types, methods and examples. QuestionPro (2021). https://www.questionpro.com/blog/qualitative-research-methods/#:~:text=Qualitative%20rese arch%20is%20defined%20as,looking%20to%20improve%20its%20patronage. Accessed: 18 Mar 2022

41. Quantitative research and analysis: Quantitative methods overview. LibGuides (2022). https://lib-guides.letu.edu/quantresearch#:~:text=Quantitative%20research%20methods%20emphasize%20objective,statistical%20data%20using%20computational%20techniques. Accessed: 18 Mar 2022

42. Bhandari, P.: An introduction to quantitative research. Scribbr (2021). https://www.scribbr.com/methodology/quantitative-research/. Accessed: 18 Mar 2022

Author Index

The manufacturer's authorised representative in the EU is Springer
Nature Customer Service Centre GmbH, Europaplatz 3, 69115 Heidelberg,
Germany. If you have any concerns regarding our products, please
contact ProductSafety@springernature.com

Printed and bound by CPI Group (UK) Ltd, Croydon, CR0 4YY

27/04/2026

02097586-0013